CISM® Review Manual

16th Edition

CISM. Certified Information Security Manager.
An ISACA® Certification

ISACA®

About ISACA

For more than 50 years, ISACA® (*www.isaca.org*) has advanced the best talent, expertise and learning in technology. ISACA equips individuals with knowledge, credentials, education and community to progress their careers and transform their organizations, and enables enterprises to train and build quality teams. Among those credentials, ISACA advances and validates business-critical skills and knowledge through the globally respected Certified Information Systems Auditor® (CISA®), Certified in Risk and Information Systems Control® (CRISC®), Certified Information Security Manager® (CISM®), Certified in the Governance of Enterprise IT® (CGEIT®) and Certified Data Privacy Solutions Engineer™ (CDPSE™) credentials. ISACA is a global professional association and learning organization that leverages the expertise of its 145,000 members who work in information security, governance, assurance, risk and privacy to drive innovation through technology. It has a presence in 188 countries, including more than 220 chapters worldwide.

Disclaimer

ISACA has designed and created the *CISM® Review Manual 16th Edition* primarily as an educational resource to assist individuals preparing to take the CISM certification exam. It was produced independently from the CISM exam and the CISM Certification Working Group, which has no responsibility for its content. Copies of past exams are not released to the public and were not made available to ISACA for preparation of this publication. ISACA makes no representations or warranties whatsoever with regard to these or other ISACA publications assuring candidates' passage of the CISM exam.

ISACA
1700 E. Golf Road, Suite 400
Schaumburg, IL 60173, USA
Phone: +1.847.660.5505
Fax: +1.847.253.1755
Contact us: https://support.isaca.org
Website: www.isaca.org

Participate in the ISACA Online Forums: https://engage.isaca.org/onlineforums

Twitter: http://twitter.com/ISACANews
LinkedIn: www.linkedin.com/company/isaca
Facebook: www.facebook.com/ISACAGlobal
Instagram: www.instagram.com/isacanews/

ISBN 978-1-60420-901-3
CISM® Review Manual 16th Edition
Printed in the United States of America

CISM® Review Manual 16th Edition

ISACA is pleased to offer the sixteenth edition of the *CISM® Review Manual*. The purpose of the manual is to provide CISM candidates with information and references to assist in the preparation and study for the Certified Information Security Manager® (CISM) exam.

The *CISM® Review Manual* is updated regularly to keep pace with rapid changes in the management of information security. As with previous manuals, the sixteenth edition is the result of contributions from many qualified authorities who have generously volunteered their time and expertise. We respect and appreciate their contributions and hope their efforts provide extensive educational value to CISM manual readers.

The sample questions contained in this manual are designed to depict the types of questions typically found on the CISM exam and to give further clarity to the content presented in this manual. The CISM exam is a practice-based exam. Simply reading the reference material in this manual will not properly prepare candidates for the exam. The self-assessment questions are included for guidance only. Scoring results do not indicate future individual exam success.

Certification has resulted in a positive impact on many careers, including worldwide recognition for professional experience and enhanced knowledge and skills. The CISM certification is designed for IT and business professionals who have hands-on experience with information security management. ISACA wishes you success with the CISM exam.

Acknowledgments

The *CISM® Review Manual 16th Edition* is the result of collective efforts of many volunteers. ISACA members from throughout the world participated, generously offering their talent and expertise. This international team exhibited a spirit and selflessness that has become the hallmark of contributors to ISACA manuals. Their participation and insight are truly appreciated.

Authors

Edward B. McCabe, CISM, CGEIT, CRISC, CDPSE, COBIT 2019, ISMS LI, ISO 27001, SABSA Chartered Security Architect, The Rubicon Advisory Group, USA
Greg Witte, CISM, CISSP-ISSEP, Palydin LLC, USA

Expert Reviewers

Andreas Abeck, CISM, ISO 27001 LI, Germany
Lisa Abshire, MBA, CISA, CISM, CRISC, CISSP, USA
Michael Allen, CISA, CISM, CDPSE, USA
Neethu Aneesh, CISA, CISM, CDPSE, CCSK, CCSP, CIPP/E, CISSP, Australia
Md. Abul Kalam Azad, CISA, CISM, CRISC, CDPSE, CISSP, Eastern Bank Ltd., Bangladesh
Bruce Borchorst, CISA, CISM, CGEIT, CRISC, CCSK, PRINCE2, ITIL Expert, USA
Alistair Cockeram, CISM, CISSP, CCSP, SCCP, MCIIS, Fidelity International, United Kingdom
Vinod A. Devathas, PhD, CISA, CISM, CGEIT, CRISC, CPIM, GCD Services Pte. Ltd., Singapore
Howard Duck, CISA, CISM, CDPSE, CISSP, Conduent Inc., USA
Sherif El-Gendy, PhD, CISM, CDPSE, C|CISO, CCIP, CEH, FBCS, ISO 27001LI, ISO 27032LCM, Egypt
Paul Ellis, CISM, Arculus Cyber Security, UK
Adham Etoom, CISM, CRISC, FAIR, GCIH, PMP, Government of Jordan/National Cyber Security Center, Jordan
Thales Fernandes, CISM, CGEIT, CISSP, COBIT 5, GLEG, HDI-SCM, ITIL Expert, ISO 20000, ISO 27001, Lean IT OCEB2, PSM-I, Spain
Aaron Franks, CISM, Department of Defense, USA
Hakim Fubara, CISA, CISM, CISSP, Cognitor Consulting Ltd., Canada
Mohamed Gohar, MBA, CISA, CISM, CGEIT, CRISC, CEH, CISSP, CLCSM, CLPTP, COBIT 5/2019, CPDE, ISO/IEC 27001 LI/LA, ISO/IEC 27005 LRM, ISO/IEC 27032 LCM, ISO/IEC 27035 LIM, ISO/IEC 27034 ASLI, ISO/IEC 38500 IT CGM, ISO 22301 LI/LA, ISO 31000 LRM, ITIL v3/v4 Expert/Pract/MP, LDRM, PECB Certified Auditor & Trainer, PeopleCert ITIL/Resilia Approved Trainer and Invigilator, PMP, Resilia Pract, SSGB, The Open Group TOGAF Authorized Trainer, TOGAF 9.2 Pract, Egypt
Stacy J. Hill, CISA, CISM, CGEIT, CRISC, CISSP, USA
Leighton R. Johnson, III, CISA, CISM, CRISC, CGEIT, CDPSE, CISSP-ISSEP, ISFMT, Inc., USA
Aileen Jones, CISA, CISM, CRISC, CISSP, ISSMP Certified, PMI/PMP, Internal Revenue Service, USA
Hasnain Ahmed Karimi, CISM, VOCUS, Australia
Robert Kendall, CISM, Capita, UK
Ashok Kumar DL, CISA, CISM, CDPSE, CFE, CISSP, CRMA, Happiest Minds Technologies Limited, India
Scott Mahoney, MBA, CISA, CISM, CRISC, USA
Muhammad Umair Mazhar, CISM, CRISC, Australia
Pedro Montalvan, CISM, PSA MARINE PERU, Peru
Ng Yen Nee, CISM, Malaysia
See Woh Ng, CISM, AIG Insurance New Zealand Limited, New Zealand
Nnamdi Nwosu, CISA, CISM, CGEIT, CRISC, CEH, University of the People, USA
Omar Olivos, CISM, GAC, Peru
Leonard Ong, CISA, CISM, CGEIT, CRISC, CDPSE, CSX-P, GE Healthcare, Singapore
Tafadzwa Padare, CISA, CISM, CCSP, CEH, CISSP, EcoCash Holdings Zimbabwe Limited, Zimbabwe

Acknowledgments *(cont.)*

Perkins Poon, CISA, CISM, CDPSE, CISSP, Hong Kong
Tabish Qureshi, CISA, CISM, CASP+, CEH v11, ITIL, MCS, MCSA, MCSE, Mic. Azure Sol. Arch Expert, Mic Azure Administrator Associate, PMP, Prince 2 Found & Pract, SAP Active Project Manager, Saudi Arabia
Md. Mushfiqur Raham, CISA, CISM, CGEIT, CRISC, CCISO, CISSP, LPT (Master), OSCP, First Security Islami Bank Limited, Bangladesh
Krishna Rajesh, CISM, India
Allan Rono, CISA, CISM, CRISC, Standard Chartered Bank, Kenya
Pativeth Ruangsuwan, CISM, MINOR Group, Thailand
Chris Sandefur, CISM, CRISC, CDPSE, CISSP, CCSP, CySA+, PMP, NewNet Communication Technologies, USA
Anne Sempa-Morrison, CISM, USA
Ling Ai Seong, CISM, Singapore
Prashanth Srinivas S, CISA, CISM, CRISC, CDPSE, AZ-900, LA & LI ISO 27001, Cognizant, India
Katalin Szenes, PhD, CISA, CISM, CGEIT, CISSP, Obuda University, Budapest, Hungary
Sridhar Vedhanabatla, CISM, Gainsight, India
Gabriel Villas, CISM, QCloud Systems, USA
Bernard Wanyama, CISA, CISM, CGEIT, CRISC, SYNTECH ASSOCIATES Limited, Uganda

ISACA has begun planning the seventeenth edition of the *CISM® Review Manual*. Volunteer participation drives the success of the manual. If you are interested in becoming a member of the select group of professionals involved in this global project, please visit *engage.isaca.org* to be notified of all upcoming CISM-related opportunities.

New—CISM Job Practice

Beginning in 2022, the Certified Information Security Manager® exam will test the new CISM job practice.

An international job practice analysis is conducted periodically to maintain the validity of the CISM certification program. A new job practice forms the basis of the CISM exam beginning in 2022.

The primary focus areas of the job practice are the current tasks performed and the knowledge used by CISMs. By gathering evidence of the current work practice of CISMs, ISACA ensures that the CISM program continues to meet the high standards set for the certification of professionals throughout the world.

The findings of the CISM job practice analysis are carefully considered and directly influence the development of new test specifications to ensure that the CISM exam reflects the most current best practices.

The new job practice reflects the areas of study to be tested. The complete CISM job practice can be found at *www.isaca.org/credentialing/CISM.*

Old CISM Job Practice	New CISM Job Practice
Information Security Governance (24%)	**Information Security Governance (17%)**
Information Risk Management (30%)	**Information Security Risk Management (20%)**
Information Security Program Development and Management (27%)	**Information Security Program (33%)**
Information Security Incident Management (19%)	**Incident Management (30%)**

Table of Contents

Page intentionally left blank

About This Manual

Overview

The *CISM® Review Manual 16th Edition* is a reference guide designed to assist candidates in preparing for the CISM examination. **The manual is one source of preparation for the exam but should not be thought of as the only source or viewed as a comprehensive collection of all the information and experience required to pass the exam.** No single publication offers such coverage and detail.

As candidates read the manual and encounter topics that are new to them or ones in which they feel their knowledge and experience are limited, additional references should be sought. The examination will be composed of questions testing the candidate's technical and practical knowledge, and ability to apply the knowledge (based on experience) in given situations.

Organization of This Manual

The *CISM Review Manual 16th Edition* is divided into four chapters covering the CISM domains tested on the exam in the percentages listed below:

Domain	Name	Percentage
Domain 1	Information Security Governance	17 percent
Domain 2	Information Security Risk Management	20 percent
Domain 3	Information Security Program	33 percent
Domain 4	Incident Management	30 percent

The manual has been developed and organized to assist in the study of these areas. Exam candidates should evaluate their strengths, based on knowledge and experience, in each of these areas.

Note: Each chapter defines the tasks that CISM candidates are expected to understand and includes a series of knowledge statements required to perform those tasks. These constitute the current practices for the IT risk practitioner. **The detailed CISM job practice can be viewed at *www.isaca.org/credentialing/CISM/CISM-job-practice-areas.***

Format of This Manual

Each chapter of the *CISM Review Manual* follows the same format:

- The Overview section provides a summary of the focus of the chapter, along with:
  - The domain exam content outline
  - Related task statements
  - Suggested resources for further study
  - Self-assessment questions
- The Content section includes:
  - Content to support the different areas of the job practice
  - Definitions of terms commonly found on the exam

Please note that the manual is written in standard American English, except for material imported from publications written in International English.

Submit suggestions to enhance the review manual or suggested reference materials to *studymaterials@isaca.org*.

Preparing for the CISM Exam

The CISM exam evaluates a candidate's practical knowledge based on experiences and application of the job practice domains as described in this review manual. We recommend that the candidate look to multiple resources to prepare for the exam, including this review manual and external publications. This section includes some tips for studying for the exam.

Read to understand which areas need more attention. See reference sources to expand knowledge and gain experience in those areas.

Actual exam questions test the candidate's practical application of relevant knowledge. At the end of each chapter, a sample self-assessment, consisting of questions, answers and explanations, introduces the question structure and general content. Remember that the sample questions may not be similar to questions appearing on the actual exam. Use reference material to find other publications that offer more detailed information on the topics addressed in this manual.

Getting Started

Having adequate time to prepare for the CISM exam is critical. Most candidates spend between three and six months studying prior to taking the exam. Set aside a designated time each week to study, and perhaps increase study time as the exam date approaches. It helps to develop a study plan for preparing for the exam.

Using the CISM Review Manual

The *CISM Review Manual* is divided into four chapters, each corresponding to a domain in the CISM job practice. While the review manual does not include every concept that could be tested on the CISM exam, it does cover a breadth of topics to provide a solid base for the exam candidate. The manual is one source of preparation for the exam and should not be thought of as the only source or viewed as a comprehensive collection of all the information and experience required to pass the exam.

Features in the Review Manual

The CISM Review Manual includes several features to help candidates navigate the job practice and enhance learning and retention of the material.

Review Manual Feature	Description
Overview	The overview provides the context of the domain, including job practice areas, applicable learning objectives and task statements.
Suggested Resources for Further Study	Because many of the concepts presented within the review manual are complex, candidates may find it useful to refer to external sources to supplement their understanding of those concepts. The suggested references for each chapter are resources to help enhance study efforts.
Self-Assessment Questions and Answers	The self-assessment questions in each chapter are not intended to measure the candidate's ability to answer questions correctly on the CISM exam for that area. The questions are intended to familiarize the candidate with question structure, and they may or may not be similar to questions that appear on the actual examination.
Glossary	The glossary included at the end of the manual contains terms that apply to: • The material included in the chapters • Related areas not specifically discussed in the manual Since the glossary is an extension of the manual text, it can point to areas the candidate may want to explore further using additional references.

Types of Questions on the CISM Exam

CISM exam questions are developed with the intent of measuring and testing practical knowledge and the application of information security management principles. All questions are presented in a multiple-choice format and are designed to elicit one best answer.

The candidate is cautioned to read each question carefully. Knowing that these types of questions are asked will go a long way toward answering them correctly. The best answer is one of the choices provided. There can be many potential solutions to the problems posed in the scenarios, depending on industry, geographical location, etc. It is advisable to consider the information provided in the question and to determine the best answer among the options provided.

Each CISM question has a stem (question) and four options (answer choices). The candidate is asked to choose the correct or best answer from the options. The stem may be in the form of a question or incomplete statement. In some instances, a scenario or description may be included. These questions normally describe a situation and require the candidate to answer two or more questions based on the information provided.

A helpful approach to these questions includes the following:

- Read the entire stem and determine what the question is asking. Look for key words such as "best," "most," "first," etc., and key terms that may indicate which domain or concept is being tested.
- Read all the options, and then read the stem again to attempt to eliminate options based on initial understanding of the question.

Reread the remaining options and bring in any personal experience that may illuminate the best answer to the question.

Preparing for the Exam

When preparing for the exam, the candidate should recognize that information security is a global profession, and the candidate's perceptions and experiences may not reflect the global position. Because the exam and CISM manuals are written for the international information security management community, the candidate must be flexible when reading about a condition that may contradict the candidate's experience.

Note that the CISM exam questions are written by experienced information security professionals from around the world. Each question on the exam is reviewed by ISACA's CISM Exam Item Development Working Group, which consists of international members. This geographic representation ensures that all exam questions are understood equally well in every country and language.

Using ISACA Exam Preparation Resources

The *CISM Review Manual* can be used in conjunction with other CISM exam preparation activities. The following products are based on the CISM job practice, and referenced job practice areas can be used to find related content within the *CISM Review Manual*. These resources include:

- *CISM Review Questions, Answers & Explanations Manual 10th Edition*
- CISM Review Questions, Answers & Explanations Database—12 Month Subscription
- CISM Online Review Course
- CISM review courses (provided by local ISACA chapters and accredited training organizations)

About the *CISM Review Questions, Answers & Explanations Manual*

Candidates may also wish to enhance their study and preparation for the exam by using the *CISM® Review Questions, Answers & Explanations Manual 10th Edition*.

The *CISM Review Questions, Answers & Explanations Manual 10th Edition* consists of 1,000 multiple-choice study questions, answers and explanations arranged in the domains of the current CISM job practice.

Questions in this publication are representative of the types of questions that could appear on the exam and include explanations of the correct and incorrect answers. Questions are sorted by the CISM domains and as a sample test. These publications are ideal for use in conjunction with the *CISM Review Manual 16th Edition*. These manuals can be used as study sources throughout the study process or as part of a final review to determine where candidates may need additional study. It should be noted that these questions and suggested answers are provided as examples; they are not actual questions from the examination and may differ in content from those that actually appear on the exam.

About the CISM Review Questions, Answers & Explanations Database

Another study aid that is available is the CISM® Review Questions, Answers & Explanations Database—12 Month Subscription. The online database consists of the 1,000 questions, answers and explanations included in the *CISM Review Questions, Answers & Explanations Manual 10th Edition*. With this product, CISM candidates can quickly identify their strengths and weaknesses by taking random sample exams of varying length and breaking the results down by domain. Sample exams can be chosen by domain, allowing for concentrated study, one domain at a time. Other sorting features, such as the omission of questions previously answered correctly, are available.

Note: When using the CISM review materials to prepare for the exam, candidates should be aware that they cover a broad spectrum of information security topics. **Candidates should not assume that reading these manuals and answering review questions will fully prepare them for the examination.** Since actual exam questions often relate to practical experiences, candidates should draw on their own experiences, other reference sources, and the experiences of colleagues and others who have earned the CISM designation.

Chapter 1:

Information Security Governance

Overview

Part A: Enterprise Governance

Part B: Information Security Strategy

Overview

This chapter reviews the body of knowledge and associated tasks necessary to develop an information security governance structure aligned with organizational objectives.

It provides an overview of what an information security manager needs to do in order to establish and maintain an information security governance framework and supporting processes to ensure that the information security strategy is aligned with organizational goals and objectives.

This domain represents 17 percent of the CISM examination (approximately 26 questions).

Domain 1 Exam Content Outline

A. Enterprise Governance

1. Organizational Culture

2. Legal, Regulatory and Contractual Requirements

3. Organizational Structures, Roles and Responsibilities

B. Information Security Strategy

1. Information Security Strategy Development

2. Information Governance Frameworks and Standards

3. Strategic Planning

Learning Objectives/Task Statements

Upon completion of this chapter, the information security manager should be able to:

- Identify internal and external influences to the organization that impact the information security strategy.
- Establish and/or maintain an information security strategy in alignment with organizational goals and objectives.
- Establish and/or maintain an information security governance framework.
- Integrate information security governance into corporate governance.
- Establish and maintain information security policies to guide the development of standards, procedures and guidelines.
- Develop business cases to support investments in information security.
- Gain ongoing commitment from senior leadership and other stakeholders to support the successful implementation of the information security strategy.
- Define, communicate and monitor information security responsibilities throughout the organization and lines of authority.
- Align the information security program with the operational objectives of other business functions.
- Integrate information security requirements into contracts and activities of external parties.
- Monitor external parties' adherence to established security requirements.
- Establish and/or maintain a process for information asset identification and classification.
- Identify legal, regulatory, organizational and other applicable compliance requirements.
- Establish and maintain processes to investigate and document information security incidents in accordance with legal and regulatory requirements.

Suggested Resources for Further Reading

Brotby, W.; IT Governance Institute; *Information Security Governance: Guidance for Information Security Managers,* ISACA, USA, 2008

Brotby, W.; *Information Security Governance: A Practical Development and Implementation Approach,* Wiley & Sons, 2009

Committee of Sponsoring Organizations of the Treadway Commission (COSO), *Internal Control—Integrated Framework,* USA, 2013

International Organization for Standardization (ISO), *ISO/IEC 27001:2013 Information technology—Security techniques—Information security management systems—Requirements,* Switzerland, 2013

ISO, *ISO/IEC 27002:2013 Information technology—Security techniques—Code of practice for information security controls,* Switzerland, 2013

ISO, *ISO/IEC 27014:2013 Information technology—Security techniques—Governance of information security,* Switzerland, 2013

ISACA, *The Business Model for Information Security,* USA, 2010

ISACA, *CMMI v2.0,* https://cmmiinstitute.com/cmmi

ISACA, COBIT, USA, *www.isaca.org/cobit*

ISACA, *COBIT 2019 Design Guide: Designing an Information and Technology Governance Solution,* USA, 2018

ISACA, *COBIT 2019 Implementation Guide: Implementing and Optimizing an Information and Technology Governance Solution*, USA, 2018

ISACA, *COBIT Focus Area: Information Security,* USA, 2020, *www.isaca.org/cobit*

National Association of Corporate Directors (NACD), *NACD Director's Handbook on Cyber-Risk Oversight,* USA, 2020, *www.nacdonline.org*

National Institute of Standards and Technology (NIST), *Integrating Cybersecurity and Enterprise Risk Management (ERM)*, USA, 2020, https://doi.org/10.6028/NIST.IR.8286

PricewaterhouseCoopers, *The Global State of Information Security Survey 2017,* www.pwc.com/gx/en/consulting-services/information-security-survey

SELF-ASSESSMENT QUESTIONS

CISM exam questions are developed with the intent of measuring and testing practical knowledge in information security management. All questions are multiple choice and are designed for one best answer. Every CISM question has a stem (question) and four options (answer choices). The candidate is asked to choose the correct or best answer from the options. The stem may be in the form of a question or incomplete statement. Many times, a CISM examination question will require the candidate to choose the most likely or best answer.

In every case, the candidate is required to read the question carefully, eliminate known incorrect answers and then make the best choice possible. Knowing the format in which questions are asked, and how to study to gain knowledge of what will be tested, will go a long way toward answering them correctly.

1. A security strategy is important for an enterprise **PRIMARILY** because it:

   A. provides a basis for determining the best logical security architecture.
   B. provides the approach to achieving the outcomes management wants.
   C. provides users guidance on how to operate securely in everyday tasks.
   D. helps IT auditors ensure compliance with rules and regulations.

2. Which of the following is the **MOST** important reason to provide effective communication about information security?

   A. It makes information security more palatable to resistant employees.
   B. It mitigates the weakest link in the information security landscape.
   C. It informs business units about the information security strategy.
   D. It helps the enterprise conform to regulatory information security requirements.

3. Which of the following approaches **BEST** helps the information security manager achieve compliance with various regulatory requirements?

   A. Rely on corporate counsel to advise which regulations are the most relevant.
   B. Stay current with all relevant regulations and request legal interpretation.
   C. Involve all impacted departments and treat regulations as just another risk.
   D. Ignore many of the regulations that have no penalties.

4. The **MOST** important consideration in developing security policies is that:

   A. they are based on a threat profile.
   B. they are complete and no detail is left out.
   C. management signs off on them.
   D. all employees read and understand them.

5. The **PRIMARY** security objective in creating good procedures is:

   A. to make sure they work as intended.
   B. that they are unambiguous and meet the standards.
   C. that they are written in plain language and are widely distributed.
   D. that compliance can be monitored.

6. Which of the following **MOST** helps ensure that assignment of roles and responsibilities is effective?

   A. Senior management is in support of the assignments.
   B. The assignments are consistent with existing proficiencies.
   C. The assignments are mapped to required skills.
   D. The assignments are given on a voluntary basis.

7. Which of the following benefits is the **MOST** important to an enterprise with effective information security governance?

   A. Maintaining appropriate regulatory compliance
   B. Ensuring disruptions are within acceptable levels
   C. Prioritizing allocation of remedial resources
   D. Maximizing return on security investments

8. From an information security manager's perspective, the **MOST** important factors regarding data retention are:

   A. business and regulatory requirements.
   B. document integrity and destruction.
   C. media availability and storage.
   D. data confidentiality and encryption.

9. Which role is in the **BEST** position to review and confirm the appropriateness of a list of approved users?

   A. Data owner
   B. Information security manager
   C. Domain administrator
   D. Business manager

10. In implementing information security governance, the information security manager is **PRIMARILY** responsible for:

    A. developing the security strategy.
    B. reviewing the security strategy.
    C. communicating the security strategy.
    D. approving the security strategy.

Answers on page 25

Chapter 1 ANSWER KEY

Self-Assessment Questions

1. A. Policies have to be developed to support the security strategy, and an architecture can only be developed after policies are completed (i.e., the security strategy is not the basis for architecture—policies are).
   B. A security strategy will define the approach to achieving the security program outcomes management wants. It should also be a statement of how security aligns with and supports business objectives. It provides the basis for good security governance.
   C. A security strategy may include requirements for users to operate securely, but it does not address how that is to be accomplished.
   D. IT auditors do not determine compliance based on strategy but, rather, on elements such as standards and control objectives.

2. A. Effective communication may assist in making information security more palatable, but that is not the most important aspect.
   B. Security failures are, in the majority of instances, directly attributable to lack of awareness or failure of employees to follow policies or procedures. Communication is important to ensure continued awareness of security policies and procedures among staff and business partners.
   C. Effective communication will allow business units to be informed about various aspects of information security, including the strategy, but it is not the most important aspect.
   D. Effective communication will assist in achieving compliance because it is unlikely that employees will be compliant with regulations unless they are informed about them. However, it is not the most important consideration.

3. A. Corporate counsel is generally involved primarily with stock issues and the associated filings required by regulators and with contract matters. It is unlikely that legal staff will be current on information security regulations and legal requirements.
   B. While it can be useful to stay abreast of all current and emerging regulations, it is, as a practical matter, nearly impossible—especially for a multinational company.
   C. Because departments such as human resources, finance and legal are most often subject to new regulations and must be involved in determining how best to meet the existing and emerging requirements, they typically would be most aware of these regulations. Treating regulations as another risk puts them in the proper perspective, and the mechanisms to deal with them should already exist. The fact that there are so many regulations makes it unlikely that they can all be specifically addressed efficiently. Many do not currently have significant consequences and may be addressed by compliance with other regulations. The most relevant response to regulatory requirements is to determine potential impact to the enterprise, just as with any other risk.
   D. Even if certain regulations have few or no penalties, ignoring them without consideration for other potential impacts (e.g., reputational damage) and whether they might be relevant to the enterprise is not a prudent approach.

4. **A. The basis for developing relevant security policies is addressing viable threats to the enterprise, prioritized by the likelihood of occurrence and their potential impact on the business. The strictest policies apply to the areas of greatest business value. This ensures that protection proportionality is maintained.**
   B. Policies are a statement of management's intent and direction at a high level and provide little, if any, detail.
   C. Management would not be asked to sign policies under development prior to their completion.
   D. Employees would not be reading and understanding the policies during development.

5. A. While it is important to make sure that procedures work as intended, their failure may not be a security issue.

B. All the answers are important, but the first criterion must be to ensure that there is no ambiguity in the procedures and that, from a security perspective, they meet the applicable standards and comply with policy.

C. Having clearly written procedures that are provided to all staff as needed is important, but it is not as important as ensuring that procedures comply with policy.

D. Compliance is important, but it is essential that compliance is achieved with a correct procedure.

6. A. Senior management support is always important, but it is not crucial to the effectiveness of employee activities.

B. The level of effectiveness of employees will be determined by their existing knowledge and capabilities—in other words, their proficiencies.

C. Mapping roles to the tasks that are required can be useful, but it is no guarantee that people can perform the required tasks.

D. While employees are more likely to be enthusiastic about a job they have volunteered for, it is not a requirement for them to be effective.

7. A. Maintaining appropriate regulatory compliance is a useful, but secondary, outcome.

B. The bottom line of security efforts is to ensure that business can continue to operate with an acceptable level of disruption that does not unduly constrain revenue-producing activities.

C. Prioritizing allocation of remedial resources is a useful, but secondary, outcome.

D. Maximizing return on security investments is a useful, but secondary, outcome.

8. **A. Business and regulatory requirements are the driving factors for data retention.**

B. Integrity is a key factor for information security; however, business and regulatory requirements are the driving factors for data retention.

C. Availability is a key factor for information security; however, business and regulatory requirements are the driving factors for data retention.

D. Confidentiality is a key factor for information security; however, business and regulatory requirements are the driving factors for data retention.

9. **A. Data owners are responsible for periodic reconfirmation of access lists for systems they own.**

B. Information security managers are in charge of coordinating user access list reviews, but they do not have any responsibility for data access.

C. Domain administrators may technically provide access, but they do not approve it.

D. Business manager is incorrect because the business managers may not be the data owners.

10. **A. The information security manager is responsible for developing a security strategy based on business objectives with the help of business process owners and senior management.**

B. The information security strategy is the responsibility of a steering committee and/or senior management.

C. The information security manager is not necessarily responsible for communicating the security strategy.

D. Final approval of the information security strategy must be made by senior management.

Part A: Enterprise Governance

Information can be defined as "data endowed with meaning and purpose." Information plays a critical role in all aspects of our lives. Information has become an indispensable component of conducting business for virtually all enterprises. In a growing number of companies, information is the business. Similarly, a broad array of technology continues to make it possible to access information. Together, IT constitutes key elements in every enterprise.

Enterprise IT is increasingly important. Because a majority of national critical infrastructures in the developed world are controlled by the private sector, much of the task of protecting critical information resources falls squarely on private corporations. In many enterprises, reponsibility for that resource protection resides within two important and distinct components—governance and management. COBIT describes them as follows:

- **Governance** ensures that the needs of various stakeholders are evaluated to determine balanced, agreed-on enterprise objectives. Those objectives are then used to set direction (through prioritization and decision making) and to monitor performance and compliance.
- **Management** plans, builds, runs and monitors activities, in alignment with the direction set by the governance body, to achieve enterprise objectives.

Given the criticality of IT, one would expect those factors to be key considerations for the governing body. However, studies show a large percentage of enterprises do not adequately address either existing or emerging security issues. Some enterprise leaders continue to believe that existing information security programs are insufficient to meet the needs of the enterprise and often feel that the security budget is inadequate to address current risk effectively.

Information security failures can be seen predominantly as a failure of governance and cannot be solved by technology alone. The need for adequate protection of information resources needs to be raised at the board level, like other critical governance functions, to lead to action. The complexity, relevance and criticality of information security and its governance mandate that it be addressed and supported at the highest organizational levels. Similarly, governance objectives increasingly include the need to determine the internal and external requirements for the enterprise's privacy programs and practices. While these objectives are distinct from information security considerations and are the jurisdiction of a data privacy engineer,[1] the governance body should ensure that both security and privacy are adequately addressed throughout the enterprise.

Ultimately, to achieve significant improvement in information security, senior management and the board of directors must be held accountable for information security governance and must provide the necessary leadership, organizational structures, oversight, resources and processes to ensure that information security governance is an integral and transparent part of enterprise governance. Because information security risk is a business risk and has direct line of sight to business objectives in most enterprises, accountability among security practitioners and business leaders regarding enterprise risk decisions needs to be balanced.

Increasingly, those who understand the scope and depth of risk to information take the position that information, as a critical resource, must be treated with the same care, caution and prudence as any other asset essential to the survival of the enterprise.

Often, the focus of protection has been on the IT systems that process and store the vast majority of information rather than on the information itself. However, this approach is too narrow to accomplish the level of integration, process assurance and overall security that are required. Information security takes the larger view that content and information, and knowledge based on it, must be adequately protected, regardless of how it is handled, processed, transported or stored. Increasingly, this protection includes the need to consider cloud-based technology and other virtual technology platforms.

Enterprises exist to create value for their stakeholders. Consequently, any enterprise—commercial or not—has value creation as a governance objective. Value creation means realizing benefits at an optimal resource cost while optimizing risk (**figure 1.1**). Benefits can take many forms, such as financial for commercial enterprises and high-quality public service for government entities.

[1] See the CDPSE job practice at www.isaca.org/credentialing/certified-data-privacy-solutions-engineer for more context.

Figure 1.1—The Governance Objective: Value Creation

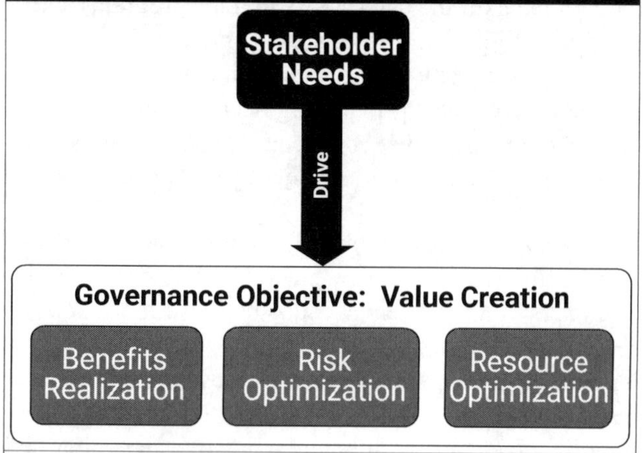

Source: ISACA, *COBIT 2019*, USA, 2018

Enterprises have many stakeholders, and "creating value" means different—and sometimes conflicting—things to each of them. Governance is about negotiating and deciding among different stakeholders' value interests. Consequently, the governance system should consider all stakeholders when making benefit, risk and resource assessment decisions. Stakeholder needs must be transformed into the enterprise's actionable strategy (for example, through the COBIT goals cascade).

Senior management is increasingly confronted by the need to stay competitive in the global economy and heed the promise of ever greater gains from the deployment of more information resources. Even as enterprises reap those gains, the increasing dependence on information and the systems that support it, and the advancing risk from an increasing host of threats, are forcing management to make difficult and often costly decisions about how to effectively address information security. In addition, scores of new and existing laws and regulations are increasingly demanding compliance and higher levels of accountability due to government efforts to address increasingly sophisticated attacks and growing losses that pose mounting threats to their national critical infrastructures.

COBIT provides some helpful principles for enterprise governance, including core requirements of a governance system for enterprise information and technology, and a governance framework that can be used to build a governance system.

It states that a governance system for enterprise IT:

- Is built from numerous components that can be of different types and that work together holistically.
- Is dynamic and adjusts to changes in the environment and the impact of those changes.
- Clearly distinguishes between governance and management activities and structures.
- Is tailored to the needs of the enterprise, using a set of design factors as parameters to customize and prioritize governance system components.
- Covers the enterprise end to end, focusing not only on the IT function but also on all the other technology and information processing the enterprise puts in place to achieve its goals, regardless of where the processing is located in the enterprise.

1.1 Importance of Information Security Governance

From an enterprise's perspective, information security governance is increasingly critical. For many, information has become essential to survival.

Information and the knowledge based on it are among the most important enterprise assets because conducting business without them would not be possible. The systems and processes that handle information are pervasive throughout enterprises globally. Reliance on information and related systems has made information security governance a critical facet of overall enterprise governance. In addition to addressing legal and regulatory requirements, effective information security governance supports good business practices. Prudent management provides a series of significant benefits, including:

- Addressing the increasing potential for civil or legal liability inuring to the enterprise and senior management as a result of information inaccuracy, insufficient information protection or inadequate regulatory compliance
- Providing assurance of policy compliance
- Increasing predictability and reducing uncertainty of business operations by lowering risk to definable and acceptable levels
- Providing the structure and framework to optimize allocations of limited security resources

- Providing a level of assurance that critical decisions are not based on faulty information
- Providing a firm foundation for efficient and effective risk management, process improvement, rapid incident response and continuity management
- Providing greater confidence in interactions with trading partners
- Improving trust in customer relationships
- Protecting the enterprise's reputation
- Enabling new and better ways to process electronic transactions
- Providing accountability for safeguarding information during critical business activities, such as mergers and acquisitions, business process recovery and regulatory response
- Effective management of information security resources

1.1.1 Outcomes of Information Security Governance

Information security governance includes the elements required to provide senior management assurance that its direction and intent are reflected in the security posture of the enterprise. This is achieved by using a structured approach to implementing a security program. Once the elements are in place, senior management can be confident that adequate and effective information security will protect the enterprise's vital information assets.

The objective of information security governance is to develop, implement and manage a security program that achieves the following six basic outcomes:

1. **Strategic alignment**—Aligning information security with business strategy to support organizational objectives, such as:
   - Security requirements that are driven by enterprise requirements and provide guidance on what must be done along with a means of measuring achievement
   - Security solutions that are compatible with enterprise processes and take into account the culture, governance style, technology and structure of the enterprise
   - Information security investments that are aligned with enterprise strategy and operations and enable development of a well-defined threat, vulnerability and risk profile
2. **Risk management**—Mitigating risk and reducing potential impacts on information resources to an acceptable level through execution of appropriate measures, such as:
   - Collective understanding of the enterprise's threat, vulnerability and risk profile
   - Understanding of risk exposure and potential consequences of compromise
   - Awareness of risk management priorities based on potential consequences
   - Risk mitigation sufficient to achieve acceptable consequences of residual risk
   - Risk acceptance/deference based on an understanding of the potential consequences of residual risk
3. **Value delivery**—Optimizing security investments in support of business objectives, such as:
   - A standard set of security practices (i.e., baseline security requirements following adequate and sufficient practices proportionate to risk and potential impact)
   - Maintaining information security overheads at a minimum level while maintaining a security program that enables the enterprise to achieve its objectives
   - Prioritization and distribution of effort to areas with the greatest risk probability and highest business impact and benefit
   - Institutionalized and commoditized standards-based solutions that provide the greatest cost-effectiveness
   - Complete solutions covering enterprise processes and technology based on an understanding of the end-to-end business of the enterprise
   - A continuous improvement culture based on the understanding that security is an ongoing process, not an event
4. **Resource optimization**—Using information security knowledge and infrastructure efficiently and effectively to:
   - Ensure that knowledge is captured and available
   - Ensure that complete processes are added to the organizational IT manual as policies and procedures

- Document security processes and practices
- Develop security architectures to define and utilize infrastructure resources efficiently

5. **Performance measurement**—Monitoring and reporting on information security processes to ensure that objectives are achieved, including:
    - A well-defined, agreed-upon and meaningful set of metrics that are properly aligned with strategic objectives and provide the information needed for effective decisions at the strategic, management and operational levels
    - A measurement process that helps identify shortcomings and provides feedback on progress made toward resolving issues
    - Independent assurance provided by external assessments and audits
    - Criteria for identifying the most useful metrics among the variety of things that can be measured
6. **Assurance process integration**—Integrating all relevant assurance factors to ensure that processes operate as intended from end to end by:
    - Determining all organizational assurance functions
    - Developing formal relationships with other assurance functions
    - Coordinating all assurance functions for more cost-effective security
    - Ensuring that roles and responsibilities between assurance functions overlap and leave no gaps in protection
    - Employing a systems approach to information security planning, deployment, metrics and management

As these elements are developed and updated, the process by which the entity will perform governance of information and technology should be instantiated as policy and shared with applicable stakeholders.

1.1.2 Scope and Charter of Information Security Governance

Information security deals with all aspects of information in any medium (e.g., written, spoken, electronic), regardless of whether it is being created, viewed, transported, stored or destroyed. It differs from IT security, which is concerned with security of information within the boundaries of the technology domain, usually in a custodial capacity. It is important to note this distinction. IT usually is not the owner of most of the information in its systems; rather, it owns the machinery that processes it. The information is in IT's care, control and custody, and IT functions as a custodian for the data owners.

Many enterprises have a corporate security function in addition to an IT security operation. Ensuring the security of the IT systems is an essential function that must be governed by the information security policies and standards. However, confidential information disclosed in an elevator conversation or sent via the postal mail would be outside the scope of IT security and would fall squarely in the purview of information security.

Cybersecurity is an area of concern and importance to information security governance and management. It includes both information and IT security. Although definitions vary widely, a common view is that cybersecurity is a subdiscipline of information security. Specific areas of concern for cybersecurity include advanced persistent threats (APTs), malware, ransomware, phishing in all its forms and the host of other threats related to cyberspace. **Figure 1.2** shows the relationship of cybersecurity to information security. **Figure 1.3** shows how these two areas differ and overlap within an enterprise. Note that in many areas there has been a convergence of cybersecurity and information security in recent years.

Figure 1.2—Relationship Between Information Security and Cybersecurity

Source: ISACA, *Cybersecurity Fundamentals Study Guide, 3rd Edition,* USA, 2021

Figure 1.3—Information Security vs. Cybersecurity

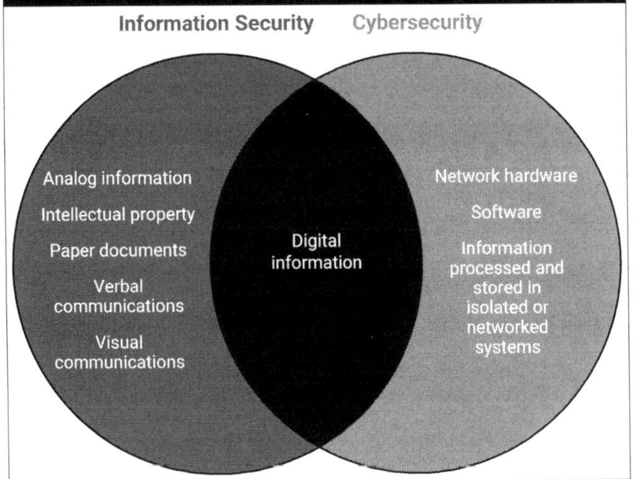

Source: ISACA, *Cybersecurity Fundamentals Study Guide, 3rd Edition*, USA, 2021

In the context of information security governance, it is important that the scope and responsibilities of information security are clearly set forth in the information security strategy and reflected in the policies. It is also essential that information security is fully supported by senior management and the various organizational units. Without clearly defined information security responsibilities, it is impossible to determine accountability.

1.2 Organizational Culture

Information security is primarily influenced through transparency and accountability throughout the enterprise culture. Culture is represented by organizational behavior, methods for navigating and influencing the enterprise's formal and informal structures to get work done, attitudes, norms, level of teamwork, existence or lack of turf issues, and geographic dispersion. Culture is impacted by individual backgrounds, work ethics, values, experiences, filters or blind spots, and the perceptions of life that individuals bring to the workplace. Every enterprise has a culture, whether it was purposely designed or simply emerged over time as a reflection of the leadership, and it must be considered in determining roles and responsibilities.

Information security primarily involves logical and analytical activities. However, building relationships, fostering teamwork and influencing organizational attitudes toward a positive security culture rely more on good interpersonal skills. The astute information security program manager will recognize the importance of developing both types of skills as essential to being an effective manager.

Building a security-aware culture depends on individuals in their respective roles performing their jobs in a way that protects information assets. All individuals, no matter what their level or role within the enterprise, should be able to articulate how information security relates to their role. For this to happen, the security manager must plan communications, participate in committees and projects, and provide individual attention to end users' and managers' needs. The security department should be able to answer the questions "What is in it for me?" and "Why should I care?" for every person in the enterprise. Once these questions have been answered, effective communications can be tailored to support the appropriate messages.

Some indicators of a successful security culture are the information security department being brought into projects at appropriate times, end users knowing how to identify and report incidents, the enterprise's ability to identify the security manager, and people knowing their role in protecting the information assets of the enterprise and integrating information security into their daily practices.

1.2.1 General Rules of Use/Acceptable Use Policy

To support a risk-aware and secure enterprise culture, all participants need to understand what behavior is acceptable, what activities are required and what actions are explicitly prohibited. An acceptable use policy provides a user-friendly summary of what personnel should do and avoid doing. This policy can detail—in everyday terms and in a straightforward, concise manner—the obligations and responsibilities of all users. It is necessary to effectively communicate the acceptable use policy to all users and ensure it is read and understood. The use policy should be provided to all new personnel who will have access to information assets, regardless of employment status.

Typically, the rules of use for all personnel include the policy and standards for access control, classification, marking and handling of documents and information, reporting requirements disclosure constraints, mobile computing, unlawful uses and enforcement. They may also include rules on email and Internet usage. The rules of use provide a general security baseline for the entire enterprise. It is often necessary to provide supplemental or additional information to specific groups in the enterprise, consistent with their responsibilities.

The information security manager should work with human resources (HR) and/or the compliance department to obtain acknowledgment from new hires that they understand and agree to fully comply with the acceptable use policy.

1.2.2 Ethics

Many enterprises have implemented ethics training to provide guidance on what the enterprise considers legal and appropriate behavior. This approach is most common when individuals are required to engage in activities of a particularly sensitive nature such as monitoring user activities, penetration testing, and accessing sensitive personal data. Information security personnel must be sensitive to potential conflicts of interest or activities that may be perceived as detrimental to the enterprise. Objectives and activities for ethical behavior should be coordinated with objectives and activities for privacy and data protection to ensure consistent and comprehensive consideration. These activities might include integration of data ethics frameworks[2] that can help define processes for appropriate and responsible data use in the enterprise.

Information security managers can set an example by sharing and adhering to their own ethical standards. The ISACA Code of Professional Ethics[3] is one example that guides the professional and personal conduct of members of the association and its certification holders. All information security personnel should refer to and acknowledge the enterprise's code of conduct or similar organizational policy for guidance on how to identify and report potential conflicts of interest. Examples of conflicts of interest include but are not limited to self-dealing, accepting gifts, improper influence, dual/multiple employment and use of corporate assets for private advantage. The signed acceptance of the code should be kept as a part of employee records.

1.3 Legal, Regulatory and Contractual Requirements

Each enterprise faces a broad array of requirements derived from local and international laws, other regulatory oversight mandates and contract-specific provisions related to information security. In preparation for creating strategy, the information security manager must gather as much information as possible about these overarching requirements. Information security is inevitably intertwined with questions of privacy; intellectual property; and contractual, civil and criminal law. Any effort to design and implement an effective information security strategy must be built on a solid understanding of the pertinent legal requirements and restrictions.

Different regions in a global enterprise may be governed by conflicting laws. For example, the level of legislative focus on privacy differs in different parts of the world, resulting in stricter privacy laws and regulations in some jurisdictions. In some countries, thorough background checks may be performed on new employees—checks that are illegal in other countries. To address these situations, the global enterprise may need to establish different security strategies for each regional division, or it can base policy on the most restrictive requirements to be consistent across the enterprise.

A number of legal and regulatory issues are associated with Internet business, global transmissions and transborder data flows (e.g., privacy, tax laws and tariffs, data import/export restrictions, warrants or subpoenas, restrictions on cryptography, warranties, patents, copyrights, trade secrets and national security). These vary depending upon the enterprise's location and may impose constraints and boundaries on security strategies. Research into these areas must be undertaken in conjunction with legal and regulatory departments and any areas of the business that may be affected.

From the perspective of the information security manager, regulatory compliance should be treated as any other risk and the extent of compliance is ultimately a business decision that must be made by senior management with input as to risk and potential impact.

[2] See the following for examples of a data ethics framework:
GOV.UK, "Guidance overview: Data Ethics Framework," 13 June 2018, www.gov.uk/government/publications/data-ethics-framework
Floridi, L.; M. Taddeo; "What is data ethics?", *Philosophical Transactions of the Royal Society A: Mathematical, Physical and Engineering Sciences*, 2016, www.turing.ac.uk/research/publications/what-data-ethics

[3] ISACA, "Code of Professional Ethics," www.isaca.org/credentialing/code-of-professional-ethics

Corporate legal departments are often primarily focused on contracts and securities or company stock-related matters. The result is that they are, in many cases, not directly tracking regulatory requirements, and the information security manager should not rely on the legal department to identify them. Typically, the impacted department will be the most knowledgeable about legal and regulatory issues. It is, however, prudent for the information security manager to request legal review and interpretation of legal requirements that have security implications to ensure clarity on the enterprise's official position on the matter. Governance, risk and compliance (GRC) automated capabilities may assist with maintaining a comprehensive catalog of legal and regulatory requirements.

In addition, the information security manager may be required to support legal standards related to privacy of information and transactions, the collection and handling of audit records, email retention policies, incident investigation procedures and cooperation with legal authorities. Legal issues must be taken into careful consideration whenever an employee of the enterprise is investigated or monitored, or when disciplinary action is taken for inappropriate behavior. Because legal and regulatory requirements differ considerably in different regions and jurisdictions, it is prudent to engage the HR and legal departments prior to taking such actions.

1.3.1 Requirements for Content and Retention of Business Records

Business records constitute a large subset of the information to be protected by the security strategy that will be developed, so it is important for the information security manager to understand the underlying requirements regarding those records. As one who provides input for creating the strategy, the information security manager must understand the business requirements regarding all types of enterprise records. Often, representatives from the enterprise legal department can help determine what types of records must be protected to ensure their confidentiality, integrity and availability. The legal affairs representatives can also provide information regarding legal and regulatory requirements for enterprise documents (including electronic messages and files).

Business requirements may exceed the legal and regulatory requirements imposed by applicable legislating bodies due to the nature of the enterprise's business. Some enterprises have business needs requiring access to data that are 10 to 20 years old, or more. This type of data can include, for example, customer records, patient records and engineering information. As a rule, the retention strategy and subsequent policy must, at a minimum, meet the legal requirements in the applicable jurisdiction and industry.

Depending upon location and industry, regulatory bodies have requirements that an enterprise must comply with, including those applicable to legal, medical and tax records.

Regulations such as Sarbanes-Oxley[4] have imposed various mandatory retention requirements for various types and categories of information, regardless of the storage medium. The enterprise's retention strategy will require the information security manager to stay current with these requirements and ensure compliance. There may also be requirements stemming from any lawful preservation order that would require an enterprise or individual to retain specific data at the behest of law enforcement or other authorities. It is also generally the case that archived information must be indexed sufficiently to be located and retrieved.

Increasingly, civil and criminal actions rely on evidence obtained from email and other electronic communications in response to a production request or subpoena. If information has been archived without being classified and cataloged, retrieving the required material can be an arduous and expensive task, as a number of high-profile cases have shown. The increasing prevalence of this type of discovery contributes to the need for careful consideration of a retention policy that limits the length of time—within the bounds of legal requirements—that certain information, such as email, is retained. Generally, the best option is to have a policy that requires destruction of any data not required to be retained by law or for specific business reasons.

The information security manager should, in conjunction with all applicable departments, enforce and maintain a data retention policy that includes a retention schedule. Additionally, certificates of destruction should be maintained as proof of compliance with secure disposal

[4] Corporate Finance Institute, "Sarbanes-Oxley Act," https://corporatefinanceinstitute.com/resources/knowledge/other/sarbanes-oxley-act/

requirements when an authorized third party eradicates any media.

1.4 Organizational Structures, Roles and Responsibilities

Enterprise governance requires responsibility and accountability from all participants. Due to their interdependencies, the organizational operating structures, the various roles defined within those structures and the responsibilities of participants in each role will constitute key inputs into an information security strategy.

COBIT points out some attributes of a successful organizational structure that should be understood by information security managers in preparation for strategy development. If these attributes are not in place, strategy activities might include working with enterprise stakeholders to incorporate them. Key considerations for an effective organizational structure:

- The organizational structure is formally established.
- The organizational structure has a clear, documented and well-understood mandate.
- Operating principles are documented and followed.
- Levels of authority and responsibilities for decision-making are defined and documented, including clear organizational charts or organigrams where possible.
- Provisions for delegation of authority are understood and implemented.
- Escalation procedures are defined and applied.
- Objectives for the performance of the organizational structures are identified, monitored and adjusted, as needed.
- Interfaces between the organizational structure and other stakeholders are managed to ensure both effective communication and clear assignment of responsibility.
- Regular evaluations result in the required continuous improvement of the organizational structure—in its composition, mandate and other parameters.

An examination of the organizational hierarchy and structure within the enterprise will enable the information security manager to understand the various stakeholders involved in the coordination, creation and management of the information security strategy. Notably, that hierarchy may not always be intuitive. The tendency to segment security into separate but related functions has created the need to integrate a variety of assurance processes found in a typical enterprise. These activities are often fragmented and segmented in silos with different reporting structures. The terminology associated with these activities generally reflects different understandings of processes and outcomes, at times with little in common. These assurance silos can include risk management, change management, internal and external audit, privacy offices, insurance offices, HR, legal and others. Evaluating business processes from start to finish (along with their controls), regardless of which particular assurance process is involved, can mitigate the tendency for security gaps to exist in various assurance functions.

Convergence is another structural consideration. Security-related activities are sometimes divided into separate divisions, such as physical security, IT security, risk management, privacy, compliance and information security. This approach has not been conducive to achieving optimal results, leading professionals and managers to reconsider this separation. The chief information security officer (CISO) may be elevated to chief security officer (CSO), with responsibility for a broad range of risk types, which can help to better integrate security elements. Integration of both the roles and infrastructure for physical security and information security is becoming commonplace. Because it is not possible to effectively deliver information security without a number of physical considerations, the evolution is natural. It is reasonable to expect that integration of many security activities will center around information security in the coming decade. As a result, integration of physical security and other assurance functions will be an increasingly relevant consideration for management.

Convergence is a holistic and encompassing approach that looks beyond assets and considers such factors as culture, organizational structure and processes. Delivering on convergence requires more than organizational integration. It is about integrating the security disciplines with the business's mission to deliver shareholder value through consistent, predictable operations while optimizing the allocation of security resources.

As new technologies emerge and threats become increasingly complex and unpredictable, senior security executives recognize the need to merge security functions throughout the entire enterprise. An incident at the Sumitomo Mitsui Bank in London, England, in which hackers attempted to steal £229 million from the bank, underlies this principle.[5] Even though the bank had strong IT security measures in place, a physical security lapse occurred. Adversaries posing as janitors installed devices on computer keyboards (i.e., keyloggers) that allowed them to obtain valuable login information. This incident highlights and reinforces the need to converge all components of an enterprise's security through an integrated and deliberate approach. To be effective, a converged approach should reach across people, processes and technology, and enable enterprises to prevent, detect, respond to and recover from any type of security incident.

In addition to the costs that companies face to deal with their immediate consequences, security incidents can cause long-term harm, such as damage to reputation and brand. Beyond the impact on market capitalization, there is the possibility that regulators may intervene if the issue threatens the public good, enacting stricter requirements for future business practices.

1.4.1 Roles and Responsibilities

Clear definitions, both of organizational roles and of the responsibilities of those who hold them, are key to effective information security governance. Because everyone in the enterprise has some information security responsibilities, it is essential to clearly define them and communicate those responsibilities throughout the enterprise on a recurring basis.

A **role** is a designation assigned to an individual by virtue of a job function or other label. A **responsibility** is a description of some procedure or function related to the role that someone is accountable to perform. Roles are important to information security because they enable responsibilities and access rights to be assigned based on the function an individual performs rather than to specific individuals. There are typically many job functions in the enterprise that support security functions, and the ability to assign access authorizations based on roles simplifies administration.

An important tool for documenting and coordinating responsibility is the RACI chart (or RACI matrix).

The name of this chart is derived from the names of the activities it describes for each role. This matrix depicts a set of roles on one axis and a set of responsibilities on another. At the intersection of each, an indication of one or more relevant role assignments is included, as follows:

- **Responsible (R)** roles take the main operational stake in fulfilling the practice and create the intended outcome. Who is getting the task done? Who drives the task?
- **Accountable (A)** roles carry overall accountability. As a principle, accountability cannot be shared. Who accounts for the success and achievement of the task?
- **Consulted (C)** roles provide input for the practice. Who is providing input?
- **Informed (I)** roles are informed of the achievements and deliverables of the practice. Who is receiving information?

Note that while the party in the accountable (A) role may delegate some or all responsibility to other participants, that party retains accountability for ensuring that a task or activity is fulfilled in an acceptable manner. Thus, while several parties may have R indications included in the matrix, there will generally be only one role with an A in each row.

RACI charts can be used effectively in defining the various roles associated with an information security program. Clear designation of roles and responsibilities is necessary to ensure effective implementation. **Figure 1.4** shows a number of typical organizational roles and related governance activities.

[5] Wattanajantra, A.; "Hackers hit bank's London offices in £229 million heist," ITPro, 22 January 2009, www.itpro.com/609610/hackers-hit-banks-london-offices-in-229-million-heist

Figure 1.4—Example RACI Chart

Decision Topic	Scope	Responsible, Accountable, Consulted, Informed (RACI)							
		Executive Committee	I&T Governance Board	Enterprise Risk Committee	Portfolio Manager	Steering (Programs/Projects) Committee	IT Management	Business Process Owners	Employees
Governance	• Integrating with enterprise governance • Establishing principles, structures, objectives	A/R	R	C			C	R	I
Enterprise strategy	• Defining enterprise goals and objectives • Deciding where and how I&T can enable and support enterprise objectives	A/R	R	C			C	R	I
I&T policies	• Providing accurate, understandable and approved policies, procedures, guidelines and other documentation to stakeholders • Developing and rolling out I&T policies • Ensuring that policies result in beneficial outcomes in accordance with guiding principles • Enforcing I&T policies	I	A	C			R	C	C
I&T strategy	• Incorporating IT and business management in the translation of business requirements into service offerings and developing strategies to deliver services in a transparent and effective manner • Engaging with business and senior management in aligning I&T strategic planning with current and future business needs • Understanding current I&T capabilities • Providing a business objectives prioritization scheme that quantifies business requirements	I	A	C	I		R	C	C

Source: ISACA, *COBIT 2019 Implementation Guide: Implementing and Optimizing an Information and Technology Governance Solution USA, 2018*

Skills

Skills must be considered when developing RACI charts. Skills are the training, expertise and experience held by the personnel in a given job function. It is important to understand the proficiencies of available personnel to ensure they map to competencies required for program implementation. Specific skills needed for program implementation can be acquired through training or from external resources. External resources, such as consultants, are often a more cost-effective choice for skills required for only a short time for specific projects.

Upon agreement that certain personnel will have specific information security responsibilities, formal employment agreements should be established that reference those responsibilities. Those agreements must be considered when screening applicants for employment.

Board of Directors

Board members need to be aware of the enterprise's information assets, risk to those assets and their criticality to ongoing business operations. The board should periodically be provided with the high-level results of comprehensive risk assessments and business impact analyses (BIAs). This information should inform board members in validating/ratifying the key assets they want protected and ensuring that protection levels and priorities are appropriate to a standard of due care.

Security expectations should be met at all levels of the enterprise. Penalties for noncompliance must be defined, communicated and enforced from the board level down.

Beyond these requirements, the board has an ongoing obligation to provide a level of oversight with respect to information security activities. Given the legal and ethical responsibility of directors to exercise due care in protecting the enterprise's key assets, which include its confidential and other critical information, an ongoing level of information security involvement and oversight is required.

There are specific reasons that mandate the board of directors involvement with and oversight of information security activities. A common concern is liability. Most enterprises, to protect themselves from shareholder lawsuits, provide specific insurance to create a level of protection for the board in exercising its governance responsibilities. However, a typical requirement of this insurance is that directors make a good faith effort to exercise due care in the discharge of their duties. Neglecting to address information security risk may constitute a failure to exercise due care and may void the protection provided by insurance.

The US Sarbanes-Oxley Act mandates that every company listed on a US stock exchange maintain an audit committee with a required level of experience and demonstrable competence. This committee is often comprised of members of the company's board of directors. One of the committee's key responsibilities is the ongoing monitoring of the enterprise's internal controls that directly affect the reliability of financial statements. Most financial controls are technical and procedural, with the technical portion generally under the scope of the information security manager. It is important for the security manager to maintain an open channel of communication with this committee.

Institutional investors and others have come to understand that the long-term prospects for an enterprise are heavily impacted by the overall state of governance. Corporate rating enterprises provide a governance rating or metric based on a number of factors. Failure to provide an adequate level of governance and support for activities that protect the major assets of the enterprise is likely to be reflected in those scores. The weight and relevance of the scores will be driven by the consequences for enterprises that suffer the loss of significant critical and sensitive information. The bottom line is that a board of directors should provide direction, oversight and requirements for appropriate metrics. A 2019 meeting of the National Association of Corporate Directors Risk Oversight Advisory Council affirmed that cyber-risk reporting to the board should evolve to keep pace with the changing needs of the enterprise and of the board itself.[6]

Senior Management

As with any other major initiative, information security must have leadership and ongoing support from senior management to succeed. An enterprise's senior management team is responsible for ensuring that needed organizational functions, resources and supporting infrastructure are available and properly used

[6] National Association of Corporate Directors, "NACD Risk Oversite Advisory Council: Current and Emerging Practices in Cyber-Risk Oversight," 4 June 2019, www.nacdonline.org/insights/publications.cfm?ItemNumber=65591

to fulfill the information security-related directives of the board, achieve regulatory compliance and meet other demands.

In addition, IT is often faced with performance pressures, while security must deal with risk and regulatory issues. These imperatives all too often fall at opposite ends of the spectrum. The result can be tension between IT and security, and it is important that senior management promote cooperation, arbitrate differences in perspective and be clear about priorities, so that performance, cost and security can be balanced appropriately.

Business Process Owners

Development of an effective information security strategy requires the involvement and cooperation of business process owners. A successful outcome is the alignment of information security activities in support of business objectives. The extent to which this outcome is realized determines the cost-effectiveness of the information security program in achieving the desired objectives of a predictable, defined level of assurance for business processes and an acceptable level of impact from adverse events.

Steering Committee

Security affects all aspects of an enterprise to some extent and must be pervasive throughout the enterprise to be effective. To ensure that all stakeholders impacted by security considerations are involved, many enterprises form a steering committee comprised of senior representatives of affected groups. The steering committee helps to achieve consensus on priorities and trade-offs. It serves as an effective communications channel and ensures the security program is aligned with business objectives. It can also be instrumental in achieving modification of behavior toward a culture more conducive to good security.

Common topics, agendas and decisions for a security steering committee include:

- Security strategy and integration efforts, especially efforts to integrate security with business unit activities
- Specific actions and progress relative to business unit support of information security program functions and vice versa
- Emerging risk, business unit security practices and compliance issues

The information security manager should make sure that the roles, responsibilities, scope and activities of the information security steering committee are clearly defined. This should include articulating clear objectives and agenda topics to avoid poor productivity or distractions from committee priorities.

It is important that materials be distributed, reviews encouraged and solution discussions held in advance of full committee meetings so that meeting participants can focus on resolving issues and making decisions. The use of subcommittees and individual action assignments is appropriate for this type of management strategy.

Chief Information Security Officer

All enterprises have a CISO, regardless of whether anyone officially holds that title. It may be the chief information officer (CIO), chief security officer (CSO), chief financial officer (CFO) or chief executive officer (CEO). For many enterprises, the CISO also works closely with the chief privacy officer (CPO) or data privacy officer (DPO) who has overall responsibility for the enterprise privacy management program.

The scope and breadth of information security is such that the authority required to make decisions and the responsibility to act will inevitably be held by a C-level officer or senior manager. Legal responsibility will extend up the command structure by default and ultimately reside with senior management and the board of directors. Failure to implement appropriate governance structures can result in senior management being unaware of this responsibility and exposed to the attendant liability. It usually results in a lack of effective alignment of security activities with organizational objectives.

While the elevation of the information security manager to an executive role is a global trend, it is not consistent across sectors and the responsibilities and authority of information security managers vary dramatically among enterprises. These responsibilities currently range from the CISO or vice president for security reporting to the CEO or board of directors, to system administrators who have part-time responsibility for security management reporting to the IT manager or CIO.

A main concern, according to PricewaterhouseCoopers, is a CISO having an inadequate budget to successfully execute the security program and provide adequate attention to end users' or managers' needs.[7] It is essential that the information security manager be able to demonstrate why an adequate budget is a necessary component to ensuring that information security programs are able to address current and emerging risk. As shown in Chapter 2, identification and quantification of risk helps the manager to build and support an effective business case.[8] Through this process, the information security manager is not simply asking for more resources, but also working with stakeholders to align objectives, resource optimization and risk management.

Risk Management Roles and Responsibilities

Managing risk effectively at an acceptable cost is the basis for the objectives and drivers of information security governance and programs to implement, develop and manage it. While risk management is ultimately a responsibility of senior management and the board of directors, everyone in an enterprise has a role to play. It is important that all risk management activities be integrated and operate under a consistent set of rules and clear objectives. This will help prevent gaps in protection, provide a more consistent level of protection, reduce needless redundant efforts and help keep different parts of the enterprise from operating at cross purposes.

The US National Institute of Standards and Technology (NIST) *Special Publication 800-30 Revision 1: Guide for Conducting Risk Assessments* describes the key roles of personnel who must support and participate in the risk management process. While the specifics in different enterprises and different countries may vary, this high-level view generally maps to most enterprises. In many enterprises, the information security manager is the CISO with executive-level status, reporting directly to senior management.

Figure 1.5 describes some relevant roles and components of organizational structures, an understanding of which helps guide information security strategy development as described in Part B.

Figure 1.5—Information Security Related Roles and Organizational Structures

Role	Description
Governing boards and senior management	Senior management, under the standard of due care and ultimate responsibility for mission accomplishment, must ensure that the necessary resources are effectively applied to develop the capabilities needed to accomplish the mission. Senior management must also assess and incorporate results of the risk assessment activity into the decision-making process. An effective risk management program that assesses and mitigates IT-related mission risk requires the support and involvement of senior management.
Chief risk officer (CRO)	The CRO is generally charged with overall enterprise risk management, which may include information security. Generally, this position includes all noninformation risk such as operational risk, environmental risk and credit risk.
Chief information officer (CIO)	The CIO is responsible for IT planning, budgeting and performance. Responsibilities often include information security components consistent with the policies and standards under the purview of the CISO or information security manager.
Chief information security officer (CISO)	The CISO generally performs most of the same functions as an information security manager but holds officer status in an enterprise, usually accompanied by greater authority. The CISO typically reports to the CEO, chief operating officer (COO) or board of directors. The position usually includes responsibility for more strategic and management elements than the typical information security manager role.
Information security manager (ISM)	Information security managers are responsible for enterprise security programs, usually including information risk management. Therefore, they play a leading role in introducing an appropriate, structured methodology to help identify, evaluate and minimize risk to information resources, including the IT systems that support enterprise missions. Information security managers generally act as major consultants in support of senior management to ensure that appropriate activities are ongoing.

7 PricewaterhouseCoopers, "The Global State of Information Security Survey 2017," www.pwc.com/gx/en/consulting-services/information-security-survey

8 Columbus, L.; "The Best Cybersecurity Predictions For 2021 Roundup," Forbes, 15 December 2020, www.forbes.com/sites/louiscolumbus/2020/12/15/the-best-cybersecurity-predictions-for-2021-roundup/

Figure 1.5—Information Security Related Roles and Organizational Structures *(cont.)*

Role	Description
System and information owners	System and information owners are responsible for ensuring that proper controls are in place to address confidentiality, integrity and availability of the IT systems and data they own. Typically, the system and information owners are responsible for changes to IT systems and are responsible for ensuring policy compliance and enforcement. Thus, they usually have to approve and sign off on changes to their IT systems and are involved in the policies and standards that govern them (e.g., system enhancement, major changes to the software and hardware, and compliance requirements). Therefore, system and information owners must understand the risk management objectives, their role in the risk management process and the requirements to provide support for the process.
Business and functional managers	The managers responsible for business operations and the IT procurement process must take an active role in the risk management process. These managers have the authority and responsibility for making the trade-off decisions essential to mission accomplishment. Their involvement in the risk management process enables the achievement of proper security for the IT systems, which, if managed properly, will provide mission effectiveness with acceptable expenditure of resources.
IT security practitioners	IT security practitioners (e.g., network, system, application and database administrators; computer specialists; security analysts; security consultants) are responsible for proper implementation of security requirements in their IT systems. As changes occur in the existing IT system environment (e.g., expansion in network connectivity, changes to the existing infrastructure and organizational policies, standards or procedures, introduction of new technologies), the IT security practitioners must support or use the risk management process to identify and assess new potential risk and ensure implementation of new security controls as needed to safeguard their IT systems.
Security awareness trainers (security/subject matter professionals)	The enterprise's personnel are the users of the IT systems. Use of the IT systems and data according to an enterprise's policies, guidelines and rules of behavior is critical to mitigating risk and protecting the enterprise's IT resources. To manage risk to acceptable levels, it is essential that system, data and application users and custodians be provided with training in security awareness and in the processes and requirements for secure operations. Therefore, the IT security trainers or security/subject matter professionals must understand the enterprise's risk management objectives and processes so they can develop appropriate training materials and incorporate risk management requirements into training programs for end users.

Key components of the governance system include culture, requirements, and roles and responsibilities, all of which provide helpful and necessary inputs into understanding enterprise needs and contribute to development of a strategy for optimizing enterprise risk and resource utilization. Activities specific to the development of a strategy are described next.

Part B: Information Security Strategy

Information security governance is the responsibility of the board of directors and senior management. It must be an integral and transparent part of enterprise governance and complement or encompass the IT governance framework. While senior management has the responsibility to consider and respond to increasingly complex and potentially destructive information security issues, boards of directors will be required to make information security an intrinsic part of governance, integrated with the processes they have in place to govern other critical organizational resources. These include monitoring and reporting processes to ensure that governance is effective and that compliance enforcement is sufficient to reduce risk to acceptable levels.

To demonstrate capability maturity model integration (CMMI®), a strategy should include methods for ensuring an integrated and repeatable approach to governance and management. To optimize value, risk and resources, everyone in the enterprise needs to work together. Many of the processes described in this guide foster collaboration among various business areas; this collaboration can be improved and maintained using many of the practices described in the integrated CMMI product suite. ISACA's CMMI models have expanded beyond software engineering to help enterprises around the world, in any industry, understand their current level of capability and performance and offer a guide to optimize business results. Thus, CMMI provides a helpful input for creating a strategy that is repeatable, predictable and consistent.

According to the developers of "The ISACA Business Model for Information Security" (see Section 1.5.5 The Desired State), "It is no longer enough to communicate to the world of stakeholders why we [the organization] exist and what constitutes success, we must also communicate how we are going to protect our existence."[9] This suggests that a clear organizational strategy for preservation is equally important to, and must accompany, a strategy for progress.

In addition to protection of information assets, effective information security governance is required to address legal and regulatory requirements and is becoming mandatory in the exercise of due care.

1.5 Information Security Strategy Development

Risk optimization is a key element of the governance and management of enterprise IT. Management activities and structures, which are distinct from and derived from governance activities, are outlined in the information security strategy. Based on the foundation described in Part A, the information security strategy will provide the plan of action by which the information security manager will accomplish enterprise needs, including those enabling the enterprise to achieve an acceptable level of risk while optimizing resources.

Each of the following elements is key to determining the necessary elements of a strategy, determining risk criteria (described in Chapter 2), and implementing a holistic information security program (described in Chapter 3).

1.5.1 Business Goals and Objectives

Corporate governance is the exercise of a set of responsibilities and practices by the board and senior management with the goals of providing strategic direction, ensuring that objectives are achieved, ascertaining that risk is managed appropriately and verifying that the enterprise's resources are used responsibly. Strategy is the plan to achieve an objective. The strategic direction of the business is defined by the objectives set forth in the strategy. To be of value to the enterprise, information security must support the business strategy and the activities that take place to achieve the objectives.

Information security governance is a subset of corporate governance. It provides strategic direction for security activities and ensures that objectives are achieved. It ensures that information security risk is appropriately managed and enterprise information resources are used effectively and efficiently.

Note that the main requirement for IT is an adequate level of performance; for information security, it is managing risk to an acceptable level. Once outcomes, requirements and the objectives that will meet the requirements are established, a high-level conceptual security architecture can be considered. The security

[9] Von Roessing, R.; "The ISACA Business Model for Information Security," 2010, https://link.springer.com/chapter/10.1007/978-3-8348-9363-5_4#citeas

architecture should simply be an overlay on the enterprise architecture, although ideally these would be created simultaneously to integrate the security elements.

When the basic information security/risk management strategy is formulated, a logical architecture showing the various functions and data flows can be developed. A road map can then be laid out with the specific steps needed to attain the goals defined in the strategy. The specifics include the control objectives necessary to achieve acceptable risk levels. Some of these objectives will best be achieved with technologies defined in the physical architecture. The physical architecture consists of specific devices, such as servers, databases, firewalls, switches and routers, along with their interconnections. Controls must be developed that are consistent with the standards, and control choices will affect the specifics of both the physical and the operational architectures. Both the strategy and information security procedures are input into the operational architecture.

Figure 1.6 shows the relationship between IT and information security governance and the sequence of the development process. Once the information security strategy has been developed, it must inform the IT strategy to ensure adequate protection for information assets and to align subsequent IT development and management processes with information security requirements.

Strategy definitions vary widely in scope, emphasis and detail, but generally align with the military concept that strategy represents "the plan to achieve an objective." As is typical, the basic concept has expanded and grown more complex, although this does not always serve to improve understanding of the concept. Two initial elements are needed to develop a plan: well-defined objectives and an understanding of the current conditions. Essentially, a strategy requires knowing where you are and where you need to go, then analyzing the gap between those two stages to determine what needs to be accomplished to bridge the gap. While a straightforward notion, numerous considerations and a host of activities must be examined both in developing the objectives and determining what is required to achieve them.

Figure 1.6—Relationship of Governance Elements

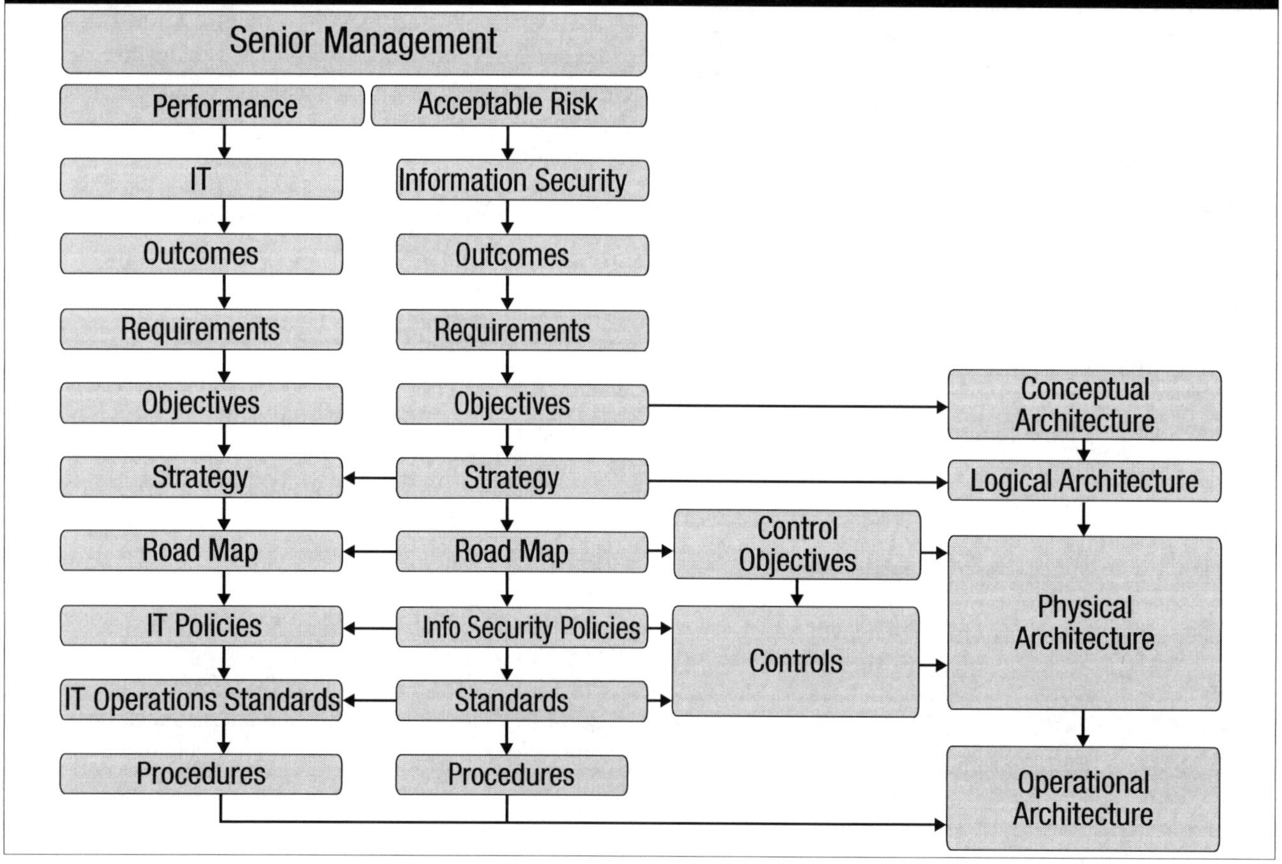

Figure 1.7 shows the participants involved in developing a security strategy and their relationships and aligns them with business objectives. The arrow marked "Business Strategy" provides the basis for a road map to achieve the "Business Objectives." In addition, it should provide one of the primary inputs into "Risk Management" plans and the "Information Security Strategy." This flow serves to promote alignment of information security with business goals. The balance among inputs comes from determining the desired state of security compared to the existing, or current, state. Business processes must be considered along with key organizational risk, including regulatory requirements, risk analysis and the associated impact analysis to determine protection levels and priorities. A constant constraint during the entire process is the enterprise's risk appetite and capacity discussed in Section 2.4.1 Determining Risk Capacity and Acceptance (Risk Appetite).

The objective of the security strategy is the desired state defined by business and security attributes. The strategy provides the basis for an action plan composed of one or more security programs that, as implemented, achieve the security objectives. The action plan must be formulated based on available resources and constraints, including consideration of relevant legal and regulatory requirements.

The strategy and action plans must contain provisions for monitoring and defined metrics to determine the level of success. This feedback allows the CISO and steering committee to make midcourse corrections and ensure that security initiatives are on track to meet defined objectives.

Figure 1.7—Information Security Strategy Development Participants

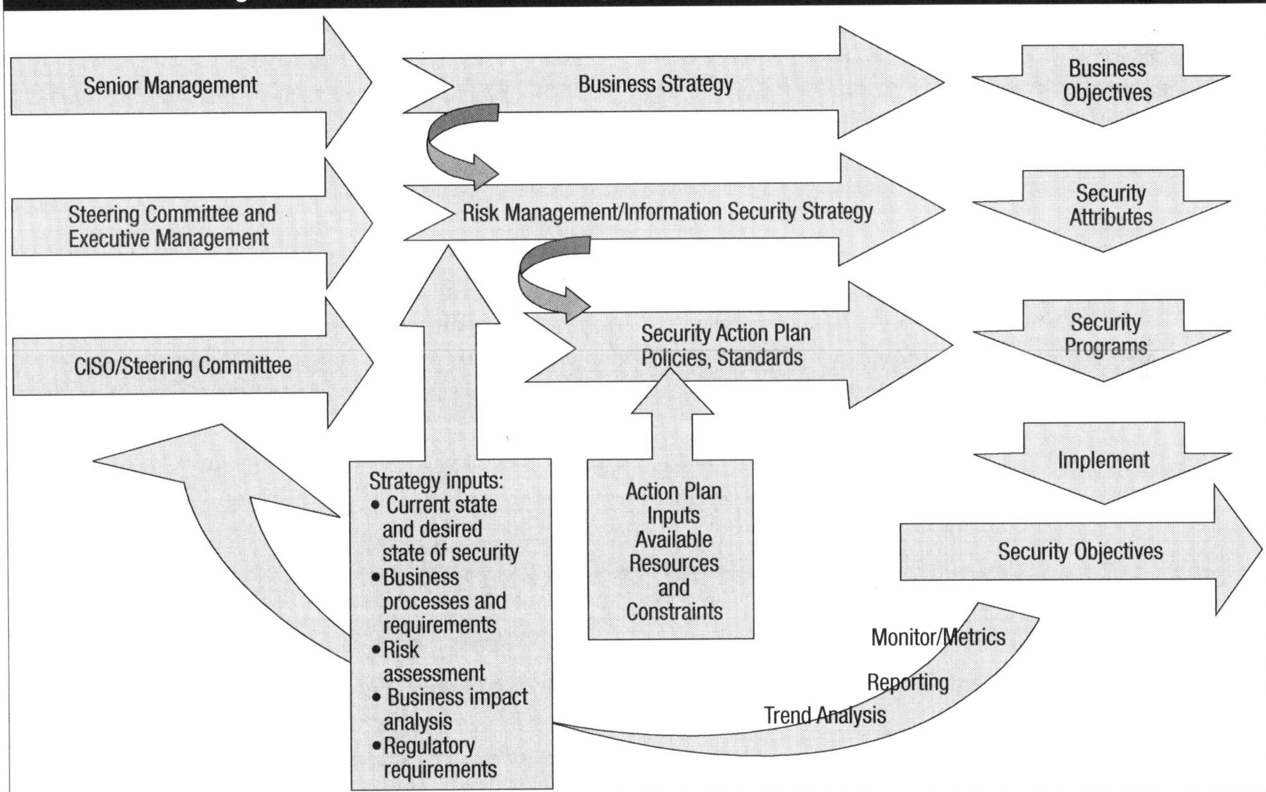

Source: ISACA, *Information Security Governance: Guidance for Information Security Managers*, USA, 2008

1.5.2 Information Security Strategy Objectives

The objectives of an information security strategy must be defined and metrics developed to determine if those objectives are being achieved. Typically, the six defined outcomes of security governance will provide high-level guidance.The six outcomes are:

- Strategic alignment
- Effective risk management
- Value delivery
- Resource optimization
- Performance measurement
- Assurance process integration

The strategy needs to address what each of the selected areas means to the enterprise, how each outcome might be achieved and what will constitute success.

Often surprisingly difficult, the first question that must be answered by an enterprise seeking to develop an information security strategy is this: What is the goal of the strategy and, ultimately, the program it enables?

Most enterprises fail to define the objectives of information security with any specificity. This may be because it seems obvious that the goal of information security is to protect the enterprise's information assets. However, that answer assumes knowledge of two things. One is that information assets are known with any degree of precision, which for most enterprises is not the case. The other is that there is an assumed understanding of what it means "to protect." Everyone understands the notion in general. It is considerably more difficult to state which assets need how much protection against what.

In part, this is because the enterprise typically has insufficient knowledge of what information exists within it. There is generally no process to purge useless, outdated or potentially dangerous information, data or unused applications. It is extremely rare to find a comprehensive catalog or index of information/processes to define what is important, what is not important or who owns what. As a result, everything typically gets saved, under the assumption that storage is cheaper than data classification, ownership assignment and the identification of users. For large enterprises, this can amount to terabytes of useless data and literally thousands of outdated and unused applications accumulated over decades.

This situation makes it difficult to devise a rational data protection plan because it makes little sense to expend resources to protect useless or dangerous data and information or unused applications. In this context, the description "dangerous data" refers to information that might be used to the detriment of the enterprise, such as damaging evidence obtained in litigation, which could have been destroyed subject to a legal and appropriate retention policy.

Assuming relevant information is located and identified, it must be classified by criticality and sensitivity or business value. Classification provides the basis for applying protective measures in proportion to the business value, resulting in more cost-effective controls. Because a great deal of a typical enterprise's data and information are neither critical nor sensitive, it is wasteful to expend substantial resources to protect them. For many enterprises, locating and classifying information assets may be a significant undertaking, and there is often a reluctance to allocate the resources necessary. However, this is a crucial step in developing a practical and useful information security strategy and a cost-effective security program.

Just as values are assigned to an enterprise's physical resources, values must be assigned to information to prioritize budget-constrained protection efforts and determine required levels of protection. Valuation of information is difficult to do with any precision. For some information, it can be the cost of creating or replacing it. In other cases, information in the form of knowledge or trade secrets is difficult or impossible to replace and may be priceless. It is obviously prudent to provide strong protection to priceless information.

One approach commonly used is to create a few rough levels of value—for example, from zero to five, with zero being of no value and five being critical. The zero-value would be assigned to information, including applications, if no owner could be determined and no use occurred for a period of time. Information of zero value could then be archived for a specified period, notices could be sent to business owners and, if there were no objections, it could be destroyed. Information deemed a five (critical) would be given the highest priority for protection efforts proportional to the other valuations.

Another approach that may be useful and substantially easier to perform is to conduct a business dependency evaluation as an indication of value. This process starts by defining critical business processes and then determining what information and physical assets are used in the process. The contribution these resources make to revenue provides a measure of the level of their criticality, which can be used as a guide for protection efforts.

Sensitivity will generally be a more subjective call. The unintended disclosure of sensitive information can have many ramifications that may be difficult to determine with any precision. The data owner is typically the best source of for determining the potential consequences of "data leakage" and is normally the individual determining the classification level for data. The classification level will subsequently provide the basis for protection efforts and access control. Most enterprises will use three or four sensitivity and criticality classifications, such as confidential, for internal use and public.

For most enterprises, asset classification is a daunting task, but one that must be undertaken for existing information if security governance is to be effective, efficient and relevant. Done correctly, classification mitigates the cost of overprotecting unimportant information and the risk of underprotecting high-value information. This task grows exponentially more onerous over time if it is not addressed. Policies, standards and processes must be developed concurrently to mandate classification moving forward and prevent related problems from getting worse. Overclassification is a serious problem for classification implementation. It can be particularly troublesome in enterprises with a blame culture, where mistakes are not well tolerated. In such environments, data owners may err on the side of caution by marking data more sensitive or critical than warranted, negating the potential benefits of classification. There is a practical solution for enterprises where IT operates on a chargeback system and IT services are a cost to the business units. In such cases, additional charges for higher classifications will tend to counteract the tendency to overclassify.

Another essential part of setting goals for information security is to ensure that all assets have a defined owner and defined accountability. This can be done effectively using RACI charts as discussed in Section 1.4.1 Roles and Responsibilities.

In summary, it will not be possible to develop a cost-effective security strategy that is aligned with business requirements prior to:

- Defining business requirements for information security
- Determining the objectives of information security that will satisfy the requirements
- Locating and identifying information assets and resources
- Valuating information assets and resources
- Classifying information assets as to criticality and sensitivity
- Implementing a process to ensure that all assets have a defined owner

1.5.3 Ensuring Objective and Business Integration

If an information security strategy is the basis for a plan of action to achieve security objectives, it is necessary to define those objectives. Defining long-term objectives in terms of a desired state of security is necessary for a number of reasons. Without a well-articulated vision of desired outcomes for a security program, it will not be possible to develop a meaningful strategy.

Without a strategy, it is not possible to develop a meaningful plan of action and the enterprise will continue to implement ad hoc tactical point solutions with nothing to provide overall integration. The resulting nonintegrated systems will be increasingly difficult to manage and will become ever more costly and difficult or impossible to secure.

Many enterprises do not allocate adequate resources to address these issues until a major incident occurs. This can result in outcomes that are far more costly than addressing issues properly in the beginning. In one case, for example, a breach of customer credit card records ultimately cost a retailer several hundred million US dollars to resolve. The numerous security governance, management and practices flaws subsequently uncovered when reviewing the event could have been remediated at a fraction of the eventual losses.

Many objectives are stated in terms of addressing risk. Information security strategy objectives should also be stated in terms of specific goals directly aimed at supporting business activities. Some risk mitigation, such as virus and other malware protection, should apply to the enterprise generally. Such protection is typically not considered a specific business enabler; rather, it supports the overall health of the enterprise by reducing adverse impacts that hinder all activities.

A review of the enterprise's strategic business plans is likely to uncover opportunities for information security activities that can enable or be directly supportive of a particular avenue of business by reducing risk, losses and potential operational disruptions. Other sources of information to guide security efforts include change management activities, audit reports and steering committee discussions. As an example, the implementation of a public key infrastructure (PKI) can enable high-value transactions between trusted trading partners or customers. Deploying virtual private networks (VPNs) may provide the sales force with secure remote connectivity, enabling strong protection for sensitive information. In other words, information security can enable business activities that would otherwise be too risky to undertake or, as frequently happens, are undertaken with the hope that nothing will go wrong.

Business Linkages

In determining strategic objectives, it is essential to ensure there are direct linkages to specific business activities and goals. These linkages can start from the perspective of a particular line of business, taking its specific objectives into account. A review and analysis of all the elements of a particular product line can illustrate how this approach might work.

Consider an enterprise that manufactures breakfast cereal. The raw materials come into the plant on a just-in-time basis via railcar. The grains are dumped into hoppers that feed the various processing machinery. The finished cereals are packaged and moved to a warehouse in a continuous, highly automated process in a matter of hours.

This relatively straightforward process relies on numerous information flows that are subject to a failure of confidentiality, integrity or availability. Any breakdown or significant disruption in the systems that support the supply chain side (e.g., ordering, tracking or payments) is likely to cause a disruption in manufacturing. All the automated processing activities in the plant are tied to data processing and information flows. Any interruption or corruption of data would cause a failure of the process, ranging from stopping manufacturing to delivering defective product. An effective information security program must be based on an understanding and consideration of all the information streams that are critical to ensuring continuous operations. Obviously, anything that can negatively affect the integrity or availability of the information needed in this continuous and interdependent process will be a problem. The linkage to the business, in this case, is the ability of an effective security program to prevent disruptions to the information systems essential to production.

An analysis of the preceding example might consider the dozens of discrete pieces of information handled and processed in the manufacturing operation. Investigation into the history of the process might reveal past failures that could reveal weaknesses in the system. Most system failures are due to human error, and the analysis might show possibilities for reducing errors, either by implementing additional or better controls or by ensuring redundancy for more reliable automated processes.

Typical errors include entry mistakes that might be avoided by range checking or other technical processes or instrumentation failure resulting in incorrect processing. Procedural changes or an entry validation process may be required to address entry errors. Instrumentation failures might be addressed by periodic self-tests or instrumentation redundancy. Information security concerns include controlling access to production systems to prevent unauthorized access, incident response and other aspects of risk management.

The development and analysis of business linkages can uncover information security issues at the operational level, which can visibly improve the value of information security by making business processes more robust, reducing errors and improving productivity.

Improving business linkages on an ongoing basis can be one of the beneficial outcomes of an information security steering group if high-level representatives of the major departments and business units are included. Linkages may also be established by regular meetings with business owners for discussion regarding security-related issues. This may present an opportunity to educate business process owners on potential benefits that added security may provide for their operation.

1.5.4 Avoiding Common Pitfalls and Bias

In preparation for strategy development, it is important to avoid some common pitfalls that may unduly influence the objectives to be met and the activities performed to fulfill enterprise goals. Experiments and studies have shown a variety of underlying causes for flawed decision making. Awareness may lead to ways to compensate for them to reduce adverse effects. Some of the main pitfalls:

- **Overconfidence**—Research shows a tendency for people to have excessive confidence in their ability to make accurate estimates. Most people are reluctant to estimate wide ranges of possible outcomes and prefer being precisely wrong, rather than vaguely right. Most also tend to be overconfident in their own abilities. For organizational strategies based on assessments of core capabilities, this can be particularly troublesome.
- **Optimism**—People tend to be optimistic in their forecasts. A combination of overconfidence and overoptimism can have a disastrous impact on strategies based on estimates of what may happen. Typically, these estimates will be unrealistically precise and overly optimistic.
- **Anchoring**—Research shows that once a number has been presented to someone, a subsequent estimate of even a totally unrelated subject involving numbers will "anchor" on the first number. While potentially useful for marketing purposes, anchoring can have serious consequences in developing strategies when future outcomes are anchored in past experiences.
- **The status quo bias**—Most people show a strong tendency toward sticking with familiar and known approaches even when they are demonstrably inadequate or ineffective. Research also indicates that concern over loss is generally stronger than excitement over possible gain. The "endowment effect" is a similar bias in which people prefer to keep what they own or know, and simply owning something makes it more valuable to the owner.
- **Mental accounting**—This is defined as "the inclination to categorize and treat money differently depending on where it comes from, where it is kept, and how it is spent."[10] Mental accounting is common even in the boardrooms of conservative and otherwise rational corporations. Some examples:
  - Being less concerned with expenses against a restructuring charge than those against the profit and loss statement
  - Imposing cost caps on a core business while spending freely on a startup
  - Creating new categories of spending such as "revenue investment" or "strategic investment"
- **The herding instinct**—It is a fundamental human trait to conform and seek validation of others. This can be observed in the "faddism" influencing security (and all other aspects of human activity), such as everyone suddenly being involved in identity management or intrusion detection. Sometimes explained as "an idea whose time has come," it is more accurately described as the herding instinct apparent among thought leaders. The implications for strategy development should be clear. It is aptly demonstrated by the statement, "For senior managers, the only thing worse than making a huge strategic mistake is being the only person in the industry to make it."
- **False consensus**—There is a well-documented tendency for people to overestimate the extent to which others share their views, beliefs and experiences. When developing strategies, false consensus can lead to ignoring or minimizing important threats or weaknesses in plans and to persisting with doomed strategies.

Research from C. F. Camerer and G. Loewenstein identifies some of common causes of flawed decision making:

- **Confirmation bias**—Seeking opinions and facts that support one's own beliefs
- **Selective recall**—Remembering only facts and experiences that reinforce current assumptions
- **Biased assimilation**—Accepting only facts that support a current position or perspective
- **Biased evaluation**—Easy acceptance of evidence that supports their own hypotheses while contradictory evidence is challenged and, almost invariably, rejected.
- **Groupthink**—Pressure for agreement in team-based cultures

There have been numerous studies on the topic of departures from rational choice during the past several decades that may be worthy of review to reduce the risk of faulty decision making. The key takeaway is that as information security managers collaborate with

[10] Outlier Allocators, "The Man in the Green Bathrobe and Mental Accounting,"19 July 2013, https://24sevenfinance.wordpress.com/2013/07/19/the-man-in-the-green-bathrobe-and-mental-accounting/

colleagues to determine the issues and objectives to be addressed by strategy, they should be careful to avoid the incorrect or exaggerated emphasis that these biases and pitfalls may introduce.

1.5.5 The Desired State

The term "desired state" is used to denote a complete snapshot of all relevant conditions at a particular point in the future. For a robust picture, it must include principles, policies and frameworks; processes; organizational structures; culture, ethics and behavior; information; services, infrastructure and applications; and people, skills and competencies.

Defining a state of security in purely quantitative terms is not possible. Consequently, a desired state of security must, to some extent, be defined qualitatively in terms of attributes, characteristics and outcomes. According to COBIT, it can include high-level objectives such as: "Protecting the interests of those relying on information, and the processes, systems and communications that handle, store and deliver the information, from harm resulting from failures of availability, confidentiality and integrity." This statement, while perhaps useful in stating intent and scope, provides little clarity in defining processes or objectives.

Qualitative elements such as desired outcomes should be defined as precisely as possible to provide guidance to strategy development. For example, if specific regulatory compliance is a desired outcome, a significant number of technical and process requirements become apparent. If characteristics include a nonthreatening compliance enforcement approach consistent with the enterprise's culture, strategy development will have limits on the types of enforcement methods to consider.

A number of useful approaches are available to provide a framework to achieve a well-defined desired state for security. These, and perhaps others, should be evaluated to determine which provides the best form, fit and function for the enterprise. It may be useful to combine several different standards and frameworks to provide a multidimensional view into the desired state.

Several respected accepted approaches are described in the following sections.

COBIT

COBIT provides a comprehensive framework for the governance and management of enterprise IT and extensively addresses IT security, governance, risk and information security in general. Because many aspects of information security involve IT and related activities, it can serve as a framework for determining the desired state for effective information security. COBIT includes several focus areas that describe a particular governance topic, domain or issue that can be addressed by a collection of governance and management objectives and their components. Examples of potential focus areas include small and medium enterprises, information security, risk, digital transformation, cloud computing, privacy and DevOps. Focus areas may contain a combination of generic governance components and variants and provide input considerations for information security governance.

COBIT is based on two sets of principles:

- Principles that describe the core requirements of a governance system for enterprise information and technology
- Principles for a governance framework that can be used to build a governance system for the enterprise

The six principles for a governance system are (**figure 1.8**):

1. Each enterprise needs a governance system to satisfy stakeholder needs and to generate value from the use of information and technology (I&T). Value reflects a balance among benefits, risk and resources, and enterprises need an actionable strategy and governance system to realize this value.
2. A governance system for enterprise I&T (EGIT) is built from a number of components, sometimes of different types, that work together in a holistic way.
3. A governance system should be dynamic. This means that each time a design factor is changed (e.g., a change in strategy or technology), the impact of the change on the EGIT system must be considered. A dynamic view of EGIT will lead toward a viable and future-proof EGIT system.
4. A governance system should clearly distinguish between governance and management activities and structures.
5. A governance system should be tailored to the enterprise's needs, using a set of design factors as

parameters to customize and prioritize the governance system components.

6. A governance system should cover the enterprise end to end, focusing not only on the IT function but on all technology and information processing the enterprise puts in place to achieve its goals, regardless of where the processing is located.

Figure 1.8—Governance System Principles

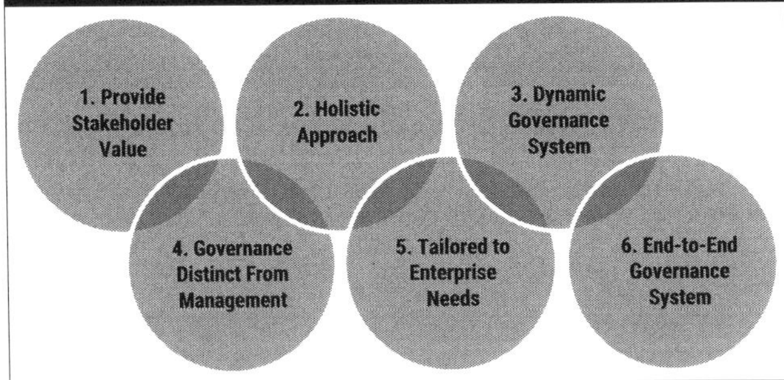

Source: ISACA, *COBIT 2019: Introduction and Methodology*, USA, 2018

The three principles for a governance framework are (**figure 1.9**):

1. A governance framework should be based on a conceptual model, identifying the key components and relationships among components, to maximize consistency and allow automation.
2. A governance framework should be open and flexible. It should allow the addition of new content and enable new issues to be addressed in the most flexible way, while maintaining integrity and consistency.
3. A governance framework should align with major related standards, frameworks and regulations.

Figure 1.9—Governance Framework Principles

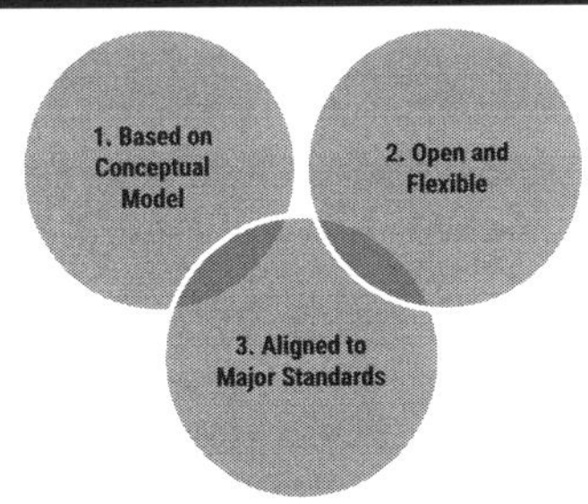

Source: ISACA, COBIT 2019: Introduction and Methodology, USA, 2018

Business Model for Information Security

The BMIS model uses systems thinking to clarify complex relationships within the enterprise to more effectively manage security. The elements and dynamic interconnections that form the basis of the model establish the boundaries of an information security program and model how the program functions and reacts to internal and external change. BMIS provides the context for frameworks such as COBIT.

A system needs to be viewed holistically—not merely as a sum of its parts—to be accurately understood. This is the essence of systems theory. A holistic approach examines the system as a complete functioning unit. Another tenet of systems theory is that one part of the system enables understanding of other parts of the system. "Systems thinking" is a widely recognized term that refers to the examination of how systems interact, how complex systems work and why "the whole is more than the sum of its parts."

Systems theory encompasses a complex network of events, relationships, reactions, consequences, technologies, processes and people interacting in often unseen and unexpected ways. Studying the behaviors and results of the interactions can assist managers to better understand the organizational system and the way it functions. While management of any discipline within the enterprise can be enhanced by approaching it from a systems thinking perspective, its implementation will certainly help with managing risk.

The success the systems approach has achieved in other fields bodes well for the benefits it can bring to security. The often dramatic failures of enterprises to adequately address security issues in recent years are due, to a significant extent, to their inability to define security and present it in a way that is comprehensible and relevant to all stakeholders. Using a systems approach to information security management will help information security managers address complex and dynamic environments and will generate a beneficial effect on collaboration within the enterprise, adaptation to operational change, navigation of strategic uncertainty and tolerance of the impact of external factors.

As illustrated in **figure 1.10**, BMIS is best viewed as a flexible, three-dimensional, pyramid-shaped structure made up of four elements linked together by six dynamic interconnections. All aspects of the model interact with each other. If any one part of the model is changed, not addressed or managed inappropriately, the equilibrium of the model is potentially at risk. The dynamic interconnections act as tensions, exerting a push/pull force in reaction to changes in the enterprise, allowing the model to adapt as needed.

Figure 1.10—BMIS Model

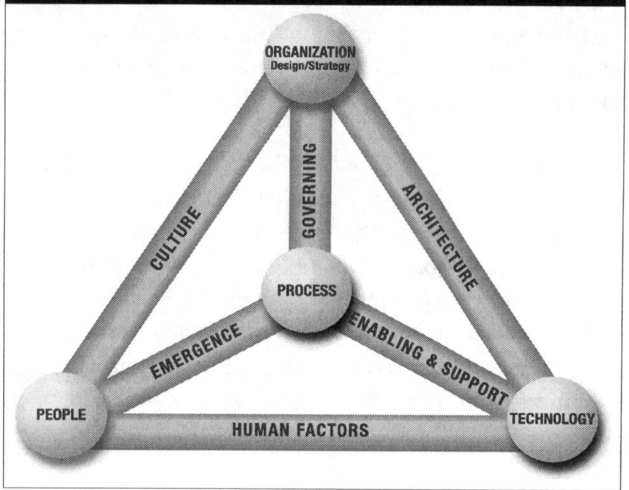

The four elements of the model are:

1. **Organization design and strategy**—An enterprise is a network of people, assets and processes interacting with each other in defined roles and working toward a common goal.
   - An enterprise's strategy specifies its business goals, the objectives to be achieved and the values and missions to be pursued. It sets the basic direction of the enterprise. The strategy should adapt to external and internal factors. Resources are the primary material to design the strategy and can be of different types (e.g., people, equipment, know-how).
   - Design defines how the enterprise implements its strategy. Processes, culture and architecture are important in determining the design.
2. **People**—This includes HR and security issues that surround them. It defines who implements (through design) each part of the strategy. It represents a human collective and must consider values, behaviors and biases.
   - Internally, it is critical for the information security manager to work with the HR and legal departments to address issues such as:
     - Recruitment strategies (access, background checks, interviews, roles and responsibilities)
     - Employment issues (location of office, access to tools and data, training and awareness, movement within the enterprise)
     - Termination (reasons for leaving, timing of exit, roles and responsibilities, access to systems, access to other employees)
   - Externally, customers, suppliers, media, stakeholders and others can have a strong influence on the enterprise and need to be considered within the security posture.
3. **Process**—This includes formal and informal mechanisms (large and small, simple and complex) to get things done and provides a vital link to all dynamic interconnections. Processes identify, measure, manage and control risk, availability, integrity and confidentiality, and they also ensure accountability. They derive from the strategy and implement the operational part of the organization element. To be advantageous to the enterprise, processes must:
   - Meet business requirements and align with policy
   - Consider emergence and be adaptable to changing requirements
   - Be well documented and communicated to appropriate human resources
   - Be reviewed periodically to ensure efficiency and effectiveness
4. **Technology**—Technology includes all the tools, applications and infrastructure that make processes more efficient. As an evolving element that experiences frequent changes, it has its own dynamic risk. Given the typical enterprise's dependence on technology, technology constitutes a core part of the enterprise's infrastructure and a critical component in accomplishing its mission.
   - Technology is often seen by the enterprise's management team as a way to resolve security threats and risk. While technical controls are helpful in mitigating some types of risk, technology should not be viewed as an information security solution.
   - Technology is greatly impacted by users and by organizational culture. Some individuals still mistrust technology; some have not learned to use it; and others feel it slows them down. Regardless of the reason, information security managers must be aware that, just as with

physical and administrative controls, some people will try to sidestep technical controls.

Dynamic Interconnections

The dynamic interconnections link the elements together and exert a multidirectional force that pushes and pulls as things change. Actions and behaviors that occur in the dynamic interconnections can force the model out of balance or bring it back to equilibrium. The six dynamic interconnections are:

1. **Governance**—Steering the enterprise and demanding strategic leadership. Governing sets limits within which an enterprise operates and is implemented within processes to monitor performance, describe activities and achieve compliance while also providing adaptability to emergent conditions. Governing incorporates ensuring that objectives are determined and defined, ascertaining that risk is managed appropriately, and verifying that the enterprise's resources are used responsibly.
2. **Culture**—A pattern of behaviors, beliefs, assumptions, attitudes and ways of doing things. It is emergent and learned, and it creates a sense of comfort. See Section 1.2 Organizational Culture for more information.
   - It is important to understand the culture of the enterprise because it profoundly influences what information is considered, how it is interpreted and what will be done with it.
   - Culture may exist on many levels, such as national (legislation/regulation, political and traditional), organizational (policies, hierarchical style and expectations) and social (family, etiquette). It is created from both external and internal factors and is influenced by and influences organizational patterns.
3. **Enablement and support**—Connects the technology element to the process element.
   - One way to help ensure that people comply with technical security measures, policies and procedures is to make processes usable and easy. Transparency can help generate acceptance for security controls by assuring users that security will not inhibit their ability to work effectively.
   - Many of the actions that affect both technology and processes occur in the enablement and support dynamic interconnection. Policies, standards and guidelines must be designed to support the needs of the business by reducing or eliminating conflicts of interest, remaining flexible to support changing business objectives, and being acceptable and easy for people to follow.
4. **Emergence**—Connotes surfacing, developing, growing and evolving, and refers to patterns that arise in the life of the enterprise that appear to have no obvious cause and whose outcomes seem impossible to predict and control. The emergence dynamic interconnection (between people and processes) is a place to introduce possible solutions such as feedback loops; alignment with process improvement; and consideration of emergent issues in system design life cycle, change control and risk management.
5. **Human factors**—Represents the interaction and gap between technology and people and, as such, is critical to an information security program. If people do not understand how to use technology, do not embrace technology or will not follow pertinent policies, serious security problems can evolve. Internal threats such as data leakage, data theft and misuse of data can occur within this dynamic interconnection. Human factors may arise because of experience level, cultural experiences and differing generational perspectives. Because human factors are critical components in maintaining balance within the model, it is important to train all the enterprise's human resources on pertinent skills.
6. **Architecture**—A comprehensive and formal encapsulation of the people, processes, policies and technology that comprise an enterprise's security practices.
   - A robust business information architecture is essential to understanding the need for security and designing the security architecture.
   - It is within the architecture dynamic interconnection that the enterprise can ensure defense in depth. The design describes how the security controls are positioned and how they relate to the overall enterprise architecture. An enterprise security architecture facilitates security capabilities across lines of businesses in a consistent and cost-effective manner and enables enterprises to be proactive with their security investment decisions.

Governance, Risk Management and Compliance

GRC is an example of the growing recognition of the necessity for convergence, or assurance process integration.

GRC is a term that reflects an approach that enterprises can adopt to integrate these three areas. Often stated as a single business activity, GRC includes multiple overlapping and related activities within an enterprise, which may include internal audit, compliance programs such as the US Sarbanes-Oxley Act, enterprise risk management, operational risk, incident management and others.

Governance is the responsibility of senior management and the board of directors and focuses on creating the mechanisms an enterprise uses to ensure that personnel follow established processes and policies.

Risk management is the process by which an enterprise manages risk to acceptable levels within acceptable tolerances. It identifies potential risk and its associated impacts, and prioritizes their mitigation based on the enterprise's business objectives. Risk management develops and deploys internal controls to manage and mitigate risk throughout the enterprise.

Compliance is the process that records and monitors the policies, procedures and controls needed to ensure that policies and standards are adequately adhered to.

It is important to recognize that effective integration of GRC processes requires having governance in place before risk can be effectively managed and compliance enforced.

Numerous GRC software products have been developed to help enterprises implement and maintain GRC processes. These are discussed in more detail in Chapter 3.

While a GRC program can be used in any area of an enterprise, it is usually focused on financial, IT and legal areas. Financial GRC is used to ensure proper operation of financial processes and compliance with regulatory requirements. In a similar fashion, IT GRC seeks to ensure proper operation and policy compliance of IT processes. Legal GRC may focus on overall regulatory compliance.

1.5.6 Information Security Strategy Development

With the information described in the previous section, a meaningful security strategy can be developed—a strategy to move from the current state to the desired state. Knowing where one is and where one is going provides the essential starting point for strategy development; it provides the framework for creating a road map. The road map essentially delineates the specific steps that must be taken to implement the strategy.

Information security objectives, coupled with available processes, methods, tools and techniques, create the means to construct a security strategy. A good security strategy should address and mitigate risk while providing an acceptable level of compliance with the legal, contractual and statutory requirements of the enterprise. It should provide demonstrable support for its business objectives and maximize value to stakeholders. The security strategy also needs to address how the enterprise will embed good security practices into every business process and area.

Often, those charged with developing a security strategy think in terms of controls as the means to implement security. Controls, while important, are not the only element available to the strategist. In some cases, reengineering a process can reduce or eliminate a risk without the need for controls. Potential impacts may be mitigated by architectural modifications rather than controls. Another consideration is that mitigating risk can sometimes reduce business opportunities to the extent that it becomes counterproductive. It is essential to consider how risk mitigation activities impact productivity so that a careful balance can be struck between security and operational efficiency/effectiveness. This can generally be accomplished by performing a cost-benefit analysis of proposed control activities.

Ultimately, the goal of security is business process assurance, regardless of the business (i.e., ensuring the continued operation of the business by supporting and minimizing disruptions to operations at an acceptable cost). This serves to protect value and value creation. While the business of a government agency may not result directly in profits, it is still in the business of providing cost-effective services to its constituency and must still protect the assets for which it has custodial care. Whatever the business, its primary operational goal is to maximize the success of business processes and minimize impediments to those processes.

1.5.7 Elements of a Strategy

What should go into a security strategy? The starting point and the destination have been defined. The next consideration must be what resources are available and what constraints must be considered when developing the road map. The resources are the mechanisms that will be used to achieve various parts of the strategy, bound by the constraints. The strategy development process should include making some realistic assumptions around effects of current and planned IT projects, evaluating ongoing business process re-engineering activities and discussing how personnel and budgets can be managed more effectively.

Road Map

The typical road map to achieve a defined, secure desired state includes people, processes, technologies and other resources. It serves to map the routes and steps that must be taken to navigate to the objectives of the strategy.

The interactions and relationships among the various elements of a strategy are likely to be complex. As a consequence, it is prudent to consider the initial stages of developing a security architecture, such as those discussed in Section 3.4.1 Enterprise Security Architectures. Architectures can provide a structured approach to defining business drivers, resource relationships and process flows. An architecture can also help ensure that contextual and conceptual elements, such as business drivers and consequences, are considered in the strategy development stage.

Achieving the secure desired state is usually a long-term goal consisting of a series of projects and initiatives. Like most large, complex projects, it is necessary to break it down into a series of shorter-term projects that can be accomplished in a reasonable time period given the inevitable resource constraints and budget cycles. The entire road map can, and should, be charted while understanding that there is no steady state for information security and some objectives will need to be modified over time. Some objectives—such as attaining a particular maturity level, reengineering high-risk processes or achieving specific control objectives—may not require modification.

Shorter-term projects aligned with long-range objectives can serve to provide checkpoints and opportunities for mid-course corrections. They can also provide metrics to validate the overall strategy.

For example, one long-term objective defined in the strategy may be data classification according to sensitivity and criticality. Because of the sheer magnitude of the effort required in a large enterprise, it is likely to require a number of years to accomplish. The strategy may include the requirement to determine that 25 percent will be targeted for completion each fiscal year using a variety of tactical approaches. A second component of the strategy might be to create policies and standards that preclude the practices that gave rise to the problem to begin with, so it does not get worse while the remediation process is underway.

Development of a strategy to achieve long-term objectives and a road map to get there, coupled with shorter-term intermediate goals, will provide the basis for sound policy and standards development in support of the effort.

Resources and Constraints—Overview

The following subsections describe the typical resources for implementing an information security strategy and some of the constraints that must be considered.

COBIT defines certain components (formerly called enablers) of the governance system as factors that individually and collectively influence whether something will work—in this case, governance and management of information security and enterprise IT. These components are driven by the goals cascade (i.e., higher-level goals define what the different enablers should achieve). The governance system components are:

- **Principles, policies and frameworks**—the vehicles to translate desired behavior into practical guidance for day-to-day management.
- **Processes**—an organized set of practices and activities to achieve certain objectives and produce a set of outputs in support of achieving overall goals.
- **Organizational structures**—the key decision-making entities in an enterprise.

- **Culture, ethics and behavior**—characteristics of individuals and the enterprise that are very often underestimated as success factors in governance and management activities.
- **Information**—all information produced and used by the enterprise. Information is pervasive throughout the enterprise and required for keeping the enterprise running and well governed, but at the operational level, information is very often the key product of the enterprise itself.
- **Services, infrastructure and applications**—the infrastructure, technology and applications that provide the enterprise with information technology processing and services.
- **People, skills and competencies**—required for successful completion of all activities and for making correct decisions and taking corrective actions.

Governance system components can function both as resources and constraints and must be considered from both perspectives.

Resources

The resources available to the enterprise need to be enumerated and considered when developing a security strategy. To the extent possible, the strategy should maximize use of existing assets and capabilities.

Resources can be considered the mechanisms, processes and systems that are available, in some optimal mix, to achieve the desired state of security over time. They include:

- Policies
- Standards
- Procedures
- Guidelines
- Architectures
- Controls—physical, technical, procedural
- Countermeasures
- Layered defenses
- Technologies
- Personnel security
- Organizational structure
- Roles and responsibilities
- Skills
- Training
- Awareness and education
- Audits
- Compliance enforcement
- Threat assessment
- Vulnerability assessment
- Business impact analysis
- Risk analysis
- Resource dependency analysis
- Third-party service providers
- Other organizational support and assurance providers
- Facilities
- Environmental security

Constraints

A number of constraints must be considered when developing a security strategy and subsequent action plan. Constraints typically include:

- **Legal**—Laws and regulatory requirements
- **Physical**—Capacity, space, environmental constraints
- **Ethics**—Appropriate, reasonable and customary
- **Culture**—Both inside and outside the enterprise
- **Costs**—Time, money
- **Personnel**—Resistance to change, resentment against new constraints
- **Organizational structure**—How decisions are made and by whom, turf protection
- **Resources**—Capital, technology, people
- **Capabilities**—Knowledge, training, skills, expertise
- **Time**—Window of opportunity, mandated compliance
- **Risk appetite**—Threats, vulnerabilities, impacts

Some constraints, such as ethics and culture, may have been dealt with in defining the desired state. Others will undoubtedly arise as a consequence of developing the road map and action plan.

Constraints can also be the magnitude of effort, challenges around legacy systems, integration with existing technologies or processes and adoption of emerging technologies such as artificial intelligence, machine learning, robotics process automation, etc.

1.6 Information Governance Frameworks and Standards

To achieve effective information security governance, management must establish and ensure maintenance of a framework to guide the development and management of a comprehensive information security program that supports the business objectives.

The governance framework will generally consist of the following:

- A comprehensive security strategy intrinsically linked with business objectives
- Governing security policies that clearly express management intent and address each aspect of strategy, controls and regulation
- A complete set of standards for each policy to ensure that people, procedures, practices and technologies comply with policy requirements and set appropriate security baselines for the enterprise
- An effective security organizational structure with sufficient authority and adequate resources, void of conflicts of interest
- Detailed workflows and structures that assist in defining responsibilities and accountability for information security governance
- Institutionalized metrics and monitoring processes to ensure compliance, provide feedback on control effectiveness and provide the basis for making appropriate management decisions

This framework provides the basis for developing a cost-effective information security program that supports the enterprise's business goals. Implementing and managing a security program is covered in Chapter 3. The objective of the program is a set of activities that provide assurance that information assets are given a level of protection commensurate with their business value or with the risk their compromise poses to the enterprise. The relationships among IT, information security, controls, architecture and the other components of a governance framework are represented in **figure 1.11**. While linkage between IT and information security may occur at various higher levels, strategy is the point where information security must integrate IT to achieve its objectives.

Figure 1.11—Prevalent Standards and Frameworks

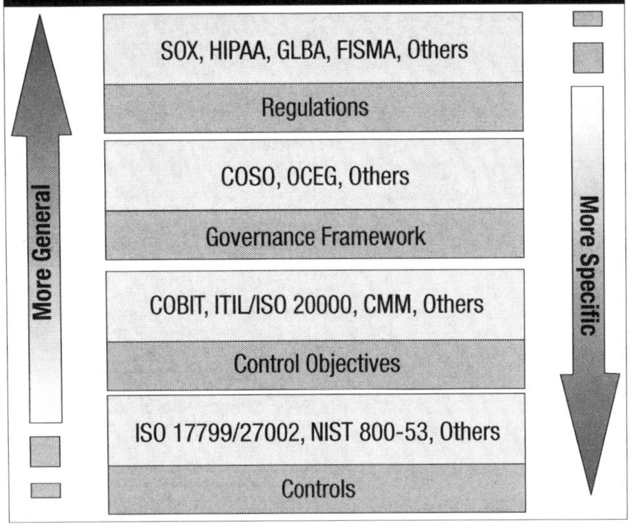

1.6.1 Balanced Scorecard

According to the Balanced Scorecard Institute, "The balanced scorecard is a strategic planning and management system used by organizations to communicate and align around strategy, prioritize, and measure performance."[11]

The balanced scorecard, as shown in **figure 1.12**, uses four perspectives. It develops metrics, collects data and analyzes the data relative to each of these perspectives:

- Learning and growth
- Business process
- Customer
- Financial

[11] Balanced Scorecard Institute, "Balanced Scorecard Solutions," https://balancedscorecard.org/solutions/bscsolution/

Figure 1.12—Balanced Scorecard Dimensions

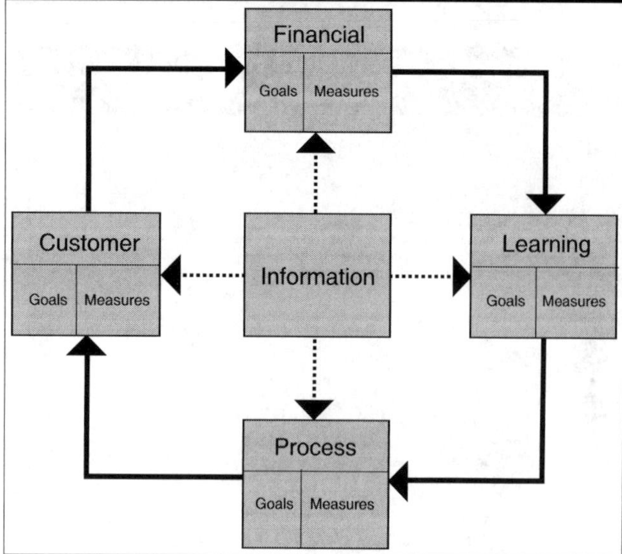

Source: ISACA, *Board Briefing on IT Governance, 2nd Edition*, USA, 2003

1.6.2 Architectural Approaches

Enterprise information security architecture (EISA) is a subset of enterprise architecture. An architecture framework can be described as a foundational structure, or set of structures, that can be used for developing a broad range of different architectures, including business process architecture—sometimes referred to as the contextual architecture—and the more traditional conceptual, logical, physical, functional and operational architectures.

Many methodologies have evolved, including process models, frameworks and ad hoc approaches favored by some consultancies. This evolution occurred as it became evident that an architectural perspective limited to IT was inadequate to address business design and development of security requirements.

A number of architectural approaches now provide linkages to the business side of information protection and methods for its design. Architectural approaches that are inclusive of business processes that may be appropriate for defining the desired state of security include (but are not limited to) framework models such as COBIT, the Open Group Architecture Framework (TOGAF), the Zachman Enterprise Architecture Framework, and the Extended Enterprise Architecture Framework (E2AF). These models can define most or all of the desired state of security, provided they are properly used to reflect and implement the organizational security strategy.

The architecture should describe a method for designing a target or desired state of the enterprise in terms of a set of building blocks, and for showing how the building blocks fit together. The target architecture is referred to as the reference architecture and serves to set the longer-term objectives for technical, systems and process design.

1.6.3 Enterprise Risk Management Frameworks

Several enterprise risk management (ERM) frameworks include elements that may be helpful in preparing for strategic planning and subsequent program development:

- The **COSO ERM Integrated Framework** defines essential enterprise risk management components, discusses key ERM principles and concepts, suggests a common ERM language, and provides clear direction and guidance for enterprise risk management.
- **ISO 31000:2018** documents principles, a framework and a process for managing risk to help enterprises increase the likelihood of achieving objectives, identifying opportunities and threats, and effectively allocating and using resources for risk treatment.
- **British Standard (BS) 31100,** the *Risk Management Code of Practice*, provides a process for implementing and maintaining the concepts described in ISO 31000, including key functions like identify, assess, respond, report and review.

1.6.4 Information Security/Cybersecurity Management Frameworks and Models

In addition to the overarching ERM practices previously described, there are several well-known frameworks that were developed with a focus on information security risk management.

ISO/IEC 27000 Series

The 14 areas of the ISO/IEC 27001:2013 standard can provide a useful framework to gauge comprehensiveness of an organizational security strategy and ensure that all relevant elements of security are addressed. It is essential to create organizational policies and standards that can track directly to each element of the standard. While it is the standard on which an enterprise may choose to be certified and assessed (as is increasingly the case globally), 27002:2013 is the code of practice for information security management that supports implementation of compliance with the standard.

The 14 security control clauses of ISO/IEC 27001:2013 are:

- A.5: Information security policies
- A.6: Organization of information security
- A.7: Human resource security (controls that are applied before, during or after employment)
- A.8: Asset management
- A.9: Access control
- A.10: Cryptography
- A.11: Physical and environmental security
- A.12: Operations security
- A.13: Communications security
- A.14: System acquisition, development and maintenance
- A.15: Supplier relationships
- A.16: Information security incident management
- A.17: Information security aspects of business continuity management
- A.18: Compliance (with internal requirements, such as policies, and with external requirements, such as laws)

Whereas ISO/IEC 27001:2013 Annex A refers to 114 "controls," they are just sections in ISO/IEC 27002:2013, many of which propose multiple security controls. ISO/IEC 27002:2013 suggests literally hundreds of good practice information security control measures that enterprises should consider in order to achieve the stated control objectives.

Like ISO/IEC 27001:2013, ISO/IEC 27002:2013 does not mandate specific controls but leaves it to the users to select and implement suitable controls, using a risk assessment process to identify the most appropriate controls for their specific requirements. Users are free to select controls that are not listed in the standard, as long as their control objectives are satisfied. The ISO/IEC standard is treated as a generic controls checklist—a menu from which enterprises select their own set.

NIST Cybersecurity Framework

Formally titled the NIST Framework for Improving Critical Infrastructure Cybersecurity, the NIST Cybersecurity Framework provides high-level guidance for aligning a cybersecurity program with enterprise objectives. In response to an increasing prevalence of cybersecurity attacks, NIST convened a series of workshops to develop a process by which an enterprise could identify opportunities for improvement in the information security program. The framework highlights the need for effective risk management integration and it broadly supports improvement in supply chain risk management.

The NIST Cybersecurity Framework does not provide controls to be applied. Instead, it guides practitioners through the process of determining gaps between the current state of practice and a desired target state that might better fulfill their enterprise mission, including risk management needs. Analysis of the gaps between states enables the use of controls-based frameworks (including those listed herein) to improve information security risk management.

NIST Risk Management Framework

The NIST Risk Management Framework (RMF) provides a process that integrates security, privacy and cyber supply chain risk management activities into the system development life cycle. Originally intended to help US government agencies to evaluate and improve information security, it has been broadened to apply to any enterprise and is available without cost. The RMF provides a risk-based approach to the categorization of relevant assets, selection and implementation of controls to achieve adequate protection, and provisions for monitoring the continued effectiveness and efficiency of risk management measures.

Other Approaches

Other approaches and methods that may be useful include other ISO standards on quality (ISO 9001:2015), the Six Sigma approach to quality and business management, publications from NIST, the Information Security Forum (ISF), and the US Federal Information Security Modernization Act (FISMA). Some of these focus more on management processes and quality management than on strategic security objectives.

However, if the objective of a security strategy is to fully implement relevant components of ISO/IEC 27001:2013 and 27002:2013, the argument can be made that most or all security requirements are likely to be met. That would probably be a needlessly expensive approach, and the standards suggest that they should be carefully tailored to the specific requirements of the adopting enterprise. Other methodologies will undoubtedly emerge in the future that may prove to be more effective that the ones mentioned. This is not meant to be an exhaustive list but merely to present some of the more widely accepted approaches currently used to arrive at well-defined information security objectives.

It may be useful to employ a combination of methods to describe the desired state to assist in communications with others and as a way to cross-check the objectives to make certain all relevant elements are considered. For example, some combination of COBIT control objectives, CMMI, balanced scorecard and an appropriate architectural model would make a powerful combination. While it may seem like overkill, each approach presents a different viewpoint, and using them in combination is likely to ensure that no significant aspect is overlooked. Since it is unlikely that an effective security program will develop from a faulty strategy, this may be a prudent approach.

1.7 Strategic Planning

Drawing from the frameworks previously described, the final step in creating an effective information security strategy is strategic planning itself. Plans for implementing and maintaining the security strategy mirror those adopted for the enterprise strategy itself: workforce and organizational structure, assurance of compliance with mandatory requirements, and specific activities to accomplish responsibilities for protecting enterprise value.

1.7.1 Workforce Composition and Skills

Personnel security is an important area of the information security strategy that must be considered as a preventive means of securing an enterprise. Because the most costly and damaging compromises are usually the result of insider activities, whether intentional or unintentional, the first line of defense is to try to ensure the trustworthiness and integrity of new and existing personnel. The processes for ensuring these attributes in the workforce (including in-house personnel and external service providers) will be implemented through the information security program, but requirements and plans should be included in the strategy.

Organizational Structure

The organizational structure will have a significant effect on the development of an information security strategy. A flexible and evolving structure is likely to be useful in developing a security strategy. In more constrained structures, efforts at developing a strategy may be perceived by various factions as a threat to their autonomy or authority. This is increasingly the case as the information security function has risen in importance and position in the organizational structure.

Although it was sufficient in the past for information security to report to the CIO, that structure has become inadequate for effectively addressing increased risk, growing losses and the sophistication of attackers. Further, it often results in a conflict of interest. As a result, information security increasingly has C-level management responsibilities and reports to the COO, CEO or the board of directors. There are several reasons for this. One is that the broad requirements of information security are outside the scope and focus of the typical CIO. Another reason is that the inherent conflict of interest resulting from information security is primarily a regulatory activity, while the CIO is often focused on cost and performance of IT. Information security, due to efforts to ensure security, is often perceived as a constraint on IT operations. CIOs and IT departments are usually under pressure to increase performance and cut costs, and a reduced security budget is usually a result of those pressures. Finally, for information security to be effective, it must be aligned with the business rather than with technology.

Centralized and Decentralized Approaches to Coordinating Information Security

An enterprise's cultural makeup will affect many aspects of the strategy, including the determination of whether a centralized or decentralized approach is more effective for the security enterprise. While many benefits can be achieved through the centralization and standardization of security, often the structure of an enterprise makes this an ineffective approach.

Multinational companies that choose a centralized approach need to carefully consider different local legal requirements in each country where they have a presence. For example, some countries may not allow business data to be stored or processed outside their national boundaries; some governments may collect taxes—such as a withholding tax for the software or hardware used by the entities within their jurisdiction, regardless of where the software or hardware is physically located.

One example of a distributed approach is an enterprise that has grown through acquisitions and operates more as a number of independent entities than as a single company. In this situation, it is not unusual for separate IT groups to exist along with different software and hardware. In this example, it would not be unusual for different security enterprises to exist with separate approaches, policies and procedures. In these situations, there may still be benefits to creating a single set of overall enterprise-wide security policies and then dealing with local differences through local standards and procedures.

A decentralized security process has advantages in that security administrators are normally closer to the users and understand local issues better. Often, they can respond more quickly to requests for changes to access rights or to security incidents. However, there are also disadvantages. For example, the quality of service may vary by location, based on the level of training provided to the local staff and the degree to which they may be encumbered with unrelated duties.

Although there are different approaches and techniques used for security, depending on whether a centralized or decentralized approach is taken, the overall responsibilities and objectives of security do not change. They must fulfill the following requirements:

- Be closely aligned with the business objectives
- Be sponsored and approved by senior management
- Have monitoring in place
- Have reporting and crisis management in place
- Have organizational continuance procedures
- Have risk management in place
- Have appropriate security awareness and training programs

Employee Roles and Responsibilities

With the many tasks employees must complete, it is important that the strategy include a mechanism that defines all security roles and responsibilities, as discussed in Section 1.4 Roles and Responsibilities, and incorporates them in employee job descriptions. Ultimately, if employees are compensated based on their adherence to meeting their job responsibilities, there is a better chance of achieving security governance objectives. An employee's annual job performance and objectives can include security-related measurements.

The information security manager should work with the HR director to define security roles and responsibilities. The related competencies required for each job position should be defined and documented.

Skills

The skills required to implement a security strategy are an important consideration. Choosing a strategy that uses skills already available is likely to be a cost-effective option, but it may be necessary to develop new skills at times or to outsource certain required activities. A skills inventory is important to determine the resources available in developing a security strategy. Proficiency testing may be useful to determine if the requisite skills are available or can be achieved through training.

Awareness and Education

Training, education and awareness are vital in the overall strategy because security is often weakest at the end-user level. It is vital to consider the need for the development of methods and processes that enable the policies, standards and procedures to be more easily followed, implemented and monitored. A recurring security awareness program aimed at end users reinforces the importance of information security and it is now required by law in some jurisdictions for a number of sectors.

In most enterprises, evidence indicates that the majority of personnel are not aware of security policies and standards, even if they do exist. Awareness and training programs provide widespread acknowledgment that security is important to the enterprise. Because security relies heavily on individual compliance, a robust security awareness program must be in place and must be considered in strategy development.

Broadening and deepening the appropriate skills of security personnel through training can do a great deal to improve an enterprise's overall security effectiveness. The challenge is to determine what the "appropriate" skills are and how they need to be improved to effectively protect the enterprise against the seemingly endless array of security risk.

Finding employees with the necessary combination of security skills to be effective in an ever-changing, diverse environment and complex regulatory climate can be difficult and expensive. One way some enterprises attempt to ensure that all needed skills are available is to hire overqualified people. The concern with this approach is that these individuals are costly to acquire and maintain and, failing to be challenged, are often dissatisfied with the work. This can lead to excessive employee turnover, unproductive attitudes or substandard performance.

Training for new or existing security personnel to equip them with the skills needed to meet specific existing and emerging security requirements can be more cost-effective. This is a strong argument for an ongoing program of training targeted to the needs of the enterprise and, at the same time, providing a career path for employees based on continuous improvement.

For training to be an effective option, it must be targeted to specific systems, processes and policies and to the enterprise's unique and specific way of doing business and its unique security context. Anything less is likely to be inadequate, and anything more wastes resources. Properly executed, this approach can seamlessly integrate into existing programs and initiatives, shore up areas of deficiency and align security processes with business processes.

1.7.2 Assurance Provisions

Because many of the governance and management objectives relate to ensuring that various enterprise and business requirements are addressed, fulfilled and monitored, strategic planning should include the methods by which oversight of those provisions will occur. Those methods will provide assurance that the strategic plan is successfully fulfilling promises made, and they will enable ongoing communication and reporting to stakeholders to confirm fulfillment of compliance objectives.

Audits

Audits—both internal and external—are one of the main processes used to determine information security deficiencies from a controls and compliance standpoint and are one of the essential resources in strategy development.

Internal audits in larger enterprises are performed by an internal audit department that generally reports to either an audit committee of the board of directors or to a senior leader. For example, the Institute of Internal Auditors' Standards Glossary describes the chief audit executive (CAE) as a senior position responsible for effectively managing the internal audit activity in accordance with the internal audit charter and the mandatory elements of the International Professional Practices Framework.[12]

Typically, a sub-unit of internal audit or an independent IT audit group will focus on IT resources. In smaller enterprises, internal IT audits or reviews may be performed by the information security manager or may be delegated to an information security officer. Typically, the focus is on the policy compliance of people, processes and technology.

External audits are most often conducted by an independent third-party and may include areas of IT and information security, depending on audit objectives. Because audits can provide powerful monitoring tools for the information security manager, it is important to ensure that the security department has access to this information. To facilitate the flow of information that is essential to effective security management, it is important for the information security manager to develop a good working relationship with other assurance providers.

Due to increased regulatory oversight, many enterprises are required to file various audit and other reports with regulatory agencies. Many of these reports have information security implications that can provide useful intelligence and monitoring information for the information security manager. For example, under compliance provisions of the US Sarbanes-Oxley Act,

[12] The Institute of Internal Auditors, "Standards Glossary," https://na.theiia.org/standards-guidance/mandatory-guidance/Pages/Standards-Glossary.aspx

the financial controls of public companies must be tested annually within 90 days of reporting to the US Securities and Exchange Commission (SEC). It is important that the results of such tests are available to the information security manager, and they should be a required component of strategy considerations.

Compliance Enforcement

Security violations are an ongoing concern for information security managers, and it is important to develop procedures for handling them as a part of developing the strategy. Senior management buy-in and backing for these procedures are critical, especially in the area of enforcement. Security managers often find that the greatest compliance problems arise with management. If there is a lack of commitment and compliance in management ranks, it may be difficult, if not impossible, to enforce compliance across an enterprise.

In an enterprise where openness and trust are valued and promoted by management, the most effective approach to compliance is likely to be a system of self-reporting and voluntary compliance based on the understanding that security is clearly in everyone's best interest. This approach usually requires that processes be carefully thought out, clearly communicated and cooperatively implemented. Determining how to accomplish these goals is an element of strategy.

An important consideration for compliance enforcement is prioritization of compliance requirements. In a typical enterprise, there are some policies and procedures that are more critical than others and, from a security perspective, may require 100 percent compliance (e.g., the operation of a nuclear power plant). Because it may not be practical, possible or cost-effective to monitor all compliance equally, prioritization of compliance requirements should focus on areas of greatest risk and impact.

1.7.3 Risk Assessment and Management

Informed by the information security models described in Part A, the information security strategy should include a comprehensive plan for identifying, assessing and treating information security risk. Strategic planning includes determination of how to achieve risk direction to protect various enterprise assets from a broad range of threats and the vulnerabilities (in the form of preexisting conditions or weaknesses) those threats might exploit.

NIST Special Publication 800-37 Revision 2 points out:[13]

> *The risk management strategy makes explicit the threats, assumptions, constraints, priorities, trade-offs, and risk tolerance used for making investment and operational decisions. This strategy includes the strategic-level decisions and considerations for how senior leaders and executives are to manage security and privacy risks (including supply chain risks) ... The risk management strategy includes an expression of organizational risk tolerance; acceptable risk assessment methodologies and risk response strategies; a process for consistently evaluating security and privacy risks organization-wide; and approaches for monitoring risk over time.*

Details regarding threat, vulnerability and risk exposure are described in Chapter 2, but these high-level factors must be included in strategic planning.

The following topics are described in depth in subsequent chapters but are introduced here as elements that should be considered in strategic planning, and subsequent implementation and operation as part of the information security program itself.

Business Impact Analysis

Risk assessment begins with an understanding of the enterprise assets that are necessary for achievement of enterprise goals—in particular, resources that are critical or sensitive. A BIA is an exercise that determines the consequences of the impact of a loss of confidentiality, integrity or availability. The consequences are sometimes expressed as financial impacts. Since risk that does not result in an appreciable impact is not always addressed, BIAs are an important component of developing a strategy that addresses potential adverse impacts. The BIA provides the basis for developing an approach to information classification and addressing business continuity requirements. See Section 4.2 Business Impact Analysis.

[13] National Institute for Standards and Technology, Special Publication 800-37 Revision 2 "Risk Management Framework for Information Systems and Organizations: A System Life Cycle Approach for Security and Privacy," December 2018, https://csrc.nist.gov/publications/detail/sp/800-37/rev-2/final

Resource Dependency Analysis

Business dependency analysis is similar to resource dependency analysis but is less granular and includes elements that would be considered in a business continuity plan, such as staples and paper clips. Resource dependency is similar to disaster recovery planning in that it considers the systems, hardware and software required to perform specific organizational functions. Resource dependency can provide another perspective on the criticality of information resources. It can, to some extent, be used instead of an impact analysis to ensure that the strategy considers resources critical to business operations. The analysis is based on determining the resources (such as systems, software, connectivity) and dependencies (such as input processes and data repositories) required by operations critical to the enterprise.

Outsourced Services

Outsourcing is common, both onshore and offshore, as companies focus on core competencies and ways to cut costs. From an information security point of view, these arrangements can present risk that may be difficult to quantify and potentially difficult to mitigate. Typically, both the resources and skills of the outsourced functions are lost to the enterprise, which in itself presents risk. Providers may operate on different standards and can be difficult to control. The security strategy should ensure that outsourced security services are not a critical single point of failure and that there is a viable backup plan in the event of service provider failure.

Increasing use of cloud services presents a host of new and often obscure sets of risk in addition to a range of potential benefits. Cloud benefits and risk are discussed further in Section 3.12.6 Cloud Computing. Risk posed by outsourcing can materialize as the result of mergers and acquisitions. Typically, significant differences in culture, systems, technology and operations between the parties present a host of security challenges that must be identified and addressed. Security is often an afterthought and the security manager must strive to gain awareness of questionable activities and assess the risk for management consideration.

Formally assessing risk is accomplished by first determining the viable threats to information resources that an enterprise faces. Among them are physical and environmental threats (e.g., flood, fire, earthquake, pandemic) and technology threats (e.g., malicious software, system failure, internal and external attacks).

The next consideration is the likelihood that these threats will materialize and their probable magnitude. This is the risk identification phase of risk assessment. For example, it may be highly likely in some areas that an earthquake will occur, but it may be that, on average, it will not be severe enough to cause damage. In this case, the infrequent major earthquakes that historically have caused damage should be considered. Some threats may be extreme but too rare to warrant consideration (e.g., a comet strike) and can be ignored.

The next step is to determine the extent of organizational weaknesses and exposure to these threats. The combination of the frequency and magnitude and the extent of the enterprise's vulnerability will determine the relative level of risk. The use of this information to calculate the resulting probable annual loss expectancy—considering frequency, magnitude and exposure—puts management in a position to decide on acceptability.

Both the frequency of occurrence and probable magnitude can be indicated by the extent to which these threats have materialized in the past and by the experiences of peer enterprises. The consideration of frequency is important, even if the magnitude is moderate. While a single event may constitute an acceptable risk, if it is a frequent occurrence, the aggregate risk may not be acceptable. For example, an enterprise may accept a US $10,000 loss once a year, but that level of loss every day may not be acceptable. See Section 2.3 Risk Analysis, Evaluation and Assessment.

Threat Assessment

While threat assessment is performed as part of overall risk assessment, it is an important element for strategic consideration by itself. One reason is that risk treatment options should consider the most cost-effective approach for addressing any particular risk. For example, mitigation measures can address threats directly, they can reduce or eliminate vulnerabilities, or they can address and compensate for impacts. The most cost-effective choice is facilitated by separately analyzing threat, vulnerability, exposure and impact.

Another reason for developing a threat profile is that the strategy should consider viable threats regardless of whether a current vulnerability is known to exist. This is a proactive approach and considers that all vulnerabilities cannot be known and new ones that may result in unacceptable risk are introduced continuously.

In addition, policy development should map to a threat profile. In a broad sense, threats are relatively constant (e.g., fire, flood, earthquake, malware, theft, fraud, attacks, mistakes), whereas vulnerabilities change frequently as a result of changes in business processes, technology and personnel. Existing policies should be reviewed as part of policy development, especially in older organizations, since there may well exist a number of policies that are no longer relevant and that do not address any conceivable threat or rational requirement. See Section 2.1.2 Threats.

Vulnerability Assessment

In most enterprises, technical vulnerability assessments using automated scans are common but by themselves are of limited value for security strategy development. Comprehensive vulnerability assessments that include physical elements—such as procedures, practices, technologies, facilities, service level agreements, and legal and contractual requirements—are essential. Processes and facilities are often the most vulnerable components; yet, because of the greater difficulty in assessing them, they are the least frequently assessed. The process of developing a strategy offers opportunities to address many vulnerabilities with a prudent, proactive approach. Even if no known or apparent threats exist for weaknesses discovered during these assessments, cost-effective opportunities to address systemic weaknesses during strategy development should be considered. See Section 2.7.11 Vulnerabilities.

Insurance

Strategy resources include the option of addressing some risk with insurance. Generally, the types of risk suitable for insuring are rare, high-impact events such as floods, hurricanes, fire, embezzlement or liability lawsuits. The most common types of insurance that can be considered include first-party, third-party and fidelity bonds. First-party insurance covers the enterprise in the event of damage from most sources, including business interruption, direct loss and recovery costs. Third-party insurance deals with potential liability to third parties. It generally includes defense against lawsuits and covers damages up to predetermined limits. Fidelity insurance or bonding involves protection against employee or agent theft or embezzlement.

Other Organizational Support and Assurance Providers

When developing a security strategy, a number of support and assurance service providers within an enterprise should be considered as part of information security resources. These can include a variety of departments, such as legal, compliance, audit, procurement, insurance, disaster recovery, physical security, training, project office and HR. Other departments or groups, such as change management or quality assurance, also have elements of assurance as a part of their operation.

Typically, these assurance functions are not well integrated. Strategic considerations include approaches to ensure that these functions operate seamlessly to prevent gaps that may lead to security compromises. The security strategy should aim to reduce or eliminate duplication of efforts and help prevent various groups working at cross-purposes (i.e., prevent the assurance activities of one group from undermining by the activities of another).

1.7.4 Action Plan to Implement Strategy

Implementing an information security strategy will typically require a number of projects or initiatives. An analysis of the gaps between the current state and the desired state for each defined metric identifies the requirements and priorities needed for an overall plan or road map to achieve the objectives and close the gaps.

Gap Analysis—Basis for an Action Plan

A gap analysis is required for various components of the strategy previously discussed, such as maturity levels, control objectives, and risk and impact objectives. The analysis will identify the steps needed to move from the current state to the desired state to achieve the defined objectives. This exercise may need to be repeated annually, or more frequently, to provide performance and goal metrics and information needed for possible mid-course corrections in response to changing environments or other factors. A typical approach to gap analysis is to work backward from the endpoint to the current state and determine the intermediate steps need to accomplish the objectives.

Some typical areas to review include:

- A security strategy with senior management acceptance and support
- A security strategy intrinsically linked with business objectives
- Security policies that are complete and consistent with strategy
- Complete standards for all relevant, consistently maintained policies
- Complete and accurate procedures for all important operations
- Clear assignment of roles and responsibilities
- An organizational structure ensuring appropriate authority for information security management without inherent conflicts of interest
- Information assets that have been identified and classified as to criticality and sensitivity
- Effective controls that have been designed, implemented and maintained
- Effective security metrics and monitoring processes in place
- Effective compliance and enforcement processes
- Tested and functional incident and emergency response capabilities
- Tested business continuity/disaster recovery plan
- Appropriate security approvals in change management processes
- Risk that is properly identified, evaluated, communicated and managed
- Adequate security awareness and training of all users
- The development and delivery of activities that can positively influence security orientation of culture and behavior of staff
- Regulatory and legal issues that are understood and addressed
- Addressing of security issues with third-party service providers
- The timely resolution of noncompliance issues and other variances

Action Plan Metrics

The plan of action to implement the strategy will require methods to monitor and measure progress and the achievement of milestones. As with any project plan, progress and costs must be monitored on an ongoing basis to determine conformance with the plan and to allow for mid-course corrections on a timely basis. There will likely be a variety of near-term goals, each requiring resources and a plan of action for achievement.

A number of approaches can be used for ongoing monitoring and measurement of progress. One or more of the methods for assessing the current state can be used on a regular basis to determine and chart how the current state has changed. For example, a balanced scorecard might be used effectively, by itself, as an ongoing means of tracking progress. Another commonly used approach is to use the CMMI to define both the current state and the objectives. The process assessment model provides a basis for performing ongoing gap analysis to determine progress toward achieving goals.

In addition, each plan of action will benefit from developing an appropriate set of key performance indicators (KPIs), defining critical success factors (CSFs) and setting agreed-upon key goal indicators (KGIs). For example, the plan of action to achieve regulatory compliance for Sarbanes-Oxley may require, among other things:

- A detailed analysis by competent legal personnel to determine regulatory requirements for affected business units
- Knowledge of the current state of compliance
- Definition by management of the required state of compliance

Key Goal Indicators

Defining clear objectives and achieving consensus on goals are essential to developing meaningful metrics. For an information security plan, the key goals could include:

- Achieving Sarbanes-Oxley controls testing compliance mandates
- Completing independent controls testing compliance validation and attestation
- Preparing the required statement of control effectiveness

For enterprises publicly traded in the US, Sarbanes-Oxley requires that all financial controls must be tested for effectiveness within 90 days of reporting. The results of testing must be signed by the CEO and CFO and must be attested to by appointed independent auditors. The results must then be included in the enterprise's public filings to the SEC.

Key Performance Indicators

Indicators of the key or critical performance factors necessary to achieve the objectives include:

- Control effectiveness testing plans
- Progress in control effectiveness testing
- Results of testing control effectiveness

For management to track progress in the testing effort, appropriate testing plans must be developed that are consistent with the defined goals and encompass the CSFs. Because of the limited time (90 days) available to perform the required tests, management will need reports on the progress and results of testing.

General Metrics Considerations

Considerations for information security metrics include ensuring that what is being measured is, in fact, relevant. Security is difficult to measure in any objective sense, and relatively meaningless metrics are often used simply because they are readily available. Metrics serve only one purpose: to provide the information necessary for making decisions. It is, therefore, critical to understand what decisions must be made and who makes them and then find ways of supplying that information in an accurate and timely fashion. Different metrics are more or less useful for different parts of the enterprise and should be determined in collaboration with business process owners and management.

Metrics will generally fall into one of three categories: strategic, tactical or operational. Senior management is typically not interested in detailed technical metrics, such as the number of virus attacks thwarted or password resets, but is very interested in information of a strategic nature (e.g., significant emerging risk that may impact the achievement of business objectives). While technical metrics may be of significance to the IT security manager, senior management typically wants a summary of information important from a management perspective—information that typically excludes detailed technical data. This includes:

- Progress according to plan and budget
- Significant changes in risk and possible impacts to business objectives
- Results of disaster recovery testing
- Audit results
- Regulatory compliance status

The information security manager may want more detailed tactical information, including:

- Policy compliance metrics
- Significant process, system or other changes that may affect the risk profile
- Patch management status
- Exceptions and variances to policy or standards

In enterprises that have an IT security manager, it is likely that most technical security data available can be useful. This includes:

- Vulnerability scan results
- Server configuration standards compliance
- Intrusion detection system (IDS) monitoring results
- Firewall log analysis

Useful information security management metrics are often difficult to design and implement. Typically, the focus is on IT vulnerabilities obtained using automated scans without knowing whether a threat exists, the extent of exposure or whether there is a potential impact. From an information security management and strategic perspective, this information is of little value.

This often results in the collection of vast amounts of data to try to ensure that nothing significant is overlooked. The result can be that the sheer volume of data makes it difficult to see the big picture, and efforts should be made to develop processes to distill technical data into information needed for effective management.

Improvements in overall monitoring can be achieved by careful analysis of available metrics to determine their relevancy. For example, it may be interesting to know how many packets were dropped by the firewalls, but this sheds little light on risk to the enterprise or potential impacts. It may be information the IT department finds useful, but it is of no value to information security management. On the other hand, knowing the amount of time it takes to recover critical services after a major incident is likely to be extremely useful to all parties.

Metrics design and monitoring activities should take into consideration:

- What is important to manage information security operations
- IT security management requirements
- The needs of business process owners
- What senior management wants to know

Communication with each of the constituencies may be helpful in determining the kinds of security reports they would find useful. Reporting processes can then be devised that provide each group with the security information they require for making informed security-related decisions.

Action Plan Intermediate Goals

For most enterprises, a variety of specific near-term goals that align with the overall information security strategy can readily be defined once the overall strategy has been completed. Based on the BIA determination of business-critical resources and the state of security as determined by the foregoing CMMI gap analysis, prioritization of remedial activities should be straightforward.

If the objectives of the security strategy are to achieve CMMI level 4 (Quantitatively Managed) compliance or certification, then an example of a near-term action (or tactical) plan may state the following:

During the next 12 months:

- Each business unit must identify current applications in use
- Twenty-five percent of all stored information must be reviewed to determine ownership, criticality and sensitivity
- Each business unit must complete a BIA for information resources to identify critical resources
- Business units must achieve regulatory compliance
- All security roles and responsibilities must be defined
- A process must be developed to ensure business process linkages
- A comprehensive risk assessment must be performed for each business unit
- All users must be educated on an acceptable use policy
- All policies must be reviewed and revised as necessary for consistency with strategic security objectives
- Standards must exist for all policies

Near-term goals and milestones are required as part of the action plans; however, the long-term desired state needs to be clearly defined to maximize potential synergies and ensure that short- or intermediate-term action plans are ultimately aligned with the end goals. For example, a tactical solution that needs to be replaced because it will not integrate into the overall plan is likely to be more costly than one that will integrate.

It is important that the strategy and long-range plan serve to integrate near-term tactical activities. This counters the tendency to implement point solutions that are typical of the "firefighting" crisis mode of operation that characterizes many security departments. As many security managers have discovered, numerous unintegrated solutions, implemented in response to a series of crises over a period of years, become increasingly costly and difficult to manage.

1.7.5 Information Security Program Objectives

Implementing the strategy with an action plan will result in an information security program. The program is, essentially, the project plan to implement and establish ongoing management of some part or parts of the strategy.

The information security program guards the interests of those relying on information and the processes, systems and communications that handle, store and deliver the information. Its objective is to protect them from harm resulting from failures of availability, confidentiality and integrity.

Emerging definitions include concepts such as information usefulness and possession (the latter to cope with theft, deception and fraud). The networked economy certainly has added the need for trust and accountability in electronic transactions.

For most enterprises, the security objective is met when:

- Information is available and usable when required, and the systems that provide it can appropriately resist attacks (availability).
- Information is observed by or disclosed to only those who have a right to know (confidentiality).
- Information is protected against unauthorized modification (integrity).
- Business transactions, as well as information exchanges between enterprise locations or with partners, can be trusted (authenticity and nonrepudiation).

The relative priority and significance of confidentiality, integrity, availability, authenticity and nonrepudiation vary according to the data within the information system and the business context in which they are used. For example, integrity is especially important relative to management information due to the impact that information has on critical strategy-related decisions. Confidentiality may be the most important, based on regulatory or legal requirements to safeguard personal, financial or medical information or to protect trade secrets.

It is important to understand that these concepts apply equally to electronic systems and physical systems. Confidentiality, for example, is as much at risk from social engineering or "dumpster diving" as it is from a successful external attack. Integrity of information can be violated at least as easily from forged physical inputs to the system as from electronic compromise.

Many significant losses occur from insider activities. Controls used to detect anomalies and ensure integrity of systems must be just as concerned with nontechnical insider attacks as with external attacks.

Case Study

The CISO of a large manufacturing company with three years' experience has begun to realize that the information security function is having less influence and information risk recommendations are increasingly being ignored by the enterprise's business units. Despite continuing efforts to communicate with managers from the various corporate departments and business units and a positively regarded security training and awareness program, she has been having little success in getting management buy-in for implementing needed controls.

The decreasing interest in information security became apparent when she was not invited to a series of meetings concerning significant changes in company operations. During subsequent budget meetings, several executives (including the CEO) said they were unsure of the value that information security contributed to the company and suggested the budget might be better allocated elsewhere. In addition, the CISO noticed that she had not been invited to a board meeting to present updates regarding the information security program in more than a year.

The company is publicly held and has been in operation for nearly 90 years. It has been profitable for all but a few years of its existence, although profits were down during the recent worldwide recession. The company has approximately 9,000 employees and a few hundred long-term contractors. It makes a wide variety of small hand and power tools and is known internationally for the wide variety of high-quality products it makes.

The CEO is also the chairman of the board of directors and appoints people to the board on the basis of their willingness to give approval for his initiatives with little delay. Consequently, the board provides little oversight and guidance to the business, and although the audit committee of the board is increasingly concerned about the unmitigated risk the enterprise faces, it has little influence on the CEO. Due to the CEO's meager appreciation of information security, the CISO is worried that her job is at risk unless she can improve management's perception of the value of information security.

An additional complication is the drop in sales of manufactured goods that occurred during the recent recession. Competitors were selling goods below cost to reduce inventories and increase cash flow. The CEO views the increase in competition and downturn in profits as further justification to reduce expenses not directly correlated with revenue production.

Business units are the backbone of this company. Except for sharing the machinery and equipment used in manufacturing, each is a fiercely independent silo with the mission of being as profitable as possible.

Business unit managers are highly valued and are placed at a fairly senior level in the organizational chart; all of them report to the COO. Each business unit often faces short deadlines to beat the competition to market with new products. As a result, business unit administrators must carefully plan their use of machinery and equipment within each plant because several business units often need machinery and equipment at the same time. Additionally, the machinery and equipment must be available on a 24/7 basis. All machinery and equipment are controlled by process automation software on computers that run in control rooms. This software is highly distributed to the point that any kind of network disruption or outage is likely to adversely affect production.

The CISO has come to realize that the information security practice set up three years ago is not adequate to deal with current ever-growing threats. Although she has made efforts to adjust the program according to changes that occurred within the enterprise, it is clear that some areas have not been sufficiently considered. One of these areas is information security metrics relevant to management's concerns. Presently, the following types of metrics are used to measure the success of the information security program:

- Percentage of Windows systems that run antivirus software that is updated daily
- Percentage of incoming network traffic that is evaluated by a firewall on an exterior gateway
- Percentage of network traffic that is monitored by an intrusion detection system
- Percentage of systems that are patched within the required time period
- Percentage of systems that are in compliance with baseline security standards
- Percentage of spam that is deleted by the company's spam wall
- The number of vulnerabilities uncovered during automated scans

The CISO realizes that metrics she considered sufficient three years ago when the program was implemented are clearly not sufficient to be useful in management's decision-making process or adequately persuasive to generate support for the information security program. She has determined that while the current metrics have been useful operationally, they are not relevant or meaningful at a tactical and strategic level and this is the underlying cause of management failing to understand the value of the information security program and the need for a number of improvements that would increase budget requirements.

1. What aspects of information security governance might the CISO use to address some of the issues and possibly improve her standing in the enterprise?

2. In what major ways and areas can information security help the business in reaching its goals?

3. How adequate is the current set of information security metrics in terms of the company's business goals and directions?

4. How can the current set of metrics be improved? Why?

Answers on page 70

Chapter 1 ANSWER KEY

Case Study

1. The following aspects could help the CISO improve her standing in the enterprise:
    - Obtaining management commitment: Obtaining management commitment in this situation would help the CISO explain the importance of information security to the enterprise and help her to influence the board of directors to consider information security in its decisions.
    - Business case development: Developing a business case is one key tool for obtaining management commitment. It provides the information required for an enterprise to decide whether a project should proceed. The business case can be used to prove the worth of IT and information security initiatives in the enterprise and provide concrete justification for the costs.
    - Information security strategy development: An information security strategy can help to ensure strategic alignment, value delivery and resource optimization for the business. It can help to define the direction of information security in terms of the business, thus ensuring that it has proven benefit to the enterprise.
    - Information security program metrics: Information security program metrics can be used to justify that the program is meeting its defined goals and providing value to the business.
2. Information security can help this business reach its goals through implementation of controls that provide assurance that security objectives are aligned with organizational goals and business strategy.
3. The current set of information security metrics does not tie well to the business's goals. The metrics are not very meaningful in the context of how information security supports the business strategy; they simply measure arbitrary factors that may not accurately portray the information security function. This set of metrics seems to be based on discussions with the CEO, who does not have a sufficient understanding of the information security function and how it can align to meet business objectives.
4. The current set of metrics can be improved by applying SMART concepts to them. They should be specific, measurable, attainable, relevant and timely. They should tie into the information security program objectives as they support the objectives of the business. Some sample objectives include:
    - Percentage of manufacturing processes per month that are uninterrupted by security problems
    - Downtime for computers used in computer-aided engineering and computer-aided manufacturing due to security problems, supported by a quantification of impact in financial terms
    - Impact on transactions with third-party entities (e.g., shippers and suppliers) that have been affected by security problems
    - Mean time per security incident from time of onset to incident closure
    - Monthly cost of interruptions in manufacturing processes due to security problems
    - Number and cost of security incidents or events that could have been prevented if certain controls were implemented
    - Number and nature of security objectives not achieved due to funding constraints or lack of business unit cooperation
    - The ratio of affirmative media reports compared to negative reports
    - Maturity level of the enterprise's information security activities

Certified Information Systems Manager. An ISACA Certification

Chapter 2:

Information Security Risk Management

Overview

Part A: Information Risk Assessment

Part B: Information Risk Response

Overview

This chapter reviews what the information security manager must understand to appropriately apply risk management principles and practices to an enterprise's information security program.

This domain represents 20 percent of the CISM examination (approximately 30 questions).

Domain 2 Exam Content Outline

A. Information Risk Assessment

1. Emerging Risk and Threat Landscape
2. Vulnerability and Control Deficiency Analysis
3. Risk Assessment and Analysis

B. Information Risk Response

1. Risk Treatment/Risk Response Options
2. Risk and Control Ownership
3. Risk Monitoring and Reporting

Learning Objectives/Task Statements

Upon completion of this chapter, the information security manager should be able to:

- Identify internal and external influences to the organization that impact the information security strategy.
- Establish and/or maintain a process for information asset identification and classification.
- Participate in and/or oversee the risk identification, risk assessment and risk treatment process.
- Participate in and/or oversee the vulnerability assessment and threat analysis process.
- Identify, recommend, or implement appropriate risk treatment and response options to manage risk to acceptable levels based on organizational risk appetite.
- Determine whether information security controls are appropriate and effectively manage risk to an acceptable level.
- Facilitate the integration of information risk management into business and IT processes.
- Monitor for internal and external factors that may require reassessment of risk.
- Report on information security risk, including noncompliance and changes in information risk, to key stakeholders to facilitate the risk management decision-making process.

Suggested Resources for Further Reading

Brotby, W.; *Information Security Management Metrics: A Definitive Guide to Effective Security Monitoring and Measurement,* Auerbach Publications, USA, 2009

Chapman, R.; *Simple Tools and Techniques for Enterprise Risk Management, Second Edition*, John Wiley & Sons Inc., USA, 2012

Committee of Sponsoring Organizations of the Treadway Commission (COSO); *Enterprise Risk Management: Understanding and Communicating Risk Appetite*, USA, 2012

COSO; *Enterprise Risk Management: Integrating with Strategy and Performance – Executive Summary,* USA, 2017

COSO; *Enterprise Risk Management for Cloud Computing,* USA, 2012

Duke, A.; *Thinking in Bets: Making Smarter Decisions When You Don't Have All the Facts,* Random House, USA, 2018

Freund, J.; J. Jones; *Measuring and Managing Information Risk,* Butterworth-Heinemann, USA, 2014

Hubbard, D.; *The Failure of Risk Management: Why It's Broken and How to Fix It.* Wiley, United Kingdom, 2020

Hubbard, D.; *How to measure anything 3rd edition,* Wiley, USA, 2014

Hubbard, D.; *How to measure anything in cybersecurity risk,* Wiley, USA 2016

International Organization for Standardization (ISO), *ISO 31000:2018 Risk management—Guidelines,* Switzerland, 2018

ISO, *ISO/IEC 27005:2018 Information technology—Security techniques—Information security risk management,* Switzerland, 2018

International Electrotechnical Commission (IEC), *IEC 31010:2019 Risk management — Risk assessment techniques*, Switzerland, 2019

ISACA, *COBIT 2019 Focus Area: Information and Technology Risk*, USA, 2021

ISACA, COBIT, *www.isaca.org/cobit*

ISACA, *COBIT® 5 for Risk,* USA, 2013

ISACA, *Cybersecurity Fundamentals Study Guide, 3rd Edition*, USA, 2021

ISACA, *Implementing and Continually Improving IT Governance,* USA, 2010

ISACA, *The Risk IT Framework 2nd Edition,* USA, 2020

ISACA, *The Risk IT Practitioner Guide 2nd Edition,* USA, 2020

Jordan, E.; L. Silcock; *Beating IT Risks,* John Wiley & Sons Inc., USA, 2005

National Institute of Standards and Technology (NIST), *NIST Special Publication 800-30 Revision 1: Guide to Conducting Risk Assessments*, USA, 2012

NIST, *NIST Special Publication 800-39 Managing Information Security Risk: Organization, Mission, and Information System View*, USA, 2011

Panko, R.; *Risk Management and Intrusion Detection,* Prentice Hall, USA, 2006

Parmenter, D.; *Key Performance Indicators: Developing, Implementing, and Using Winning KPIs,* Wiley, Germany, 2015

Rodriguez, A.; V. Chadha; *Key Risk Indicators*, Risk Books, United Kingdom, 2015

Snyder, W.; F. Swiderski; *Threat Modeling,* Microsoft Press, USA, 2004

Taleb, N.; *The Black Swan Second Edition: The impact of the Highly Improbable,* Random House, USA, 2010

Vose, D.; *Risk Analysis: A Quantitative Guide,* Wiley, Germany, 2008

Westerman, G.; R. Hunter; *IT Risk: Turning Business Threats Into Competitive Advantage,* Harvard Business School Press, USA, 2007

SELF-ASSESSMENT QUESTIONS

CISM exam questions are developed with the intent of measuring and testing practical knowledge in information security management. All questions are multiple choice and are designed for one best answer. Every CISM question has a stem (question) and four options (answer choices). The candidate is asked to choose the correct or best answer from the options. The stem may be in the form of a question or incomplete statement. Many times a CISM examination question will require the candidate to choose the most likely or best answer.

In every case, the candidate is required to read the question carefully, eliminate known incorrect answers and then make the best choice possible. Knowing the format in which questions are asked, and how to study to gain knowledge of what will be tested, will go a long way toward answering them correctly.

1. The overall objective of risk management is to:

   A. eliminate all possible vulnerabilities.
   B. reduce risk to the lowest possible level.
   C. manage risk to an acceptable level.
   D. implement effective countermeasures.

2. The information security manager should treat regulatory compliance as:

   A. an organizational mandate.
   B. a risk management priority.
   C. a purely operational issue.
   D. another risk to be managed.

3. To address changes in risk, an effective risk management program should:
   A. ensure that continuous monitoring processes are in place.
   B. establish proper security baselines for all information resources.
   C. implement a complete data classification process.
   D. change security policies on a timely basis to address changing risk.

4. Information classification is important to properly manage risk **PRIMARILY** because:
   A. it ensures accountability for information resources as required by roles and responsibilities.
   B. it is a legal requirement under various regulations.
   C. it ensures adequate protection of assets commensurate with the degree of risk.
   D. asset protection can then be based on the potential consequences of compromise.

5. Vulnerabilities discovered during an assessment should be:
   A. handled as a risk, even though there is no threat.
   B. prioritized for remediation solely based on impact.
   C. a basis for analyzing the effectiveness of controls.
   D. evaluated for threat, impact and cost of mitigation.

6. Indemnity agreements can be used to:
   A. ensure an agreed-upon level of service.
   B. reduce impacts on organizational resources.
   C. transfer responsibility to a third party.
   D. provide an effective countermeasure to threats.

7. Residual risk can be determined by:
   A. assessing remaining vulnerabilities.
   B. performing a threat analysis.
   C. conducting a risk assessment.
   D. implementing risk transfer.

8. Data owners are **PRIMARILY** responsible for creating risk mitigation strategies to address which of the following areas?
   A. Platform security
   B. Entitlement changes
   C. Intrusion detection
   D. Antivirus controls

9. A risk analysis should:
   A. limit the scope to a benchmark of similar companies.
   B. assume an equal degree of protection for all assets.
   C. address the potential size and likelihood of loss.
   D. give more weight to the likelihood versus the size of the loss.

10. Which of the following is the **FIRST** step in selecting the appropriate controls to be implemented in a new business application?
   A. Business impact analysis
   B. Cost-benefit analysis
   C. Return on investment analysis
   D. Risk assessment

Answers on page 75

Chapter 2 ANSWER KEY

Self-Assessment Questions

1. A. It is not possible to eliminate all vulnerabilities, and vulnerabilities that have no impact or exposure do not require the expenditure of resources to remediate or achieve elimination.

   B. Reduction of risk to the lowest level generally is more costly and unnecessarily restrictive. The goal is to achieve control objectives that will result in acceptable levels of risk.

   C. The objective of risk management is managing risk to a level acceptable to the enterprise.

   D. Countermeasures are a targeted control and a part of the risk treatment process to achieve the overall objective of risk management.

2. A. A regulatory requirement, regardless of whether it is mandated by the enterprise, should be treated as any other risk.

   B. A regulatory requirement is a priority to the extent the level of risk compares to other risk. Priorities for risk management are usually based on probability and impact—the more likely the compromise and the more severe the consequences, the higher the priority.

   C. Regulatory compliance is not just an operational issue, but a management issue.

   D. There are numerous regulations that may affect an enterprise. Priority will be a management decision based on those regulations with the greatest level of enforcement (risk) and the most severe sanctions (consequences or impact) in addition to the cost of compliance (mitigation), just as with any other risk. In some cases, management may decide that the cost of potential sanctions will be less than the cost of compliance. While it is generally preferable to be as compliant as reasonably possible, the extent of regulatory compliance is a management decision, not a security decision. All risk must be prioritized, and compliance may not pose the greatest risk.

3. **A. Risk changes as threats, vulnerabilities or potential impacts change over time. The risk management program must have processes in place to monitor those changes and modify countermeasures, as appropriate, to maintain acceptable levels of residual risk.**

   B. Security baselines are set to achieve acceptable levels of particular levels of identified risk. Baselines do not address changes in risk and may need to be changed when risk changes.

   C. Data classification is based on business value of the data (i.e., the data's sensitivity or criticality) and does not address changes in risk.

   D. Policies should not require changes as a result of changes in risk. Standards and procedures may need to be changed to address significant changes in risk.

4. A. Classification does not ensure accountability.

   B. Classification is not generally a legal requirement.

   C. Classification is not based on risk.

   D. Classification is based on potential impact or consequences of compromise.

5. A. Vulnerabilities may not be exposed to potential threats. Also, there may be no threat or possibly little or no impact even if exploited. While threats are always evolving, without additional information, the appropriate treatment cannot be determined.

   B. Vulnerabilities should be prioritized for remediation based on probability of compromise (which is affected by the level of exposure), impact and cost of remediation.

   C. Vulnerabilities discovered will, to some extent, show whether existing controls are in place to address a potential risk, but they do not indicate the controls' effectiveness.

D. Vulnerabilities uncovered should be evaluated and prioritized based on whether there is a credible threat, the impact if the vulnerability is exploited and the cost of mitigation. If there is a potential threat but little or no impact if the vulnerability is exploited, there is little risk, and it may not be cost-effective to address it.

6. A. Indemnity agreements are not used to define service levels; they are provided by service level agreements.

   B. Indemnity agreements serve to reduce financial impacts by providing compensation for adverse events in the scope of the agreement.

   C. Legal responsibility cannot be transferred by indemnity agreements or any other instrument.

   D. Indemnity agreements are not a countermeasure to threats, but they can be considered a compensating control.

7. A. Determining remaining vulnerabilities after countermeasures are in place says nothing about threats; therefore, risk cannot be determined.

   B. Risk cannot be determined by threat analysis alone.

   C. Regardless of whether risk is residual, it is determined by a risk assessment.

   D. Transferring all risk is not relevant to determining residual risk.

8. A. Platform security is the responsibility of IT.

   B. Data owners are concerned with, and responsible for, who has access to their resources; therefore, they need to be concerned with the strategy of how to mitigate risk of data resource usage.

   C. Intrusion detection is the responsibility of IT.

   D. Antivirus controls are typically IT security concerns.

9. A. A risk analysis would not normally consider the benchmark of similar companies as providing relevant information other than for comparison purposes.

   B. Assuming an equal degree of protection would be rational only in the rare event that all assets are similar in sensitivity and criticality.

   C. A risk analysis deals with the potential size and likelihood of loss.

   D. Because the likelihood determines (on an annualized basis) the size of the loss, both elements must be considered in the calculation.

10. A. If the risk is determined to be unacceptable, a business impact analysis (BIA) can be used to determine the level of mitigation necessary.

    B. A cost-benefit analysis can be used to determine whether mitigation cost is appropriate, considering the potential impact after a BIA has been performed.

    C. Return on investment analysis focuses on the business value of the control compared to its cost over time.

    D. It is necessary to first consider the risk and determine whether it is acceptable to the enterprise. Risk assessment can identify threats and vulnerabilities and calculate the risk. Controls are evaluated by comparing the cost of the control against the potential impact if the risk were exploited.

Part A: Information Risk Assessment

Risk management is a process aimed at achieving an optimal balance between realizing opportunities for gain, minimizing vulnerabilities and reducing the potential for loss. This is usually accomplished by ensuring that the impact of threats exploiting vulnerabilities is within acceptable limits at an acceptable cost. Risk management is different from managing risk, which is often used synonymously with risk mitigation or risk response/risk treatment.

In practical business terms, risk management means that risk is managed so it does not materially impact the enterprise or catastrophically degrade a business process to a point beyond what has been deemed as acceptable. Risk is inherent in all activities; typically, a higher level of strategic risk will be taken to attempt to achieve higher returns. However, each enterprise needs to define its risk appetite and tolerance levels and ensure they are appropriate in order to achieve the organizational goals it wants to accomplish.

The foundation for effective risk management is a comprehensive risk assessment, based on a solid understanding of the enterprise risk universe, which is ever-changing. It is not possible to devise a practical and relevant risk management program if there is no common understanding of the nature and extent of risk to information resources and the potential impact on the enterprise's activities. The structure of an enterprise's risk function can be centralized or decentralized. Mature enterprises generally manage risk through an enterprise risk management (ERM) group or department to ensure consistency. There may be instances in which enterprises have a separate IT risk department, whereas others have IT risk as a team under the ERM group. In some cases, the information security management, business resiliency and incident management programs may be integrated into an existing risk management program. In others, risk is managed by several departments and operational units, necessitating efforts to ensure continuity and integration of risk management activities.

Because risk management decisions typically have major financial implications and can require changes across the entire enterprise, it is imperative that senior management is supportive of the process and fully understands and agrees with the results of the program.

Risk management can mean different things to different people in the enterprise. For example, senior management may be looking only at the risk that would prevent the enterprise from executing its strategy and may have a difficult time justifying investing in controls to address threats that are perceived to have a low probability of occurrence. Business line managers might only look at threats to their operations and ability to meet their performance targets. An IT auditor's view may be that risk management means the prevention of loss, whereas an insurance manager could define it as cost-effective risk financing. It is critically important that the enterprise clearly provide its definition of risk management.

The effectiveness of risk management depends largely on the degree to which it is a part of an enterprise's culture and the extent to which risk management becomes everyone's responsibility.

The design and implementation of an effective risk management program will be influenced by the enterprise's:

- Culture
- Mission and objectives
- Organizational structure
- Support from senior leadership
- Ability to absorb losses
- Products and services
- Management and operation processes
- Specific organizational practices
- Physical, environmental and regulatory conditions

Effective risk management efforts not only work toward reducing the impact and probability of a risk event occurring, but also enable the decision-making process. This is important, as risk management efforts will allow informed decisions to be made about how much or how little risk the enterprise is willing to take on, which investments will yield the highest benefits, and how to prioritize limited resources in order to achieve the enterprise's strategy. Risk management establishes the foundation for sound governance.

One of the outcomes of good governance is effective risk management. This includes executing appropriate measures to respond to risk and to reduce potential impacts on information resources to an acceptable level, providing:

- An understanding of the enterprise's threat, vulnerability and risk profiles
- An understanding of risk exposure and potential consequences of compromise
- Awareness of risk management priorities based on potential consequences
- An organizational risk mitigation strategy sufficient to achieve acceptable consequences from residual risk
- Organizational acceptance/deference based on an understanding of the potential consequences of residual risk
- Measurable evidence that risk management resources are used in an appropriate and cost-effective manner
- An understanding of the enterprise's processes and information assets and their need for protection
- An understanding of the enterprise's operating environment emerging risk

2.1 Emerging Risk and Threat Landscape

The environment an enterprise operates in is constantly changing in multiple aspects, including business, geopolitical, regulatory, statutory and how technologies are being used. The potential threats and resulting risks to the enterprise are also evolving. For example, the COVID pandemic triggered the wide-scale movement of employees from workplaces to working remotely. The information security manager should be aware of and monitor these changes in terms of how they may impact the enterprise's information assets, business processes, ability to demonstrate compliance, privacy, security and risk overall.

2.1.1 Risk Identification

Before an enterprise can look into potential and emerging risk, it is important to know how to identify risk. Risk identification is the process by which the type and nature of viable threats are determined and the enterprise's vulnerabilities that are subject to those threats are examined. The vulnerabilities that may be exploited by the identified threats constitute identified risk. The process of risk identification is essential to effective risk management because only identified risk can be assessed and treated appropriately.

It is necessary to identify all information assets, including those that may reside with third parties (e.g., service providers, outsourcers, contractors). (See Chapter 3 for more information.) Viable threats, both potential and realized, must be determined. The viability of a threat considers the following two elements: The threat exists or could reasonably be expected to materialize; and the threat is subject to some form of control (e.g., administrative, technical or physical).

Risk identification is often accomplished through a knowledgeable group developing a variety of risk scenarios or brainstorming sessions (i.e., structured what-if techniques, diagramming techniques). These exercises assume that all significant vulnerabilities of the enterprise are known and the type and nature of threats that could exploit them are identified. Vulnerabilities take many forms. They may be commonly understood technical weaknesses, or they may be obscured by business processes or unmonitored procedures. A lack of awareness by staff can also create vulnerabilities, such as exposure of information via conversations in public spaces (e.g., elevators or restaurants) that could be overheard or via leaks to social media. Outsourced services are a source of vulnerabilities that may be difficult to determine.

It is difficult to identify all viable threats. As determined and well-financed attackers think of ever more sophisticated schemes to compromise enterprises, determining the range of potential threats is a formidable challenge for even the most experienced defenders.

All the identified vulnerabilities must be evaluated in terms of viable threats that might compromise them and result in an impact. This exercise will generate a list of identified risk for subsequent analysis to determine likelihood and the extent of potential impacts. Significant vulnerabilities not subject to an identified threat should be added to the analysis list, as a possible threat may not have been uncovered or may develop in the future. A prudent approach may be to consider that what can go wrong eventually will, and the process itself is subject to human error.

Despite these challenges, the odds of a successful attack can be significantly reduced by the diligent effort of a knowledgeable group identifying possible risk and remediation options on an ongoing basis. This is typically accomplished by brainstorming with members of the various organizational units.

High-quality information and thorough knowledge of the enterprise and its internal and external environments are very important in identifying risk. Historical information about the enterprise or similar enterprises may also prove very useful because the information can lead to reasonable predictions about current and evolving issues that have not yet been faced by the enterprise.

Identifying what may happen is rarely sufficient. The fact that there are many ways an event can occur makes it important to study all reasonably possible and significant causes and scenarios. Methods and tools used to identify risk and its occurrence include threat modeling, checklists, judgments based on experience and records, flowcharts, brainstorming, systems analysis, scenario analysis and systems engineering techniques.

In selecting a risk identification methodology, the following techniques should be considered:

- Workshops, which can prove effective in building commitment and making use of different experiences
- Structured techniques, such as flowcharting, system design review, systems analysis, hazard and operability studies, and operational modeling
- What-if and scenario analysis for less clearly defined situations, such as the identification of strategic risk and processes with a more general structure, as shown in **figure 2.1**
- Threats identified internally and externally mapped to identified and suspected vulnerabilities

Figure 2.1—Risk Scenario Approaches

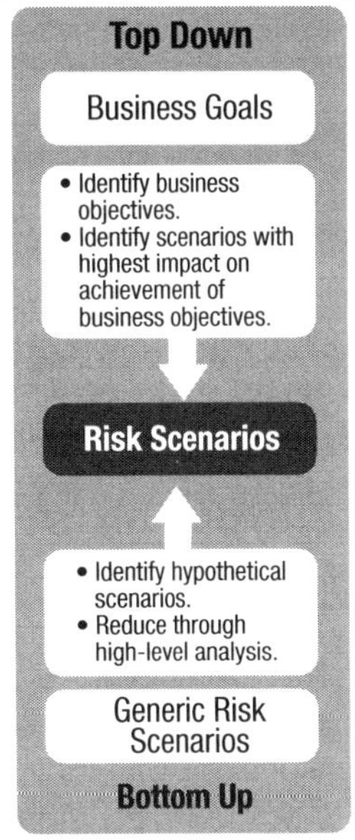

Source: ISACA, *COBIT 5 for Risk*, USA, 2013

2.1.2 Threats

Threats to information resources and the likelihood that they will exploit an existing vulnerability must be assessed. In this context, threats are any circumstances or events with the potential to cause harm to an information resource by exploiting vulnerabilities in the system.

Threats may be the result of accidental actions, intentional/deliberate actions or natural events. Threats may originate from either internal or external sources, and actual attacks may leverage a combination of both internal and external sources. They may be caused by natural events or political, economic or competitive factors. Threats always exist and are typically beyond the direct control of the enterprise. Not all conceivable threats need to be considered by every enterprise. For example, an enterprise that operates in a region with a seismic rating of zero might not be inclined to invest their efforts in documenting exposure to volcanoes or earthquakes. However, it is important to identify the various types of threats that do apply and may compromise systems or otherwise affect the enterprise.

Threats may be divided into multiple categories, including:

- Physical
- Natural events

- Loss of essential services
- Disturbance due to radiation
- Compromise of information
- Technical failures
- Unauthorized actions
- Compromise of functions

The information security manager should document all the threats that may apply to the systems and business processes under review. This requires using the resources noted previously but should also include examining the cause of past failures, audit reports, media reports, information from national computer emergency response teams (CERTs), data from security vendors and communication with internal or peer groups.

Where threats may be directed by individual agents, the information security manager should know and remain aware that such threat agents tend to be imaginative, creative and determined and will explore new methods and avenues of attack. To counter threat agents, the information security manager must also be determined and creative and seek to discover as many threats as possible. An unidentified threat is one for which the enterprise is more likely to be unprepared and vulnerable than a threat that is well documented.

Sources for information regarding threats are:

- Assessments
- Audits
- Business continuity plans
- Cybersecurity advisory organizations
- Finance
- Government publications
- Human resources
- Insurance companies
- Management
- Media
- Product vendors
- Security companies
- Service providers
- Threat monitoring agencies
- Users

Internal Threats

Although many enterprises label their employees and other staff as their best asset, they may be unhappy if inadequately trained, treated poorly or not given enough time to do their jobs properly. Disillusionment and resentment can lead to a higher risk of errors, negligence and more conscious actions such as theft. Key personnel may be drawn to another company and leave serious gaps in the knowledge and skills needed to operate systems effectively.

Employees are the cause of a significant number of business impacts, which can be intentional and unintentional. A disgruntled employee may intentionally compromise systems or release data that expose the enterprise to legal or reputational risk. Employees may be convinced, bribed or threatened to disclose trade secrets for ideological or economic reasons. Many employees have a level of access to systems and data that far exceeds their actual job requirements, which can be used and exploited in an attack. The solution to the employee problem, therefore, lies at least in part in the application of need-to-know and least privilege and segregation of duties (SoD), but this is an imperfect solution. Any system has trusted insiders, and one of them choosing to violate trust is difficult to either predict or prevent.

The typical profile of a malicious insider is a current or former employee, contractor or other business partner who has or once had authorized access to an enterprise's network, system or data and intentionally intercepted, exfiltrated, interrupted, modified or fabricated data on the enterprise's information systems. The first step in addressing personnel threats is to start with the hiring process and review the qualifications and attitude of prospective employees. Employment candidates may submit incorrect information on job applications and claim education, certification or experience they do not actually possess. A review of references and performance of background checks may be worthwhile to the extent permitted by law. At the time of hiring, the employee should be required to sign a nondisclosure agreement (NDA) and be advised of the ethics and policies of the enterprise.

Throughout employment, employees should be reminded of organizational policies and their responsibilities through awareness sessions and regular management reviews. One of the best employee-based controls is to actively engage with employees to understand any frustrations, complaints or issues they may be facing and then seek to resolve those issues. During times of strike, layoffs, mergers, acquisitions, relocation and reorganization, an employee's threat profile is more likely to increase—and by extension, the associated risk. An employee who has been recently demoted or bypassed for a promotion may also pose a risk.

At the end of employment, the enterprise should ensure that the employee returns all organizational assets, including identification badges, equipment (e.g., laptops, mobile phones, access cards) and uniforms so that they cannot be used to gain unauthorized access in the future. In addition, systems, network and facility access should be disabled or removed immediately prior to the employee's departure to minimize the potential for crimes of opportunity.

Enterprises should implement continuous monitoring across all business systems. Anomalous behavior of staff and other insiders should be flagged through use of artificial intelligence and machine learning.

External Threats

In a networked environment, where data is stored offsite or hosted by cloud service providers, threats to information systems from outside the enterprise can originate from anywhere and may take several forms, including, but not limited to:

- Criminal acts
- Data corruption
- Disease (epidemic/pandemic)
- Espionage
- Facility flaws (freezing pipe/pipe burst)
- Fire
- Flooding
- Hardware flaws
- Industrial accidents
- Stolen assets
- Mechanical failures
- Power surge/utility failure
- Sabotage
- Seismic activity
- Severe storms
- Software errors
- Supply chain interruption
- Terrorism
- Theft

Natural events such as floods, storms, earthquakes or tornadoes are unpredictable and may be extremely damaging. The use of governmental data and weather monitoring services may identify the threats associated with natural events and allow the risk practitioner to take necessary steps to be prepared.

An external personnel threat includes a hacker, a thief or an advanced persistent threat (APT) that is skilled and determined to break into systems, normally for military, political or economic purposes.

Most breaches are the result of targets of opportunity, not determined attacks. As seen in the annual reports from Verizon[14] and others, many enterprises were breached because they were discovered to be easy targets and threat agents took advantage of their vulnerabilities.

Advanced Persistent Threats

Advanced persistent threats (APTs) refers to advanced, highly skilled attackers who are sufficiently motivated to exploit systems and networks. The increased skills available to the hacking community and the effectiveness of the tools they possess make the risk of compromise much more significant. APTs may be sponsored by governments, organized crime or competitors. The information security manager must be aware that APTs pose a significant risk to enterprises of virtually all types globally and ensure that appropriate steps are in place to detect and identify this threat.

APT is defined by the US National Institute of Standards and Technology (NIST) as follows[15]:

> *An APT is an adversary that possesses sophisticated levels of expertise and significant resources which allow it to create opportunities to achieve its objectives using multiple attack vectors (e.g., cyber, physical and deception). These objectives typically include establishing*

[14] Verizon, "2021 Data Breach Investigations Report," www.verizon.com/business/resources/reports/dbir/

[15] National Institute of Standards and Technology (NIST), Special Publication 800-39 "Managing Information Security Risk: Organization, Mission, and Information System View," March 2011, https://csrc.nist.gov/publications/detail/sp/800-39/final

and extending footholds within the IT infrastructure of the targeted organizations for purposes of exfiltrating information, undermining or impeding critical aspects of a mission, program or organization; or positioning itself to carry out these objectives in the future. The advanced persistent threat: (i) pursues its objectives repeatedly over an extended period of time; (ii) adapts to defenders' efforts to resist it; and (iii) is determined to maintain the level of interaction needed to execute its objectives.

Typical APT attacks have generally exhibited the following life cycle:

- **Begin initial compromise**—Attackers use social engineering and spear phishing via email, using zero-day viruses. They may plant malware on a website that the victimized employees are likely to visit.
- **Establish foothold**—Attackers may plant remote administration software in the victim's network and/or create network backdoors and tunnels that allow stealth access to network infrastructure.
- **Escalate privileges**—APTs use exploits and password cracking to acquire administrator privileges over the victim's computer and possibly expand it to Windows domain administrator accounts.
- **Perform internal reconnaissance**—Attackers collect information on surrounding infrastructure, trust relationships and Windows domain structure.
- **Move laterally**—They expand control to other workstations, servers and infrastructure elements and perform data harvesting on them.
- **Maintain presence**—APTs ensure continued control over access channels and credentials acquired in previous steps.
- **Complete mission**—Attackers exfiltrate stolen data from the victim's network.

Figure 2.2 shows the typical sources of APT. Due to the required sophistication, expertise, time and costs involved, these efforts are normally mounted only against high-value targets.

Figure 2.2—Typical Sources of APT

Threat	What They Seek	Business Impact
Intelligence agencies	Political, defense or commercial trade secrets	Loss of trade secrets or commercial, competitive advantage
Criminal groups	Money transfers, extortion opportunities, personal identity information or any secrets for potential onward sale	Financial loss, large-scale customer data breach or loss of trade secrets
Terrorist groups	Production of widespread terror through death, destruction and disruption	Loss of production and services, stock market irregularities and potential risk to human life
Activist groups	Confidential information or disruption of services	Major data breach or loss of service
Armed forces	Intelligence or positioning to support future attacks on critical national infrastructure	Serious damage to facilities in the event of a military conflict

Source: ISACA, *Advanced Persistent Threats: How to Manage the Risk to Your Business*, USA, 2013

2.1.3 Defining a Risk Management Framework

To develop an enterprise's systematic risk management program, a reference model should be used and adapted to the circumstances of the enterprise. The reference model will reflect the desired state discussed in Chapter 1 (i.e., a snapshot of a future state that meets all risk management objectives). Several publications/standards are available to provide guidance on information technology and security risk management approaches. Examples include:

- COBIT
- NIST Special Publication 800-39 Managing Information Security Risk: Organization, Mission and Information System View

- NIST Special Publication 800-39 Managing Information Security Risk: Organization, Mission and Information System View

The standards referenced in the list have similar risk management requirements, including:

- **Policy**—An enterprise's senior management/executive leadership needs to define and document its policy for risk management, including its objectives and level of commitment. The policy must be relevant to the enterprise's strategic context, goals, objectives and the nature of its business. Management should ensure that the policy is understood, and that standards are developed, implemented and maintained at all levels in the enterprise.
- **Planning and resourcing**—Responsibility, authority, accountability and interrelationships of personnel who perform and verify work affecting risk management must be defined and documented (see Section 1.4 Organizational Structures, Roles and Responsibilities). The enterprise must identify resource requirements and facilitate the implementation of risk management programs, through the assignment of trained personnel to manage ongoing work activities and verify activities for internal review.
- **Implementation program**—The enterprise must define the steps required to implement an effective risk management system.
- **Management review**—Executive management must ensure periodic review of the risk management system to ensure its continuing stability and effectiveness in satisfying requirements of the program. Records of such reviews must be maintained.
- **Risk management process**—Risk management can be applied at both strategic and tactical levels in the enterprise: products/services, business/IT processes, projects, decisions, applications and platforms. The enterprise must prioritize individual risk treatment according to its business objectives, risk appetite and regulatory environment for the industry.
- **Risk management documentation**—For each stage of the process, adequate records must be kept that are sufficient to satisfy an independent audit.

The framework for risk management establishes the basic parameters within which risk must be managed are defined, including the criteria for acceptable risk and control objectives. Consequently, the scope for the rest of the risk management process is also set. It includes the definition of basic assumptions for the enterprise's external and internal environment and the overall objectives of the risk management process and activities. Although the definition of scope and framework are fundamental for the establishment of risk management, they are independent of the particular structure of the management process, methods and tools to be used for the implementation.

In order to define an efficient framework, it is important to:

- Understand the background of the enterprise and its risk (e.g., its core processes, valuable assets, competitive areas)
- Understand the threats the enterprise potentially faces (i.e., threat actor motivations and capabilities)
- Understand the efficacy of controls present within the enterprise (i.e., whether the controls actually reduce residual risk to acceptable levels)
- Evaluate existing risk management activities and criteria for acceptable risk levels
- Develop a structure and process for the development of risk management initiatives and controls sufficient to achieve acceptable risk levels (control objectives)

This approach is useful for:

- Clarifying and gaining common understanding of the organizational objectives
- Identifying the environment in which the objectives are set
- Specifying the main scope and objectives for risk management, applicable restrictions or specific conditions, and the outcomes required
- Developing a set of criteria against which risk will be measured
- Defining a set of key elements for structuring the risk identification and assessment process

The risk management program must be integrated with the enterprise's overall management system and, whenever possible, must adapt various elements—such as policies, organizational processes, accountability, resources and communication methods—to its specific needs.

Many enterprises' existing management practices and processes include elements of risk management, and many enterprises have already adopted a risk management process for particular types of risk or circumstances. These processes should be critically reviewed and assessed to determine whether they meet current control objectives and other requirements (e.g., efficiency, user acceptance, cultural compatibility, regulatory requirements).

Defining the External Environment

Defining the external environment includes specifying the environment in which the enterprise operates. The external environment typically includes:

- The global/local market; the industry; and the competitive, financial and political environments
- The legal and regulatory environment
- Social and cultural conditions
- External stakeholders

It is important that both the perceptions and values of the various stakeholders and any externally generated threats or opportunities are properly evaluated and taken into consideration.

Defining the Internal Environment

Key areas that must be evaluated to provide a comprehensive view of the enterprise's internal environment include:

- Key business drivers (e.g., market indicators, competitive advantages, product attractiveness)
- The enterprise's strengths, weaknesses, opportunities and threats
- Internal stakeholders
- Organizational structure and culture
- Assets in terms of resources (i.e., people, systems, processes, capital)
- Goals and objectives, and the strategies already in place to achieve them
- The amount of loss the enterprise is willing to accept in pursuit of organization's strategy
- The acceptable and unacceptable risk criteria for programs/projects at operational and tactical levels

2.1.4 Emerging Threats

Indications of emerging threats may include unusual activity on a system, repeated alarms, slow system or network performance, or new or excessive activity in logs. In many cases, compromised enterprises have evidence of emergent threats in their logs well in advance of the actual compromise, but the evidence is not noticed or acted on. Lack of effective monitoring, when combined with a threat, can lead to a breach.

Most technologies are built with an emphasis on function and purpose without due consideration for the security implications. As a result, new technology tends to be a source of new vulnerabilities and may even itself be a threat agent within an information system. The information security manager must be alert to the emergence of new technologies and prepare for their introduction into the enterprise, particularly if the technologies promise cost savings or competitive advantage.

Bring your own device (BYOD) is an example of a revolution in the way enterprises view technology assets. It is an opportunity with self-evident risk, yet it has tempted a wide variety of enterprises by promising to greatly reduce the cost of initial procurement of IT assets and the rate at which they need to be refreshed. A threat strategy that emphasizes rejection of new technology is unlikely to remain in place for long after it gains executive sponsorship.

Information security managers need to be aware of the ever-changing threat landscape and how it affects their enterprise. As infrastructures evolve, new threats often arise in the least assuming areas.

The adoption of cloud computing in the form of as-a-service models for platform (PaaS), infrastructure (IaaS) and software (SaaS) and the interconnection between these new models and legacy technology require careful consideration to changing the risk profile. New sets of risk-reducing processes, staff and technologies that had not been previously considered may be required to reduce residual risk to acceptable levels.

The explosive growth of various smart technologies, Internet of Things (IoT)-enabled devices and edge computing enable a model in which devices are located and information is processed in the periphery of the network, physically closer to user locations. This decentralized model differs from the traditional data center paradigm, and information security managers need to take into account the associated risk and consider the required controls to address and reduce risk and ensure it aligns with the enterprise's defined risk appetite and tolerance.

2.1.5 Risk, Likelihood and Impact

The International Organization of Standardization (ISO) defines risk as "the effect of uncertainty on objectives."[16] This means that outcomes could have either a positive or negative result. In this publication, risk will be considered from primarily a negative perspective, where negative risk is defined as "the probability of an event (uncertainty) and its consequences (impact to objectives)."

The likelihood, or probability, is a measure of the frequency that an event may occur. When identifying risk, likelihood is used to calculate the level of risk based on the frequency of events, combined with the impact of those events that may occur in a given time period (e.g., a year). The likelihood or frequency combined with the magnitude (of impact) is used in determining annual loss expectancy (ALE). The greater the frequency, the greater the likelihood and, consequently, the greater the risk. See Section 2.3.8 Risk Analysis for more information.

When discussing risk, it is important to acknowledge the subtle differences between likelihood and probability. Likelihood is an expected frequency of occurrence, meaning how many times an event may occur over a specified interval (weeks, months, years). Probability is described in a range from 0 to 1; in other words, an event may or may not occur. When identifying risk, the level of risk is calculated based on its likelihood and probability, in combination with the impact that may occur within a given time period (e.g., a year). The greater the likelihood (or frequency of occurrence) and the resulting outcome (or consequence/impact), the greater the risk.

Determining likelihood requires consideration of a variety of factors, including:

- **Volatility**—The probability of a risk may vary depending on the volatility of the situation. When conditions vary a great deal, there may be times when the risk is greater than at other times, increasing unpredictability and, therefore, requiring a higher estimation of risk.
- **Velocity**—In this context, velocity is a consideration of the extent of prior warning of an event and the amount of time between an event's occurrence and the subsequent impact.
- **Proximity**—This is a term used to indicate the time between an event and the impact (i.e., the greater the velocity, the closer the proximity).
- **Interdependency**—It is important to consider risk not in isolation, but rather in the organizational context and in relationship to other assets and functions. The materialization of several types of risk might affect the enterprise differently depending in part on whether the risk events occur concurrently or sequentially.
- **Motivation**—The extent of an attacker's motivation will affect the chances of success. The nature of the motivation affects, to some extent, the type of assets at risk (i.e., politically motivated nation states will typically target different assets than criminals seeking financial gain will target, thereby affecting the risk to particular assets).
- **Skill**—The level of skill of potential attackers will typically determine the type and value of assets attacked (i.e., high-value assets are likely to attract more skilled attackers).
- **Visibility**—High-visibility targets are more likely to be attacked.

The information security manager must understand the business risk profile (normally in the negative sense) of the enterprise in terms of adversely affecting the ability to achieve its objectives.

No single model provides a complete picture of all possible risk, but logically categorizing the risk areas of an enterprise (as illustrated in **figure 2.3**) facilitates a focus on key risk management strategies and decisions. It also enables the enterprise to develop and implement risk treatment approaches that are relevant to the business and cost-effective.

[16] International Organization for Standardization (ISO), ISO Guide 73:2009 "Risk Management – Vocabulary," November 2009, www.iso.org/standard/44651.html

Figure 2.3—Operational Risk Categories

Operational Risk Area	Description	Information or IT Mapping
Facilities and operating environment risk	Loss or damage to operational capabilities caused by problems with premises, facilities, services or equipment	Business continuity management for IT facilities
Health and safety risk	Threats to the personal health and safety of staff, customers and members of the public	Confidentiality of home addresses, travel schedules, etc.
Information risk	Unauthorized disclosure or modification of information, loss of availability of information, or inappropriate use of information	All aspects of information and IT security
Control frameworks risk	Inadequate design or performance of the existing risk management infrastructure	Business process analysis to identify critical information flows and control points
Legal and regulatory compliance risk	Failure to comply with the laws of the jurisdictions in which business operations are carried out; failure to comply with any regulatory, reporting and taxation standards; failure to comply with contracts; or failure of contracts to protect business interests	Compliance with applicable data protection legislation, cryptographic control regulations, etc.; accuracy, timeliness and quality of information reported to regulators; and content management of all information sent to other parties
Corporate governance risk	Failure of directors to fulfill their personal statutory obligations in managing and controlling the enterprise	Information security policy making, performance measurement and reporting
Reputation risk	The negative effects of public opinion, customer opinion and market reputation, and the damage caused to the brand by failure to manage public relations	Controlling the disclosure of confidential information; presenting a public image of a well-managed enterprise
Strategic risk	Failure to meet the long-term strategic goals of the business, including dependence on any estimated or planned outcomes that may be in the control of third parties	Managing the quality and granularity of information on which strategic business decisions are based (e.g., mergers, acquisitions, disposals)
Processing and behavioral risk	Problems with service or product delivery caused by failure of internal controls or information systems, lack of employee integrity, errors and mistakes, or through weaknesses in operating procedures	All aspects of information systems security and the security-related behavior of employees in carrying out their tasks
Technology risk	Failure to plan, manage and monitor the performance of technology-related projects, products, services, processes, staff and delivery channels	Failure of information and communications technology systems and the need for business continuity management

Figure 2.3—Operational Risk Categories *(cont.)*		
Operational Risk Area	Description	Information or IT Mapping
Project management risk	Failure to plan and manage the resources required for achieving tactical project goals, leading to budget overruns, time overruns or both, or leading to failure to complete the project; the technical failure of a project or the failure to manage the integration aspects with existing parts of the business and the impact that changes can have on business operations	Management of all information security-related projects
Criminal and illicit acts risk	Loss or damage caused by fraud, theft, willful neglect, gross negligence, vandalism, sabotage, extortion, etc.	Provision of security services and mechanisms to prevent all types of cybercrime
Human resources risk	Failure to recruit, develop or retain employees with the appropriate skills and knowledge or to manage employee relations	Need for policies protecting employees from sexual harassment, racial abuse, etc., through corporate email systems, etc.
Supplier risk	Failure to evaluate adequately the capabilities of suppliers leading to breakdowns in the supply process or substandard delivery of supplied goods and services; failure to understand and manage supply chain issues	Outsourced service delivery of IT or other business information processing activities
Management information risk	Inadequate, inaccurate, incomplete or untimely provision of information to support the management decision-making process	Managing the accuracy, integrity, currency, timeliness and quality of information used for management decision support
Ethics risk	Damage caused by unethical business practices, including those of associated business partners. Issues include racial and religious discrimination, exploitation of child labor, pollution, environmental issues, negative behavior toward disadvantaged groups, etc.	Ethical collection, storage and use of information; management of information content on websites, intranets, and in corporate emails and instant messaging systems
Geopolitical risk	Loss or damage in some countries caused by political instability, poor quality of infrastructure in developing regions, or cultural differences and misunderstandings	Managing all aspects of information security and IT systems' security in regions where the enterprise has business operations but where there is special geopolitical risk
Cultural risk	Failure to deal with cultural issues affecting employees, customers or other stakeholders. These include language, religion, morality, dress codes and other community customs and practices.	Management of information content on websites, intranets, and in corporate emails and instant messaging systems
Climate and weather risk	Loss or damage caused by unusual climate conditions, including drought, heat, flood, cold, storm, winds, etc.	Business continuity management for IT facilities
Source: Copyright SABSA Institute, *www.sabsa.org*. Reproduced with permission.		

A high-level categorization of risk is an inherent part of business and, because it is impractical and costly to attempt to eliminate all risk (risk can never be eliminated), every enterprise has a level of risk it will accept (risk appetite). The level of acceptable risk is a decision that must be made by senior management, although the information security manager may need to assist management in developing a concrete set of criteria. Approaches to assist in determining the level of acceptable risk are discussed in detail in Section 2.4.1 Determining Risk Capacity and Acceptance Risk (Risk Appetite).

The essential concept is that the cost of protection should be proportional to the value of the asset and not exceed the value of the asset being protected. With most remedial activities, there is a point of diminishing returns at which costs of additional controls rise faster than the benefits derived.

Many factors will affect what the enterprise ultimately considers acceptable based on considerations such as culture, the ability of the enterprise to absorb losses (sometimes referred to as risk appetite), the effects and costs of mitigation, the extent and kind of potential impacts and possibly contractual and other legal requirements. In terms of culture, the enterprise may be generally risk-averse and opt for tighter security and higher control costs, or the enterprise may be risk-aggressive and choose to take more chances.

For most enterprises, the failure to adequately identify, analyze, evaluate and respond to risk results in risk management efforts not being properly allocated and directed at situations with the greatest probability of compromise and the greatest impact.

The primary enterprise risk management efforts are typically directed at controlling unauthorized system access—which, on average, represents a relatively small proportion of losses. The majority of losses from other identified causes—such as outsourced services, electronic backup, lost or stolen laptops, and paper records—generally receive less attention.

For the prevalent sources of compromise, the information security manager needs to consider how to allocate resources for the greatest benefit. Because many of the most significant threats can be addressed directly (e.g., employees and former employees, service providers, consultants, suppliers), it is prudent to consider the specific controls addressing the risk. Strong access controls, limiting access to need-to-know, network segmentation, effective termination procedures and good monitoring will all contribute to reducing an enterprise's risk.

It is important to recognize that the major risk to enterprises does not come from technology and cannot always be solved by technology. Most risk is largely a management and personnel problem.

2.1.6 Risk Register

During the process of identifying risk and its components, a risk register should be established. The register should serve as a central repository for all information security risk, including specific threats, vulnerabilities, exposures and assets affected. It should include the asset owner, the risk owner and other stakeholders.

As the risk register is a living repository, content within the risk register should be filled out as the assessment process gets underway. Once the identification, analysis, evaluation and risk response efforts have been completed and other pertinent information has been entered into the register, it will serve as an authoritative reference point for all risk management-related activities.

Risk registers enhance accountability by assigning risk to risk owners and provide a tracking mechanism for ensuring risk has been mitigated according to the agreed action plans and within the agreed timelines. Without a risk register, there is lack of accountability.

The risk register provides the narrative of the enterprise's risk profile. A risk profile is an essential element for effective information risk management. It will serve to provide a comprehensive overview of the overall (known) risk to which the enterprise is exposed along with other pertinent information. A variety of approaches are available to accomplish this requirement, including the detailed and effective COBIT process (**figure 2.4**).

<table>
<tr><th colspan="2">Figure 2.4—I&T Risk Profile</th></tr>
<tr><th>Type of Content</th><th>Specification</th></tr>
<tr><td>Description</td><td>The comprehensive view of I&T risk</td></tr>
<tr><td>Goals and quality criteria</td><td>
<ul>
<li>Source information is accurate (confirmed through audit) and aggregated in the risk management application according to fixed rules.</li>
<li>Information is based on verifiable facts and substantiations, using the common risk view established throughout the enterprise.</li>
<li>The risk profile is structured as defined and the recipient confirms the relevancy of information provided.</li>
<li>The risk profile covers the full enterprise scope and the full risk register. However, some information might not be available, and assumptions need to be made and substantiated.</li>
<li>The volume of information is appropriate to the recipient's needs and defined during the design.</li>
<li>In order for stakeholders to make informed decisions, the risk profile should be understood by all relevant stakeholders.</li>
<li>Access to the risk profile is determined by the risk function, and is restricted as follows:
<ul>
<li>Write access: risk function (based on input from contributors)</li>
<li>Read access: all other stakeholders</li>
</ul></li>
</ul></td></tr>
<tr><td>Structure/High-level content</td><td>A risk profile is a description of the overall (identified) I&T risk to which the enterprise is exposed. An I&T risk profile consists of:
A. Risk register
A risk register provides detailed information on:
<ul>
<li>Each identified risk, such as risk owner, details of the scenario and assumptions. A risk scenario is a detailed description of an IT-related risk that can lead to a business impact when it occurs. It includes elements such as:
<ul>
<li>Actor/threat community</li>
<li>Intent/motivation</li>
<li>Threat event</li>
<li>Assets/resource</li>
<li>Effect</li>
<li>Timing</li>
<li>Affected stakeholders</li>
<li>Causes/indicators</li>
<li>Information on the detailed scores (risk ratings) on the risk analysis</li>
<li>Detailed information on the risk response (e.g., action owner) and the risk response status (e.g., time frame for action)</li>
<li>Related projects</li>
<li>Risk tolerance level</li>
</ul></li>
</ul>
See figure 2.5 for a sample risk register template.
B. Risk action plan
The risk action plan provides a framework that documents the priority order in which individual risk actions shall be implemented and how they shall be implemented. An action plan should be discussed with appropriate stakeholders and clearly document:
<ul>
<li>Risk scenarios that will be mitigated by the identified actions</li>
<li>Root cause of the scenario (root cause analysis [RCA])</li>
<li>The reasons for selection of action options based on the control evaluation criteria</li>
<li>Those who are accountable for approving the plan and those who are responsible for implementing the plan</li>
<li>Proposed actions</li>
</ul></td></tr>
</table>

Figure 2.4—I&T Risk Profile *(cont.)*	
Type of Content	Specification
	• Resource requirements, including contingencies • Performance measures and constraints • Cost vs. risk reduction benefit • Reporting and monitoring requirements • Timing and schedule **C. Loss events (historical and current)** A loss event is a risk event that results in a loss. For example, an error in systems processing/timing of trades can result in a loss or negative position. It should include information on root cause and actual cost of the event, ideally subdivided by the enterprise's standard loss forms. **D. Risk factors** A risk factor is a condition that can influence the frequency, impact and, ultimately, the business impact of IT-related events/scenarios. Risk factors can also be interpreted as causal factors of the scenario that is materializing, due to vulnerabilities or weaknesses. These factors include: • External context • Internal context • Risk management capabilities • IT-related capabilities **E. Independent assessment findings** This is an audit report that contains findings of assessments that should be taken into consideration during risk identification and analysis activities.
Source: ISACA, COBIT Focus Area: Information & Technology Risk, USA, 2021	

Figure 2.5 contains a sample template for a risk register entry, which is a part of the risk profile.

Figure 2.5—Example of a Risk Register Template				
Part I—Summary Data				
Risk statement				
Risk owner				
Date of last risk assessment				
Due date for update of risk assessment				
Risk category	Strategic	Program	Project	Operational
Risk classification (copied from risk analysis results)	▢ LOW	▢ MEDIUM	▢ HIGH	▢ VERY HIGH
Risk response	▢ ACCEPT	▢ TRANSFER	▢ MITIGATE	▢ AVOID

Figure 2.5—Example of a Risk Register Template *(cont.)*						
Part II—Risk Description						
Title						
High-level scenario (from list of sample high-level scenarios)						
Detailed scenario description—Scenario components	**Actor**					
	Threat Type					
	Event					
	Asset/Resource					
	Probability					
	Consequences					
Other scenario information						
Part III—Risk Analysis Results						
Frequency of scenario (number of times per year)	0	1	2	3	4	5
	N ≤ 0,01 ▢	0,01 < N ≤ 0,1 ▢	0,1 < N ≤ 1 ▢	1 < N ≤ 10 ▢	10 < N ≤ 100 ▢	100 < N ▢
Comments on frequency						
Impact of scenario on business	0	1	2	3	4	5
1. Productivity	**Revenue Loss Over One Year**					
Impact rating	I ≤ 0,1% ▢	0,1% < I ≤ 1% ▢	1% < I ≤ 3% ▢	3% < I ≤ 5% ▢	5% < I ≤ 10% ▢	10% < I ▢
Detailed description of impact						
2. Cost of response	**Expenses Associated With Managing the Loss Event**					
Impact rating	I ≤ 10k$ ▢	10K$ < I ≤ 100K$ ▢	100K$ < I ≤ 1M$ ▢	1M$% < I ≤ 10M$ ▢	10M$ < I ≤ 100M$ ▢	100M$ < I ▢
Detailed description of impact						
3. Competitive advantage	**Dropin Customer Satisfaction Ratings**					
Impact rating	I ≤ 0,5 ▢	0,5 < I ≤ 1 ▢	1 < I ≤ 1,5 ▢	1,5 < I ≤ 2 ▢	2 < I ≤2,5 ▢	2,5 < I ▢
Detailed description of impact						
4. Legal	**Regulatory Compliance—Fines**					
Impact rating	None ▢	< 1M$ ▢	< 10M$ ▢	< 100M$ ▢	< 1B$ ▢	> 1B$ ▢
Detailed description of impact						
Overall impact rating (average of four impact ratings)						
Overall rating of risk (obtained by combining frequency and impact ratings on risk map)	▢ LOW	▢ MEDIUM	▢ HIGH	▢ VERY HIGH		
Part III—Risk Response						
Risk response for this risk	▢ ACCEPT	▢ TRANSFER	▢ MITIGATE	▢ AVOID		
Justification						

Figure 2.5—Example of a Risk Register Template *(cont.)*			
Detailed description of response (NOT in case of ACCEPT)	**Response Action**	**Completed**	**Action Plan**
	1.	▢	▢
	2.	▢	▢
	3.	▢	▢
	4.	▢	▢
	5.	▢	▢
	6.	▢	▢
Overall status of risk action plan			
Major issues with risk action plan			
Overall status of completed responses			
Major issues with completed responses			
Part IV—Risk Indicators			
Key risk indicators for this risk	1.		
	2.		
	3.		
	4.		
Source: ISACA, *COBIT 5 for Risk*, USA, 2013, figure 62			

2.2 Vulnerability and Control Deficiency Analysis

The term vulnerability, also referred to as weakness, is often used for a binary condition. Something is vulnerable or it is not vulnerable. In most cases, assets are vulnerable to varying degrees (i.e., a particular control condition represents a high degree of vulnerability, while another control condition represents a lower degree of vulnerability). The extent of exposure must be considered, as it affects the probability that a vulnerability is compromised. These distinctions become critical in the process of prioritizing risk management efforts, when determining the level of risk within a scenario, and also when explaining conclusions and recommendations to management.

The NIST *Special Publication 800-30 Revision 1: Guide to Conducting Risk Assessments* provides a list of vulnerabilities to consider, along with predisposing conditions that may lead to the rapid or unpredictable emergence of new vulnerabilities. Many vulnerabilities are conditions that exist in systems and must be identified before they can be addressed. The purpose of vulnerability identification is to find the problems before they are found by an adversary and exploited, which is why an enterprise should conduct regular vulnerability assessments and penetration tests to identify, validate and classify its vulnerabilities. An assessment of vulnerabilities must consider process and procedural weaknesses along with logical ones. Where vulnerabilities exist, there is potential for risk.

Note: Other sources of vulnerabilities include:

- National Vulnerability Database at *nvd.nist.gov*
- Common Weakness Enumeration at *nvd.nist.gov/cwe.cfm*
- Common Vulnerabilities and Exposures at *cve.mitre.org*
- Exploit Database at *exploit-db.com*
- The Community Driven Vulnerability Database at *vulndb.org*
- Vulnerability Database Catalog at *www.first.org/global/sigs/vrdx/vdb-catalog*
- Packet Storm Security at *packetstormsecurity.com*
- Rapid7's Vulnerability and Exploit Database at *rapid7.com/db*
- CXSecurity Free Vulnerability Database at *cxsecurity.com/exploit/*
- Vulnerability Lab at *vulnerability-lab.com*
- 0day.today at *https://0day.today*
- Harmonized Threat and Risk Assessment at *www.cse-cst.gc.ca*
- Contingency Planning and Management at *contingencyplanning.com*
- Open Web Application Security Project (OWASP) at *www.owasp.org*

Estimating the degree of vulnerability can be accomplished through various forms of testing or through subject matter expert estimates. As with other valuations, estimates can be quantitative or qualitative. Whatever the approach, it is important to communicate the nature of these estimates, so management is not misled. Effective approaches for reflecting uncertainty in values include using ranges or distributions to indicate both unlikely maximums and values that are more probable.

Determining the ultimate relevancy of a weak control requires an understanding of the other controls in place that may mitigate the overall exposure. It would be inaccurate and a disservice to portray a control as a severe problem when, in fact, the combination of controls is relatively robust.

Many IT system weaknesses are identified using automated scanning equipment, and these can serve as leading indicators of potential compromise. Process and performance vulnerabilities are more difficult to ascertain and may require careful review and analysis to uncover. To be effective, the assessment must consider process, procedural and physical vulnerabilities in addition to technology weaknesses.

Consider the enterprise that does not have a formal information security training and awareness program. One set of vulnerabilities in this instance would stem from a lack of user awareness of security policies, standards and guidelines. Absent such awareness training, an enterprise is considerably more likely to suffer compromise from social engineering attacks such as phishing. Vulnerabilities can spring from numerous causes, ranging from a vast variety of technical issues, such as a lack of processes for configuration control, to countless human factors, such as poor personnel morale.

It may be useful to consider vulnerabilities in the following categories because the approach will vary for different areas:

- Network vulnerabilities
- Physical access
- Applications and publicly accessible services
- Utilities
- Supply chain
- Processes
- Equipment
- Cloud computing
- IoT
- BYOD

Audits, security reviews, vulnerability scans and penetration tests are among the approaches that are usually helpful in identifying vulnerabilities. Some typical examples of vulnerabilities include:

- Defective software
- Improperly configured hardware/software
- Inadequate or inconsistent compliance enforcement
- Poor network design (i.e., flat networks)
- Uncontrolled, unmonitored or defective processes
- Inadequate governance or management
- Insufficient staffing levels
- Lack of knowledge to support users or operations
- Lack of security functionality
- Lack of proper hygiene and maintenance

- Poor choice of passwords
- Transmission of unprotected communications
- Lack of redundancy
- Poor management communications

2.2.1 Security Control Baselines

Controls are designed as part of the information security risk management framework, which incorporates policies, standards, procedures, practices and organizational structures. It is designed to provide reasonable assurance that business objectives are achieved and the potential impacts of undesired events are sufficiently addressed. The framework must consider people, processes and technology and encompass the physical, technical, contractual and procedural aspects of the enterprise. It must take into account the strategic, programmatic, operational and tactical components of the enterprise to be effective.

Safeguards include any practice, procedure, process or other instrumentation that serves to reduce risk through the application of a precautionary measure to protect a business asset. Safeguards are considered proactive controls in that they are applied and used in an attempt to prevent an event from occurring. Some examples of proactive controls or safeguards include employee background checks, intrusion prevention systems (IPSs) and turnstile gates.

Countermeasures include practices, procedures, processes or other instrumentation used to respond to an event that has occurred. Countermeasures typically respond to a threat or vulnerability once it has been identified. The implementation and integration of countermeasures can take a variety of forms and can range from modifying architecture or reengineering processes, to reducing or eliminating internal threats to technical vulnerabilities, to creating an employee awareness program to target social engineering and promote early recognition and reporting of security incidents.

There is a wealth of information available from NIST, COBIT, ISO and security vendors regarding standards for information security controls. However, the information security manager must keep in mind that every enterprise has its own needs and priorities. While NIST, ISO, COBIT and vendors can provide starting points of support for developing controls, specific analysis should always be performed.

Controls suitable for the enterprise must be developed based on a variety of factors—such as culture, ethics, organizational structure, staffing, skills and available supporting infrastructure—in the context of the enterprise's defined risk appetite and tolerance. When defining the risk analysis program, it is important to consider people and processes in addition to technology. The information security manager needs to develop procedural and physical security baselines. This will often present a challenge due to some areas typically being outside the control of the information security department. Appropriate standards approved by the steering committee, as described in Chapter 1, can be the most effective approach to address this issue. Internal audit and regular security reviews can help provide assurance of conformance required by the governing authority.

Implementing baselines for security processes sets the minimum security requirements throughout the enterprise so they are consistent with acceptable risk levels. Different baselines must be established for different security classifications, with more stringent security controls required for the higher classification levels of the more critical or sensitive assets. If the enterprise has not implemented a classification scheme, it will be difficult for the information security manager to develop a rational basis for setting baselines without the risk of overprotecting some resources and underprotecting others.

In order to formulate a baseline of security controls, some measurement of the effectiveness and efficiency of controls is necessary. A baseline is not established on a single test of controls, but on the overall capacity of controls to collectively mitigate risk to acceptable levels.

To set control baselines, security managers can refer to many of the published standards that may be implemented within the enterprise. Based on these standards, a test of the control can be performed multiple times to establish an evaluation of the effectiveness and efficiency of the control required by the standard.

Setting security baselines for an enterprise has a number of benefits. It standardizes the minimum number of security measures that must be employed throughout the enterprise; this not only results in positive benefits for risk management but also allows operational management according to classification level instead of a per system or per asset basis. It provides a convenient point of reference to measure changes to security and identify corresponding effects on risk.

Working in conjunction with the enterprise architecture group, an information security technology baseline of controls can be developed that is appropriate for the enterprise's operating environment.

There is a consensus among many vendors, security organizations, information security professionals and systems auditors about security configuration specifications that represent a prudent level of due care. These cooperative efforts continue to define consensus-based, good practice security configurations for various systems and platforms. The information security manager should examine these specifications and, if appropriate, should tailor them for incorporation into organizational security baselines.

While it is important for information security managers to be aware of industry standard baselines, they must assess the level of security that should be employed in various areas of the enterprise. The commingling of different technologies, data and users/consumers can often introduce new risk and change a secure system or platform into one that has new vulnerabilities. A tailored risk assessment that recognizes these interactions and dependencies will enable the information security manager to determine whether security processes and procedures above the defined baselines are necessary to provide adequate security commensurate with the enterprise's defined levels of acceptable risk. Some enterprises and industries may require higher baselines, such as highly regulated industries. That may also be the case for an enterprise that handles information that is classified as highly critical or sensitive. In both of these cases, the enterprise must have control mechanisms that provide a high level of security commensurate with these requirements.

Standards must be developed or modified to set the appropriate boundaries of protection for each security domain. Standards provide the basis for measurement and testing approaches for evaluating whether security baselines are being met by existing controls. The objective is for residual risk across the security domain to be at a consistent acceptable level. This should be validated by periodic risk assessments to address the ever-changing nature of threats, vulnerabilities and technologies.

Selecting relevant metrics among the numerous available choices can be achieved by using a set of criteria. Effective metrics for risk management, including controls for evaluation, can be selected based on the best ranking of the following characteristics:

- **Specific**—Based on a clearly understood goal; clear and concise
- **Measurable**—Able to be measured; quantifiable (objective), not subjective
- **Attainable**—Realistic; based on important goals and values
- **Relevant**—Directly related to a specific activity or goal
- **Timely**—Grounded in a specific time frame
- **Meaningful**—Understood by the recipients
- **Accurate**—Reasonably accurate
- **Cost-effective**—Not too expensive to acquire or maintain
- **Repeatable**—Able to be acquired reliably over time
- **Predictive**—Indicative of outcomes
- **Actionable**—Clear to the recipient regarding what action to take

Example: To establish a baseline for antivirus processes, the information security manager requires periodic (weekly, monthly) reports of infected systems, virus alerts, virus incidents reported to the help desk, definition file updates and other pertinent information. Based on this information, it is possible to evaluate the effectiveness of the control and based on additional information—such as staff resource hours required, software costs, remediation/response expenses, and residual risk—to evaluate the efficiency of the antivirus process as an IT control. This demonstrates how metrics can be used to monitor the effectiveness of established baselines and provide a basis for adjusting them as necessary to manage risk.

2.2.2 Events Affecting Security Baselines

A number of factors may change the risk, probability or impact equation, necessitating that baseline security be changed. Baseline security is determined by the collective ability of controls to protect the enterprise's information assets. Baseline security is essentially controlled by the least restrictive aspect of collective standards and is the minimum level of security across the enterprise. Baseline security levels should also be reflected in control objectives.

Any incident can be attributed to either a control failure or the lack of a control. Any significant incident will require a risk reassessment and performing a root cause analysis of the failure, which may require increasing or modifying baseline security by changing the relevant policies, processes, procedures, standards or controls.

Information security managers need to monitor and assess events that affect security baselines and, thus, might affect the enterprise's security posture. Based on this assessment, the information security manager must determine if the enterprise's security strategy, roadmap and test plans require modification to address changing risk.

Security baselines may be modified for various reasons. For example, a vendor may identify a parameter in its software or hardware that must be changed to achieve or maintain the desired protection levels. Another reason for modification could be an outside event that necessitated an increase in the established baselines. For example, a protest or other civil unrest near an enterprise facility might warrant an increase in the baseline for physical security for a period until the threat passed. Other drivers include new or changing laws or regulations, identification of unacceptable risk levels because of new or changing threats, degradation of controls over time, and system changes creating new vulnerabilities.

2.3 Risk Analysis, Evaluation and Assessment

Risk management consists of a series of processes that take into account the end-to-end requirements of identifying, analyzing, evaluating and maintaining risk at acceptable levels. These include weighing policy alternatives in consultation with interested parties, considering risk assessment and other factors, and selecting appropriate prevention and control options that have acceptable costs and impacts on the enterprise's ability to operate efficiently.

Risk management functions usually include performance of a number of the following processes:

- **Establish scope and boundaries**—A process for the establishment of global parameters for the performance of risk management within an enterprise. Both internal and external factors have to be taken into account to provide context.
- **Identify assets and valuation**—A complete asset inventory and valuation process to determine assets at risk and potential impacts from incidents
- **Perform risk assessment**—A process consisting of risk identification, analysis and evaluation, including:
  - Identifying viable threats, vulnerabilities and exposures
  - Analyzing the level of risk, in the context of probability and potential outcomes
  - Evaluating whether the risk meets the criteria for acceptance
- **Recommend risk treatment or response**—A process of selecting strategies to deal with identified risk that exceeds the acceptable level. Risk treatment strategies are avoiding, by cessation of risky activities; mitigating, by developing and implementing controls; transferring risk to a third party, either inside or outside the enterprise; and accepting. Risk is usually accepted if the risk is below the defined risk appetite and tolerance criteria.
- **Accept residual risk**—The decision and approval by management to accept the remaining risk after any required treatment process is concluded (i.e., the risk may be accepted after evaluation shows it is within acceptable limits or if no effective treatment option is available)
- **Communicate about and monitor risk**—A process to exchange and share information related to risk and review the effectiveness of the whole risk management process. Communication of risk is usually performed among decision makers and other stakeholders inside and outside the enterprise. Through communication and monitoring, the scope, boundaries, evaluated risk and action plans remain relevant and updated.

Developing a systematic, analytical and continuous risk management process, as shown in **figure 2.6,** is critical to any successful security program and must be implemented as a formal process. Determining the correct or appropriate level of security is dependent on the potential risk that an enterprise faces, the potential impact, and the enterprise's ability to accept or otherwise mitigate risk. Risk is unique to each enterprise.

Figure 2.6—Continuous Risk Management Steps

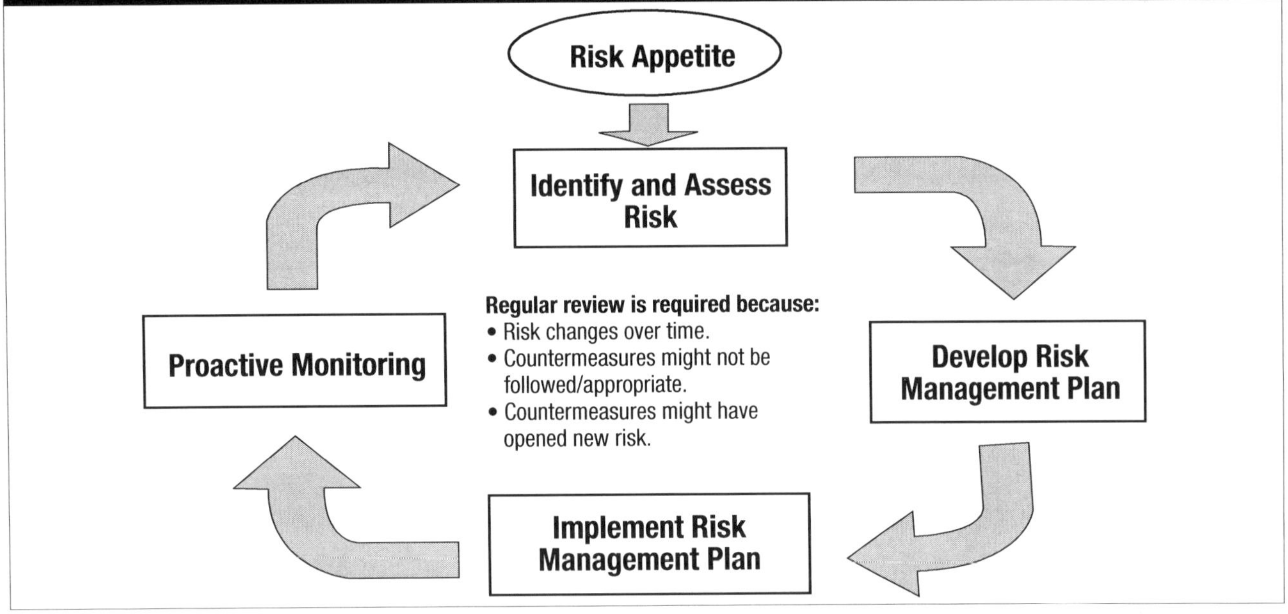

The information security manager should set up a regular, formal process in which risk assessments are performed at the organizational, system and application levels, including business processes both logical and physical. Ensuring that there are appropriate measurements (metrics) in place to assess the risk and the effectiveness of security measures is part of the information security manager's ongoing responsibility. The effectiveness of security measures or controls should be assessed against control objectives and security baselines. The information security manager should explore continuous manual and automated techniques to monitor risk and make recommendations to risk and control owners. This risk assessment process is important because it focuses the enterprise's security activities on issues that have the greatest likelihood, impact and significance.

Overgeneralization by applying risk factors across industries or regions should be avoided. Furthermore, the effectiveness of an information security program is frequently challenged by organizational, technological and business/operational change. These changes can be monitored, to a large extent, through links to all change management processes in the enterprise. Risk management should be a continuous and dynamic process to ensure that changing threats and vulnerabilities are addressed in a timely manner.

Processes must be developed to monitor the status of security controls and countermeasures to determine their ongoing effectiveness. Controls usually degrade over time and are subject to failure, mandating ongoing control monitoring and periodic testing.

There are three distinct phases within risk assessment:

- Risk identification
- Risk analysis
- Risk evaluation

The output of these three phases is the overarching risk assessment, which then can be used to inform risk treatment.

In risk identification, a set of threat scenarios is developed based on a thorough assessment of the threat landscape. It combines appropriate threat modeling and supporting vulnerability assessments (both logical and physical, including consideration of exposures) to understand and determine credible threats to the enterprise. See Section 2.1 Emerging Risk and Threat Landscape for more information.

Among the variety of available methodologies for assessing risk, some are more complex than others. Whichever approach is used, the outcome should be similar. The choice of methodologies, unless mandated by management or a regulatory body, should be based on the best fit for the enterprise.

The COBIT approach to performing a risk assessment, which aligns with ISO/IEC 27005:2018, includes identification, analysis and evaluation (**figure 2.7**).

Figure 2.7—Information Security Risk Management Process

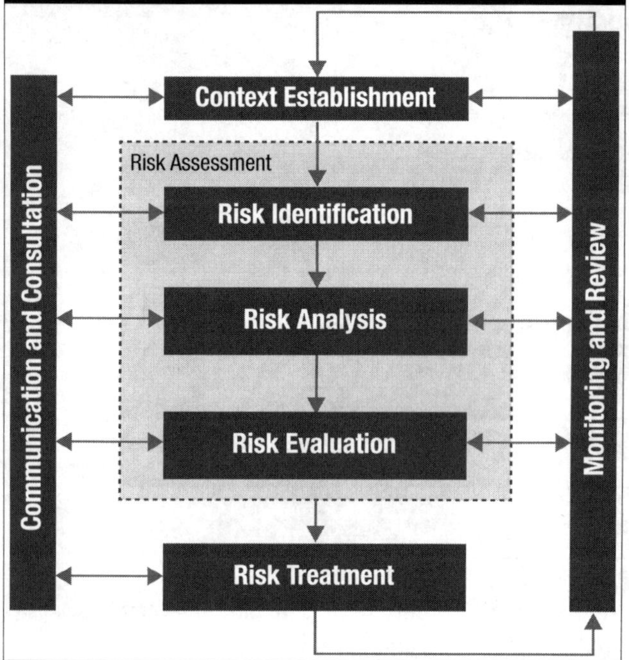

Source: ISACA, *COBIT 5 for Risk*, USA, 2013

There is no single best approach to risk assessment. The enterprise should define an approach that best aligns with its goals and objectives in determining the relative risk rating of assets and processes critical to the business. It is essential to identify as much significant risk as possible. An approach to achieving this is to develop risk scenarios.

2.3.1 Determining the Risk Management Context

In business terms, the process of managing risk must provide a balance between benefits and costs. The context defines the scope of risk management activities and the environment in which risk management operates, including the organizational structure, principles, culture, people, skills and infrastructure.

Determining the risk management context involves defining the:

- Range of the enterprise and the processes or activities to be assessed
- Full scope of the risk management activities
- Roles and responsibilities, not only pertaining to the various parts of the enterprise participating in the risk management process, but also with regard to risk and control ownership
- Organizational culture in terms of risk-averseness or -aggressiveness

The criteria for evaluating risk must be determined and agreed upon. Deciding whether risk treatment is required is usually based on operational, technical, financial, regulatory, legal, social or environmental criteria or combinations thereof. The criteria should be in line with the scope and analysis of the enterprise's internal policies and procedures and must support its goals and objectives.

Important criteria to be considered are:

- **Impact**—The kinds of consequences that will be considered
- **Likelihood**—The probability of a negatively impacting event occurring
- **Cost-benefits analysis**—To determine the best approach for mitigation versus transferring impact of a risk event
- **Risk appetite/risk tolerance**—The rules that determine whether the risk level is such that further treatment activities are required

These criteria may need to change during later phases of the risk management process due to changing circumstances or as a consequence of the risk assessment and evaluation process itself.

2.3.2 Operational Risk Management

Operational risk is defined as the risk of loss resulting from ineffective, inefficient, inadequate or failed processes, people and systems, or from external events. Interruption to business operations is a major concern, and preventing it should be a primary focus of risk management. In most cases, incident management is adequate to managing materialized risk, minimizing significant disruption to operations and potential impacts. In some cases, incidents will escalate to disasters and fall under the purview of business continuity and disaster recovery. In either circumstance, the backstop to limit risk and ensure it is managed is the understanding and capability to address relevant issues sufficiently to ensure the survival of the enterprise. The following section covers the main elements that must be addressed by the information security manager and other organizational units to manage risk effectively under most foreseeable circumstances.

2.3.3 Risk Management Integration with IT Life Cycle Management Processes

Ensuring that risk identification, analysis, evaluation, assessment and response activities are integrated into life cycle processes is an important task for information security management.

The need to minimize the negative impact on an enterprise and to establish a sound basis for decision making are the fundamental reasons enterprises implement a risk management process for their IT systems. Effective risk management must be fully integrated into the system development life cycle (SDLC). An IT system's SDLC has five phases: initiation, development or acquisition, implementation, operation or maintenance, and disposal. In some cases, an IT system may occupy several of these phases at the same time. However, the risk management methodology is the same, regardless of the SDLC phase for which the assessment is being conducted. Risk management is an iterative process that can be performed during each major phase of the SDLC. See Section 3.6.3 Life Cycle Principles Supporting the Road Map for more information.

Enterprises typically have change management procedures that can provide the information security manager with an approach to implementing risk management processes on an ongoing basis. Because changes to any information resource are likely to introduce new vulnerabilities and change the overall risk equation, it is important that the information security manager be aware of proposed modifications within the environment. With distributed computing having become the norm, changes are made more easily in a dispersed environment by people with limited knowledge. Enterprises often experience a lack of standardization in their hardware and software environments. Management in many enterprises has therefore instituted more robust change management procedures and, as a consequence, has begun to achieve better control over enterprise information resources. This is a moving target, and enterprises with remote operations are, in some cases, still finding effective change management an elusive goal.

Change management processes may already be established for other business areas and activities. One benefit is that many enterprises now have change management procedures that span the entire enterprise. The information security manager must be aware of these change management activities and ensure that security is properly integrated with business operations so changes are not made without considering the implications to the overall security of the enterprise's information assets. One method of helping to ensure this is for information security management to participate as a member of the change management committee and ensure that all changes are subject to review and approval by security, and that proposed changes meet policy and standards requirements. Any proposed deviations should be identified and documented for further analysis.

While the normal change management focus is on hardware and software changes (testing, sign-offs, etc.) and security impact, the change management process should extend well beyond the system owners and IT population. The change management process must include facilities management with respect to data center infrastructure and any other area that may impact overall information security (e.g., physical access control of sensitive or critical areas).

The impact of change management on system and facilities maintenance windows must be addressed with facilities personnel (often outsourced) and business continuity management. Often, changes are not documented on a timely basis within these areas. Facilities may not have current single-line drawings and blueprints. Correspondingly, computer infrastructure/configuration management may not have the changes properly documented or updated on a timely basis. Business continuity may lag when relevant updates occur in cycles. Emergency response and business continuity may suffer communications lapses when current and changing processes are not reviewed within facility infrastructure areas.

Facilities personnel often have access to environmental monitoring and control systems (building management system [BMS]/supervisory control and data acquisition [SCADA] systems) for heating, ventilating and air conditioning (HVAC), water and electricity, or even physical access control systems (PACS). These are often programmed for remote computer access, an area that often escapes information security oversight. Physical security and control systems have been designed within the context of their deployment within a closed/controlled environment.

Closed-circuit camera systems once configured to transmit data over the backbone network are often integrated with the IT infrastructure, introducing the risk of compromise to these systems from IT facilities and the network.

IT systems can also be compromised due to vulnerabilities in the physical security system. Physical security and control systems, because of their importance in the protection of facilities and people, may be part of the enterprise's critical infrastructure. The means of protecting these systems, their system codes and data need to be integrated into the enterprise security classification schemes. Facility service contracts in support of physical and control systems often have emergency response clauses. Those contracts should be reviewed, because they may lack adequate service level agreements or fail to provide sufficient details and accountability for an adequate emergency response. A high-availability application may suffer unforeseen business impacts as a result of facilities failures.

Internal or external parties managing the facilities are sometimes overlooked from a risk management perspective, even though human beings pose the greatest threat to information security. Human beings may be negligent in complying with established processes, ignorant of known threats, willing to engage in collusion or subject to emotional behavior. It is important to include the human factor in assessing the risk associated with critical information assets. Internal parties include operators whose job roles grant them direct physical access to the systems and facilities. External parties include servicing agents (e.g., cleaning or maintenance crew). Possible controls are background screening, employment terms, annual confirmation (via signature) of compliance to code of conducts, or contractual terms in the case of external parties.

It is not uncommon for enterprises to leverage or rely on third-party services in a number of different areas, not just IT services. Facility management may be outsourced to a third party, as may certain business activities and processes. The enterprise must ensure that risk acceptance and tolerance levels are not exceeded in areas outsourced to a third party. Risk management needs to be integrated in all phases of third-party management, including identification of requirements, evaluation and selection of suppliers, contracting, and regular review, in addition to onboarding and offboarding.

By integrating risk identification, analysis, assessment and response activities into change management (life cycle processes), the information security manager can ensure that critical information resources are adequately protected. This is a proactive approach, enabling the information security manager to better plan and implement security policies and procedures in alignment with the business goals and objectives of the enterprise. It permits the interjection of information security controls into an activity that holds the greatest potential for degrading existing controls.

Because risk management is a continuous process, the information security manager should view risk management itself as having a continuous life cycle. This life cycle includes assessment, treatment and monitoring phases, as illustrated in **figure 2.8**. Employing a life cycle-based risk management approach that is integrated with change management limits costs in that a full risk assessment does not have to be performed periodically. Instead, updates may be made to the risk assessment and risk management processes on an incremental basis.

Figure 2.8—The IT Risk Management Life Cycle

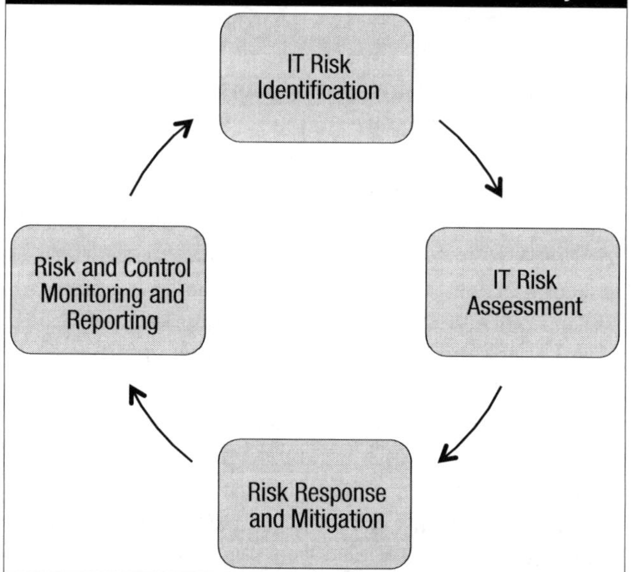

Source: ISACA, *CRISC Review Manual, 7th Edition*, USA, 2021

2.3.4 Risk Scenarios

Risk analysis consists of the thorough analysis of credible risk scenarios using various techniques (i.e., FAIR™ or HARM™ methodologies) to decompose the respective elements of the scenario and understand their relationships. Determination of the potential frequency and outcome of a specific risk event occurring is determined during this phase.

The main areas to focus on for developing risk scenarios are shown in **figure 2.9**.

Figure 2.9—Risk Scenario Technique Main Issues/Attention Points

Issue/Attention Point	Summary Guidance
Maintain currency of risk scenarios and risk factors.	Risk factors and the enterprise change over time; hence, scenarios will change over time, over the course of a project or over the evolution of technology. For example, it is essential for the risk function to develop a review schedule and for the chief information officer (CIO) to work with the business lines to review and update scenarios for relevance and importance. Frequency of this exercise depends on the overall risk profile of the enterprise and should be done at least on an annual basis, or when important changes occur.
Use generic risk scenarios as a starting point and build more detail where and when required.	One technique of keeping the number of scenarios manageable is to propagate a standard set of generic risk scenarios through the enterprise and develop more detailed and relevant scenarios when required and warranted by the risk profile only at lower (entity) levels. The assumptions made when grouping or generalizing should be well understood by all and adequately documented because they may hide certain scenarios or introduce confusion to risk response. For example, if the term insider threat is not well defined within a scenario, it may not be clear whether the threat includes both privileged and non-privileged insiders. The differences between various aspects of a scenario can be critical in trying to understand the frequency and impact of events and identify mitigation opportunities.
Ensure the number of scenarios are representative and reflect business reality and complexity.	
Use generic risk scenario structure to simplify risk reporting.	For risk reporting purposes, entities should not report on all specific and detailed scenarios, but they can use the generic risk scenario structure to do so. For example, an entity may have taken a generic risk scenario (project quality), translated it into five scenarios for its major projects, subsequently conducted a risk analysis for each of the scenarios, then aggregated or summarized the results and reported back using the generic risk scenario header "project quality."
Ensure adequate people and skills requirements for developing relevant risk scenarios.	Developing a manageable and relevant set of risk scenarios requires: • Expertise and experience to avoid overlooking relevant scenarios and being drawn into highly unrealistic or irrelevant scenarios. While the avoidance of scenarios that are unrealistic or irrelevant is important in properly utilizing limited resources, some attention should be paid to situations that are highly infrequent and unpredictable, but which could have a cataclysmic impact on the enterprise. • A thorough understanding of the environment. This includes the IT environment (e.g., infrastructure, applications, dependencies among applications, infrastructure components), the overall business environment, and the means used in IT environments to support the business environment and understand the business impact. • The intervention and common views of all parties involved—senior management, which has the decision power; business management, which has the best view on business impact; IT, which has the understanding of what can go wrong with IT; and risk management, which can moderate and structure the debate among the other parties. The process of developing scenarios usually benefits from a brainstorming/workshop approach, which usually requires performance of a high-level assessment to reduce the number of scenarios to a manageable, but relevant and representative, number.

<table>
<tr><th colspan="2">Figure 2.9—Risk Scenario Technique Main Issues/Attention Points (cont.)</th></tr>
<tr><th>Issue/Attention Point</th><th>Summary Guidance</th></tr>
<tr><td>Use the risk scenario building process to obtain buy-in.</td><td>Scenario analysis is not just an analytical exercise involving risk analysts. A significant additional benefit of scenario analysis is achieving organizational buy-in from enterprise entities and business lines, risk management, IT, finance, compliance, and other parties. Gaining this buy-in is one reason scenario analysis should be a carefully facilitated process.</td></tr>
<tr><td>Involve the first line of defense in the scenario building process.</td><td>Scenario building should be coordinated with management, and selected members of the staff who are familiar with detailed operations should be included in discussions, where appropriate. Staff whose daily work is in the detailed operations are often more familiar with vulnerabilities in technology and processes that can be exploited.</td></tr>
<tr><td>Do not limit focus to rare and extreme scenarios.</td><td>The focus of scenario development should not be limited to worst-case events because they rarely materialize; less severe incidents occur more often.</td></tr>
<tr><td>Deduce complex scenarios from simple scenarios by showing impact and dependencies.</td><td>Simple scenarios, once developed, should be fine-tuned into more complex scenarios, showing cascading and/or coincidental impacts and reflecting dependencies. For example:<ul><li>A scenario of involving a major hardware failure can be combined with a scenario of a failed disaster recovery plan.</li><li>A scenario of a major software failure can trigger database corruption and, in combination with poor data management backups, can lead to serious consequences, or at least consequences of a different magnitude than a software failure alone.</li><li>A scenario of a major external event can lead to a scenario of internal apathy.</li></ul></td></tr>
<tr><td>Consider systemic and contagious risk.</td><td>Attention should be paid to systemic and contagious risk scenarios:<ul><li>Systemic—Something happens to an important business partner, affecting a large group of enterprises within an area or industry. An example would be a nationwide air traffic control system that goes down for an extended period of time, such as six hours, affecting air traffic on a very large scale.</li><li>Contagious—Events occur at several of the enterprise's business partners within a very short time frame. An example would be a clearinghouse that is fully prepared for any sort of emergency by having very sophisticated disaster recovery measures in place, but is temporarily out of business when a catastrophe takes place because no transactions are sent by its providers.</li></ul></td></tr>
<tr><td>Use scenario building to increase awareness for risk detection.</td><td>Scenario development also helps to address the issue of detectability, moving away from a situation in which an enterprise does not know what it does not know. The collaborative approach for scenario development assists in identifying risk the enterprise otherwise would not have recognized (and hence would not have addressed with countermeasures). After the full set of risk items is identified during scenario generation, risk analysis assesses the frequency and impact of the scenarios.</td></tr>
<tr><td></td><td>Questions to be asked include:<ul><li>Will the enterprise ever detect that the risk scenario has materialized?</li><li>Will the enterprise notice something has gone wrong so it can react appropriately?</li></ul>Generating scenarios and creatively thinking of what can go wrong will automatically raise and, hopefully, generate responses to questions of detectability. Detectability of scenarios includes two steps: visibility and recognition. The enterprise must be in a position to observe anything going wrong, and it needs the capability to recognize an observed event as something wrong.</td></tr>
<tr><td colspan="2">Source: ISACA, Risk IT Practitioner's Guide, 2nd Edition, USA, 2020</td></tr>
</table>

Technical methods, including software, can be used for identifying and tracking risk and providing reporting tools to record the analysis of risk. As with any process, the best tool to use is the one that is best suited to meet the unique needs of the enterprise. In applying risk identification and analysis methods, the information security manager should define resource requirements and establish a budget and timetable for carrying out the most important tasks.

Once an inventory of information assets is completed, a comprehensive list of sources of threats, vulnerabilities, exposures and risk can be generated as a list of events that might have an impact on the ability of the enterprise to achieve its identified objectives, defined by scope and framework. These threats might prevent, degrade, delay or enhance achievement of the enterprise objectives.

In general, a risk can be related to or characterized by:

- **Actor (origin)**—Threat actors exist internally (e.g., hostile employees, employees who have not been properly trained) or externally (e.g., competitors, governments, business partners) and as acts of nature.
- **Type of threat (driver, intent and motivation)**—The type of threat experienced by an enterprise, i.e., was there malicious intent or was the cause accidental? Did hardware fail or was it the result of some act of nature?
- **Resulting event (specific reason for its occurrence)**—System design error, human intervention, prediction of—or failure to predict—competitor activity
- **Asset/resource (what we need to protect)**—Encompassing both the tangible and intangible, assets and resources are the things the enterprise has determined to be of value and worth protecting. Assets and resources can vary from the classic confidentiality, integrity and availability of systems, to public confidence and trust, to the ability to meet strategic goals and objectives.
- **Consequences, results or impact (what happens should this occur)**—The range of outcomes should the event occur. The outcomes can be either negative or positive. Examples include service unavailability, a loss or increase of market share/profits, increase in regulation, increase or decrease in competitiveness, fines and penalties, and enterprise efficiency gains.
- **Frequency (how likely it is this will happen in the next...)**—Forecasting the chances of when an event may occur. When considering all the known and unknown factors, making an estimated projection of when the event will be realized, given a defined period of time. For example: estimating the rate of occurrence during a year on a weekly (52 times), monthly (12 times), semi-annually (six times), annually (one time) or biennially (.5 times) basis.

Additionally, the following elements should be considered:

- **Protective mechanisms and controls (estimated effectiveness)**—Consisting of all applicable controls, based upon both their effectiveness and integration into the environment; examples of controls range from physical access control systems to network intrusion detection systems, policies, two-person integrity, logging and monitoring, security training, market research and surveillance of market.
- **Exposure (where)**—Defining where the asset or resource is most susceptible to an adverse event occurring. Is the asset located internally within the enterprise network behind multiple firewalls and security zones, or is it publicly available on the Internet with minimal controls in place? What is the business value of the resource, and are the applied controls commensurate with its value?

The development of risk scenarios is based on describing a potential risk event and documenting the factors and areas that may be affected by the risk event. Risk events may include system failure, loss of key personnel, theft, network outages, power failures, natural disasters or any other situations that could affect business operations and mission. Each risk scenario should be related to a business objective or impact experienced by the enterprise. The key to developing effective scenarios is to focus on real and relevant potential risk events. Examples are developing a risk scenario based on a radical change in the market for an enterprise's products, a change in government or leadership, or a supply chain failure. **Figure 2.10** shows an example of the many inputs that are required to develop risk scenarios.

Figure 2.10—Risk Scenario Components

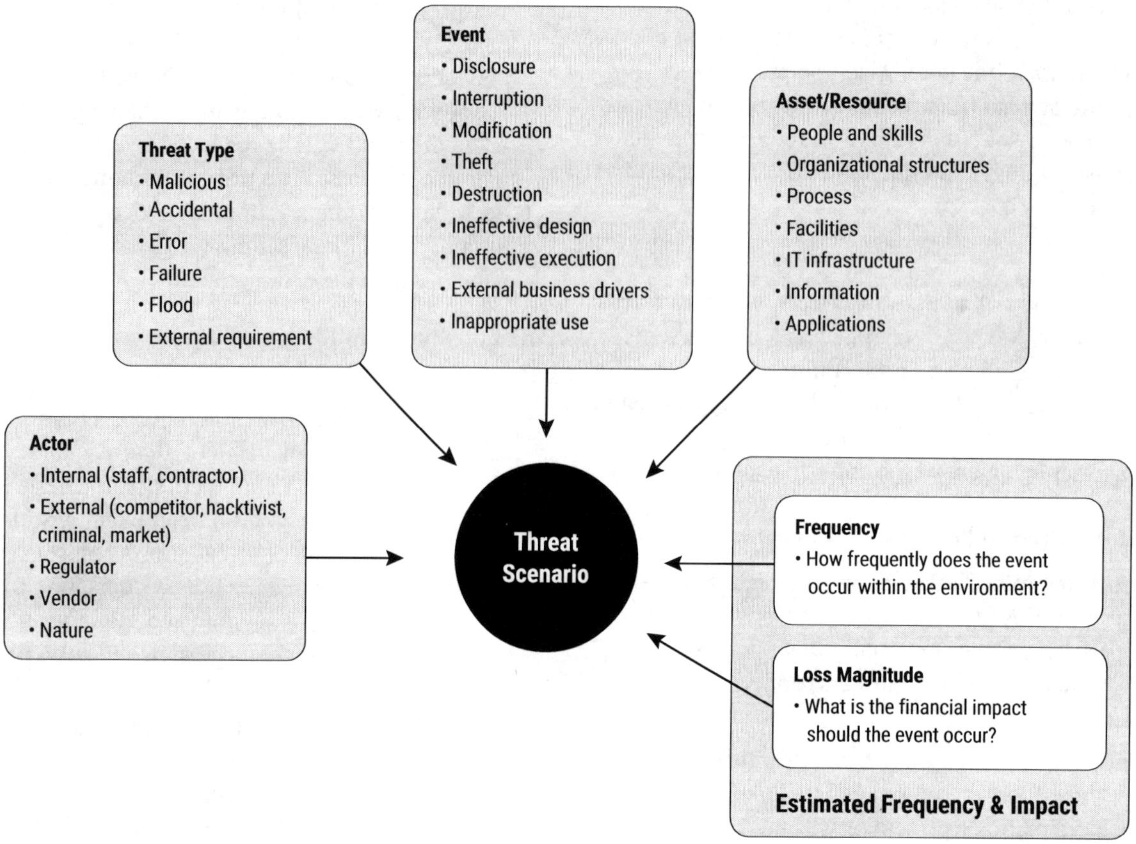

Source: ISACA, *CRISC Review Manual, 7th Edition*, USA, 2021

2.3.5 Risk Assessment Process

Risk assessment—coupled with either a business impact analysis or information asset classification process to determine criticality or sensitivity and subsequent analysis—is used as a basis for identifying appropriate and cost-effective controls or countermeasures to mitigate identified risk. Sensitivity or criticality is often stated as business value.

Most risk assessment approaches have four discrete phases. These include:

- **Risk identification**—the process for determining and documenting the risk an enterprise faces.
- **Risk analysis**—a process by which frequency and magnitude of IT risk scenarios are estimated. It also includes analyzing the value of assets to the business, identifying threats to those assets and evaluating how vulnerable each asset is to those threats. Risk analysis can include an evaluation of the probable frequency of a particular event and the probable impact of that event. Analysis may include statistical computations to gain greater insight into risk distribution (i.e., the maximum risk and probable risk and potential consequences [impact]).
- **Risk evaluation**—the process of comparing the results of the risk analysis in the context of the defined risk appetite and tolerance criteria. Deciding the appropriate risk response is usually based on operational, technical, financial, regulatory, legal, social or environmental criteria, or combinations of criteria. The criteria should be in line with the scope and analysis of the enterprise's internal policies and procedures and must support its goals and objectives.
- **Risk assessment**—the process of determining the recommended course of action based upon the results of the risk analysis in the context of the risk evaluation process. This forms the basis for the

recommended course of action the enterprise should take to address the specific risk scenario.

Figure 2.11 shows the practical application of the IT risk assessment process, taking a risk-driven business approach for selecting an appropriate risk response. In this example, the asset to be protected is identified as sensitive/regulated data.

Assuming an asset is of significant value, the next step is to determine what vulnerabilities to loss or damage exist. If vulnerabilities exist, an assessment of viable threats must be performed. If the asset has value and vulnerabilities susceptible to viable threats, then there is a risk. To clarify, it is obvious that vulnerabilities for which no threats exist pose no risk (although threats are dynamic and may arise at any time). Another way to look at it is that the greater the value, and the greater the number and degree of vulnerabilities coupled with a greater number of viable threats, the greater the risk of loss.

Figure 2.11—Risk-Driven Approach

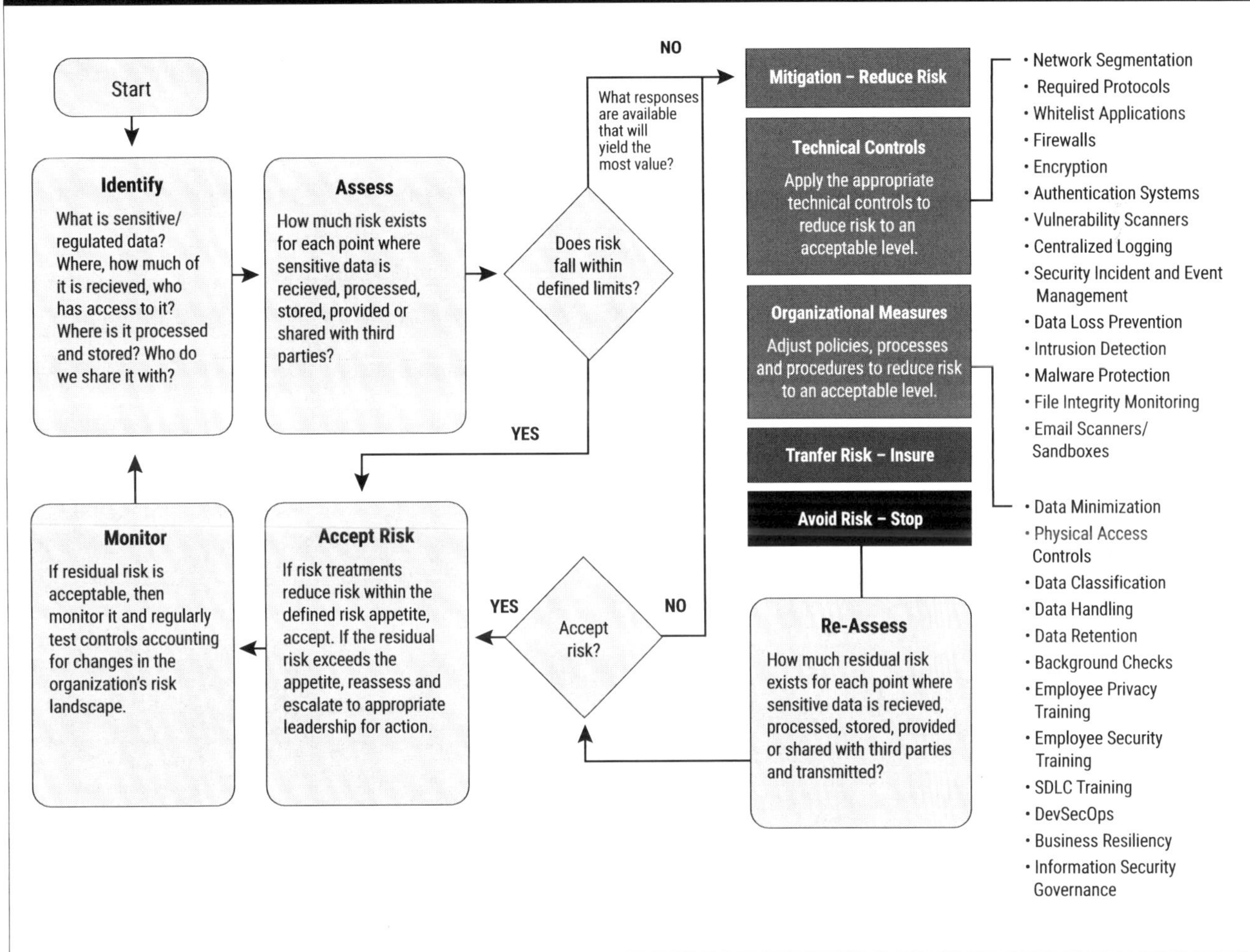

Source: ISACA, *CRISC Review Manual, 7th Edition*, USA, 2021

2.3.6 Risk Assessment and Analysis Methodologies

Numerous risk management models and assessment approaches are available to the information security manager. The approach selected should be determined by the best form, fit and function. The approaches include COBIT, OCTAVE®, NIST 800-39, HB 158-2010, ISO 27005:20018, ISO/IEC 31000, ITIL® and CRAMM. Other approaches—such as Factor Analysis of Information Risk (FAIR), Holistic Approach to Risk Management (HARM), risk factor analysis and value at risk (VAR)—may be more suitable, depending on the enterprise and the specific requirements.

In the COBIT approach, risk scenarios involve the process of identifying risk, followed by analysis. Risk evaluation is the next step to determine whether risk exceeds acceptable levels. These three steps allow the risk assessment to generate a recommendation of the appropriate risk response, or risk treatment. Response (treatment) priorities are based on a cost-benefit and risk-level analysis, with high cost-benefit and high likelihood/high impact taking the highest priority.

Note: Information security managers should have broad knowledge of the existence of various methodologies to determine the most suitable approach or combination of approaches for their enterprise. Specific approaches will not be tested in the CISM examination.

NIST Risk Assessment Methodology

The NIST risk assessment methodology encompasses nine primary steps:

- Step 1—System (or general domain) characterization
- Step 2—Threat identification
- Step 3—Vulnerability identification
- Step 4—Control analysis
- Step 5—Likelihood determination
- Step 6—Impact analysis
- Step 7—Risk determination
- Step 8—Control recommendations
- Step 9—Results documentation

Steps 2, 3, 4 and 6 can be conducted in parallel after step 1 has been completed.

Figure 2.12 depicts these steps and the inputs to and outputs from each step.

Figure 2.12—NIST Risk Assessment Methodology

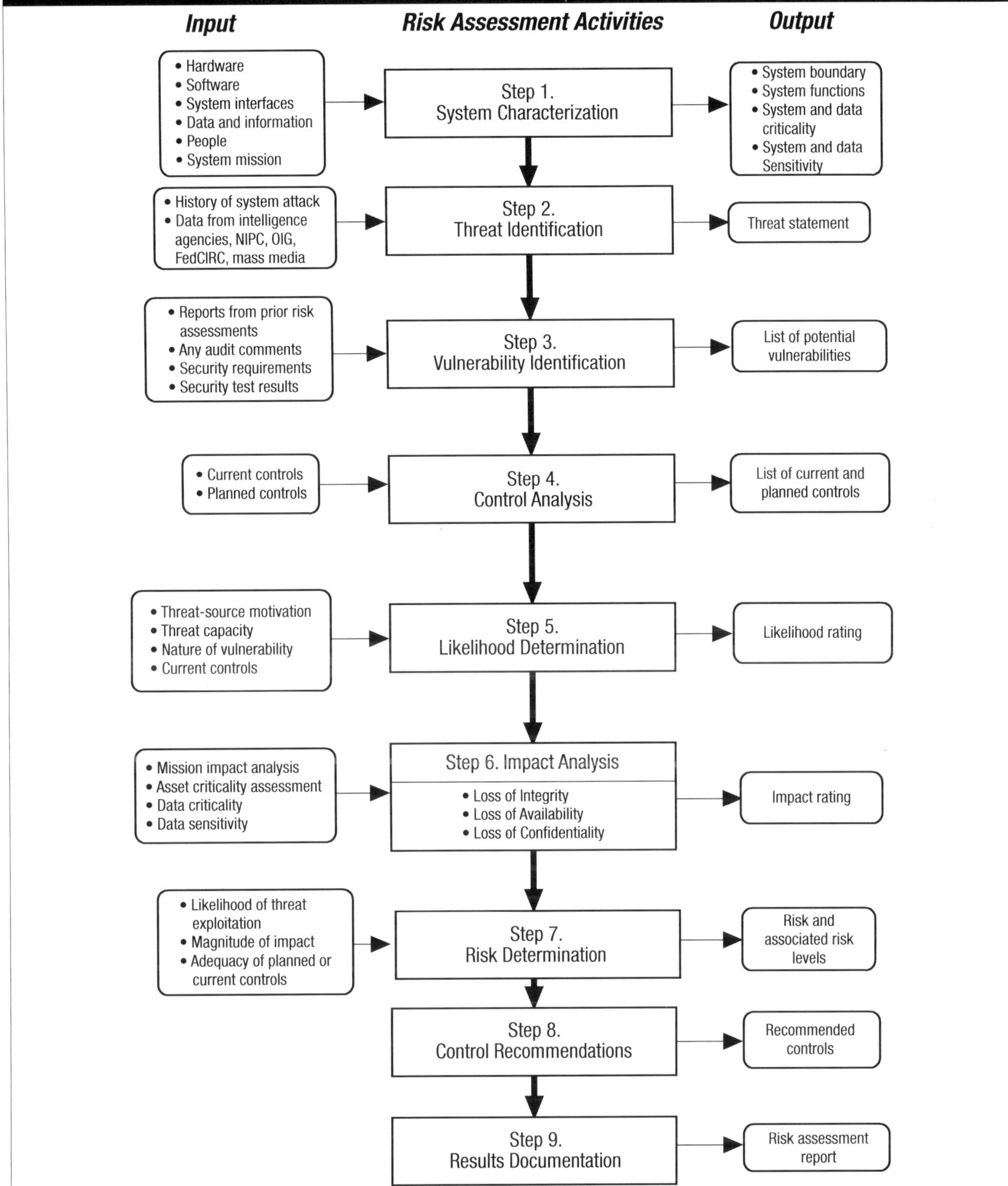

Source: National Institute of Standards and Technology, *Special Publication 800-30, Revision 1: Guide for Conducting Risk Assessments*, USA, 2012. Reprinted courtesy of the NIST, US Department of Commerce. Not copyrightable in the United States of America.

ISO/IEC Process Steps

Figure 2.13 shows the ISO/IEC 27005 process steps for risk assessment and their relation to COBIT.

Figure 2.13—ISO/IEC 27005 Process Steps Covered by *COBIT 5 for Risk*

ISO/IEC 27005 Process Step	Important Concepts of the Component	*COBIT 5 for Risk* Coverage
Context Establishment	This process step includes: • Setting the basic criteria necessary for information security risk management (ISRM) • Defining the scope and boundaries • Establishing an appropriate organization operating the ISRM	This process step is included in the enabler dimension goal. More specifically, contextual quality: the extent to which outcomes of the enabler are fit for purpose given the context in which they operate.
Risk Assessment	Risk assessment determines the value of the information assets, identifies the applicable threats and vulnerabilities that exist (or could exist), identifies the existing controls and their effect on the risk identified, determines the potential consequences, and finally, prioritizes the derived risk and ranks it against the risk evaluation criteria set in the context establishment. This process step consists of the following activities: risk identification, risk analysis and risk evaluation.	Appendix B.3 describes risk assessment as one item of the Information enabler.
Risk Identification	Risk identification includes the identification of: • Assets • Threats • Existing Controls • Vulnerabilities • Consequences The output of this process is a list of incident scenarios with their consequences related to assets and business processes.	The sequence used in ISO/IEC 27005 to identify risk is partly aligned to the *COBIT 5 for Risk* approach. The identification of risk comprises the following elements in *COBIT 5 for Risk*: • Control • Value • Threat condition that impose a noteworthy level of IT risk *COBIT 5 for Risk* also uses scenario development for identifying risk. Key attributes of potential and known risk events are stored in a repository. Attributes may include name, description, owner, expected/actual frequency, potential/actual magnitude, potential/actual business impact, disposition, etc.
Risk Analysis	The risk estimation process step includes the following important concepts: • Assessment of consequences • Assessment of incident likelihoods • Determination of level of risk	Risk analysis is the process whereby frequency and impact of IT risk scenarios are estimated.
Risk Evaluation	In this step, levels of risk are compared according to risk evaluation criteria and risk acceptance criteria. The output is a prioritized	• Addresses this process step intrinsically as a part of 'risk aggregation'. It evaluates the risk

Figure 2.13—ISO/IEC 27005 Process Steps Covered by *COBIT 5 for Risk* (cont.)

ISO/IEC 27005 Process Step	Important Concepts of the Component	*COBIT 5 for Risk* Coverage
	list of risk elements and the incident scenarios that lead to the identified risk elements.	according to 'risk tolerance of the management with regard to the risk appetite of the board'. • Uses a risk map for ranking and graphically displaying risk by defined ranges for frequency and impact.
Risk Treatment	Risk treatment options include: • Risk modification • Risk retention • Risk avoidance • Risk sharing	The treatments of identified risk is described in section 2B. These are: • Risk avoidance • Risk reduction/mitigation • Risk sharing/transfer • Risk acceptance
Information Security Risk Acceptance	The input is a risk treatment plan and the residual risk assessment subject to the risk acceptance criteria. This step comprises the formal acceptance and recording of the suggested risk treatment plans and residual risk assessment by management, with justfication for those that do not meet the enterprise's criteria.	Covers risk acceptance process step in section 2B, subsection 5.2 Risk Response. If an enterprise adopts a risk acceptance stance, it should carefully consider who can accept the risk— even more so with IT risk. IT risk should be accepted only by business management (and business process owners), in collaboration with and supported by IT, and acceptance should be communicated to senior management and the board.
Information Security Risk Communication and Consultation	This is a transversal process—information about risk should be exchanged and shared between the decision maker and other stakeholders throughout all the steps of the risk management process.	• Principle 1: Meeting stakeholder needs. • The Information enabler includes specific information to be communicated between the stakeholders.
Information Security Risk Monitoring and Review	Risk and its influencing factors should be monitored and reviewed to identify any changes in the context of the organization at an early stage and to maintain an overview of the complete risk picture.	Includes goals and metrics that can be used to measure performance and a maturity model to set a road map for improving risk management processes.

Source: ISACA, *COBIT 5 for Risk*, USA, 2013

Cascading Risk

Cascading risk can manifest unacceptable impacts as a result of one failure leading to a chain reaction of failures. An example of this occurred on the East Coast of the United States when a failure at a small power utility in the Midwest caused a cascade of failures across the power grid, ultimately encompassing most of the northeastern quarter of the United States. Similarly, to the extent that portions of the enterprise's IT and other operations have closely coupled dependencies, the information security manager must consider how any particular failures or combinations of failures will affect dependent systems.

This is often realized when numerous minor vulnerabilities that individually are acceptable and may not by themselves result in an event are combined and chained together, resulting in a significant impact to the enterprise.

Vulnerabilities can exist outside the technical realm and will often be chained together to allow threat actors to pursue their objectives. For example, a vulnerability was discovered in large food distributor's accounts payable process. The process allowed an invoice submitted under a certain dollar amount to be paid 1) without a corresponding purchase order assigned to it, and 2) without being reconciled with the department being charged. While properly implemented technical controls were in place, they only flagged invoices over a specific dollar amount. This allowed the enterprise to receive, process and pay a number of fraudulent invoices (in excess of $250,000). None of the transactions had been questioned, detected or flagged for alerts on by the technical controls or accounts payable team. The defined individual associated processes and supporting technical controls worked as designed, but when chained together they were successfully abused.

2.3.7 Other Risk Assessment Approaches

Developments over the past few decades have resulted in notable improvements in defining the bounds of probable risk. However, few directly address information risk effectively. Some of these developments are being adopted in the information security field and it is likely that the use of more sophisticated techniques and methods will continue to be developed. Some of these methods are described in the following sections.

Factor Analysis of Information Risk (FAIR)

FAIR is a recognized industry approach for decomposing risk and understanding its components. The approach offers a reasoned, detailed analysis process that is designed primarily as a complement to other assessment approaches with the objective of increasing accuracy (**figure 2.14**).

FAIR provides a reasoned and logical framework for the following:

- A taxonomy of the factors that make up information risk. This taxonomy provides a foundational understanding of information risk, without which one could not reasonably carry out the process. It also provides a set of standard definitions for the necessary terms.
- A method for measuring the factors that drive information risk, including threat event frequency, vulnerability and loss.
- A computational engine that derives risk by mathematically simulating the relationships among the measured factors.
- A simulation model that allows one to apply the taxonomy, measurement method and computational engine to build and analyze risk scenarios of virtually any size or complexity.

The four primary components of risk taxonomy that identify threat agent characteristics affect:

- The frequency with which threat agents come into contact with an enterprise or assets
- The probability that threat agents will act against an enterprise or assets
- The probability of threat agent actions being successful in overcoming protective controls
- The probable nature (type and severity) of impact to assets

Figure 2.14—FAIR Methodology

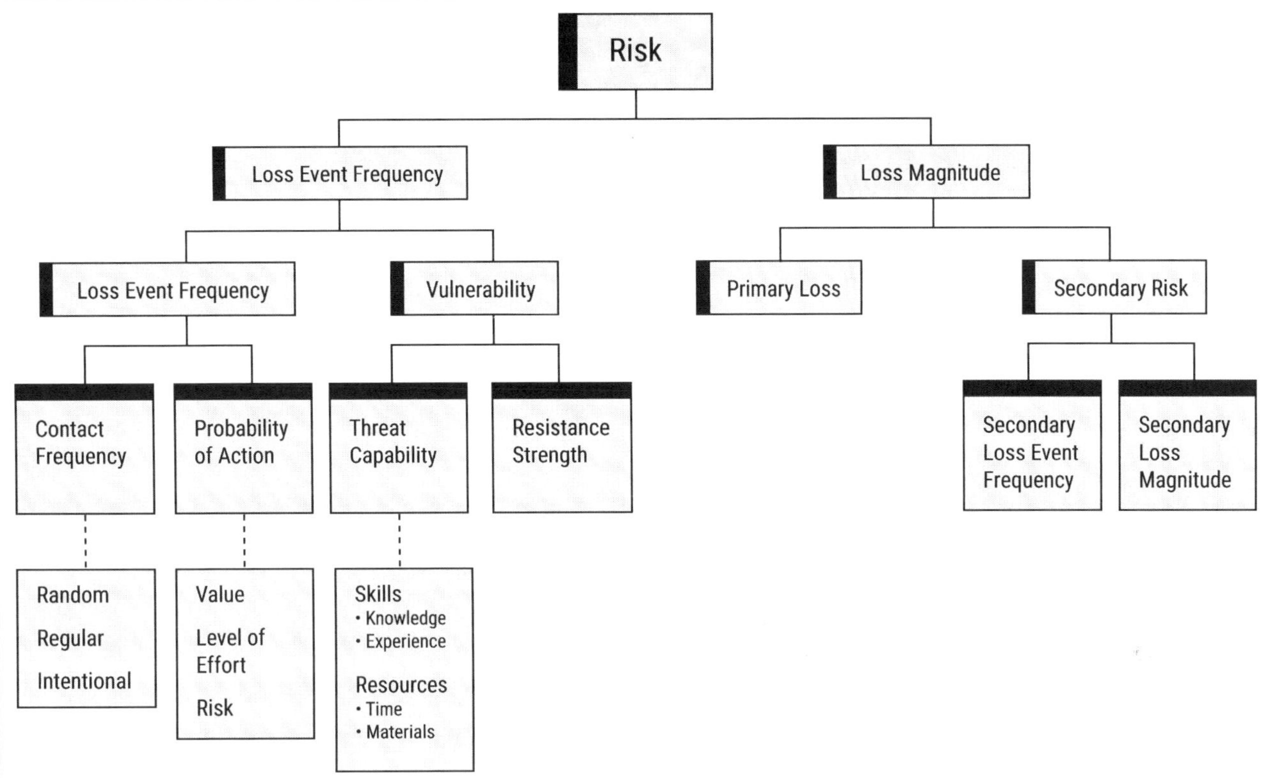

Source: The FAIR Institute, https://www.fairinstitute.org/

Holistic Approach to Risk Management (HARM)

A methodology designed and developed to support and normalize an enterprise's approach relating to performing risk analysis. Designed to leverage the FAIR™ risk analysis model, HARM's focus is to:

1. Refine the estimation process
2. Remove subjectivity from analysis
3. Provide an appropriate level of assurance
4. Define a repeatable method to ensure consistent results
5. Provide a defensible method for risk analysis efforts

Benefits of using the HARM methodology include:

- Consistency in results through use of repeatable, well-defined processes
- Confident estimations
- Ability to demonstrate due care
- Reasonable assurance
- Ability to make better-informed decisions
- Higher confidence in results
- Defensible results

HARM is not meant to be a replacement for FAIR; rather, it provides the information security manager the ability to mature risk analysis efforts, providing confidence in analysis results in addition to the ability to provide the appropriate level of assurance desired by many enterprises.

Figure 2.15—Core Processes of HARM

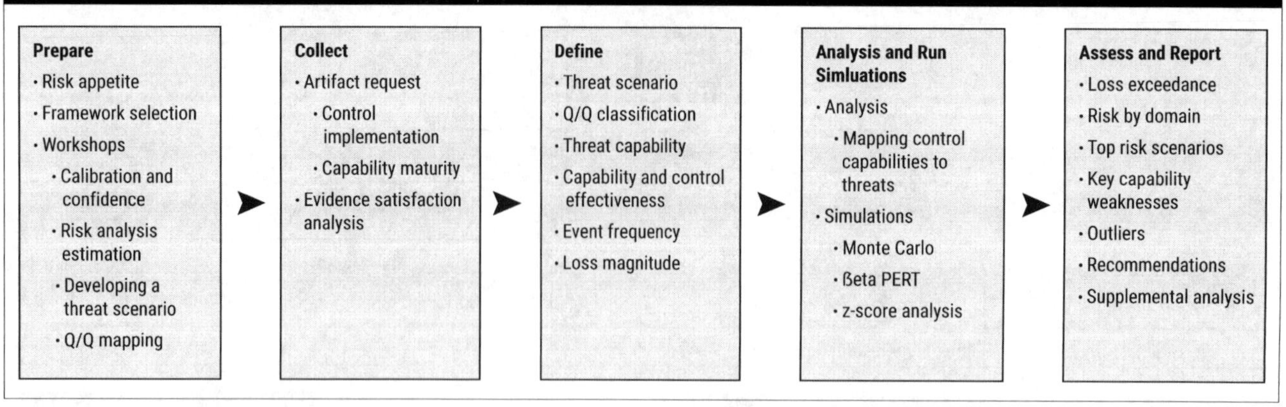

Probabilistic Risk Assessment

Probabilistic risk assessment (PRA) has emerged as an increasingly popular analysis tool, especially during the last decade. PRA is a systematic and comprehensive methodology to evaluate risk associated with every life cycle aspect of a complex engineered technological entity, from concept definition through design, construction and operation, and up to removal from service. Developed for use by the US National Aeronautics and Space Administration (NASA) and the nuclear power industry, the approach is complex and time-consuming, but it may see increasing application in cases that require high network security.

The approach aims to answer three questions:

- What can go wrong?
- How likely is it?
- What are the consequences?

The answers are based on a thorough deconstruction of all the elements at risk in a particular set of circumstances, followed by systematically identifying, modeling and quantifying scenarios that can lead to adverse consequences based on probability and statistical theory, reliability engineering, decision theory and other information. Elements that go into assessing a possible chain of events include hardware and software failure, human actions, control failures and other possible interactions that can lead to serious consequences.

2.3.8 Risk Analysis

Risk analysis is the phase in which potential probability and resulting outcomes are calculated and determined. This phase includes determining threat actor capabilities and motivations, the effectiveness of existing controls, and the extent to which they may influence a particular identified risk.

Risk analysis involves:

- Thorough examination of the risk sources (threats and vulnerabilities) determined in the risk identification phase
- The extent to which information assets have exposure to potential threats and the effect on likelihood
- The potential negative consequences (impact) if the assets are successfully attacked
- The likelihood that those consequences may occur and the factors that affect them
- Inclusion of applicable existing controls or processes that tend to minimize negative risk or enhance positive outcomes (these controls may derive from a wider set of standards, controls or good practices selected according to an applicability statement [i.e., the application of controls identified in the risk register] and may also come from previous risk treatment activities)

The level of risk can be estimated in various ways, including using statistical analysis and calculations combining impact and likelihood. Impact may not be clear unless BIAs have been performed to provide an understanding of the cost to the enterprise as the result of the loss of a particular function or asset.

Any formulas and methods for combining impact and likelihood must be consistent with the criteria defined when establishing the risk management context, because an event may have multiple outcomes and affect different objectives. Therefore, consequences and likelihood need to be combined to calculate the level of risk. If no historical or statistically reliable data are available (e.g., incident data kept for an incident database), other estimates based on impacts affecting other enterprises may be made, but they must be appropriately communicated to and approved by the decision makers.

Information used to estimate impact and likelihood usually comes from:

- Experience or data and records (e.g., incident reporting)
- Reliable practices, international standards or guidelines
- Market research on other enterprises and analysis
- Experiments and prototypes
- Economic, engineering or other models
- Specialist and expert advice

Risk analysis techniques vary and may include:

- Interviews with experts in the area of interest and questionnaires
- Use of existing models and simulations
- Statistical and other analysis

Risk analysis may vary in detail according to the risk, the purpose of the analysis, and the required protection level of the relevant information, data and resources. Analysis may be qualitative, semi-quantitative (hybrid), or quantitative. In any case, the type of analysis performed should be consistent with the criteria developed as part of the definition of the risk management context, and consensus should be gained on the approach used.

Gap Analysis

Gap analysis in the context of risk management refers to determining the gap between existing controls and control objectives. Control objectives based on acceptable risk should have been defined as an outcome of developing an information security governance and management strategy as discussed in Chapter 1.

Control objectives should lead to controls that result in residual risk falling into acceptable levels, ensuring that the established information security baseline is maintained.

Control objectives may change as a part of risk management activities as exposures, business objectives, operations, contractual obligations or regulations change, potentially creating a gap between the existing control and its revised objectives. Periodically analyzing the gap between controls and their objectives should be a standard practice. This is normally accomplished as a part of the process of controls testing for effectiveness. To the extent that effectiveness of controls fails to meet the control objective and achieve acceptable risk, the controls may need to be modified, redesigned or supplemented with additional control activities. For more information on the relationship between controls and control objectives, see Chapter 3.

Qualitative Analysis

In qualitative analysis, the magnitude and likelihood of potential consequences are presented and described in detail. The scales used can be formed or adjusted to suit the circumstances, and different descriptions may be used for different risk. Qualitative analysis may be used:

- As an initial assessment to identify risk that will be the subject of further, detailed analysis
- If nontangible aspects of risk are to be considered (e.g., reputation, culture, image)
- If there is a lack of adequate information and numerical data or resources necessary for a statistically acceptable quantitative approach

A common approach to qualitative analysis can be accomplished by using a risk map, as shown in **figure 2.16**.

Figure 2.16—Risk Map Indicating Risk Appetite Bands

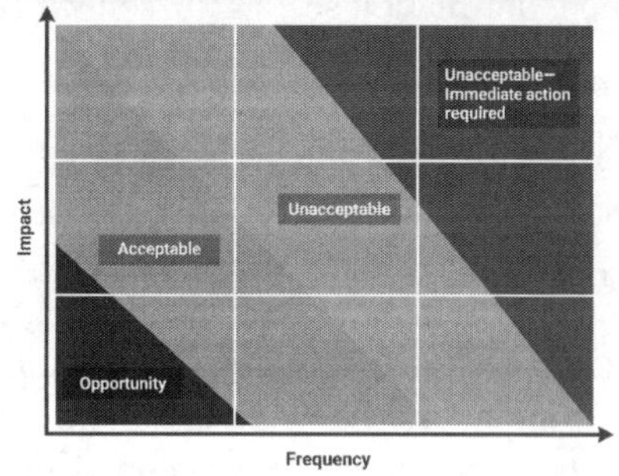

Source: ISACA, *Risk IT Practitioner Guide, 2nd Edition*, USA, 2020

Semi-quantitative (Hybrid) Analysis

In semi-quantitative analysis, the objective is to define a set of agreed-upon ranged values that are wide enough to allow risk to be estimated consistently. The goal is to provide sufficient accuracy to allow for the understanding, comparison and prioritization of risk. Qualitative terms are usually subjective; the ability to define and map them to quantitative values normalizes basic definitions used to forecast potential outcomes.

For this approach to be useful, the values selected should be generally indicative and sufficient for the prioritization of one risk above another risk. For any process to operate successfully there should be a common understanding of the values and the terms employed. Definitions already in use within the enterprise can be substituted for those that follow. It may be possible to use a subset from the ERM framework if one exists.

Example values for impact are:

- Insignificant (value = 1): No meaningful impact or of limited consequence
- Minor (value = 2): Impact on a small part of the business only or less than US $1 million impact
- Major (value = 3): Impact on the enterprise's brand or more than US $1 million impact
- Material (value = 4): Impact of more than US $200 million and requiring external reporting
- Catastrophic (value = 5): Failure or significant downsizing of the enterprise

Example values for likelihood are:

- Rare (value = 1)
- Unlikely (value = 2): Not seen within the last five years
- Moderate (value = 3): Seen within the last five years but not within the last year
- Likely (value = 4): Seen within the last year
- Frequent (value = 5): Occurs on a regular basis

These values should be sufficient to allow risk prioritization according to a semi-quantitative approach.

Typically, the risk probability and consequences are calculated as:

- Risk = impact × likelihood

An example is Risk = 4 (material) × 3 (moderate) = 12.

Quantitative Analysis

In quantitative analysis, numerical values are assigned to both impact and likelihood. These values are derived from a variety of sources. The quality of the entire analysis depends on the accuracy of the assigned values and the validity of the statistical models used. Impact can be determined by evaluating and processing the various results of an event or by extrapolation from experimental studies or past data.

Consequences may be expressed in various terms of:

- Monetary
- Technical
- Operational
- Human impact criteria

The specification of the risk level is not unique. Impact and likelihood may be expressed or combined differently, according to the type of risk and the scope and objective of the risk management process.

Annual Loss Expectancy

Quantitative risk assessments attempt to arrive at a numerical value, usually expressed in financial terms. The most common form is either single loss expectancy (SLE) or annual loss expectancy (ALE). SLE is the product of the asset value (AV) multiplied by the exposure factor (EF): SLE = AV × EF.

EF represents the percentage of loss that a realized threat could have on a specific asset when the specific threat matches up with a specific vulnerability. Said another way, EF is the proportion of an asset's value that is likely to be destroyed by a particular risk, expressed as a percentage.

ALE is the annual expected financial loss to an asset, resulting from one specific threat. ALE adds the annualized rate of occurrence (ARO) to the equation with the result that multiple occurrences will result in greater potential losses. ALE is usually expressed as: ALE = SLE × ARO. The result is that the greater the asset value, coupled with a greater probability and greater magnitude of impact, the greater the potential risk of loss.

ARO is the number of times a threat on a single asset is estimated to occur. The higher the risk associated with the threat, the higher the ARO. For example, if insurance data suggest that a serious fire is likely to occur once in 25 years, then the annualized rate of occurrence is 1/25 = 0.04.

Value at Risk

Another approach required in certain financial sectors is value at risk (VAR), which can also have general risk management utility and benefit. This approach has been studied by various researchers, suggesting its suitability for information security management.

VAR is a computation based on historical data of the probability distribution of loss for a given period of time at a certainty factor, typically of 95 percent or 99 percent. The probability distribution is arrived at using Monte Carlo simulations, typically run through thousands of iterations with random variables based on historical information.

Other Risk Analysis Methods

A number of other analysis options may prove useful, although they are typically more sophisticated than most enterprises employ. Some of the more common approaches include:

- **Bayesian analysis**—A Bayesian analysis is a method of statistical inference that uses prior distribution data to determine the probability of a result. This technique's effectiveness and accuracy rely on the accuracy of the prior distribution data.
- **Bow tie analysis**—A bow tie analysis provides a diagram to communicate risk assessment results by displaying links among possible causes, controls and consequences. The cause of the event is depicted in the middle of the diagram (the knot of the bow tie). Triggers, controls, mitigation strategies and consequences branch off the knot.
- **Delphi method**—The Delphi method uses expert opinion, which is often received using two or more rounds of questionnaires. After each round of questioning, the results are summarized and communicated to the experts by a facilitator. This collaborative technique is often used to build a consensus among the experts.
- **Event tree analysis**—An event tree analysis is a forward-looking, bottom-up model that uses inductive reasoning to assess the probability of different events resulting in possible outcomes.
- **Fault tree analysis**—A fault tree analysis uses deductive reasoning and starts with an event and examines possible means for the event to occur (top down) and displays these results in a logical tree diagram. This diagram can be used to generate ways to reduce or eliminate potential causes of the event.
- **Markov analysis**—A Markov analysis is used to analyze systems that can exist in multiple states. The Markov model assumes that future events are independent of past events.
- **Monte-Carlo analysis**—According to IEC 31010:2019:[17]

Monte Carlo simulation is used to establish the aggregate variation in a system resulting from variations in the system, for a number of inputs, where each input has a defined distribution and the inputs are related to the output via defined relationships. The analysis can be used for a specific model where the interactions of the various inputs can be mathematically defined. The inputs can be based upon a variety of distribution types according to the nature of the uncertainty they are intended to represent. For risk assessment, triangular distributions or beta distributions are commonly used.

[17] ISO, International Electrotechnical Commission, IEC 31010:2019 "Risk Management—Risk Assessment Techniques," 2019, www.iso.org/standard/72140.html

2.3.9 Risk Evaluation

During the risk evaluation phase, decisions are made concerning how the enterprise responds to and prioritizes risk, based on the foregoing analysis, with allowances made for the likely margin of error, which may be considerable if reliable data are not available. This is done in the context of the enterprise's defined risk appetite, tolerance criteria and capacity—establishing a method to advise a reasonable and appropriate risk response.

If the risk meets the acceptable risk criteria, the treatment option is likely to be acceptance. If the risk exceeds the acceptable level and is not within the tolerance variance, then treatment will most likely be some form of mitigation. The mitigation options include modification or addition of controls or business process reengineering that would render a process less risky. A system redesign can serve to reduce technical risk (e.g., eliminating a single point of system failure), or risk transfer (or sharing) might be the most cost-effective option. If there are no cost-effective options for mitigating excessive risk, management may decide that the activity is not worth the risk, or it may decide to accept the risk if the benefits are sufficiently high.

Typically, risk transfer is selected for risk that has low likelihood and high impact. If risk is mitigated through the use of controls, control risk must also be considered (i.e., control risk is the probability the control will fail or be inadequate).

The risk evaluation may lead to a decision to undertake further analysis if the results are ambiguous or are considered inaccurate or misleading.

The criteria used by the risk management team must also take into account the organizational objectives, the stakeholder views, and the scope and objective of the risk management process itself and its probable margins of error. The decisions made are usually based on the level of risk but may be related to thresholds specified in terms of:

- Consequences (e.g., impacts)
- The likelihood of events
- The cumulative (aggregated) impact of a series of events that could occur simultaneously
- The effect of cascading risk (domino effect) in closely coupled systems
- The cost of treatment
- The ability of the enterprise to absorb losses

2.3.10 Risk Ranking

The risk practitioner uses the results of risk assessment to place risk in an order that can be used to help the risk owner direct the risk response efforts. Risk ranking is derived from a combination of all the components of risk, including the recognition of the threats and the characteristics and capabilities of a threat source, the severity of a vulnerability, the likelihood of occurrence when considering effectiveness of controls, control risk, and the impact to the enterprise should the risk be realized. Taken together, these indicate the level of risk associated with a threat.

Part B: Information Risk Response

Once risk is identified, analyzed and evaluated, the risk assessment is concluded, and a reasonable recommendation can be made on how to suitably respond to a specific risk.

Figure 2.17 provides an example of a risk response workflow.

Figure 2.17—Sample Risk Response Workflow

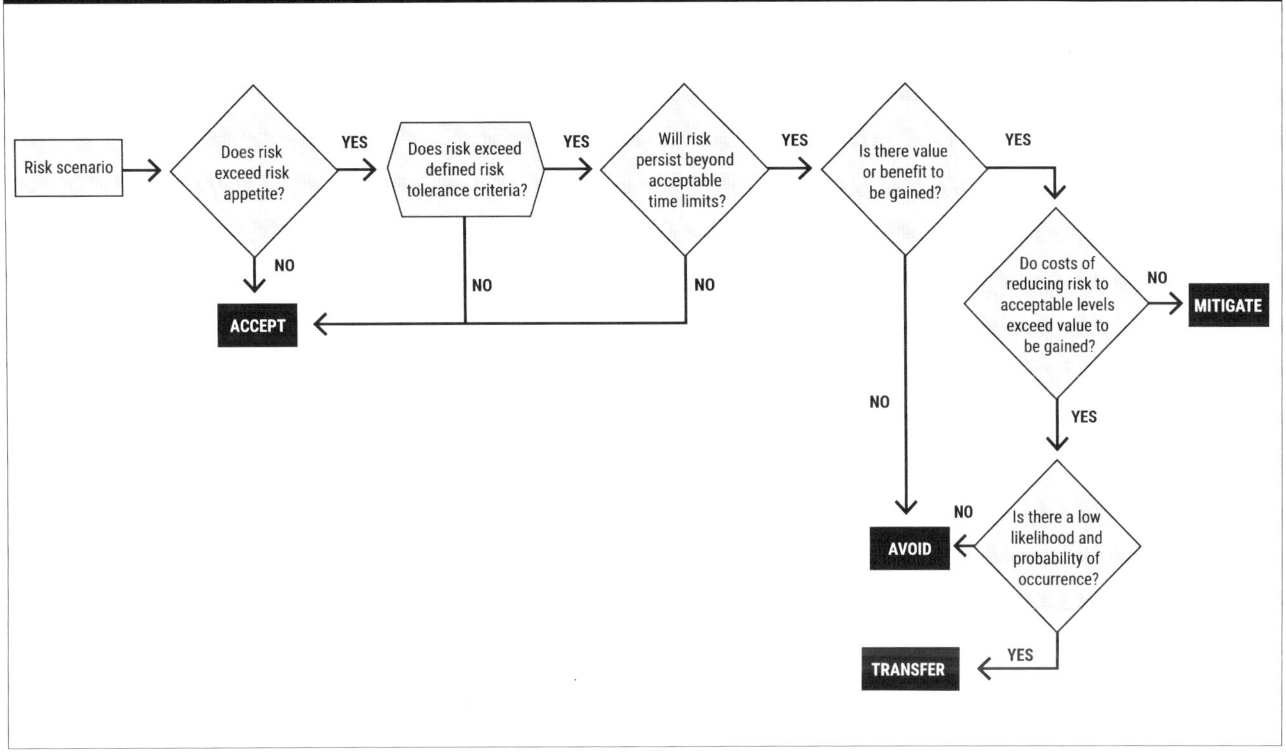

A key to understanding the appropriate risk response is to understand the enterprise's desired state of security, as discussed in Chapter 1. A major input into defining the desired state is the enterprise's defined risk appetite, tolerance criteria and capacity—that is, what management considers acceptable risk, tolerable deviations from acceptable risk levels, and total amount of risk that does not jeopardize the enterprise's viability to operate. This is another critical step, since defined acceptable risk translates into the control objectives or other risk mitigation measures employed and the criteria by which risk can be evaluated for acceptability. The defining of control objectives is instrumental in determining the type, nature and extent of controls and countermeasures the enterprise employs to manage risk. **Figure 2.18** presents the relationship between risk, control measures and the cost of controls.

Figure 2.18—Relationship Between Cost and Level of Control

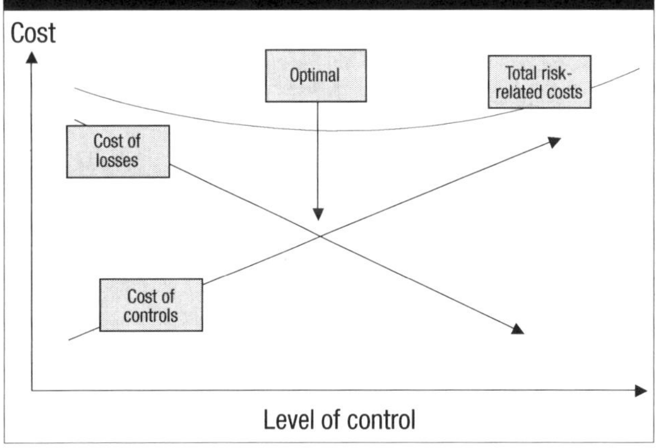

Without a reasonably clear definition of acceptable risk, it is difficult to determine whether information security is meeting its objectives and if the appropriate resources have been applied.

The definition of some risk—and ultimately what the enterprise defines as being acceptable—can be quantified by using the business continuity approach of developing recovery time objectives (RTOs). Using a summary approach to determining RTOs may provide adequate input for strategy development. This can be an informal determination by business process owners of the amount of time critical systems can be inoperative without serious business consequences. This provides the basis for approximating costs of achieving recovery. If costs are considered too high, iteration of the process will arrive at an acceptable recovery time at an acceptable cost. This may be considered the acceptable risk.

Acceptable risk can also be approximated by examining the amount of business interruption insurance the enterprise carries, the amount of the deductible and its cost (i.e., annual premiums). For example, if the enterprise has US $1 million of insurance with a $10,000 deductible at an annual cost of $50,000, the argument can be made that it is reasonable to spend up to $50,000 in control activities to reduce a $1 million risk to an acceptable risk level of $10,000 (i.e., the residual risk).

Developing the appropriate strategy objectives usually needs to be an iterative approach based on analysis of costs to achieve the desired state and achieve acceptable risk levels. It is likely that lowering the level of acceptable risk will be more costly. However, the approach to achieving the desired state will have a significant bearing on costs as well.

For example, risk may exist because of certain practices that are not necessary or useful to the enterprise or are detrimental to its operation. This could include practices that might be considered discriminatory or contrary to law, posing the risk of a lawsuit. Such practices, when examined, may have resulted from outmoded attitudes or approaches that can be efficiently changed at a lower cost, resulting in elimination or mitigation of the risk. In other cases, it may be possible to reengineer certain processes or provide better architectures to reduce inherent risk. In other words, the approach to addressing or treating specific risk has a significant impact on costs.

The information security manager must understand that technical controls (e.g., firewalls, intrusion detection systems [IDSs]) are merely one dimension to be considered. Physical, process and procedural controls may be more effective and less costly. In most enterprises, process risk poses the greatest hazard and technical controls are unlikely to adequately compensate for poor management or faulty processes.

Once objectives have been clearly defined, there will be several ways to architect solutions that will vary significantly in costs and complexity. Whichever process is used, the objective is to define, in meaningful, concrete terms, the desired overall state of security at some future point.

2.4 Risk Treatment/Risk Response Options

Selecting the appropriate response must be done in the context of the enterprise's defined risk appetite and tolerance criteria. Risk can then be quickly categorized and prioritized.

There are often multiple risk appetites within an enterprise. The enterprise's risk appetite is the total amount of risk the enterprise is willing to take on, which should encompass the risk appetites of subordinate business units. A simple example to illustrate this is provided in **figure 2.19**.

Figure 2.19—Risk Appetites Within an Organization

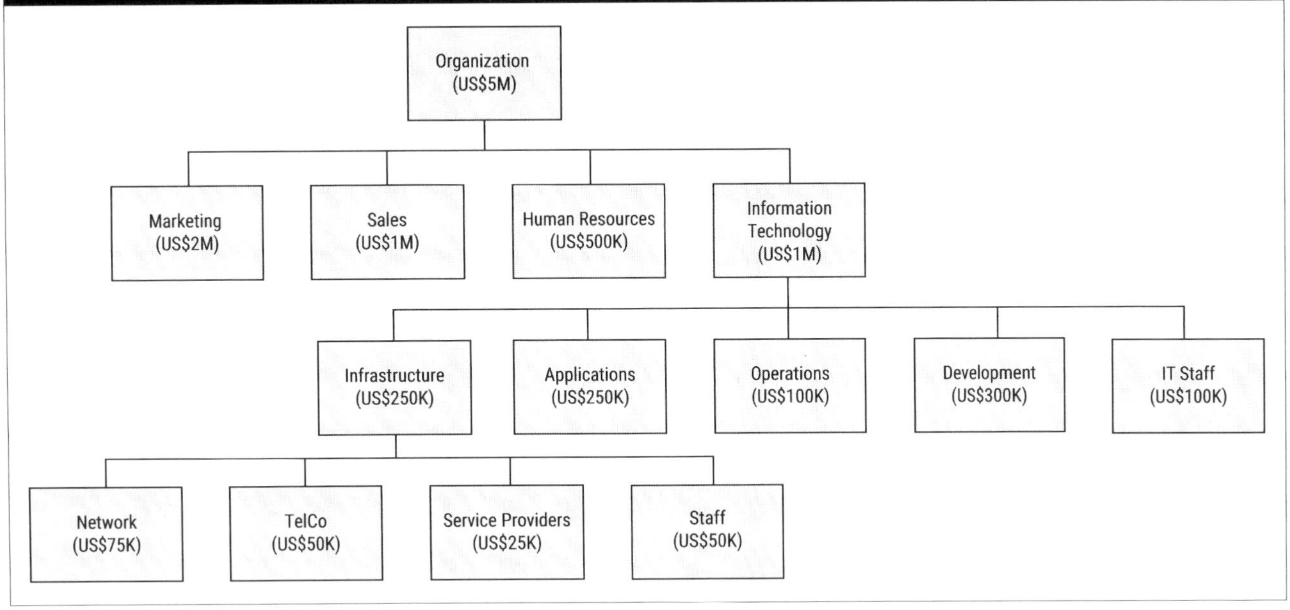

As illustrated, the enterprise's risk appetite is US $5 million. This is disbursed across the business units, with IT having a risk appetite of US $1 million, which is distributed across the various functional areas within that department. In this example, for a manager from the network group, a risk below US $75,000 could be accepted; however, approval would be required from an authority in the Infrastructure unit for acceptance of any risk exceeding that amount.

Regardless of the action taken on the risk, it should be documented in the risk register, and the enterprise should continue to monitor it for any changes in the environment that might cause that risk to become unacceptable. Accepted risk is another form of debt the enterprise carries and is responsible for, a debt that can be called upon for payment at any time.

When selecting a risk response, the information security manager may recommend an appropriate risk response, acting in the role of an internal advisor or consultant. Ultimately the risk owner is accountable for the risk and will make the final decision as to the desired action.

When concluding the risk assessment and making recommendations as to the appropriate risk response, the information security manager must clearly communicate to the risk owner how and why the response option was provided, with sufficient detail to allow an informed decision to be made.

2.4.1 Determining Risk Capacity and Acceptable Risk (Risk Appetite)

Every enterprise has a particular risk capacity, defined as the objective amount of loss an enterprise can tolerate without its continued existence being threatened. Subject to the absolute maximum imposed by this risk capacity, the owners or board of directors of an enterprise set the risk appetite for the enterprise. Risk appetite is defined as the amount of risk, on a broad basis, that an entity is willing to accept in pursuit of its mission. In some cases, the board of directors may delegate setting the risk appetite to senior management as part of strategic planning.

Acceptable risk determination or risk appetite and the criteria for assessment are essential to virtually all aspects of information security and most other aspects of organizational activities. Risk appetite will determine many aspects of strategy including control objectives, control implementation, baseline security, cost-benefit calculations, risk management options, severity criteria determinations, required incident response capabilities, insurance requirements and feasibility assessments, among others.

Risk appetite is translated into a number of standards and policies to contain the risk level within the boundaries set by the risk appetite, which need to be regularly adjusted or confirmed. Within the boundaries, risk may be accepted, a formal and explicit process that affirms that the risk requires and warrants no additional response by the enterprise as long as the specific risk and the risk environment stay substantially the same and accountability for the risk is assigned to a specific owner.

Risk acceptance generally should not exceed the risk appetite of the enterprise, but it must not exceed the risk capacity (which would threaten the continued existence of the enterprise). Risk tolerance levels are risk appetite deviations that are not desirable but are known to be sufficiently below the risk capacity that acceptance of risk is still possible when there is compelling business need and other options are too costly. Risk tolerance may be defined using IT process metrics or adherence to defined IT procedures and policies, which are a translation of the IT goals that need to be achieved. Like risk appetite, risk tolerance is defined at the enterprise level and reflected in the policies created by senior management. Exceptions can be tolerated at lower levels of the enterprise as long as the overall exposure does not exceed the risk appetite at the enterprise level.

2.4.2 Risk Response Options

Faced with risk, information security managers can advise enterprises as to four strategic options:

- Avoid the risk by terminating the activity that gives rise to it.
- Transfer risk to another party (note that risk transfer usually results from a transfer of impact).
- Mitigate risk with appropriate control measures or mechanisms.
- Accept the risk.

One thing to keep in mind is that while the information security manager is bound to recommend one of the four risk responses listed above, the enterprise may choose to ignore the risk, which can be dangerous. The distinction between ignoring and accepting risk is that acceptance means understanding the likelihood, probability and consequences and making an informed decision to accept the risk under the circumstances. Ignoring a risk may lead to a serious underestimation of both the likelihood and possible magnitude of the impact, with severe or disastrous consequences. Accordingly, this is an inadvisable course of action. The only time it may be prudent to ignore an identified risk is when the impact is so great and rare that there is no possibility of addressing it (e.g., a comet strike).

Terminate the Activity

There are often ways activities might be modified or processes reengineered that can serve to mitigate or manage risk to acceptable levels. Analysis of the activity could also lead to the conclusion that it is not worth the risk. In this circumstance, even though the enterprise has decided to terminate the product or service, the liability remains as long as the product or service is being used.

Transfer the Risk

An example of risk transference is purchasing insurance to address areas of risk. When an enterprise buys insurance, some risk is transferred to the insurance company in exchange for premium payments that reflect the insurance company's assessment of the degree of risk it is assuming. However, the risk is actually not transferred; rather, the impact to the enterprise is reduced to the extent that insurance covers some or all of the costs associated with a compromise.

Risk can be transferred by outsourcing IT functionality to a third party, provided indemnification clauses are in the contracts. However, in transferring operational risk, third-party agreements and contracts must specifically address the liability and responsibilities of both parties in specific indemnification clauses.

Indemnity agreements that can be part of an outsourced service agreement provide a level of protection against harmful incidents. While some possible financial impacts associated with the risk can be transferred, the legal responsibility for the consequences of compromise generally cannot be transferred.

Risk is typically transferred to insurance companies when the probability of an incident is low, but the impact is high.

An example would be earthquake or flood insurance. For the information security manager, this means that a well-managed risk program must interface with other organizational assurance providers, such as the insurance department, to establish what risk is covered and to what extent. If some identified risk is adequately managed by other entities, duplication of effort is generally not warranted.

Mitigate the Risk

Risk can be mitigated in a variety of ways, such as through implementing or improving security controls, instituting countermeasures, or modifying or eliminating risky processes. Preventive controls can directly address the risk, or it may be possible to reduce exposure, thereby reducing risk. In some cases, risk can be reduced through appropriate countermeasures that reduce or eliminate the probability of a threat.

Potential impact may be reduced through compensating or corrective controls, including contractual, procedural or technical processes. See Section 3.8.3 Controls and Countermeasures for more information.

Accept the Risk

A defined risk may be accepted in a variety of circumstances. If a risk has been identified as below the defined risk acceptance levels (both the defined risk appetite and risk tolerance criteria), the risk should be accepted and monitored moving forward. There are a few limited cases in which it may not be feasible to effectively mitigate a risk for which there is low likelihood of realization or low potential impact. This effectively results in increasing the risk acceptance level for a specific risk for a defined duration or financial amount. However, it is not intended to be, nor should it be treated as, the perpetual acceptance of that risk.

Elements such as customer trust and confidence, legal liability or breach of regulatory requirements need to be considered as well. In any case, the information risk management procedure should enable accurate and appropriate documentation of the risk so that a business manager can decide whether to accept the risk based on sufficient knowledge and understanding. Acceptance of risk should be regularly reviewed to ensure that the rationale for the initial acceptance is still valid within the current business context.

2.4.3 Risk Acceptance Framework

A risk acceptance framework can be a useful tool used to set the criteria for the acceptance of risk and the level at which management acceptance is executed.

An example risk acceptance framework is shown in **figure 2.20**.

Figure 2.20—Example Risk Acceptance Framework

Risk Level	Level Required for Acceptance
Low	Risk acceptance possible by business unit level (e.g., manager)
Medium	Risk acceptance possible at the division level (e.g., director)
High	Risk acceptance possible at the department level (e.g., CFO, COO, CIO)
Severe	Risk acceptance only at board/governing body level. Risk reduction is mandatory through rigorous controls and monitoring. Management notification process is required

2.4.4 Inherent and Residual Risk

The risk level or exposure without taking into account the actions that management has taken or might take (e.g., implementing controls) is called inherent risk. The risk that remains after controls have been implemented is called residual risk. Risk can never be eliminated, as a certain level of residual risk always remains even with the application of appropriate controls. It should be noted that reducing one risk inevitably introduces another risk, hopefully of a lesser nature. For example, requiring dual control to access sensitive information introduces the risk that two individuals collude to provide unauthorized access.

The objective is to ensure that residual risk is equal to the enterprise's criteria for acceptable risk or meets risk tolerance criteria. Risk tolerance is defined as the allowable deviation from acceptable risk and is usually described as a percentage (e.g., plus or minus 10 percent) or range (e.g., a project exceeding planned duration by four weeks). Acceptable residual risk should be the outcome of meeting the defined control objectives and be equivalent to the defined security baselines for the enterprise.

Residual risk reported through a subsequent risk assessment can be used by management to identify areas in which more control is required to further mitigate risk. Acceptable levels of risk are established as part of an information security strategy, as described in Chapter 1. If a strategy is not developed, management must determine the acceptable risk levels, usually in terms of allowable potential impacts. Residual risk in excess of the acceptable level should be further treated with the option of additional mitigation through implementing more stringent controls. Risk below the acceptable level should be evaluated to determine whether the controls being applied are still warranted, and whether a cost savings can be achieved by removing or modifying them. Final acceptance of residual risk takes into account:

- Cost and effectiveness of implementing controls
- Acceptable levels of potential impacts
- Organizational culture and maturity, relating to risk
- Organizational policies and standards
- Sensitivity and criticality of relevant assets
- Uncertainty inherent in the risk assessment approach
- Regulatory compliance

In judging the appropriateness of controls, the full life cycle cost must be considered, including the total cost of ownership relating to the implementation, ongoing operation and maintenance of the various measures and mechanisms used to balance the risk and potential impacts being addressed.

2.4.5 Impact

Ultimately, all risk management activities are designed to reduce impacts to acceptable levels to create or preserve value for the enterprise. An impact results when any vulnerability exploited by a threat causes a loss. Threats and vulnerabilities that do not cause an impact are usually irrelevant and generally not considered risk.

In commercial enterprises, impact is generally quantified as a direct financial loss in the short term or an ultimate (indirect) financial loss in the long term. Examples of such losses can include:

- Direct loss of money (cash or credit)
- Criminal or civil liability
- Loss of reputation/goodwill/image
- Reduction of share value
- Conflict of interest for staff, customers or shareholders
- Breach of confidence/privacy
- Loss of business opportunity/competition
- Loss of market share
- Reduction in operational efficiency/performance
- Interruption of business activity
- Noncompliance with laws and regulations, resulting in penalties

As with risk calculations, impact calculations can be made either qualitatively or quantitatively. Some impacts lend themselves to quantitative representation, such as the range of possible financial impacts. Others, such as loss of reputation or market share, may appear to be more difficult to quantify and may be adequately presented by qualitative statements if they are well defined and communicated prior to use.

Impacts may be determined by performing activities such as a BIA or subsequent analysis (such as privacy impact analysis or a security impact analysis). These activities generally may include gathering industry statistics or information from previous events and incidents the enterprise has experienced.

The results of these types of analysis should determine both the criticality and sensitivity of information assets. They can then provide the basis not only for establishing business continuity plan requirements, such as RTOs, RPOs, maximum tolerable outages (MTOs), service delivery objectives (SDOs) and acceptable interruption window (AIW), but also for establishing requirements for minimal safeguards and countermeasures, ranging from access control to notification requirements.

These various analysis activities often serve as a method to prioritize risk management. Coupled with asset valuations, they can provide a basis for the levels and types of protection required and a basis for the development of a business case for controls. See Chapter 4 for more information.

2.4.6 Controls

A control is any technology, process, practice, policy, standard or procedure that serves to regulate an activity to mitigate or reduce risk. It can be of an administrative, technical, management or legal nature. Controls are discussed in detail in Chapter 3.

Because it is normal to find a number of different controls in different parts of a typical process, it is important to understand the entire risk mitigation process from end to end. While layering of controls is a prudent approach, using an excessive number of controls that address the same risk is wasteful and usually reduces productivity. It is important to ensure that the various controls are not subject to the same risk, which defeats the purpose of layering them. For risk assessments to be effective and reasonably accurate, it is necessary to ensure that they are conducted from the beginning of a process to the end. This approach will facilitate understanding if upstream controls minimize or eliminate some risk that may preclude the need for subsequent controls. It will also help determine whether there is unnecessary control redundancy or duplication.

2.4.7 Legal and Regulatory Requirements

Legal and regulatory requirements must be considered in terms of risk and impact. This is necessary for senior management to determine the appropriate level of compliance and priority. Regulations must first be evaluated by legal/general counsel to determine the exposure the enterprise is subject to by the regulation and the present level at which the enterprise can demonstrate compliance. If it is found that the enterprise is noncompliant, then the regulations must be evaluated to determine the level of risk they pose to the enterprise. The enterprise must take into consideration the level of enforcement and its relative position in relation to its peers, because enforcement actions are usually initiated against those that are least compliant. The potential impact of full compliance, partial compliance and noncompliance, in both direct financial and reputational terms, must be evaluated as well. These evaluations provide the basis for senior management to determine the nature and extent of compliance activities appropriate for the enterprise. The information security manager must be aware that senior management may decide that risking sanctions is less costly than achieving compliance, or that because enforcement is limited, or even nonexistent, compliance is not warranted. This is a management decision that should be based on risk and impact.

2.4.8 Costs and Benefits

When controls are planned, an enterprise should consider the costs and benefits. If the costs of specific controls (control overhead) exceed the benefits of mitigating a given risk, the enterprise may choose to accept the risk rather than incur the cost of mitigation.

Cost-benefit analysis helps provide a financial view of risk and helps determine the cost of protecting what is important. However, cost-benefit analysis is also about making smart choices based on potential risk mitigation costs versus potential losses. Both concepts tie directly back to good governance practices.

Unfortunately, most information security crime and loss metrics are not as established as traditional robbery and theft statistics. For example, the annual Verizon Data Breach Report has been one source involving losses in the information security realm. A number of practitioners suggest that Verizon's loss figures are still understated, as they only reflect customers directly involved with the company.

Rather than debate the validity of the metrics reported, it may be more useful to focus on a few that most enterprises can quantify with some accuracy. Three common measurements of potential losses are employee productivity impacts, revenue losses and direct cost loss events. Virus and worm incidents are the ones most frequently cited when discussing impact on productivity. Another is the result of the compromise of personally identifiable information.

Revenue losses can also be determined in a similar manner. If a business has an e-commerce website that is producing US $1 million of revenue each day, then a denial of service (DoS) attack that lasts half a day creates a US $500,000 loss. It is debatable whether this type of attack merely forces customers to delay their purchases or whether they go to competitors. However, any public perception of an enterprise being the victim of a hacking attack, whether sensitive information is compromised or not, often results in the loss of customer trust.

While productivity, response and organizational costs are considered direct losses, indirect losses include competitive advantage, legal expenses (fines and penalties), damaged reputation and impaired growth as a result of the incident.

The total cost of ownership (TCO) must be considered for the full life cycle of any control or countermeasure that may be implemented. This can include such elements as:

- Acquisition costs
- Deployment, implementation and integration costs
- Recurring maintenance costs
- Testing and assessment costs

- Compliance monitoring and enforcement
- Inconvenience to users
- Reduced throughput of controlled processes
- Training in new procedures or technologies as applicable
- End-of-life decommissioning

2.5 Risk and Control Ownership

Who owns the risk? This is a commonly asked question and the answer is, it depends. From a strategic standpoint, all risk ultimately is owned by senior management. As a matter of practicality and from an operational standpoint, ownership is delegated to the individuals who have the authority and responsibility for managing risk in accordance with the criteria established by the governing body within their respective business areas, driving ownership of both risk and controls to the relevant business process owner (i.e., the business).

2.5.1 Risk Ownership and Accountability

Risk requires ownership and accountability. After a risk has been identified, analyzed and evaluated, a manager or senior official within the enterprise must be identified as its owner. A risk owner is accountable for accepting risk based on the organizational risk appetite and tolerance criteria, and should be someone with the capability (e.g., budget, authority, resources) to select the appropriate risk response based on analyses and guidance provided by the information security manager. This accountability extends to approving controls when mitigation is the chosen risk response. Types of controls are examined in more detail in Chapter 3. However, the concept is to create a direct link, so that all risk is addressed through appropriate treatment and all controls are justified by the risk that mandates their existence. **Figure 2.21** illustrates the relationship between risk and control.

The owner of a risk should also own any controls associated with that risk and be held accountable for ensuring the monitoring of their effectiveness, due to the shared relationship between risk and controls. In areas where there are regulations or laws that apply to risk, the risk owners may have to prepare standard reports on the status of risk, any incidents that may have occurred, the level of risk currently faced by the enterprise and the tested effectiveness of controls.

Figure 2.21—Relationship Between Risk and Control

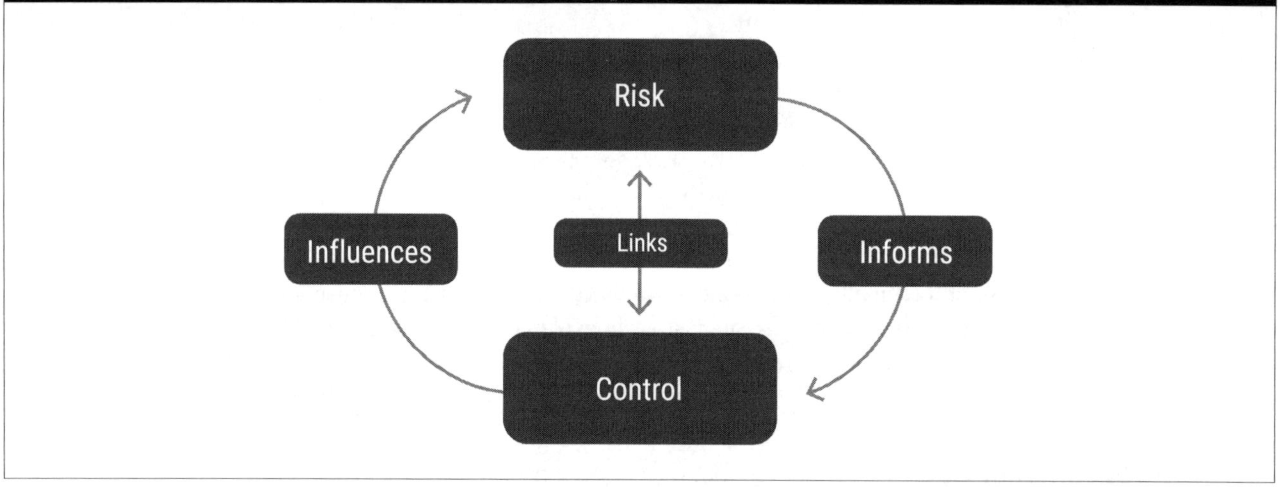

2.5.2 Risk Owner

The term risk owner can be defined as the person to whom the enterprise has granted the authority and accountability for making risk-based decisions and who owns the loss associated with a realized risk scenario. From a strategic aspect, senior management (e.g., chief executive officer, president, founder) is the risk owner who is ultimately accountable for risk response for the entirety of the enterprise. From an operational and management perspective, directors, vice presidents, managers, etc., are the individuals who have the authority and responsibility, and should be held accountable, for making decisions relating to risk as a part of routine operations.

Confusion arises with respect to risk associated with information technology, as it is common within enterprises to attempt to place the accountability and responsibility for that risk with the IT department. While IT personnel serve as custodians/stewards of systems to support business operations, the risk ownership falls to the individual within the business who requires and consumes those services in order to carry out their business functions.

2.5.3 Control Owner

Control owner, like its counterpart risk owner, is a term that often gets confused. The control owner is the individual to whom the enterprise has granted the authority and accountability for making control-related decisions. The control owner and the risk owner are normally the same individual, as any modifications to or removal of a control will impact the risk being treated, potentially leading to the risk exceeding the defined risk appetite.

Just as with risk ownership, control ownership falls to individuals within the enterprise who have the authority to make decisions related to the controls and who will be held accountable for how risk is managed. IT staff may serve as the custodians/stewards of the controls; however, it is ultimately the business unit that bears accountability if a control should be ineffective in properly treating risk.

There are instances in which the business unit will not be the control owner. Technology controls, including intrusion detection/prevention systems, email filters, data loss prevention platforms and end-point detection are typically enterprise-wide controls that are configured and managed by the enterprise's security operations staff.

2.6 Risk Monitoring and Reporting

Implementing an effective risk management program requires regular monitoring and effective communication. Monitoring the effectiveness of controls is an ongoing effort required to manage risk. Communication channels must be established both for reporting and disseminating information relevant to managing risk and for providing the information security manager with information about risk-related activities throughout the enterprise, which includes reporting significant changes in risk and training in awareness.

2.6.1 Risk Monitoring

An important component of the risk management life cycle is continuously monitoring, evaluating, assessing and reporting risk. The results and status of this ongoing analysis need to be documented and reported to senior management on a regular basis. To facilitate such reporting, visual aids such as graphs or charts and summarized overviews can be useful. **Figure 2.22** shows a risk report format from COBIT that can serve as a standard approach for communicating risk status.

Figure 2.22—Risk Report

A risk report includes information on current risk management capabilities and actual status and trends with regard to risk. This report will be based on the risk profile and will be tailored to the requirements of recipients.

Life Cycle and Stakeholders	Life Cycle Stage	Internal Stakeholder	External Stakeholder	Description/Stake
	Information planning	Risk function		Risk management capabilities, actual status and trends are communicated timely and accurately to the right people, based on their needs and requirements.
	Information design	Risk function		Risk management capabilities, actual status and trends are communicated timely and accurately to the right people, based on their needs and requirements.
	Information build/acquire	Risk function, business process owners/CIO		Ensure that the risk report includes the latest information on risk management capabilities, latest status and trends with regard to risk of the entire organisation.
	Information use/operate: store, share, use	Board, executive management, CIO, risk function, business process owners/CIO, compliance, internal audit	External audit, regulator	Effective utilisation and availability of information item by all involved stakeholders.

Figure 2.22—Risk Report *(cont.)*

Life Cycle and Stakeholders		**Information monitor**	Board, risk committee, audit committee, risk function, business process owners/ CIO	External audit	Verifies that information remains actual and alerts on changes.
Life Cycle and Stakeholders		**Information dispose**	Risk function		Ensures information is disposed of in a timely, secure and appropriate manner.
Goals		**Quality Subdimension and Goals**	**Description—The extent to which information is...**	**Relevance**	**Goal—The risk report...**
Goals	Intrinsic	**Accuracy**	correct and reliable	High	should accurately define the risk management capabilities and actual status and trends with regard to risk, in such a way that it does not arouse confusion
Goals	Intrinsic	**Objectivity**	unbiased, unprejudiced and impartial	High	information is based on the enterprise's risk culture and confirmed by observations.
Goals	Intrinsic	**Believability**	regarded as true and credible	Medium	should be realistic and accurate
Goals	Intrinsic	**Reputation**	regarded as coming from a true and credible source	High	source information is collected from competent and recognised sources.
Goals	Intrinsic	**Relevancy**	applicable and helpful for the task at hand	High	is tailored according to the requirements of the target audience
Goals	Intrinsic	**Completeness**	not missing and is of sufficient depth and breadth for the task at hand	High	typically covers the end-to-end enterprise structure as well external stakeholders
Goals	Intrinsic	**Currency**	sufficiently up to date for the task at hand	High	is typically not older than one year because it should be kept up to date
Goals	Intrinsic	**Amount of information**	appropriate for the task at hand	High	should contain an appropriate amount of information, based on the requirements of the recipients
Goals	Intrinsic	**Concise representation**	compactly represented	Medium	depends on the target audience
Goals	Intrinsic	**Consistent representation**	presented in the same format	High	shall always be presented according to the predefined formats/ templates
Goals	Intrinsic	**Interpretability**	in appropriate languages, symbols, and units, and the definitions are clear	High	should be understandable for target audience
Goals	Intrinsic	**Understandability**	easily comprehended	High	should be comprehensible for target audience
Goals	Intrinsic	**Manipulation**	easy to manipulate and apply to different tasks	Medium	information can be manipulated to present in different types of risk reports
Goals	Security	**Availability**	available when required, or easily and quickly retrievable	High	shall be available at required frequency to the stakeholders
Goals	Security	**Restricted access**	restricted appropriately to authorised parties	High	access is determined by the risk function, and is restricted as follows: • Write access: Risk function • Read access: All other stakeholders

Figure 2.22—Risk Report *(cont.)*

	Attribute	Description	Value
Good Practice	**Physical**	Information carrier/media	The information carrier for the risk report can be an electronic and/or printed document.
	Empiric	Information access channel	The risk report is accessible through the ERM portal and/or printed in a specific location.
	Syntactic	Code/language	The risk report contains the following subparts: • Status of risk items • Action items (risk response) • Risk capabilities
Good Practice	**Semantic**	Information type	Information (risk) reports
		Information currency	Information should be current for organisational use.
		Information level	Depends on target audience; for board and risk committee function level a status of risk and a risk capability presentation. For process owners a detailed risk analysis report.
	Pragmatic	Retention period	According to data retention policy (and taking into account local legal retention requirements).
		Information status	The information produced would be current. Once replaced it becomes historical.
		Novelty	It is current as the risk status is updated in time.
		Contingency	Enterprise risk portal should provide as and when required.
	Social	Context	This information item should be used in context of IT risk communication plan.

Source: ISACA, *COBIT®5 for Risk, USA, 2013, figure 64, page 155*

Senior management will typically have little interest in technical details and will likely want an overview of the current status and indicators of any immediate or impending threat that requires attention.

Security dashboards, heat charts or stoplight charts are often used to show an overall assessment of the security posture. Depending on the recipients, other representations of security status, such as bar graphs or spider charts, may be more effective at conveying trends. Whatever the form of reporting, the information security manager is responsible for managing this reporting process to ensure that it takes place, and that the results are analyzed adequately and acted on appropriately in a timely manner. This responsibility includes identifying the types of events that will trigger reporting required by regulatory agencies or law enforcement and advising management of requirements.

2.6.2 Key Risk Indicators

One approach seeing increasing use is to report and monitor risk through the use of key risk indicators (KRIs). KRIs can be defined as measures that indicate when an enterprise is subject to risk that exceeds a defined risk level. Typically, these indicators emerge from trends in factors known to increase risk and are generally developed based on experience. They can be as diverse as increasing absenteeism or turnover in key employees or rising levels of security events or incidents.

KRIs can provide early warnings on possible issues or areas that pose particular risk.

A variety of risk indicators can be developed for various parts of an enterprise as a means of ongoing monitoring. In addition to experience, selection of KRIs can be based on sources such as industry benchmarks, external threat-reporting services, or any other factor that can be monitored that indicates changes in risk to the enterprise.

KRIs are specific to each enterprise, and their selection depends on a number of parameters in the internal and external environment—such as the size and complexity of the enterprise, whether it operates in a highly regulated market and its business strategy. Identifying useful risk indicators involves the following considerations:

- Including all stakeholders in the enterprise. Risk indicators should not focus solely on the operational or the strategic side of risk. Rather, they should be identified for all stakeholders. Involving the right stakeholders in the selection of risk indicators will ensure greater buy-in and ownership.
- Balancing the selection of risk indicators to gain insight. Balance should be maintained between performance indicators that indicate risk after an event has occurred (lag indicators), lead indicators that indicate what capabilities are in place to prevent events from occurring, trends based on analyzing indicators over time, and other correlating indicators.
- Ensuring that the selected indicators drill down to the root cause of events rather than just focusing on symptoms.

It is important to determine which measures are likely to serve as effective KRIs. These are differentiated by being highly relevant and possessing a high probability of predicting or indicating a significant change in risk. The criteria for selecting effective KRIs include:

- **Impact**—Indicators for risk with high potential impact are more likely to be KRIs.
- **Effort to implement, measure and report**—Among indicators of equivalent sensitivity to changing risk, the ones that are easier to measure are preferred.
- **Reliability**—The indicator must possess a high correlation with the risk and be a good predictor or outcome measure.
- **Sensitivity**—The indicator must be representative of the risk and capable of accurately indicating variances in the risk level.

Because the enterprise's internal and external environments are constantly changing, the risk environment is also highly dynamic, and the set of KRIs will more than likely change over time. Each KRI is related to risk appetite and tolerance so trigger levels can be defined that will enable stakeholders to take appropriate action in a timely manner.

2.6.3 Reporting Changes in Risk

As changes occur in an enterprise, the risk assessment must be updated to ensure its continued accuracy. Reporting changes to the appropriate levels of management (e.g., risk/control owners) at the proper time is a primary responsibility of the information security manager. The information security manager should have periodic meetings with the appropriate, relevant stakeholders to present a risk status and with senior management on the enterprise's overall risk profile, including changes in risk level and the status of any open (untreated) risk.

In addition, the security program should include a process in which a significant security breach or security event will trigger a report to senior management and a reassessment of risk and applicable controls because all security events or incidents are the result of the failure of, or lack of, controls. The information security manager should have defined processes for evaluating security events based on impact to the enterprise. This evaluation may warrant a special report to inform upper management of the event, the impact, and the steps being taken to mitigate the risk. Refer to Chapter 4 for more detailed information on establishing and managing an incident response program.

An example IT risk indicator dashboard is illustrated in

2.6.4 Risk Communication, Awareness and Consulting

For risk management to become part of the enterprise's culture, it is necessary to communicate and create awareness of the issues across the enterprise at each step of the risk management process.

Communication should involve consultation with all relevant stakeholders and focus on development of a common understanding of the objectives and requirements of the risk management program. This approach will allow variations in needs and perceptions to be identified and addressed more effectively. A template for risk communication is shown in **figure 2.24**.

Figure 2.23—Example of IT Risk Indicator Dashboard

Indicator Metric	Value	Trend
Business Impact Indicators		
Monetary value of losses due to IT risk (YTD)	$30,000	→
# of customers affected by IT risk incidents (YTD)	$20,000	↗
# of regulator notifications (YTD) (figure D.2)	3	→
Risk Indicators		
# of non-compliance incidents (YTD) (figure D.3)	10	→
% of critical system availability (Current Month)	95%	↘
# of significant IT risk incidents (YTD)	50	↗
Control Indicators		
% of control environment effectiveness (Current Month) (figure D.4)	80%	↗
# of control issues (YTD) (figure D.5)	50	↗
# of overdue management actions (Current Month)	3	↘
# of policy reviews (YTD)	10	→
% of staff trained (YTD)	75%	↗

Source: ISACA, *COBIT Focus Area: Information and Technology Risk*, USA, 2021

Figure 2.24—Risk Communication Plan

Type of Content	Specification
Description	A risk communication plan defines the frequency of reporting, types of information about I&T risk and recipients of that information. The main purpose of the plan is to reduce the overload of irrelevant information (avoiding the likelihood of risk noise).
Goals and quality criteria	The risk communication plan: • Should accurately define the type, frequency and recipient of communications • Ensure that information is based on the enterprise's risk culture • Should be based on input from both the risk function and business process owners, making the devised risk communication plan appropriate • Shall be aligned to the needs of the recipients • Shall cover both the end-to-end enterprise structure and external stakeholders • Shall not be older than one year • Should contain communication frequencies, types and recipients • Should ensure that information is always presented according to the predefined formats/templates • Should be understandable for the target audience

	• Shall be available at the required frequency to key stakeholders; should be available to the risk function 24/7
	• Should indicate that access to this information item is determined by risk function and is restricted as follows:
	  ■ Write access: risk function
	  ■ Read access: all other stakeholders

Structure/High-level content	The risk communication plan contains the following subparts: • Frequency/timing of communication • Type of communication • Target audience and distribution

Source: ISACA, *COBIT Focus Area: Information & Technology Risk*, USA, 2021

Risk Awareness

Awareness is a powerful tool in creating the culture, shaping ethics and influencing the behavior of the members of an enterprise. The risk and security awareness program should include communication of risk and security information, periodic testing as a metric for awareness, and a channel for staff to report risk and security issues. The staff and operational teams of an enterprise are often the first to be aware of any problems or abnormal activities. Through awareness programs, it is possible to develop a team approach to risk management that enables every member of an enterprise to identify and report on risk and work to defend systems and networks from attacks. Each member of the team can help identify vulnerabilities, suspicious activity and possible attacks. This may enable a faster response and better containment of a risk when an attack happens. Risk awareness acknowledges that risk is an integral part of the business. Because not all risk can be avoided or eliminated, it aims to ensure that:

- Risk is well understood and known.
- Information risk is identifiable.
- Employees recognize that organizational risk can affect them personally.
- The enterprise recognizes and uses the available means to manage risk.

A risk awareness program creates an understanding of overall risk, risk factors and the various types of risk that an enterprise faces. An awareness program should be tailored to the needs of the individual groups within an enterprise and deliver content suitable for each group. The program should not disclose vulnerabilities or ongoing investigations unless the problem has already been addressed. Using examples and descriptions of the types of attacks and compromises that other enterprises have experienced can reinforce the need for diligence and caution when addressing risk.

Awareness education and training can mitigate some of the most significant weaknesses contributing to organizational risk and achieve the most cost-effective improvements in security and risk management. Awareness can generally be achieved by educating an enterprise's staff in required procedures and policy compliance, and ensuring that staff can identify and understand the risk that threatens the enterprise. Training must effectively communicate the risk and its potential impact so staff can understand the justification for the seemingly inconvenient extra steps that risk mitigation and security controls often require.

The development of awareness and training programs that will be effective in the environment depends on the information security manager's ability to understand the enterprise's structure, culture and most-effective types of communication. Periodically changing risk awareness messages and the means of delivering them will help maintain a higher level of risk awareness. Procedural and technical controls can be complex, and it is essential to provide training as needed to ensure that staff understands the procedures and can correctly perform the required steps.

Awareness of information security architecture, policies, standards and procedures by all personnel is essential to achieving effective risk management. Employees cannot be expected to comply with policies or standards they are not aware of or follow procedures they do not understand. The information security manager should use a standardized approach, such as short computer- or paper-based quizzes, to gauge awareness levels. Periodic use of a standardized testing approach provides metrics for awareness trends and training effectiveness. Further training needs can be determined by a skills assessment or through testing. Indicators for additional training requirements can come from various sources, such as tracking help desk activity, operational errors, security events and audits.

An awareness program for management should highlight the need for management to play a supervisory role in protecting systems and applications from attack. Managers have the responsibility to oversee the actions of their staff and direct compliance with the policies, procedures and practices of the enterprise.

Awareness training for senior management should highlight liability, need for compliance, due care and due diligence, and the need to reflect the tone and culture of the enterprise through policy and good practice. Senior managers may need reminders that they are ultimately the ones who own the risk and bear the responsibility for determining risk acceptance levels.

2.6.5 Documentation

Appropriate and readily available documentation regarding risk management policies, standards, services, infrastructure and applications, in addition to other relevant risk-related matters, is required to effectively manage risk. Decisions concerning the nature and extent of documentation involve costs and related benefits. The risk management strategy, policy and program define the documentation needed. Specifically, at each stage of the risk management process, documentation should include:

- Objectives
- Audience
- Information resources
- Assumptions
- Decision criteria

A risk management policy and process document includes information such as:

- Objectives of the policy and rationale for managing risk
- Scope and charter of information risk management
- Links between the risk management policy and the enterprise's strategic and corporate business plans
- Extent and range of issues to which the policy applies
- Guidance on what is considered acceptable risk levels
- Criteria for deviations from acceptable risk levels
- Risk management responsibilities
- Support expertise available to assist those responsible for managing risk
- Level of documentation required for various risk management-related activities (e.g., change management)
- A plan for reviewing conformance and compliance with the risk management policy
- Incident and event severity levels
- Risk reporting and escalation procedures, format and frequency. In some circumstances, a compliance and due diligence statement may be required to ensure that managers formally acknowledge their responsibility to comply with risk management policies and procedures.

Typical documentation for risk management should include

- A risk register (see Section 2.1.6 Risk Register) that records, for each risk identified, the:
    - Source of risk—Where is the risk originating from (e.g., the threat actor/community)?
    - Nature of risk—What happens if the risk is realized (i.e., unauthorized access, interruption, theft)?
    - Risk owner—Who is the individual who is accountable and has the authority to make decisions about the identified risk?
    - Risk ranking by severity—How will the enterprise be impacted (i.e., high/medium/low, immaterial/moderate/significant/material/catastrophic)?
    - Selected treatment option—Do we accept, avoid, mitigate or transfer the risk?
    - Existing controls—What controls do we have already, how are they currently implemented, and how do existing controls presently integrate with the business?
    - Recommended controls not implemented and the reasons why they should be implemented—What logical, physical or administrative controls would reduce the residual risk to an acceptable level?
- Consequences and likelihood of compromise, including:
    - Organizational—New business processes, personnel or technologies needed to sufficiently address the risk, or losses requiring unplanned capital investments (e.g., replacing assets) or operational expenses (e.g., bringing in a third party for an audit or assessment)
    - Productivity—Failure to achieve key targets, loss of staff productivity, loss resulting from an operational inability to achieve defined targets.
    - Response costs—Costs directly associated with responding to a risk event having occurred (e.g., contractors, consultants, hardware/software, public relations firm, external legal counsel)
    - Legal risk—Costs resulting from litigation (e.g., fines, penalties, summary judgements) that need to be paid as a result of a risk event occurring

  - Competitive advantage—Losses resulting in competitors gaining an advantage due to a loss in confidence or trust in the enterprise, loss of intellectual property or key personnel
  - Impaired growth—Losses resulting in delays to new lines of business, new offerings, new ventures or other strategic initiatives
  - Damaged reputation—Negative publicity gained due to an event occurring, leading to regulatory disapproval/censure, increased scrutiny/oversight by a regulatory body, or geographic litigation, and losses resulting from the external stakeholder perspective that the enterprise's value has decreased or its liability has increased.
- Vulnerability to external/internal factors
- An inventory of information assets, including IT and telecommunication assets, that lists:
  - Description of the asset
  - Technical specifications
  - Number/quantity
  - Location
  - Special licensing requirements if any
  - System (business) owner
  - System (technical) steward/custodian
- A risk mitigation and action plan, providing:
  - Who is accountable for successfully reducing the residual risk
  - Who has responsibility for implementing the plan
  - Resources to be utilized (e.g., staff, technology, third party)
  - Budget allocation
  - Timetable for implementation
  - Details of mechanism/control measures
  - Policy compliance requirements
- Monitoring and audit documents, which include:
  - Outcomes of audits/reviews and other monitoring procedures
  - Follow-up of review recommendations and implementation status

Finally, it is essential that all documentation be subject to an effective version control process in addition to a standard approach to marking and handling. Documentation should be labeled with classification level, revision date and number, effective dates and document owner. The risk management policy should be approved by the board of directors to give it a solid foundation for gaining support from all stakeholders in the enterprise.

Case Study

A major retailer was compromised, resulting in the loss of about 45 million credit and debit card records. Estimates of the ultimate total costs to the retailer were up to US $18 billion, including costs incurred due to banks having to replace the cards and cover the resultant fraudulent charges. The total included the possible costs of lawsuits, governmental sanctions and fines levied by the major credit card organization for failure to be PCI-compliant. The retailer suffered a 46 percent decrease in holiday sales when the breach was made public.

Upon analysis of the incident, it was discovered that the breach was facilitated initially by a phishing email to one of the retailer's service providers—a HVAC company. The retailer had a service provider and vendor portal to facilitate purchasing and billing. Once the hackers gained access to the service company, they used the retailer's portal to gain access to the retailer's network. Although the portal was in a segmented portion of the network, the intruders managed to bridge the segment and gain access to the internal network. From there, they gained access to the point-of-sale (POS) system. They were able to install malware on the POS terminals that captured credit and debit card transactions because the POS traffic was in cleartext to avoid the system overhead associated with encryption.

The unencrypted customer information intercepted was stored on the compromised retailer's server and then subsequently exfiltrated to a series of Internet service providers before finally being sent to overseas in an effort to hide the trail. To mask the exfiltration, the data were sent only during normal business hours. Analysis discovered that the exfiltration did not start until several weeks after the malware had been installed.

The retailer had previously contracted with FireEye to monitor its systems for intrusions and malware. Almost immediately, FireEye sent several alerts to the retailer's security department indicating which of the servers were compromised as per the agreement with the retailer. No immediate action was taken by the security group. No action was taken until several weeks later when the retailer received notification from a government agency that it had been compromised.

1. From a risk management standpoint, who in the enterprise should bear primary responsibility for this event?

   A. Board of directors
   B. CEO
   C. Information security manager
   D. IT manager

2. What could have been done to ensure the most effective action was taken when the company's security department was notified by FireEye that servers had been compromised?

   A. Investigate and analyze the potential impact of the compromised servers.
   B. Isolate the POS devices.
   C. Initiate a tested incident management plan.
   D. Locate and remove the malware on the POS devices.

3. What could the information security manager suggest from a risk management standpoint to prevent a similar incident from occurring in the future?

Answers on page 134

Chapter 2 ANSWER KEY

Case Study

1. **A. It is the responsibility of the board of directors to ensure that executive management adequately addresses significant risk to the enterprise. These and other systemic failures in various departments were the result of lack of oversight, resources, authority or competency, or perhaps inadequate integration or communication. Whichever the case or combination of causes, this catastrophic event inevitably is a failure of governance, and responsibility for the string of failures that led to it resides with the board of directors.**

   B. The CEO would be responsible for aspects of the information security program and the circumstances leading up to the event; however, this incident was primarily caused by failures in governance.

   C. The information security manager would be responsible for aspects of the information security program and the circumstances leading up to the event; however, this incident was primarily caused by failures in governance.

   D. The IT manager is responsible for certain aspects of the retailer's IT program; however, this incident was primarily caused by failures in governance.

2. A. Isolating the affected servers and implementing encryption would have prevented the POS transactions, resulting in significant revenue loss unless backup servers in a recovery facility could have been brought on line to handle the traffic.

   B. Once the POS devices were compromised, there were few good options available. Taking them offline would have had a massive impact on revenues. Because the credit and debit information was being stored for several weeks before being exfiltrated, isolating those servers while investigating and analyzing them would have thwarted the impact of the attack.

   C. If a tested incident management plan had existed, it is likely that the risk and impact scenario would have been considered and tested, and it can be assumed that some level of preventive action would have been initiated.

   D. Locating the malware on the POS devices would have been feasible, but removing it from tens of thousands of devices would have posed a major problem unless it could have been automated.

3. A more robust training and awareness program regarding potential information security risk to inform all parties, from vendors to senior management, would better position the enterprise to recognize and respond to potential risk events. Awareness training has a positive impact on risk management.

   The information security manager may also want to suggest better third-party management, including ensuring that the outsourcers contractually adhere to the information security policies of the enterprise and that third parties are granted the appropriate level of access to systems. Compliance with PCI DSS would be another important suggestion to help prevent further incidents, as it would set requirements for security to which the enterprise should adhere.

Chapter 3:

Information Security Program Development and Management

Overview

Part A: Information Security Program Development

Part B: Information Security Program Management

Overview

This chapter reviews the diverse areas of knowledge needed to develop and manage an information security program.

This domain represents 33 percent of the CISM examination (approximately 50 questions).

Domain 3 Exam Content Outline

A. Information Security Program Development

1. Information Security Program Resources

2. Information Asset Identification and Classification

3. Industry Standards and Frameworks for Information Security

4. Information Security Policies, Procedures and Guidelines

5. Information Security Program Metrics

B. Information Security Program Management

1. Information Security Control Design and Selection

2. Information Security Control Implementation and Integrations

3. Information Security Control Testing and Evaluation

4. Information Security Awareness and Training

5. Management of External Services

6. Information Security Program Communications and Reporting

Learning Objectives/Task Statements

Upon completion of this chapter, the information security manager should be able to:

- Identify internal and external influences to the organization that impact the information security strategy.
- Integrate information security governance into corporate governance.
- Establish and maintain information security policies to guide the development of standards, procedures and guidelines.
- Define, communicate and monitor information security responsibilities throughout the organization and lines of authority.
- Compile and present reports to key stakeholders on the activities, trends and overall effectiveness of the information security program.
- Evaluate and report information security metrics to key stakeholders.
- Establish and/or maintain the information security program in alignment with the information security strategy.
- Align the information security program with the operational objectives of other business functions.
- Establish and maintain information security processes and resources to execute the information security program.
- Establish, communicate and maintain organizational information security policies, standards, guidelines, procedures and other documentation.
- Establish, promote and maintain a program for information security awareness and training.
- Integrate information security requirements into organizational processes to maintain the organization's security strategy.
- Integrate information security requirements into contracts and activities of external parties.
- Monitor external parties' adherence to established security requirements.
- Define and monitor management and operational metrics for the information security program.
- Identify legal, regulatory, organizational, and other applicable compliance requirements.
- Determine whether information security controls are appropriate and effectively manage risk to an acceptable level.
- Facilitate the integration of information risk management into business and IT processes.
- Monitor for internal and external factors that may require reassessment of risk.
- Report on information security risk, including noncompliance and changes in information risk, to key stakeholders to facilitate the risk management decision-making process.

- Establish and maintain an incident response plan, in alignment with the business continuity plan and disaster recovery plan.
- Establish and maintain communication plans and processes for internal and external entities.

Suggested Resources for Further Reading

Brotby, W.; G. Hinson; *PRAGMATIC Security Metrics: Applying Metametrics to Information Security,* Auerbach Publications, USA, 2013

Cloud Security Alliance (CSA), www.cloudsecurityalliance.org

Cloud Security Alliance (CSA), ISACA; *Certificate of Cloud Auditing Knowledge Study Guide,* USA, 2021

ISACA, *CMMI Performance Solutions, https://cmmiinstitute.com/*

ISACA, *COBIT,* www.isaca.org/cobit

ISACA, *Implementing the NIST Cybersecurity Framework Using COBIT 2019*, USA, 2019

ISACA, *IT Risk, www.isaca.org/resources/it-risk*

ISACA, *The Business Model for Information Security,* USA, 2010

ISACA, *IT Audit Framework 4th Edition,* USA, 2020

National Association of Corporate Directors, *NACD Director's Handbook on Cyber-Risk Oversight,* USA, 2020

National Initiative for Cybersecurity Education (NICE), *NICE Workforce Framework*, www.nist.gov/nice

National Institute of Standards and Technology (NIST), *Computer Security Resource Center,* http://csrc.nist.gov/publications

NIST, *Framework for Improving Critical Infrastructure Cybersecurity,* USA, 2014, *www.nist.gov/cyberframework*

NIST, *NIST Risk Management Framework, https://csrc.nist.gov/Projects/risk-management/about-rmf*

Otero, A.; *Information Technology Control and Audit, Fifth Edition,* CRC Press, USA, 2018

SANS Institute, *www.sans.org*

Wysocki, R.; *Effective Project Management: Traditional, Agile, Extreme, 8th Edition,* Wiley Publishing Inc., USA, 2019

SELF-ASSESSMENT QUESTIONS

CISM exam questions are developed with the intent of measuring and testing practical knowledge in information security management. All questions are multiple choice and are designed for one best answer. Every CISM question has a stem (question) and four options (answer choices). The candidate is asked to choose the correct or best answer from the options. The stem may be in the form of a question or incomplete statement. Many times, a CISM examination question will require the candidate to choose the most likely or best answer.

In every case, the candidate is required to read the question carefully, eliminate known incorrect answers and then make the best choice possible. Knowing the format in which questions are asked, and how to study to gain knowledge of what will be tested, will go a long way toward answering them correctly.

1. When implementing an intrusion detection system for Internet traffic, the information security manager should recommend that it be placed:

   A. outside the firewall.
   B. on the firewall server.
   C. on a screened subnet.
   D. on the external router.

2. Which of the following is the **BEST** metric for evaluating the effectiveness of security awareness training? The number of:

   A. password resets
   B. reported incidents
   C. incidents resolved
   D. access rule violations

3. Security monitoring mechanisms should **PRIMARILY:**

   A. focus on business-critical information.
   B. assist owners to manage and control risk.
   C. focus on detecting network intrusions.
   D. record all security violations.

4. When contracting with an outsourcer to provide security administration, the **MOST** important contractual element is the:

   A. right-to-terminate clause.
   B. limitations of liability.
   C. service level agreement.
   D. financial penalties clause.

5. Which of the following is **MOST** effective in preventing security weaknesses in operating systems?

   A. Patch management
   B. Change management
   C. Security baselines
   D. Configuration management

6. Which of the following is the **MOST** effective solution for preventing internal users from modifying sensitive and classified information?

   A. Baseline security standards
   B. System access violation logs
   C. Role-based access control
   D. Background investigations

7. Which of the following is the **MOST** important consideration when implementing an intrusion detection system?

   A. Tuning
   B. Patching
   C. Encryption
   D. Packet filtering

8. Which of the following practices is **BEST** used to remove system access for contractors and other temporary users when it is no longer required?

   A. Log all account usage and send regular reports to their managers.
   B. Establish predetermined automatic expiration dates.
   C. Require managers to email the security department when the user leaves.
   D. Ensure that each individual has signed a security acknowledgment.

9. Which of the following is **MOST** important for a successful information security program?

   A. Adequate training on emerging security technologies
   B. Open communication with key process owners
   C. Adequate policies, standards and procedures
   D. Executive management commitment

10. An enterprise is implementing an information security program. During which phase should metrics be established to assess the effectiveness of the program over time?

   A. Testing
   B. Initiation
   C. Design
   D. Development

Answers on page 139

Chapter 3 ANSWER KEY

Self-Assessment Questions

1. A. Placing an intrusion detection system (IDS) on the Internet side of the firewall is not usually advised (except to assess the traffic hitting the firewall) because the system will generate alerts on all malicious traffic—even though most traffic will be stopped by the firewall and never reach the internal network.

   B. Because firewalls should be installed on hardened servers with minimal services enabled, it would be inappropriate to install an IDS on the same physical device.

   C. An IDS should be placed on a screened subnet, which is a demilitarized zone.

   D. If placing it on the external router were feasible, it would not be advised (except to assess the traffic hitting the firewall) because the system will generate alerts on all malicious traffic—even though most traffic will be stopped by the firewall and never reach the internal network.

2. A. Password resets may or may not have anything to do with awareness levels.

   B. Reported incidents will provide an indicator of the awareness level of staff. An increase in reported incidents could indicate that the staff is paying more attention to security.

   C. The number of incidents resolved may not correlate to staff awareness.

   D. Access rule violations may or may not have anything to do with awareness levels.

3. **A. Security monitoring must focus on business-critical information to remain effectively usable by and credible to business users.**

   B. Control risk is the possibility that controls would not detect an incident or error condition and, therefore, is not a correct answer because monitoring would not directly assist in managing this risk.

   C. Network intrusions are not the only focus of monitoring mechanisms.

   D. Although ideally all security violations should be recorded, this is only one objective of security monitoring.

4. A. Right to terminate is usually a part of the service level agreement (SLA) that can be invoked on failure of the outsourcer to meet the terms of the SLA.

   B. The element of limitations of liability is also typically covered as a part of the SLA.

   C. SLAs provide metrics to which outsourcing firms can be held accountable and will typically cover the other choices as well. This is the most encompassing answer.

   D. Financial penalties are covered by the SLA in the event of failure of performance as specified in the SLA.

5. **A. Patch management is a preventive control in that it corrects discovered weaknesses by applying a patch to the original program code that eliminates the weakness preventing exploitation.**

   B. Change management controls the process of introducing changes to systems that may introduce new vulnerabilities.

   C. Security baselines provide minimum recommended settings to provide a consistent minimum level of security across the enterprise.

   D. Configuration management ensures that incorrect configuration does not result in increased risk and controls the updates to the production environment.

6. A. Baseline security standards may require access controls, but alone do not prevent unauthorized access.

   B. Violation logs are detective and do not prevent unauthorized access.

   C. Role-based access control helps ensure that users have access only to files and systems appropriate for their job role and is a preventive control.

   D. Background checks are not a preventive control although they may be predictive based on past events.

7. **A. If an intrusion detection system (IDS) is not properly tuned, it will generate an unacceptable number of false positives and/or fail to sound an alarm when an actual attack is underway.**

   B. Patching is more related to system hardening and typically a part of maintenance activities.

   C. Encryption is not a significant consideration when implementing an IDS.

   D. Packet filtering is not used in an IDS.

8. A. Logging account usage does nothing to remove access for temporary employees.

   B. Predetermined expiration dates that automatically remove access are the most effective means of removing systems access for temporary users.

   C. Reliance on managers to promptly send in termination notices cannot always be counted on and by itself does not ensure access termination.

   D. Requiring each individual to sign a security acknowledgment would have little effect in this case.

9. A. Adequate training on new technologies is one of many requirements for an effective security program, but it is not as crucial as management support.

   B. Open communication with process owners is an important element, but by itself it is not sufficient to ensure a successful program.

   C. Adequate policies, standards and procedures are essential, but they will not be effective absent management support for adequate resources and enforcement.

   D. Sufficient executive management support is the most important factor for the success of an information security program.

10. A. The testing phase is too late because the system has already been developed and is in production testing.

    B. In the initiation phase, the basic security objective of the project is acknowledged, but it is premature to consider where security checkpoints should be located in the development of a test plan.

    C. In the design phase, security checkpoints are defined and a test plan is developed.

    D. Development is the coding phase and is too late to consider security test points and test plans.

Part A: Information Security Program Development

An information security program encompasses all the activities and resources that collectively provide information security services to an enterprise. The program is the project plan to implement and establish ongoing management of the information security strategy as mentioned in Chapter 1. Primary program activities include design, development and integration of enterprise-wide controls related to information security, along with the ongoing administration and management of these controls. Controls can range from simple policies and processes to highly complex technology solutions. Depending on the size and nature of the enterprise, these activities can be executed by a single individual or a chief information security officer (CISO) managing a large staff with diverse skills. While information security program development has clear goals and provides a road map for large enterprises, it is not as easy and smooth for small and medium scale enterprises (SMEs) because the business needs vary in the short and near term. Hence, the security program needs to be more flexible concerning business needs for SMEs.

In some instances, the information security manager may be required to initiate an information security program from its inception or to restart a program after a corporate merger or other significant change. Often, the information security manager modifies and improves an existing program. In either case, it is important for the information security manager to have a solid understanding of the many aspects and requirements of effective program design, implementation and management.

3.1 Information Security Program Overview

Successful security program management is not significantly different from management of any other organizational activity. The primary difference is that, despite increased visibility, information security remains a somewhat ill-defined and frequently misunderstood discipline.

Often, information security managers have a technical background. Many did not embark on a management career; rather, they were technologists who found themselves increasingly faced with management functions and responsibilities. In many cases, the shift of information security toward a broader management role is driven by the increased desire of a business to understand why specific security controls are required, and how the business will benefit specifically from them. In short, senior management wants to understand the specific risk the information security program is addressing and why the controls it mandates are a sound investment and actually benefit the business. As a result, many information security professionals have had to expand their view beyond technology and develop a greater understanding of the business activities they are seeking to protect.

The dual trends of growing security organizations and increased pressure from the business to ensure that the security program is aligned with the business objectives have combined to broaden the body of knowledge security managers must master. An extensive range of business knowledge and understanding must now be added to the base of information security knowledge that all security professionals should possess. This presents an opportunity for the information security manager to establish an effective bridge between the organizational business needs and the needs of the information technology and security teams. Implementing and executing a program that manages information risk in a cost-effective manner—at the same time enabling business initiatives while protecting organizational interests—supports enterprise awareness and improvement.

3.1.1 Information Security Management Trends

In an increasing number of enterprises, the information security manager is a member of senior leadership, designated as vice president of security, CISO or chief security officer (CSO), as detailed in Section 1.4.1 Roles and Responsibilities. Also, a number of security functions may report to an independent corporate-level security organization. These functions include physical and information security, IT security, compliance, privacy, business continuity planning/disaster recovery and security architecture. In some large multinational enterprises, many or all these functions are currently included under a senior corporate risk manager or chief risk officer (CRO). Irrespective of the reporting structure of the CISO or information security manager, the critical requirement is to ensure the board of directors or the top decision-making board of the enterprise gets periodic updates from the security organization. Without such updates, business leadership of the enterprise has insufficient visibility of the information security posture.

The benefits of this trend are apparent. All these functions serve the basic need of ensuring the safety and preservation of the enterprise and are interdependent. Aggregating these assurance activities under a single corporate function is likely to gain favor as it becomes increasingly apparent that a disintegrated, stovepipe approach to security is inefficient, costly and ineffective.

In addition, many enterprises have recognized the value of including IT risk along with other enterprise risk that must be evaluated, treated and monitored. As various risk response results from across the enterprise are integrated and combined with results from other risk management categories, senior leaders are able to gain a comprehensive risk awareness.

However, in other companies, information security continues to be a fragmented, low-level IT effort. In many sectors, such as manufacturing, the food industry and retail, information security is seen as primarily a technical activity largely dealing with compliance issues as opposed to a vital strategic business activity.

Regardless of trends and optimal considerations for security, the reality in the majority of enterprises is something less than optimal, but security must still be managed on an ongoing basis.

IT functions, including security elements, are increasingly performed by external partners or vendors. Where critical functions such as software development, IT operations and security monitoring are provided by third parties, the information security manager must also consider the additional supply chain risk inherent in those circumstances.

In addition to understanding security concepts and technologies, information security managers will increasingly need to gain expertise in a range of management functions such as budgeting, planning, business case development, recruiting and other personnel-related functions.

3.1.2 Essential Elements of an Information Security Program

Three elements are essential to ensure successful security program design, implementation and ongoing management:

1. The program must demonstrate execution of a well-developed information security strategy that is closely aligned with and supports organizational objectives.
2. The program must be well-designed with cooperation and support from management and stakeholders.
3. Effective metrics must be developed for program design and implementation phases and the subsequent ongoing security program management phases to provide the feedback necessary to guide program execution to achieve the defined outcomes.

Many frameworks recommend that the risk assessment serve as the starting point for developing an information security strategy. While this may be adequate in some cases, it is not optimal and does not address the balance of important outcomes for information security, including strategic alignment, resource management, value delivery, assurance process integration and performance measurement. See Chapters 1 and 2 for more information.

A comprehensive approach to security strategy development, as presented in Chapter 1, goes beyond just addressing risk by defining overall objectives for information security. These objectives should be explicitly linked to organizational objectives. The outlined approach also describes methodologies for defining the desired state of security and provides the basis for developing a comprehensive and effective strategy to achieve those objectives. Beyond focusing solely on managing risk, this approach considers how information security should link to and actively support the enterprise's strategic objectives, ensure its preservation, and optimize security resources and activities.

Many enterprises are not ready to undertake the costs and efforts to implement information security governance. In these circumstances, the information security manager may need to tailor objective development. Use of a standard framework—such as COBIT or ISO/IEC 27001:2013—in conjunction with

Capability Maturity Model Integration (CMMI®) or a process assessment model (PAM) will allow the information security manager to assess the current state of the information security program, set specific goals and determine a strategy to achieve them.

The information security manager must define objectives for the information security program, thus supporting management and stakeholder consensus. Without defined objectives for information security, it will be impossible to devise effective information security management metrics because there may be misalignment. Without a link to stakeholder objectives, it becomes difficult to demonstrate progress toward organizational goals, thereby hampering progress and resulting in ad hoc and haphazard results.

Regardless of how the objectives and strategy of information security are devised, the goals of an information security program are to implement the strategy and achieve the defined objectives. Once developed, the information security program should clearly represent the elements of the strategy.

Information security program development entails a variety of activities, projects and initiatives involving people, processes and technology over a protracted period of time. The information security manager should keep in mind that the objectives and expected benefits of the information security program are most useful when they are defined in business terms to help nontechnical stakeholders understand and endorse the program goals. This is also more likely to promote feedback and participation from business owners that will make it more likely that the security program will be aligned with overall organizational objectives. The information security manager should also consider that programs and initiatives that do not have specific identifiable business or organizational benefits should be carefully examined to determine whether they are justified or if resources can produce greater benefits elsewhere.

3.1.3 Importance of the Information Security Program

Information security program management is an ongoing requirement that serves to protect information assets, satisfy regulatory obligations, lead appropriate response to incidents, and minimize potential legal and liability exposures.

Achieving acceptable levels of information security at a reasonable cost requires good planning, an effective strategy and capable management. Properly designed, implemented and managed, the information security program provides critical support for many business functions that simply would not be feasible without it.

To be of any use, a strategy must be implemented and made operational through processes that achieve the strategic objectives. The security program is the process by which the enterprise's security systems are designed, engineered, built, deployed, modified, managed, monitored and maintained until they are removed from service. This critical aspect of the information security manager's responsibilities covers a broad area and requires substantial expertise and technical and managerial skills.

A well-executed security program is one that is effectively designed, implemented, managed and monitored, transforming strategy into actuality. While providing the capabilities to meet security objectives, the program also accommodates the inevitable changes in security requirements and risk landscape. The program takes advantage of security expertise, tools and techniques that are available in the infrastructure and draws upon partnerships (such as with external vendors and service providers) to support ongoing requirements. The well-designed security program increases the likelihood that the efforts are well integrated, decreasing costs of maintenance and administration while providing a consistent level of security across the enterprise.

It should be clear that an effective security program requires a great deal of planning along with expertise and resources. Effective planning can be significantly aided through application of an enterprise security architecture at the conceptual, logical, functional and physical levels. Well-defined models and frameworks that can assist in this process are detailed in Section 3.6 Defining an Information Security Program Road Map.

3.1.4 Applying the Security Program Business Case

Development of major information security program initiatives and projects is based upon the business case described in Chapter 1. That business case should provide a clear statement of the value proposition (or cost benefit) based on the identified needs of the enterprise.

The need from an information security perspective is to identify the risk that must be addressed and to consider both the potential impacts if the project is not undertaken and the potential reduction in risk and resulting impacts if the project is carried out. To be effective, the business case must make it evident that there is a significant potential return on the proposed investment, that the project is feasible and practical, and that the impact on productivity is acceptable.

As Chapter 1 shows, budgeting is an essential part of information security program management and can have a significant impact on the program's success. Effective preparation and defense of a budget can mean the difference between having or not having sufficient staff and other resources to accomplish the objectives of the information security program.

As with many business activities, self-education and advance preparation are key factors in successfully navigating this frequently challenging process. Well before the budget cycle begins, the information security manager should become familiar with the budgeting process and methods used by the enterprise, including the timing of the various stages of the enterprise's budget cycle.

Another key consideration before beginning the budgeting process is the information security strategy. All budget expenditures for information security should be derived from and supported by the information security strategy. Ideally, detailed elements of the security strategy are laid out in a security road map, as discussed previously in this section. The strategy and security road map are informed by an assessment of the risk posture of the enterprise in the context of the business objectives. This risk quantification supports the effective balance among IT benefits, resource optimization and risk management.

Having consensus on the strategy objectives and the strategy communicated and approved by management before entering into the budgeting process is key to creating a successful budget proposal.

Many costs associated with an information security program are straightforward. Expenses such as personnel (salaries, training, etc.), basic hardware and software, and subscription services fall into this category. In addition to the typical program startup and yearly operational costs, short- and long-term projects represent various objectives on the security road map. These projects consume resources over the course of months (or years) and must be accounted for in the budget as accurately as possible. The information security manager should collaborate with the enterprise's project management office (PMO) and the appropriate subject matter experts to help estimate costs for projects that will start within the fiscal year. Elements of each project that should be considered include:

- Employee time
- Contractor and consultant fees
- Equipment (hardware, software) costs
- Space requirements (data center rack space, etc.)
- Testing resources (personnel, system time, etc.)
- Training costs (staff, users, etc.)
- Travel
- Creation of supporting documentation
- Ongoing maintenance
- Contingencies for unexpected costs
- License/subscription costs
- Cyberinsurance

While it will be impossible to be completely accurate, engaging the appropriate SMEs and skilled project managers can be invaluable in arriving at a fairly accurate estimate.

Some aspects of an information security program are not entirely predictable and can incur unanticipated costs—particularly in the area of incident response. These costs often result from the need for external resources to assist with a security event that exceeds the skills or bandwidth of the enterprise's staff. One approach to budget for these situations is to use historical data from incidents and remediation costs of previous security events that required unbudgeted external resources.

Even if the enterprise has recently initiated its security program, prior events may have necessitated external resources. If the planned program does not anticipate having those skills on staff, it is likely that external resources will be needed again in the future. For example, if during the past three years the enterprise has engaged external forensic consultants to assist with security events because the required skill sets were not on staff, the security manager should consider adding a line item in the budget to account for this situation. Costs can be estimated based on the average costs over the previous years as a starting point. If this information is not available, industry statistics from peer enterprises may be useful as an indicator of risk and remediation costs.

3.1.5 Outcomes of Information Security Program Management

Effective information security program management should achieve the objectives defined in the security strategy discussed in Chapter 1. As with other management activities, the goals must be defined in specific, objective and measurable terms. Appropriate metrics must then be established to determine whether the goals have been achieved and, if not, by how much they were missed and how performance might be improved.

Regardless of whether formal information security governance has been implemented, the objectives of an effective information security program should be based upon acceptable achievement of the following six outcomes:

- Strategic alignment
- Risk management
- Value delivery
- Resource management
- Performance measurement
- Assurance process integration

Strategy development and the definition of the information security program attributes are primarily conceptual and logical exercises. Development of the security program will require transforming these concepts and logical relationships into technologies and processes. From an architectural perspective, that transformation will require development of the physical, functional and operational components necessary to achieve the defined objectives.

For a major initiative, a full security architecture should be developed to ensure that the goals and desired outcomes are realized. If an enterprise architecture already exists, then a security architecture should be incorporated into it. As with any complex structure with numerous moving parts, architecture can serve to define logical, physical and operational component and process relationships. It can also clarify potential issues and provide traceability from concept to implementation and operation.

Strategic Alignment

Effective alignment of information security with business or mission objectives requires regular interaction with business owners and an understanding of their plans and objectives. This synergy often depends on garnering input from the major operating units within the enterprise and building consensus. In the realm of the information security manager, achieving consensus requires an understanding of:

- Organizational information risk
- Selection of appropriate control objectives and standards
- Gaining agreement on acceptable risk and risk tolerance
- Definitions of financial, operational and other constraints

Strategic alignment can be accomplished through a security steering committee, if business owners or their delegates are members and active participants. The security program can support the alignment of business objectives and information security by implementing processes that ensure that defined business objectives provide the ongoing input to guide security activities.

Both old and new issues requiring attention should be tracked and communicated regularly. Action items related to issue investigation, resolution and disposition should be monitored and reported as organizational security performance metrics. A regular information security strategy report should be delivered to executive management to provide visibility into successes and setbacks around strategic alignment. This information can range from progress on projects of interest to new risk or capabilities that may affect a particular line of business.

Day-to-day operational interactions provide powerful opportunities for building rapport and cooperation throughout the enterprise and clarifying accountability lines. In addition to facilitating timely action on information security issues, active relationships fostered by the information security manager can increase awareness and a sense of responsibility around information security.

If the enterprise has a strategic business planning unit, active participation in its activities may also provide insight into future business directions and ensure that security considerations are included in the planning process. This interaction may provide opportunities to orient security activities to support business objectives and identify potential risk.

Efforts to align information security with business objectives must include consideration of security solutions that are a good fit for current and planned business initiatives. Alignment must also consider enterprise processes, cost, culture, governance, existing technology and structure of the enterprise.

Risk Management

Managing the risk to information assets is a primary responsibility of the information security manager and provides the foundation and rationale for virtually all information security activities. Risk analysis must be based on business requirements and an understanding of the enterprise's processes, culture and technology. To effectively manage risk, the information security manager must develop a comprehensive understanding of threats the enterprise faces, its vulnerabilities, its risk profile and the level of risk that management determines is acceptable. The potential impacts of threats that can materialize must be evaluated and used to establish treatment priorities. Risk must be managed to a level that is acceptable to the enterprise. However, the risk landscape is always changing, and new risk will inevitably arise during program development and administration. It is important that a continuous process of risk management be maintained during program development, implementation and evolution.

See Chapter 2 for more information.

Value Delivery

Value delivery as an objective requires information security to deliver the required level of security effectively and efficiently. The execution of the security program can have a considerable effect on achieving this goal. Good planning and project management skills are needed to implement the strategy efficiently.

Security investments should be managed to optimize support of business objectives and deliver clear value to the enterprise. The information security manager should direct efforts toward achievement of a standard set of security practices and establishment of security baselines proportionate to risk. Protection efforts must be prioritized to allocate limited resources to areas of greatest need and benefit.

Continued delivery of value requires that security solutions be institutionalized as normal and expected practices based on standards. Solutions must comprehensively address logical, technical, operational and physical concerns based on an understanding of the end-to-end operating processes of the enterprise. Security management cannot remain static; it must embody a culture of continuous improvement.

Resource Management

Developing and managing a security program require people, technology and processes. The information security manager must endeavor to use human, financial, technical and knowledge resources efficiently and effectively. An important aspect of resource management is to ensure that knowledge is captured and made available to those who need it.

Security processes and practices must be documented, and they must be consistent with standards and policies. Project planning, technology selection and skill acquisition or development significantly factor into the effectiveness of resource management. These considerations include the acquisition and maintenance of external resources. Security architectures should be developed to define and use infrastructures to achieve security objectives efficiently. These efforts help promote recognition of resource needs and shortfalls and provide the basis for good resource management.

Performance Measurement

If an information security strategy has been developed, it should identify a variety of important monitoring and metrics requirements. It is likely that during the evolution and management of a security program, additional opportunities to develop meaningful metrics or points of useful monitoring will become apparent. There may be opportunities to roll up groups of metrics to provide a more holistic picture for managing security. This topic is covered in greater detail in Section 3.7 Information Security Program Metrics.

The development and implementation of the security program itself will require a means of measuring progress and monitoring activities. An effective information security program results in processes designed to achieve governance objectives and provide measurable artifacts that demonstrate whether the objectives are met. Security processes should be designed with measurable control points that allow independent auditors to attest that the program is in place and effectively managed.

The information security manager must develop monitoring processes and associated metrics to provide continuous reporting on the effectiveness of information security processes and controls. Good metrics design and implementation require an understanding of the information needed by various constituencies for effective management. Metrics must be developed at multiple levels, including strategic, tactical and operational levels. The metrics used should be defined, agreed on by management and aligned with strategic objectives. Care must be taken to ensure that metrics provide useful information relevant to managing security activities to achieve defined objectives. These measurement processes help identify shortcomings and failures of security activities and provide feedback on progress made in resolving issues.

Assurance Process Integration

It is important for the information security manager to be aware of and understand all organizational assurance functions because they invariably have significance for information security. The information security manager should develop formal relationships with other assurance providers and endeavor to integrate relevant activities with information security activities. In the typical enterprise, these providers might include physical security, risk management, privacy office, quality assurance, audit, change management, insurance, human resources (HR), business continuity and disaster recovery. Other groups may also have a role to play.

As dictated by the governance objectives discussed in Chapter 1, an information security manager should seek to increase information assurance and the predictability of business operations through mitigation measures that reduce information-related risk to defined and agreed-upon levels of acceptability. The information security manager can use results from business and privacy impact assessments to identify enterprise assets that are most critical to strategic objectives and provide key performance indicators (KPIs) that will demonstrate adequate and effective protection.

In other cases, acceptable risk may be determined in terms of reliability, integrity, performance levels, confidentiality, acceptable downtimes and financial impacts.

3.2 Information Security Program Resources

To support continued alignment and consistent management of the information security program, the information security manager typically has access to numerous organizational resources. Application of these resources further supports the governance framework principles (such as those described in COBIT) by helping to ensure that the program:

- Is based upon a conceptual model with identified key components and relationships.
- Applies an open and flexible approach that can be adjusted based upon priorities and adjustments from key stakeholders while maintaining integrity and consistency.
- Supports ongoing alignment with relevant standards, frameworks and regulations.

Use of program resources also supports alignment with the architectural elements previously described, supporting a consistent organizational and communication approach to managing and reporting IT risk.

3.2.1 Information Security Program Objectives

The objective of the information security program is to implement the strategy in the most cost-effective manner possible, while maximizing support of business functions and minimizing operational disruptions. Chapters 1 and 2 explain how governance and risk management objectives for a security program are defined and incorporated into an overall strategy. The success of these initial steps will determine the degree of clarity in understanding the information security program development objectives.

For a well-developed security strategy, the primary task will be turning high-level strategy into logical and physical reality through a series of projects and initiatives. Even with a well-developed security strategy, elements will need to be modified or reconsidered during program design, development and ongoing administration. Adjustments may be required for a variety of reasons, such as changes in business requirements, underlying infrastructure, topology, technologies or risk level. Another possibility is that better solutions may become available during the course of program development or subsequently. Unanticipated resistance from those affected by the new or modified security program can drive significant alterations in its design, implementation or operation.

Whether a strategy has been developed in significant detail or only to the conceptual level, a great deal of planning and design will be required to achieve working project plans. It is likely that standard system development life cycle (SDLC) approaches will be useful, including feasibility, requirements and design phases. Collaboration during development of plans is important to gain consensus and cooperation from various stakeholders and to minimize subsequent implementation and operational problems.

Defining Objectives

An information security manager is rarely faced with a situation in which no information security activity is present in an enterprise. Therefore, only rarely will the information security program need to be built from scratch. More often, developing the information security program will be a process of comparing the existing program to what is required to reach the desired information security state of the enterprise. This is achieved by performing a gap analysis. As noted in Chapter 1, the IT organization should have identified this at a high level, but it may be necessary to further define these objectives at a more concrete and practical level. This may require a substantial amount of effort, but it is a critical component in developing the security program.

It is essential to determine the forces that drive the business need for the information security program. Primary drivers for an information security program include:

- The ever-increasing requirements for regulatory compliance
- Higher frequency and cost related to security incidents
- Concerns over reputational damage
- Adoption of industry best practices and standards
- Business processes or objectives that may increase organizational risk

Determining the drivers will help clarify objectives of the program and provide the basis for development of relevant metrics.

Once the security program objectives have been clearly defined, security program development activities are used to develop processes and projects that close gaps between the current state and desired state. Typically, much of the basic work is to identify necessary controls, implement them, develop suitable metrics, and then monitor control points in support of control objectives.

An example implementation of this process is provided by the US National Institute of Standards and Technology (NIST) Framework for Improving Critical Infrastructure Cybersecurity, commonly referred to as the NIST Cybersecurity Framework. This program, developed through a series of collaborative community workshops, supports a comparison of the current program state with a defined target (or desired) state that will achieve acceptable levels of risk. Comparing these two states results in a gap assessment that can inform security program objectives. Users may be further assisted by ISACA's implementation guidance that combines application of the NIST Cybersecurity Framework with COBIT's governance and management objectives.

Whether there is an existing information security program or not, there are some basic building blocks that need to be in place to support control activity and ensure that it is effective. The first step is to determine management objectives for information security, develop key goal indicators (KGIs) that reflect those objectives, and then develop ways to measure whether the program is heading in the right direction to meet those objectives.

3.2.2 Information Security Program Concepts

As an information security program is created, the developers must keep in mind the fundamental purpose of the security program (i.e., to implement the security strategy and achieve the defined outcomes, as detailed in Chapter 1).

If security governance has not been implemented and/or a strategy has not been developed, it will still be necessary to define overall objectives for security activities. Off-the-shelf, ready-made objectives can include conforming to a particular set of standards or achieving a defined maturity level based on the CMMI model.

A security program implementation effort should include a series of specific control objectives, such as those defined in COBIT or the ISO 27000 family of standards. It is likely that any security program will consist largely of designing, developing and implementing controls, whether technical, procedural or physical. As these controls are developed, monitoring and metrics must also be considered. Processes to measure control effectiveness and determine control failure will be essential. Some metrics development approaches and processes are detailed in Section 3.7 Information Security Program Metrics.

Implementation will typically consist of a series of projects and initiatives. It generally involves project management skills, including resource utilization, budgeting, scheduling and time management skills (i.e., meeting timelines and milestones), quality assurance and user acceptance testing (UAT).

Many projects involve unusual or complex technical elements and may require detailed specification, design and engineering efforts. Because they often requires skills outside the information security manager's capabilities, it is generally prudent to consider engaging the services of consultants or contractors with subject matter expertise.

Management and Process Concepts

Implementing and managing a security program will require the information security manager to understand and have a working knowledge of a number of management and process concepts including:

- Architectures
- Budgeting, costing and financial issues
- Business case development
- Business process reengineering
- Communications
- Compliance monitoring and enforcement
- Contingency planning
- Control design and development
- Control implementation and testing
- Control monitoring and metrics
- Control objectives
- Critical thinking
- Deployment and integration strategies
- Documentation
- Personnel issues
- Problem resolution
- Project management
- Quality assurance
- Requirements development
- Risk management
- Software development life cycles
- Specification development
- Supply chain management
- Threat intelligence
- Training needs assessments and approaches
- Variance and noncompliance resolution

Technology Resources

An information security program involves a variety of technologies in addition to processes, policies and people. The information security manager must be qualified to make decisions with respect to technology, including the viability and applicability of available solutions in terms of the program's goals and objectives. It is essential that the information security manager understand where a given technology fits into the basic prevention, detection, containment, reaction and recovery framework, and how it will serve to implement strategic elements.

Some technologies related directly to information security that the information security manager should be familiar with include:

- Antivirus/antimalware systems
- Application security methodologies (including secure software development and application testing)
- Authentication and authorization mechanisms (one-time passwords [OTPs], challenge-response, public key infrastructure [PKI] certificates, multifactor authentication, biometrics)

- Backup and archiving approaches such as redundant array of inexpensive disks (RAID)
- Cloud-based resource provisioning and management techniques
- Cryptographic techniques (e.g., PKI, Advanced Encryption Standard [AES], Transport Layer Security/Secure Sockets Layer [TLS/SSL])
- Cyberthreat information sharing methodologies and techniques
- Data integrity controls (e.g., backups, data snapshots, data replication, RAID), storage area network [SAN] real-time replication)
- Data leak prevention methodologies (e.g., removable media security, content filtering) and associated technologies
- Digital signatures
- Identity and access management systems
- Firewalls
- Intrusion monitoring and detection, including host-based and network-based intrusion detection systems (IDSs) and intrusion prevention systems (IPSs)
- Log collection, analysis and correlation tools (i.e., security information and event management [SIEM])
- Mobile device operations, security, and management
- Remote access methodologies (virtual private networks [VPNs], etc.)
- Secure cloud access techniques (secure access service edge [SASE], cloud access request broker [CASB])
- Security features inherent in networking devices (e.g., routers, switches)
- Vulnerability scanning and penetration testing tools
- Web security techniques
- Wireless security methodologies

While many of these technologies are specifically related to security (and most function as controls), the information security manager must recognize that virtually all deployed technologies will have security implications.

In addition to technologies that are security-related, the information security manager must be familiar with the broader aspects of IT including, but not limited to:

- Application servers
- Bring your own device (BYOD)
- Cloud computing
- Containerization
- Cryptocurrency
- Cyber-physical systems
- Databases
- DevOps/DevSecOps
- Enterprise architectures (two- and three-tier client servers, messaging, etc.)
- Internet and network protocols (e.g., TCP/IP, BGP)
- Internet of things (IoT)
- Local area networks (LANs)
- Machine learning
- Middleware
- Network routing concepts and protocols
- Operating systems
- Red team/blue team
- Servers
- Storage area networks (SANs)
- Virtualization (system and network level)
- Web-related technologies and architectures
- Wide area networks (WANs)

Note: These lists are not meant to be comprehensive; instead, they are representative of the areas and types of technologies the information security manager should be familiar with to successfully manage an information security program. Any CISM candidate who is unfamiliar with any of the terms listed should review the glossary at the end of this manual. CISM candidates can also refer to the Resources section of the ISACA website for additional information on trends and topics in information security.

3.2.3 Scope and Charter of an Information Security Program

Whether forming a new information security program or coming into an existing one, the information security manager will need to determine the scope, responsibilities and charter of the program. These elements are often less clearly defined than technical elements (e.g., firewalls, IDSs and virus detection). The scope of the information security program primarily depends on how roles of responsibilities are designed. Often, asset processes are owned by one department while they are managed or operated by another department. Therefore, it is useful to develop a well-aligned RACI (responsible, accountable, consulted, informed) matrix before the preparation of information security program. Without clearly defined responsibilities, the security manager will find it difficult to determine what to manage or how well a given security function is meeting objectives.

Information security managers coming into new situations should take the time to gain an understanding of the relevant responsibilities, scope, authority, budgets, reporting requirements, etc., from those they will be reporting to. It will be useful to specifically document these elements and obtain agreement with management.

In terms of the chain of command, it is vital to understand where the information security function fits into the overall organizational structure. In many situations, there will be inherent structural conflicts that the manager should be aware of and carefully consider. It may also be prudent to discuss any potential conflicts of interest with management and understand how they will be handled.

The information security department largely performs an internal regulatory function, and its ability to operate effectively precludes reporting to those it is supposed to regulate. While there may be exceptions, information security managers who report in the technology chain of command or to other operational managers tend to be limited in their ability to provide effective information security across the enterprise.

If a program is established and has been functioning well, it is likely that many security program functions will already be accepted practice. Nevertheless, it will be useful to determine whether responsibilities are clearly defined and well documented. In many instances, a prior manager will have assumed a variety of functions and taken on responsibilities that were not formally defined and documented. Such managers may have been effective through being persuasive and influential rather than through defined and documented processes and structures. If the prior manager is available for orientation, it would be prudent to use whatever time is available to gain insight into the existing situation. If the prior manager is not available, it may take a thorough investigation to determine what the manager's responsibilities were and how tasks were accomplished.

The ability to be effective in a particular enterprise will be heavily impacted by culture and the information security manager's understanding of it. Security is often politically charged, and success may hinge more on developing the right relationships than on any particular expertise. To a varying extent, enterprises do not operate in the manner defined by organizational charts, but by undocumented relationships and influence. Much as a search engine determines relative importance by the number of links to a particular site, the influence of individuals is affected by their relationships to other people within the enterprise.

It is also essential to gain a thorough understanding of the current state of security functions in the enterprise. This may include the assessment elements such as risk assessment and business impact analysis (BIA). The state of governance and strategy will need to be ascertained, as will the condition of policies and standards, compliance, etc. Reviews of recent audits, incidents and other pertinent reports will be useful as well. Once these assessments and reviews are completed, the balance of the elements identified in Chapter 1 can be considered, and the information security manager will have a basis for moving forward with implementation of an information security management framework.

Figure 3.1 shows a summary of the steps in developing an information security program. While many of these tasks will fall to the information security manager, some may be under the purview of other departments.

Figure 3.1—Steps to Developing an Information Security Program

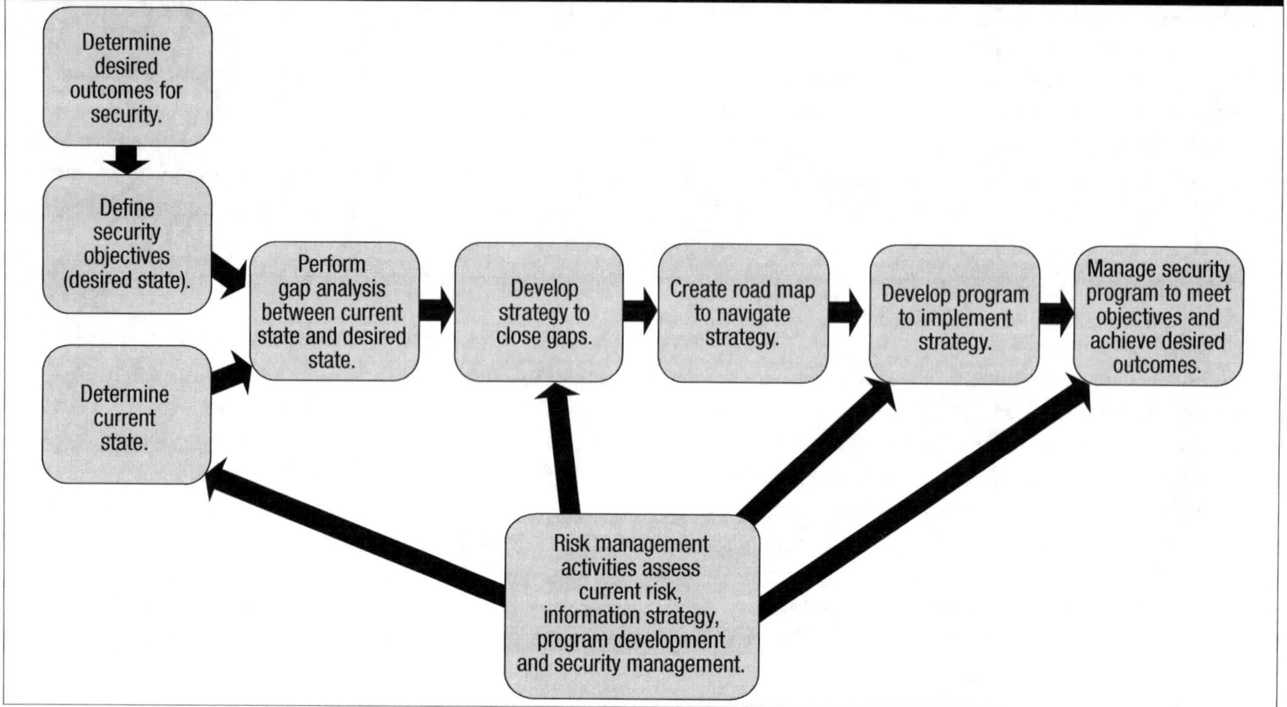

The scope of an information security program is established by the development of a strategy as discussed in Chapter 1, in combination with risk management responsibilities covered in Chapter 2. The extent to which management supports the implementation of the strategy and risk management activities determines the charter.

Implementation of a security program impacts an enterprise's established way of doing things. Within an existing structure of people, processes and technology, the information security manager must strive to integrate changes to established processes and policies. Inevitably, this will result in some degree of resistance to change, which the information security manager should plan to address.

In the absence of an adopted information security strategy and where no formal charter is documented, an information security manager can fall back on industry standards, such as a customized version of ISACA's description of a mature information security program, which might read:

> *Information security is a joint responsibility of business, information security and IT management and is integrated with corporate business objectives. Information security requirements are clearly defined, optimized and included in a verified security plan. Security functions are integrated with applications at the design stage and end users are increasingly accountable for managing security. Information security reporting provides early warning of changing and emerging risk, using automated active monitoring approaches for critical systems. Incidents are promptly addressed with formalized incident response procedures supported by automated tools. Periodic security assessments evaluate the effectiveness of implementation of the security plan. Information on new threats and vulnerabilities is systematically collected and analyzed, and adequate mitigating controls are promptly communicated and implemented. Intrusion testing, root cause analysis of security incidents and proactive identification of risk are the basis for continuous improvements. Security processes and technologies are integrated enterprise-wide.*

This approach, coupled with COBIT or ISO/IEC 27001's requirements descriptions, can serve as the basis for a strategy and help define the scope and charter of the information security program.

3.2.4 Common Information Security Program Challenges

Initiating, refining or expanding a security program will often result in a surprising array of unexpected impediments for the information security manager. These include:

- Organizational resistance due to changes in areas of responsibility introduced by the program
- A perception that increased security will reduce access required for job functions
- Overreliance on subjective metrics
- Failure of strategy
- Assumptions of procedural compliance without confirming oversight
- Ineffective project management, delaying security initiatives
- Previously undetected, broken or buggy security software
- Poor management or monitoring of vendor/third-party security activities
- Lack of program alignment with business goals and objectives

There are always cultural and organizational challenges in any job function and the path is not cleared for the information security manager simply by virtue of gaining senior management support. To implement a truly successful program, the cooperation of many others in the enterprise is important as well.

Figure 3.2 identifies some constraints inherent in road map development for three different organizations. An information security manager must be aware of the type of constraints inherent in the organization when designing control activities and strive to minimize their impact on the information security program objectives. Note that the information in the table is provided for illustrative purposes only, as no two enterprises are exactly the same.

Figure 3.2—Constraints on Developing an Information Security Road Map

	Organization 1	Organization 2	Organization 3
Legal and regulatory requirements	Compliance requires major changes in application data flow.	Frequent spot checks interrupt progress on longer-term projects.	Restrictions exist on the sharing of data with service providers.
Physical and environmental factors	Computer room is located on easily accessible floor and subject to flooding.	Data center operation is outsourced.	Data center on fourth floor is a suitable environment control.
Ethics	Attitude is "if I see it on my screen, it is mine."	Attitude is "if I can use it to make money, it should be mine."	Attitude is "if I need it, my request should be approved."
Culture/regional variances	Culture promotes freedom of information sharing.	Turf wars forestall policy approval processes.	The tone at the top promotes information security goals.
Costs	Company is in bankruptcy and cannot spend money on IT.	All information security projects must be cost-justified.	Information security budget is approved and adequate.
Personnel	Former hackers are hired by departments seeking competitive information.	Background checks are done sporadically based on human resources risk assessments.	Personnel screening processes are uniformly implemented.
Logistics	The information security manager is located in a branch with limited network access.	The information security manager is located at headquarters and has no data center access.	The information security manager is well situated between headquarters and the data center.
Resources	No staff or equipment is dedicated to security.	The information security manager staff lacks technical skills.	The information security manager staff has IT experience and daily access to technology.
Capabilities	Documentation only	Process coordination	Control implementation

The last line in **figure 3.2** shows the information security program capabilities that result from the set of constraints associated with the corresponding organization. Organization 1 is the most resource-constrained with regard to the implementation of a successful information security program. In contrast, Organization 3 has abundant resources and strong management and technical support in place—all of which are conducive to developing an effective program. These examples are contrasted to demonstrate that the ability of information security managers to produce effective information security programs is almost totally dependent on the environments in which they operate.

Historically, some enterprise leaders have failed to recognize information security risk as requiring the same level of governance and oversight as other critical risks, and instead have viewed IT risk as a low-level, technology-based cost center. While universally recognized as necessary, information security has been viewed as an impediment to getting the job done. In the past, this viewpoint was accentuated by information security personnel who failed to achieve balance between risk treatment and efficient operations. Thankfully, this trend is diminishing, yet in many enterprises this historic misunderstanding may have produced a challenging environment for an information security manager. A few common manifestations of such an environment include lack of management support, poor resource levels for information security, a shortsighted approach to strategy and poor cooperation from other business units. Typically, the information security manager in this situation reports far down in the hierarchy and has the daunting task of trying to drive security up the organizational structure.

The situation is gradually changing for the better for a number of reasons, including legal and regulatory mandates that require improved security as a matter of national security and commercial necessity. Expectations of customers and business partners are an important consideration that has provided a positive push toward enhanced security. Another is the credit card industry's rigorous security requirements from the PCI DSS council for enterprises that process credit card information. Since these requirements impact a very wide range of enterprises, they are likely to significantly improve many aspects of information security globally. Matching the rate of adoption and improved security to the pace of increasingly sophisticated and profitable criminal elements remains a challenge.

Future drivers include the likelihood of increased litigation resulting in substantial damage awards, which already has occurred following adoption of the European Union's General Data Protection Regulation (GDPR). Also, the emergence of the necessity for cyber insurance, with the attendant requirements of insurers for adequate risk management, will be a driver for better, more effective security. This outcome will likely be realized gradually, just as insurance gradually improved automobile, product and fire safety.

Although the overall situation in terms of security is improving, the information security manager must deal with the situation as it exists. Regardless of organizational circumstances, a persuasive information security manager with a clear vision of the role of information security in the enterprise can often improve the overall security posture with an ongoing campaign to educate stakeholders in the role and relevance of information security. This includes defining and seeking agreement on information risk control objectives, determining the enterprise's risk appetite and identifying mission-critical information assets.

It is beneficial for information security activities to align with and support defined business objectives. This is most effective if it is an ongoing effort and suitably communicated to stakeholders. Developing meaningful KPIs and metrics is also useful in supporting information security objectives. Each information security manager must determine the appropriate breadth and depth of metrics for the enterprise to provide the information needed for management. Information security managers should also implement some form of consistent reporting to promote awareness of the importance of information security management for the achievement of organizational objectives.

Other issues the information security manager may need to deal with occur in situations in which the role of information security has been elevated within an enterprise. Even for mature information security programs, requirements and demands are rapidly changing, driven by technical and regulatory pressures. The challenges described in the following sections do not represent an exhaustive list, but they do illustrate methods for assessing and addressing several of the most common concerns. The information security manager should be cognizant of common challenges to effective information security management, the reasons behind those challenges and the strategies for addressing them.

Management Support

Lack of management support is most common in smaller enterprises or in those of any size that are not in security-intensive industries. Such enterprises often have no compulsory requirement to address information security and, therefore, often view it as a marginally important issue that adds cost with little value. Those views often reflect a misunderstanding of the enterprise's dependence on information systems, the threat and risk environment, or the impact the enterprise may face or could already be unknowingly experiencing.

In such circumstances, the information security manager must use resources such as industry statistics, organizational impact and dependency analyses and reviews of common threats to the enterprise's specific information processing systems. In addition, management may require guidance on what actions are expected and information on approaches industry peers are taking to address information security. Even if initial education does not result in immediate strengthening of support, ongoing education should still be conducted to develop awareness of security needs.

It is important that the information security program strategy include provisions for managing changes and updates. Management support requires an ongoing dialogue with periodic review of objectives and strategy. Without regular updates, changes to business priorities may reduce the actual or perceived alignment of security priorities with those business needs and objectives.

Funding

Inadequate funding for information security initiatives is one of the most frustrating and challenging issues the information security manager must address. While this issue may be a symptom of an underlying lack of management support, there are often other factors the information security manager is able to influence. Some funding-related issues that may need to be addressed by the information security manager include:

- Management not recognizing the value of security investments
- Security being viewed as a low-value cost center
- Management not understanding where existing money is going
- The organizational need for a security investment not being understood
- The need for more awareness of industry trends in security investment

If additional funding to close financial gaps is not available, the information security manager must exercise strategies that minimize the impact of the financial shortfall on the enterprise's information risk posture. Some common strategies that can be applied include:

- Leveraging the budgets of other organizational units (e.g., product development, internal audit, information systems) to implement needed security program components
- Improving the efficiency of existing information security program components
- Working with the information security steering committee to reprioritize security resource assignments, and providing senior management with an analysis of which security components will become under-resourced and the associated risk implications

The information security manager should pay close attention to funding issues and work on them on an ongoing basis. It is often too late for analyzing needs and educating management once the actual budgeting process begins, delaying needed investments by months or years.

It is also important for the information security manager to understand that financing an information security program is often difficult. If the program is working successfully, management may not see where the money is going and may wonder why so much is being spent. If the program is not successful, management may not understand the need to budget significant amounts of money for systems that are still being compromised. It is essential for the information security manager to find ways to show that security is important, functional and business-related.

Staffing

The root cause of funding issues is often inadequate staff to meet security program requirements. Obstacles to obtaining effective staffing levels might include:

- Poor understanding of what activities new resources will do
- Questioning the need or benefit of new resource activities

- Lack of awareness of existing staff utilization levels or activities
- Belief that existing staff are underutilized
- Desire to examine outsourcing alternatives

When presented with these issues, the information security manager should use workload management procedures to generate personnel workload analyses, utilization reports and other metrics that demonstrate the level of effort currently expended. In addition, charts that associate specific information security roles or teams with the protection they provide to enterprise information systems are helpful. High or growing levels of productivity also help demonstrate that the information security program is utilizing resources effectively and efficiently.

If the enterprise is unable to allocate additional HR to the program, the information security manager may wish to consider implementing the following strategies to minimize the impact of understaffing on information security program effectiveness:

- Collaborate with other business units to determine if they can assume more information security responsibilities; delegate appropriate tasks with oversight.
- Analyze outsourcing possibilities, especially for high-volume operational activities; be prepared to demonstrate how freed resources would be immediately redeployed to higher-value activities.
- Work with the information security steering committee to reprioritize security personnel assignments; provide senior management with an analysis of what security activities will not be addressed with current staff, and communicate risk implications.

3.2.5 Common Information Security Program Constraints

In addition to the challenges mentioned, there are numerous overarching constraints that should be considered while developing an information security program. They will set the boundaries for the options available and should be thoroughly understood before initiating program development.

Physical

A variety of physical and environmental factors may influence or constrain an information security program. The obvious ones include capacity, space, environmental hazards and availability of infrastructure. The security strategy and program should make certain that provisions are made for the consideration of environmental hazards and adequate infrastructure capacity. Consideration should include physical requirements for recovery in the case of a disaster.

The strategy must include consideration of personnel and resource safety.

Ethics

The perception that customers and the public at large have of the enterprise's ethical behavior can have a major impact on the enterprise and affect its value. These perceptions are often influenced by location and culture, and an effective program will include ethical considerations in the areas of the enterprise's operations.

Culture

The enterprise's internal culture must be considered when developing a security program. The culture in which the enterprise operates must also be considered. A program that is at odds with cultural norms may encounter resistance and may be difficult to implement successfully.

Organizational Structure

Organizational structure will have a significant impact on how a governance strategy can be devised, implemented and translated into an information security program. Often, various assurance functions exist in silos that have different reporting structures and authority. Cooperation among these functions is important and typically requires senior management buy-in and involvement.

Costs

The development and implementation of a strategy consumes resources including time and money. The most cost-effective way to implement a program is an important consideration.

Enterprises often justify spending based on a project's value. With security projects, however, control of specific risk and compliance with regulations are typically the primary drivers.

Generally, from a business perspective, a cost-benefit or other financial analysis is the most accepted approach to justifying expenditures and should be considered when developing a program.

A traditional, but speculative, approach is to consider the value of avoiding specific risk by estimating the potential losses incurred by a specific event and multiplying by the probability of it occurring in a given year. This results in an annual loss expectancy (ALE). Thus, the cost of the controls required to preclude such an event can be compared to the ALE to determine the return on investment (ROI).

Risk exposure can include losses that are challenging to quantify, so it can be difficult to directly calculate ROI. For example, calculating the benefit of controls to support compliance with regulatory provisions may include intangible consequences, such as prison sentences and large fines for senior executives. The ROI on programs to prevent such penalties can be difficult to quantify, although a subjective value from the affected executives should be readily obtainable.

Technological advances, such as single sign-on and user access provisioning technologies and procedures, have resulted in savings in time and cost over traditional manual administration techniques, which may provide a reasonable basis for ROI calculations. There are many examples that compare the costs of traditional processes against the newer procedures, which can be used in developing a business case.

Personnel

A security strategy must consider what resistance may be encountered during implementation. Resistance to significant changes, along with possible resentment against new constraints possibly viewed as making tasks more difficult or time-consuming, should be expected.

Resources

An effective strategy must consider available budgets; the total cost of ownership (TCO) of new or additional technologies; and the manpower requirements of design, implementation, operation, maintenance and eventual decommissioning. Typically, the TCO must be developed for the full life cycle of technologies, processes and personnel.

Capabilities

The resources available to implement a strategy should include the known capabilities of the enterprise, including expertise and skills. A strategy that relies on demonstrated capabilities is more likely to succeed than one that does not.

Time

Time is a major constraint in developing and implementing a strategy. There may be compliance deadlines that must be met or support for certain strategic operations, such as a merger, that must be accommodated. There may be windows of opportunity for particular business activities that mandate specific timelines for implementation of certain strategies.

Technology

Technological complexities may constrain the implementation of a security strategy consistently across the enterprise. There may be existing legacy and unsupported systems that are unable to support the security control implementation until they are decommissioned. Exemption processes may be developed to consider and manage the risk arising from these constraints.

3.3 Information Asset Identification and Classification

Because the key purpose of the information security program is to ensure cost-effective protection of valuable resources, commensurate with stakeholder expectations, it is important that the information security program provide for adequate and consistent identification and classification of the assets to be protected. Notably, assets include the broad array of data, personnel, devices, systems, facilities and other resources that enable the enterprise to achieve business objectives. The identification and classification activities should include a determination of those assets' relative importance to organizational objectives and the enterprise's risk strategy.

3.3.1 Information Asset Identification and Valuation

An important step for the information security program is to identify and inventory information assets and determine their relative or approximate business value (i.e., criticality or sensitivity). This is necessary because the business value is a part of the risk determination (i.e., risk exists only if there is likelihood of impact and consequences [risk = likelihood × consequences]). In addition, it is not possible to determine vulnerability and the extent of exposure of unidentified assets. The business value will also be needed for classification purposes and to provide justification for the level of protection required.

The process of valuation, which consists of relating all values in a common financial form, is straightforward for some assets. Hardware can be easily valued based on replacement costs. The value of information, in some cases, is the cost of recreating or restoring it, or it may be based on the contribution to generating revenues. In other cases, the value is related to the consequential costs and possible regulatory sanctions stemming from the exposure of confidential information or the loss of trade secrets.

The impact or consequences of a breach of personally identifiable information (PII) can be regulatory sanctions. Other potential impacts can arise if the individuals suffering identity theft losses file lawsuits for damages, or if attorneys file class-action lawsuits on behalf of thousands of victims. Another consequence is possible reputational damage, often resulting in loss of share value. In this case, the damage assessment cannot be based on the intrinsic value of the information, which may be low or zero. Rather, valuation must be based on the total range of potential losses and other impacts.

Marketing materials—another type of information with no intrinsic value—can nevertheless create unintended liabilities and, therefore, risk that must be considered. Inaccurate representations of products or services or information leading to wrong investor decisions can result in significant losses as a consequence of various legal actions. Therefore, a prudent enterprise must consider ensuring systematic review and control of information to manage the risk of potential liability created by publicly released information.

Categories of typical information assets that must be assigned a value and protected include, but are not limited to:

- Proprietary information and processes of all types, including information that can damage the enterprise
- Current financial records and future projections
- Acquisition or merger plans
- Strategic marketing plans
- Trade secrets
- Patent-related information
- Privacy-related information, including PII and protected health information (PHI)
- Customer data, including payment card information (PCI)

3.3.2 Information Asset Valuation Strategies

Some enterprises may avoid asset valuation due to the complexity of agreeing about relative priorities and mission importance. Many enterprises do not have an accurate list of information assets, and the effort to inventory and categorize their assets can appear to be a daunting task. Another reason is that even if assets are known, it is often difficult to place an exact value on less tangible assets, such as PII or trade secrets. However, a high degree of accuracy is not necessary.

In most cases, effective resource valuation is best based on loss scenarios. Information can be classified and put into a matrix with each loss scenario to make a complex problem more manageable and understandable. Loss scenario considerations should include an evaluation of the potential impact of a loss of confidentiality, integrity or availability, as described in Chapter 2. See **figure 3.3.**

Figure 3.3—Matrix of Loss Scenarios

Scenario	Type of Data	Size of Loss	Reputation Loss	Lawsuit Loss	Fines/Reg Loss	Market Loss	Expected Loss per Year	Notes
Hacker steals data, publicly blackmails company.	Customer data	1K records 10K records	US $1M US $10M	US $1M US $10M	US $1 US $35M	US $1M US $5M	US $10 M	Regulatory loss of ability to make acquisitions for 1 year
Employee steals data, sells data to competitors.	Strategic plan	3-year plan	Minimal	Minimal	Minimal	US $20M	US $2M	Competitor duplicates new products, brings them to market faster.
Contractor steals data, sells data to hackers.	Employee data	10K records	US $5M	US $10M	Minimal	Minimal	US $200,000	
Backup tapes and data are found in garbage, makes front-page news.	Customer data	10M records	US $20M	US $20M	US $10M	US $5M	US $200,000	

The accuracy of the valuation is not as critical as having a consistent approach to prioritize efforts. Values within the same order of magnitude as the actual loss (should it occur) are sufficient for planning purposes. Media reports contain many well-documented loss scenarios and loss amounts on which to base a valuation.

Information asset valuation methodologies include many variables, including the level of technical complexity and the level of potential direct and consequential financial loss. Quantitative valuation methodologies are generally the most precise but can be quite complex once actual and downstream impacts have been analyzed.

Another valuation methodology, which is qualitative in nature, involves making an independent decision based on business knowledge, executive management directives, historical perspectives, business goals and environmental factors. There are situations in which quantitative data are not available and this alternative method is the only option. Many information systems managers use a combination of techniques. In some cases, simply assigning value based on a subjective scale of low, medium and high may be satisfactory.

The most straightforward approach is based on the monetary value—the purchase price, replacement cost or book value—if it represents the asset's importance to the organization. If not, other approaches must be considered. For an asset that directly or indirectly generates revenue, a computed value such as net present value (NPV) may be a reasonable approach.

Another approach is to consider value-add or other intangible values. For example, an e-commerce application and server may have hardware and software costs of only US $50,000 but are essential components for generating millions in revenue every month. In this situation, value may be computed in terms of revenue generation or the financial impact of any unanticipated downtime.

Intangible assets are usually comprised of intellectual property such as trade secrets, patents and copyrights, knowledge base, brand reputation, corporate culture, customer loyalty and trust and innovation. Intangible assets that may prove difficult to quantify are the enterprise's reputation and consumer trust. Although a hacking incident itself may not create any direct losses, customers may leave due to lack of confidence in the enterprise, especially if there are strong competitors. Auditors may represent intangible assets under the heading of goodwill.

For example, when customers' personal credit data are stolen, the enterprise could incur the costs of notifying a large number of people about the incident. Additionally, this type of incident could result in potential costs related to legal defense; for example, those affected may file a lawsuit. In the case of credit card compromise, the affected banks typically insist on recovering the costs of reissuing new cards in addition to any fraud costs they covered. This typically is in the range of US $10 or more for each card.

In a publicly traded company, intangible assets represent the difference between the tangible assets as recorded in the financials and the company's market capitalization value. For example, a company with a US $5 billion market capitalization has US $1 billion in tangible assets and US $4 billion in intangible assets. Therefore, 80 percent of the company's value (US $4 billion) is made up of intangible assets. For the purpose of protecting and preserving their value, most of these intangible assets fall under the purview of information security.

The information security manager needs to be aware of ongoing changes in the enterprise and should alter the use of valuation methodologies to best meet any needs that result from these changes. If quantitative data are outdated and cannot be updated in a reasonable time frame, it may be desirable to use qualitative data, either in place of or to augment the quantitative data.

While a detailed discussion on methods of establishing intangible asset values is beyond the scope of this manual, it is important for the information security manager to understand valuation approaches and the necessity for this activity.

3.3.3 Information Asset Classification

Information asset classification is required to determine the relative sensitivity and criticality of information assets, sometimes referred to collectively as business value. Criticality is determined by the impact on the enterprise as a result of the loss of an asset (i.e., how important the asset is to the business). Sensitivity is based on the potential damage to the enterprise as a result of unauthorized disclosure. It provides the basis for protection efforts, business continuity planning and user access control. For larger enterprises, information asset classification can be a daunting task because there are likely to be vast amounts of electronic data, warehouses of documents and thousands of individuals and devices. Yet, without determining the business value, sensitivity and criticality of information resources (and, increasingly, their related legal and regulatory requirements), it is not possible to develop an effective risk management program that provides appropriate protection proportional to business value or sensitivity and criticality.

If comprehensive classification is not possible due to resource constraints or for other reasons, a less effective option is a business dependency assessment. It can be used to allocate proportional protective activities based on the information resources critical business functions use.

The first step in the classification process is to ensure the information asset inventory is complete, including identification of the location and purpose of each asset. Because this is also a necessary step in the risk identification phase of a risk assessment, it is an essential activity. In many enterprises, it may prove difficult to carry out, because there is often no comprehensive inventory of information-related assets. This is especially true in larger enterprises with multiple independent business units lacking a strong centralized security function. The identification process must determine the location of the data, the data owners, data users and data custodians. The security manager must also determine what data are housed by external service providers including cloud-hosted environments and Software as a Service applications like payroll services or health insurance administration. Service providers may also include media vaulting and archival firms, mailing list processors, firms that process mail containing company information, firms that act as couriers or transporters of information, and third-party service providers.

Coordination with business unit managers should include determination of the appropriate information classification based on business value or levels of sensitivity and criticality of information assets. It should ensure that all business and IT stakeholders have the opportunity to review and approve the established guidelines for access control levels. The number of levels should be kept to a minimum, and classifications should be simple—e.g., designations by differing degrees for sensitivity and criticality. End-user managers, in coordination with the security administrator, can use these classifications in their risk and impact assessment process and to determine access levels of users. The information security manager must be aware that in a risk-averse enterprise or one with a blame culture there will be an incentive to overclassify, and it will be necessary to consider controls to limit this tendency.

A major benefit of information asset classification is the fact that tying security to business objectives reduces the risk of either underprotection or costly overprotection of information assets. The long-term benefits to the enterprise are substantial; the alternative is to provide all information assets with the same level of protection, which is unlikely to be cost-effective. If the enterprise is risk-averse and requires a high level of security, providing the same high level of protection to all assets can be very costly.

A number of questions should be asked in any information asset classification model, including but not limited to:

- How many classification levels are suitable for the enterprise?
- How will information be located?
- What process is used to determine classification?
- How will classified information be identified?
- How will it be marked?
- How will it be handled?
- How will it be transported?
- How will confidential information be stored and archived?
- What is the life cycle of the information (create, update, retrieve, archive, dispose)?
- What are the processes associated with the various stages in the information asset life cycle?
- How will it be retained according to policy or law?
- How will it be safely destroyed at the end of the retention period?
- Who has ownership of information?
- Who has access rights?
- Who has authority for determining access to the data?
- What approvals are needed for access?

Information classification requires more than applying a classification label to each piece of information. An important part of the process is identifying security measures that can consistently be applied at each level. As the level of sensitivity or criticality increases, security measures should increase in rigor so that, at the highest level, security mechanisms are the most restrictive or provide the greatest level of protection. Sensitivity and criticality require different security mechanisms and processes. For any piece of information, an owner may have to make both a sensitivity and a criticality decision.

3.3.4 Methods to Determine Criticality of Assets and Impact of Adverse Events

A number of methods exist to determine the sensitivity and criticality of information resources and the impact of adverse events. A BIA is the usual process to identify the impact of adverse events. Methods outlined within COBIT, NIST and other frameworks are representative of the resources the information security manager may use.

It is a generally accepted practice to focus on the impact that a loss of information assets has on the enterprise rather than on a specific adverse event. Because numerous adverse events could occur, it is not practical or cost-effective to list them all. It is important, however, to ensure that considerations include both the direct impact (such as a service outage or information disclosure) and any downstream consequences (like regulatory penalties or loss of customer confidence).

The first step to determine information asset importance is to break the corporate or organizational structure into business units or departments (**figure 3.4**). Under the corporate or top-level organizational structure, each of the business units should be rated by its importance or value to the business.

In **figure 3.4**, Business Unit B is given a number one rating because it is the most important. The importance usually equates with revenue, but the value may equate with critical functions being performed and the sensitivity of the information stored/managed/processed. There can be as many units or departments as exist, but it may be more manageable to stay at a higher level.

Figure 3.4—Top Layer of Business Risk Structure

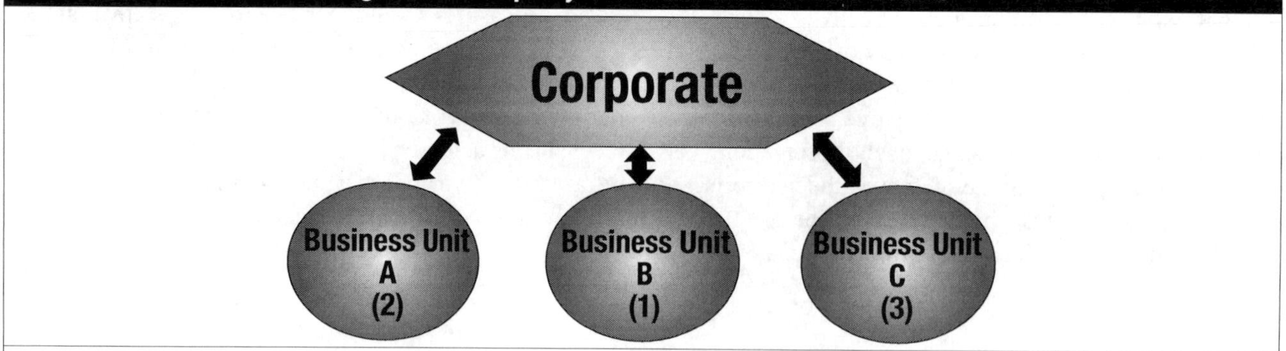

Source: Courtesy of Kenneth D. Biery

The rating should be done by the senior management team, based on its understanding of the enterprise. Ratings are the foundation for establishing the risk management structure. The relative importance or value of the business units or departments will flow down into critical functions, assets and resources.

The next step is identifying the critical organizational functions. The focus for each business unit or department is to define what tasks are important to the unit in achieving its goals. There can be a two-level structure within the critical function layer to represent complex operations. The critical business functions are also numerically rated against each other to help with prioritization of subsequent risk remediation efforts.

Once critical functions are identified, as shown in **figure 3.5**, the basic structure of the enterprise is mapped. It is important to recognize that this structure focuses only on operational elements, not technologies, applications or data. This progressive drill-down structure—which looks similar to a BIA, which is performed when conducting business continuity planning—will provide a management-level view of risk and where it resides in the enterprise.

Figure 3.5—Critical Function Layer of Business Risk Structure

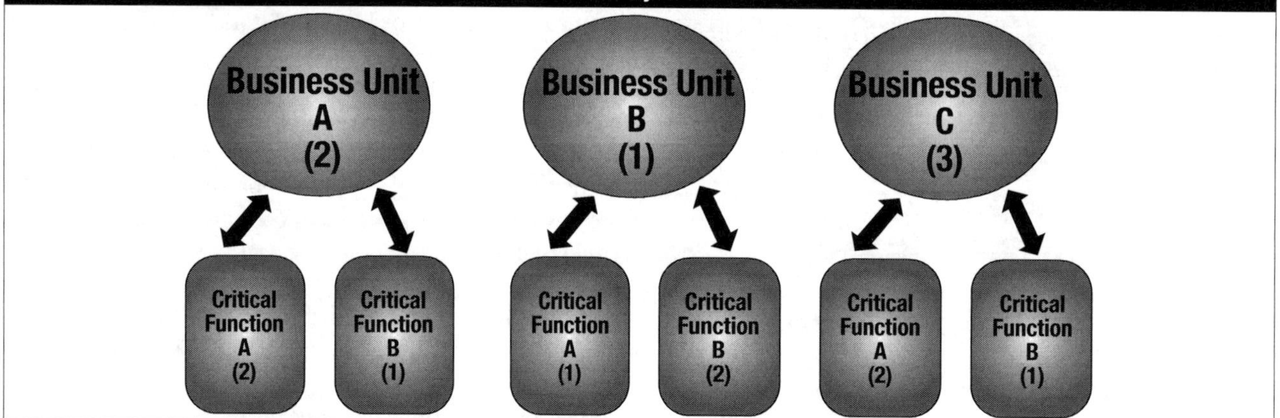

Source: Courtesy of Kenneth D. Biery

In the structure shown in **figure 3.6**, assets and resources are the containers of risk. Because there are vulnerabilities identified with the assets that can be exploited by threats, there is risk. Assets, like business units and critical functions, are numerically rated.

Because assets are associated with the critical business functions they support, they will be rated against each other from the most important to the least important in their group.

Figure 3.6—Aligning Assets to the Critical Function Layer

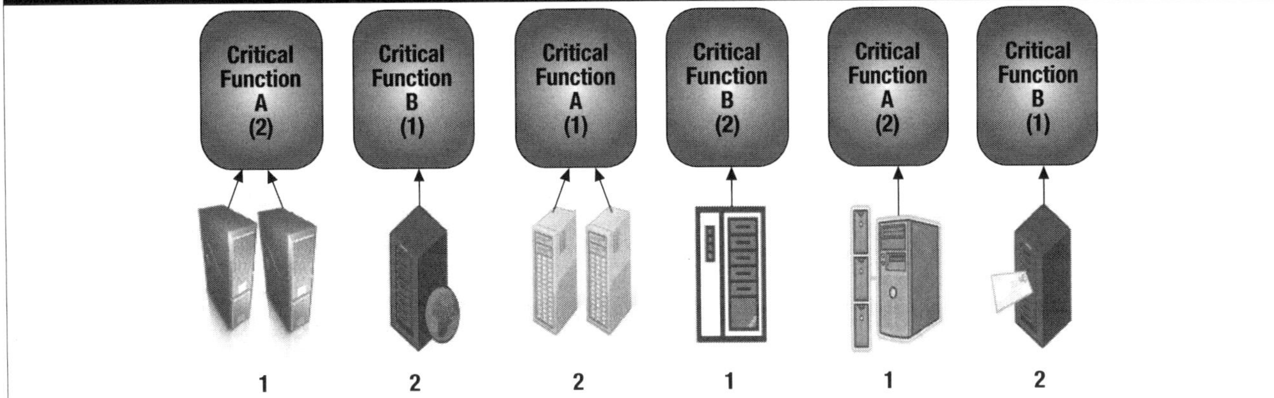

Source: Courtesy of Kenneth D. Biery

The risk represented in **figure 3.7** is the composite of vulnerabilities that a threat can exploit to cause a negative impact to an asset. With the approach represented in the preceding figures, an enterprise can see where risk originates and how it can potentially impact business operations. The roll-up and drill-down nature of this approach is useful for management throughout the enterprise. For example, business owners may want to see their critical functions' level of risk to be able to set a schedule for fixing vulnerabilities or prioritizing protection efforts.

Figure 3.7—Asset Vulnerabilities

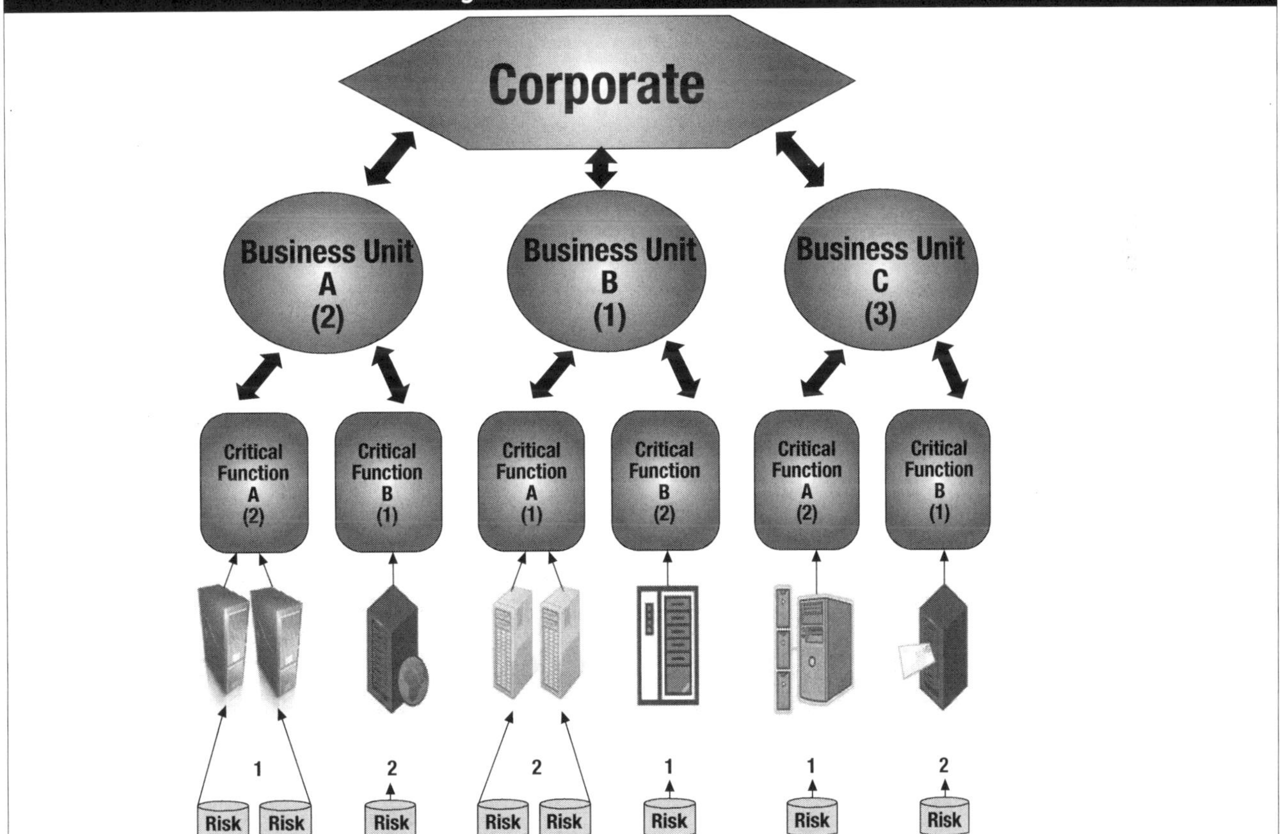

Source: Courtesy of Kenneth D. Biery

The information asset classification is not a one-time activity. It must be repeated periodically to ensure that the classification levels and the levels of protection are appropriate to the business objectives. Furthermore, given the amount of information processing required for identification and classification, tooling and automation can be used to avoid human subjectivity in the process.

3.4 Industry Standards and Frameworks for Information Security

Several internationally recognized standards and frameworks provide a common reference and guide for managing an information security management program. Because of that recognition, they provide helpful normative (or informative) guidance to aid in the implementation and management of an information security program. In addition to broad management frameworks, there are numerous industry-specific standards as well.

3.4.1 Enterprise Information Security Architectures

An enterprise information security architecture (EISA) can be a powerful tool for the development, implementation and integration of a strategy. The effectiveness of an EISA depends on it being an integral part of enterprise architecture (EA). It helps ensure that proper controls are implemented and integrated throughout the enterprise's infrastructure, processes and technologies.

The failure of enterprises to embrace the notion of security architecture appears to have several identifiable causes. One is that such projects are expensive and time-consuming, and there is little or no understanding or appreciation at most organizational levels for the necessity or the potential benefits.

It may also be that there are few competent security architects with sufficiently broad and deep experience to address the wide range of issues necessary to ensure a reasonable degree of success. This lack of architecture over time has resulted in functionally less security integration and increasing vulnerability across the enterprise even though technical security has significantly improved. This lack of integration contributes to the increasing difficulty in managing enterprise security efforts effectively. Given the complexity of implementing an information security architecture as a framework to manage the complexity, it is recommended that the information security manager obtain assistance from enterprise architects. Guidance from those with expertise and understanding of architecture development will help ensure that the complex integration with information and technology will remain relevant and pragmatic as conditions evolve.

The objectives of information architecture approaches include:

- Provide overarching structure, coherence and cohesiveness.
- Serve as a program development road map.
- Ensure strategic alignment between business and security.
- Support and enable achievement of business strategy.
- Implement security policies and strategy.
- Ensure traceability back to business strategy, specific business requirements and key principles.
- Provide a level of abstraction independent of specific technologies and preferences.
- Establish a common language for information security within the enterprise.
- Allow many individual contributors to work together to achieve objectives.

Several architectural approaches have been developed for the enterprise, all of which include essential aspects of security and some of which deal exclusively with security. While a detailed discussion of each of these approaches is beyond the scope of this manual, it should be noted that these approaches fall into three basic categories: process approaches, frameworks and reference models. Frameworks such as COBIT, the Zachman framework, Sherwood Applied Business Security Architecture (SABSA) and The Open Group Architecture Framework (TOGAF) allow a great deal of flexibility in how each element of the architecture is developed. The essence of the frameworks is to describe the elements of architecture and how they must relate to each other. Process models are more directive in the processes used for the various elements. Reference models are a small-scale representation of the actual implementation. While the objectives of all the models are essentially the same, their approaches vary widely.

However, a number of these approaches are similar, having evolved from the development of enterprise architecture. For example, the Zachman framework approach of developing a who, what, why, where, when and how matrix is shared by SABSA and E2AF. See **figure 3.8.**

Figure 3.8—SABSA Security Architecture Matrix

	Assets (What)	Motivation (Why)	Process (How)	People (Who)	Location (Where)	Time (When)
Contextual	The Business	Business Risk Model	Business Process Model	Business Organization and Relationships	Business Geography	Business Time Dependencies
Conceptual	Business Attributes Profile	Control Objectives	Security Strategies and Architectural Layering	Security Entity Model and Trust Framework	Security Domain Model	Security-related Lifetimes and Deadlines
Logical	Business Information Model	Security Policies	Security Services	Entity Schema and Privilege Profiles	Security Domain Definitions and Associations	Security Processing Cycle
Physical	Business Data Model	Security Rules, Practices and Procedures	Security Mechanisms	Users, Applications and the User Interface	Platform and Network Infrastructure	Control Structure Execution
Component	Detailed Data Structures	Security Standards	Security Products and Tools	Identities, Functions, Actions and ACLs	Processes, Nodes, Addresses and Protocols	Security Step Timing and Sequencing
Operational	Assurance of Operational Continuity	Operational Risk Management	Security Service Management and Support	Application and User Management and Support	Security of Sites, Networks and Platforms	Security Operations Schedule

Source: Copyright SABSA Institute, ww.sabsa.org. Reproduced with permission.

TOGAF addresses the following four interrelated areas of specialization, called architecture domains:

- Business architecture, which defines the business strategy, governance, organization and key business processes of the enterprise
- Applications architecture, which provides a blueprint for the individual application systems to be deployed, the interactions among the application systems, and their relationships to the core business processes of the enterprise with the frameworks for services to be exposed as business functions for integration
- Data architecture, which describes the structure of an enterprise's logical and physical data assets and the associated data management resources
- Technical architecture, or technology architecture, which describes the hardware, software and network infrastructure needed to support the deployment of core mission-critical applications

The objectives of the various approaches are essentially the same. The framework details the organization, roles, entities and relationships that exist, or should exist, to perform a set of business processes. The framework should provide a rigorous taxonomy that clearly identifies what processes a business performs and includes detailed information about how those processes are executed and secured. The end product is a set of artifacts that describe, in varying degrees of detail, exactly what and how a business operates and what security controls are required.

The choice of approaches may be limited by an existing organizational standard, but if one does not exist, the choice should be made based on form, fit and function. In other words, a particular approach may be more consistent with existing organizational practices or may be more suitable for a particular situation. The various approaches may also entail considerably greater efforts and resources. Some are more oriented to or limited to technical architectures and will not be well suited for governance purposes.

While a specific security architecture may be of considerable benefit, it is essential that it be guided by, and tightly integrated with, the overall enterprise architecture. A current enterprise architecture, such as TOGAF (**figure 3.9**), will address security as an essential component of the overall design and, in most cases, will be the preferred approach to ensure effective integration.

Figure 3.9—Structure of the TOGAF Document

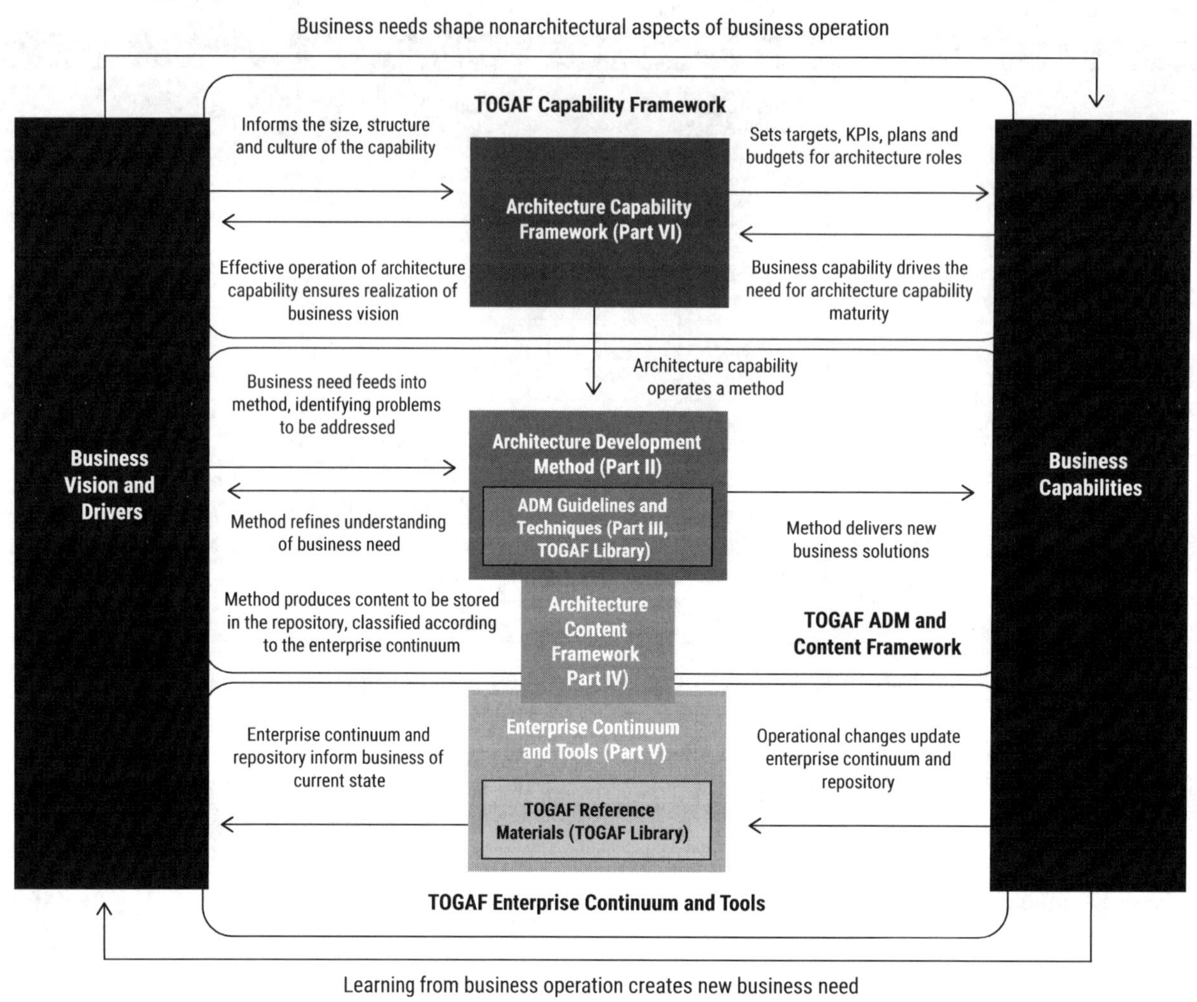

Source: The Open Group, *TOGAF® Standard v9.2*, United Kingdom, 2018

The TOGAF Architecture Development Method (ADM) phases, as shown in **figure 3.10**, include:

- **Preliminary phase**—Deals mainly with the definition of the architecture framework and the architecture principles. In addition, the overall scope, constraints, objectives and assumptions are identified.
- **Architecture vision**—Deals with defining the vision and scope of the architecture and specific segments of work to be performed.
- **Business architecture**—Addresses the description of the as-is business architecture domain, the development of the to-be business architecture and the gap analysis between the two.
- **Information systems architecture**—Provides the description of the as-is and to-be data, applications domains and conducting the gap analyses.
- **Technology architecture**—Deals with the description of the as-is and to-be technology domains and conducting a gap analysis.
- **Opportunities and solutions**—Deals with the formulation of a high-level implementation and migration strategy to transform the as-is architecture into the to-be architecture.
- **Migration planning**—Deals with formulation of a detailed implementation and migration road map, including the analysis of costs, benefits and risk.

- **Implementation governance**—Ensures that the implementation projects conform to the defined architecture.
- **Architecture change management**—Deals with keeping the architecture up-to-date and ensures that the architecture responds to the needs of the enterprise as changes arise.
- **Requirements management**—Ensures that the architecture projects are based on business requirements and the business requirements are validated against the architecture.

Figure 3.10—The TOGAF Architecture Development Method

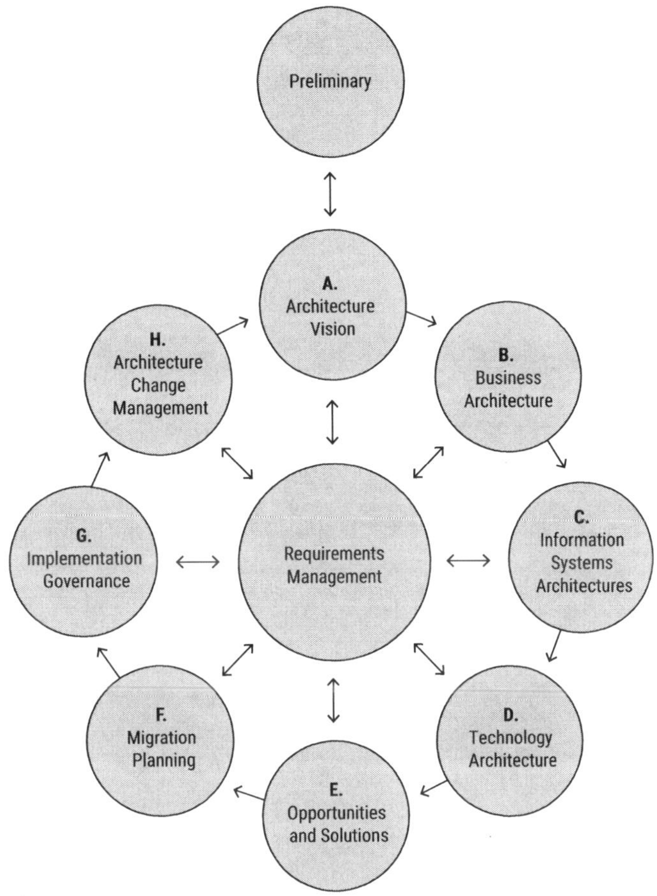

Source: The Open Group, *TOGAF® Standard v9.2*, United Kingdom, 2018

Alternative Enterprise Architecture Frameworks

The choice of an architectural approach should be based on factors such as form, fit, function and, in some enterprises, mandate. In addition to those mentioned, approaches to enterprise and security architecture include the following:

- AGATE French Délégation Générale pour l'Armement Atelier de Gestion de l'ArchiTEcture des systèmes d'information et de communication
- Integrated Architecture Framework of Capgemini
- Interoperable Delivery (of European government services to public) Administrations, Business and Citizens (IDABC)
- Method for an Integrated Knowledge Environment (MIKE2.0), which includes an enterprise architecture framework called the Strategic Architecture for the Federated Enterprise (SAFE)
- Model-driven Architecture (MDA) of the Object Management Group

- NIH Enterprise Architecture Framework
- OBASHI business and IT methodology and framework (OBASHI)
- Open Security Architecture
- SAP Enterprise Architecture Framework, an extension of TOGAF, to better support commercial off-the-shelf programs and service-oriented architecture
- Service-Oriented Modeling Framework (SOMF)
- United Kingdom Ministry of Defence Architecture Framework (MODAF)
- United States Department of Defense Architectural Framework (DoDAF)
- United States Office of Management and Budget Federal Enterprise Architecture (FEA)

Enterprise Architecture Domains

There are four commonly accepted subsets of an overall enterprise architecture:

- A business (or business process) architecture defines the business strategy, governance, organization and key business processes.
- A data architecture describes the structure of an enterprise's logical and physical data assets and data management resources.
- An applications architecture provides a blueprint for the individual application systems to be deployed, their interactions, and their relationships to the core business processes of the enterprise.
- A technology architecture describes the architectural principles, component relationships, and hardware and software infrastructure intended to support the deployment of core, mission-critical applications.

Whatever architectural approach is chosen, an effective approach must start with the enterprise business architecture. The subsequent designs—such as application, security and data architectures—function as subsets to ensure alignment with and support of business strategy and objectives.

The complexity of developing and implementing some approaches has proven to be a hindrance to adoption. For example, some notions of information security architecture frameworks include six layers, from contextual to physical. Like a building architecture, the highest or contextual level defined in SABSA and the Zachman frameworks is the "business" or utility layer (i.e., what the structure is to be used for). A theater is designed very differently from an office building because the buildings are used for different purposes. The design, or architecture, is tightly aligned with the purpose (i.e., linked to the business objective). The contextual architecture serves to define the relationships among various required business attributes. These include who, what, when, where and how, which drive the next layer—the conceptual layer—which integrates the architectural design concepts with the business requirements.

The next layer, the logical architecture, describes the same elements in terms of the relationships of logical elements. It is followed by the physical layer, which identifies the relationships among various security mechanisms that will execute the logical relationships and the component architecture, consisting of the actual devices and their interconnections. Finally, there is the operational architecture, describing how security service delivery is organized.

While arguably comprehensive, the SABSA and Zachman frameworks are often complex and costly to develop. Many enterprises that have implemented them find them difficult to maintain as they experience rapid change and define new business objectives.

The important consideration, regardless of the approach, is that at the point of the development and implementation of an information security program, some form of high-level architecture or design should be in place. This is particularly the case for major implementations comprised of many parts and projects that must integrate well to achieve program objectives. Although many enterprises do not have them, the adoption of an appropriate enterprise or security architecture can be essential to developing and implementing an effective information security program.

Objectives of Information Security Architectures

One of the key functions of architecture as a tool is to provide a framework for successfully managing complexity. As a project grows in size and complexity, many designers and design influences must work as a team to create something that has the appearance of being created by a single design authority.

As the complexity of the business environment grows, many business processes and support functions must integrate seamlessly to provide effective services and management for the business, its customers and its partners. Architecture provides a means to manage that complexity.

3.4.2 Information Security Management Frameworks

The information security management framework is a conceptual representation of an information security management structure. It should define the technical, operational, managerial, administrative and educational components of the program; the organizational units and leadership responsible for each component; the control or management objective that each component should deliver; the interfaces and information flow among the components; and each component's tangible outputs. Although formats and detail levels vary, the framework should fundamentally describe the information security management components (e.g., roles, policies, standard operating procedures [SOPs], management procedures, security architectures) and their interactions in broad strokes. This is, in essence, an operational architecture as described in Section 3.4.1 Enterprise Information Security Architectures.

Other outcomes of an effective security management framework focus on shorter-term needs. For example, organizational decision makers require awareness of risk and mitigation options in support of corporate initiatives such as external hosting of information systems. Implementers of solutions often require the services of technical security subject matter experts, which the information security manager should facilitate either through internal or external resources. Ensuring that initiatives and existing operations adhere to policies and standards is also a responsibility that the information security manager and the security department are expected to manage.

The information security manager is typically expected to craft information security management options that deliver outcomes that are less direct, but no less important, to achieving security goals. These objectives include demonstrating, both directly and indirectly, that:

- The program adds tactical and strategic value to the enterprise.
- The program is being operated efficiently and with concern for cost issues.
- Management has a clear understanding of information security drivers, activities, benefits and needs.
- Information security knowledge and capabilities are growing as a result of the program.
- The program fosters cooperation and goodwill among organizational units.
- There is facilitation of information security stakeholders' understanding of their roles, responsibilities and expectations.
- The program includes provisions for the enterprise's continuity of business.

These soft goals revolve around directly and indirectly demonstrating to security steering committees, senior management and boards of directors that the information security program is delivering results and the information security manager is managing the program effectively.

There are a number of different frameworks that can be used by the information security manager for developing the information security program. After understanding various frameworks to manage information security, it is key to understand that no framework can be adopted as-is for any enterprise. An incremental adoption approach will help in implementing a program tailored to the enterprise.

> **Note:** Multiple frameworks are available for information security managers to use. The following sections do not constitute an exhaustive list of frameworks, but they provide an overview of some commonly used frameworks. The CISM exam will not test any specific framework or standard, but candidates should understand how to apply a framework in their enterprises. Information security managers should be aware of frameworks applicable to their industries or specific enterprises.[18]

COBIT

Chapter 1 illustrates how COBIT provides a comprehensive framework with a focus on helping enterprises create optimal value from IT by maintaining a balance between realizing benefits and optimizing risk

[18] One such framework is HITRUST. For more information, see https://hitrustalliance.net/.

levels and resource use. COBIT enables IT and information to be governed and managed holistically for the enterprise, addressing the business and IT functional areas of responsibility, and considering the information-related interests of internal and external stakeholders.

COBIT is based on two sets of principles: 1) principles that describe the core requirements of a governance system for enterprise information and technology; and 2) principles for a framework that can be used to build a governance system for the enterprise.

COBIT, including the information security focus area, provides tools to help understand, use, implement and direct core information security-related activities and make more-informed decisions. It enables information security professionals to effectively communicate with business and IT leaders and manage risk associated with information, including risk related to compliance, continuity, security and privacy.

COBIT includes numerous focus areas that describe certain governance topics, domains or issues that can be addressed by a collection of governance and management objectives and their components. Examples of potential focus areas include small and medium enterprises, information security, risk, digital transformation, cloud computing, privacy and DevOps.

The major drivers for the COBIT information security focus area include:

- The need to describe information security in an enterprise context, including:
  - The full end-to-end business and IT functional responsibilities for information security
  - Key aspects that lead to effective governance and management of information security, such as organizational structures, policies and culture
  - The relationship and alignment of information security with enterprise objectives
- An ever-increasing need for the enterprise to:
  - Achieve and maintain information risk at an acceptable level; protect information from unauthorized disclosure, unauthorized or inadvertent modification and possible intrusion; and protect technology assets from damage and destruction
  - Ensure that services and systems are continuously available to internal and external resources for whom it is appropriate to have access, leading to user satisfaction with IT engagement and services
  - Ensure cybercrime resilience within the enterprise
  - Comply with relevant laws and regulations, contractual requirements and internal policies on information and systems security and protection, and provide transparency regarding compliance
  - Achieve all of the above while containing the cost of IT services and technology protection
- The need to connect to and, where relevant, align with other major frameworks and standards in the marketplace
- The need to link major ISACA research, frameworks and guidance, with a primary focus on the Business Model for Information Security (BMIS) and COBIT, but also on other relevant focus areas, such as the IT Assurance Framework (ITAF)

ISO/IEC 27001:2013

The security standards *ISO/IEC 27001:2013: Information technology—Security techniques—Information security management systems—Requirements* and *ISO/IEC 27002:2013: Information technology—Security techniques—Code of practice* for information security controls provide a widely accepted framework and approach to information security management. The 114 controls in the 14 domains of ISO/IEC 27001:2013 can be generally mapped to COBIT, but they are less business-oriented and comprehensive and do not provide complete tool sets. These standards do provide high-level comprehensive requirements for information security programs. Based on the British Standard (BS7799), this standard has been slightly expanded to include 14 broad control areas:

- A.5: Information security policies
- A.6: Organization of information security
- A.7: Human resource security (controls that are applied before, during or after employment)
- A.8: Asset management
- A.9: Access control
- A.10: Cryptography
- A.11: Physical and environmental security
- A.12: Operations security

- A.13: Communications security
- A.14: System acquisition, development and maintenance
- A.15: Supplier relationships
- A.16: Information security incident management
- A.17: Information security aspects of business continuity management
- A.18: Compliance (with internal requirements, such as policies, and with external requirements, such as laws)

The ISO/IEC 27000 series of standards covers virtually all aspects of security at a high level. The series includes:

- ISO/IEC 27000 Information technology—Security techniques—Information security management systems—Overview and vocabulary
- ISO/IEC 27001 Information technology—Security techniques—Information security management systems—Requirements
- ISO/IEC 27002 Information technology—Security techniques—Code of practice for information security controls
- ISO/IEC 27003 Information technology—Security techniques—Information security management system implementation guidance
- ISO/IEC 27004 Information technology—Security techniques—Information security management—Measurement
- ISO/IEC 27005 Information technology—Security techniques—Information security risk management
- ISO/IEC 27006 Information technology—Security techniques—Requirements for bodies providing audit and certification of information security management systems
- ISO/IEC 27007 Information technology—Security techniques—Guidelines for information security management systems auditing
- ISO/IEC TR 27008 Information technology—Security techniques—Guidelines for auditors on information security controls
- ISO/IEC 27010 Information technology—Security techniques—Information security management for inter-sector and inter-organizational communications
- ISO/IEC 27011 Information technology—Security techniques—Information security management guidelines for telecommunications organizations based on ISO/IEC 27002
- ISO/IEC 27013 Information technology—Security techniques—Guidance on the integrated implementation of ISO/IEC 27001 and ISO/IEC 20000-1
- ISO/IEC 27014 Information technology—Security techniques—Governance of information security
- ISO/IEC TR 27015 Information technology—Security techniques—Information security management guidelines for financial services
- ISO/IEC TR 27016 Information technology—Security techniques—Information security management—Organizational economics
- ISO/IEC TR 27019 Information technology—Security techniques—Information security management guidelines based on ISO/IEC 27002 for process control systems specific to the energy utility industry
- ISO/IEC 27031 Information technology—Security techniques—Guidelines for information and communication technology readiness for business continuity
- ISO/IEC 27032 Information technology—Security techniques—Guidelines for cybersecurity
- ISO/IEC 27033 Parts 1 to 5 Information technology—Security techniques—Network security
- ISO/IEC 27034-1 Information technology—Security techniques— Application security—Part 1: Overview and concepts
- ISO/IEC 27035 Information technology—Security techniques—Information security incident management
- ISO/IEC 27036-3 Information technology—Security techniques—Information security for supplier relationships—Part 3: Guidelines for information and communication technology supply chain security
- ISO/IEC 27037 Information technology—Security techniques—Guidelines for identification, collection, acquisition and preservation of digital evidence
- ISO 27799 Health informatics—Information security management in health using ISO/IEC 27002

NIST Cybersecurity Framework

Formally titled the NIST Framework for Improving Critical Infrastructure Cybersecurity, this model provides high-level guidance for aligning a cybersecurity program with enterprise objectives. In response to an increasing prevalence of cybersecurity attacks, NIST convened a series of workshops to develop a process by which an enterprise could identify opportunities for improvement in the information security program. The framework highlights the need for effective risk management integration and it broadly supports improvement in supply chain risk management.

The NIST Cybersecurity Framework does not provide controls to be applied. Instead, it guides practitioners through the process of determining gaps between the current state of practice and a desired target state that might better fulfill enterprise mission, including risk management needs. Analysis of the gaps between states enables the use of controls-based frameworks (including those listed herein) to improve information security risk management.

Components of the NIST Cybersecurity Framework include:

- The Framework Core—a set of cybersecurity-related outcomes organized in terms of five concurrent functions: Identify, Protect, Detect, Respond, Recover. When considered together, these functions provide a high-level, strategic view of the life cycle of an enterprise's management of cybersecurity risk. The Framework Core then identifies underlying key categories and subcategories for each function. To provide clarity regarding the intended outcomes of each subcategory, NIST provides examples (or informative references) from well-known standards, guidelines and practices, including several mentioned previously.
- Framework Implementation Tiers—a set of four levels that help an enterprise determine the level of diligence required for its information security risk management program, risk management integration into enterprise operations, and sharing of information security information with external parties. The tiers characterize an enterprise's practices over a range from Partial (Tier 1) to Adaptive (Tier 4). These tiers reflect a progression from informal, reactive responses to approaches that are agile and risk-informed. Coordination with enterprise stakeholders to select a desired tier supports discussions about the extent to which these characteristics should be included in the information security program.
- Framework Profile is a representation of how an enterprise (or subset thereof) has implemented or desires to implement the outcomes described in the core. By iterating through each of the categories and subcategories in the core, based on business drivers and information security risk assessment, users can document the current state of the information security program and can evaluate opportunities for improvement.

NIST Risk Management Framework

The NIST Risk Management Framework (RMF) provides a process that integrates security, privacy, and cyber supply chain risk management activities into the system development life cycle. Originally intended to help US government agencies to evaluate and improve information security, it has been broadened to apply to any enterprise and is available without cost. The RMF provides a risk-based approach to the categorization of relevant assets, selection and implementation of controls to achieve adequate protection, and provisions for monitoring the continued effectiveness and efficiency of risk management measures.

The RMF consists of seven steps:

- **Prepare** for applying the framework by determining enterprise goals and objectives, relevant risk management roles, enterprise risk strategy and policy directives, organizational artifacts regarding risk assessment (existing and planned) and methods for monitoring and communicating risk activities and results.
- **Categorize** the system and information processed, stored and transmitted based on an analysis of the impact of the loss of confidentiality, integrity and availability of that system or information.
- **Select** the set of security and privacy controls (generally published in NIST Special Publication 800-53) that will achieve the appropriate risk management objectives in light of the categorization. Baseline sets of controls are provided in a separate document as a starting point, and they can then be tailored to achieve risk management objectives. Similar processes are available for shared controls that may be used by various entities throughout the enterprise.

- **Implement** the controls as described in a detailed system security plan and update relevant documentation, as needed.
- **Assess** the efficacy and efficiency of the implemented controls through a disciplined security control analysis process, based on detailed criteria described in NIST Special Publication 800-53A. That document recommends methods for examining evidence, interviewing stakeholders, and testing actual operation of implemented controls.
- **Authorize** the system for operation, based on a determination from a senior official that the steps above adequately provide a risk management condition that is acceptable for the enterprise, based upon the potential impact of a loss as determined in Step 1. If the risk is not found to be acceptable, the system may be denied authority to operate, or the system owner may be directed to correct deficiencies.
- **Monitor** the system (or common control infrastructure) through ongoing assessment of the effectiveness of implemented controls, including determination of major changes to the system or the risk landscape that might trigger a need for additions or changes to the system security plan.

Numerous industry-specific standards provide their own specific criteria and conformance specifications. Examples include:

- PCI DSS—supports specific security controls to protect the security of payment card and cardholder information
- Health Insurance Portability and Accountability Act of 1996 (HIPAA)— requires particular protections to safeguard electronic protected health information (e-PHI) that represents individually identifiable health information that a covered entity creates, receives, maintains, or transmits in electronic form
- North American Electric Reliability Corporation (NERC) Critical Infrastructure Protection (CIP)—a set of requirements designed to secure the assets required for operating North America's bulk electric system.

In addition to these international and industry-sector standards, many local, regional and national standards provide additional requirements and guidelines for management of information security programs.

3.4.3 Information Security Framework Components

Most standard frameworks for information security show the development of an information security program as starting with risk assessment and the identification of control objectives and key controls defined by standards such as COBIT and ISO/IEC 27001 and 27002. While guidance is provided by these standards, control objectives must be based on individual organizational objectives and risk appetite and tolerance tailored to achieve the desired outcomes. As the program develops and matures and conditions change, control objectives may need to be changed and additional or modified controls may be required to address new conditions, emerging risk, evolving regulations or contractual obligations.

The various components that make up the management framework can be broken down into their functional elements (i.e., technical, operational, managerial, administrative and educational components). This can be helpful in ensuring that each aspect is adequately represented in the framework and given appropriate security consideration.

Technical Components

Information security is typically involved in most or all of the technical IT components of an enterprise, including providing and maintaining suitable security standards, reviewing procedures for policy compliance, designing and implementing appropriate security metrics, and providing general oversight. Many of the key controls identified in the framework address risk associated with the technical components, including their configuration, monitoring, maintenance and operation. While IT may own the systems, IT is typically not the data owner and serves as custodian with a requirement to provide adequate protection and compliance with the enterprise's information security policies by operating within the applicable standards. In other cases, the business owner may actually own the systems supporting the business operation but, in either case, IT will still serve as custodian. It is essential that all technology components have an identified owner and that there are no orphan systems. This is necessary to ensure responsibility and accountability for maintaining all systems in compliance with security policies and for ownership and proper treatment of associated risk to acceptable levels.

From an information security perspective, the vast majority of the enterprise's information will reside with IT and will be a major focus of the information security framework. The information security function must adequately regulate the IT function and provide oversight to ensure policy compliance sufficient to achieve acceptable risk levels consistent with the information security strategy objectives.

Operational Components

Operational components of a security program are the ongoing management and administrative activities that must be performed to provide the required level of security assurance. These operational components include items such as SOPs, business operation security practices, and maintenance and administration of security technologies. They are generally conducted on a daily to weekly timeline.

The information security manager must provide ongoing management of the operational information security components. Because it is common for many of these components to fall outside the direct control of the information security department (e.g., operating system patching procedures), the information security manager must work with and provide oversight for IT, business units and other organizational groups to ensure that operational security needs are covered. Examples of common operational components include:

- Identity management and access control administration
- Security event monitoring and analysis
- System patching procedures and configuration management
- Change control and release management processes
- Security metrics collection and reporting
- Maintenance of supplemental control technologies and program support technologies
- Incident response, investigation and resolution
- Retirement and sanitization of data processing and media storage equipment

For each operational component related to information security, the information security manager needs to identify the owner and collaborate with the owner to document key information needed for management of the necessary functions. This information includes the component ownership and execution roles, activity schedules or triggers, needed information or data inputs, actual procedural steps, success criteria, failure escalation procedures, and approval/review processes. It also includes processes for providing suitable management metrics for the feedback necessary for effective ongoing management.

The information security manager should ensure that procedures for log maintenance, issue escalation, management oversight, periodic risk assessment and quality assurance reviews are developed and implemented. The information security manager must update the roles and responsibilities documentation as new tasks arise in operational component development. For example, a new operational procedure that requires a monthly chief operating officer (COO) review of security issues related to business activities needs to be added to the appropriate task lists and schedules.

Management Components

In addition to a variety of ongoing technical and operational security tasks, the information security manager needs to consider a number of management components. These typically include strategic implementation activities such as standards development or modification, policy reviews, and oversight of initiatives or program execution. These are activities that generally take place less frequently than operational components, perhaps on a timeline measured in months, quarters or years.

Management objectives, requirements and policies are key in shaping the rest of the information security program, which, in turn, defines what must be managed. The information security manager must ensure that the program development process is executed with appropriate consideration to legal, regulatory, risk and resource issues, and a suite of metrics necessary for decision support.

Ongoing or periodic analysis of assets, threats, risk and organizational impacts must continue to be the basis for modifying security policies and developing or modifying standards. Early versions are often too permissive, too restrictive or misaligned with operational realities. As a result, the information security manager is well advised to exercise flexibility in making adjustments to standards and policy interpretation during the initial stages of a security program's implementation.

Ongoing communication with business and operational units is critical to providing the feedback that can provide guidance to information security management, ensure program effectiveness, and maintain alignment with and support for the objectives of the enterprise.

During development of operational and technical management components, it is important that there is management oversight ensuring fulfillment of requirements and consistency with strategic direction. This oversight often occurs in the form of management reviews of program components (for example, the CIO, chief executive officer [CEO], steering committee or executive committee performing a quarterly review of security operations). Topics for review include modifications to operational or technical components, general effectiveness of program components, review of metrics and KPIs, root cause analysis of detrimental events such as outages or compromises, issues hampering component effectiveness that require management attention, and review of action items and commitments from previous review sessions.

Administrative Components

As the scope and responsibilities of the information security management function grow, so do the resources, personnel and financial aspects involved. This means that information security management must address the same business administration activities as other business units. The information security manager in charge of such an operation must ensure that financial, HR and other management functions are effective.

Financial administration functions generally consist of budgeting, timeline planning, TCO analysis/management, ROI analysis/management, acquisition/purchasing and inventory management. These functions, particularly budgeting and timeline planning, often require updates throughout the fiscal year as financial realities and organizational goals change. The information security manager should establish a working rapport with the enterprise's finance department to ensure a strong working relationship, support, and compliance with financial policies and procedures.

HR management functions generally include job description management, organizational planning, recruitment and hiring, performance management, payroll and time tracking administration, employee education and development, and termination management. The information security program should account for the time and resources needed for these activities, particularly as program staffing grows over time. Those charged with management of larger information security programs must also address the need to develop an efficient organizational structure with appropriate layers of management and supervisory personnel. In all issues related to HR management, it is important for the information security manager to work closely with HR leadership and adhere to established procedures to prevent legal liabilities and other types of risk.

Effective management functions require the information security manager to balance project efforts and ongoing operational overhead with staff head count, utilization levels and external resources. Rarely does any information security program have an optimal number of resources, and it is always necessary to prioritize efforts. The information security manager should work with the steering committee and executive management to determine priorities and establish consensus on what project items may be delayed because of resource constraints. Spikes in activity or unexpected project efforts can often be addressed with third-party resources such as contractors. The information security manager should maintain relationships with the vendors most likely to be engaged in such cases.

It is not unusual for the information security manager to be under pressure to shortcut security management, quality assurance (QA) and development processes or to divert resources from daily operations to accelerate project efforts. It is the role of the information security manager to document and ensure that executive management understands the risk implications of moving an initiative ahead without full security diligence; it is up to executive management to decide if the initiative is important enough to warrant the risk. If this situation occurs, the information security manager should make every effort to utilize the first available opportunity to revisit systems or initiatives that are not certified or accredited.

To ensure that the existing security environment operates as needed, security operational resources should be diverted to project efforts only if they are not fully utilized. Even in this situation, it needs to be clearly communicated that operational security resources are provided ad hoc, and a spike in operational activities (e.g., an intrusion) requires the immediate attention of the operational staff.

Educational and Informational Components

Employee education and awareness regarding security risk is often integrated with employee orientation and initial training. General organizational policies and procedures, such as acceptable use policies and employee monitoring policies, should be communicated and administered at the enterprise's HR level. Issues and responsibilities that are specific to an employee's role or enterprise (e.g., call center authentication of customers) should be communicated and administered at the business unit level. Interactive education techniques, such as online testing and role-playing, are often more effective than a purely informational approach. Examples of these types of training include incident response and contingency plan training and exercises. In all cases, the information security manager should collaborate with HR and business units to identify information security education needs. Pertinent metrics (e.g., average employee quiz scores, average time elapsed since last employee training) should be tracked and communicated to the steering committee and executive management.

3.5 Information Security Policies, Procedures and Guidelines

There is a broad range of interpretation of policy, standards, procedures and guidelines. The definitions used in this manual agree with the major standards bodies and should be adopted to preclude miscommunication. Policies and standards are considered tools of governance and management, respectively, and procedures and guidelines the purview of operations. For clarity, the four are defined in the following subsections.

3.5.1 Policies

Policies are the high-level statements of management intent, expectations and direction. Well-developed high-level policies in a mature enterprise can remain fairly static for extended periods.

An example of an effective high-level policy statement on access control could be: "Information resources shall be controlled in a manner that effectively precludes unauthorized access."

Policies must be clearly aligned with and support the strategic security objectives of the enterprise.

An exception process must be created for situations in which policy compliance cannot be obtained. The exception process must include formal documented governance oversight acknowledging acceptance of the risk created by not adhering to the information security policy.

Policy Development

One of the most important aspects of the action plan to execute the strategy is to create or modify policies and standards as needed. Policies must capture the intent, expectations and direction of management. As a strategy evolves, it is vital that supporting policies are developed to articulate the strategy. For example, if the objective is to become ISO/IEC 27001:2013-compliant over a three-year period, then the strategy must consider which elements are addressed first, which resources are allocated, how the elements of the standard can be accomplished and so forth. The road map should show the steps and the sequence, dependencies and milestones. The action plan is essentially a project plan to implement the strategy following the road map.

If the objective is ISO/IEC 27001:2013 compliance, each of the relevant 14 domains and major subsections must be the subject of one or more policies. In practice, this can be effectively accomplished with about two dozen specific policies for even large institutions. Each of the policies is likely to have a number of supporting standards typically divided by security domains. In other words, a set of standards for a high-security domain will be more stringent than the standards for a low-security domain. Other standards may need to be developed for different business units, depending on their activities and regulatory requirements.

The completed strategy provides the basis for creation or modification of existing policies. The policies should be directly traceable to strategy elements. If they are not, either the strategy is incomplete or the policy is incorrect. It should be apparent that a policy that contradicts the strategy is counterproductive. The strategy is the statement of intent, expectations and direction of management. The policies must be consistent with and support the intent and direction of the strategy.

Most enterprises have some information security policies. Typically, they have evolved over time, are usually created in response to a security problem or regulations, and are often inconsistent and sometimes contradictory. These policies generally have no relationship with a security strategy (if one exists) and only a coincidental relationship with business activities.

Policies are one of the primary elements of governance. They must be properly created, accepted and validated by the board and senior management and broadly communicated throughout the enterprise. There may be occasions when sub-policies must be created to address unique situations separate from the bulk of the enterprise. For example, a separate part of the enterprise might be performing highly classified military work. Policies that reflect the specific security requirements for classified military work may exist as a separate set.

There are several attributes of good policies that should be considered:

- Security policies should be an articulation of a well-defined information security strategy and capture the intent, expectations and direction of management.
- Each policy should state only one general security mandate.
- Policies must be clear and easily understood by all affected parties.
- Policies should rarely be more than a few sentences long.
- There should rarely be a reason to have more than two dozen policies.

Most enterprises create security policies prior to developing a security strategy. Indeed, most enterprises still have not developed a security strategy. In many cases, policy development has not followed the previously defined approach and has been ad hoc in a variety of formats. Often, these policies have been written to include standards and procedures in lengthy, detailed documents compiled in large, dusty volumes relegated to the stock room.

In many cases, especially in smaller enterprises, effective practices have been developed, but they may not be reflected in written policies. Existing practices that adequately address security requirements may usefully serve as the basis for policy and standards development. This approach minimizes organizational disruptions, communications of new policies, and resistance to new or unfamiliar constraints.

3.5.2 Standards

Standards, in this context, are the criteria used to determine whether procedures, processes or systems meet policy requirements. Metrics show whether a procedure complies with a standard or does not. Boundaries are set in terms of allowable limits on processes, people and technologies.

A standard for passwords used for access control could be: "Passwords for medium- and low-security domains shall be composed of no fewer than eight characters consisting of a mixture of upper- and lower-case letters and at least one number and one punctuation mark."

The standard for access control for employees on the premises can include password composition requirements, minimum and maximum password length, frequency of password changes, and rules for reuse. Generally, a standard must provide sufficient parameters or boundaries, so that it can be unambiguously determined whether a procedure or practice meets the requirements of a relevant policy or does not. Standards must be carefully crafted to provide only the necessary limits to ensure security while maximizing procedural options.

Standards must change as requirements and technologies change. Multiple standards will usually exist for each policy, depending on the security domain or classification level. For example, the password standard would be more restrictive when accessing high-security domains.

Standards Development

Standards are powerful security management tools. They set the permissible bounds for procedures and practices of technology and systems, and for people and events. Properly implemented, they are the law to the constitution of policy. They provide the measuring stick for policy compliance and a sound basis for audits. They govern the creation of procedures and guidelines. Standards set the security baselines, reflect acceptable risk and control objectives, and are the criteria for evaluating risk as being acceptable.

Standards are the predominant tool for implementing effective security governance, and they must be owned by the information security manager. They must be carefully crafted to provide only necessary and meaningful boundaries without unnecessarily restricting procedural options. Standards serve to interpret policies and must reflect the intent of policy. Standards must be unambiguous, consistent and precise as to scope and audience. Standards must exist for the creation of additional standards and policies regarding format, content and required approvals.

Standards must be disseminated both to those governed by them and to those impacted. Review and modification processes must be developed as well.

Exception processes must be developed for standards not readily attainable for technological or other reasons. A process for implementing mitigating controls must be developed for out-of-compliance situations.

3.5.3 Procedures

Procedures are the responsibility of operations, including security operations, but they are included here for clarity. Procedures must be unambiguous and include all necessary steps to accomplish specific tasks. They must define expected outcomes, displays and required conditions precedent to execution. Procedures must also contain the steps required when unexpected results occur.

Procedures must be clear and unambiguous, and terms must be exact. For example, the words "must" and "shall" are used for any task that is mandatory. The word "should" must be used to mean a preferred action that is not mandatory. The terms "may" or "can" must be used only to denote a purely discretionary action. Discretionary tasks should appear in procedures only if necessary, since they dilute the procedures' messages.

Procedures for passwords include the detailed steps required for setting up password accounts and for changing or resetting passwords.

3.5.4 Guidelines

Guidelines for executing procedures are the responsibility of operations. Guidelines should contain information that will be helpful in executing procedures, such as clarification of policies and standards, dependencies, suggestions and examples, narratives clarifying the procedures, background information that may be useful, and tools that can be used. Guidelines can be useful in many other circumstances as well, but they are considered here in the context of information security governance.

Policies, procedures, standards and guidelines should cross-reference each other, so they can be easily understood, referenced when needed and maintained. It is always advisable to have an intranet or some other means to store them so the appropriate audience can access them when necessary.

3.6 Defining an Information Security Program Road Map

The key goals of strategic alignment, risk management, value delivery, resource management, assurance process integration and performance measurement are universal and are defined to some extent in the development of a security strategy. The process of program development requires that each of the six key goals is considered in detail and clarified in light of the evolving road map. As specific project plans for various parts of the road map develop, approaches to best achieve each key goal should become apparent.

These may be concepts that are not well understood by management and other stakeholders, which could lead to unrealistic expectations and poor outcomes. To maximize the chances for success, it may be most effective to develop a road map for the information security program in stages, starting with relatively simple objectives designed to demonstrate the value of the program and provide feedback on achievement of the key goals.

For example, the first stage might be to create the subcomponent of the program that is necessary to demonstrate the extent of strategic alignment and suggest approaches to improvements. To get started, an information security manager can interview stakeholders—such as department heads in HR, legal, finance and major business units—to determine important organizational issues and concerns. Information taken from such interviews will point to candidates for information security steering committee members. In stage 2, that forum can be used to draft basic security policies for the implementation of an information security program for approval by upper management. Because members of the information security steering committee, by definition, represent business interests, the forum can be used to list specific business goals for security with reference to business processes (and, thus, also to systems, as depicted in **figure 3.11**). In stage 3, members of the information security steering committee hold functional roles that can promote awareness of the policy and conduct internal security reviews to see if they are in compliance. In stage 4, the compliance gaps identified in the security reviews can be used to effect change, and an approach to monitor the organizational policy compliance strategy can be simultaneously developed. From that foundation, the information security manager can begin the work of building consensus around roles and responsibilities, processes, and procedures in support of the policy.

Figure 3.11—Information Security Management System Controls Process

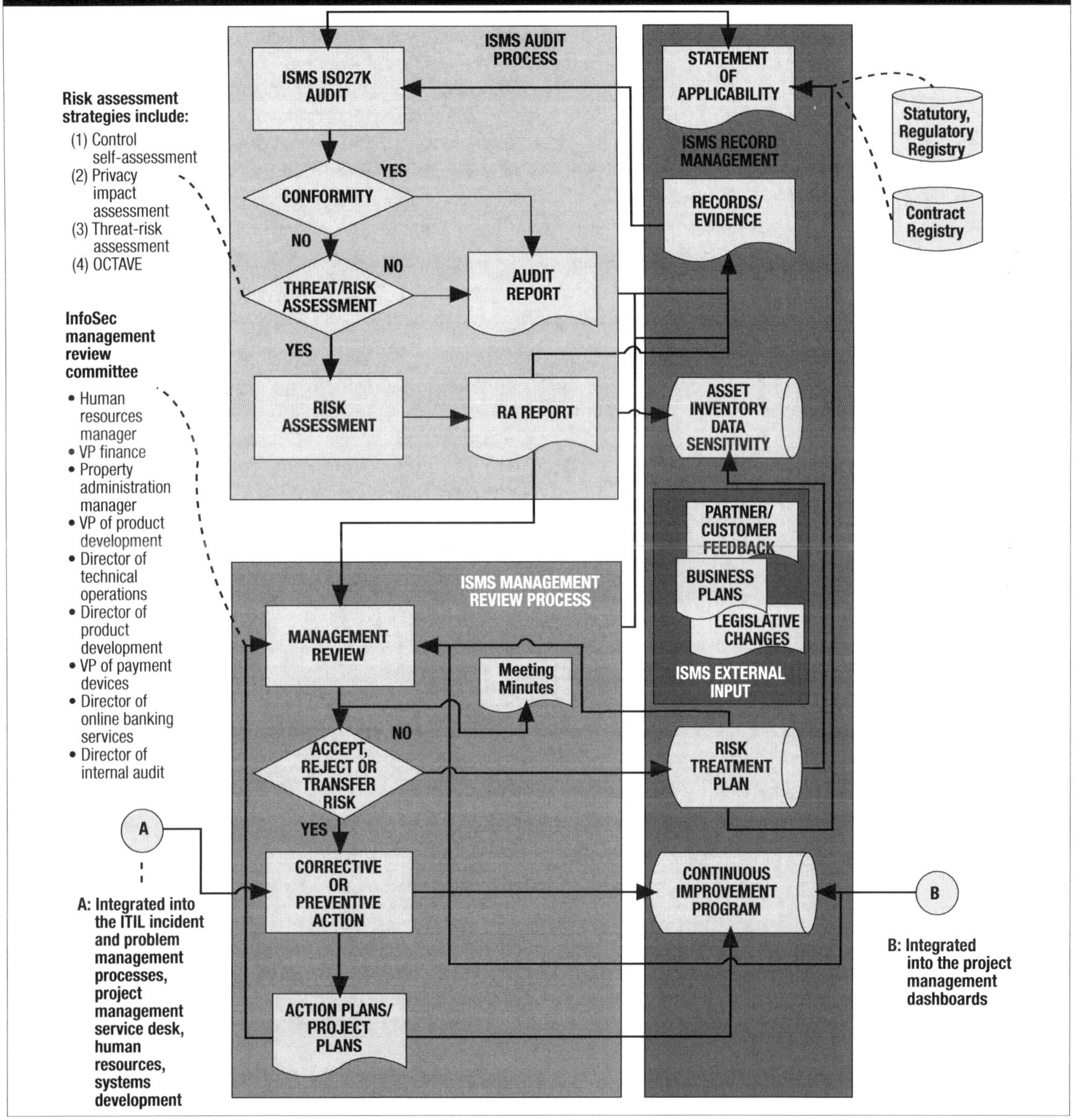

3.6.1 Applying Frameworks and Architectures to Create a Program Road Map

Architecture also acts as a road map for a collection of smaller projects and services that must be integrated into a single homogeneous whole. It provides a framework within which many members of large design, delivery and support teams can work harmoniously and toward which tactical projects can be migrated.

Simplicity and Clarity Through Layering and Modularization

In the same way that conventional architecture defines the rules and standards for the design and construction of buildings, information systems architecture addresses issues for the design and construction of computers, communications networks and the distributed business systems that are required for the delivery of business services. Information systems architecture must, therefore, take account of:

- The goals that are to be achieved through the systems
- The environment in which the systems will be built and used
- The technical capabilities of the people to construct and operate the systems and their component subsystems

Business Focus Beyond the Technical Domain

Information systems architecture is concerned with much more than technical factors. It is concerned with what the enterprise wants to achieve and with the environmental factors that will influence those achievements. The word enterprise implies not just a large organization, but one in which all the parts exhibit a joined-up quality and which, at the highest level, is viewed as a single entity with an integrated mission and purpose.

In some enterprises, this broad view of information systems architecture is not well understood. Technical factors are often the main influences on the architecture, which can result in failure of the architecture to deliver what the business expects and needs.

Architecture and Control Objectives

When considering security control objectives, a systems architect can use combinations of technologies to provide control points in a system's infrastructure. Combined with control activities and associated procedures, these control points may be used to ensure that policy compliance is preserved as new systems that use the infrastructure are deployed. For example, if a network is structured so there is only one connection to the Internet, then all network traffic destined for the Internet must travel through that connection. This would allow technology to be deployed in one place where all documents destined for the Internet could be inspected to ensure authorization to send the information contained in the document to an external entity. Often, no technology will be specified by the architecture, leaving a wide range of design choices for control points for inspection of documents being sent to the Internet.

Architecture Implementation

Some enterprises have enough experience with combinations of technologies used for a specific purpose that they elevate architectural decisions to the policy level. That is, choices of combinations of technology used for a given purpose are mandated by policy, because certain combinations allow easy implementation of security features that accomplish specific control objectives. Often, architectural policies are warranted if potential damage from data exposure warrants redundant controls. Some examples of architecture policy domains are:

- Database management systems (to restrict application access)
- Telecommunications (to mitigate threats of phone fraud)
- Web application access

For example, web applications are often protected from unauthorized access via user IDs and passwords. Yet inherent vulnerabilities in communicating on publicly available networks have prompted security architects to require the use of transport layer security (TLS) on web servers that host applications that exchange sensitive information with clients.

This configuration is often mandated by policy to ensure that traffic between client and server is encrypted to prevent the user ID and password, and the subsequent data flow, from being observed on the public network. However, such a policy does not provide any assurance that the client has not been compromised or the user password has not been stolen. Mitigation of this impersonation threat requires a technology control in addition to passwords and basic TLS encryption.

There are multiple alternatives that an application may employ to achieve the level of client identification necessary to mitigate the risk of impersonation. In financial applications such as online banking, regulators require that banks use some form of multifactor authentication to provide additional assurance of the identity of the individual initiating the client request. Applying this requirement uniformly on all applications (making it part of the enterprise's security architecture) allows the enterprise to mitigate the impersonation threat in a uniform, efficient and supportable manner. A number of approaches to architecture for components of information systems exist (e.g., architectures for data and databases, servers, technical infrastructures, identity management). However, few enterprises have developed an overall comprehensive enterprise security architecture, structured its management, and defined its relationship to business objectives. This is somewhat analogous to a situation in which separate, unintegrated designs for aircraft wings, engines, navigational equipment, passenger seats, etc., exist, but there are no designs for the complete aircraft showing how the various components fit together. The result would be unlikely to function well, if at all, and the outcome would be untrustworthy. Admittedly, information systems are designed to operate in a far more loosely coupled fashion, but the point is, nevertheless, relevant.

A number of architectural frameworks have been developed during the past decade to address this issue, and they offer useful insight and approaches to dealing with many current design, management, implementation and monitoring issues. Some specific approaches are listed in Section 3.4.1 Enterprise Information Security Architectures.

The framework approaches offer a great deal of flexibility in using a variety of standards and methods such as COBIT, ITIL and ISO/IEC 27001. It is true that many of the approaches may be more sophisticated and complex than many enterprises are prepared to take. However, the growing reliance on increasingly complex systems, coupled with the escalating problems of manageability and security, eventually will leave enterprises with little choice but to get organized.

For the information security manager, the approach may be helpful in developing long-term objectives or suggesting approaches to address current issues. Some enterprises have adopted elements of the architectural approach piecemeal, with the long-term objective of full implementation over time.

Security Program Management and Administrative Activities

Information security program management includes directing, overseeing and monitoring activities related to information security in support of organizational objectives. Management is the process of achieving the objectives of the business organization by bringing together human, physical and financial resources in an optimum combination with process and technology and making the best decision for the enterprise while taking into consideration its operating environment.

In the typical enterprise, information security program management includes short- and long-range planning and day-to-day administration in addition to directing various projects and initiatives. It also includes a variety of risk management activities and incident management and response functions and a variety of oversight and monitoring functions. Program management typically includes aspects of governance—whether in terms of policy and standards development or procedural controls and general rules of use for end users. As with other aspects of information security, governance cannot remain static in a changing risk environment and must evolve to be effective.

The information security manager has the responsibility for managing information security program activities to achieve the outcomes listed in Section 3.1.2 Outcomes of Information Security Program Management. It is the responsibility of senior management to support those objectives and provide adequate resources and authority to ensure that they are achieved. In addition, the roles and responsibilities of other assurance providers must be clearly defined to prevent gaps in protection.

As the scope of the information security manager's responsibilities continues to expand, there is the risk that important security elements may be overlooked or neglected. It may be useful for the information security manager to consider the following checklist of components of a comprehensive, well-managed security program:

- A security strategy intrinsically linked with business objectives that has senior management acceptance and support
- Security policy and supporting standards that are complete and consistent with strategy
- Complete and accurate security procedures for all important operations
- Clear assignment of roles and responsibilities
- Established method to ensure continued alignment with business goals and objectives, such as a security steering committee
- Information assets identified and classified by criticality and sensitivity
- Security architecture complete and consistent with strategy and in line with business objectives
- Effective controls that are well-designed, implemented and maintained
- Effective monitoring processes in place
- Tested and functional incident and emergency response capabilities
- Tested business continuity/disaster recovery plans
- Appropriate information security involvement in change management, SDLC and project management processes
- Established processes to ensure that risk is properly identified, evaluated, communicated and managed
- Established security awareness training for all users
- Established activities that create and sustain a corporate culture that values information security
- Established processes to maintain awareness of current and emerging regulatory and legal issues
- Effective integration with procurement and third-party management processes
- Resolution of noncompliance issues and other variances in a timely manner
- Processes to ensure ongoing interaction with business process owners
- Business-supported processes for risk and business impact assessments, development of risk mitigation strategies and enforcement of policy and regulatory compliance
- Established operational, tactical and strategic metrics that monitor utilization and effectiveness of security resources
- Established methods for information capture and dissemination
- Effective communication and integration with other organizational assurance providers

Note: This list is not comprehensive, nor will it fit all enterprises. It is simply meant to demonstrate the range of activities and established practices that would constitute a mature security program. This list must be tailored for the size and nature of each enterprise.

Program Administration

Administration of a security program typically involves a series of repetitive functions similar to those required in other organizational units. There will be differences in administration of program development projects and the ongoing administration of the operations aspects of the program, which need to be considered.

Ongoing administration might include such tasks as:

- Personnel performance, time tracking and other record keeping
- Resource utilization
- Purchasing and acquisition
- Inventory management
- Project monitoring and tracking
- Awareness program development
- Budgeting, financial management and asset control
- Business case development and financial analysis
- HR administration and personnel management
- Project and program management
- Operations and service delivery management
- Implementation and administration of metrics and reporting
- IT development life cycle management

There may be a number of technical administrative and operational requirements as well. These include:

- Cryptographic key management
- Log reviews and monitoring
- Change request review and oversight
- Configuration, patch and other life cycle management reviews and oversight
- Vulnerability scanning

- Threat monitoring
- Compliance monitoring
- Penetration testing

An effective information security manager should be familiar with existing frameworks and major international standards for IT and security management (e.g., COBIT, ISO/IEC 27001 and 27002) and be able to extract relevant elements to use for the management approach best suited to the enterprise. Some may prove to be a better fit than others, depending on organizational structure, culture, available resources, business sector, etc.

The information security manager has many responsibilities, and one may be as a facilitator to help resolve competing objectives between security and performance. As an active facilitator, the information security manager gains senior management support and organizational acceptance and is likely to achieve greater compliance with information security program policies, standards and procedures. Through a facilitative approach, the information security manager can work with the different departments to discuss information security risk and suggest solutions that address both security requirements and ways to minimize the impact on business activities. The information security manager also needs to ensure that the enterprise's life cycle processes incorporate information security. By working in a consultative role, the information security manager can facilitate the enterprise's information security program while staying informed about activities that may impact information security.

3.6.2 Developing an Information Security Program Road Map

A road map to implement the information security strategy must consider several factors. If a well-developed strategy exists, then a high-level road map to achieve the strategy objectives should also exist. Objectives, resources and constraints will have been defined. The remaining work will be to transform the conceptual or logical architecture or design into a physical one. Construction of specific projects and initiatives must be planned, along with budgets, timetables, personnel and other tactical project management aspects that will result collectively in achieving the strategy objectives. It is similar to the differences between the architecture of a house and the tasks required to build the house.

However, if a strategy is not developed and risk management objectives are not defined, there is a risk that the diverse elements that must be developed for the information security program will not be integrated or prioritized. In addition, there will be a lack of useful metrics and, over time, the results likely will be less than optimal.

Much of an information security program development effort will involve designing controls that meet control objectives, and then developing projects to implement, deploy and test the controls. One factor to consider is the ability of the enterprise to absorb new security activities to address control weaknesses and meet new objectives. Consideration must be given to the extent that these activities are disruptive to other organizational activities. See Section 3.12 Controls and Countermeasures.

An important skill to have in developing an information security program road map is the ability to thoroughly review the security level of existing data, applications, systems, facilities and processes, which will provide insight into the specific projects required to meet strategic objectives.

An implementation road map can essentially be a high-level project plan (or set of project plans) or an architectural design that can serve the same purpose. Either can serve to define the steps necessary to achieve a particular objective of the program. The purpose is to have an overall view of the steps required and their sequence. In more complex projects, it can be a benefit to have both. A road map should include various milestones that will provide KGIs, indicate KPIs and define critical success factors (CSFs).

Gap Analysis as the Basis for an Action Plan

Once the organizational roles and responsibilities seem appropriately established and inventory is taken of the required versus existing technology and processes, an information security manager can identify where control objectives are not adequately supported by controls. The information security manager should work with the appropriate personnel to identify control points and assist in developing processes to monitor them. Those executing new processes and procedures should concentrate on KGIs and KPIs, frequently validating that control objectives are being met and that progress toward control objectives aligns with information security program goals. It is more important that the procedure for monitoring achievement of control objectives is established than it is that all processes are right on the first pass. It is this monitoring that, if effective, will provide a basis for the security program to evolve and mature.

3.6.3 Life Cycle Principles Supporting the Road Map

Because operating an information security program, including risk management activities, is a continuous process, the information security manager should view the program as having a life cycle. This life cycle includes assessment, treatment and monitoring phases, as illustrated in **figure 3.12**. Employing a life cycle-based approach integrated with change management contributes to resource optimization, enabling program and risk management process updates to be performed incrementally.

Figure 3.12—Characteristics of the SDLC Phases

SDLC Phase	Phase Characteristics	Support From Risk Management
Phase 1—Initiation	The need for an IT system is expressed and the purpose and scope of the IT system are documented.	Identified risk is used to support the development of the system requirements, including security requirements and a security concept of operations (strategy).
Phase 2—Development or Acquisition	The IT system is designed, purchased, programmed, developed or otherwise constructed.	Risk identified during this phase can be used to support the security analyses of the IT system that may lead to architecture and design trade-offs during system development.
Phase 3—Implementation	The system security features should be configured, enabled, tested and verified.	The risk management process supports implementation against its requirements and within its modeled operational environment. Decisions regarding risk identified must be made prior to system operation.
Phase 4—Operation or Maintenance	The system performs its functions. Typically, the system will undergo periodic updates or changes to hardware and software; the system may also be altered in less obvious ways due to changes to organizational processes, policies and procedures.	Risk management activities are performed for periodic system reauthorization (or reaccreditation or whenever major changes are made to an IT system in its operational production environment (e.g., new systems interfaces).
Phase 5—Disposal	This phase may involve the disposition of information, hardware and software. Activities may include moving, archiving, discarding or destroying information, and sanitizing the hardware and software.	Risk management activities are performed for system components that will be retired or replaced to ensure that the hardware and software are properly disposed of, that residual data are appropriately handled, and that system migration is conducted in a secure and systematic manner.

3.7 Information Security Program Metrics

A metric is defined as a quantifiable entity that allows measurement of the achievement of a process goal. Security is the protection from or absence of harm. Therefore, security metrics should tell us about the state or degree of safety relative to a reference point. It may be useful to clarify the distinction between managing the technical IT security infrastructure at the operational level and the overall management of an information security program.

Technical metrics are useful for the tactical operational management of technical security systems (i.e., IDSs, proxy servers, firewalls, etc.). They can indicate that the infrastructure is operating soundly and technical vulnerabilities are identified and addressed. However, these metrics are of little value from a strategic management or governance standpoint. Technical metrics say nothing about strategic alignment with organizational objectives or how well risk is being managed. They provide few measures of policy compliance or whether objectives for acceptable levels of potential impact are being reached, and they provide no information on whether the information security program is headed in the right direction and achieving the desired outcomes.

From a management perspective, technical metrics cannot provide answers to questions such as:

- How secure is the enterprise?
- How much security is enough?
- How do we know when we have achieved an adequate level of security?
- What are the most cost-effective security solutions?
- How do we determine the degree of risk?
- How well can risk be predicted?
- Is the security program achieving its objectives?
- What impact is lack of security having on productivity?
- What impact would a catastrophic security breach have?
- What impact will security solutions have on productivity?

Attempts to provide meaningful answers to these questions can ultimately be addressed only by developing relevant measures—metrics that specifically address the requirements of management to make appropriate decisions about the enterprise's safety.

Full audits and comprehensive risk assessments are typically the only activities enterprises undertake that provide this breadth of perspective. While important and necessary from a security management point of view, they provide only history or a snapshot—not what is ideally needed to guide day-to-day security management and supply the information needed to make prudent decisions.

3.7.1 Effective Security Metrics

It is difficult or impossible to manage any activity that cannot be measured. The fundamental purpose of metrics, measures and monitoring is decision support. For metrics to be useful, the information they provide must be relevant to the roles and responsibilities of the recipient so that informed decisions can be made. Anything that results in a change can be measured. The key to effective metrics is to use a set of criteria to determine which of the nearly infinite number of metrics candidates are the most suitable. Good metrics are SMART:

- Specific—Based on a clearly understood goal; clear and concise
- Measurable—Able to be measured; quantifiable (objective), not subjective
- Attainable—Realistic; based on important goals and values
- Relevant—Directly related to a specific activity or goal
- Timely—Grounded in a specific time frame

Additional considerations include[19]:

- Accurate—A reasonable degree of accuracy is generally adequate.
- Cost-effective—The measurements cannot be too expensive to acquire or maintain.
- Repeatable—The measure must be reliably available over time.
- Predictive—Measurements should be indicative of outcomes.
- Actionable—It should be clear to the recipient what action must be taken.

Standard security metrics include things such as downtime due to malware, number of system penetrated in an assessment, application system recovery time results, number of vulnerabilities uncovered with network scans, and percentage of servers patched. While these measures can be indicative of aspects of security and perhaps are useful to IT operations, none provide any actual information about how secure the enterprise is and probably will not satisfy the aforementioned criteria.

There is an increasing understanding that the lack of useful metrics is an area of information security that has hindered effective management. This has led to development of a variety of approaches to address this issue during the past few years. Some major efforts include:

- **ISO/IEC 27004:2009 Information technology—Security techniques—Information security**

[19] Brotby, W.; *Information Security Management Metrics*, Auerbach Publications, USA, 2009

management—Measurement—This standard is a part of the growing ISO/IEC 27XXX series of security standards that includes ISO/IEC 27001:2013 Information security management and ISO/IEC 27002:2013 Information technology—Security techniques—Code of practice for information security controls. ISO/IEC 27004 "provides guidance on the development and use of measures and measurement in order to assess the effectiveness of an implemented information security management system and controls or groups of controls as specified in ISO/IEC 27001."[20] This standard has not seen wide acceptance and suffers a number of deficiencies. As a result, it is currently being rewritten to address many of the issues raised by the information security community.

- **COBIT**—COBIT offers several sample metrics for each of 13 suggested enterprise goals, 13 alignment goals, and associated processes. In particular, *COBIT Focus Area: Information Security* provides example information security metrics for many governance and management processes. However, there is currently a lack of guidance on actual development and implementation in terms of relevant and achievable metrics.
- **The Center for Internet Security (CIS)**—*The CIS Security Metrics* offers a comprehensive approach to developing and implementing information security metrics. It is based on the consensus of 150 industry professionals regarding relevant metrics and the approach to implementation and includes 28 metrics definitions with a number of possible metrics for seven major business functions.
- ***NIST Special Publication 800-55 Revision 1: Performance Measurement Guide for Information Security***—This document is aligned with the security controls provided in NIST SP 800-53 to assist with the assessment of information security program implementation. It offers a comprehensive approach to selection, development and implementation of a metrics approach primarily aimed at supporting the Federal Information Security Modernization Act (FISMA), which is a high-level policy document for US federal agencies and has value for the commercial environment.

Operational risk and security are not readily measured in any absolute sense; rather, probabilities, exposures, attributes, effects and consequences are normally the gauge. Various approaches that may be useful include value at risk (VAR), return on security investment (ROSI) and ALE. VAR is used to compute maximum probable loss in a defined period (day, week, year) with a confidence level of typically 95 percent or 99 percent. ROSI is used to calculate the return on investment based on the reduction in losses resulting from a security control compared to the cost of the control. ALE provides the likely annualized loss based on probable frequency and magnitude of security compromise. These often speculative numbers can then be used as a basis for allocating or justifying resources for security activities.

Some enterprises attempt to determine the maximum impacts of potential adverse events as a measure of security. Measuring security by consequences and impacts is similar to gauging how tall a tree is by how loud a noise it makes when it falls. In other words, adverse events would have to occur to determine if security is working. An absence of adverse events does not confirm a state of security. It may mean that defenses worked, that no one attacked or that a vulnerability was not discovered. Simulated attacks with penetration testing can provide some measure of the effectiveness of defenses against specific attacks. However, unless a statistically relevant percentage of all possible attacks is attempted, no prediction can be made about the state of security and the enterprise's ability to resist attack.

It may be that all that can be stated with certainty about security is that:

1. Some enterprises are attacked more frequently and/or suffer greater losses than others.
2. There is a strong correlation between good security management and practices and relatively fewer incidents and losses.

Good management and good governance are inextricably linked. Measuring effective information security governance and management with any precision may be more difficult than measuring security. Metrics will, in most respects, be based on attributes, costs and subsequent outcomes of the security program. **Figure 3.13** presents components of an information security governance program and demonstrates that the actual course of governance and the ability to measure and report performance are required.

[20] International Organization for Standardization, *ISO/IEC 207004:2009 Information technology—Security techniques—Information security management—Measurement,* Switzerland, 2009

Figure 3.13—Components of Security Metrics

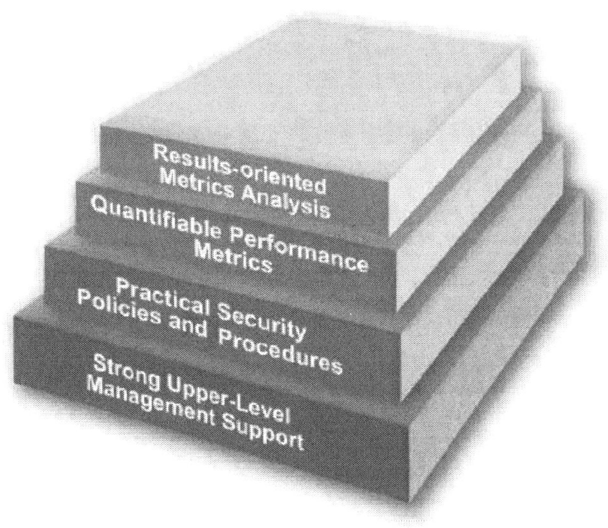

Source: National Institute of Standards and Technology (NIST); *NIST Special Publication 800-55 Revision 1: Performance Measurement Guide for Information Security,* USA, 2008. Reprinted courtesy of the NIST, US Department of Commerce. Not copyrightable in the United States of America.

Because security governance is difficult to measure by a set of objective metrics, there is a tendency to use metrics that are available, regardless of demonstrated relevancy. A typical example is the use of vulnerability scans as an indication of overall security. Arguably, if it were possible to eliminate all or most vulnerabilities (which is not possible), most risk could be avoided. The fallacy is the assumption that something can be determined about risk, threat or impact by measuring just technical vulnerabilities without considering viable threats, exposure and possible impacts.

While there is no universal objective scale for security or security governance, effective metrics can be designed to guide program development and management if there are clear information security objectives. Essentially, metrics can be reduced to any measure of the results of the information security program progressing toward the defined objectives, which serve as the reference points. Different metrics are required to provide information at the strategic, tactical and operational levels. Strategic metrics will be oriented toward high-level outcomes and business objectives for the information security program.

Governance Implementation Metrics

Implementing an information security governance strategy and framework can require a significant effort. It is important that relevant metrics are in place during the implementation of an information security program. Performance of the overall security program will be too far downstream to provide timely information on implementation and another approach must be used. KGIs and KPIs can be useful to provide information about the achievement of process or service goals and can determine whether organizational milestones and objectives are being met. Because implementation of various aspects of governance will typically involve projects or initiatives, standard project measurement approaches can serve metrics requirements (e.g., achieving specific milestones or objectives, budget and timeline conformance).

Strategic Alignment Metrics

Strategic alignment of information security in support of organizational objectives is essential to the ultimate success of the information security program in providing value to the enterprise. It should be clear that the cost-effectiveness of the security program is inevitably tied to how well it supports the objectives of the enterprise and at what cost. Without organizational objectives as a reference point, any other gauge, including good practices, may be overkill, or may be inadequate or misdirected. From a business perspective, adequate and sufficient practices proportionate to the requirements are likely to be more cost-effective than best practices. They are also likely to be received better by cost-conscious management.

The best overall indicator that security activities are in alignment with business (or organizational) objectives is the development of a security strategy that defines security objectives in business terms and ensures that the objectives are directly articulated from planning to implementation of policies, standards, procedures, processes and technology. The litmus test is to be able to track the reverse order evaluation of a specific control to a specific business requirement. Any control that cannot be tracked directly back to a specific business requirement is suspect and should be analyzed for relevancy and possible elimination.

Indicators of alignment include:

- The extent to which the security program demonstrably enables specific business activities
- Business activities that have not been undertaken or have been delayed because of inadequate capability to manage risk
- A security enterprise that is responsive to defined business requirements based on business owner input
- Organizational and security objectives that are defined and clearly understood by all involved in security, and related assurance activities measured by awareness testing
- The percentage of security program activities mapped to organizational objectives and validated by senior management
- A security steering committee consisting of key executives with a charter to ensure ongoing alignment of security activities and business strategy

Risk Management Metrics

Risk management is the ultimate objective of all information security activities and organizational assurance efforts. While risk management effectiveness is not subject to direct measurement, some indicators correlate with a successful approach. A successful risk management program can be defined as one that efficiently, effectively and consistently meets expectations and attains defined objectives in maintaining risk at levels acceptable to management.

Once again, it is a requirement that expectations and objectives of risk management be defined. Otherwise, there is no basis for determining whether the program is succeeding or heading in the right direction and whether resource allocations are appropriate.

Indicators of appropriate risk management can include:

- Organizational risk appetite and tolerance defined in terms relevant to the enterprise
- The completeness of an overall security strategy and program for achieving acceptable levels of risk
- The number of defined mitigation objectives for identified significant risk
- Processes for management or reduction of adverse impacts
- Coverage of all business-critical systems by a systematic, continuous risk management processes
- Trends of periodic risk assessment indicating progress toward defined goals
- Trends in impacts
- Results from tested incident response and business continuity/disaster recovery plans
- The completeness of the asset inventory, valuation and assignment of ownership
- The percentage of BIAs of all critical or sensitive systems
- The extent of a complete and functioning asset classification process
- The ratio of security incidents from known risk compared to those from unidentified risk

The key goal of information security is to reduce adverse impacts on the enterprise to an acceptable level. Therefore, a key metric is the adverse impacts of information security incidents experienced by the enterprise and the extent to which they do or do not exceed criteria for acceptable risk and impact. An effective security program will show a trend in reduced incident frequency and impact. Quantitative measures include trend analyses of impacts over time in financial terms.

Value Delivery Metrics

Value delivery occurs when security investments are optimized in support of organizational objectives. Value delivery is a function of strategic alignment of security strategy and business objectives—in other words, when a business case can be convincingly made for all security activities. Optimal investment levels occur when strategic goals for security are achieved and an acceptable risk posture is attained at the lowest cost.

Key indicators (KGIs and KPIs) include:

- Security activities that are designed to achieve specific strategic objectives in a cost-effective manner
- The cost of security being proportional to the value of assets
- Security resources that are allocated by degree of assessed risk and potential impact
- Protection costs that are aggregated as a function of revenues or asset valuation

- Controls that are well-designed based on defined control objectives and that achieve those control objectives and are fully utilized
- An adequate and appropriate number of controls to achieve acceptable risk and impact levels
- Control cost-effectiveness that is determined by periodic testing
- Policies in place that require all controls to be periodically reevaluated for cost, compliance and effectiveness
- The use of controls. Controls that are rarely used are not likely to be cost-effective.
- The number of controls to achieve acceptable risk and impact levels. Fewer effective controls can be expected to be more cost-effective than a greater number of less-effective controls.
- The effectiveness of controls as determined by testing. Marginal controls are not likely to be cost-effective.

Resource Management Metrics

Information security resource management describes the processes to plan, allocate and control information security resources, including people, processes and technologies, for improving the efficiency and effectiveness of business solutions.

As with other organizational assets and resources, information security resources must be managed properly. Knowledge must be captured, disseminated and available when needed. Providing multiple solutions to the same problem is inefficient and indicates a lack of resource management. Controls and processes must be standardized, when possible, to reduce administrative and training costs. Problems and solutions must be well documented, referenced and available.

Indicators of effective resource management include:

- Infrequent problem solution rediscovery
- Effective knowledge capture and dissemination
- The extent to which security-related processes are standardized
- Clearly defined roles and responsibilities for information security functions
- Information security incorporated into every project plan
- The percentage of information assets and related threats adequately addressed by security activities
- The proper organizational location, level of authority and number of personnel for the information security function
- Resource utilization levels
- Staff productivity
- Cost per user for security services

Performance Measurement

Measuring, monitoring and reporting on information security processes are required to ensure that organizational objectives are achieved. Methods to monitor security-related events across the enterprise must be developed; it is critical to design metrics that provide an indication of the performance of the security machinery and, from a management perspective, information needed to make decisions to guide the security activities of the enterprise.

Indicators of effective performance measurement include:

- The time it takes to detect and report security-related incidents
- The number and frequency of subsequently discovered unreported incidents
- Benchmarking comparable enterprises for costs and effectiveness
- The ability to determine the effectiveness/efficiency of controls
- Clear indications that security objectives are being met
- Results of internal/external audits
- The absence of unexpected or undetected security events
- Knowledge of evolving and impending threats
- Effective means of determining organizational vulnerabilities
- Methods of tracking evolving risk
- Consistency of log review practices
- Results of business continuity planning/disaster recovery tests
- The extent to which key controls are monitored
- The percentage of metrics achieving defined criteria (metametrics)

3.7.2 Security Program Metrics and Monitoring

In the process of information security program management, several aspects of metrics must be considered. First, are the metrics necessary to track and guide program development itself at the project, management and strategic levels? Second, will the development of metrics be needed for ongoing management of the results of the program? Because one of the essential elements of controls selection is whether they can be effectively monitored and measured, it is critical to consider this aspect during program design and development. Key controls that cannot be monitored pose an unacceptable risk and should be avoided.

The security of an enterprise involves much more than specific technical controls like firewalls, passwords, intrusion detection and disaster recovery plans. It also includes processes that surround technical controls and people issues that make it a complex system involving many components.

For any complex system, applying basic system engineering concepts will improve the performance of the system. The concepts of design, planned implementation, scheduled maintenance and management can significantly increase the effectiveness and performance of a security program. One of the fundamental principles of systems engineering is the ability to measure and quantify. Measurement enables proper design, accurate implementation to specifications, and effective management activities including goal setting, tracking progress, benchmarking and prioritizing. In essence, measurement is a fundamental requirement for security program success.

An effective security program involves design and planning, implementation and ongoing management of the people, processes and technology that impact all aspects of security across an enterprise.

It may be useful to clarify the distinction between managing the technical IT security systems at the operational level and the overall management of an information security program. Technical metrics are useful for the purely tactical operational management of the technical security infrastructure (e.g., antivirus servers, intrusion detection devices, firewalls). They can indicate that the infrastructure is operated in a sound fashion and technical vulnerabilities are identified and addressed. However, these metrics are of less value from a strategic or overall security program management standpoint. That is, they say nothing about strategic alignment with organizational objectives or how well risk is being managed; they provide few measures of policy compliance or whether objectives for acceptable levels of potential impact are being reached. They also provide no information on information security program direction, velocity or objective proximity.

From a management perspective, despite improvements in technical metrics, they are often incapable of providing answers to business-related questions from key stakeholders. For this reason, the information security program requires both technical metrics (to track and report control effectiveness) and broader metrics to report on program effectiveness and resource optimization.

3.7.3 Metrics Tailored to Enterprise Needs

The information security governance process should produce a set of goals for the information security program—goals that are tailored to the enterprise. As discussed in Section 3.2.2 Information Security Program Concepts, these goals generate control objectives and corresponding planning activity designed to achieve the objectives, resulting in the desired outcomes. Information security program metrics that directly correspond to these control objectives are essential for managing the program.

It should be evident that it will not be possible to develop meaningful security management metrics without the foundation of governance to set goals and create points of reference. That is to say, measurements without a reference in the form of objectives or goals are not metrics and are not likely to be useful in program guidance.

Ultimately, metrics serve only one purpose: decision support. The enterprise measures to manage. It measures to provide the information upon which to base informed decisions relative to what it is trying to accomplish (i.e., the goals).

Several considerations are key to developing useful and relevant metrics in the course of program development. Because the purpose of metrics is decision support, it is essential to know what decisions are made at various levels of the enterprise and, consequently, what metrics information is needed to make those decisions correctly. That means roles and responsibilities have to be defined to know what information is required by whom. The primary parameters of metrics design can be summed up as:

- Who needs to know?
- What do they need to know?
- When do they need to know it?

Metrics need to provide information at one or more of the following three levels:

- Strategic
- Management
- Operational

Strategic

Strategic metrics are often a compilation of other management metrics designed to indicate that the security program is on track, on target and on budget to achieve the desired outcomes. At the strategic level, the information needed is essentially navigational (i.e., determining whether the security program is headed in the right direction to achieve the defined objectives leading to the desired outcomes). This information is needed by both the information security manager and senior management to provide appropriate oversight.

Management

Management (or tactical) metrics are those needed to manage the security program, such as the level of policy and standards compliance, incident management and response effectiveness, and manpower and resource utilization. At the security management level, information on compliance, emerging risk, resource utilization, alignment with business goals and other topics is needed to make the decisions required for effective management.

The information security manager also requires a summary of technical metrics to ensure that the machinery is operating properly in acceptable ranges, much as the driver of an automobile wants to know there is fuel in the tank and the oil pressure and water temperature are in an acceptable range. While these metrics will not ensure that the car is heading in the right direction or that it will arrive at its destination, they can indicate that the destination will not be reached.

Operational

Operational metrics are the more common technical and procedural metrics, such as open vulnerabilities and patch management status. Purely technical metrics are primarily useful for IT security managers and system administrators. These include the usual malware mitigation measures, firewall configuration data, syslog reviews and other operational matters.

There are a number of additional considerations for developing , including:

- **Manageable**—This attribute suggests that the data should be readily collected, condensed, sorted, stored, correlated, reviewed and understood.
- **Meaningful**—This attribute suggests that the data should be understandable to the recipient and relevant to the objectives and provide a basis for the decisions needed to manage.
- **Actionable**—Just as a compass makes it clear to a pilot which direction to head to stay on course, so should management metrics make it clear whether to turn left or right. Information that merely invites further investigation may just be clutter.
- **Unambiguous**—Information that is not clear is not likely to be useful.
- **Reliable**—It is essential to be able to rely on the various feedback mechanisms and on their consistency in providing the same result for the same conditions each time they are measured. For example, when the gas tank is actually empty, the gauge should indicate it every time it is measured. In addition, to be reliable, the metric must measure what you think it is measuring, not an unrelated event or spurious artifact.
- **Accurate**—Showing a heading of north when going south is worse than having no information at all. The degree of accuracy depends on how critical the measure is, and it varies considerably. Qualitative metrics may be approximations, but nevertheless may be adequate in many situations. Quantitative metrics need to be accurate to be of any use (e.g., if the gauge shows 10 gallons of fuel, but the actual amount is only five, the metric can be dangerous).
- **Timely**—To be useful, feedback must occur when needed. It is better to know that the barn door is open before the horse escapes.

- **Predictive**—To the extent possible, leading indicators are very valuable.
- **Genuine**—Metrics subject to manipulation are less reliable and may suffer from inaccuracy as well.

These attributes can be used as a measure of metrics themselves, serving to rank the metrics and determine which are most useful. Any metric that substantially fails to meet these criteria is suspect. In many cases, the metrics in use by most enterprises will not rate well on these criteria, but nevertheless may be the best available. Even well-rated metrics can fail. A prudent approach is to strive to create a system of metrics that cross-reference each other for the purpose of validation. This can be accomplished by measuring two separate aspects of the same thing and ensuring agreement between them. For example, if an engine consumes five gallons (~19 liters) of fuel each hour, a 10-gallon (~38 liters) tank should last two hours. After one hour, the fuel gauge should indicate that half the tank remains, assuming it was full at the start. In a similar manner, discrepancies between internal measures of compliance and the results of an audit must be investigated to determine which measure is faulty. If they both indicate a similar level of compliance, it serves to validate the measures.

A number of other descriptive attributes can be developed, but the ones listed previously in this section are the most significant. The question then becomes whether these attributes can be prioritized or whether any metrics or combinations of metrics that do not include most or all of the characteristics listed should be discarded.

Security management metrics must be implemented to determine the ongoing effectiveness of security to meet the defined objectives at the strategic, management and operational levels. The information required to make decisions about security will be different for each level, as will be the metrics to capture it.

Monitoring processes are required to ensure compliance with applicable laws and regulations to which the enterprise is subject. Monitoring of all relevant metrics is required to ensure they are operating and that the information they provide is properly distributed and handled.

In recent years, a number of industries have become subject to specific regulations to ensure the security and privacy of sensitive information, especially in financial and healthcare enterprises, and to reduce operational risk in national critical infrastructure enterprises. Compliance failure in these cases can have adverse legal implications, so adequate monitoring is a requirement.

To assess the effectiveness of an enterprise's security program, the information security manager must have a thorough understanding of how to monitor security programs and controls on an ongoing basis. Some monitoring is technical and quantitative in nature while other aspects are, by necessity, imprecise and qualitative. Technical metrics can be used to provide quantitative metrics for monitoring and can include elements such as the number or percentage of:

- Unremediated vulnerabilities
- Open or closed audit items
- User accounts in compliance with standards
- Perimeter penetrations
- Unresolved security variances

Qualitative metrics that should be monitored and used to determine trends can include such things as:

- CMMI levels at periodic intervals
- KGIs
- KPIs
- KRIs
- Business balanced scorecard
- Six Sigma quality indicators
- ISO 9001:2015 quality indicators
- PAM results (ISO 33020:2019)

Other relevant measures of significance can include the cost-effectiveness of controls and the extent of control failures.

Other monitoring activities relate to organizational compliance with security policies and procedures established by the enterprise as a security baseline. As information resources change over time, the security baseline and the resources must adapt to changing threats and new vulnerabilities. All stakeholders should be aware of these changes and an appropriate consensus reached.

Part B: Information Security Program Management

Many of the elements described in Part A establish a firm foundation for planning, implementing, operating and maintaining an effective information security program. Having gained an understanding of the objectives and expectations of the enterprise's senior leaders, and having established a business-based strategy for managing risk to the enterprise's security and privacy objectives, the information security manager is then prepared to build and maintain that comprehensive architecture. The program draws upon a cross-functional team to build, run, monitor and maintain a cost-effective and practical approach to protecting the enterprise's resources.

While many of the program techniques include technical components, the vast majority relate to managing risk to, through and from human beings. In the same way that the enterprise itself depends upon people for innovation, decision-making and skilled task execution, the information security program helps ensure that the human factor strengthens risk management activities. Effective support for the human factor, combined with effective and efficient technical and administrative processes, provides the basis for fulfilling the promises established in the information security manager's business case and program management plan.

3.8 Information Security Control Design and Selection

Controls are the means of managing risk. They are comprised of many of the elements described previously (including policies, procedures, guidelines, practices and organizational structures) and represent the primary components to consider when developing an information security program.

Controls are implemented to achieve particular objectives, and they work together to enable the stakeholder goals through the strategic program plan. Control objectives support the alignment between security and privacy goals and achievement. Control objectives are defined as a statement of the desired result or purpose to be achieved by implementing control procedures in a particular process. For example, a set of control objectives for access control might be designed to "provide reasonable assurance that logical access to programs, data, and computer resources is restricted to authorized and appropriate users, and such users are restricted to performing authorized and appropriate actions" and that "physical access to computer and other resources is restricted to authorized and appropriate personnel."[21] Aligning the control objectives with organizational objectives helps to support a cost-effective approach that balances IT Value with resource and risk optimization. The following sections describe mechanisms for evaluating, managing and monitoring risk to an acceptable level.

3.8.1 Managing Risk Through Controls

Controls can be physical, technical or administrative. The choice of controls must be based on a number of considerations including ensuring their effectiveness, their cost or potential restriction to business activities, and their optimal form of control.

IT Controls

Because information and technology have a key role in the operations of many enterprises, IT controls constitute most of the controls they require. While they include technical controls, many IT controls are technical and administrative controls.

Non-IT Controls

The information security manager must be aware that information security controls also must be developed for non-IT-related information processes, including secure marking, handling and storage requirements for physical information and considerations for handling and preventing social engineering. Environmental controls must be taken into account so that otherwise secure systems are not subject to simply being stolen, as has occurred in some well-publicized cases.

Layered Defenses

Layering defenses, or applying defense in depth, is an important concept in designing an effective information security strategy or architecture. The layers must be

[21] Association of International Certified Professional Accountants, "Information for management of a service organization in a SOC 1 engagement," 2019, https://us.aicpa.org/content/dam/aicpa/interestareas/frc/auditattest/downloadabledocuments/info-for-mgmt-of-serv-org-in-soc-engagement.pdf

designed so that the cause of failure of one layer does not cause failure of the next layer.

The number of layers needed will be a function of asset sensitivity and criticality, the reliability of the defenses and the degree of exposure. Excessive reliance on a single control is likely to create a false sense of confidence. For example, a company that depends solely on a firewall can still be subject to numerous attack methodologies. A further defense may be the creation through education and awareness of a human firewall, which can constitute a critical layer of defense. Segmenting the network can constitute another defensive layer.

Technologies

In the past few decades numerous security technologies have been developed to address the ever-growing threats to information resources. Technology is one of the cornerstones of an effective security strategy. The information security manager must be familiar with how technologies can serve as controls in achieving the desired state of security. Technology cannot compensate for management, cultural or operational deficiencies, however, and the information security manager is cautioned to not place excessive reliance on it. As **figure 3.14** demonstrates, to achieve effective defenses against security incidents, a combination of policies, standards and procedures must come together with technology.

Figure 3.14—Defense in Depth by Function

Defenses Against System Compromise	Policies, Standards, Procedures, Technology
Prevention	Authentication Authorization Awareness and training Data labeling/handling/retention Encryption Firewalls Intrusion prevention Management Personnel security Physical security
Containment	Authorization Data privacy Firewalls/security domains Network segmentation Physical security
Detection/notification	Auditing/logging Honeypots Intrusion detection Measurements/metrics Monitoring Virus detection
Reaction	Additional security mechanisms Incident response New/better controls Policy/procedure change

Figure 3.14—Defense in Depth by Function *(cont.)*

Defenses Against System Compromise	Policies, Standards, Procedures, Technology
Evidence collection/event tracking	Auditing/logging Forensics Management/monitoring Nonrepudiation
Recovery/restoration	Backups/restoration Business continuity/disaster recovery Failover/remote sites

Source: W. Krag Brotby

A number of technologies with security mechanisms can play a critical role in the success of an enterprise's security strategy. Given the ongoing and rapid development of technology in this area, the prudent information security manager will utilize available resources to stay current on the latest developments.

3.8.2 Controls and Countermeasures

In designing the information security program, planning must include both general and system-level controls to achieve control objectives. General, or common, controls are control activities that support the entire enterprise in a centralized fashion as part of the security infrastructure. Because infrastructure is often shared among different departments in the same enterprise, the term general controls is often used to describe all controls in the infrastructure. These include control activities in support of an operating system, network and facility security. These controls typically include centralized user administration policies, standards and procedures, and technical elements such as access controls, firewalls and IDSs. These general controls can then be inherited by subordinate system-level activities to achieve control objectives.

Where specific, decentralized business information processing is protected by technology, the controls that are specific to providing security to a system or application are often referred to as system-level controls. In most enterprises, general controls and system-level controls are managed by different groups (i.e., technical infrastructure is managed by IT while specific financial controls are managed by the finance department). Some enterprise IT systems may also be hosted in external environments (e.g., cloud-hosted infrastructure), so system-level controls may extend beyond the enterprise's physical boundaries.

The information security manager must ensure that security-related roles and responsibilities are identified for these and all other groups. The roles and responsibilities should be documented to ensure a collective understanding across the enterprise.

A major part of security management is the design, implementation, monitoring, testing and maintenance of controls. Controls are defined as the policies, procedures, practices, technologies and organizational structures designed to provide reasonable assurance that business objectives are achieved and undesirable events are prevented or detected and corrected.

Controls are essentially any process—whether physical, technical or procedural—necessary to achieve objectives. The choice of controls is based on a number of considerations, including effectiveness, cost, restrictions to business activities and optimal form.

Controls are one of the primary methods of managing information security risk and a major responsibility of information security management. Controls for physical elements, such as administrative processes and procedures, are just as critical as controls applied to technology. Many security failures can ultimately be attributed to failures of management, and management problems typically do not have technical solutions. Inevitably, people and physical processes at each end of technical processes constitute the greatest risk to information security. The information security manager must be careful not to place excessive focus and reliance on technology.

The information security manager must be aware that standards or procedures that are too restrictive or that prevent the enterprise from meeting its business objectives reduce the value of organizational IT and are likely to be circumvented. The objective is to balance the need for controls with the requirements of the business. Therefore, the information security manager must have a good business perspective, understand the risk to the enterprise's information resources, interpret the information security policies, and implement security controls that consider all aspects. The information security manager should use the approach that is least restrictive and disruptive to the business that nevertheless meets the criteria for acceptable risk at an acceptable cost. The optimal trade-off between the greatest security and least impact on business activities is the fine balance that the effective information security manager must strive to achieve.

Information security controls must be developed for both IT- and non-IT-related information processes, including secure marking, handling, transport and storage requirements for physical information and considerations for handling and preventing social engineering. Environmental controls must also be considered, so that otherwise secure systems are not subject to theft or to destruction by some physical hazard.

A number of standards and guides available for information security management should be familiar to the information security manager. Two of the most accepted references for information security are COBIT and ISO/IEC 27001 and 27002. Numerous other sources of guidance are available, such as various frameworks published by NIST and the *Standard of Good Practice for Information Security* published by the Information Security Forum.

3.8.3 Control Categories

To support creation of a defense-in-depth strategy, and to ensure comprehensive achievement of control objectives, controls should be implemented across several control categories, including:

- **Preventive**—Preventive controls inhibit attempts to violate security policy and include such controls as access control enforcement, encryption and authentication. Preventive controls directly address risk.
- **Detective**—Detective controls warn of violations or attempted violations of security policy and include such controls as audit trails, intrusion detection methods and checksums.
- **Corrective**—Corrective controls remediate impact. Backup and restore procedures are a corrective measure as they enable a system to be recovered if harm is so extensive that processing cannot continue without recourse to corrective measures.
- **Compensating**—Compensating controls are internal controls that reduce the risk of an existing or potential control weakness resulting in errors and omissions; for example, adding a challenge response component to weak access controls can compensate for the deficiency, and insurance can compensate for breach losses. Corrective and compensating controls address impact.
- **Deterrent**—Deterrent controls provide warnings that can deter potential compromise. Examples include warning banners on login screens or rewards offered for the arrest of hackers. Deterrent controls address threat.

Controls and their effects are shown in **figure 3.15**. Note that compensating and corrective controls are often combined because they both address impact.

Figure 3.15—Control Type and Effect

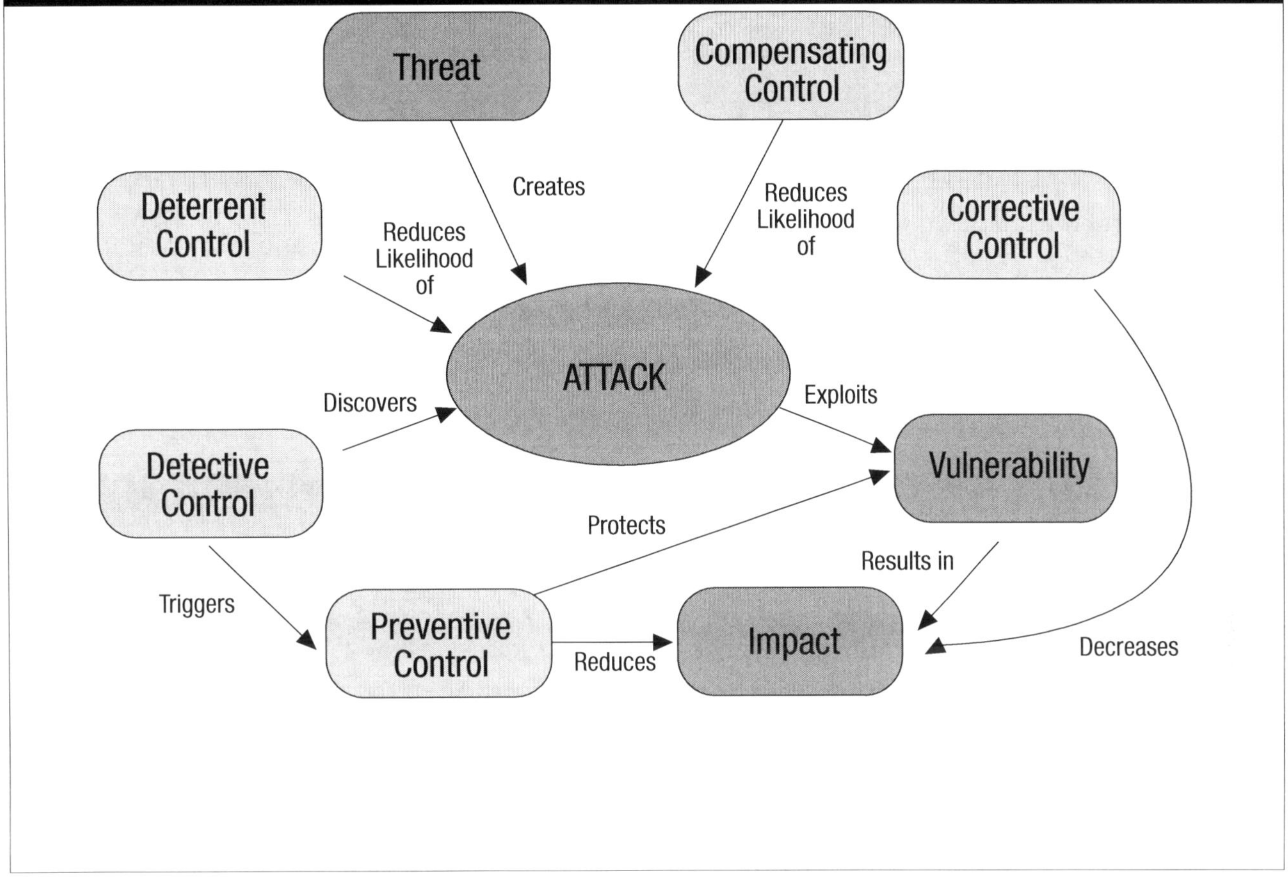

3.8.4 Control Design Considerations

To ensure comprehensive and practical design, controls and countermeasures are most efficient when based on a top-down, risk-based approach. This is because control objectives are essentially determined by management's defined acceptable risk levels. The acceptable risk levels are the objectives the controls must be designed to achieve. The control objectives are consequently both the design goal and the subsequent control metric for effectiveness (i.e., the primary control effectiveness metric is the extent to which the control meets the objectives).

Defining the control objectives is essential in program development and is pertinent to physical, administrative and technical controls.

Achieving control objectives requires combinations of several control types. For example, a technical control such as a firewall may require a physical protection control, a configuration procedural control and oversight via an administrative control.

As with other security activities, it is usually best to base selection of options on cost-effectiveness comparisons of those that are available, but this is only one among many criteria. Other selection elements that may need to be considered include:

- Impacts on productivity/inconvenience to users
- Acquisition and implementation costs
- Training costs
- Operational costs
- Maintenance and testing costs
- User acceptance
- Cultural and ethical acceptability
- Legal and regulatory requirements and restrictions
- Adaptability to changing risk
- Scalability
- Ability to monitor
- Ability to provide notification
- Robustness
- Resilience

- Reliability
- Ease of testing
- Self-testing capability
- Acceptable failure mode
- Tamper resistance

3.8.5 Control Methods

Security controls encompass the use of technical and nontechnical methods, including administrative, technical and physical controls (**figure 3.16**). Technical controls are safeguards that are incorporated into computer hardware, software or firmware (e.g., access control mechanisms, identification and authentication mechanisms, encryption methods, intrusion detection software). Nontechnical controls are management and operational controls such as security policies, standards, operational procedures and personnel, and physical and environmental security. For example, multifactor authentication can include technical and manual processes (e.g., smart cards with a technical security certificate supported by a human knowledge element in the form of a personal identification number). Adequate physical controls are an essential requirement for achieving acceptable overall risk levels.

Figure 3.16—Control Methods

Category	Description
Managerial (administrative)	Controls related to the oversight, reporting, procedures and operations of a process. These include policies, procedures, balancing, employee development and compliance reporting.
Technical	Controls (also known as logical controls) provided through the use of a technology, piece of equipment or device. Examples include firewalls, network or host-based intrusion detection systems (IDSs), passwords and antivirus software. A technical control requires proper managerial (administrative) controls to operate correctly.
Physical	Controls such as locks, fences, closed-circuit TV (CCTV) and devices that are installed to physically restrict access to a facility or hardware. Physical controls require maintenance, monitoring and the ability to assess and react to an alert should a problem arise.

Source: ISACA, *CISA Review Manual 27th Edition*, USA, 2019

Countermeasures

In addition to establishing the general safeguards that standard controls provide, the information security manager may occasionally require a control against a specific threat. Such a control is called a countermeasure. Countermeasures often provide specific protection, making them more effective, but less efficient, than broader, more general safeguards—although not necessarily less cost-effective, depending on the original and residual ALE associated with the threat being countered.

Countermeasures are controls put into place in response to a specific threat that is known to exist. They may be preventive, detective or corrective, or any combination of the three. They are not recognized in ISO/IEC 27001:2013 and can be considered a form of targeted control. Countermeasures can be nontechnical as well, such as offering a reward for information leading to the arrest of hackers.

Countermeasures deployed to narrowly address specific threats or vulnerabilities are often expensive, both operationally and financially, and can become a distraction from core security operations. Their deployment should commence only with clear justification and due caution and only when an existing or more general control cannot adequately mitigate the threat.

Countermeasures can be used just like any other control. Because they are implemented in response to a specific threat, they are applied as incremental enhancements to existing controls. For example, an enterprise that scans all email to block incoming viruses may encounter a threat to its email infrastructure due to an influx of spam. It may implement a countermeasure to the spam attacks by enhancing the virus scanner to block incoming mail from a list of known spammers.

An information security program must be flexible enough to implement a countermeasure with very little warning. Emergency changes may need to bypass standard change control processes, but they must be used with caution and be thoroughly documented. They must still pass through the change management process, even if it is after the fact. Countermeasures are commonly deployed in response to specific threats. A technical countermeasure might be a cellphone jammer to prevent phone usage in sensitive areas.

Physical and Environmental Controls

All efforts to protect information have as their foundation a strong physical barrier protecting the physical media on which the information resides. In many enterprises, physical security is a service provided as part of facilities management. The physical security organization may set requirements on a building-by-building basis and enforce those requirements using a combination of physical security technology measures and manual procedures. An information security manager should validate technology choices in support of physical security processes and must ensure that policies and standards are developed to ensure adequate physical security.

Physical and environmental controls are a specialized set of general controls on which all computing facilities and personnel depend. In addition, some technologies have features that allow physical mechanisms to override logical controls. For example, unauthorized physical access to technology devices may allow unauthorized access to information. Though the information security manager is often not responsible for physical access controls, it is important to assign roles and responsibilities with respect to these controls and to define an escalation path to ensure that requirements are met. It must be impossible for an unauthorized person to physically connect equipment to the network. In addition, equipment and removable media (including documents and discarded items) must be protected from theft.

Methods to keep unauthorized individuals from gaining access to tangible information resources include identification badges and authentication devices such as smart cards or access controls based on biometrics, security cameras, security guards, fences, lighting, locks and sensors. Many types of intrusion sensors are available, including vibration sensors, motion detectors and others.

Physical controls are intended to prevent or mitigate damage to facilities and other tangible resources that might be caused by natural or technological events. For example, backup power sources can sustain operations if a hurricane damages the power lines serving the facility or if the power grid fails. Environmental controls include air conditioning, water drainage, fire suppression and other measures designed to ensure that system storage facilities are designed to meet the physical requirements of computer system operation. Without adequate environmental controls to prevent, detect and recover from physical damage to information systems, other general and application control activities could be rendered ineffective or useless.

In a large and geographically dispersed enterprise, an IT operations manager may be assigned at each site to ensure that all equipment is inventoried and configured to policy-compliant standards. An information security manager may establish this role and responsibility as a resource to interface with local physical security organizations on behalf of the information security program.

Control Technology Categories

When determining the types of control technologies that must be considered by the information security manager, it may be useful to consider operational authority and the types of controls available. Because the majority of technical controls are the direct responsibility of the IT department, consideration must be given to how security will be maintained. Technologies typically fall into one of three different categories in terms of the type of controls that are available: native, supplemental or support control technologies. In some cases, operational authority may be split between IT and the security department.

Native Control Technologies

Native control technologies are out-of-the-box security features that are integrated with business information systems. For example, most web servers include functions providing authentication capabilities, access logging and Secure Sockets Layer (SSL) transport encryption. All these controls would be considered native to the web server technology.

Although the policies and standards governing their use are established by the information security function, most native control technologies are generally configured and operated by IT. This is because native controls often directly impact production operations. Further, providing information security staff with configuration rights to core production systems often violates the segregation of duties (SoD) principle and can create risk by complicating change control processes and system ownership issues.

Native technology controls exist on all information technology devices including:

- Servers
- Databases
- Routers
- Switches

Supplemental Control Technologies

Supplemental control technologies are usually components that are added to an information systems environment. They often provide some function that is not available from native components (e.g., network intrusion detection) or that is more appropriate to implement outside of primary business application systems for architectural or performance reasons (e.g., a single network firewall vs. individual host-based network filtering).

Supplemental control technologies tend to be more specialized than native control technologies and, therefore, they are often operated by security specialists. Even when technical security specialists are resources of the information security group, technical security operations can benefit by leveraging the support of information technology units. In some cases, it may be appropriate to share responsibility for a particular supplemental control technology, particularly if it is deeply embedded in both the security and business application domains. Federated identity and access management are common examples of supplemental technologies for which responsibilities are shared across the security and technology organizations. Typical supplemental control technologies include:

- Federated identity management systems
- Single sign-on
- IPSs
- Firewalls
- Zero trust networks
- Device trust systems

Management Support Technologies

Management support technologies serve to automate a security-related procedure, provide management information processing, or otherwise increase management efficiency or capabilities. A few examples include SIEM tools, security event analysis systems and compliance monitoring scanners. These technologies are primarily used by the security organization, and they do not directly impact the production environment. For these reasons, and to help enforce SoD, technologies that support security operations are commonly implemented and operated by the information security group in relative independence from the IT department.

Security-related procedures can frequently be automated to increase the information security program's efficiency or capabilities. The use of these supporting technologies to increase resource productivity is an important strategy in developing an efficient and effective program. Some of the most common supporting technologies include:

- Compliance monitoring and management tools
- Access management workflow systems
- Vulnerability scanning tools
- Security configuration monitoring tools
- Policy management and distribution systems
- SASE
- SIEM systems and security orchestration, automation and reporting (SOAR) platforms

Technical Control Components and Architecture

Information security management includes dealing with a wide range of technical components that have been previously categorized as native control technologies, supplementary control technologies and management support technologies.

Native control and support technologies collectively form the technical security architecture. This construct can be applied to individual business applications or to the enterprise as a whole, with the objective of revealing how the interaction of individual technical components provides for overall enterprise or application security. This holistic view of technical component capabilities prevents a point solution perspective that leads to poor overall security. Technical security architecture analysis should be coordinated closely with reviews and analysis of threat and risk factors. The information security manager must ensure that the components of the technical security architecture are aligned with the enterprise's risk and threat postures and its business requirements. Provided that the technical architecture is in alignment with the higher levels of architecture (i.e., logical, conceptual), alignment with business objectives should occur naturally.

When analyzing technical security architecture, the information security manager should use a clearly defined set of measurable criteria to enable tracking of performance metrics. A common approach to the development of metrics is to pose questions that need to be answered and then develop methods to provide answers. A few possible criteria for analyzing technical security architecture and components and developing suitable metrics and monitoring are:

- Control placement
  - Where are the controls located in the enterprise?
  - Are controls layered?
  - Is control redundancy needed?
  - Are controls on or near the perimeter efficient providers of broad access protection?
  - Are there uncontrolled access channels to processing services or data? (Consider physical, network, system-level, application and message access vectors.)
- Control effectiveness
  - Are controls reliable?
  - Are controls the minimum required?
  - Do controls inhibit productivity?
  - Are controls automated or manual?
  - Are key controls monitored? In real time?
  - Are control easily circumvented?
- Control efficiency
  - How broadly do the controls protect the environment?
  - Are controls specific to one resource or asset?
  - Can they and should they be more fully utilized?
  - Is any particular control a single point of application failure?
  - Is any particular control a single point of security failure?
  - Is there unnecessary redundancy in controls?
- Control policy
  - Do controls fail secure or fail open?
  - Do controls implement a restrictive policy (e.g., denial unless explicitly permitted) or a permissive policy (e.g., permission unless explicitly denied)?
  - Is the principle of least-needed functionality and access enforced?
  - Does the rationale for the control configuration align with policy, corporate expectations and other drivers?
- Control implementation
  - Is each control implemented in accordance with policies and standards?
  - Are controls self-protecting?
  - Will controls alert security personnel if they fail or detect an error condition?
  - Have controls been tested to verify that they implement the intended policy?
  - Are control activities logged, monitored and reviewed?
  - Do controls meet defined control objectives?
  - Are control objectives mapped to organizational goals?
- Control measurement
  - Who is responsible for measuring the control?
  - How should the control outcome be reported and to whom? At what frequency?
  - Will the control be tested by the control owner or some other team (e.g., compliance)?
  - What are the thresholds for reporting any error or normal condition?

Details of specific security technologies, technical control architecture and analysis of technical control requirements are an important component of information security program development and ongoing management and administration. The information security manager should be well versed in the technologies of the technical security architecture and have access to technical specialists who will be responsible for installing, configuring and maintaining them.

3.9 Information Security Control Implementation and Integration

Controls provide the core component of strategy implementation. Implementing a strategy largely consists of designing, developing, testing and implementing controls of various types in various combinations. Development of the strategy includes determining acceptable risk and risk tolerance, as discussed in Chapters 1 and 2. Acceptable risk levels are used to determine control objectives that set the main requirements for the controls. Controls are also subject to some or all of the criteria described in the previous section.

Effective information security requires controls that will affect all aspects of an enterprise, including people, technology and processes. Often, a combination of controls is required to achieve the control objectives. The options for controls are essentially unlimited, which adds to the challenge.

For example, access control is a preventive control that prevents unauthorized access that may result in harm to systems. Intrusion detection is a detective control because it enables the detection of unauthorized access. Backup and restoration procedures are a corrective control that enables a system to be recovered if harm is so extensive that data are lost or irreparably damaged, thereby resulting in impact. Compensating controls (e.g., insurance) are similar to corrective controls and compensate for an impact as the result of a compromise.

Security products often provide various combinations of different types of controls. A typical control is a firewall, which is a product that filters network traffic to limit what protocols (or ports) can be used to enter or exit an internal network, and what address or address range is allowed as a source and destination. This is a preventive control because it prevents access to specific network ports, protocols or destinations not specifically allowed. The same firewall may have more advanced features that allow it to examine inbound network traffic for malware and send alerts to an operations center if suspect traffic passes through the device. This is a detective control. The firewall may also have a feature that allows operations to divert incoming traffic to a backup site if, upon responding to the virus alert, it is found that a virus has reduced the capacity at the primary site. (However, this would typically be accomplished by making changes to the Internet router.) This is a recovery, or corrective, control because it allows the systems to resume normal operations. The proxy service that runs on the firewall may be capable of displaying a warning banner as a deterrent control against unauthorized access.

Note that the deterrent, preventive, detective or corrective (or compensatory) control features of the firewall are fully describable, technically, without using the word firewall. The point is that the information security manager must recognize the security value of technology product features independently of the label given to a product by the product vendor. It is the features and how they are used in achieving the control objectives and enabling control points to be established that are important, not the choice of product or its name.

Controls should be automated as much as possible so that it is technically infeasible to bypass them. (See the Countermeasures subsection.) Some common control practices that make it hard for users to bypass controls are mechanisms that embody these principles:

- **Access (logical) control**—Users of information should be identified, authenticated and authorized prior to accessing information. There are various ways to implement access control. Most access control models fall into one of two types: mandatory access control (MAC) or discretionary access control (DAC). MAC refers to a means of restricting access to data based on security requirements for information contained in the data and the corresponding security clearance of users. MAC is typically used for military applications where, for example, a secret clearance is required to access data classified as secret. There is generally also a second requirement of need-to-know for access authorization. DAC refers to means of restricting access to objects based on the identity of subjects or groups to which they belong. The controls are discretionary in the sense that rules may allow a subject with certain access permission to pass that permission on to another subject. The choice of appropriate access control mechanisms in a given situation depends on organizational requirements for data protection.
- **Secure failure**—A device design to shut down and stop processing information whenever a malfunction that may affect its access control mechanisms is detected. Secure failure as a control policy must be carefully considered because it affects availability. It may also pose a hazard when electrically controlled

physical access fails in a locked condition, preventing egress in the case of fire or other disaster.

- **Principle of least privilege**—A resource access design strategy that provides administrative capability to partition resource access so that those requiring fewer resources than others have the minimum system privileges they require to accomplish their responsibilities.
- **Compartmentalizing to minimize damage**—The capacity of system architecture to contain access to subsets of system resources by requiring a separate set of authorization controls per subset. For example, a system in which administrative privileges are not granted when they are requested on certain network interfaces can be combined with network port restrictions to lock Internet users out of administrative functions.
- **Segregation of duties (SoD)**—The ability of software to restrict a user from having two functions that are meant to provide supervisory or oversight features. For example, software should prevent a person who has the ability to print checks from being able to change the name of the check recipient before and after it is printed.
- **Transparency**—Providing the average layperson with the ability to understand how system security is supposed to work so that all stakeholders can easily see what effect their activities have on systems security. Users, administrators, engineers and architects should be able to converse about system controls in a way that verifies they are working as expected. Transparency is often achieved by keeping the technology design as simple as possible to avoid confusion as to system functionality.
- **Trust**—A design strategy that includes the existence of a security mechanism that determines a user's identity based on the user's relationship to an identity provider that is trusted by a relying party. The relying party has some mechanism for determining the authenticity of a connection from the identity provider and relies on that information to allow the identity provider to pass on the identity of the user. A typical application uses a trusted third party in PKI architecture, known as the certificate authority (CA), to attest to the identity of an entity by issuing a certificate.
- **Zero trust**—A scenario in which there is no implicit trust granted to assets or user accounts based solely on their physical or network location (i.e., local area networks versus the Internet) or based on asset ownership (enterprise or personally owned).[22] In light of recent industry trends involving remote users, mobile devices and cloud-based resources, the zero trust practice recognizes that it is no longer practical to implement controls simply based on perimeter boundaries or user associations.

Automation alone will not necessarily result in a cohesive and trustworthy solution. The information security manager may wish to apply a SOAR solution. SOAR generally refers to any security solution or group of preexisting tools that allows enterprises to streamline incident response, security operations, and threat and vulnerability management. Like SIEMs, SOAR ingests multiple sources of data and assists with ingesting external data sources such as threat intelligence feeds. SOAR is popular with security teams because they can orchestrate SOAR data sources (i.e., SIEM, EDR, antimalware) to automate incident response.

3.9.1 Baseline Controls

Defined baseline security controls should be a standing requirement for all new systems development. Baseline security requirements should be defined and documented, usually in standards, as an essential part of the system documentation. Adequate traceability of the security requirements should be ensured and supported across the different phases of the life cycle. A few examples include authentication functions, logging, role-based access control and data transmission confidentiality mechanisms. The information security manager must understand the enterprise's risk appetite and should refer to industry and regional sources to determine a baseline set of security functions appropriate to organizational policies and acceptable risk levels. Supplemental controls may be warranted based on vulnerability, threat and risk analysis, and these controls should be included in the requirements-gathering process.

The information security team may be consulted during the design and development phases to evaluate how well solution options fulfill acceptable risk requirements. Rarely is a perfect solution found, and there will always

[22] National Institute for Standards and Technology, Special Publication 800-207: "Zero Trust Architecture," August 2020, https://csrc.nist.gov/publications/detail/sp/800-207/final

be trade-offs among security requirements, performance, costs and other demands. It is important that the information security manager exercise diligence in identifying and communicating solution deficiencies and developing mitigating or compensating controls to achieve control objectives. The information security manager should also employ internal or external resources to review coding practices and security logic during development to ensure that the practices are adequate.

During the quality and acceptance phases, the information security manager should coordinate testing of originally established functional security requirements in addition to testing system interfaces for vulnerabilities. This testing should verify that the system's security mechanisms meet control objectives and provide the information security team with needed administrative and feedback functions. If functional security shortcomings, coding vulnerabilities or exploitable logic flaws are identified, the information security manager should work with the project team to prioritize and resolve issues. If issues cannot be repaired or mitigated prior to planned rollout, the senior management team should review security issues and associated risk to decide if the system should be deployed prior to resolution of identified vulnerabilities. If the system is to be deployed with unresolved security issues, the security manager should ensure that the issues are documented and that there is an agreed-on timetable to resolve issues. If there is no viable resolution available, the information security manager must track and periodically reassess the situation to be aware of a viable resolution as soon as one becomes available.

The information security manager should ensure that appropriate segregation of duties is considered throughout the SDLC. Testing and QA plans must be subject to review by the information security manager to ensure that the security elements are properly tested and certified. In some cases, for software developed for critical operations, it may be necessary to perform a code review in addition to the QA testing process to ensure there are no unexpected vulnerabilities. Code reviews are often outsourced to ensure independence.

3.10 Information Security Control Testing and Evaluation

After controls have been implemented, the next step is to evaluate the extent to which they achieve their intended purpose. As with other elements of the security strategy and program, the goal is not to ensure that the controls completely eliminate any risk, but rather to ensure that the layers of controls implemented achieve the agreed-upon acceptable level of risk.

Testing and evaluation of the various management, technical and physical controls will continue in an ongoing manner throughout the operation of the security program, including system-specific controls that will be continually assessed during the system life cycle. Because changes occur to risk objectives, threat landscape, and system operation, the evaluation process must continually evolve to ensure continued achievement of control objectives, including those related to cost-effectiveness and mission alignment. Testing and evaluation are implemented through the following methods.

3.10.1 Control Strength

Strength of controls can be measured by the type of control being evaluated (preventive, detective, manual, automated, etc.) and its quantitative and qualitative compliance testing results. Although an automated control is typically preferable to a manual control, detailed analysis may reveal that a manual control is better. An automated control design may create alerts and generate automatic reports. However, careful evaluation of the process may determine that no evidence of review can be produced and subsequent response actions up to and including resolution cannot be measured. In this scenario, the control fails. On the other hand, if handwritten notes are recorded within IDS log reports on a daily basis with initials and dates, and if the same notes contain analysis, action plans, ticket numbers and resolution, then the manual control is far more effective than the automated one. Of course, no final conclusion can be reached as to the strength of the control until it has been adequately tested.

The strength of a control can be measured in terms of its inherent, or design, strength and the likelihood of its effectiveness. An example of an inherently strong control is balancing the books to account for all cash and segregating accounting responsibilities among multiple employees. An example of an inherently strong control by design is requiring dual control to access sensitive areas or materials.

To demonstrate value and alignment with business objectives, risk mitigation must be tied to supported business functions. This ensures that information security and IT governance initiatives are inherently followed, and cost justification for the treatment process is readily available and self-explanatory.

In many cases, assessment of control effectiveness is provided by an independent reviewer. For example, the NIST RMF Assess Step, as described in NIST Special Publication 800-37 Revision 2, recommends that an enterprise might use an internal security control assessor for a self-assessment, or could employ an independent assessor. It states, "An independent assessor is an individual or group that can conduct an impartial assessment. Impartiality means that assessors are free from perceived or actual conflicts of interest with respect to the determination of control effectiveness or the development, operation, or management of the system, common controls, or program management controls."

The enterprise can also define the criteria by which control strength will be assessed. The RMF Assess steps include assessment criteria for security and privacy controls along with an explanation of how to use the criteria to assure that risk mitigation has been applied in accordance with approved security and privacy plans.

An additional independent review may be performed in the form of penetration testing. Penetration testing is a specialized type of assessment that simulates the actions of a malicious threat actor. Test personnel are often highly skilled in network, operating system and application-level security and are able to evaluate the effectiveness of system defenses. This independent and agile assessment helps to identify previously unknown (or underestimated) vulnerabilities that might otherwise increase the likelihood of a risk event.

While security control assessments and penetration testing may be conducted infrequently, many enterprises apply an ongoing assessment model in which automated tools continuously evaluate the state of technical controls. This continuous monitoring process provides near real-time feedback about potential changes to the controls implemented or to the environment in which those controls are deployed. It enables rapid notification of applicable information security personnel who may then take appropriate action.

3.10.2 Control Recommendations

Elements of controls that should be considered when evaluating control strength include whether the controls are preventive or detective, manual or automated, and formal (documented in procedure manuals and evidence of their operation is maintained) or ad hoc. During this step of the process, controls that could mitigate or eliminate the identified risk (as appropriate to the enterprise's operations) to an acceptable level are provided. The following factors should be considered in recommending controls and alternative solutions to achieve control objectives:

- Effectiveness of recommended options
- Compatibility with other impacted systems, processes and controls
- Relevant legislation and regulation
- Organizational policy and standards
- Organizational structure and culture
- Operational impact
- Safety and reliability
- Measurement

The control recommendations are the results of the risk assessment and analysis process and provide input to the risk treatment process. During the risk treatment process, the recommended procedural and technical security controls are evaluated, prioritized and implemented. To determine which ones are required and appropriate for a specific enterprise, a cost-benefit analysis should be conducted for the proposed controls to demonstrate that the costs of implementing the controls can be justified by the reduction in the level of risk or impact. For effective outcomes, the control implementation process should seek input from the appropriate business unit owner.

3.10.3 Control Testing and Modification

Changes to the technical or operational environment can often modify the protective effect of controls or create new weaknesses that existing controls are not designed to mitigate. Periodic testing of controls is mandatory in most publicly traded enterprises and should be implemented as a regular practice in all enterprises to ensure that procedural controls are being carried out consistently and effectively.

Changes to technical or operational controls must be made with caution. Changes to technical controls should be made according to change control procedures and with stakeholder approval. The information security manager should analyze the proposed control environment to determine if new or recurring vulnerabilities exist in the design and to ensure that the control is properly designed (i.e., self-protecting, contains a failure policy, can be monitored). Upon implementation, acceptance testing must be conducted to ensure that prescribed policies are enforced by the mechanisms.

Changes to operational procedures should also undergo review and approval through the appropriate change management process. Requisite changes to process inputs, activity steps, approvals or reviews, and process results should be considered and modifications to related processes and technologies should be coordinated. Workloads should also be taken into consideration to ensure that changes to operational controls do not overload resources and impact operational quality. If additional staff training is required to implement changes, it should be coordinated and completed prior to implementation of the change. The operational control should be reviewed in the form of a walkthrough shortly after implementation to ensure that all elements are understood and appropriately implemented.

Extensive information is available on developing control objectives and implementing specific controls from COBIT and other sources such as NIST guidance and ISO/IEC 27001 and 27002 standards.

3.11 Information Security Awareness and Training

A large percentage of security incidents are caused by human errors, either through a lack of understanding of expected behavior or through accidental mistakes. The most effective control for managing these human factors is a thorough information security awareness and training protocol. An effective action plan to implement a security strategy must consider an ongoing program of security awareness and training. In most enterprises, evidence indicates that the majority of personnel are not aware of security policies and standards, even if they do exist. To ensure awareness of new or modified policies, all impacted personnel must be trained appropriately, so they can see the connection between the policies and standards and their daily tasks. Information should be tailored to individual groups to ensure that it is relevant, and it must be presented in terms that are clear and understood by the intended audience. For example, presenting new standards on hardening servers is not likely to be meaningful to the shipping department. In addition to providing information to those affected by changes, it is important to educate staff members involved in the various aspects of implementing the strategy. Their training should focus on understanding the objectives of the strategy (KGIs), the processes and performance metrics for the various activities (KPIs), and the critical success factors (CSFs), which are the elements or events that must occur to achieve the KGIs.

3.11.1 Security Awareness Training and Education

Risk that is inherent in using computing systems cannot be addressed purely through technical security mechanisms. An active security awareness program can greatly reduce risk by addressing the behavioral element of security through education and consistent application of awareness techniques. Security awareness programs should focus on common user security concerns such as password selection, appropriate use of computing resources, email and web browsing safety and social engineering. The programs should be tailored to specific groups. In addition, users are the front line for the detection of threats that may not be detectable by automated means (e.g., fraudulent activity and social engineering). Employees should be educated on recognizing and escalating such events to enhance loss prevention.

An important aspect of ensuring compliance with the information security program is the education and awareness of the enterprise regarding the importance of the program. In addition to being informed about the need for information security, all personnel must be trained in their specific responsibilities that are related to information security.

Employee awareness should start from the point of joining the enterprise (e.g., at onboarding training) and continue regularly. Techniques for delivery need to vary to prevent them from becoming stale or boring. They may also need to be incorporated into other organizational training programs.

Security awareness programs should consist of training (often administered online); simple quizzes to gauge retention of training concepts; security awareness reminders such as posters, newsletters or screen savers;

and a regular schedule of refresher training. In larger enterprises, there may be a sufficient population of middle and senior management to warrant special management-level training on information security awareness and operations issues.

All employees of an enterprise and, where relevant, third-party users must receive appropriate training and regular updates on the importance of security policies, standards and procedures in the enterprise. Their training should include security requirements, legal responsibilities, business controls and instruction in the correct use of information processing facilities (e.g., login procedures, use of software packages). For new employees, this should be a part of new employee orientation and, therefore, should occur before access to information or services is granted.

3.11.2 Developing an Information Security Awareness Program

The information security manager should take a methodical approach to developing and implementing the education and awareness program, and consider such aspects as:

- Who is the intended audience (e.g., senior management, business managers, IT staff, end users)?
- What is the intended message (e.g., policies, procedures, recent events)?
- What is the intended result (e.g., improved policy compliance, behavioral change, better practices)?
- What communication method will be used (e.g., computer-based training [CBT], all-hands meetings, intranet, newsletters)?
- What is the organizational structure and culture?

A number of different mechanisms available for raising information security awareness include:

- Computer-based security awareness and training programs
- Email reminders and security tips
- Written security policies and procedures (and updates)
- Nondisclosure statements signed by employees
- Use of different media in promulgating security (e.g., company newsletters, web pages, videos, posters, login reminders)
- Visible enforcement of security rules
- Simulated security incidents for improving security
- Rewards for employees who report suspicious events
- Job descriptions
- Performance reviews

By applying these various methods to inform and reinforce security understanding, employees and partners will learn how to fulfill expectations and how to minimize the likelihood that a security incident will occur through human error or malfeasance.

3.11.3 Role-Based Training

While all employees and third-party partners will require general training in organizational policies and practices, the security program should also include training that is specific to the responsibilities for those in security-specific work roles, including leadership roles. This type of training should include more detailed descriptions of how behaviors and practices are intended to reduce the likelihood or impact of particular risk scenarios. Specific considerations include:

- Training for executives, leaders and managers to help them understand their responsibilities for establishing risk expectations (such as through risk appetite direction, risk tolerance statements and key indicators). Those in an executive or management role should understand their responsibility to set the tone for adherence to security objectives and ethics from the top of the enterprise and to support the security program as a component of the overall enterprise risk management activities.
- Training for those in roles with elevated privileges (e.g., access control management, administrative roles for critical or sensitive assets, managing privacy-related information) should focus on specific methods to safeguard valuable resources. Training for privileged personnel should reinforce the additional responsibility entrusted to staff in those roles, and, if applicable, inform them about additional consequences for failure to abide by organizational processes.
- Training for physical security personnel targets those who bear the responsibility for physical protection, including environmental factors, that support the confidentiality, integrity and availability of important organizational assets.

Training, both general and role-specific, should be updated regularly. It may be helpful to use previous lessons learned—either from actual internal security incidents or those that have occurred elsewhere—to identify opportunities for improvement. Since policies, processes, regulations and technologies change, and since the risk landscape is ever evolving, it is important that the security program include periodic reviews to ensure that all awareness and training activities, including documentation of successful training completion, are kept current.

3.11.4 Training and Education Metrics

To ensure that all necessary staff receive the appropriate training, there should be a systematic approach to measuring and tracking delivery of the various courses and the results of that delivery. Considerations for such tracking include:

- **Coverage**—The key metric for success of any training program is the coverage of applicable personnel (including external participants if that condition is applicable). Tracking coverage helps to monitor the number of recipients, including those within particular groups (e.g., within a particular role, department or organization level). A target coverage level (usually expressed as a percentage) should be defined, after which progress toward a specific goal can be tracked, reported and maintained.
- **Grading**—While enterprises are not required to grade members based on training, it is a good practice to follow up with employees who score below the expected level of competence for certain training or awareness programs. For example, an SLA or a regulatory requirement might require that a given percentage of applicable personnel receive a particular passing score.
- **Automation and deployment**—Deployment of a learning management system (LMS) can provide automation that supports creation, delivery, tracking and reporting capabilities. Use of an LMS supports monitoring of adherence to awareness and education requirements, enabling both conformance management and overall information security improvement.

3.12 Integration of the Security Program With IT Operations

The information security program is a partnership with other elements of enterprise information and technology governance and management. The information security manager collaborates with many of the stakeholders described in Chapter 1 who established the information security strategy and methodology as part of an integrated approach. These partnerships serve to ensure that information security processes do not unnecessarily hinder operations and that they help to reinforce understanding and buy-in from non-security personnel.

3.12.1 Personnel, Roles, Skills and Culture

The information security manager allocates personnel resources based on the technical and administrative skills required to effectively operate the program. Staff members include security engineers, QA and testing specialists, access administrators, project managers, compliance liaisons, security architects, awareness coordinators, auditors and policy specialists. The information security manager should develop positions in accordance with specific program needs, even merging responsibilities of multiple roles into one personnel position for small enterprises.

The information security manager must ensure that personnel within the security organization and other responsible organizations maintain the appropriate skills needed to carry out program functions. Each organization's skill requirements will vary, generally revolving around the existing information systems and security technologies implemented.

Personnel requirements for information security program development differ after the program is implemented. For example, the personnel involved in the construction of a security program are likely not the same personnel who will administer systems once they are functioning normally. Skills that are only rarely needed are best acquired through engagement of service providers such as integrators or consulting firms. When faced with the need for a specialized skill, the information security manager should analyze the cost, timing and intellectual capital implications of hiring or training staff versus using an external service provider. Additionally, in some enterprises there may be a need for background checks, especially if classified, confidential or highly sensitive information is involved with the job. The HR department should be involved in and conduct background checks, because there are privacy regulations that limit the extent of investigation in some jurisdictions.

Project management is a normal activity in managing the development of a security program. Larger enterprises usually have a project management office (PMO), which may be available to the information security manager to assist in development and implementation projects. Existing functions within the enterprise should be used whenever possible both to maximize organizational involvement in the program and leverage existing capabilities.

Roles

A role is a designation assigned to an individual by virtue of a job function or other label. A responsibility is a description of some procedure or function related to the role that someone is accountable to perform. Roles are important to information security because they allow responsibilities and access rights to be assigned based on functions performed rather being assigned to individual people. Because there are typically fewer roles than staff members and the roles change less often, administrative costs are consequently reduced. In addition, roles can be assigned during the onboarding process by HR, which further streamlines the process.

RACI charts can be used effectively in defining the various roles associated with aspects of developing an information security program. Clear designation of roles, responsibilities and accountability is necessary to ensure effective implementation and management.

Skills

Skills are the training, expertise and experience held by personnel in given job functions. It is important to understand the proficiencies of available personnel to ensure that they map to competencies required for program implementation. Specific skills needed for program implementation can be acquired through training or by utilizing external resources. External resources such as consultants are often a more cost-effective choice for skills required for only a short time or for specific projects.

Once it has been agreed that certain personnel will have specific information security responsibilities, formal employment agreements should be established that reference those responsibilities. These must be considered when screening applicants for employment.

Documentation

Oversight of the creation and maintenance of security-related documentation is an important administrative component of an effective information security program. Documents that commonly pertain to the program include:

- Policies, standards, procedures and guidelines
- Technical diagrams of infrastructure, architectures, applications and data flows
- Training and awareness documentation
- Risk analyses, recommendations and related documentation
- Security system designs, configuration policies and maintenance documentation
- Operational records such as shift reports and incident tracking reports
- Operational procedures and process flows
- Organizational documentation such as organizational charts, staff performance objectives and RACI models

Each document should be assigned an owner who is responsible for updating documentation (or templates in the case of operational records). Changes should be made under the recommendations of management or the security steering committee; the person or group should also approve changes prior to their distribution. The owner is responsible for ensuring that access to documentation is appropriate, controlled and auditable.

The information security manager should ensure the availability of governance system components (**figure 3.17**) (formerly called enablers) that address creation, approval, change, maintenance, controlled distribution and retirement of documentation. In many cases, these services are provided as part of a larger enterprise document management system, an ideal situation considering that the information security manager does not necessarily maintain custodianship of all security-related documentation. The information security manager should ensure that sensitive technical and operational documents are protected by controls and practices equal to or stronger than those implemented for other sensitive corporate information assets. Security documentation must follow the organizational standards for appropriate classification and labeling.

Figure 3.17—COBIT Components of a Governance System

Source: ISACA, *COBIT 2019: Introduction and Methodology*, USA, 2018

A number of documents will be required to design, initiate and implement an information security program. Documentation requirements will change at various stages and it is important to make sure they are current. Updates to standards and procedures must address changes in risk, technology, business activities or baselines, but must remain consistent with published policies, which typically change with far less frequency.

Version control is essential to ensure that all parties are operating from the same document revisions, and that a reliable notification and publication process is required.

Some of the required documentation includes:

- Program objectives
- Road maps
- Business cases
- Required resources
- Controls
- Budgets
- Systems designs/architectures
- Policies, standards, procedures, guidelines
- Project plan milestones, timelines
- KGIs, KPIs, CSFs and other metrics
- Training and awareness requirements
- Business impact and risk analysis
- SLAs
- Severity criteria

Document Maintenance

Documentation typically needs to be updated as the information security program is implemented and as the enterprise evolves. The information security manager must establish procedures for adding, modifying and, in some cases, retiring information security policies, standards, procedures and other documentation.

An important consideration for all documentation activities is to ensure that an appropriate version control process is in place so that all recipients are using current documentation. Processes should be developed to retire documentation that has been superseded by later releases. Automated systems using a single source for all documentation help to ensure that only current policies, standards and procedures are being used. Also, all documentation must have standardized markings, including effective release date, version, owner and classification.

A process for change proposals can be based on policy reviews or initiated as stakeholders recognize the need for a policy change. The information security manager should track proposed changes to policies for review in the appropriate forums.

Modification of standards will probably occur more frequently than modification of policies. These changes are often driven by changes in technology such as availability of new security capabilities, changes in risk, evolution of the technical infrastructure, and requirements of new business initiatives. Proposed standards should be reviewed by the steering committee or by departments impacted by the proposed standards. The opportunity to provide input and suggested modification should be afforded, to optimize cooperation and compliance. Standards should be reviewed periodically or as warranted by environmental changes, changing risk, request of stakeholders or audit determination of insufficiency. Changes to standards should be managed in a similar manner to policy changes and should also include technical or operational risk analysis relative to the proposed change in standards.

Modifications to policies or standards should trigger procedures to modify compliance monitoring tools and processes. Changes should be periodically shared with auditors and compliance personnel who are not already involved in the change management process to ensure awareness and acceptance of changes prior to auditing activities.

Changes in standards will necessitate a review of procedures that may require modification to help maintain compliance. Other documentation, such as acceptable use policies, guidelines, QA and procurement processes may also require modification.

3.12.2 Information Security Liaison Responsibilities

The typical information security program has several operational responsibilities in addition to providing various security-related services. The operations and services vary considerably among enterprises; however, the following section describes those most typically found in larger enterprises.

Since information security is a subdomain of corporate risk management, information security has extensive liaison with corporate risk management. Information security will closely work with other managers of broad risk types like reputation risk, market risk and especially operation risk. Information security risk management should be well integrated with overarching enterprise risk management, through methods that are well-documented within enterprise governance and management processes.

In addition to overseeing the roles discussed previously, it is essential for an effective information security manager to maintain ongoing relationships with several other groups and departments in the enterprise. These other organizational functions have a great impact on the ability of the information security manager to be effective in implementing and managing the security program. While the names of these departments may vary, enterprises typically have most of these functions. While the information security program will achieve greater success by integrating assurance activities with the following departments to the extent possible, effective integration with IT is essential.

Physical/Corporate Security

Most large enterprises have a corporate security department charged with physical security responsibilities. These departments are typically managed by individuals from law enforcement and often have limited exposure to information security. In many small enterprises, physical security is handled as a part of facilities management. In either case, physical security issues invariably impact information security, so a close working relationship between the two departments is important. It is essential for the information security manager to understand the physical security operation, including the relevant policies, standards, procedures and practices, to avoid a situation in which inadequate physical security undermines the information security program.

IT Audit

Either IT or internal audit is generally charged with providing assurance of policy compliance and identifying risk. Often, especially in the absence of complete policies and standards, the auditors will have findings on information security based on what they consider good or acceptable practices. Depending on the expertise of the auditors, their findings may or may not agree with the information security manager's perspective, and this underscores the necessity for complete governance documentation. Because internal audit activities invariably impact the information security program, it is essential for the information security manager to develop and maintain a good working relationship with internal audit. A good relationship with internal audit can provide considerable support for achieving information security objectives.

Information Technology

IT staff play a critical role in information security program development and management as the hands-on implementers and operators of information processing systems. It is important for the information security manager to develop a strong working relationship with the IT department to foster rapport, trust, understanding of common goals and open communication. This can be a challenge, because IT often perceives security as an impediment to its efforts.

IT often has conflicting requirements to ensure that policies and standards are met while performance and efficiency requirements are being addressed. This conflict between safety and performance can result in sacrificing security to meet operational objectives.

Typically, security requirements encompass implementation of control mechanisms in the network, systems and application environments and ensure that technology operations address security requirements. This can be a challenging task for IT because it must fulfill security needs while addressing issues such as functionality, accessibility, performance, capacity and scalability. The information security manager should work with IT to determine solutions that fulfill security requirements and still meet performance requirements. IT management must understand that a serious compromise will severely affect its ability to meet those performance requirements.

In addition to configuring security within the actual technical environment, many enterprises use IT to design, deploy and operate security systems such as firewalls, identity management systems and encryption technologies (e.g., virtual private networks, SSL accelerators). Effective oversight, monitoring and good communication are critical to achieve information security objectives.

The separation of operational responsibilities between the information security department and IT is often based on the impact that a particular security system has on the production technology environment. Typically, any system that directly affects production will be operated by IT. For example, failure of a passive control such as IDS is unlikely to create a system-wide outage, but the failure of an in-line system such as a firewall could cause the Internet or critical business partner connections to go down.

Business Unit Managers

The information security manager should engage business unit management when developing the information security program and continue to develop relationships in ongoing security management activities. These interactions will provide the basis for ensuring the ongoing alignment of information security with business objectives. They will also provide assurance that business unit managers responsible for front-line business operations meet security requirements, and that they understand their responsibility for identifying and escalating security incidents and other risk concerns.

Most enterprises benefit from having an information security steering group composed of representatives of the business units and other main organizational units (i.e., finance, legal, IT, information and physical security, etc.). This forum can provide the information security manager consistent information on such things as business direction, emerging risks, control effectiveness and other matters related to information security. It is also useful in ensuring that principal stakeholders are informed about information security activities and issues.

In addition to daily operational business units, most enterprises have business units responsible for the development of new products or services targeted at internal users, an external marketplace or both. It is important that the information security manager engage in the development process for any products or services related to the enterprise's information resources—in other words, virtually all such initiatives. The product development business unit should use an established baseline of standing security requirements (e.g., authentication controls, activity logging) for any new development project and work with the information security manager to develop additional controls to safeguard against application-specific risk. Early involvement in the product development cycle and standard baseline information security requirements helps the information security manager ensure that resources and time are allocated for effective controls implementation. By working with the security architecture team, if one exists, the information security group gains an understanding of the effects on the architecture and possible requirements for modifications.

Human Resources

The HR department within most enterprises has significant information security responsibilities regarding employee policy distribution, background checks, education and enforcement. The information security manager should work with HR leadership to establish the best means to administer employee education on, and in agreement with, computer resource usage policies and procedures.

The information security manager must ensure that the HR and legal departments are intimately involved in any action involving monitoring of an employee's actions or suspected abuse of computing resources. Because of the legal implications involved with personnel actions in most locales, cooperation is crucial. The information security manager should establish procedures and escalation as part of incident management, so all involved parties understand their roles and responsibilities and are prepared for immediate action when an event does occur. A senior representative of the HR department should be assigned to the information security steering committee.

Legal Department

Information security issues are frequently related to compliance, liability, corporate responsibility and due diligence. In most enterprises, these areas are the domain of the legal department. Another major area that falls to the legal department includes contracts for outsourcing and service providers. While these areas are primarily in the purview of the legal department, it is essential that the information security manager be kept in the loop to ensure inclusion of adequate security considerations. The information security manager should liaise with a representative of the legal department, who should also be on the security steering committee. The information security manager can help protect the enterprise from legal liability by ensuring that the legal department has ongoing awareness of information security issues and that the information security manager is acting with the legal department's consensus.

Employees

Employees serve as the first line of defense in the security of information. It is essential that appropriate security training on relevant policies, standards and applicable procedures is provided periodically or as needed. Testing should be used to confirm understanding, and signed acknowledgment of the training should be kept with personnel records.

Once trained, it is the responsibility of all employees to follow policies, standards and procedures. Employees should be trained to report potential threats and incidents and offer suggestions for improvement to the information security program, based on their day-to-day involvement with the program.

Procurement

Most enterprises use a formal procurement process that can have consequences for information security in terms of product acquisitions. The information security manager must have visibility into the process and be able to provide input into acquisition practices. Mature enterprises have an approved equipment list that has been evaluated for policy and standards compliance to manage and minimize vulnerabilities introduced as a result of new equipment acquisitions. In the absence of such a process, it is important for the information security manager to be advised of proposed acquisitions and provided the opportunity to determine what risk may be introduced as a result.

Compliance

As a consequence of the increasingly complex legal and regulatory landscape that enterprises must navigate, many enterprises have implemented a compliance office that may be an independent department or a part of the legal department. Because there may need to be policy, standards and procedural recognition of applicable legal and regulatory requirements, it is necessary for the information security manager to establish a working relationship with the compliance office.

Privacy

Privacy regulations have become increasingly common and restrictive in many parts of the world. In response, many enterprises have instituted a privacy office or a privacy officer. In some cases, it is a part of the compliance office, or it may be a separate function. In any event, privacy requirements in some jurisdictions are vigorously enforced and compliance must be a major focus of information security. To ensure requirements are met, the information security manager must maintain coordination with the privacy office to avoid sanctions that have grown increasingly severe.

Training

Many larger enterprises have a separate training and education department. The information security manager should have contact with this function for assistance in providing security awareness training and education in needed security skills.

See Section 3.11 Information Security Awareness and Training for more information.

Quality Assurance

QA must include acceptable levels of security-related controls. Understanding the QA process and ensuring that it includes testing of security-related aspects are important considerations for information security. The information security manager should maintain a relationship with the QA department to ensure that risk is addressed as a standard part of the process.

Insurance

Most enterprises maintain various insurance policies, such as business interruption coverage, that have relevance for information security activities related to incident response, business continuity and disaster recovery. It is incumbent on the information security manager to understand the kinds and extent of insurance the enterprise has in order to include it in risk analysis and management and recovery planning, because it serves as a compensating control.

Third-party Management

Third-party management includes outsourced functions and services. Some services, such as outsourced IDS monitoring, may be under the direct control of information security but most are likely to be managed by other departments. It is important that the information security manager understand not only what functions or services are provided by external parties but also the associated risk. Managing risk to acceptable levels in these situations can pose a challenge and may require a variety of preventive, detective and compensatory controls including oversight and monitoring.

Project Management Office

The information security organization should maintain a strong relationship with any PMOs within the enterprise. It is important that the information security manager or representatives have an awareness of all projects, particularly IT projects, across the enterprise. Creating and maintaining a relationship with the PMO helps to ensure that the information security team will be able to review projects to provide insight into any potential risk or required security measures. This relationship also provides insight into which project managers have the best qualifications for the information security projects as the program develops.

3.12.3 Cross-Organizational Responsibilities

The information security manager is directly responsible for many critical aspects of the information security program. It is important to be aware that there can be SoD issues if the same manager is responsible for overlapping aspects of policy, implementation and monitoring. Although in smaller enterprises it may be difficult to achieve an optimal level of separation, the information security manager must be aware of the risk presented and endeavor to provide compensating controls to the extent feasible. It also generally falls to the information security manager to provide assurance that these areas of responsibility are appropriately assigned across senior managers within the enterprise to avoid possible conflicts of interest. A typical set of roles and responsibilities, with a sample approach for KPIs, is illustrated in **figure 3.18**. There a many other possible KPIs that can be considered. However, for the KPIs to be useful as a management tool, KGIs must also be defined. This approach supplies the most useful metric as it shows the extent to which the goal or objective has been achieved. It shows whether there is adequate progress or if additional efforts are required to achieve the goal.

Figure 3.18—Information Security Roles and Responsibilities

Role	Information Security Process Responsibility	Sample Key Performance Indicator
Executive management	Security strategy oversight and alignment	Organizational responsibility for executing all security program elements is assigned.
Business risk management	IT risk assessment	Prioritized list of IT risk that needs to be addressed is maintained and periodically updated.
Department manager	Security requirements sign-off and acceptance testing	Security features to be incorporated into application are formally approved.
	Access authorization	Individuals or groups to have access to data are formally approved.
Legal advisor to executive management	Information protection counsel	Information protection policies are consistent with applicable laws and regulations and formally approved, and those affected are aware of them.
IT operations management	Security monitoring	Security incidents are identified before they cause damage.
	Incident response	Appropriate responses to security incidents are embedded in operational procedures.
	Crisis management	Recovery procedures are periodically and successfully tested.
	Site inventory	All purchased computing devices are accounted for and correlate with a business purpose.
Quality manager	Security review participation	Security-policy-compliant systems are configured.
	Security requirements capture	Business requirements for confidentiality, integrity and availability are documented.
	Application security design	Technical implementation plans for meeting business process security requirements are established.
	Change control	Secure archival, retrieval and compilation plans of enterprise-maintained source code and product customizations are established.
	Security upgrade management	Testing and application of security software fixes are ensured.
Purchasing	Security requirements capture	Formal requirements for security in all requests for product information and proposals are established.
	Contract requirements	Business requirements for confidentiality, integrity and availability in information service provider and technology maintenance contracts are established.

As each phase of a security program is developed, executive management, managers with risk management responsibilities and department management should be made aware of the content of the information security program so activities can be coordinated and specific areas of responsibility confirmed.

Information security programs typically cross numerous department boundaries; therefore, fostering awareness and getting consensus early in the process are important.

To achieve this, the information security manager often becomes an ambassador for the information security program. The information security manager must work closely with management to ensure that those in various departments and business units understand, accept and have the resources necessary to implement their part of the information security program.

Where individual business units have key product lines or offerings, the organizational structure might include a dedicated business information security officer (BISO). Personnel in this role might help to map organizational security requirements to that business unit's specific requirements of customers or prospects. The BISO might help ensure effective alignment and implementation of security controls within the unit's products and services and might ensure that customer-specific requirements are incorporated in the overall security roadmap. The BISO may also work closely with implementation teams of new customers to ensure effective deployment and tracking of security controls.

One strategy for incorporating the ideas and support of the enterprise's management includes the formation of an information security steering committee or an executive security council, as discussed in Chapter 1. These committees can also serve to coordinate activities among groups involved in other aspects of risk management and assurance functions, thereby helping to achieve assurance process integration and strategic alignment. The members of these committees are selected for their ability to support the information security program and represent the enterprise's interests. They help ensure that information security requirements are identified and that enterprise-wide support is achieved. The steering committee typically owns the information security strategy and is commonly designated as the group empowered to approve changes to policies or standards.

3.12.4 Issue Resolution through the Information Security Program

In addition to practices related to information security event management, the information security program includes elements related to an effective problem management approach. Problem management is focused on ascertaining the root causes of issues. This typically requires a systematic approach to understanding the various aspects of the issue, defining the problem, designing an action program, assigning responsibility and assigning due dates for resolution. A reporting process should be implemented for tracking the results and ensuring that the problem is resolved.

As the information systems environment continually undergoes changes via updates and additions, it is not unusual for a security control in place to develop a problem and not work as intended. It is at this point that the information security manager must identify the problem and assign a priority.

The information security manager should also be familiar with mitigating controls that may have to be employed if the primary security control fails. Rather than allowing the security vulnerability to put the enterprise at risk, it may be necessary for the information security manager to take alternative actions to protect the information resources until the problem is resolved. For example, if a firewall fails, the information security manager may decide to disconnect the system from the outside until the firewall problem is corrected. While this would protect the information resources from outside risk, it would likely affect the enterprise's ability to perform business. Therefore, it is important that specific authority and limits are established by management.

Vendor Management

An ongoing management and administrative responsibility for the typical information security manager is the oversight and monitoring of external providers of hardware and software, general supplies, and various services. This is to provide assurance that risk introduced in acquisition processes, implementation and service delivery is managed appropriately. Other organizational units involved in aspects of managing vendors include legal, finance, procurement and some business units.

Security service providers are a common feature of many information security programs and often represent the most cost-effective approach to various monitoring and administrative functions. They can provide the information security manager with specialist skills as needed, longer-term staff augmentation while recruiting for open positions, and even offloading of routine tasks. Outsourced security service providers can deliver a range of services such as assessment and audit, engineering, operational support, security architecture and design, advisory services and forensics support.

Security service providers can free up internal resources to focus on projects or operations where preservation of intellectual capital is at a premium. The use of external security resources can also provide an objective, fresh perspective on the information security program. If the information security manager uses an outsourced security provider, the capabilities and approaches the vendor takes should align with the enterprise's information security program.

The use of external parties to provide security-related functions usually creates risk that must be managed by the information security manager. Issues such as financial viability, quality of service, adequate staffing, adherence to the enterprise's security policies and right to audit must be addressed.

Physical and Environmental Factors

The confidentiality, integrity and availability of information can be compromised through unauthorized physical access and damage or destruction to physical components. The level of security surrounding any IT hardware and software, or any physical information assets such as documents or other media, should depend on the criticality of the systems, sensitivity of the information that can be accessed, the significance of applications processed, the cost of the equipment and the availability of backup equipment. Control of physical security may reside with a separate security department or sometimes with facilities management, but increasingly, this function falls to the information security group.

Regardless of who is responsible for physical security, the information security manager must ensure that physical security policies, standards and activities are sufficient to avoid jeopardizing information security efforts. A wide range of physical security controls—such as electronic locks, motion detectors, cameras, steel wire caging and radio frequency tracking devices—are available to implement physical security.

Physical security policies and standards must be established in addition to control processes. Physical control of access to computing resources should be applied based on the sensitivity of information accessed, processed and stored. Access should be provided on an as-needed basis.

Location within facilities and environmental factors are also concerns. Locating critical systems in areas with unstable environments or in proximity to water pipes or other potential hazards should be avoided. Computing environments should incorporate systems to monitor and control environmental factors such as temperature, humidity and electrical power quality.

Personal computers are often used in less secure user areas and may require special consideration to ensure adequate levels of security. If a workstation has a particularly sensitive function or is required to store sensitive information, isolating it may be desirable. Other physical workstation controls can include physically securing the device to prevent theft, locking the chassis to prevent tampering, removing or disabling external device interfaces (e.g., universal serial bus [USB], serial ports), and enforcing LAN-based storage to minimize sensitive data on workstation disks.

Laptops and portable devices require special consideration, particularly given the significant risk of theft or loss. The information security manager should consider the use of whole disk encryption to protect sensitive information in the event of loss.

Security of electronic and print media should also be protected. Disclosure of sensitive information on paper, microfilm, tape, CD-ROM or other physical media is as great a risk to the enterprise as an online compromise, and the media must be stored in secure locations. The transport and storage of backup tapes, if not encrypted, can also present significant risk, particularly when stored offsite. The information security manager should consider a clean desk policy to prevent unauthorized access to sensitive information in less secure office areas.

Geographic concerns need to be considered, particularly where organizational facilities and disaster recovery sites are involved. Regions with a risk of earthquakes, hurricanes, flooding or other natural disasters should be avoided when selecting facility sites. Proximity to facilities that present special risk (e.g., nuclear power plants, chemical production facilities, airports) should be considered. Primary processing facilities, disaster recovery sites and offsite data storage facilities should be located far enough from one another to ensure that a disaster event does not impact more than one site.

Cultural and Regional Variances

The information security manager should be aware of differences in perceptions, customs and appropriate behavior across different regions and cultures and recognize that what is viewed as reasonable in one culture may not be acceptable in another. The information security manager needs to identify the audience and those who will be affected by the information security activities.

In addition, laws in different countries restrict certain sharing of personal information. The information security manager needs to be aware of these complications and work to develop an information security program that meets the individual needs of the enterprise.

Policies, controls and procedures should be developed and implemented with respect to these differences. Elements that might be culturally offensive to others must be avoided, particularly if alternative elements are available that meet control requirements. If in doubt, the information security manager should work with the legal and HR department to develop appropriate strategies for addressing differences across the regions and cultures represented within the enterprise to identify potential conflicts and work toward solutions.

Logistics

The information security manager must address logistical issues effectively, particularly given the significant amount of interaction with other business units and individuals that is required by an effective information security program. Some logistic issues the information security manager needs to be able to manage include:

- Cross-organizational strategic planning and execution
- Project and task management
- Coordination of committee meetings and activities
- Development of schedules of regularly performed procedures
- Resource prioritization and workload management
- Coordination of security resources and activities with larger projects and operations

Existing corporate resources, such as online scheduling and resource management systems, can assist with these concerns. In addition, the information security manager should develop logistics management skills through training, self-study or mentoring.

3.12.5 Integration With IT Processes

It is important to provide defined interfaces between the enterprise's security-related functions and other organizational assurance functions and ensure that there are clear channels of communication. For example, information security risk management activities should integrate well with the activities of an organizational risk manager to ensure continuity and efficiency of efforts. Business continuity planning is often a separate function that must integrate with incident response activities of the information security department.

Integration

The information security manager must ensure that the information security program interfaces effectively with other organizational assurance functions. This will help drive the enterprise to the strategic outcome of business assurance process integration, discussed in Chapter 1. It will serve to reduce security gaps and duplication of efforts, situations in which poor practices in one area serve to undermine information security efforts, or assurance process providers (e.g., compliance, QA, change and configuration management, legal, audit, physical security) working at cross-purposes. These interfaces are often bidirectional; that is, security-related information is received from these departments and, in turn, information security provides relevant information to these units. The assurance functions provide input, requirements and feedback to the information security program, which, in turn, provides metrics and evaluation data for assurance evaluation. It is important that the enterprise's assurance units are part of the steering committee to ensure broader awareness of security issues. Broad ongoing involvement also helps prevent the unintegrated silo effect created when assurance functions operate in isolation.

To be effective, information security must be pervasive, affecting every aspect of the enterprise. The range of responsibilities for effective security management is broad and, in most cases, exceeds the direct authority of the information security manager. As a result, the information security manager is most likely to be successful by operating in a collaborative fashion, being a good communicator and developing a persuasive business case for security initiatives.

System Development Life Cycle Processes

Achieving effective information systems security is easiest when risk and protection considerations are included in the SDLC. While some enterprises focus on SDLC as the *software* development life cycle, the integration process is important for any system to be secured.

Because SDLC activities are usually the responsibility of other departments but have significant impact on security, the information security manager must develop approaches to integrating these functions with information security activities. It is also critical to create a process to convey any proposed change to the information security manager, who can then ensure the associated risk is assessed and appropriate treatment is provided.

The SDLC typically includes a planning phase, design phase, implementation phase, test phase and maintenance phase (**figure 3.19**).

Figure 3.19—Software Development Life Cycle

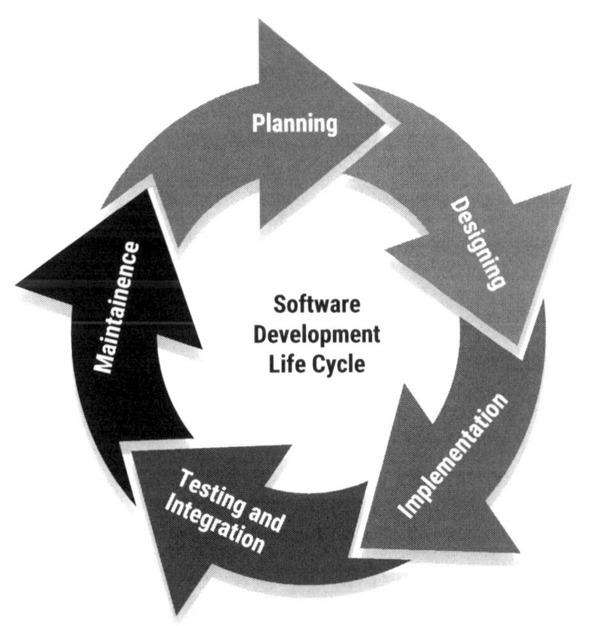

Source: ISACA, *Software Development Fundamentals Study Guide*, USA, 2021

Each of these phases includes detailed stages for ensuring that the system is functional, reliable and secure, from initial requirements through system end-of-life. The SDLC provides a significant opportunity to ensure that security requirements are considered and included in the system engineering process. Collaboration among IT and security personnel during each of the stages helps to ensure that design and deployment of controls are an integral part of the SDLC process.

This integration also provides organizational benefits, since prevention techniques through inclusion of controls have been proven to be more effective than security that is added at the end of the cycle. Failure to integrate security in the design of a system or application is one of the major contributing factors to cybersecurity vulnerabilities, making it easier for systems to be compromised. Too often, security is an afterthought, and controls are retrofitted in an ad hoc way only after security weaknesses are identified. This is less than satisfactory and is often time-consuming and costly to the enterprise. Security and risk mitigation should be part of the formal design criteria in any SDLC process and start with threat and risk assessment of the proposed system, identification of controls, implementation of those controls, testing and review.

Another opportunity for integration is during operations and maintenance of the system. Integration of security considerations should be built into procedures for operating the system securely, including application of the various controls described elsewhere in this guide. That application includes secure system upgrades, during which system components are replaced with newer versions. As they are aligned with flaw remediation and change management, system upgrades and updates should include effective security oversight, documentation and risk management.

While the general life cycle follows the pattern described previously, there are numerous models for applying the SDLC. While there are many methodologies to choose from, this guide focuses on the two best-known methods in software development: waterfall and Agile. All methodologies include some form of planning, designing, testing and maintenance.

Waterfall—named for its linear, sequential execution, much like a waterfall's top-down flow—includes a set of constituent activities. These typically include a concept phase, requirements phase, implementation phase, test phase and installation and checkout phase. These are performed generally in that order with little or no iteration.

Agile provides a flexible and collaborative approach and represents an umbrella term for a set of frameworks and practices for creating software. Agile software development provides an opportunity to continually integrate security considerations in a dynamic way. Because of the numerous, iterative planning and feedback loops that might occur within days, weeks and months, this SDLC method presents additional opportunities for security integration with the IT team.[23]

DevOps and DevSecOps

Integrated development and operations (DevOps) combines the concepts of Agile development, Agile infrastructure, and flexible operations to enable rapid and continuous releases and ongoing improvement in IT value creation. The DevOps movement was built out of frustration of IT groups with the dysfunction and deficient tools and processes, with the aim of making software development and operations more efficient and less painful.

DevOps breaks large projects into smaller deliverables and multiple deployments, which are easier to manage from design to deployment and operations. Iterative and frequent deployments can be orchestrated to move seamlessly from one group to the next until they are promoted to production with minimal risk of disruptions. Small deployments are easier to debug along the development process and are stabilized after they are in operation.

Some business performance benefits of DevOps include:

- Reduced time to market
- Faster return on investment
- High performance
- Increased quality
- Customer satisfaction
- Reduced IT waste
- Improved supplier and business partner performance
- Reduction to the human factor threat

Challenges to using DevOps include:

- Misconception about what DevOps means
- Belief that DevOps is not concerned with compliance and security
- Need for automation
- Lack of skills
- Organizational culture
- Fear of change
- Silo mentality

DevOps is the natural evolution of the Agile methodology, which counters the flaws in a traditional waterfall SDLC approach. Agile improves efficiency and typically relies on popular open source tools for a continuous integration/continuous development (CI/CD) pipeline that makes rapid feedback and deployment of code possible, enabling enterprises to achieve daily software deployments if they desire.

Although reduced time to market makes business and product teams very happy, cybersecurity professionals have concerns—vulnerable code, if not checked, can also be deployed faster. The traditional way of providing security assurance cannot keep up and does not work in a CI/CD world, which sparked the DevSecOps movement. DevSecOps applies the same principles to cybersecurity that DevOps applies to traditional IT processes to improve efficiency, removing manual intervention wherever possible. DevSecOps aims to shift security to the left by incorporating security assurance at every stage of the CI/CD pipeline and making it as essential a success criterion as development and testing. This shift is achieved by building and automating security into the CI/CD pipeline. It requires a cultural change that must be endorsed by top-level management to succeed.

The information security manager should ensure effective integration of security processes with CI/CD tools as part of the DevSecOps environment. The policies, procedures and SLAs for software security assurance should be reviewed to ensure they can be adapted to work in a high-speed CI/CD world.

Change Management

Most enterprises employ some form of change management process, whether formal or informal.

[23] ISACA, *Software Fundamentals Study Guide,* https://store.isaca.org/s/store#/store/browse/detail/a2S4w000004KokfEAC

Security needs to be an integral part of the change management process because new vulnerabilities may be introduced as a result of system or process changes. The information security manager should identify all change management processes used by the enterprise and establish a notification process when changes that may impact security take place.

The information security manager needs to implement processes to ensure that security implications are considered as a standard practice. This is generally accomplished by a requirement that risk and potential impact of the proposed change is assessed prior to implementation and appropriately treated if risk exceeds the acceptable level. A part of the assessment is analysis of the extent to which existing controls may mitigate any change in risk. As changes are made to systems and processes over time, it is important to consider that there is often a tendency for existing security controls to become less effective. Therefore, it is critical for the security manager to ensure that information security controls and countermeasures are tested regularly as part of the change management process and, if needed, updated and adapted or modified to address changes in risk or impact.

A decentralized enterprise can pose a special challenge to the security manager in terms of change management. Often, many divisions are highly autonomous, and it may be difficult to monitor and ensure compliance with corporate policies and procedures. It is important to understand the organizational structure during development and implementation of a security program to establish an effective change management approach.

To maintain accountability for policy compliance through inevitable system, environment, business and risk changes, an information security program must identify where in the enterprise IT changes are initiated, funded and deployed. The information security manager must negotiate hooks into these processes so those in job functions that specify, purchase and deploy new systems have policy compliance as part of their job functions. This includes providing timely notification so the information security manager can understand potential vulnerabilities in new systems or devices, identify new risk presented by the systems, and assist the implementation team in developing policy-compliant standards that can be handed to a release manager as preapproved for production deployment. This is one key element of effectively integrating the security program into the day-to-day work of the enterprise.

Configuration Management

Incorrect configuration is the major enabler of security breaches to information systems. As a consequence, it is essential that strong procedural and technical controls are implemented to effectively manage this risk by ensuring proper configuration prior to system or device activation on the network.

The typical underlying causes for failure to properly configure systems include a lack of clear standards or procedures for configuration and overburdened staff failing to properly follow procedures or taking improper shortcuts. The information security manager must ensure that proper documentation exists on correct configuration, adequate oversight is provided, and IT staff has sufficient training in performing these activities. If proper tested and validated procedural documentation does exist and adequate skills exist, then the workload of those responsible should be examined to see if time is the issue or if some form of compliance enforcement is required to ensure correct configuration.

Release Management

When properly implemented, release management reduces the chances of operational failure by ensuring adequate security testing has been performed and required conditions exist for the correct operation of new software, devices or systems. The information security manager should ensure that proper standards and procedures exist so that products are not deployed to production prematurely. In addition, it is important to provide adequate monitoring and oversight to ensure that procedures are followed to avoid unexpected production system failure.

3.12.6 Cloud Computing

Cloud computing represents a significant portion of enterprise IT and merits special attention within the information security program. NIST defines cloud computing as "a model for enabling convenient, on-demand network access to a shared pool of configurable computing resources (e.g., networks, servers, storage, applications, and services) that can be rapidly provisioned and released with minimal management effort or service provider interaction."[24]

The defining characteristic of cloud computing is that processing and data are somewhere in the cloud as opposed to being in a specific known location. Cloud computing can be provided as either public hosting for a number of unrelated entities or private hosting, in the case of large enterprises wanting greater control over the environment.

The five essential characteristics of the cloud include:

- **On-demand self-service**—Computing capabilities can be provisioned without human interaction from the service provider.
- **Broad network access**—Computing capabilities are available over the network and can be accessed by diverse client platforms.
- **Resource pooling**—Computer resources are pooled to support a multitenant model.
- **Elasticity**—Resources can scale up or down rapidly and, in some cases, automatically, in response to business demands.
- **Measured service**—Resource utilization can be optimized by leveraging charge-per-use capabilities.

As cloud computing has become pervasive, these characteristics have been applied through various models to support enterprise needs.

Cloud Service Models

The cloud model can be thought of as being composed of three primary service models (**figure 3.21**). As cloud services have evolved, a variety of services, platforms and software have become available.

Figure 3.20— Cloud Computing Service Models

Service Model	Definition	To Be Considered
Infrastructure as a Service (IaaS)	IaaS is the capability to provision processing, storage, networks and other fundamental computing resources, offering the customer the ability to deploy and run arbitrary software that may include operating systems and applications. IaaS puts these IT operations into the hands of a third party.	Options to minimize the impact if the cloud provider has a service interruption
Platform as a Service (PaaS)	PaaS is the capability to deploy onto the cloud infrastructure customer-created or acquired applications using programming languages and tools supported by the provider.	• Availability • Confidentiality • Privacy and legal liability in the event of a security breach, as databases housing sensitive information will be hosted offsite • Data ownership • Concerns around e-discovery
Software as a Service (SaaS)	Capability to use the provider's applications running on cloud infrastructure. The applications are accessible from various client devices through a thin client interface such as a web browser (e.g., web-based email).	• Who owns the applications? • Where do the applications reside?

Source: ISACA, *Cloud Computing: Business Benefits With Security, Governance and Assurance Perspectives*, USA, 2009, *www.isaca.org/Knowledge-Center/Research/ResearchDeliverables/Pages/Cloud-Computing-Business-Benefits-With-Security-Governance-and-Assurance-Perspective.aspx*

[24] NIST, Special Publication 800-145: "The NIST Definition of Cloud Computing," September 2011, https://csrc.nist.gov/publications/detail/sp/800-145/final

Note: The Cloud Security Alliance (CSA) is a nonprofit organization with a mission to promote best practices for providing security assurance with cloud computing and can be considered a main source of information on this topic.

Advantages

Cloud computing is viewed as a significant change to the platform in which business services are translated, used and managed. Many consider it to be as large a shift in IT as the advent of the personal computer or Internet access. However, a major difference between the cloud and those technologies is that the introductions of those earlier technologies encompassed a slower development phase. With the cloud, the required pieces have come together more rapidly for implementation. Some drivers bringing the cloud to the attention of enterprise decision makers are:

- **Optimized resource utilization**—Enterprises typically use just 15 to 20 percent of server computing resources. This means that they have five times the computing capacity than is typically used. By using a pay-as-you-go cloud solution, resources become available when needed and are liberated when no longer needed; there is near-perfect alignment with actual demand.
- **Cost savings**—Increased server utilization plus the transition of computational capability from acquired and maintained computers to rented cloud services change the computing cost paradigm from a capital expenditure (CAPEX) to an operational expenditure (OPEX), with potentially significant up-front and total cost savings. Indeed, flexible, on-demand services enable solution testing without significant capital investments and provide transparency of usage charges to drive behavioral change within enterprises.
- **Better responsiveness**—On-demand, agile, scalable and flexible services that can be implemented quickly provide enterprises with the ability to respond to changing requirements and peak periods.
- **Faster cycle of innovation**—Innovation is handled a lot faster in the cloud than within the enterprise. Patch management and upgrades to new versions become more flexible. For the cloud user, upgrading to a new software version is often nothing more than typing a different uniform resource locator (URL) into the web browser.
- **Reduced time for implementation**—Cloud computing provides processing power and data storage as needed and at the capacity needed, in near-real time, not requiring the weeks or months (or funding) that are necessary when a new business initiative is brought online in a traditional IT enterprise.
- **Resilience**—A large, highly resilient environment reduces the potential for system failure. The failure of one component of a cloud-based system has less impact on overall service availability and reduces the risk of downtime.

Depending on business needs, any or all of the foregoing benefits could be a sufficient reason to consider a cloud computing solution. The world economy recently has pushed many enterprises to be more fiscally conservative. In the IT space, cloud computing presents a potentially significant savings by enabling enterprises to maximize dynamic computing on a pay-per-use basis.

As with any evolving technology, cloud computing offers the possibility of high reward in terms of containment of costs and features such as agility and provisioning speed. However, it also brings the potential for unknown and potentially high risk. Cloud computing introduces a level of abstraction between the physical infrastructure and the owner of the information being stored and processed. Traditionally, data owners have had direct or indirect control of the physical environment affecting their data. In the cloud, this is no longer the case. Due to this abstraction, there is already a widespread demand for greater transparency and a robust assurance approach of the cloud computing supplier's security and control environment.

After it has been determined that cloud services are a plausible solution for an enterprise, it is important to identify the business objectives and risk that accompany a cloud implementation. This will assist enterprises in determining what types of data should be trusted to the cloud, and which applications and services might deliver the greatest benefit. For many enterprises, prudence dictates initially entrusting only relatively low-value, noncritical services to the cloud.

Evaluation of Cloud Service Providers

As is the case with many outsourced services, the primary driver for cloud computing is usually cost. Depending on the criticality of the services provided, selection of a vendor based on cost alone could pose an excessive risk to the enterprise. Therefore, it is incumbent on the enterprise to conduct a thorough evaluation of the potential service providers based on the enterprise's security posture and risk appetite. It must be considered that the services provided are under the control of a number of other enterprises, including the data center provider, backbone transport and Internet service provider, among others. Failure of any of these providers results in loss of possibly critical operations. Thorough evaluation of all providers can serve to quantify this risk to some extent and provide an informed basis for the decision to use these services.

3.13 Management of External Services and Relationships

In addition to cloud services, enterprises increasingly rely on other external partners to supply, host and operate information and technology. While not a new challenge, risk inherent to the supply chain has drawn increasing scrutiny from security personnel and regulators alike. The enterprise gains great benefits from the use of third-party providers; as with other information and technology aspects, that value should be balanced with resource and risk optimization to achieve stakeholder risk objectives.

3.13.1 Governance of Third-Party Relationships

An important aspect of information security governance are the rules and processes employed when dealing with third-party relationships. These parties include:

- Service providers
- Outsourced operations
- Trading partners
- Merged or acquired enterprises

The ability to effectively manage security in these relationships poses a significant challenge for the information security manager. This is particularly true in the case of enterprises being merged. These challenges include cultural differences that may result in approaches to security and behavior that are not acceptable to the security manager's enterprise. There may be technology incompatibilities between the enterprises, process differences that do not integrate well or inadequate levels of baseline security. Other areas of concern can involve incident response, business continuity and disaster recovery capabilities.

To ensure that the enterprise is adequately protected, the information security manager must assess the impacts of any of the reasonably possible security failures of any third party that may become involved with the enterprise. It is important to have an adequate understanding and a plan to manage any such potential failures effectively, so the potential impacts are within a range acceptable to management.

The responsibilities of the information security manager to address the potential risk and possible impacts of third-party relationships should be clear and documented. Policies, standards and procedures establishing the involvement of information security should be developed prior to the creation of any third-party relationship so risk can be determined and management can decide whether it is acceptable or must be mitigated. Finally, there should be a formalized engagement model between the information security organization and those groups that establish and manage third-party relationships for the enterprise

3.13.2 Third-Party Service Providers

A typical enterprise uses many information resources in support of its business processes. These resources can originate within the enterprise or be provided by entities external to the enterprise. Most enterprises will use a combination of the two. The information security manager needs to be aware of the location and access permissions for all information resources because they all require protection regardless of who is processing them.

The information security manager has several considerations to address when outsourcing, including:

- Ensuring that the enterprise has appropriate controls and processes in place to facilitate outsourcing
- Ensuring that there are appropriate information risk management clauses in the outsourcing contract
- Ensuring that a risk assessment is performed for the process to be outsourced

- Ensuring that an appropriate level of due diligence is performed prior to contract signature
- Managing the information risk for outsourced services on a day-to-day basis
- Ensuring that material changes to the relationship are flagged and new risk assessments are performed as required
- Ensuring that proper processes are followed when relationships are ended

Considerations when outsourcing services include the following:

- Outsourcing or planning to outsource business-critical functions generally increases information risk.
- The complexity of managing information risk is increased in outsourcing arrangements by the separation of responsibility for control specification and control implementation.
- The separation of responsibility for control specification and control implementation is bridged by the outsourcing contract. This underlines the contract's importance as the primary method through which the enterprise can manage its information risk.
- Where the outsourced business function operates within a regulated industry, the outsourcing contract needs to explicitly address regulatory requirements.
- The complexity of information risk assessment is increased in outsourcing arrangements because there are three different areas of information risk to assess: the business function, the outsourcing provider and outsourcing itself.
- The style of the overall contract and the amount of innovation contributed by the provider have a major impact on the way information risk management requirements are specified.
- The relationship between the enterprise and the outsourcing provider often contributes more to effective information risk management in an outsourcing arrangement than the contract.
- Because few businesses remain static, information risk management within the outsourcing arrangement must evolve so that it continues to be relevant to the enterprise's needs.
- The exit strategy for the outsourcing arrangement is at least as important as the initial transition. It should be developed at the planning stage and included in the contract to facilitate the continued availability of the outsourced business function. The exit strategy is far too important to leave until the outsourcing arrangement comes to its conclusion.

The information risk management requirements for outsourced business functions are different from those for in-house functions and, in many instances, they are greater. After the information risk has been analyzed and the controls have been identified, these controls need to be defined within the contract for the provider to implement. Outsourcing results in a disconnection between setting the controls and their implementation. **Figure 3.21** provides a simplistic view of this separation of the responsibilities of the enterprise versus those of the provider.

Figure 3.21—Disconnect of Responsibilities with Outsourced Providers

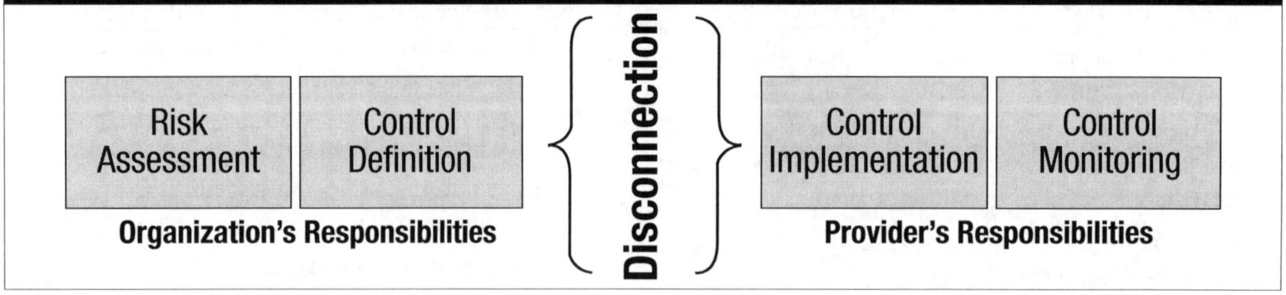

Although the enterprise can outsource information risk management to a third party, it generally cannot outsource responsibility.

The disconnection between control definition and control implementation makes managing the risk associated with outsourcing business functions complex and renders the outsourcing contract essential in managing information risk. The challenge for the information security manager is in how to define and implement information risk management controls in different outsourced business functions throughout the enterprise.

The business problem is the need to define and implement information risk management measures to protect the information within business functions that have been handed to a third party to operate on a day-to-day basis.

Information risk recommendations for outsourcing initiatives include ensuring the following:

- Timely involvement of information risk management professionals to ensure the risk assessment and controls definition
- Negotiation of key information risk management controls within the contract
- Mechanisms to negotiate small changes to information risk management controls as they may be costly
- Avoidance of difficult and complicated changes to information risk management controls
- Mechanisms to get information on whether information risk is being managed effectively
- Mechanisms to compensate for the lack of trust in the provider's staff

Outsourcing and Service Providers

The two types of outsourcing that an information security manager may encounter are third-party providers of security services and outsourced IT or business processes that must be integrated into the overall information security program. Most of the security requirements are similar, depending on criticality and sensitivity of assets and extent of services involved, but the ownership is different. The information security manager is normally the process owner for outsourced security services whereas other outsourced services are typically the responsibility of the process owner. The risk posed by third parties connected to the enterprise's internal network can be substantial and must be carefully considered.

Economics are the primary driver of outsourcing. As a result, early engagement by the information security manager is essential to ensure that those making the decisions do not unduly compromise security for the sake of cost. It is also important to understand the TCO of outsourcing over the duration of the contract. Typically, over an extended contract, there is very little, if any, overall economic benefit. This may be due to the fact that service levels are usually contracted for at a specific level while circumstances may result in a contraction of the business and require fewer services with no commensurate reduction of costs. It is also possible that a growth in the business will require additional services with the potential result that the outsourcer demands much higher fees. Either event can increase cost per unit of service provided, reducing or eliminating any initial cost savings. Some enterprises have also found that it takes a considerable amount of time to negotiate increased service levels, which adversely affects the enterprise's agility to meet changing business needs. Finally, the costs of repatriation of outsourced services at the end of the contract period, in the event the enterprise chooses to insource, must be considered as well. This may occur because the enterprise finds the constrictions imposed by outsourcing are not acceptable or the costs associated with a new agreement are too high.

Other important and possibly adverse considerations when evaluating outsourcing options include:

- Loss of essential skills
- Lack of visibility into security processes
- New access and other control risk
- Viability of the third-party vendor
- Complexity of incident management
- Cultural and ethical differences
- Unanticipated costs and service inadequacies

Whether considering outsourcing entire operations or evaluating service providers, the adequacy of the vendor's controls needs to be audited and monitored through the life of the contract to ensure that security measures are not marginalized over time as a result of cost pressures. This can be accomplished by independent audit or onsite visits at the third-party facility to ensure that the proper controls are in place.

The existence and enforcement of privacy laws to protect a company's data also need to be considered. This is particularly true as individuals in different cultures may treat information differently (i.e., what a firm in one country considers sensitive information may not be considered sensitive in another country).

While technical controls for the IT component of outsourced processes may seem obvious, arrangements that deal with business processes require that training, awareness, manual controls and monitoring be put in place to ensure that employees in third-party facilities are treating the processes and physical and electronic data to acceptable standards.

Third-party security providers are a viable strategy that the information security manager can use to assist in the design and operation of the enterprise's information security program or to provide other IT services. One of the main concerns for security is the extent that the third-party provider can and will meet the enterprise's security policies and standards on an ongoing, verifiable basis. This can affect security breaches.

The maturity of a vendor's security program and the vendor's assurance of compliance with the contracting enterprise's security policies should be high on the list of decision factors when selecting a vendor. This proposal and evaluation process is also applicable when evaluating whether to use an enterprise's autonomous division or subsidiary for certain security services.

The issues associated with outsourcing that require attention are broad and must be enumerated based on the scope, type and risk associated with the initiative. Some common issues include:

- Isolation of external party access to resources
- Integrity and authenticity of data and transactions
- Protection against malicious code or content
- Privacy/confidentiality agreements and procedures
- Security standards for transacting systems
- Data transmission confidentiality
- Identity and access management of the third party
- Incident contact and escalation procedures
- Compliance enforcement of critical sole source vendors
- Alignment of security processes
- Ability to influence security and compliance standards and processes across vendors
- Data residing offshore

3.13.3 Outsourcing Challenges

Outsourced information resources may present an information security manager with other challenges, including external enterprises that may be reluctant to share technical details on the nature and extent of their information protection mechanisms. This makes it critical to ensure that adequate specified levels of protection are included in SLAs and other outsourcing contracts. One common approach is to specify requirements for specific audits such as SOC 2[25] or ISO 27001:2013 certification. It is also important to analyze SOC 2 or other audit reports upon receipt for third-party auditor comments and, if present, comments about customer control effectiveness and policy compliance. Note that SOC 2 reports are often not sufficient on their own because the criteria have been defined by the enterprise in question. For high-risk relationships, it is

[25] AICPA, *AICPA Guide for Supply Chain: Reporting on an Examination of Controls Relevant to Security, Availability, Processing Integrity, Confidentiality, Privacy in a Production, Manufacturing, or Distribution System*,www.aicpa.org/interestareas/frc/assuranceadvisoryservices/soc-for-supply-chain.html

generally preferable to rely on periodic compliance assessments conducted directly by the sourcing enterprise or a contracted third party.

From a risk management perspective, it is important that incident management and response, business continuity planning/disaster recovery planning and testing include all important outsourced services and functions. Among them are implementing a well-defined and tested incident detection, escalation and response plan in concert with the outsourcing entities.

For regulated enterprises such as financial institutions, a time frame for notification of regulatory agencies regarding suspicious events involving regulated information is often in place. Contracts with third parties must ensure that processes are established to support such notifications.

Third-party vendor financial viability is another consideration. Because outsourcing contracts are often awarded to low-cost bidders, the risk of the outsourcing enterprise to continue to operate according to the contract and to honor any indemnity agreements may be a function of its financial capabilities. Financial information can be obtained from a variety of sources including credit reports, US Securities and Exchange Commission filings of publicly traded firms, and annual reports. If such certifications are not available, information must be obtained from providers—information sufficient to determine how external entities are securing information assets.

Some portion of risk associated with outsourced information services can be transferred by incorporating indemnity clauses in SLAs. Key clauses that should be part of a third-party contract must include, but are not restricted to:

- Right to source code in event of default of provider (e.g., source code escrow)
- Requirement that the vendor remain timely with compliance to industry and regulatory requirements
- Right to audit the vendor's books of accounts and premises
- Right to review the vendor's processes
- Defined SOPs
- Right to assess the skill sets of the vendor resources
- Advance information if the resources deployed are to be changed

An SLA should also be developed and formally agreed that explains timeliness of response (system and human), scanning expectations and other key issues.

3.13.4 Outsourcing Contracts

The fundamental purpose of contracts is twofold: 1) to ensure that the parties to the agreement are aware of their responsibilities and rights within the relationship; and 2) to provide the means to address disagreements once the contract is in force. Within that framework, the information security manager should be familiar with certain provisions for security and information protection. While the information security manager may or may not be included in contract reviews, the following issues should be addressed with the legal department to ensure an understanding of security requirements that should be covered.

The most common security provision addresses confidentiality or nondisclosure. Each party will typically agree that any confidential or sensitive information it receives as part of the agreement, or about the other party, will be kept confidential through appropriate measures. This may also include the requirement to return or destroy any proprietary or confidential information upon termination of the contract or after a specified period of time. The information security manager will need to determine the specific level of destruction that will be required (e.g., document shredding, disk and tape degaussing).

The contract may also stipulate that either or both parties must maintain security controls to ensure that the systems and information used under the agreement are protected by appropriate means. The contract should explicitly define what is meant by appropriate, and the requirements for demonstrating the effectiveness of those protections. Whether it is through the production of a current third-party audit report (e.g., SSAE16) or compliance with an industry-standard security framework (such as ISO/IEC 2700X or COBIT), the standards by which the program will be judged should be defined in the contract. Additionally, if the contracted product or service includes network connectivity between the buyer and the seller, the contract should address responsibility for the security of that connection. Specifications as to the level of security expected (e.g., firewalls, intrusion detection/prevention, monitoring) or specific technical requirements should also be addressed.

A contract with a service provider that has been determined (through a risk assessment) to be beyond a predetermined risk threshold should always contain provisions concerning right-to-audit and a right-to-inspect without notice. This would typically be for any third party that accesses, stores or processes any sensitive or otherwise business-critical information; provides mission-critical services; or connects to the network infrastructure of the contracting enterprise. The right-to-audit clause should allow the customer, upon proper notice, the right to conduct an in-depth audit of the third party's security program and processes to verify the effectiveness of all associated controls. The right-to-inspect without notice, although not generally favored by service providers, can provide greater incentive to adhere to contractual requirements on an ongoing basis. If these provisions are included in the contract, the parameters for an audit, such as compliance criteria, notification, scope limitations, frequency and responsibility for incurred costs, should be explicit. The right to inspect should ideally have few, if any, constraints.

In the event that a security breach happens at either party, the contract should specify the roles each party will play in the investigation and remediation process. Issues such as which party will lead the investigation, notification procedures and responsibilities (including law enforcement or regulatory notifications), and timing must all be addressed. During an active incident, pressure is high, tempers can flare and fairness and equity are much harder to come by, so addressing these issues in the contract is easier and can be done much more equitably.

Finally, the contract should contain indemnity clauses that ensure compensation for impacts caused by the service provider. Service providers will typically attempt to limit compensation for their failure to specific amounts or, in some cases, to the amount of fees paid to them for a specific period, such as the past 12 months. Such limits are not in the best interests of the contracting enterprise. Another consideration is what are called choice of law provisions, which require that any potential litigation take place in certain jurisdictions, typically favorable to the service provider. While these elements are in the purview of the legal department (if there is one, which may not be the case in a small enterprise), it is useful for the information security manager to have an understanding of these issues.

The contract between the parties is a key element of establishing an appropriate level of control of the enterprise's information processing facilities (IPFs). Depending on the business processes and operational needs of the enterprise requiring the services of third-party vendor outsourcing, contracts may need to deal with a number of complex security questions. Points that should be covered in the contract (from the perspective of the information security manager) can include, but are not limited to:

- Detailed specification of outsourced service
- Specific security requirements
- Restrictions for copying information and securing assets
- Prohibiting access without explicit authorization and maintaining a list of individuals who have access
- Right to audit and inspect
- Indemnity clauses to mitigate impacts caused by the service provider
- Requirements for incident response plans (IRPs) and business continuity plans (BCPs)
- Level of service quality
- Integrity and confidentiality of business assets
- Nondisclosure agreements to be signed by the employees/agents of third parties
- Protection of intellectual property
- Ownership of information
- Requirement that applicable legal and regulatory requirements are met
- Return or destruction of information/assets at the end of the contract
- Duration for maintenance of confidentiality
- Requirement that employees or agents of the third party must comply with security policies of the enterprise
- Escalation processes
- Predetermined reductions or increases in costs associated with changing service levels
- Response and implementation times for changing service requirements
- Conditions and circumstances for contract cancellation and associated costs

3.13.5 Third-Party Access

Third-party access to the processing facilities of the information security manager's enterprise under any circumstances should be controlled based on risk assessment and must be clearly defined in an SLA. Access should be granted based on the principles of least privilege, need-to-know and need-to-do. It is important to bear in mind that third parties may have a different business culture and set of ethics, which must be considered in terms of risk.

Providing access to third parties must be based on clearly defined methods of access, access rights and levels of functionality, and access must require the approval of the asset owner.

Access usage should be fully logged and reviewed by the security manager on a regular basis. The review frequency should be decided based on factors such as:

- Criticality of information to which access rights are given
- Criticality of privileges given
- Period of contract

Anomalies noticed should be immediately reported to the asset owner and escalation conditions specified wherever required. The access rights given to third parties should be removed immediately after the contract expires.

Network and information access should not be granted to a third party until the contract is signed. The contract should define the terms for access and control requirements and make allowances for assurance that appropriate safeguards are in place and will remain in place for the duration of the contract.

3.14 Information Security Program Communications and Reporting

Among the most important outcomes of the information security program are effective communications and reporting regarding the successful achievement of security and privacy objectives, ongoing risk status, and opportunities for improvement. Senior leaders have a responsibility to remain aware of various risk factors. For some, failure to stay current could result in prison or financial penalties. Through various assessment, monitoring and reporting techniques, the information security manager can fulfill the commitments made in the business case, demonstrate successful implementation of the security strategy, and ensure that relevant stakeholders are always informed regarding results of ongoing monitoring.

3.14.1 Program Management Evaluation

Certain situations call for the information security manager to assess the current state of an existing information security program (e.g., if promoted or hired into an existing CSO role). It is also important for the information security manager to periodically reevaluate the effectiveness of the program relative to the changes in organizational demands, environments and constraints. The results of such analysis should be shared with the information security steering committee or other stakeholders for review and development of needed program modifications.

While the information security manager must determine the most appropriate scope for current state assessment, the following section outlines several critical areas for evaluation.

Program Objectives

The information security manager must evaluate the documented security objectives established for the program. Key considerations include:

- Has an information security strategy and development road map been developed?
- Have criteria for acceptable risk and impact been determined?
- Do complete and current policies, standards and procedures exist?
- Are program goals aligned with governance objectives?
- Are objectives measurable, realistic and associated with specific timelines?
- Do program objectives align with organizational goals, initiatives, compliance needs and operational environment?
- Is there consensus on program objectives? Were objectives developed collaboratively?
- Have metrics been implemented to measure program objective successes and shortfalls?

- Are there regular management reviews of objectives and accomplishments?

Compliance Requirements

Alignment with and fulfillment of compliance requirements are among the most visible indications of security management status. Because many standards establish program management requirements, the information security manager must evaluate the management program itself—framework and components—against compulsory and voluntary compliance standards. Key considerations include:

- Has management determined the level of compliance the enterprise will undertake along with timelines and milestones?
- Is there facilitation of close communication between compliance and information security groups? Are information security compliance requirements clearly defined?
- Does the information security program specifically integrate compliance requirements into policies, standards, procedures, operations and success metrics?
- Do the program's technical, operational and managerial components align with the components required by regulatory standards?
- What were the results of recent audit and compliance reviews of the information security program?
- Are program compliance deficiencies tracked, reported and addressed in a timely way?
- Are compliance management technologies used to increase the efficiency of fulfilling security compliance demands?

Program Management

Evaluation of program management components reveals the extent of management support and the overall depth of the existing program. Very technical, tactically driven security programs tend to implement fewer management components, whereas strategic programs driven by standards, compliance and governance implement a more comprehensive set of management activities to ensure that requirements are established and fulfilled. Considerations for program management components include:

- Is there thorough documentation of the program itself? Have key policies, standards and procedures been reduced to accessible operating guidelines and distributed to responsible parties?
- Do responsible individuals understand their roles and responsibilities?
- Are roles and responsibilities defined for members of senior management, boards, etc.? Do these organizations understand and engage in their responsibilities?
- Are responsibilities for information security represented in the business managers' individual objectives and are they part of their individual performance ratings?
- Are policies and standards complete, formally approved and distributed?
- Are business unit managers involved in guiding and supporting information security program activities? Is there a formal steering committee?
- How is the program positioned within the enterprise? To whom is the program accountable? Does this positioning impart an appropriate level of authority and visibility for the objectives the program must fulfill?
- Does the program implement effective administration functions (e.g., budgeting, financial management, HR management, knowledge management)?
- Are meaningful metrics used to evaluate program performance? Are these metrics regularly collected and reported?
- Are there forums and mechanisms for regular management oversight of program activities? Does management regularly reassess program effectiveness?

Security Operations Management

The information security manager must evaluate the effectiveness with which the information security program implements security operational activities, both within the security organization and in other organizational units. Some key considerations include:

- Are security requirements and processes included in security, technology and business unit SOPs?
- Do security-related SOPs provide for accountability, process visibility and management oversight?

- Are there documented SOPs for security-related activities such as configuration management, access management, security systems maintenance, event analysis and incident response?
- Is there a schedule of regularly performed procedures (e.g., technical configuration review)? Does the program provide for records of scheduled activities?
- Is there SoD among system implementers, security administrators and compliance personnel?
- Does the program provide for effective operational, tactical and strategic metrics reporting that gives management needed information for oversight? Are other oversight mechanisms in place?
- Does management regularly review security operations? Is there a forum for operational issues to be escalated to management for resolution?

Technical Security Management

Management of the technical security environment is critical to ensuring that information processing systems and security mechanisms are implemented effectively. In addition to evaluating the current technical environment, the information security manager should consider the following issues regarding management of technical security concerns:

- Are there technical standards for the security configuration of individual network, system, application and other technology components?
- Do standards exist that address architectural security issues such as topology, communication protocols and compartmentalization of critical systems?
- Do standards support and enforce high-level policies and requirements? Are standards a collaborative effort among technology, operations and security staff?
- Are technical standards uniformly implemented? Do procedures exist to regularly evaluate and report on compliance with technical standards? Is there a formal process to manage exceptions?
- Is there continuous monitoring of key controls? Do controls provide notification on failure?
- Is separation of development, test and production environments enforced?
- Do systems enforce SoD, especially where high levels of administrative access are concerned?
- Is there reliable and comprehensive visibility (logging) into system activities, configurations, accessibility and security-related events? Is this visibility continual or intermittent?
- Are proper decommissioning processes in place to prevent data leakage?
- Is there a clear communications and escalation path or channel for cross team priorities or responsibilities?
- Is there an acceptable RACI for various security operations?

Resource Levels

The information security manager must assess the level of financial, human and technical resources allocated to the program. Areas of deficiency must be identified and escalated to senior management or the steering committee. Considerations include the following areas:

- Financial resources:
  - What is the current funding level for the program?
  - Is a comprehensive capital and operating budget maintained?
  - Do financial allocations align with program budget expectations?
  - Are there linkages between resource allocation and business objectives?
  - Are functions within the program prioritized in terms of financial allocation?
  - Which functions are likely to suffer from underfunding?
- HR:
  - Does the program implement a workload management methodology?
  - What is the current staffing level for the program?
  - Are existing resources fully utilized in terms of time and skills?
  - Are existing resources adequately skilled for the roles they are in?
  - Are there low-value tasks that other resources could be leveraged to complete?
  - What other human resources (e.g., IT staff) is the program dependent on to operate effectively? Is information security a formal part

of these resources' job descriptions and activity plans?
    - Is the training road map for the staff in alignment with the strategic plan?
- Technical resources:
    - What technologies currently support information security program objectives?
    - Is the capacity of supporting technologies sufficient to support current demands? Will these technologies scale to meet future needs?
    - Does the program account for maintenance, administration and eventual replacement of supporting technologies?
    - Are there other technologies that could make the program more efficient or effective?

3.14.2 The Plan-Do-Check-Act Cycle

The information security program is based on the effective, efficient management of controls designed and implemented to treat or mitigate threats, risk, vulnerabilities and impacts. The unique dependency on the effective, efficient management of a business process such as information security lends itself to the concepts and methodologies encompassed within the total quality management (TQM) system.

An important TQM outcome, originally developed by American physicist Walter Shewhart during the 1920s, was a four-step problem-solving iterative technique used to improve business processes. That cycle was adapted and popularized by quality control pioneer W. Edwards Deming in the 1950s. The cycle, which Deming called the Shewhart Cycle after his mentor, became the now famous tailored plan-do-check-act (PDCA) process. PDCA comprises four quality assessment and improvement processes, as depicted in **figure 3.22**.

Figure 3.22—PDCA Methodology

The PDCA methodology is an iterative process model.

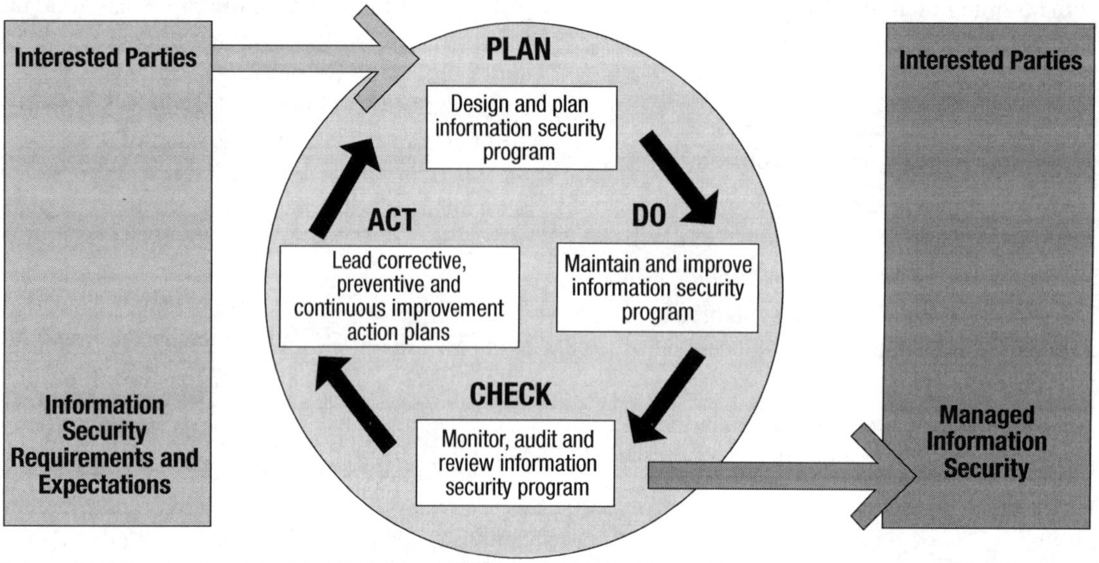

PLAN	Design, plan and initiate the information security program. These activities include creating a strategy; socialization concepts; and policies, goals, objectives and practices as necessary to manage risk. The activities include creating a strategy; socialization concepts; and policies, goals, objectives and practices as necessary to manage risk."
DO	Execute and control the information security strategy including the integration into organizational practices.
CHECK	Facilitate semiannual audits to determine conformance to the statement of applicability and identify opportunities for improvement. Wherever appropriate, develop and integrate performance matrices which support information security program goals and objectives.
ACT	Upon the discovery of nonconformities and/or opportunities, create and track corrective, preventive and continuous improvement action plans. Present findings from internal/external audit and risk assessments to the management review committee for decisions regarding the acceptance, rejection or transfer of risk and the commitment of resources and capital to facilitate subsequent efforts.

The TQM approach, combined with a governance methodology that focuses on strategic program alignment with organizational goals, provides information security managers with tools that they can use to implement and maintain a highly effective, efficient program. As described in Chapter 1, the basic elements of a governance methodology include a strategic vision, objectives, KGIs, CSFs, KPIs, and key actions or tactical and annual action plans. These elements are defined as follows and depicted in **figure 3.23**:

- Vision is a broadly defined, clear and compelling statement about the enterprise's purpose. It should include the desired outcomes of the information security program.
- Strategic objectives are a set of goals that are necessary and sufficient to move the enterprise toward its vision. These goals should be reflected in KGIs.
- CSFs are a set of circumstances or events that are necessary to achieve the strategic objectives.
- KPIs are concrete metrics tracked to ensure that the CSFs are being achieved.
- Key actions, including tactical and annual action plans, are the initiatives to be delivered to achieve the strategic objectives and KGIs.

Figure 3.23—Strategic Objectives, CSFs, KPIs, Key Actions

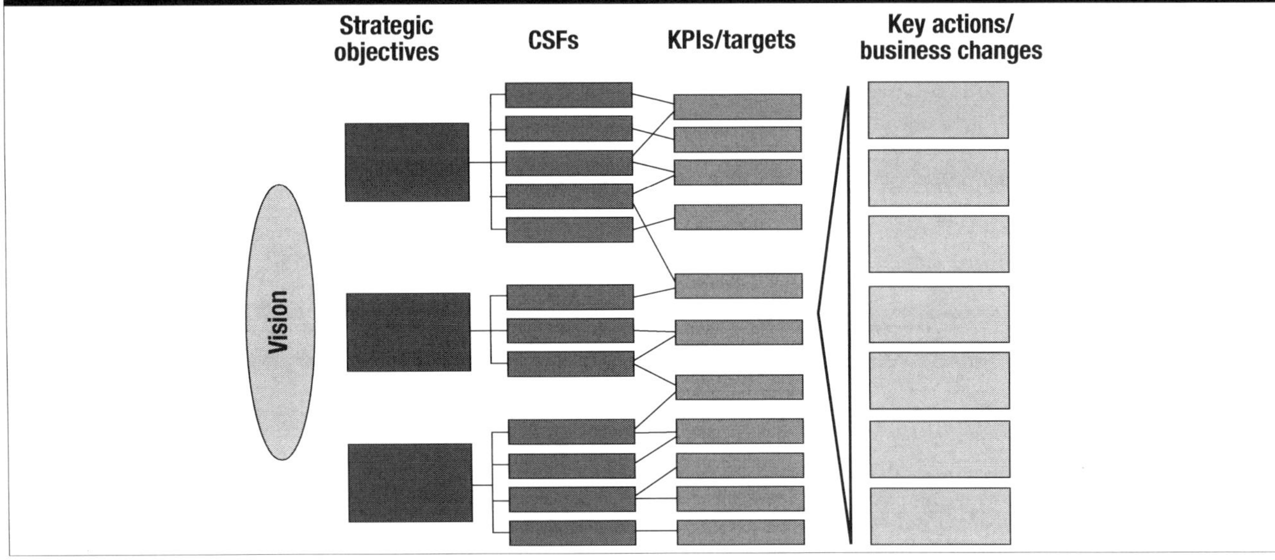

3.14.3 Security Reviews and Audits

During the development and management of an information security program, it is essential for the manager to have a consistent standardized approach to assessing and evaluating the state of various aspects of the program. Using a consistent approach will provide trend information over time and can serve as a metric for improvements to the information security program. This can be accomplished using a security review process similar to an audit. Like standard approaches to auditing, security reviews have:

- **Objective**—A review objective is a statement of what is to be determined in the course of a review. For example, the objective of a review may be to determine whether an Internet banking application can be exploited to gain access to internal systems. Objectives define what the information security manager wants to get out of the review. Usually, it is to determine whether a given systems environment meets some security standard. In the preceding example, the review objective is that of a typical external penetration study (i.e., to make sure that users of web services cannot exploit system vulnerabilities to gain access to the systems that host those services).
- **Scope**— Scope refers to the mapping of the objective to the aspect that is to be reviewed. Thus, the review objective dictates scope. For example, the review objective in the previous example dictates that the scope includes the Internet access points of the application and all the underlying technology that enables that access. If the scope is hard to describe, the review objective should be clarified to ensure that the result of the review are well-defined and actionable.
- **Constraint**—A constraint is the situation within which reviewers operate that may impact aspects of conducting a review. It may or may not hinder their ability to review the entire scope and complete the review objective. In the example, a constraint may be a prohibition on accessing the application during business hours. The ability to fulfill the objective of the review in the context of constraints is something an information security manager must evaluate.
- **Approach**—An approach is a set of activities that cover the scope in a way that meets the objective of the review, given the constraints. There are usually alternative sets of activities that can cover the scope and objective. The idea is to identify the set that is hampered by the fewest constraints. In the previous example, a constraint could be that the information security manager would not be given the credentials necessary to create a web session as an authorized user of the application under review. (In this example, the objective requires the reviewer to provide a determination on whether application Internet access can be exploited to gain access to internal systems.) To meet this objective, the review must have application Internet access as part of the scope. An information security manager, in this situation, should identify the lack of authorization

for application access as a constraint and find some other way to achieve the same objective. One approach could be to set up the system in a test environment where access authorization is not an issue.

- **Result**—A result is an assessment of whether the review objective has been met. It is an answer to the question, "Is this secure?" If it is not possible to answer the question with any level of assurance, the review should be declared incomplete. This would occur in the example case if the application access required for covering the scope were not achieved.

Figure 3.24 depicts some common types of reviews and the objective, scope, constraint and approach results of each.

Figure 3.24—Security Review Alternatives

Review Type	Control Self-Assessment	Security Architecture or Design Review	Security Spot Check
Objective	To establish that the controls implemented are sufficient to maintain security in the systems environment required to effect security	To establish that a system is capable of securing data and to identify configuration parameters	To decide whether a given security process is working
Scope	Documentation of the system security mechanisms in the systems environment housing the data that an enterprise is charged to secure	Network and operating system placement diagrams, as well as detailed technical design	Process description, system security parameters of system directly supporting the process
Constraint	• Unknowns or lack of expertise in security mechanisms in third-party products • Time • The possible bias of participants who are also responsible for system maintenance	• Unknowns or lack of expertise in security mechanisms in third-party products • Time	Reliance on assumptions with respect to systems interfaces and supporting systems (e.g., data feeds, network, OS)
Approach	• Identify risk, exposures and potential perpetrators. • Evaluate ability of controls to protect, detect or recover from exploits.	Compare settable parameters of all system components to known secure configurations or security policies.	• Review all system security procedures and settings. • Identify expected user community. • Evaluate whether expected controls are in place.
Result	List of control weaknesses	List of issues to address, iterative process	Yes or no

While performing security reviews, an information security manager can gather data not only about policy and process at various levels of the enterprise, but also about specific control weaknesses that may put information at risk. This data can be used to help prioritize program development efforts.

Audits

Like security reviews, audits have objectives, scopes, constraints, approaches and results. The professional practice of information systems audit is based on an approach in which auditors identify, evaluate, test and assess the effectiveness of controls. Effectiveness is judged based on whether controls meet a given set of control objectives, such as compliance with policies and standards. In performing an audit, an audit team assembles documentation that: 1) maps controls to control objectives, 2) states what the team did to test those controls and 3) links those test results to the final assessment. This documentation, called work papers, may or may not be delivered with the final report.

When an information security program has established policies and standards, an audit is extremely useful in identifying whether those policies and standards have been fully implemented. However, when an information security program is under development, those policies and standards may not yet be finalized. In this situation, an information security manager may select an externally published standard and engage an audit team to determine the extent to which the enterprise is in compliance. An external standard or framework, such as COBIT or ISO/IEC 27001 and 27002, provides a structure for control objectives that enables an audit team to organize its examination of existing controls. The work papers from such an audit can often be more useful than the final report. The value in the analysis of existing controls and their mapping to a set of external standards is most useful if the set of external standards closely resembles those the information security manager intends to put in place as part of the information security program.

Different standards focus on different aspects of controls. The following examples start with the most comprehensive in scope and are followed by those whose scope narrows into specific technology domains:

- COBIT lists control objectives and control practices for each control objective.
- The Standard of Good Practice for Information Security catalogs information security management practices and lists corresponding requirements for resources and responsibilities.
- ISO/IEC 27001 and 27002 list control practices in the domain of IT security, followed by an appendix listing security-related control objectives and control practices for each control objective.

Auditors

It is essential for the information security manager to develop a good working relationship with the auditors, whether internal or external. While it is not unusual for auditors to be viewed in a negative light by IT and information security staff and others in the enterprise, effective information security managers understand that audits are both an essential assurance process and a critical and influential ally in achieving good security governance and compliance. They can be instrumental in implementing security standards by providing feedback to senior management through audit findings that can serve to influence the tone at the top and create high-level support for security activities. Involving auditors in overall security management can be a powerful tool for improving an enterprise's security culture.

The information security program must integrate with internal and external auditing activities. Some audits are compulsory, such as those required to establish compliance with a regulatory standard. Others are voluntary, as when an independent auditor makes an attestation to compliance with an industry standard.

The information security manager should coordinate with organizational audit coordinators to ensure that time and resources are allocated to address audit activities. Procedures should be established in advance for scheduling, observation of employee activities, and provision of configuration data from technical systems.

In some cases, a deficiency identified by an auditor may not be applicable to the information security manager's specific enterprise. If concerns are identified during an audit, the information security manager should work with the auditors to agree on associated risk, mitigating factors and satisfactory control objectives. With this information in hand, the information security manager may craft one or more potential solutions that fit the enterprise's operational, financial and technical environment. Any combination of mitigating or compensating controls that enforce the agreed-on control objectives should satisfy the issue.

Audit findings provide strong, independent feedback for the steering committee and management to use in assessing the effectiveness of the information security program.

3.14.4 Compliance Monitoring and Enforcement

Compliance enforcement processes must be considered during program development to ensure subsequent effectiveness and manageability once the program is implemented. Compliance enforcement refers to any activity within the information security program that is designed to ensure compliance with the enterprise's security policies, standards and procedures.

Compliance, especially with procedural controls, may pose one of the major challenges for managing a security program and must be given careful attention when designing controls during program development. Ease of monitoring and enforcement is often one of the essential factors in control selection. Complex control processes that are not readily enforceable or are difficult to monitor for compliance are generally of little value and may pose a considerable risk themselves.

Enforcement procedures should be designed to assume that control activities are in place in support of control objectives. These procedures provide an added layer of control to ensure that the procedures established by management are actually followed. For example, in a password reset procedure, an enforcement procedure may consist of a supervisor listening to randomly selected help desk calls and listing any help desk staff who neglected to ask a user for a security identification code prior to resetting a password. The enforcement procedure would be to use the list first to warn and then to discipline any help desk staff member who did not follow the password reset procedure.

Policy Compliance

Policies form the basis for all accountability with respect to security responsibilities throughout the enterprise. Policies must be comprehensive enough to cover all situations in which information is handled, yet flexible enough to allow different processes and procedures to evolve for different technologies and still be in compliance. Except in very small enterprises, an information security manager will not have direct control over SDLC activities of all information systems in the enterprise. Consequently, it is necessary to designate formal security roles that establish which department head is responsible for putting processes in place that maintain security policy compliance and meet the appropriate standards for a given set of information systems.

It is the responsibility of the information security manager to ensure that, in the assignment process, there are no orphan systems or systems without policy compliance owners. It is also the responsibility of the information security manager to provide oversight and ensure that policy compliance processes are properly designed. An information security manager can accomplish this oversight via a combination of security review, metrics gathering and reporting processes.

Information security management literature often refers to a policy exception process. This is a method by which business units or departments can review a policy and decide not to follow it based on various factors. Several justifications can exist for policy exceptions. An exception may be based on a risk/reward decision in which the benefit of not following the policy justifies the risk. It may be financially or technically infeasible to comply with specific policies or standards. Such trade-offs should be considered in the policy development process, when possible, to minimize the need for subsequent exceptions. As part of the program development, a formal waiver process should be implemented to manage the life cycle of these exceptions to ensure they are periodically reviewed and, when possible, closed. Any such policy exceptions must be assessed for risk and impact prior to implementation and the identified risk accepted by appropriate levels of management.

Standards Compliance

Standards provide the boundaries of options for systems, processes and actions that still comply with policy. The standards must be designed to ensure that all systems of the same type within the same security domain are configured and operated in the same way based on criticality and sensitivity of the resources. These will allow platform administration procedures to be developed using standards documents as references to ensure that policy compliance is maintained. Standards also provide economy of scale; the configuration mapping to policy needs to be done only once for each security domain, and technology and process engineering efforts are reused for systems of the same type.

As much as possible, compliance with standards should be automated to ensure that system configurations do not, either intentionally or unintentionally, deviate from policy compliance. However, as policies should state only management intent, direction and expectations to allow flexibility for different standards to develop, and provide many options to comply, exceptions to standards should always be reviewed to see if they deviate from the intent of the policy. It may also be that a business situation justifies a deviation from existing standards but, nevertheless, may be determined to fall within the intent of the policy. As with policy exceptions, standards exceptions must include risk assessment and acceptance by appropriate management. If exceptions are required to go through the change management process (assuming one is in place), assessing the risk of the change will be a standard part of the process.

Resolution of Noncompliance Issues

Noncompliance issues may result in risk to the enterprise, so it is important to develop specific processes to deal with them in an effective and timely manner. Depending on how significant a risk is, various approaches can be taken to address it. If a particular noncompliance event is a serious risk, then resolution needs to occur quickly. The security manager benefits from a method of determining criticality and then implementing a risk-based response process.

Typically, a timetable is developed to document each noncompliance item and responsibility for addressing it is assigned and recorded. Regular follow-up is important to ensure that any noncompliance issues and other variances are satisfactorily addressed in a timely manner. Noncompliance issues and other variances can be identified through a number of different mechanisms, including:

- Normal monitoring
- Audit reports
- Security reviews
- Vulnerability scans
- Due diligence work

Compliance Enforcement

Compliance enforcement is an ongoing set of activities that endeavor to ensure policy and, by default, standards requirements that are not being met are brought into compliance. Audits are a snapshot of compliance in time; compliance enforcement is an ongoing process that helps reduce risk and ensure positive audit opinions.

Compliance enforcement responsibilities are usually shared across organizational units and the results are commonly shared with executive management and the board's audit or compliance committees. The legal and internal audit departments often have responsibility for assessment of business strategies and operations, respectively. The information security unit is often responsible for implementing independent evaluation of technical standards, preferably using automated tools. In larger enterprises and heavily regulated industries, an independent compliance organization may be established to handle and coordinate these activities.

The information security program itself is also a target of compliance evaluation and performance. The information security manager should be prepared to work closely with compliance and internal audit personnel to demonstrate compliance of the information security program with pertinent standards and regulations. As with a formal audit, issues identified should be defined in terms of risk, mitigating factors and acceptable control objectives. Depending on the magnitude of the issue, the information security manager may address the concern independently or may collaborate with executive management and/or the security steering committee to create acceptable solutions.

3.14.5 Monitoring Approaches

It is important for the security manager to develop a consistent, reliable method to determine the overall ongoing effectiveness of the program. One way is to regularly conduct risk assessments and track improvements over time. Another standard tool is the use of external and internal scanning and penetration testing to determine system vulnerabilities, although this will indicate the effectiveness of only one facet of the overall program. Doing so on a regular basis and tracking the results can be a useful indicator of trends in technical security. Most enterprises conduct regular vulnerability scans to determine if open vulnerabilities are addressed and new ones appear. Steady improvement is the hallmark of an effective program, although it is of limited value from a management perspective unless it is accompanied by information about viable threats and potential impacts to provide enough information to inform appropriate security decisions.

In addition to monitoring automated security activities, the enterprise's change management system should feed the information security's monitoring program. Metrics are important, but of little use if adverse trends are not dealt with in a timely manner. The information security manager should have a process in place whereby metrics are reviewed on a regular basis and any unusual activity is reported. An action plan to react to the unusual activity should be developed.

Monitoring Security Activities in Infrastructure and Business Applications

Because an enterprise's vulnerability to security breaches likely exists at all times, continuous monitoring of security activities is a prudent business practice (and increasingly a regulatory requirement) that the information security manager should implement. A great deal of this monitoring will be technical and may be performed by IT personnel. In this case, the monitoring requirements must be defined in suitable operating standards along with severity criteria and escalation processes.

Continuous monitoring of IDSs and firewalls can provide real-time information on attempts to breach perimeter defenses. Training help desk personnel to escalate suspicious reports that may signal a breach or an attack can serve as an effective monitoring and early warning system. This information can be critical to taking corrective action in a timely manner.

Determining Success of Information Security Investments

It is important for the information security manager to have processes in place to determine the overall effectiveness of security investments and the extent to which objectives have been met. There is always competition for resources in enterprises, and senior management will seek to obtain the best ROIs and justify costs.

During the design and implementation of the security program, the information security manager should ensure that KPIs are defined and agreed to, and a mechanism to measure progress against those indicators is implemented. The information security manager can then assess the success or failure of various components of the security program and whether they are cost-justifiable. This will be helpful when developing a business case for other elements of the security program.

Actual costs for various components of a security program need to be accurately calculated to determine cost-effectiveness. The concept of TCO is useful for evaluating the various components of a security program. In addition to initial procurement and implementation costs, it is important to include:

- Costs to administer controls
- Training costs
- Maintenance costs
- Monitoring costs
- Update fees
- Consultant or help desk fees
- Fees associated with other interrelated systems that may have been modified to accommodate security objectives

3.14.6 Measuring Information Security Management Performance

The information security manager should understand how to implement processes and mechanisms that provide the ability to assess the successes and shortcomings of the information security program. Measuring success consists of defining measurable objectives, tracking the most appropriate metrics, and periodically analyzing results to determine areas of success and improvement opportunities. The specific objectives of the information security program will vary according to the scope and operating level of the security department, but they must be conceptually and chronologically aligned with business goals.

An information security program generally includes a core set of common objectives:

- Achieve acceptable levels of risk and loss related to information security issues.
- Support achievement of overall organizational objectives.
- Support organizational achievement of compliance.
- Maximize the program's operational productivity.
- Maximize security cost-effectiveness.
- Establish and maintain organizational security awareness.
- Facilitate effective logical, technical and operational security architectures.
- Maximize effectiveness of program framework and resources.
- Measure and manage operational performance.

While each enterprise must develop its specific goals, the following sections cover the most common objectives and suggested methodologies for measuring their successful delivery.

Measuring Information Security Risk and Loss

The primary objective of an information security program is to ensure that risk is managed appropriately and impacts from adverse events fall within acceptable limits. Attaining perfect security while retaining system usability is virtually impossible. Determining whether the security program is functioning at a suitable level—balancing operational efficiency against adequate safety—can be approached in a number of ways from different perspectives.

The following are possible approaches to periodically measuring the program's success against risk management and loss prevention objectives:

- The technical vulnerability management approach poses the following questions:
  - How many technical or operational vulnerabilities exist?
  - How many have been resolved?
  - What is the average time to resolve them?
  - How many recurred?
  - How many systems (critical or otherwise) are impacted by them?
  - How many have the potential for external exploit?
  - How many have the potential for gross compromise (e.g., remote privileged code execution, unauthorized administrative access, bulk exposure of sensitive printed information)?
- The risk management approach is concerned with the following questions:
  - How many high-, medium- and low-risk issues are unresolved? What is the aggregate annualized loss expectancy (ALE)?
  - How many were resolved during the reporting period? If available, what is the aggregate ALE that has been eliminated?
  - How many issues were completely eliminated versus partially mitigated versus transferred?
  - How many were accepted because no mitigation or compensation method was tenable?
  - How many remain open because of inaction or lack of cooperation?
  - The loss prevention approach is concerned with the following questions:
  - Were there loss events during the reporting period? What is the aggregate loss, including investigation, recovery, data reconstruction and customer relationship management?
  - How many events were preventable (i.e., risk or vulnerability identified prior to the loss event)?
  - What was the average amount of time taken to identify loss incidents? To initiate incident response procedures? To isolate incidents from other systems? To contain event losses?

In addition to these quantitative metrics, a number of qualitative measures can be applied to risk management success monitoring. Some of these include:

- Do risk management activities occur as scheduled?
- Have incident response plans (IRPs) and business continuity plans (BCPs) been tested?
- Are asset inventories, custodianships, valuations and risk analyses up to date?
- Is there consensus among information security stakeholders as to acceptable levels of risk to the enterprise?
- Do executive management oversight and review activities occur as planned?

Measuring Support of Organizational Objectives

The information security program must support core organizational objectives. Measuring this set of objectives is largely subjective and organizational objectives can change rapidly in the face of evolving operational pressures and market conditions. The following qualitative measures can be reviewed by the information security steering committee and executive management:

- Is there a documented correlation between key organizational milestones and the objectives of the information security program?
- How many information security objectives were successfully completed in support of organizational goals?
- Were there organizational goals that were not fulfilled because information security objectives were not met?
- How strong is consensus among business units, executive management and other information

security stakeholders that program objectives are complete and appropriate?

The information security manager should recognize that much of a successful measure's value is in analysis of why an objective was or was not met. Qualitative measures such as those represented by support of organizational objectives should be handled as such. For missed objectives, the reasons they were not accomplished should be analyzed and the feedback used to guide ongoing optimization of the information security program.

Measuring Compliance

An essential, ongoing and primary concern for information security program management is policy and standards compliance. Given that most security failures are the result of personnel failing to follow procedures in compliance with standards, compliance is an essential element of security management. Criticality and sensitivity must be known, as they mandate the level of compliance that must be achieved to manage risk to acceptable levels. Anything less than 100 percent compliance is unacceptable when piloting passenger jets or operating nuclear power plants because impacts are likely to be catastrophic. For any activity that is not life- or enterprise-threatening, the cost and level of compliance efforts must be weighed against the benefits and potential impacts.

Measuring compliance with technical standards is often straightforward and can frequently be automated. Compliance with procedural or process standards is generally more difficult and may pose a challenge. Because this is frequently the area of failure leading to security compromise, it requires careful consideration. Some compliance requirements are sufficiently critical to warrant direct continuous monitoring, such as access controlled by guards and sign-in procedures. In other cases, detective controls such as logging and checklists may suffice.

Compliance requirements may be statutory, contractual or internal. If the enterprise must comply with compulsory or voluntary standards involving information security, the information security manager must ensure that program goals are aligned with those requirements. Likewise, the policies, procedures and technologies implemented by the program must fulfill requirements of adopted standards. Measurements of compliance achievement are often tied to the results of internal or external audits. The information security manager may wish to implement automated or manual compliance monitoring with higher frequency and/or broader scope than achievable with incremental audits. In addition to actual point-in-time compliance, the program should be measured on the effectiveness of resolving identified compliance issues.

It should be noted that compliance and security are not necessarily synonymous. Many enterprises have wrongly approached legal, regulatory or contractual compliance as the chief goal of the security program. An enterprise that has properly aligned security and privacy approaches with all relevant organizational objectives will naturally fulfill requirements related to compliance obligations.

Measuring Operational Productivity

No information security program has unlimited resources. It is crucial for the information security manger to maximize operational productivity, especially in light of the rapid growth of IT enterprises.

Ways productivity can be improved include using automation technologies, outsourcing low-value operational tasks and leveraging the activities of other organizational units. Security management automation technologies can act as workforce multipliers, increasing the accomplishment of operational tasks many times over. Vulnerability scanning tools are an outstanding example of this effect: Manual vulnerability assessment that once took several individuals several weeks can now be accomplished in hours or days. The personnel cost savings can often justify the expense of such tools.

Productivity measures are most useful when employed in a time-based comparison analysis. This approach provides a powerful demonstration of security automation value by showing productivity before and after application of a productivity-boosting technology. Using this approach, the information security manager can demonstrate returns on security investments.

Productivity is a measure of work product generated per resource. For example, if analysis of event log entries is the work product and a security analyst is the resource, the measure of productivity is event log entries analyzed per analyst. Productivity measures can be applied to technology resources in addition to personnel (e.g., network packets processed per IDS node).

The information security manager should set periodic goals for increasing the productivity of the information security program through specific initiatives. These goals should be reviewed to determine the productivity gains achieved. Where possible, the information security manager should analyze data such as hourly employee cost and effort expended per task to demonstrate the financial value of productivity improvement initiatives to senior management.

Measuring Security Cost-Effectiveness

It is important for the information security program to be financially sustainable because financial constraints are a common reason for security lapses, including failure to plan for ongoing maintenance requirements. The information security manager must work to maximize the value of each security investment to control information security expenses and ensure sustainable achievement of objectives.

This process begins with accurate cost forecasting and budgeting. The success of this activity is generally established by monitoring budget utilization versus original projections and can help identify issues with security cost planning. In addition to measuring budgeting effectiveness, the information security manager should implement procedures to measure the ongoing cost-effectiveness of security components, most often accomplished by tracking cost-result ratios. This approach establishes cost-efficiency goals for new technologies and improvement goals for existing technologies by measuring the total cost of generating a specific result.

To be accurate, costs must include maintenance, operations and administration costs for the period analyzed (e.g., month, quarter, year). Including all pertinent costs provides the information security manager with the TCO for the security investment being analyzed. Ratios of result-units per currency-unit (e.g., 7,400 network packets analyzed per US dollar annually) or vice versa (€0.04 per thousand emails scanned annually) can be used to demonstrate cost-efficiency and cost of results. Other examples include:

- Costs of vulnerability assessment per application
- Costs of workstation security controls per user
- Costs of email spam and virus protection per mailbox

Technology purchase and deployment efforts represent only a fraction of full life cycle costs. The information security manager must regularly consider the total costs of maintaining, operating and administering technical security components. In addition, the personnel costs associated with ongoing operational and management activities should be considered. These analyses should be shared with the security steering committee to help identify areas of opportunity for improving cost-effectiveness and to assist in forecasting future resource needs.

Measuring Organizational Awareness

Even in a tightly controlled technical environment, personnel actions can present threats that can be mitigated only through education and awareness. It is important for the information security program to implement processes for tracking the ongoing effectiveness of awareness programs.

Tracking organizational awareness is most commonly achieved at the employee level. The information security manager should work with the HR department to implement metrics for tracking organizational awareness success. Records of initial training, acceptance of policies and usage agreements, and ongoing awareness updates are useful metrics relative to the actual training program. In addition to identifying individuals in need of training, this helps identify organizational units that may not be fully engaged with the security awareness program.

Another measure of awareness program effectiveness is employee testing. The information security manager should develop tools such as short online or paper examinations that are administered immediately following training to determine the effectiveness of the training. Conducting additional surveys on a random sampling of employees several months after training will help determine the long-term effectiveness of awareness training and other efforts (e.g., information security newsletters).

Measuring Effectiveness of Technical Security Architecture

The technical security architecture is often one of the most tangible manifestations of an information security program. It is important for the information security manager to establish quantitative measures of the effectiveness of the technical control environment. The range of possible technical metrics is quite broad, and the information security manager should identify those metrics most meaningful to the identified recipients. Technical security metrics can be categorized for reporting and analysis purposes by protected resource and geographic location. Some examples of technical security effectiveness metrics include:

- Probe and attack attempts repelled by network access control devices; qualify by asset or resource targeted, source geography and attack type
- Probe and attack attempts detected by IDSs on internal networks; qualify by internal versus external source, resource targeted and attack type
- Number and type of actual compromises; qualify by attack severity, attack type, impact severity and source of attack
- Statistics on viruses, worms and other malware identified and neutralized; qualify by impact potential, severity of larger Internet outbreaks and malware vector
- Amount of downtime attributable to security flaws and unpatched systems
- Number of messages processed, sessions examined and kilobytes (KB) of data examined by IDSs

In addition to the foregoing quantitative success metrics, a number of important qualitative measures apply to the technical control environment. Some examples include the following:

- Individual technical mechanisms have been tested to verify control objectives and policy enforcement.
- The security architecture is constructed of appropriate controls in a layered fashion.
- Control mechanisms are properly configured and monitored in real time, self-protection is implemented, and information security personnel are alerted to faults.
- All critical systems stream events to information security personnel or to event analysis automation tools for real-time threat detection.

Although these measures and metrics are useful for IT and information security management and other individuals, most will have little meaning or interest to senior management. A composite summary indicating the security department is performing according to expectations will probably be much more useful to senior and executive management.

Measuring Effectiveness of Management Framework and Resources

Efficient information security management maximizes the results produced by the components and processes it implements. Mechanisms for capturing process feedback, identifying issues and opportunities, tracking consistency of implementation, and effectively communicating changes and knowledge help maximize program effectiveness. Methods of tracking the program's success in this area include:

- Tracking the frequency of issue recurrence
- Monitoring the level of operational knowledge capture and dissemination
- Standardizing process implementations
- Documenting information security roles and responsibilities clearly and completely
- Incorporating information security requirements into every project plan
- Making the program more productive and cost-effective
- Monitoring overall security resource utilization and trends
- Alignment with and supporting organizational objectives

The information security manager should implement such mechanisms with the goal of extracting additional latent value from the framework, procedures and resources that make up the program.

Measuring Operational Performance

Measuring, monitoring and reporting on information security processes help the information security manager ensure that operational components of the program effectively support control objectives. Measures of security operational performance include:

- Time to detect, escalate, isolate and contain incidents

- Time between vulnerability detection and resolution
- Quantity, frequency and severity of incidents discovered after their occurrence
- Average time between vendor release of vulnerability patches and their application
- Percentage of systems that have been audited within a certain period
- Number of changes that have been released without full change control approval

The information security manager should determine the most appropriate metrics for tracking security operations within all organizational units. These metrics should be compiled, analyzed and distributed to stakeholders and responsible management on a regular basis. Performance issues should be analyzed for root cause by the security steering committee and improvement solutions implemented.

3.14.7 Ongoing Monitoring and Communication

There are several monitoring considerations in implementing or managing a security program, regardless of its scope. New or modified controls, in addition to numerous other design considerations, require methods to determine if they are operating as intended. Monitoring technical controls often consists of reviewing logs and checking various alerts, such as IDSs or firewalls, for potential security vulnerabilities or emerging threats.

Procedural and process controls are typically just as important but more difficult to implement. Technical monitoring of physical processes is likely to be most efficient and effective. Personnel usually interface with information systems at various points in typical processes and these will be the most promising control points to monitor. Monitoring earlier processes, in addition to watching for suitable outcomes, can provide earlier warnings of impending problems.

Monitoring of information systems security is a critical operational component of any information security program. The information security manager should consider the development of a central monitoring environment that provides analysts visibility into all enterprise information resources. A broad range of security events are logged and could be monitored, and each enterprise needs to determine which events are the most pertinent in terms of affected resources and event type. Some commonly monitored event types include:

- Failed attempts to access resources
- Processing faults that may indicate system tampering
- Outages, race conditions and faults related to design or other issues
- Changes to system configurations, particularly security controls
- Privileged system access and activities
- Technical security component fault detection

Procedures for analyzing events and taking appropriate responsive actions must be developed. Security monitoring analysts should be trained on these procedures, and monitoring supervisors should have response procedures to address anomalies. Usually, response procedures involve analyzing related events and system states, capturing additional event-related information, investigating suspicious activity, and escalating the issue to senior analysts or management. The escalation path for security events and incident initiation should be tested regularly.

In addition to real-time monitoring, the information security manager should periodically conduct an analysis of trends in security-related events, such as attempted attack types or most frequently targeted resources. The longer view associated with this type of analysis can often reveal threat and risk patterns that would otherwise go unrecognized. Key controls should be monitored in real time whenever possible. Detective controls, such as log reviews, tend to be useful only to determine how something that has already happened might have unfolded. Even IDS alerts are reactive; depending on tuning, an IDS may not be effective as a means of triggering rapid response.

Results of ongoing monitoring may be rolled up to assure management that security is providing the appropriate levels of operational assurances and control objectives are being met.

Page intentionally left blank

Case Study

At the start of a multinational corporation's financial year, a new information security manager was hired to oversee the firm's information security program. The information security manager requested and obtained policies and procedures, prior year internal audits, and results from the most recent external audits.

Upon reviewing information provided by internal audit, the information security manager focused on the change management component of the overall information security program. In assessing the control design effectiveness for the change management process, the manager noted, through interviews with key IT personnel, that the firm used a proprietary change control system (dubbed GLASS) to enter change requests and then track them through the change management process—taking into account approvals and plans for both rolling out and backing out changes. GLASS keeps a record of all changes made to the billing system, along with the associated date, using unique identifiers for each change and audit logs that capture other billing system activities.

To determine operational effectiveness for the control process, the information security manager conducted interviews with technology owners for the billing system and the firm's audit personnel, then used a random sample of changes taken from the proprietary change control system. The sampling methodology that was used concurred with the firm's internal audit policies. The resulting control assessment involved in the audit was conducted, along the parameters required by the firms' policies and procedures. The change control system passed and no exceptions were found.

However, the firm's external audit determined that there were changes to the system that did not have the required approvals. Reviewing the policies and procedures, the information security manager could not find any obvious reason for missing the changes during the internal audit. Through subsequent investigation with the audit team and personnel responsible for migrating changes into one of the production systems, the information security manager determined that GLASS was not the sole point of entry for change requests but could be bypassed.

The firm was then tasked to develop a monitoring solution to examine all billing system and database system activity, then compare it against approved functionality (called VIEW). This tool would then alert IT security of any actions that did not reflect those permitted by change management policies and procedures, such as a change that did not have approvals being migrated into production.

1. When evaluating control design effectiveness, reviewing the audit program and making inquiries with staff, what are some mistakes the information security manager made?

2. What type of control does the implementation of the VIEW tool represent?

   A. Compensating
   B. Corrective
   C. Detective
   D. Preventive

Answers on page 248

Chapter 3 ANSWER KEY

Case Study

1. The information security manager's review and sampling methods were flawed. First, although not be primarily involved in the audit function, the information security manager could consult the audit reports to gather additional information. Second, interviews should be supported with additional research because interviews can be unreliable; employees may omit information or not be forthcoming with information for a variety of reasons. As seen in the case study, interviews did not uncover the more significant issues of the occurrence of changes that bypassed the system. When inquiring about a process that has a built-in version control and monitoring system, it is important to note all possible entry points. Since it is the supplemental control technology, GLASS, that recorded activity, it was important to note whether there was a way around this system. The closer the information security manager can get to the native control technology of a system, the closer the manager will be to accessing core functionality. The information security manager missed this part of the investigation.

2. A. A compensating control is an internal control that reduces the risk of an existing or potential control weakness, resulting in errors and omissions. The VIEW reacts to attempted violations and logs the information but does not react to the actions of other controls and correct errors; therefore, it is detective.

   B. A corrective control would have the power to remediate impact. In the case of the VIEW tool, it is a monitor against activity and sends out alerts when a breach of acceptable activity occurs.

   C. A detective control warns of violations or attempted violations of security policy—in this case, logging of system activity and comparing it against authorized actions. The VIEW tool can react only once an action has occurred; therefore, it is detective.

   D. The VIEW reacts to the activity already implemented within the targeted systems; therefore, it cannot be a preventive tool. For it to be preventive, the tool would have to be empowered with preventing users from completing an action that was not authorized.

Chapter 4:

Incident Management

Overview

Part A: Incident Management Readiness

Part B: Incident Management Operations

Overview

This chapter reviews the essential knowledge necessary to establish an effective incident management program to respond to and subsequently manage incidents that threaten an enterprise's information systems and infrastructure.

This domain represents 30 percent of the CISM examination (approximately 45 questions).

Domain 4 Exam Content Outline

A. Incident Management Readiness

1. Incident Response Plan
2. Business Impact Analysis
3. Business Continuity Plan
4. Disaster Recovery Plan
5. Incident Classification/Categorization
6. Incident Management Training, Testing and Evaluation

B. Incident Management Operations

1. Incident Management Tools and Technologies
2. Incident Investigation and Evaluation
3. Incident Containment Methods
4. Incident Response Communications
5. Incident Eradication and Recovery
6. Post-Incident Review Practices

Learning Objectives/Task Statements

Upon completion of this chapter, the information security manager should be able to:

- Identify internal and external influences to the organization that impact the information security strategy.
- Establish and maintain an incident response plan, in alignment with the business continuity plan and disaster recovery plan.
- Establish and maintain an information security incident classification and categorization process.
- Develop and implement processes to ensure the timely identification of information security incidents.
- Establish and maintain processes to investigate and document information security incidents in accordance with legal and regulatory requirements.
- Establish and maintain incident handling process, including containment, notification, escalation, eradication and recovery.
- Organize, train, equip and assign responsibilities to incident response teams.
- Establish and maintain communication plans and processes for internal and external entities.
- Evaluate incident management plans through periodic testing and review, including table-top exercises, checklist review and simulation testing.
- Conduct post-incident reviews to facilitate continuous improvement, including root-cause analysis, lessons learned, corrective actions and reassessment of risk.

Suggested Resources for Further Reading

Alberts, C; A. Dorofee; G. Killcrece; R. Ruefle; M. Zajicek; *Defining Incident Management Processes for CSIRTs: A Work in Progress,* Carnegie Mellon University, USA, 2004

Bace, R.; *Intrusion detection*; Macmillan Technical Publishing, United Kingdom, 2000

Brown, R.; S. Roberts; *Intelligence-Driven Incident Response: Outwitting the Adversary,* O'Reilly Media, Inc., USA, 2017

Burtles, J.; *Principles and Practice of Business Continuity: Tools and Techniques,* Rothstein Associates Inc., USA, 2007

Carnegie Mellon University, Software Engineering Institute, *Create a CSIRT,* https://resources.sei.cmu.edu/library/asset-view.cfm?assetid=485693

Cloud Security Alliance (CSA), *Top Threats to Cloud Computing V1.0*, USA, 2010

CSA, *Top Threats to Cloud Computing: Egregious Eleven Deep Dive,* USA, 2020

CSA, *Top Threats to Mobile Computing,* USA, 2012

Federal Emergency Management Agency, www.fema.gov

Hiles, A.; *The Definitive Handbook of Business Continuity Management, 3rd Edition*, John Wiley & Sons Inc., USA, 2011

International Organization for Standardization (ISO), *ISO 22301:2019 Security and resilience — Business continuity management systems — Requirements,* Switzerland, 2019

Johansen, C.; *Digital Forensics and Incident Response Second Edition,* Packet Publishing Ltd, United Kingdom, 2020

Kabay, M.; *CSIRT Management*, USA, 2009, www.mekabay.com/infosecmgmt/csirtm.pdf

Lucas, J.; B. Moeller; *The Effective Incident Response Team*, Addison-Wesley, USA, 2004

Lucas, M.; *Network Flow Analysis,* No Starch Press, USA, 2010

Luttgens, J.; M. Pepe; K. Mandia; *Incident Response & Computer Forensics, 3rd Edition,* McGraw Hill Education, USA, 2014

Maiwald, E.; W. Sieglein; *Security Planning and Disaster Recovery,* McGraw-Hill Education, UK 2002

Marcus, E., *The Resilient Enterprise: Recovering Information Services from Disasters*, Veritas Software Corporation, USA, 2002

Middleton, B.; *Cyber Crime Investigator's Field Guide, 2nd Edition*, Auerbach Publications, USA, 2005

National Institute of Standards and Technology (NIST), *NIST Special Publication 800-61 Revision 2 Computer Security Incident Handling Guide,* USA, 2012

NIST, *NIST Special Publication 800-83 Revision 1 Guide to Malware Incident Prevention and Handling*, USA, 2013

NIST, *NIST Special Publication 800-86 Guide to Integrating Forensic Techniques into Incident Response*, USA, 2006

Nelson, B.; A. Philips; C. Stuart; *Guide to Computer Forensics and Investigations, 6th Edition,* Cengage Learning, USA, 2018

Nikkel, B.; *Practical Forensic Imaging: Securing Digital Evidence with Linux Tools,* No Starch Press, USA, 2016

Rajnovic, D.; *Computer Incident Response and Product Security,* Pearson Education, USA, 2010

Sanders, C.; *Practical Packet Analysis: Using Wireshark to Solve Real-world Network Problems*, No Starch Press, USA, 2017

Solomon, M.; E. Tittel; N. Broom; D. Barrett; *Computer Forensics Jump Start, 2nd Edition,* Wiley Publishers, USA, 2011

Snedaker, S.; *Business Continuity & Disaster Recovery Planning for IT Professionals, 2nd Edition*, Syngress Publishing Inc., USA, 2013

Toigo, J.; *Disaster Recovery Planning,* Prentice Hall PTR, United Kingdom, 2002

SELF-ASSESSMENT QUESTIONS

CISM exam questions are developed with the intent of measuring and testing practical knowledge in information security management. All questions are multiple choice and are designed for one best answer. Every CISM question has a stem (question) and four options (answer choices). The candidate is asked to choose the correct or best answer from the options. The stem may be in the form of a question or incomplete statement. Many times, a CISM examination question will require the candidate to choose the most likely or best answer.

In every case, the candidate is required to read the question carefully, eliminate known incorrect answers and then make the best choice possible. Knowing the format in which questions are asked, and how to study to gain knowledge of what can be tested, will go a long way toward answering them correctly.

1. The **PRIMARY** goal of a post-incident review is to:
   A. gather evidence for subsequent legal action.
   B. identify individuals who failed to take appropriate action.
   C. prepare a report on the incident for management.
   D. derive ways to improve the response process.

2. Which of the following is the **MOST** appropriate quality that an incident handler should possess?
   A. Presentation skills for management report
   B. Ability to follow policy and procedures
   C. Integrity in all actions
   D. Ability to cope with stress

3. What is the **PRIMARY** reason for conducting triage?
   A. To prioritize limited resources when handling incidents
   B. To align with mandatory process steps in the incident handling process
   C. To mitigate the change of an incident occurring
   D. To detect an incident before it can spread further

4. Which of the following is **MOST** important when deciding whether to build an alternate facility or subscribe to a hot site operated by a third party?
   A. Cost to rebuild information processing facilities
   B. Incremental daily cost of losing different systems
   C. Location and cost of commercial recovery facilities
   D. Estimated annual loss expectancy from key risk

5. Which of the following documents should be contained in a computer incident response team manual?
   A. Risk assessment
   B. Severity criteria
   C. Employee phone directory
   D. Table of all backup files

6. Which of the following types of insurance coverage would protect an enterprise against dishonest or fraudulent behavior by its own employees?
   A. Fidelity
   B. Business interruption
   C. Valuable papers and records
   D. Business continuity

7. Which of the following practices would **BEST** ensure the adequacy of a disaster recovery plan?
   A. Regular reviews of recovery plan information
   B. Tabletop walkthrough of disaster recovery plans
   C. Regular recovery exercises using expert personnel
   D. Regular audits of disaster recovery facilities

8. Which of the following procedures would provide the **BEST** protection if an intruder or malicious program has gained super user (e.g., root) access to a system?
   A. Prevent the system administrator(s) from accessing the system pending investigation of the incident.
   B. Inspect the system and intrusion detection output to identify all changes and then undo them.
   C. Rebuild the system using original media.
   D. Change all passwords, then resume normal operations.

9. Which of the following is likely to be the **MOST** significant challenge when developing an incident management plan?
   A. Misalignment between plan and organizational goals
   B. Implementation of log centralization, correlation and event tracking
   C. Development of incident metrics
   D. Lack of management support and organizational consensus

10. If a forensics copy of a hard drive is needed, which of the following would be the **MOST** defensible from a legal standpoint if used?

    A. A compressed copy of all contents of the hard drive
    B. A copy that includes all files and directories
    C. A bit-by-bit copy of all data
    D. An encrypted copy of all contents of the hard drive

Answers on page 254

Chapter 4 ANSWER KEY

Self-Assessment Questions

1. A. Forensic evidence should have been gathered earlier in the process.

   B. A post-incident review should not focus on finding and punishing individuals who did not take appropriate action or learning the identity of the attacker.

   C. Although a post-incident review can be used to prepare a report/presentation to management, it is not the primary goal.

   D. The primary goal of a post-incident review is to derive ways in which the incident response process can be improved.

2. A. Presentation skills are useful for preparing management reports but not the most essential quality.

   B. The ability to follow policy and procedures is important, but incidents are unanticipated and chaotic. It is likely that there are no specific policies or procedures to deal with them, and if the individual cannot cope with the stress of an incident, the ability is of little value.

   C. Integrity is an essential quality, but if an employee lacks it, they probably should not be employed by the enterprise.

   D. Incident handlers work in high-stress environments when dealing with incidents. Incorrect decisions are likely made if the person is unable to cope with stress; thus, the primary quality of incident handlers is to cope with stress.

3. **A. The primary reason for conducting triage is that incident handling resources are limited, and they must be used to the greatest benefit. With categorization, prioritization and assignment of incidents based on their criticality, resources can be allocated more efficiently.**

   B. Triage is not generally considered a mandatory process in incident handling.

   C. Triage does not mitigate an incident, but applies available resources most effectively to address the impact.

   D. Triage does not serve to detect incidents.

4. A. The cost of rebuilding the primary processing facility is not a factor in choosing an alternate recovery site.

   B. The daily cost of losing systems is the same whether the alternate site is built or rented.

   C. The decision whether to build an alternate facility or rent hot site facilities from a third party should be based entirely on business decisions of cost and ensuring the location is not susceptible to the same environmental risk as the primary facility.

   D. Annual loss expectancy is not a factor in choosing to build or rent an alternate site.

5. A. Risk assessments would be available to the response team. However, they typically change at least annually, so it would not make sense to include them in the manual.

   B. Severity criteria will remain relatively static and is the only one of the choices that is appropriate for the manual. The other choices will change frequently, and it would not make sense to reprint the manual every time phone numbers or backup files change.

   C. A phone directory will change frequently and would not be included in the manual.

   D. A table of backup files would typically be very large and change frequently and would not be included in the manual.

6. **A. Fidelity coverage means insurance coverage against loss from dishonesty or fraud by employees.**

   B. Business interruption insurance protects against losses from events that prevent the business from operating.

   C. Valuable papers and records insurance protects against the costs associated with the destruction of business records due to fire, flood or other incident.

   D. Business continuity insurance is similar to business interruption coverage, but generally provides broader protection.

7. **A. The most common failure of disaster recovery plans is a lack of maintaining the current essential operational information.**
   B. Tabletop walkthroughs are useful only if the information about systems and versions is current and up to date.
   C. Recovery exercises are critical for testing plans and procedures, but expert personnel have the knowledge to recover systems without using the plans and written procedures, which makes the recovery test less useful because there is no assurance that in a real disaster those individuals would be available.
   D. Audits can be helpful, but they are typically infrequent and use sampling; therefore, they provide limited and only occasional assurance that information in recovery plans is current and up to date.

8. A. Preventing access by system administrator(s) provides no protection and does nothing to restore the system.
   B. Root access makes it possible to initiate changes that are difficult or impossible to locate and is not an acceptable choice to resolve the issue.
   C. If someone, or a malicious program, gains superuser privileges to a system without authorization, the enterprise never really knows what the perpetrator or program has done to the system. The only way to assure the integrity of the system is to wipe it clean by either performing a low-level format on the hard disk or replacing it with a new one (usually after making a bit copy backup for the purpose of further analysis and to prevent the destruction of data that may not exist elsewhere) and starting over again by reinstalling the operating system and applications using original media.
   D. Changing passwords provides no protections against any malicious changes made to the system.

9. A. The incident management plan is a subset of the security strategy, which already aligns to organizational goals and, therefore, does not represent a major challenge.
   B. Implementation of log centralization, correlation and event tracking is required, but it is not the most significant challenge.
   C. Incident metrics must be developed, but they are straightforward and not a significant challenge.
   D. Getting senior management buy-in is often difficult, but it is the necessary first step to move forward with any incident management plan.

10. A. Whether a copy is compressed is irrelevant, and a straight copy operation will not include everything on the hard disk that is not identified by the operating system as a standard file.
    B. A copy of all files and directories will not be an image of the hard disk and will fail to copy a variety of data, including data between the end of a file and the end of the disk sector (slack space) and deleted files that have not been overwritten.
    C. There is no alternative to making a bit-by-bit copy. For legally sufficient evidence, only a bit copy will result in a true image of the hard drive.
    D. Whether the data are encrypted is not relevant, and copying all files and folders will miss certain data such as data between the end of a file and the end of the disk sector (slack space).

Part A: Incident Management Readiness

Note: For the purpose this review manual, an incident management program will focus predominantly on security risk and the subsequent incidents faced by an enterprise. Incidents may range from the mundane—such as a losing a key individual to a competitor, a shift in the market that threats strategic goals, loss of Internet connectivity due to a fiber seeking backhoe—to the near disastrous, such as a fire or flood at the primary data processing facilities.[26]

4.1 Incident Management and Incident Response Overview

An incident management program is a subset of risk management, with a focus on the planning, preparation and identification of events that deviate from normal, planned operations. The desired goal is to: 1) reduce the impact felt by an enterprise and 2) recover and resume operations at acceptable levels. The speed with which an enterprise can identify, analyze, respond to and recover from an incident reduces the impact felt by the enterprise and ultimately the costs associated with the incident. This normally results in senior management understanding that the enterprise needs an effective and efficient means of responding to an incident.

Individual program activities and resources vary based upon an enterprise's maturity, industry, strategic goals, compliance requirements, geographic operations, staffing levels and expressed desire or need to address incidents. Mature enterprises in highly regulated industries may have more capabilities, infrastructure, and resources dedicated to incident management in contrast to enterprises that do not have the same or similar drivers. Each enterprise must decide on the structure and operations that are reasonable and appropriate; there is no one-size-fits-all answer for incident management. What works for one team may not work for another based upon various constraints and operational requirements.

A number of contributing factors come into play and must be considered when developing an incident management program. Working with relevant stakeholders and constituents served by the enterprise is just as critical to the success of the overall program as is senior management's support. As the subject matter expert relating to information security management, the information security manager may be asked to establish an incident management program from the ground up. Our an information security manager may be asked to review the existing capabilities, skills and instrumentation to address any potential gaps or to otherwise enhance, augment and mature an existing program to meet the needs of an enterprise based on changes to its operating environment.

Ensuring successful development (and ultimately management) of an enterprise's incident management program is not unlike ensuring the success of other existing management programs. Key processes need to be identified, practices and activities need to be defined, staff need to be trained to the appropriate skill levels, and once operationalized, they must be managed to ensure the proper support and alignment with the enterprise's strategic goals and objectives.

4.1.1 The Relationship Between Incident Management and Incident Response

Subtle differences and nuances exist between incident management and incident response functions. **Incident management** is the ability to provide and ensure the start-to-finish management of an incident within the enterprise. This means identifying how tasks and processes relate to one another, how information is exchanged (internally and externally) and what actions need to be coordinated to successfully manage an incident. **Incident response** includes the processes, procedures and activities performed when responding to an incident and focuses on the identification, triage, containment, eradication and recovery actions taken to resume normal, planned operations.

Briefly, incident management includes all the processes, practices and activities that take place prior to, during and after an incident. In contrast, incident response is a subset of activities performed when an incident is declared by the enterprise.

Together, incident management and incident response capabilities are the operationalization of emergency operations in light of an adverse event that impacts an enterprise. Both are components of overall organizational resiliency and risk management. Incident

[26] For this chapter, the author reached out to Brandon McCrillis, SANS Institute instructor and principal consultant at Qualified Cyber, LLC, to collaborate on the topic of incident management and incident response.

management and response capabilities help to ensure risk to the enterprise is properly managed and addressed. Achieving this aim requires not only acknowledgment by senior management, but also reasonable and appropriate commitments to ensure that risk is sufficiently addressed and efficiently and effectively managed to the acceptable risk tolerance level.

4.1.2 Goals of Incident Management and Incident Response

Incidents can originate from a wide spectrum of potential sources, including large-scale cyberattacks, losses associated with natural disasters, the loss of key personnel, workplace accidents or any other unexpected adverse events that occur as a result of a shift in the threat landscape. Efforts need to include managing and responding to incidents as they relate to information security, regardless of what medium (logical, physical, human) originated the incident.

How an enterprise prepares itself to respond and manage incidents will greatly influence its ability to recover and resume normal business operations. This outcome requires a consistent, coordinated approach that is aligned with the enterprise to ensure that when an incident does occur, impacts and costs to the enterprise will be minimal.

As the old saying goes, "It's not a question of if, but when." No enterprise is exempt from experiencing an incident, and each enterprise needs to understand that its strategy and solution need to be tailored to provide suitable incident management and response capabilities that meet the needs of its stakeholders and ensure that efforts are properly aligned with the enterprise's needs. The approach adopted depends on a variety of factors, including:

- **Constituency to be served**—Who are the consumers of this capability?
- **Enterprise mission, goals and objectives**—Is the approach properly aligned with the enterprise?
- **Services to be provided**—What services are committed to meet constituent needs?
- **Organizational model and the relationship with various stakeholders**—Who is the enterprise accountable and responsible to?
- **Funding for startup costs and ongoing operations**—How will this capability be funded?
- **Resources needed by the computer security incident response team (CSIRT)** —What is needed to deliver the desired capabilities to the constituents served?

Numerous organizations—such as the Carnegie Mellon University Software Engineering Institute (CMU SEI), the US National Institute of Standards and Technology (NIST), the International Consortium for Organizational Resilience (ICOR), the SANS Institute and ISACA — provide varying degrees of information, approaches and methodologies to develop incident management and response capabilities.

Incident management involves all the actions taken prior to, during and after an information security incident occurs. Incident management includes program management (planning, training, testing), operational (processes, procedures, protocols) and tactical (evidence collection, triage, initial analysis) practices, and individual activities.

Incident management practices need to be designed to mitigate the impact of an incident and ensure efficient and effective recovery with the following goals in mind:

- Support the overall enterprise strategy.
- Provide an effective means of addressing the situation so it minimizes the impact to the enterprise.
- Provide management with sufficient information to decide on appropriate courses of action.
- Maintain or restore continuity of enterprise services in line with business continuity and disaster recovery plans.
- Provide an initial defense against subsequent attacks.
- Provide additional deterrence through the use of technology, investigation and prosecution.

Incident management includes coordination of both business and technical resources who have been assigned as part of the enterprise's incident management team. In addition to security and IT, members may include representatives from legal, finance/accounting, human resources (HR), public relations (PR), corporate communications, and the impacted lines of business, in addition to the resources who are actively responding to the incident, such as hardware vendors or service providers.

Having an effective incident management capability in place is an important part of the deployment and implementation of any system. Enterprises now realize that active communication and collaboration between the business (e.g. system, risk and control owners), its technical counterparts (e.g., the application developers, system and network administrators, information and cybersecurity) and staff performing and supporting incident management activities provide the best insight for developing approaches to security baselines, better defensive practices, and more streamlined response processes to identify, detect, prevent, respond and recover from the growing variety of threats being faced. At the same time, an effective incident management capability increases overall organizational resiliency efforts in time of need.

The extent of incident management and response capabilities must be carefully balanced with baseline security, business continuity (BC) and disaster recovery (DR) requirements defined by the appropriate stakeholders. The level of incident management capability must also be considered in the context of BC planning and DR planning. At some point it may be more cost effective to use alternative processing options than to maintain a high level of incident management and response capability.

The goals of incident management and response activities can be summarized as the following:

- Identify and detect incidents quickly.
- Diagnose incidents accurately.
- Contain and minimize damage.
- Restore affected services.
- Determine root causes.
- Implement improvements to prevent recurrence.
- Document and report.

4.1.3 Incident Handling and Incident Management Life Cycle

Incident handling is one service that involves all the processes or tasks associated with handling events and incidents. It involves multiple functions:

- **Detection and reporting**—The ability to receive and review event information, incident reports and alerts
- **Triage**—The actions taken to categorize, prioritize and assign events and incidents to maximize the effectiveness of limited resources
- **Analysis**—The attempt to determine what happened, the impact and threat, the damage that resulted, and the recovery or mitigation steps that should be followed
- **Incident response**—The actions taken to resolve or mitigate an incident, coordinate and disseminate information, and implement follow-up strategies to prevent recurring incidents

The incident management life cycle is described in **figure 4.1**.

Figure 4.1—Incident Management Life Cycle Phases

Phase	Activities
Planning and preparation	• Creating policies, acquiring management support, developing user awareness, building a response capability • Conducting research and development • Building checklists and acquiring necessary tools • Developing a communication plan and awareness training • Ensuring stakeholder buy-in and commitment to an incident response program
Detection, triage and investigation	• Defining events vs. incidents, and notification process • Detecting and validating incidents • Prioritizing and rating incidents • Implementing intrusion detection systems, intrusion prevention systems and security information event monitoring

Figure 4.1—Incident Management Life Cycle Phases *(cont.)*

Phase	Activities
Containment, analysis, tracking and recovery	• Executing containment strategy for various incidents • Performing forensic analysis according to evidence-handling processes • Executing recovery procedures in line with enterprise business continuity plans and disaster recovery plans • Determining the source of the incident

Post-incident assessment	• Conducting postmortem
	  ■ Exactly what happened and at what time?
	  ■ How well did staff and management perform in dealing with the incident? Were the documented procedures followed? Were they adequate?
	  ■ What corrective actions can prevent similar incidents in the future?
	• Reporting on incident management-related metrics (e.g., mean-time-to-incident-discovery, cost of recovery)
	• Providing feedback on lessons learned

Incident closure	• Conducting incident response postmortem analysis • Submitting reports to management and stakeholders

Source: ISACA, *Incident Management and Response*, USA, 2012

By definition, incidents are unexpected events. The ability to detect, identify and assess the situation, determine the causes and quickly arrive at solutions can mean the difference between an inconvenience and a disaster. An important consideration is recognizing the point at which an incident becomes a problem and, subsequently, when the inability to adequately address a problem calls for the declaration of a disaster. The time to make those determinations is not in the middle of a crisis. The progression of a disaster is shown in **figure 4.2**.

Figure 4.2—Progression of a Disaster

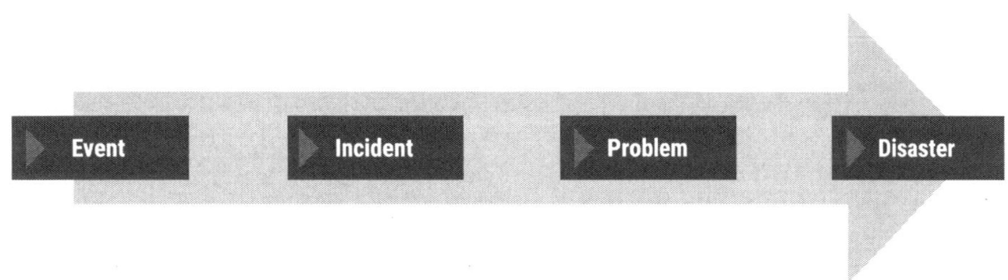

Rigorous planning and commitment of resources are necessary to adequately plan for such events. As with other aspects of security, it is critical to achieve stakeholder consensus and senior management support for an effective incident management capability. Support can be gained as a result of unacceptable impacts of prior incidents to the enterprise or from developing a persuasive business case detailing examples of similar events in other enterprises that show the consequences of inadequate incident management. Incident management and response can lead to lower overall security costs by setting baselines to address common events and providing protection with an adequate response, containment and recovery capability. This is similar to the common approach for protecting against fire by a combination of reasonable preventive controls, coupled with an effective fire detection system, evacuation plans and triggers for fire department response, complemented with insurance policies in the event that incident management and response measures fall short. While a totally fireproof structure could be built, optimal cost-effectiveness uses a combination of risk management approaches developed through trial and error.

Many enterprises have a separate department responsible for BC planning and DR and the extent of information security involvement and authority varies widely. Regardless of how these departments are structured, it is essential that they work together closely and that the plans are complementary and well-integrated. The individuals in charge of various types of events must be clearly defined and there must be clear severity and declaration criteria.

Severity criteria should be consistent, concisely described and easy to understand so severity levels of similar events are uniformly determined. Escalation and incident declaration criteria must also be established so it is clear who has the authority to determine the response level, activate the teams, declare an incident or disaster and mobilize the appropriate teams to initiate containment and recovery processes. Severity criteria and their use must be widely published and communicated to all relevant parties. Personnel must be trained to recognize potential incidents and provide proper classification, and they must be trained in notification, reporting and escalation requirements. The information security manager must be aware that, regardless of how well incidents are planned for and handled, there is always the possibility that events will escalate to a disaster.

4.2 Incident Management and Incident Response Plans

Effective incident management ensures that incidents are identified, detected, recorded and managed to limit impacts. Recording incidents is required so incident response activities can be tracked, information can be provided to aid planning activities and no aspect of an incident is inadvertently overlooked. Recording is required to properly document information, potentially including forensics data that can be used to pursue disciplinary or legal options. Incidents must be classified to ensure that they are correctly prioritized and routed to the correct resources. Incident management includes initial support processes that allow new incidents to be checked against known errors and problems so that any previously identified workarounds can be quickly identified.

Incident management provides a structure for investigating, diagnosing, resolving and then closing incidents. The process ensures that the incidents are owned, tracked and monitored throughout their life cycle. There may be occasions when major incidents require a response above and beyond what is provided through the normal incident process, and they may require activation of C/DR capabilities.

Incident response is the last step in an incident-handling process that encompasses the planning, coordination and execution of appropriate containment, eradication and recovery activities and may include the development of recommendations or lead to follow-on mitigation activities identified during the lessons learned.

The information security manager must be aware of nontechnical incidents to be planned for and addressed. These incidents can include social engineering, lost or stolen backup tapes or devices, physical theft of sensitive materials and natural disasters.

4.2.1 Importance of Incident Management

As enterprises increasingly rely on information processes and systems and significant disruption to those activities results in unacceptably severe impacts, the criticality of effective incident management and response has grown. Some factors that intensify the necessity of effective incident management include:

- The trend of both increased occurrences and escalating losses resulting from information security incidents (e.g., ransomware)
- The increase of vulnerabilities in software or systems affecting large parts of an enterprise's infrastructure and impacting operations
- Failure of security controls to prevent incidents
- Legal and regulatory mandates requiring the development of an incident management capability
- Growing sophistication and capabilities of threat actors
- Advanced persistent threats (APTs)
- Exploitation of poorly managed IT processes and practices
- Increasing zero-day attacks

4.2.2 Outcomes of Incident Management

Outcomes of good incident management and response include the following:

- The enterprise can deal effectively with unanticipated events that might threaten to disrupt the business (e.g., recovery time objective [RTO] and recovery point objective [RPO]).

- The enterprise will have sufficient detection and monitoring capabilities to ensure that incidents are detected in a timely manner.
- Well-defined severity and declaration criteria will be in place, as will defined escalation and notification processes.
- Personnel will be trained in the recognition of incidents, the application of severity criteria, and proper reporting and escalation procedures.
- The enterprise will have response capabilities that demonstrably support the business strategy by being responsive to the criticality and sensitivity of the resources protected.
- The enterprise will serve to proactively manage the risk of incidents appropriately in a cost-effective manner and will provide integration of security-related organizational functions to maximize effectiveness.
- The enterprise will provide monitoring and metrics to gauge performance of incident management and response capabilities, and it will periodically test its capabilities and ensure that information and plans are updated regularly, and are current and accessible when needed.

The monitoring and metrics activities will ensure that:

- Information assets are adequately protected and the risk level is within acceptable limits.
- Properly trained and equipped incident management and response teams are in place.
- Effective incident response plans (IRPs) are in place and understood by relevant stakeholders (e.g., management, IT departments, end users, incident handlers).
- Incidents are quickly identified, correctly categorized and contained, and the root cause is addressed to allow recovery within defined recovery objectives.
- Communication flows to different stakeholders and external parties are well controlled, as documented in the communication plan.
- Lessons learned are documented and shared with stakeholders to increase the level of security awareness and serve as a basis for improvement.
- Assurance is provided to internal and external stakeholders (e.g., customers, suppliers, business partners) that the enterprise has adequate control and is prepared to ensure business survivability in the long term.

4.2.3 Incident Management Resources

A number of internal and external resources may be used in the development of an incident management and response plan. In a typical enterprise, these resources may include, but not be limited to, the following:

- Compliance office
- Facilities management
- HR
- Industry and national community emergency response teams
- Information sharing and analysis centers
- Insurance provider
- Internal audit
- IT department
- Law enforcement
- Legal department
- Local government
- Physical security
- Privacy officer
- Public relations
- Risk management
- Sales and marketing
- Senior management
- Third-party providers
- Training partners
- Trusted advisors
- Vendors/suppliers

As with other aspects of information security, it is essential to develop a clear scope, objectives and implementation strategy. The strategy must consider the elements needed to move from the current state of incident management to the desired state, as defined by the enterprise. It should clarify what resources are required and how they must be deployed.

4.2.4 Policies and Standards

The incident response plan (IRP) must be supported by well-defined policies, standards and procedures. A documented set of policies, standards and procedures is important to:

- Ensure that incident management activities are aligned with the incident management team (IMT) mission.
- Set correct expectations.
- Provide guidance for operational needs.
- Maintain consistency and reliability of services.
- Clearly understand roles and responsibilities.
- Set requirements for identified alternative personnel for all important functions.

4.2.5 Incident Management Objectives

At its core, incident management exists to address the inevitable events that threaten the operation of any enterprise. It serves as the next-to-last safety net after controls have failed to prevent or contain an incident. The primary purpose is to respond to and contain security incidents and restore normal operations as quickly as possible in the event of an incident. Failing to do so will often result in the declaration of a disaster, and the need for recovery operations. This may include the move to an alternative site to restore operations as defined within the BC/DR plans.

The objectives of incident management are to:

- Handle incidents when they occur so the exposure can be contained or eradicated to enable recovery within recovery time objectives (RTOs) and recovery point objectives (RPOs).
- Restore systems and business processes to normal operation.
- Prevent incidents from recurring by documenting and learning from past incidents.
- Deploy proactive countermeasures to prevent/minimize the probability of incidents occurring in the future.
- Deploy safeguards to protect and reduce impact to assets in the event of an incident occurring.

Ideally, incident management and response capabilities must effectively address a wide range of possible unexpected events. Enterprises need to ensure not only that they have well-developed monitoring capabilities for key controls in order to provide early detection of potential problems, but also that these capabilities are accessible to the appropriate incident management personnel. Personnel should be trained in assessing the situation, conducting triage and managing effective responses that maximize operational continuity and minimize impacts. Incident managers will have provisions in place to capture all relevant information and apply previously learned lessons. They will be prepared for a disaster through well-defined criteria, experience, knowledge and authority to invoke the disaster recovery processes necessary to maintain or recover operational status.

4.2.6 Strategic Alignment

Similar to many other support functions, incident management must be aligned with an enterprise's strategic plan. The following components may help to accomplish this alignment:

- **Constituency**—To whom does the incident management team (IMT) provide services? It is important to know who the stakeholders are for this function and identify their expectations and information needs. For example, senior management in financial institutions may be bound by Basel III or another regulation. Thus, the IMT should meet applicable performance and reporting requirements.
- **Mission**—The mission defines the purpose of the team and the primary objectives and goals that are provided by the IMT. An example of a possible IMT mission statement follows: "The mission of the incident management team is to develop, maintain and deliver incident management capabilities and services to safeguard the enterprise's information assets against computer incidents. We strive to provide assurance to our stakeholders that risk and cyber- or IT-related incidents are dealt with in an efficient and effective manner and that we will prevent/minimize losses resulting from such incidents."
- **Services**—Services provided by the IMT should be clearly defined to manage stakeholder expectations. Services offered in enterprises may differ significantly, and normally have a positive correlation with the size of the enterprise and the extent of senior management support. At a high level, these services include functions such as incident management, vulnerability management,

situational awareness, knowledge transfer and event management.[27]

- **Organizational structure**—The structure of the IMT should effectively support the enterprise's structure. For multinational companies, a geography-based structure may be the best. For enterprises with multiple subsidiaries, one IMT may be developed for each major subsidiary. The best structure would provide the business with the maximum availability of IMT services on the most cost-effective basis.
- **Resources**—Sufficient qualified staffing is needed for both effectiveness and efficiency. Because incident management can include a wide range of services, most of the time it is not possible to have all the resources available within one IMT. Ways to solve this issue include establishing virtual team members and complementing the team with external resources.
- **Funding**—The IMT usually consists of highly specialized members. The training, equipment and systems used in the course of providing their services tend to be very specialized, requiring greater capital expenditures. Sufficient funding is required to ensure the continuity of critical incident response services.
- **Management support**—Senior management buy-in is essential for establishing a successful incident management capability within an enterprise. A lack of support can result in a number of issues. For example, the inability to respond to an incident due to existing silos within the enterprise, untrained team members due to underfunding, insufficient budget allocation to allow for effective and efficient response, or to attract or retain qualified personnel. Without the commitment of senior management, the incident management and response capabilities will rely on personal heroics at best or introduce a variety of legal risk (e.g., the spoliation or mishandling of evidence).

4.2.7 Response and Recovery Plan

Enterprises should have a formal, focused and coordinated approach to responding to incidents, including an incident response plan (IRP) that provides the road map for implementing the incident response capability. Each enterprise needs a plan that meets its unique requirements, which relate to the enterprise's mission, size, structure and functions. The plan should lay out the necessary resources and management support. The IRP should include the following elements:

- Mission
- Strategies and goals
- Senior management approval
- Organizational approach to incident response
- Key decision-making personnel and responsibilities
- Communication with the rest of the enterprise and with other enterprises
- Metrics for measuring the incident response capability and its effectiveness
- Road map for maturing the incident response capability
- How the program fits into the overall enterprise

The enterprise mission, strategies and goals for incident response should help in determining the structure of its incident response capability. The incident response program structure should also be discussed within the plan. Once an enterprise develops a plan and gains management approval, the enterprise should implement the plan and review it at least annually (or when there is any significant change that could introduce unplanned risk) to ensure the enterprise is following the road map for maturing its capability and fulfilling its goals for incident response.

The following section covers the necessity for incident response capabilities and the typical responsibilities of an information security manager. These responsibilities can vary significantly in different enterprises and, in some cases, may include some DR and BC activities.

4.2.8 The Role of the Information Security Manager in Incident Management

The role the information security manager has within BC, DR planning and incident response is going to be influenced by multiple factors, such as the enterprise's size, the industry, applicable regulatory requirements and the maturity of BC, DR and incident response capabilities. The information security manager typically is responsible for responding to information security-related incidents.

[27] FIRST, "FIRST CSIRT Services Framework" Version 2.1, www.first.org/standards/frameworks/csirts/csirt_services_framework_v2.1

In smaller enterprises, the information security manager may be involved in all BC, DR and incident response functions—assisting the business units in completing their business impact analyses (BIAs), working with the IT department to identify suitable backup and recovery solutions, coordinating incident response efforts as events are escalated, and delivering normal information security services needed by the enterprise.

In larger enterprises, BC, DR and incident response business functions may be separate departments, each with their own dedicated staff and budgets needed to support operations. Here, the role of the information security manager may be an internal consultant, advising as a subject matter expert in any of the related functions. The information security manager may be a general contributor—supporting and augmenting existing operations and delivering services in support of business need—or may function purely as a business peer, with security incidents being reported for the purposes of monitoring, prioritization and remediation, and with response efforts performed by the incident response department.

Regardless of the environment the information security manager is operating in, it is important to have a good conceptual and practical understanding of what is required to adequately address related responsibilities. In addition, there must be a good understanding of the BC and DR processes. This is to ensure that incident management and response plans and activities integrate well with the overall BCP and DRP in the event that an incident escalates to a disaster.

4.2.9 Risk Management

Effective incident management and response capabilities are necessary for successful outcomes of risk management. Any risk that materializes and is not prevented by the enterprise's internal controls constitutes an incident that must be managed and responded to with the intent that it does not escalate into a disaster.

4.2.10 Assurance Process Integration

The type and nature of incidents the information security manager may deal with often require the involvement of a number of other organizational functions, such as physical security, HR and legal. It is important to ensure that incident management and recovery plans actively incorporate and integrate those functions as required. An effective outcome is a set of plans that define which departments are involved in various incident management and response activities and specify that those linkages have been tested under realistic conditions.

4.2.11 Value Delivery

Incident management capabilities must be closely integrated with business functions and provide the last line of defense to support cost-effective risk management. Incident management involves more than the technology controls to prevent or respond to incidents; it includes a set of processes that can provide an optimal balance between prevention, containment and restoration.

To deliver value, incident management should:

- Integrate with business processes and structures as seamlessly as possible.
- Improve the capability of businesses to manage risk and provide assurance to stakeholders.
- Integrate with the business continuity plan (BCP).
- Become part of an enterprise's overall strategy and effort to protect and secure critical business functions and assets.
- Provide the backstop and optimize risk management efforts

4.2.12 Resource Management

Resource management encompasses time, people, budget and other factors to achieve objectives efficiently under given resource constraints. Incident management and response activities consume resources that must be managed to achieve optimal effectiveness. This is accomplished by ensuring appropriate oversight, monitoring of resources and regular reporting. When it is not possible to achieve all objectives, effective resource management ensures that the most important priorities are addressed first. In terms of incident response, effective triage capabilities ensure that limited resources are applied most effectively to contain and limit damage. This is based on quickly identifying compromised assets that cannot be quickly addressed, the assets that are unaffected and can wait, and the ones that can most efficiently be restored with the available resources.

4.2.13 Defining Incident Management Procedures

There is no single, fixed, one-size-fits-all set of incident management procedures for every enterprise. However, there are a number of good practices that most enterprises adopt and customize to meet their own specific needs. Commonly adopted approaches are available from CMU SEI and the SANS Institute, among others.

4.2.14 Detailed Plan of Action for Incident Management

There are a number of approaches to developing the incident management plan and IRP.

CMU/SEI's *Defining Incident Management Processes* describes the following approach (**figure 4.3**):[28]

1. **Prepare (prepare/improve/sustain)**—This process defines all program preparation work that has to be completed prior to having any capability to respond to incidents. It contains subprocesses to evaluate incident-handling capability and postmortem review of incidents for improvements. Subprocesses include:
   - Coordinate planning and design:
     - Identify incident management requirements.
     - Establish vision and mission.
     - Obtain funding and sponsorship.
     - Develop implementation plan.
   - Coordinate implementation:
     - Develop policies, processes and plans.
     - Establish incident-handling criteria.
     - Implement defined resources.
     - Evaluate incident management capability.
     - Conduct postmortem review.
     - Determine incident management process changes.
     - Implement incident management process changes.
2. **Protect (reputation/brand/infrastructure/data)**—From the business perspective, the goal is to protect the enterprise's reputation and brand. From a technology perspective, the goal is a process that aims to protect and secure critical data and computing infrastructure and its constituency when responding to incidents. It also proposes improvement on a predetermined schedule while keeping the appropriate security context in consideration. Subprocesses include:
   - Implement changes to computing infrastructure to mitigate an ongoing or potential incident.
   - Implement infrastructure protection improvements from postmortem reviews or other process improvement mechanisms.
   - Evaluate computing infrastructure by performing proactive security assessment and evaluation.
   - Provide input to detect process on incidents/potential incidents.
3. **Detect (events/incidents/anomalies)**—The detect process identifies unusual, suspicious or malicious activity that might impact critical business functions or infrastructure. Subprocesses include:
   - Proactive detection—The detect process is conducted regularly prior to an incident. The IMT monitors various types of information from online/periodic vulnerability scanning, network monitoring, antivirus and firewall alerts, security information and event management (SIEM) products, file integrity management products, data loss prevention products, third-party monitoring service alerts, commercial vulnerability alert services, risk analysis threat intelligence reports and security audit/assessments.
   - Reactive detection—The detect process is conducted when there are reports from system users or other enterprises. Users may notice unusual or suspicious activity and report it to the IMT. It is also possible that another enterprise's IMT will provide advisories when its system has received malicious activity from an enterprise.
   - For the IMT to receive the report promptly, there should be multiple communication channels from end users to the IMT. This can be in the form of phone calls, faxes, email messages, web-form reporting, team collaboration suites, or automated intrusion detection systems (IDSs).

[28] Alberts, C; A. Dorofee; G. Killcrece; R. Ruefle; M. Zajicek; *Defining Incident Management Processes for CSIRTs: A Work in Progress,* Carnegie Mellon University, USA, 2004

4. **Triage**—Triage is a process of sorting, categorizing, correlating, prioritizing and assigning incoming reports/events into (typically three) categories: the problems that cannot be readily resolved, those that can wait and those that can be efficiently addressed with the resources available. It is an essential element of any incident management capability to ensure maximum effectiveness of limited resources. When there are multiple incident reports coming into the IMT, triage allows events to be prioritized appropriately, thus maximizing response effectiveness. It can also serve as a single point of entry for any IMT communication and information.
   - Properly organized, triage can provide a snapshot of the current status of all incident activity reported, a central location for incident status reporting and an initial assessment of incoming reports for further handling. Triage prioritization can be done at two levels:
     - Tactical—Based on a set of criteria
     - Strategic—Based on the activity's impact on the ability to achieve business goals and objectives
   - Subprocesses include:
     - Categorization—This is the use of predetermined criteria to classify all incoming reports/events. There are many ways to categorize events, such as:
       - Denial of service (DoS)
       - Malicious code
       - Unauthorized access
       - Inappropriate usage
       - Login successes and failures
       - Elevation of account privileges
       - Privileged account access
       - Data extraction
       - Extended account use
       - Remote access patterns
       - Changes in logging/audit settings
       - Phishing attacks, viruses, worms, etc.
     - Correlation—This subprocess correlates a report/event with other relevant information. A higher correlation of a report/event provides more information that is useful for the IMT to decide on the appropriate response. For example, a specific event may be the cause of an incident whereas another may be a consequence and dealing with it would not resolve the issue.
       - Prioritization—In an ideal world, every undesirable event is followed up as soon as possible. However, resources are limited, and it may not always be possible. To ensure minimal impact to critical business functions or information assets, incidents are usually prioritized based on their potential impact rather than a specific set of criteria. Remediation efforts obviously start with the highest priority and then move down to the lowest priority.
     - Assignment—When an incident or potential incident has been identified, it is assigned to the IMT to initiate the response effort. Assignment may be based on:
       - Workload of IMT members
       - IMT members who have handled similar incidents
       - Category or priority of the event
       - Relevant business unit
5. **Respond**—The response process includes steps taken to address, resolve or mitigate an incident. CMU SEI defines three types of response activities:[29]
   - Technical response—It is appropriate for technical IMT members, such as incident handlers and IT representatives, to analyze and resolve an incident. Technical response forms include the following:
     - Collecting data for further analysis
     - Analyzing incident-supporting information such as log files
     - Researching corresponding technical mitigation strategies and recovery options
     - Consulting telephone or email technical assistance
     - Securing onsite assistance
     - Analyzing logs
     - Developing and deploying patches and workarounds

[29] *Ibid*

- Management response—The management response includes activities that require supervisory or management intervention, notification, interaction, escalation or approval as part of the response effort. This response activity is normally executed by business managers, senior management and members of the affected business units.
- Legal response—The legal response is associated with activity that relates to investigation, prosecution, liability, copyright and privacy issues, laws, regulations and nondisclosure agreements. Because this response may require in-depth knowledge on legal matters, it is usually referred to the corporate legal team.

Figure 4.3—Incident Response Workflow

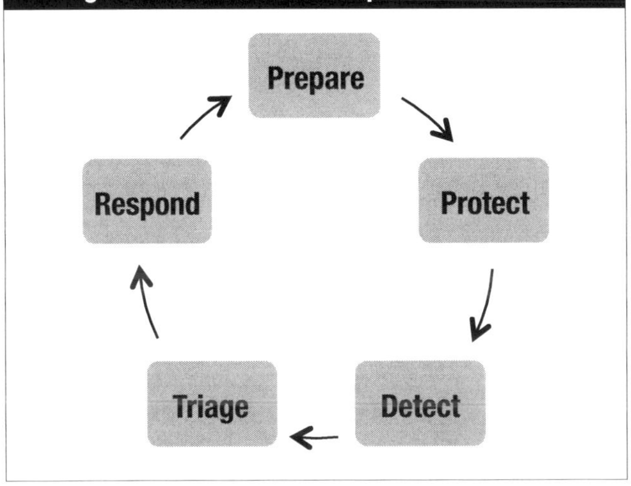

4.2.15 Current State of Incident Response Capability

Most enterprises have some sort of ad hoc or formal incident response capability. The information security manager must identify what is already in place as a basis for understanding the current state. There are many ways to do this, including:

- **Survey of senior management, business managers and IT representatives**—Uses input from senior management, business line managers and technology representatives, employee surveys and focus groups to gather information to help determine the past performance and perception of the IMT and its process capabilities.
- **Self-assessment**—Self-assessment is conducted by the IMT against a set of criteria to develop an understanding of current capabilities. This is the easiest method because it does not require participation from many stakeholders. The disadvantage of this method is that it may provide only a limited view of current capabilities and other aspects that stakeholders may consider important.
- **External assessment or audit**—This is the most comprehensive option, and it combines interviews, surveys, simulation and other assessment techniques in the assessment. This option is normally used for an enterprise that already has an adequate incident management capability but is further improving it or reengineering the processes.

These techniques will help to determine if the current state is effective and, if not, will help with determining the desired state of the incident response capability.

History of Incidents

Past incidents (both internal and external) can provide valuable information on trends, types of events and business impacts. This information is used as an input for the assessment of types of incidents that must be planned for and considered.

A sample of historical information maintained following an incident is shown in **figure 4.4**. Note that this represents a few sample items to track and is not meant to be a complete list.

Figure 4.4—Sample Historical Information to Track Regarding Security Incidents								
Org Incident #	Vendor Incident #	Start Date and Time	End Date and Time	Outage Duration	Description	Root Cause	Solution	Business Impact
12345	Z12111	1/14/2021 4:00 p.m. ET*	1/14/2021 5:00 p.m. ET	1 hr	Describes a specific event in an order entry system that caused a loss of functionality. Includes details depending on the business.	Describes the root cause of a functionality lost from the order entry system. This represents the key reason(s) for the function(s) becoming unavailable.	What was done specifically to solve the problem? Includes the group that performed the action and the system to which the action was directed.	Includes specific function lost, affected geographical or business areas and number of affected users (if applicable).
12346	Z12156	2/23/2021 7:00 a.m. ET	2/23/2021 7:31 a.m. ET	31 min	Describes a specific event in the enterprise's billing system that caused a loss of functionality. Includes details depending on the business.	Describes the root cause of a functionality lost from the billing system. This represents the key reason(s) for the function(s) becoming unavailable.	What was done specifically to solve the problem? Includes the group that performed the action and the system to which the action was directed.	Includes specific function lost, affected geographical or business areas and number of affected users (if applicable).
12347	None	4/16/2021 4:30 a.m. ET	4/17/2021 5:00 a.m. ET	24 hrs 30 min	Describes the DoS attack and the related system(s) affected. The key is detailing the functionality lost by this event.	Describes the root cause of a functionality lost from the system affected by the DoS attack. This represents the key reason(s) for the function(s) becoming unavailable.	What was done specifically to solve the problem? Includes the group that performed the action and the system to which the action was directed.	Includes specific function lost, affected geographical or business areas and number of affected users (if applicable).
* ET = Eastern Time Zone, United States of America								

Threats

Threats are any event that may cause harm to an enterprise's assets, operations or personnel. There are a number of threats that must be considered, including:

- **Environmental**—Environmental threats include natural disasters. While natural disasters vary among locations, some natural disasters may occur for prolonged periods of time and others may occur annually. Some potentially catastrophic threats are rare enough and impractical to address effectively, so they are either generally disregarded (e.g., comet strike) or might be addressed with some type of business interruption insurance.

- **Technical**—Technical threats include fire; electrical failure; heating, ventilating and air conditioning (HVAC) failure; information system and software issues; telecommunications failure; and gas/water leakage. Technical threats are normally found in every enterprise and are quite common. With sufficient planning, most technical threats can be managed adequately. The exceptions may be advanced persistent threats and zero-day attacks.
- **Human driven**—Threats that arise from human-initiated actions may include damage by disgruntled employees, accidents in the workplace, taking shortcuts to save time, and political instability, which may degrade or severely impact business functions. Many of these threats may be easy to identify while some, such as corporate sabotage/espionage or embezzlement, will be far more difficult.

Vulnerabilities

A weakness in a system, technology, process, person or control that can be exploited and result in compromise is a vulnerability. A vulnerability that can be exploited by threats results in risk. One aspect of risk management is managing vulnerabilities to maintain risk within acceptable limits as determined by the enterprise's risk appetite and tolerance criteria. Vulnerability management is part of the incident management capability; it is the proactive identification, monitoring and repair of any weaknesses.

4.2.16 Developing an Incident Response Plan

The IRP is the operational component of incident management. The plan details the actions, personnel and activities that take place in case adverse events result in the loss of data, information systems or processes. The plan should include the formation, management and maintenance of the incident response team.

Elements of an Incident Response Plan

A common approach to developing an IRP is to base it on a six-phase model of incident response that covers preparation, identification, containment, eradication, restoration and follow-up. Those stages are defined as follows:

1. **Preparation**—This phase prepares an enterprise to develop an IRP prior to an incident. Sufficient preparation facilitates smooth execution. Activities in this phase include:
   - Establishing an approach to handle incidents
   - Establishing policy and warning banners in information systems to deter intruders and allow information collection
   - Establishing a communication plan for stakeholders
   - Developing criteria on when to report an incident to authorities
   - Developing a process to activate the IMT
   - Establishing a secure location to execute the IRP
   - Ensuring equipment needed is available
   - Establishing a capability to create a baseline for information security risk metrics
   - Establishing a capability to automate rapid collection, analysis and escalation of information security risk status
2. **Identification**—This phase aims to verify if an incident has happened and to find out more details about it. Reports on possible incidents may come from information systems, end users or other enterprises. Not all reports are valid incidents; they may be false alarms or may not qualify as an incident. Activities in this phase include:
   - Assigning ownership of an incident or potential incident to an incident handler
   - Verifying that reports or events qualify as an incident
   - Establishing chain of custody when handling potential evidence
   - Determining the severity of an incident and escalating it as necessary
3. **Containment**—After an incident has been identified and confirmed, the IMT is activated and information from the incident handler is shared. The team will conduct a detailed assessment and contact the system owner or business manager of the affected information systems/assets to coordinate further action. The action taken in this phase is to limit the exposure. Activities in this phase include:
   - Activating the IMT/IRT to contain the incident
   - Notifying appropriate stakeholders affected by the incident
   - Obtaining agreement on actions taken that may affect availability of a service or risk of the containment process

- Getting the IT representative and relevant virtual team members involved to implement containment procedures
- Obtaining and preserving evidence
- Documenting actions and making backups from this phase onward
- Controlling and managing the PR team's communications to the public

4. **Eradication**—When containment measures have been deployed, it is time to determine the root cause of the incident and eradicate it. Eradication can be done in a number of ways: restoring backups to achieve a clean state of the system, removing the root cause, improving defenses and performing a vulnerability analysis to identify any additionally impacted systems with the same root cause. Activities in this phase include:
   - Determining the signs and cause of incidents
   - Locating the most recent version of backups or alternative solutions
   - Removing the root cause. In the event of worm or virus infection, it can be removed by deploying appropriate patches and updating antivirus software.
   - Improving defenses by implementing protection techniques
   - Performing a vulnerability analysis to discover related vulnerabilities identified during root cause analysis
5. **Recovery**—This phase ensures that affected systems or services are restored to a condition specified in the service delivery objectives (SDO) or BCP. The time constraint up to this phase is documented in the RTO. Activities in this phase include:
   - Restoring operations as defined in the SDO
   - Validating that actions taken on restored systems were successful
   - Getting involvement of system owners to test the system
   - Facilitating system owners to declare normal operation
6. **Lessons learned**—At the end of the incident response process, a report should always be developed to share what has happened, what actions were taken, and the results after the plan was executed. Part of the report should contain lessons learned that provide the IMT and other stakeholders valuable learning points on what could have been done better. These lessons should be developed into a plan to enhance the incident management capability and the documentation of the IRP. Activities in this phase include:
   - Creating the incident report
   - Analyzing issues encountered during incident response efforts
   - Proposing improvement based on issues encountered
   - Presenting the report to relevant stakeholders

Gap Analysis—Basis for an Incident Response Plan

A gap analysis provides information on the gap between current incident response capabilities and the desired level determined by senior management. Comparing the two levels allows improvements in capabilities, skills and technology to be identified, including:

- Processes that need to be improved to be more efficient and effective
- Resources needed to achieve the objectives for the incident response capability

The resulting gap analysis report can be used for planning purposes to determine the steps needed to close the gaps between the current state and the desired state. It can also be useful in determining the most effective strategy to achieve the objectives and prioritize efforts. The priorities should be based on the areas of greatest potential impact and on the best cost benefit.

Logistics

The plan must include provisions for all logistical support necessary for continuing normal business activities during the recovery effort. This includes detailed, up-to-date hard-copy procedures that can be followed easily by staff and contract personnel who are unfamiliar with the standard and recovery operations. This ensures that the plan can be implemented, even if members of the regular staff are unavailable. Also, a supply of special forms, such as check stock, invoice forms and order forms, should be secured at an offsite location.

If the data entry function is dependent on certain hardware devices or software programs, these programs and equipment, including specialized electronic data interchange (EDI) equipment and programs, must also be provided at the recovery site.

4.2.17 Incident Management and Response Teams

The plan must identify teams and define their assigned responsibilities ahead of an incident occurring. To implement the strategies that have been developed for business recovery, key decision-making, technical and end-user team leaders need to be designated and trained. Depending on the size of the business operation, the team may consist of a single person. The involvement of these teams depends on the level of the disruption of service and the types of assets lost, compromised, damaged or endangered. A matrix should be developed that indicates the correlations among the functions of the different teams. This will facilitate estimating the magnitude of the effort and activating the appropriate combination of teams. Examples of the kinds of teams usually needed include:

- **Emergency action team**—Designated first responders whose function is to deal with fires or other emergency response scenarios.
- **Damage assessment team**—Qualified individuals who assess the extent of damage to assets and make an initial determination regarding what is a complete loss versus what is restorable or salvageable.
- **Emergency management team**—Responsible for coordinating the activities of all other recovery teams and handling key decision-making.
- **Relocation team**—Responsible for coordinating the process of moving from the affected location to an alternative site or to the restored original location.
- **Security team**—When no designated/formal capability is defined by the enterprise, the security team will often become the de facto CSIRT. It is responsible for monitoring the security of systems and communication links, containing any ongoing security threats, resolving any security issues that impede the expeditious system recovery and ensuring the proper installation and functioning of every security software package.

A number of key decisions must be agreed on during the planning, implementation and evaluation phases of the response and recovery plan. These include:

- Goals/requirements/products/services for each phase
- Key goal indicators (KGIs)/key performance indicators (KPIs)
- RTO/RPO
- Reporting criteria
- Critical success factors and critical path aspects of implementation
- Alternative facilities in which tasks and operations can be performed
- Critical information resources to deploy (e.g., data and systems)
- Decision authority and persons responsible for completion
- Available resources—including financial, personnel and technical—to aid in deployment
- Scheduling of activities with established priorities

4.2.18 Organizing, Training and Equipping the Response Staff

Training the response teams is not only essential but also critical. The information security manager should develop reasonable, real-world event scenarios and test the response and recovery plans to ensure that team participants are familiar with their tasks and responsibilities. Through this process, the teams will identify the resources they require for response and recovery. An added value of training is detecting and modifying ambiguous procedures to achieve clarity and determining recovery resources that may not be adequate or effective.

IMT members should undergo the following training program:

- **Induction to the IMT**—The induction should provide the essential information required to be an effective IMT member.
- **Mentoring team members regarding roles, responsibilities and procedures**—Existing IMT members can provide valuable knowledge to aid new members after induction. To facilitate effective mentoring, the buddy system can be used, pairing new members with experienced members.
- **On-the-job training**—This may serve to provide an understanding of company policies, standards, procedures, available tools and applications, acceptable codes of conduct, etc.

- **Formal training**—Team members may require formal training to attain an adequate level of competence necessary to support the overall incident management capability.

4.2.19 Incident Notification Process

Having an effective and timely security incident notification process is a critical component of any security program. The information security manager should understand how obtaining timely and relevant information can help the enterprise respond quickly and efficiently and will ultimately limit the potential loss and damage that may occur as the result of an incident. Notification mechanisms that enable an automated detection system or monitor to send email or phone messages should be used whenever possible. The following functions are most likely to need information concerning incidents when they occur:

- Application development
- Business process owners
- Cybersecurity
- HR (when an incident appears to involve insiders)
- IT department
- Legal/general counsel
- Network operations
- Physical and information security
- Privacy department (when an incident appears to impact privacy)
- PR/corporate communications
- Risk management
- Senior management
- Threat intelligence team

Notification activities are effective only if knowledgeable personnel understand their responsibilities and perform them in an efficient and timely manner. The information security manager therefore needs to define the responsibilities and communicate them to key personnel. It can also be effective to work with HR to determine how responsibilities can be documented in employees' job descriptions.

4.2.20 Challenges in Developing an Incident Management Plan

When developing and maintaining an incident management plan, there may be unanticipated challenges as the result of:

- **Lack of management buy-in and organizational consensus**—Most challenges result from a lack of management buy-in and consensus among the business units. When an incident occurs, the management response may not be provided as expected, thus hindering incident management efforts. This may happen when senior management and other stakeholders or constituents are not involved in incident management planning and implementation. Challenges can also result from the lack of regular meetings between the IMT and constituents. A sense of ownership among constituents in incident management helps to ensure that sufficient resources and support are available for the IMT.
- **Mismatch to organizational goals and structure**—Business operates at an accelerated rate and may change significantly over a short period of time. Incident management may not be able to cope with the speed or nature of changes happening within the enterprise. Consider a situation in which the business expands to emerging countries. The presence in new countries may grow at a significant rate; however, it may be difficult to expand incident management capabilities. A round of discussions may be needed to identify critical business functions and local stakeholders and understand local regulations. Senior management is usually occupied with business matters at this stage and may not be able to invest time in incident management. It is the responsibility of the IMT to identify any critical issues and make them known to executive management.
- **IMT member turnover**—Developing an incident management plan may take a significant amount of time and involve frequent interaction with various stakeholders. The champion of incident management, who is normally either a member of senior management or the information security manager, may leave the enterprise unexpectedly, causing any planning or development efforts to come to a halt. The lack of a champion is likely to reduce the focus and resources devoted to implementing the plan.

- **Lack of communication process**—Ineffective communication processes may result either in under-communication or over-communication. In the case of under-communication, relevant stakeholders may not receive the information they need. This may result in different understandings about the need for incident management planning; the benefits that can be obtained; or their role in developing, implementing and maintaining an incident management capability. Over-communication may turn stakeholders against incident management because they may feel that the plan is too much to handle or it competes with priorities they have established.
- **Complex and broad plan**—The proposed plan may be good and cover many issues, but it may be too complex and too broad. Constituents may not be prepared to participate and commit to plans that appear overreaching.

4.3 Business Impact Analysis

A BIA is performed to determine the impact to an enterprise of losing the availability of any resource. It establishes the escalation of that loss over time, identifies the minimum resources needed to recover, and prioritizes the recovery of processes and supporting systems. The BIA is often thought of in the context of BC and DR. Other methods aside from the BIA may be used to determine potential impact. Impact is the bottom line of risk, and the range of severity in terms of the enterprise must be determined to provide the information needed and to guide risk management activities. Although high probability events with little or no individual impact are not necessarily a cause for alarm, they should not be entirely dismissed without understanding the role of the event within the larger system it supports.

Unfortunately, it is common for these assessments to focus on only a worst-case outcome, which represents a minority of events. As a result of this impact inflation, management often discounts these assessments as unrealistic and excessively pessimistic.

A more effective approach involves performing a reasonably small set of scenario analyses with key stakeholders, where a range of potential outcomes is determined. This range of outcomes is then used to define a quantitative distribution of impact magnitudes, including minimum, maximum and most likely, including values and a confidence level. These values can then be used as inputs to quantitative (e.g., Monte Carlo simulations to determine probability distribution) and qualitative analysis methods that provide management with more accurate descriptions of the real impact potential.

The other advantage this approach provides is that it more closely resembles the type of impact data that management receives from other business risk domains (e.g., investment, marketing, credit). This alignment improves management's ability to make a consistent comparison and well-informed risk decisions.

Before beginning the impact analysis of a specific set of assets, it is necessary to obtain the following information:

- System mission (e.g., objectives of the processes performed by the IT system or personnel)
- System (manual or technical) and data criticality (e.g., the system's value or importance to an enterprise)
- System, personnel and data criticality (the impacts associated with unintended disclosure)
- Supporting infrastructure (what the system relies upon to operate as planned)

This information can be obtained from performing a BIA or from organizational documentation such as a mission impact analysis report or asset criticality assessment report, if they exist. A mission impact assessment and analysis or BIA prioritizes the impact levels associated with the compromise of an enterprise's information assets based on a qualitative or quantitative assessment of the criticality of those assets. An asset criticality or resource dependency assessment identifies and prioritizes the critical information assets (e.g., hardware, software, systems, services and related technology assets) that support the enterprise's critical missions.

If this documentation does not exist or such assessments for the enterprise's information assets have not been performed, the system and data sensitivity can be determined based on the level of protection required to maintain the availability, integrity and confidentiality of the system and data.

The adverse impact of a security event can be described in terms of loss or degradation or any combination of confidentiality, integrity, availability and safety:

- **Loss of confidentiality**—In this context, confidentiality refers to the protection of information from unauthorized disclosure. The impact of unauthorized disclosure of confidential information can range from the jeopardizing of national security to the disclosure of private consumer data. Unauthorized, unanticipated or unintentional disclosure of private consumer or other regulated data can result in loss of public confidence, loss of customer base and legal action against the enterprise.
- **Loss of integrity**—System and data integrity refers to the requirement that information be protected from improper modification. Integrity is lost if unauthorized or erroneous changes are made to the data or IT system by either intentional or accidental acts. If the loss of system or data integrity is not corrected, continued use of the contaminated system or corrupted data could result in broader corruption, fraud or misinformed decisions. Also, violation of integrity may be the first step in a successful attack against system availability or confidentiality.
- **Loss of availability**—If a mission-critical IT system or process is unavailable to its end users, the enterprise's mission may be affected. Loss of system functionality and operational effectiveness, for example, may result in loss of productive time, thus impeding the end users' performance of their functions in supporting the enterprise's mission.

Some tangible impacts can be measured quantitatively in lost revenue, the cost of repairing the system, or the level of effort required to correct problems caused by a compromise. Other impacts (e.g., loss of public confidence, loss of credibility, damage to an enterprise's interest) cannot be measured in specific units but can be described qualitatively in terms of high, medium and low impacts.

In conducting an impact analysis, consideration should be given to the advantages and disadvantages of quantitative versus qualitative assessments. The main advantage of the qualitative impact analysis is that it prioritizes the risk and identifies areas for immediate improvement in addressing the vulnerabilities. The disadvantage of the qualitative analysis is that it does not provide specific quantifiable measurements of the magnitude of the impacts, therefore making a cost-benefit analysis of any recommended controls difficult.

The major advantage of a quantitative impact analysis is that it provides a measurement of the impacts' magnitude, which can be used in the cost-benefit analysis of recommended controls.

The disadvantage is that, depending on the numerical ranges used to express the measurement, the meaning of the quantitative impact analysis may be unclear, requiring the result to be interpreted in a qualitative manner. Additional factors must also be considered to determine the magnitude of impact, such as the range of possible errors in estimations or computations.

A BIA must:

- Determine the loss to the enterprise resulting from a function being unavailable
- Establish the escalation of that loss over time
- Identify the minimum resources needed for recovery
- Prioritize the recovery of processes and supporting systems

BIAs have three primary goals:

- **Criticality prioritization**—Every critical business unit process must be identified and prioritized. The impact of an incident must be evaluated—the higher the impact, the higher the priority.
- **Downtime estimation**—The assessment is also used to estimate the maximum tolerable downtime (MTD) or maximum tolerable outage (MTO) the business can endure and still remain viable. This can also mean the maximum period of time a system can be unavailable before compromising the achievement of the enterprise's business objectives (i.e., the acceptable interruption window [AIW]).
- **Resource requirement**—Resource requirements for critical processes are also identified at this time, with the most time-sensitive and highest-impact processes receiving the highest priority for resource allocation.

An assessment includes the following activities:

- **Gathering assessment material**—The initial step of the BIA is to identify which business units are critical to an enterprise. This step can be drilled down to the critical tasks that must be performed and the resources needed to ensure business survival.
- **Analyzing the information compiled**—During this phase, several activities take place, such as

documenting required processes and resources, identifying interdependencies, and determining the acceptable period of interruption. Tasks in this phase include:

- Identify interdependencies among the functions and departments classified as critical or high impact.
- Discover all possible disruptions that could affect the mechanism necessary to allow the departments to function together.
- Identify and document potential threats that could disrupt interdepartmental communication.
- Gather quantitative and qualitative information pertaining to those threats.
- Provide alternative methods of restoring functionality and communication.
- Provide a brief statement of rationale for each threat and corresponding information.

- **Documenting the result and presenting recommendations**—The last step of an assessment is documenting assessment results from the previous activities and creating a report for business units and senior management.

Another way of viewing a BIA is that it is a business function designed to identify the resources that are most important to an enterprise and the impact resulting from disruption or availability loss. It should also result in an understanding of process flows in the enterprise needed to optimize recovery priorities based on system dependencies and interdependencies. When conducted properly, a BIA facilitates understanding the amount of potential loss (and various other unwanted effects) that could occur from certain types of events. Potential loss includes direct financial loss and less tangible types of loss, such as reputational damage or failure to achieve regulatory compliance.

Despite the high level of importance of understanding the business impact of incidents on the business process, many enterprises fail to undertake this assessment. Another common problem is the failure to update BIAs when systems and business functions are added or changed. A BIA is a part of risk assessment insofar as the degree of risk exposure will correlate to the potential for an event resulting in an impact. The BIA is also used to determine the consequences, whereas the risk determination calculates both the probability and consequences.

4.3.1 Elements of a Business Impact Analysis

The way BIAs are conducted varies from enterprise to enterprise. However, there are commonalities. In general, BIAs:

- Describe the business mission of each particular business/cost center.
- Identify the functions that characterize each business function.
- Determine dependencies such as required inputs from other operations.
- Determine subsequent operations dependent on the function.
- Identify critical processing cycles (in terms of time intervals) for each function.
- Estimate the impact of each type of incident on business operations.
- Determine required recovery time (i.e., RTO).
- Identify the resources and activities required to restore an acceptable level of operation.
- Determine the amount of data that can be lost and must be recreated to determine RPOs.
- Determine workaround possibilities, such as manual or PC-based operation or workload shifting.
- Estimate the amount of time that recovering from each type of incident is likely to take in relation to the RTO. If the estimated time is greater than the RTO, additional resources may be needed to ensure recovery objectives are met or revisited to validate business need. This effort needs to consider not only the system being reviewed, but also the restoration of all required dependencies the system relies upon.

A typical BIA includes obtaining the following information from the enterprise's functional units:

- **Function description:** What is the function of the business unit?
- **Dependencies:** What is dependent upon this function? What has to happen or needs to be available before the function can be performed?
- **Impact profile:** Is there a specific time, day, week or month that the function would be more vulnerable to risk/exposure or the impact to the business would be greater if the function were not performed?
- **Operational impacts:** When would operational impact to the business be realized if the function were not performed?

- **Financial impacts:** When would financial impact to the business be realized if the function were not performed?
- **Work backlog:** At what point will the backlog of work start to impact the business?
- **Recovery resources:** What kind of resources are needed to support the function, how many are needed, and how soon are they needed after a disruption (e.g., phones, desks, PCs)?
- **Technology resources:** What software and applications (both internally and externally provided) are needed to support the function?
- **Standalone PCs or workstations:** Does the function require a standalone PC or workstation?
- **Network accessibility:** Does the function require access to networked services? (e.g., local area network [LAN], cloud, etc.)
- **Workaround procedures:** Are there currently manual workaround procedures in place that would enable the function to be performed in the event that IT was unavailable? If so, how long could the workarounds be used to continue the function?
- **Remote work:** Can the function be performed remotely/from home?
- **Workload shifting:** Is it possible to shift workloads to another part of the business that might not be impacted by the disruption?
- **Business records:** Are there business records needed to perform the function and, if so, are they backed up? How? With what frequency?
- **Regulatory reporting:** Are regulatory documents created as a result of the function?
- **Work inflows:** What input is received, either internally or externally, that is needed to perform the function?
- **Work outflows:** Where does the output go after it leaves the functional area or, in other words, who would be impacted if the function were not performed?
- **Business disruption experience:** Has there ever been a disruption of the function? (If so, provide a brief description.)
- **Competitive analysis:** Would there be a competitive impact if the function were not performed? If so, when would the impact occur and when would a potential loss of the customer occur?
- **Other issues and concerns:** What are other issues or concerns relevant to the success of performing the function?

Collecting and analyzing this information for all significant functions across an enterprise provides a detailed picture of workflows, dependencies and interdependencies that determine options for the required order of restoration efforts (i.e., resources dependent on other functions require the restoration of those functions before they can be operational). It provides information on restoration and emergency operation options, critical timing, options for workarounds or other operational choices in the event of function failure, and other essential information needed to develop effective IRPs, DRPs and BCPs.

4.3.2 Benefits of Conducting a Business Impact Analysis

Conducting BIAs produces several important major benefits, including:

- Increasing the understanding of the amount of potential loss and various other undesirable effects that could occur from certain types of incidents resulting from the loss of a particular function, including catastrophic events that can place survival of the business at risk
- Prioritizing restoration activities and understanding recovery options
- Understanding dependencies of various functions and their interdependencies
- Raising the level of awareness for response management within an enterprise

4.4 Business Continuity Plan

Disruptions to the business are likely to happen. The ability to work through those disruptions requires the enterprise to establish the capability to continue delivering its services or products, even in a diminished capacity as defined by the enterprise, with the goal to reduce and limit the overall impact. This requires a plan that outlines how the enterprise will continue to operate during an unplanned disruption. It should include a comprehensive set of plans that consider every aspect of the enterprise that could be affected during a crisis inclusive of key processes, personnel, information and technology assets along with required third parties. The

BCP should inform the development of DR procedures, as the enterprise defines and prioritizes critical processes and systems that are absolutely vital to function, even in a diminished capacity, to enable the enterprise to recover and resume normal operations.

4.4.1 Integrating Incident Response With Business Continuity

Effective integration of incident response and BC/DR planning requires the relationships among RTO, RPO, SDO and MTO to be carefully considered as the transition from incident response to disaster recovery operations for any solutions aside from mirrored or duplicate processing sites will require time. This is important to consider as RTOs, MTOs and AIWs are directly influenced by recovery capabilities and the failure to plan accordingly often results in the inability to achieve target objectives.

DR historically comprises the plan to recover an IT-processing facility or the plan by business units to recover an operational facility. With the continued growth and widespread adoption of cloud services, there is a movement away from thinking of IT in terms of facilities toward viewing IT as a capability. The incident management and recovery plan must be consistent with and support the overall IT plan of the enterprise. BC planning, DR and incident response do not necessarily have to be combined into a single plan; however, each must be consistent with the other and integrated so that the transition to declaration of a disaster is effective.

4.4.2 Methods for Providing Continuity of Network Services

Methods for providing continuity of network services include:

- **Redundancy**—Achieving redundancy involves a variety of solutions, including:
  - Providing extra capacity with a plan to use the surplus capacity should the normal primary transmission capability not be available. In the case of a local area network, a second cable could be installed through an alternate route for use in the event that the primary cable was damaged.
  - Providing multiple paths between routers.
  - Using special dynamic routing protocols such as the Open Shortest Path First (OSPF) and External Gateway Routing Protocol (EGRP).
  - Providing failover devices to avoid single points of failure in routers, switches, firewalls, etc.
  - Saving configuration files for recovery of network devices, such as routers and switches, in the event that they fail.
- **Alternative routing**—Alternative routing means routing information via an alternative medium such as copper cable or fiber optics. This involves use of different networks, circuits or end points, if the normal network is unavailable. Most local carriers are deploying counter-rotating fiber-optic rings. These rings have fiber-optic cables that transmit information in two directions and in separate cable sheaths for increased protection. Currently, these rings connect through one central switching office. However, future expansion of the rings may incorporate a second central office in the circuit. Some carriers are offering alternative routes to different points of presence or alternative central offices. Other examples include dial-up circuits as an alternative to dedicated circuits, a cellular phone and microwave communications as alternatives to land circuits and couriers as alternatives to electronic transmissions.
- **Diverse routing**—This is the method of routing traffic through split cable facilities or duplicate cable facilities. This can be accomplished with different or duplicate cable sheaths. If different cable sheaths are used, the cable may be in the same conduit and therefore subject to the same interruptions as the cable it is backing up. The communication service subscriber can duplicate the facilities by having alternative routes, although the entrance to and from the customer's premises may be in the same conduit. The subscriber can obtain diverse routing and alternative routing from the local carrier, including dual entrance facilities; however, acquiring this type of access is time-consuming and costly. Most carriers provide facilities for alternative and diverse routing, although most services are transmitted over terrestrial media. These cable facilities are usually located in the ground or the basement of buildings that house computer equipment. Ground-based facilities are at risk due to the aging infrastructures of cities. In addition, cable-based facilities usually share space with mechanical and electrical systems

that can impose risk due to human error and disastrous events.

- **Long-haul network diversity**—Many vendors of recovery facilities provide diverse long-distance network availability, using high-speed data circuits among the major long-distance carriers. This ensures long-distance access if any single carrier experiences a network failure. Several of the major carriers have now installed automatic rerouting software and redundant lines that provide instantaneous recovery if a break in their lines occurs. The information security manager should confirm that the recovery facility has these vital telecommunications capabilities.
- **Last-mile circuit protection**—Many recovery facilities provide a redundant combination of local carrier high-speed data circuits, microwave and coaxial cable access to the local communications loop. This enables the facility to have access during a local carrier communication disaster. Alternative local carrier routing is also used.
- **Voice recovery**—Many service, financial and retail industries depend on voice communication. Therefore, their recovery plans should provide for redundant cabling and alternative routing for voice and data communication lines.
- **Telephony recovery**—With the increased use of network based Voice over Internet Protocol (VoIP)-based telephony, careful attention and consideration needs to be given to business functions that require high availability and accessibility to telephony services. This is especially true if the enterprise is in a time-sensitive industry or provides critical services, such as healthcare or emergency services. While it may appear cost-effective to reduce and consolidate the number of providers to provide both network and telephony over the provider's data circuits, this carries the risk of creating a single point of failure. Information security managers should advise proper diversification of carriers and use of plain old telephone service (POTS) lines to reduce the impact and chances associated with a total communication failure if the data services should be interrupted.

4.4.3 High-Availability Considerations

The loss or disruption of servers managing sensitive and critical business processes could have catastrophic effects on an enterprise. Plans should include operational failover methods to prevent servers from going offline for an extended period of time. Server recovery should be included in the DRP. Some techniques for providing failover or fault-tolerant capabilities include the use of universal power supplies (UPSs) and failover systems to prevent power failures of varying levels.

Direct attached storage (DAS) is a data storage and availability solution in which the storage device (e.g., disk drive) is directly attached to a server or client. In order for multiple users to access the DAS, each needs to have direct access to the server that is housing the storage device. If the need for more storage arises, the server or client needs to be taken offline so additional drives can be installed, which affects availability.

Network attached storage (NAS) is a dedicated network attached data storage appliance with its own operating system (e.g., TrueNAS). File storage and user accessibility are provided through an existing Ethernet network. Adding storage to the NAS causes minimal downtime, because the connection is to the network rather than the server; therefore, availability is not necessarily impacted as storage needs increase. Connectivity and access to files are typically facilitated through a variety of protocols such as Network File Share or Server Message Block. The ability to access files via a web browser, dedicated application or command line tools may also be available in NAS appliances.

A storage area network (SAN) is a high-speed, special-purpose network that provides mass storage using remote interconnected devices—such as disk arrays, tape libraries or optical jukeboxes—with associated data servers that function as if they were attached locally. SANs are typically part of the overall network of computing resources for larger enterprises but may also serve as remote resources for backup and archival storage. SANs typically support disk mirroring, backup and restore functions, data migration between storage devices, and the sharing of data among different servers in one or more networks.

Compatible with DAS, NAS and SAN storage solutions, a redundant array of inexpensive (or independent) disks (RAID) provides performance improvements and fault-tolerant capabilities via hardware or software solutions, breaking up data and writing them to a series of multiple disks to improve performance and save large files simultaneously. These systems provide the potential for cost-effective continuous data availability onsite or offsite.

Strategies to ensure data availability and recreation in the event of an incident are dependent on the RPOs and RTOs, as discussed previously. An illustration of techniques implemented in relation to RTOs and RPOs is seen in **figure 4.5.**

Figure 4.5—Techniques Implemented in Relation to RTOs and RPOs

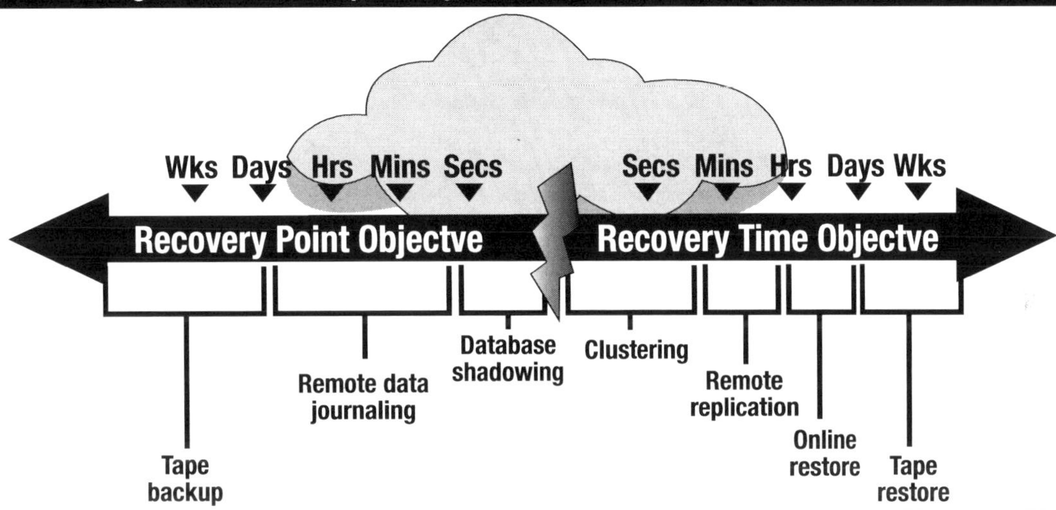

Source: Global Knowledge, https://www.globalknowledge.com

After an incident involving data loss, the acceptable time before a system must be restored/recreated (i.e., RTO) and degree of completeness, or the acceptable limit of data loss for the recreated system (i.e., RPO), are business requirements that are enabled through the use of high-availability or fault-tolerant solutions. Their use depends on the needs of the business and varies among industries.

If the RTO is instantaneous and the RPO is equally stringent (i.e., the goal is for users to experience no downtime), then a fault-tolerant storage solution is established. Fault-tolerant servers provide for fail-safe redundancy through mirrored images of the primary server. Using this approach also entails distributed processing of a server load—a concept referred to as load balancing or clustering—where all servers take part in processing. In this arrangement, an intelligent cluster unit provides for load balancing for improved performance. This type of server architecture is transparent to users. The only thing that may be noticeable to a user is performance degradation if a server fails.

The information security manager must be aware of the costs associated with fault-tolerant solutions and difficulties in achieving this state of data availability. For example, in a virtual environment, multiple instances (copies) of a virtual machine (VM) running in parallel must exist. Any change in the state of the primary VM (such as modification of a file) must be applied on all the secondary VMs in real time.

If the RTO and RPO are more flexible (i.e., the business will tolerate a limited amount of downtime), then a high-availability storage solution is established. An example of high availability is a set of servers that have a fail-over relationship. When an application is running and the primary server fails, the application is restarted in the failover server. In this arrangement, the most current work in progress may be lost; however, the application could be up and running within seconds. High availability solutions are less costly to implement than those designed for 100 percent fault tolerance. See **figure 4.6.**

Figure 4.6—Relationship of RTOs, RPOs, High Availability and Fault Tolerance

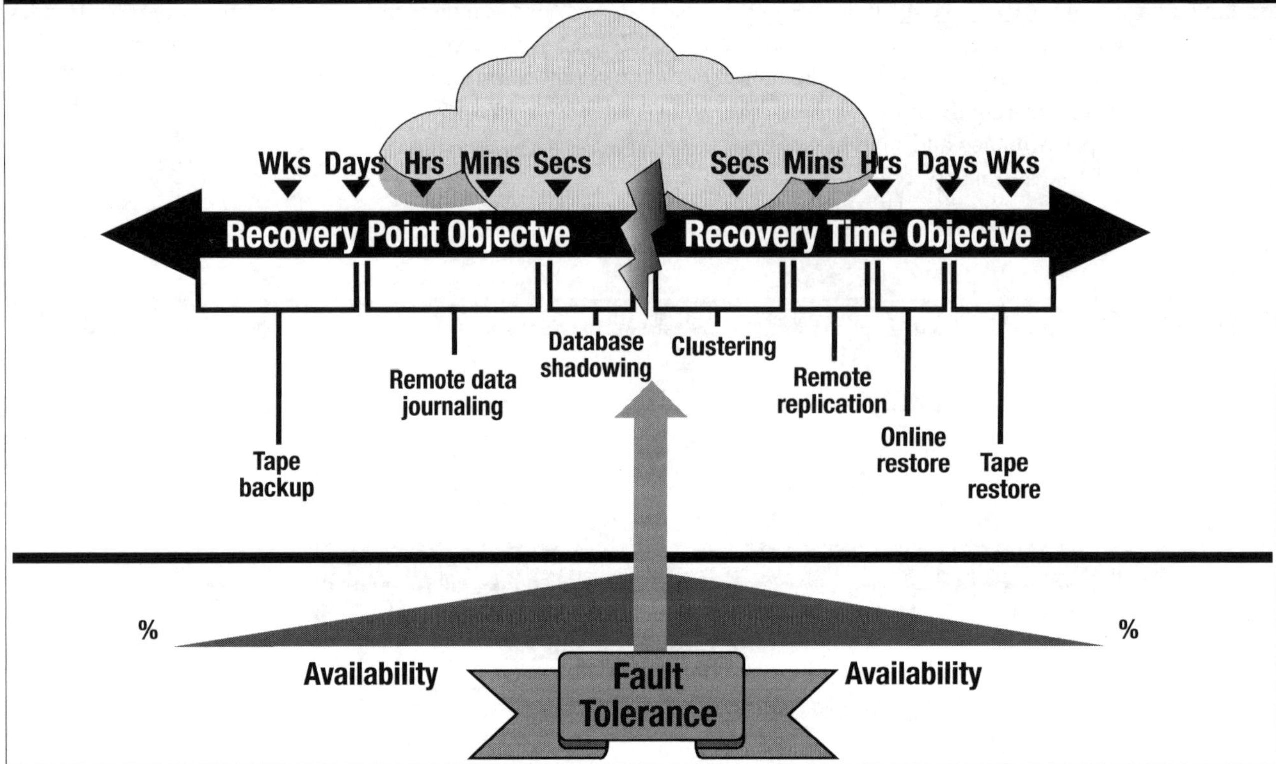

Source: Adapted from Global Knowledge, https://www.globalknowledge.com

4.4.4 Insurance

The IRP should include information regarding the enterprise's insurance plans, including general coverage, cyber insurance or IT-related insurance. Some elements of the enterprise's coverage, such as a business interruption policy, may provide some level of protection and should be considered as part of the plan. Current information systems processing insurance policies usually require a multi-peril policy designed to provide various types of IT coverage. These policies should be constructed modularly, so they can be adapted to the insured's particular IT environment.

An enterprise typically cannot insure against failure to comply with legal and regulatory requirements or any other breach of the law. There are usually a number of other exclusions and deductibles, and careful review by the information security manager is required to gain a clear understanding of the actual protection provided.

Some specific types of coverage that are available include:

- **IT equipment and facilities**—Coverage of physical damage to the information processing facility (IPF) and owned equipment. An enterprise should also insure leased equipment if it is obtained when the lessee is responsible for hazard coverage. The information security manager should review these policies carefully; many policies are worded so that insurers are obligated to replace damaged or destroyed equipment with like kind and quality, not necessarily the identical brand and model.
- **Media (software) reconstruction**—Covers damage to computer-related media that are the property of the insured and for which the insured may be liable. Insurance is available for on-premises, off-premises or in-transit disasters and covers the actual reproduction cost of the property. Considerations in determining the amount of coverage needed are programming costs to reproduce the media damaged, backup expenses, and physical replacement of media devices such as tapes, cartridges and disks.
- **Cybersecurity**—Covers cyberattacks of various kinds, including ransomware, denial of service

(DoS) distributed DoS (DDoS), and losses associated with breaches.

- **Professional and commercial liability**—Protection from third-party claims for losses and damages caused by the insured.
- **Extra expense**—Designed to cover the extra costs of continuing operations following damage or destruction at the IPF. The amount of insurance needed is based on the availability and cost of backup facilities and operations. Extra expense can also cover the loss of net profits caused by computer media damage. This provides reimbursement for monetary losses resulting from suspension of operations due to the physical loss of equipment or media as is the case when IPFs are on the sixth floor and the first five floors are burned out. In this case, operations would be interrupted even though the IPF remained unaffected.
- **Business interruption**—Covers the loss of profit due to the disruption of the activity of the company caused by any covered IT malfunction or security-related event in which an attacker or malicious code caused loss of availability of computing resources.
- **Valuable papers and records**—Covers the actual cash value of papers and records (not defined as media) on the insured's premises against unauthorized disclosure, direct physical loss or damage.
- **Errors and omissions**—Provides legal liability protection in the event that the professional practitioner commits an act, error or omission that results in financial loss to a client. This insurance originally was designed for service bureaus, but it is now available from several insurance companies for protecting against actions of systems analysts, software designers, programmers, consultants and other information systems personnel.
- **Fidelity coverage**—Usually takes the form of banker's blanket bonds, excess fidelity insurance and commercial blanket bonds, and covers loss from dishonest or fraudulent acts by employees. This type of coverage is prevalent in financial institutions operating their own IPF.
- **Media transportation**—Provides coverage for potential loss or damage to media in transit to off-premises IPFs. Transit coverage wording in the policy usually specifies that all documents must be filmed or otherwise copied. When the policy does not specifically require that data be filmed prior to being transported and the work is not filmed, management should obtain from the insurance carrier a letter that specifically describes the carrier's position and coverage in the event data is destroyed.

4.5 Disaster Recovery Plan

The information security manager must understand the basic processes required to recover operations from information system incidents resulting in security breaches and system failures, natural disasters, and other probable events that potentially could disrupt business operations.

DR has traditionally been defined as the recovery of IT systems after disruptive events that cause major system failures, such as hurricanes and floods resulting in inaccessibility or prolonged power or communication outages. Business recovery is defined as the recovery of all the critical business processes necessary to continue or resume operations. Business recovery includes DR and all other required operational aspects.

Planning includes documenting the requirements for declaring a disaster (i.e., determining when an incident cannot be resolved by the available recovery processes). The declaration of a disaster pursuant to defined declaration criteria generally requires moving operations to the alternative processing site.

Not all events, incidents or critical disruptions should be classified as security incidents. For example, disruption in service can be caused by system malfunctions or accidents. Regardless of the cause of operational disruption, satisfactory resolution requires prompt action to maintain or recover operational status. Actions may, among other things, necessitate restoration of hardware, software and data files.

Each of these planning processes typically includes several main phases, including:

- Conducting a risk assessment and BIA
- Defining a response and recovery strategy
- Documenting response and recovery plans
- Training that covers response and recovery procedures
- Updating response and recovery plans
- Testing response and recovery plans
- Auditing response and recovery plans

Prior to creating a detailed BCP, it is important to perform BIAs to determine the incremental daily cost of losing different systems. This provides the basis for deciding on appropriate RTOs and associated costs. This, in turn, affects the location and cost of offsite recovery facilities and the composition and mission of individual response and recovery teams, which are key to disaster recovery.

4.5.1 Business Continuity and Disaster Recovery Procedures

There are several considerations when developing response and recovery plans, including available resources; expected services; and the types, kinds and severity of threats faced by the enterprise. The state of monitoring and detection capabilities must be known, and the level of risk the enterprise is willing to accept must be determined, as discussed in Section 2.4.1 Determining Risk Capacity and Acceptable Risk (Risk Appetite). An effective strategy for recovery plans strikes the most cost-effective balance among risk management efforts, incident management and response and BC/DR planning.

ISACA defines business continuity as "preventing, mitigating and recovering from disruption. The terms 'business resumption planning,' 'disaster recovery planning' and 'contingency planning' also may be used in this context; they focus on recovery aspects of continuity."

The International Consortium for Organizational Resilience[30] defines business continuity as "a management process that identifies potential threats to an organization and the impacts to business operations if those threats are realized." Therefore, the relationship between BC and DR is such that the DRP is a subset of the BCP. Specifically, while BCP goals include incident prevention and mitigation, the DRP is focused on what must be done to restore operations after an incident has already taken place. A BCP may be seen as a continuous process that is actively implemented in business-as-usual scenarios, while the DRP is reactive in nature and is implemented only upon satisfaction of a specific set of conditions (i.e., the business has incurred an incident).

4.5.2 Recovery Operations

Once the enterprise is up and running in recovery mode (which is usually from a DR site in the case of damage or inaccessibility of the primary facility), the BC teams should monitor the restoration progress at the primary site. This is done to assess when it is safe to return and perform tests to evaluate whether the primary data center and facilities are accessible, operational and capable of functioning at normal capacities and processing load.

The teams that were responsible for relocating to the alternative site and making it operational perform a similar operation to return to the primary site. On complete restoration of the primary facility and data processing capabilities, the recovery teams update the BC leader, who will then declare normalcy in consultation with the crisis management team and migrate operations back to the primary site.

In the event that the primary site is completely destroyed or severely damaged, the enterprise may make a strategic decision to transform the alternative recovery site to the primary operations site or identify, acquire and set up another site where operations will eventually be restored and which will function as the primary site. This is especially true for cases in which the enterprise subscribes to a third-party disaster recovery site because the costs of operating from such a site for an extended period may prove to be prohibitively high.

To ensure effective and comprehensive contingency planning, enterprises setting up a BCP should address the processes, roles and responsibilities involved in identifying an incident, declaring a disaster and managing operations in a disaster mode, but it should also define processes to restore operations at the primary site and announce the return to normalcy. A cold site may be identified during the strategy phase to be upgraded to a primary operating facility in the event that the incident renders the primary facility useless.

It is important to remember that information resources must still be protected, even during the potentially chaotic environment of a business interruption or disaster. The information security manager must ensure that information security is incorporated into all response and recovery plans. The security manager should carefully review these plans to ensure that their execution does not compromise information security

[30] International Consortium for Organizational Resilience, https://www.build-resilience.org/

standards and requirements. If such a compromise is unavoidable, other mitigation options should be explored. Minimally, a focused risk assessment should be conducted to make management aware of the extent and potential impacts of the security risk introduced by execution of the plan.

In the likely event that the crisis is not catastrophic and the enterprise has switched to disaster recovery mode for only a limited time, it is important that the disaster recovery site be restored to an acceptable state of readiness after operations are reinstated at the primary facility.

Lessons learned and gaps identified in the plan when either switching to the disaster recovery site or reverting to the primary facility should be recorded and recommendations should be implemented to enhance the effectiveness of the plan. A realistic plan should cover all aspects of reestablishing the operations at the primary site, including people, facilities and technology areas.

4.5.3 Evaluating Recovery Strategies

Various strategies exist for recovering critical information resources. The most appropriate strategy is likely to be the one that demonstrably addresses probable events with acceptable recovery times at a reasonable cost.

The total cost of a recovery capability includes the cost of preparing for possible disruptions (e.g., purchasing, maintaining and regularly testing redundant computers; maintaining alternative network routing; and training and personnel costs) and the cost of putting these into effect in the event of an incident. Impacts of disruptions can, to some extent, be mitigated by various forms of business interruption insurance, which should be considered as a strategy option.

Depending on the size and complexity of the enterprise and the state of recovery planning, the information security manager should understand that the development of an incident management and response plan is likely to be a difficult and expensive process that may take considerable time. It may require the development of several alternative strategies, encompassing different capabilities and costs, to be presented to management for a final decision. Each alternative must be sufficiently developed to provide an understanding of the trade-offs among scope, capabilities, risk and cost. It may be prudent to consider outsourcing some or all of the needed capabilities and determine associated costs for the purpose of comparisons. Once the decision is made on which strategy best meets management's objectives that strategy provides the basis for the development of detailed incident management and response plans.

4.5.4 Addressing Threats

Some proactive strategies that may be considered in incident management when responding to threats include:

- **Eliminate or neutralize a threat**—Although removing or neutralizing a threat might seem like the best alternative, it can be unrealistic with external threats. If the threat is internal and specific, it may be possible to eliminate it. For example, the threat of a particular activity creating a security incident might be addressed by ceasing the activity.
- **Minimize the likelihood of a threat's occurrence**—The best alternative is often to minimize the likelihood of a threat's occurrence by reducing or eliminating vulnerabilities or exposure. This goal can be achieved by implementing the appropriate set of physical, environmental and security controls. For example, deploying firewalls, IDSs and strong authentication methods might substantially reduce the risk of a successful attack. Reducing exposure may be achieved by compartmentalization, such as network segmentation.
- **Minimize the effects of a threat if an incident occurs**—There are a number of ways to minimize impact if an incident occurs, such as effective incident management and response, insurance, redundant systems with automatic failover, or other compensating or corrective controls.

Each critical information processing system requires an approach to restoring operations in the event of disruption. There are many alternative strategies that can be considered both in terms of the incident management and response capability and from a DR perspective. These can range from redundant and mirrored systems to ensuring a high degree of system or process resilience and robustness.

4.5.5 Recovery Sites

The most appropriate alternatives for a recovery site must be based on the probability of major outages occurring, the nature and extent of impact on the enterprise's ability to continue operations, and overall cost. Lengthier and more costly outages or disasters that impair the primary physical facility are likely to require offsite backup alternatives. The types of offsite backup facilities that can be considered include:

- **Hot sites**—Hot sites are configured fully and ready to operate within several hours. The equipment, network and systems software must be compatible with the primary installation being backed up. The only additional needs are staff, programs, data files and documentation.
- **Warm sites**—Warm sites are complete infrastructures but are partially configured in terms of IT, usually with network connections and essential peripheral equipment such as disk drives, tape drives and controllers. Sometimes a warm site is equipped with a less powerful central processing unit (CPU) than the primary site.
- **Cold sites**—Cold sites are a viable option only when enterprises can afford a relatively long downtime. Cold sites have only the basic environment (electrical wiring, air conditioning, flooring, etc.) to operate an IPF. The cold site is ready to receive equipment but does not offer any components at the site in advance of the need. Activation of the site may take several weeks. Because data and software are required for these strategies, special arrangements need to be considered for their backup to removable media and their safe, secure storage offsite. Two options for equipping a cold site include:
    - Vendor or third party—Hardware vendors are usually the best source for replacement equipment. However, this may often involve a waiting period that is not acceptable for critical operations. It is unlikely that any vendor will guarantee a specific reaction to a crisis. Vendor arrangements are used best when an enterprise plans to move from a hot site to a warm or cold site, so advance planning is critical. Another source of equipment replacement is the used hardware market. This market can supply critical components or entire systems on relatively short notice, often at a substantially reduced cost. If the entity is considering purchasing used hardware, vetting of the dealers and supply chain should be performed in advance to prevent purchasing of counterfeit or hardware devices that have been maliciously modified or tampered with. Establishing relationships with dealers well in advance of any actual emergency is critical.
    - Off-the-shelf—Such components are often available from the inventory of suppliers on short notice but may require special arrangements. To make use of this approach, several strategies must be used, including:
        - Avoiding the use of unusual and hard-to-get equipment
        - Regularly updating equipment to keep current
        - Maintaining software compatibility to permit the operation of newer equipment
- **Mobile sites**—Mobile sites are specially designed trailers that can be quickly transported to a business location or an alternative site to provide a ready-conditioned IPF. These mobile sites can be attached to form larger work areas and can be preconfigured with servers, desktop computers, communications equipment, and microwave and satellite data links. They are a useful alternative when there are no recovery facilities in the immediate geographic area. They are also useful in case of a widespread disaster and may be a cost-effective alternative for duplicate IPFs for a multisite enterprise.
- **Duplicate sites**—These facilities are dedicated recovery sites that are functionally similar or identical to the primary site that can quickly take over for the primary site. They range from a standby hot site to facilities available through a reciprocal agreement with another company. The assumption is that there are fewer problems in coordinating compatibility and availability in the case of duplicate sites. Large enterprises with multiple data facilities can often develop failover capabilities among their own geographically dispersed data centers provided the following principles are considered:
    - The site chosen should be located so it is not subject to the same disaster event as the primary site. For example, if the primary site is in an area subject to hurricanes, the recovery site should not be subject to the same hurricanes.

  - Coordination of hardware/software strategies is necessary. A reasonable degree of hardware and software compatibility must exist to serve as a basis for backup.
  - Resource availability must be assured. The workloads of the sites must be monitored to ensure that sufficient availability for emergency backup use exists.
  - There must be agreement concerning the priority of adding applications (workloads) until all the recovery resources are fully used.
  - Regular testing is necessary. Whether duplicate sites are under common ownership or under the same management, testing of the backup operation on a regular basis is necessary to ensure that it will work in the event of a disaster.
- **Mirror sites**—If continuous uptime and availability are required, a mirror site may be the best option. By definition, a mirror site is very similar or identical to the primary site. The mirror site is operational in concert with the primary site on a load-sharing basis. Typically, applications are launched by an automatic scheduler that balances the loads between the sites based on available operational capacity, and applications can be executed in either one. Provided that sufficient reserve capacity exists, applications are seamlessly switched between the sites without interruption. Enterprises with multiple data facilities can often develop this capability among their own geographically dispersed data centers.
- **Disaster recovery as a service (DRaaS)**—With the growth and availability of cloud service providers, DRaaS is a category of cloud computing used for protecting a system or data from disruptions at an IPF by enabling a full recovery within a cloud environment. This differs from a cloud-based backup/storage service by providing the necessary IT capabilities on demand (pay as you go) and ensuring systems are recovered and operate as needed, reducing overhead investment costs associated with mirror, hot and warm sites.
- **Reciprocal agreements**—Note: Reciprocal agreements are not as common as they once were. Under the typical agreement, participants promise to provide computing time and network operations to each other when an emergency arises. If the recovery strategy is to use reciprocal agreements with one or more internal or external entities, it is essential that similar equipment and applications are available. It is important to consider that IT resources are generally used in a manner that approaches their maximum capacity, and they may not be able to support the requirements of recovery operations. Enterprises do not generally have sufficient reserve resources to satisfy even fairly small recovery requirements related to central processing units, network bandwidth or storage capacity. The availability of competent personnel at an alternative facility must also be considered. It is likely that in the event of a serious incident or disaster, the availability of staff resources will be adversely affected. Extra expenses, integrating external personnel into operations and additional threats to physical security are some of the difficult and immediate problems inherent in this type of solution. Additionally, creating a contract that provides adequate protection can be a difficult task, and the cost of dealing with changes over time is likely to be significant. It is important that contractual provisions for the use of third-party sites should cover important issues such as configuration of third-party hardware and software, speed of availability, reliability, duration of usage, nature of inter-site communications and period of usage.

The type of site most suitable will largely be based on operational requirements determined by the BIA, the costs and benefits, and the risk appetite of management. It may be determined that some critical operational aspects must be mirrored to meet service level requirements while others can be adequately supported by hot, warm or cold site capabilities at the same or other facilities.

Additionally, part of the recovery of IT facilities involves telecommunications, for which the strategies usually considered include elements of network disaster prevention:

- Alternative routing
- Diverse routing
- Long-haul network diversity
- Protection of local resources
- Voice recovery
- Availability of appropriate circuits and adequate bandwidth
- Availability of out-of-band communications in case of failure of primary communications methods
- Alternative telecommunication carriers

After a strategy for the recovery of sufficient IT facilities to support critical business processes has been developed, it is critical that the strategies work for the entire period of recovery until all facilities are restored. The strategies may include:

- Doing nothing until recovery facilities are ready.
- Using manual procedures.
- Focusing on the most important customers, suppliers, products, systems, etc., with the resources that are still available.
- Using PC-based systems to capture data for later processing or performing simple local processing.

4.5.6 Basis for Recovery Site Selections

The type of site selected for a response and recovery strategy should be based on the following considerations:

- **AIW**—Acceptable interruption window. The total time that the enterprise can wait from the point of failure to the restoration of critical services/applications. After this time, the cumulative losses caused by the interruption may threaten the existence of the enterprise.
- **RTO**—Recovery time objective. The length of time from the interruption to the time that the process must be functioning at a service level sufficient to limit financial and operational impacts to an acceptable level. Some enterprises express it as partial moments (i.e., from point of failure to technical recovery or point of disaster declaration to full operations).
- **RPO** —Recovery point objective. The age of the data the enterprise needs to be able to restore in the event of a disaster (i.e., the amount of data that can be lost and need to be recreated). Sometimes this is expressed as the point of last known good data. This will be the starting point for operations at the recovery site. If full backups are infrequent, it may take too much time to recreate the amount of data lost and the result would be RTOs not being met.
- **SDO**—Service delivery objective. Level of services to be supported during the alternative process mode until the normal situation is restored. This must be directly related to business needs.
- **MTO**—Maximum tolerable downtime. The maximum time the enterprise can support processing in the alternative mode. Various factors will determine the MTO, including increasing backlogs of deferred processing. This, in turn, is affected by the SDO if it is less than that required during normal operations.
- **Proximity factors**—The distance from potential hazards, which can include flooding risk from nearby waterways, hazardous material manufacturing or storage, or other situations that may pose a risk to the operation of a recovery site
- **Location**—Sufficient distance needed to minimize the likelihood of both the primary and recovery facilities being subject to the same occurrence of an environmental event. When planning, consideration should be given to the typical impact area of the types of events that have a higher likelihood of occurrence for a given location. For example, in the case of hurricanes vs. tornadoes, the impact area of a hurricane is typically much larger than the impact area of a tornado, requiring greater distance between sites for a location where hurricanes frequently occur.
- **Nature of probable disruptions**—This must be considered in terms of the MTO. For example, a major earthquake is likely to render a primary site inoperable for a number of months. Clearly, the MTO in an area subject to this disruption must be greater than the probable duration of such an event.

To prepare a suitable recovery strategy, the information security manager must balance all these parameters with the capabilities of different types of recovery sites, their costs, locations and the skills and capabilities of the enterprise staff.

The complexity and cost of the response and recovery plans, along with the type and cost of the recovery site, are proportionally inverse to these time objectives. An interruption window of two hours, for instance, dictates a hot or mirrored solution that is generally very expensive, but the corresponding recovery process is likely to be simple and inexpensive. In contrast, an interruption window of a month may permit the use of a cold site that is inexpensive, but the associated recovery process is likely to be complex and expensive.

4.5.7 Response and Recovery Strategy Implementation

Based on the response and recovery strategy selected by management, a detailed response and recovery plan should be developed. It should address all issues involved in recovering from a disaster. Various factors should be considered while developing the plan, including:

- Preincident readiness
- Evacuation procedures
- How to declare a disaster
- Transition steps to DR if incident response fails
- Identification of the business processes and IT resources that should be recovered
- Identification of individuals with decision authority and responsibilities in the plan
- Identification of the people (and alternatives) responsible for each function in the plan
- Identification of contact information
- The step-by-step explanation of the recovery options
- Identification of the various resources required for recovery and continued operations
- Ensuring that other logistics such as personnel relocation and temporary housing are considered

The response and recovery plan should be documented and written in simple language that is clear and easy to read. It is also common to identify teams of personnel who are responsible for specific tasks in case of incidents or disasters. Most BCPs are created as a set of procedures that accommodate system, user, application and network recovery strategies. Copies of the plan must be kept offsite to ensure that it is available when needed; this includes at the recovery facility, the media storage facility and the homes of key decision-making personnel.

4.6 Incident Classification/Categorization

The ability to identify, classify and categorize responding to an incident is a common practice as not all incidents are necessarily equal, nor does the enterprise have the ability to leverage limited resources simultaneously.

As a result, the need to effectively and properly triage incidents that do occur enables the enterprise to respond to the incidents that have the greatest impact using the limited resources available.

How an enterprise responds should be defined in advance of an incident occurring; the approach to defining the classification and categorization of an incident needs to be tailored to the environment and commitments the enterprise has established.

Examples of incident classification and categorization are illustrated in **figures 4.7** and **4.8**.

Figure 4.7—Incident Classification

Urgency	Enterprise Impact: Low	Medium	High
High	3	2	1
Medium	4	3	2
Low	5	4	3

Figure 4.8—Incident Categorization

Priority	Resolution
1	2 hours
2	8 hours
3	24 hours
4	36 hours
5	160 hours

4.6.1 Escalation Process for Effective Incident Management

The information security manager should work with management to define and implement an escalation process to establish the events to be managed (i.e., in the event of a telecommunications shutdown). Events that appear routine can be related to a security compromise and constitute an incident (e.g., data corruption may not be due to an application problem, but rather to a virus or worm infection). As part of the emergency management and incident management policies and procedures, a detailed description of the escalation process and who must authorize various recovery actions or disaster declaration must be clear and documented.

For every credible and actionable event, a list of actions should be described in the sequence to be performed. Every action listed should identify the responsible person, alternatives in case of unavailability and an estimated time for execution.

When all the actions have been completed successfully, the process should continue in the section dedicated to end of emergency. If any action cannot be executed or if the estimated time is reached, the process should continue in the next action. Each unsuccessful action wastes time. If the accumulated elapsed time reaches a predetermined limit, the emergency status may change to an alert condition (i.e., low, medium, high). An alert situation prompts notification of individuals and enterprises who have authoritative decision-making responsibilities, as appropriate and defined by the incident. Entities and personnel that may receive an alert notification include, but are not limited to, the following:

- Backup facilities
- Business partners
- Customer support representatives
- Customers
- General counsel/legal
- HR
- Insurance companies
- Internal audit
- Investors/shareholders
- Network operations
- Privacy department
- Public relations
- Regulators
- Response and recovery teams
- Risk management
- Security operations
- Senior management
- Vendors/suppliers

The process should continue until the emergency is resolved or the last alert has occurred. At this point, the emergency management team meets to evaluate the damages and mitigation alternatives, decide whether to declare a disaster or launch the response and recovery plan, and determine the appropriate strategy. The information security manager should develop a communication plan in consultation with PR, legal counsel and appropriate senior management to ensure the appropriateness of any information disclosures.

After the escalation process, tasks such as notifying personnel, activating backup facilities, containing security threats to information resources, making transportation arrangements and carrying them out, retrieving and unloading data, and testing must be executed. The total elapsed time should be in accordance with the established RTO.

The escalation process includes prioritizing event information and the decision process for determining when to alert various groups, including senior management, the public, shareholders and stakeholders, legal counsel, HR staff, vendors and customers.

The information security manager should develop these escalation processes and decision authority through consultation with PR, legal counsel and appropriate senior management. This process should include vendors and utility services.

Many enterprises define the level of events and the escalation procedures differently for each level. These levels can be based on the severity of the event and the number of enterprises that may be affected by the event and their specific need to be notified. The information security manager should also have mechanisms to communicate crisis or event information. These mechanisms may include using email (if computing systems and networks are operational), cellular phones, fax machines, electronic pagers, websites, or an emergency telephone number at which a message can be placed. Note that some types of communication, such as email messages, are by default in clear text, making them subject to potential interception. The information security manager should also develop methods to encrypt email and other communications used in relaying crisis or event-related information to ensure that information is released only as prudent or according to plans.

4.6.2 Help/Service Desk Processes for Identifying Security Incidents

The information security manager should have processes defined for help/service desk personnel to distinguish a typical request from a possible security incident. The help/service desk is likely to receive the first reports indicating a security-related problem. Prompt recognition of an incident in progress and quick referral to appropriate parties are critical to minimizing the damage resulting from such incidents.

By defining appropriate criteria and improving the awareness of help/service desk personnel, the information security manager develops another important method to detect a security incident. Proper training also helps to reduce the risk that the help/service desk could be successfully targeted in a social engineering attack designed to obtain access to accounts, such as a perpetrator pretending to be a user who has been locked out and requires immediate access to the system. In addition to identifying a possible security incident, help/service desk personnel should be aware of the proper procedures to report and escalate a potential issue.

4.7 Incident Management Training, Testing and Evaluation

Given that an incident may occur at any time, the information security manager should ensure that staff are properly trained in how the enterprise handles incidents, whether they manage an incident from end-to-end, and if it is managed by a third-party or a combination of the two.

Training should be inclusive of all roles involved in incident management—both technical and nontechnical. This is to ensure proper understanding of the duties and the foundational capabilities and skills needed to respond throughout the life cycle of an incident. Training can take many forms, ranging from formal instructor-led classes to on-the-job training. The skills needed for each role need to be clearly defined and kept current with the current operating environment of the enterprise.

To ensure and validate the effectiveness in managing incidents within the operating environment, regular testing should be performed. This is to ensure both that individuals know and understand their responsibilities and to determine the effectiveness of the plan itself.

To determine efficiency and conformance with the plan, independent and objective evaluation of processes, practices and activities should be conducted at least annually or when there are significant changes to the environment. Evaluation against the enterprise's defined standard of practice for incident management should consider not only the processes, but also the individual capabilities and skill levels, but also relevancy of the plan itself, supporting infrastructure and overall ability to achieve defined targets as planned.

4.7.1 Incident Management Roles and Responsibilities

The incident management capability in an enterprise acts as the first responder for a variety of incidents, including information processing and processes. It responds to and manages incidents to contain and minimize damage, limit disruptions to business processes and restore operations as quickly as possible. Poorly managed incidents have the capacity to become disasters.

Incident management is, nominally, a component of risk management and can be considered the operational and reactive element. If managing risk is insufficient to prevent a threat from materializing and causing an impact, incident management and response capabilities should be available to react appropriately to limit the damage and restore operations.

The information security manager should understand the various activities involved in a response and recovery program. This includes meeting with emergency management officials (e.g., federal, state/provincial, municipal/local) to understand what governmental capabilities are available. These officials are likely to have information concerning the nature of the risk to which the location or area is susceptible. Most countries and governments have civil defense and emergency management agencies that are tasked with advising and assisting the population in dealing with a wide range of natural and human-initiated threats. This will provide insight into historical events that will inform the enterprise on the sorts of events it must plan to manage.

Emergency management activities typically focus on the activities immediately after an incident. These events may require prompt action to recover operational status. Actions may necessitate restoration of hardware, software and data files. Emergency management activities include measures to ensure the safety of personnel, such as evacuation plans and creation of a command center from which emergency procedures can be executed. It is important that information about an incident be communicated only on a need-to-know basis to control exposure of potentially sensitive information.

Understanding the hierarchy and organizational structure associated with the various roles common within incident management is important. Each role needs to be clearly defined and communicated to reduce miscommunication in a time of crisis.

The roles associated with incident management will vary enterprise to enterprise. Common roles normally involved in incident management activities include, but are not limited to, the following:

- Affected business unit representation
- Corporate communications
- Executive sponsor
- General counsel
- Human resources
- Incident communications lead
- Incident coordinator (documentation and timeline)
- Incident response team lead
- Information security manager
- Internal audit
- Lead investigator
- Public relations
- Risk management
- Security analysts
- Technical subject matter experts (e.g., applications, infrastructure, engineering)
- Technology analysts
- Threat intelligence analysts

Senior Management Commitment

As is the case with other aspects of information security, senior management's commitment is critical to the success of incident management and response activities.

A business case can show that, under many circumstances, effective incident management and response may be a less costly option than attempting to implement controls for all possible conditions. Tested incident management and response may also allow the enterprise greater business opportunities by allowing higher levels of acceptable risk based on a demonstrated capacity and capability to handle security incidents. Sufficient incident response, in combination with effective information security, is likely to offer the most cost-effective risk management approach and may be the most prudent resource management decision. These points should be included in the business case, which can be used to gain senior management commitment needed to ensure the program's success.

Responsibilities

There are a number of incident management responsibilities that the information security manager must undertake, including:

- Developing information security incident management and response plans.
- Handling and coordinating information security incident response activities effectively and efficiently.
- Validating and reporting safeguard or countermeasure solutions, either logical, physical or administrative.
- Planning, budgeting and program development for all matters related to information security incident management and response.

The approach to incident response varies depending on the situation and types of events that may occur, but the goals are constant and include:

- Maintaining incident response readiness.
- Containing and minimizing the effects of the incident so damage and losses do not escalate out of control.
- Notifying the appropriate people for the purpose of recovery or to provide needed information.
- Recovering quickly and efficiently from security incidents.
- Responding systematically and decreasing the likelihood of recurrence.
- Balancing operational and security processes.
- Dealing with legal and law enforcement-related issues.

The information security manager also needs to define what constitutes a security-related incident. Typically, security incidents include:

- Malicious code attacks
- Unauthorized access to IT or information resources
- Unauthorized use of services
- Unauthorized changes to systems, network devices or information
- DoS attacks
- DDoS attacks
- Misuse/abuse of resources
- Surveillance and espionage

- Hoaxes/social engineering
- Ransomware

Many incidents that initially appear to be malicious instead turn out to be the result of human error. Typically, enterprises experience nearly double the number of incidents due to human error than are caused by externally initiated security breaches.

4.7.2 Incident Management Metrics and Indicators

Incident management metrics, measures and indicators are the criteria used to measure the effectiveness and efficiency of the incident management function. Metrics based on KPIs and program goals (KGIs) established for incident management should be presented to senior management as a basis of justification for continuous support and funding. They enable senior management to understand the incident management capability of the enterprise and areas of risk that need to be addressed.

KPIs are a quantifiable activity measure (e.g., the number of incidents per year resolved within two minutes of occurrence). KGIs are either quantitative or qualitative, depending on the situation, and are intended to show progress toward a predefined goal. For example, a business goal for the year is to have 1,000 incidents resolved within two minutes of incident occurrence. At the point of measurement, the KPI of incidents currently resolved in the target time frame is 100; therefore, the KGI at the point of measurement is 10 percent (100 incidents resolved out of 1,000 target incidents).

Incident management reports and measures are useful for the IMT for self-assessment and to understand what has been done satisfactorily and where improvements need to be made. Common criteria that are used as part of incident management metrics may include:

- Total number of reported incidents
- Total number of detected incidents
- Number of days without incident
- Average time to respond to an incident relative to the RTO
- Average time to resolve an incident
- Total number of incidents successfully resolved
- Incidents not resolved successfully
- Proactive and preventive measures taken
- Total number of employees receiving security awareness training
- Total damage from reported and detected incidents if incident response was not effective or not performed
- Total savings from potential damages from incidents resolved
- Total resources involved in responding to incidents
- Detection and notification times

Recovery Time Objectives

The information security manager must understand RTOs and how they apply to the enterprise's information resources as part of the overall evaluation of risk. The enterprise's business needs will dictate the RTO, which is usually defined as the amount of time to recover an acceptable level of normal operations. The acceptable level is defined by the SDO. The information asset's functional criticality, recovery priorities and interdependencies offset by costs are variables that will determine the RTO.

Determining RTOs can depend upon a number of factors including the cyclical need (e.g., time of day, week, month or year) of the information and enterprise, interdependencies among the information and the enterprise's requirements, and the cost of available options. The enterprise's requirements can be based on customer needs, contractual obligations or service level agreements (SLAs) and, possibly, regulatory requirements.

The information security manager should consider that the RTO may vary with the timing of the month or year. Financial information may not be as critical at the beginning of the month when the new fiscal month is being opened. This same information is likely to be highly critical at the end of the month when the monthly financial reports are being prepared and the accounting period is being closed. The timing of business cycles and their dependence on information need to be considered as part of information classification.

RTOs are determined by performing a BIA in coordination with developing a BCP. The interconnection of systems and their dependencies will generally require a BIA for most or all systems related to critical business functions as this will affect the order of restoration.

The BIA is generally conducted by interviewing information owners to obtain their perspective on the cost associated with an interruption in service for a business system or process. Often there are two perspectives for RTOs. One is the perspective of the individuals whose job it is to use the information, and the other is the view of senior management who must consider costs and may need to arbitrate among business units competing for resources. An information asset that a divisional supervisor may believe is critical may not be critical in the eyes of the vice president of operations, who is able to include the overall organizational risk in the evaluation of the RTO.

The information security manager should understand that both perspectives are important and work toward an RTO that considers both. The result will factor into the BCP, the scope of the services to be restored and priority order for the recovery of systems. In the end, the final decision is that of senior management. Senior management is in the best position to arbitrate the needs and requirements of the different components of the business—such as the regulatory requirements to which the enterprise is subject—and to determine which processes are the most critical to the continued survival of the business, in addition to determining acceptable costs.

RTO and Its Relation to Business Continuity Planning and Contingency Planning Objectives and Processes

Knowledge of the RTO for information systems and their associated data is needed for an enterprise to develop and implement an effective BC program. Once the RTOs are known, the enterprise can identify and develop contingency strategies that will meet the RTOs of the information resources. The RTOs will drive the order of priority for restoration of services and, in certain cases, the selection of specific recovery technologies in situations where the RTO is short.

One critical factor when developing contingency processes is cost. System owners invariably prefer shorter RTOs, but the tradeoffs in cost may not be warranted. Near-instantaneous recovery can be achieved, where needed, using technologies such as mirroring of information systems, so that, in the event of a disruption, the information systems are always available quickly. In general, the cost of recovery is less if the RTO for a given resource is longer.

There is a break-even point in the time period to determine the RTO, where the impact of the disruption begins to be greater than the cost of recovery. The length of this time period depends on the nature of the business disruption and the assets involved. Qualitative and quantitative issues must be taken into consideration because loss of customer confidence, even if it cannot be estimated, can have a long-term negative impact on the enterprise. Most enterprises can reduce their RTOs, but there is an associated cost.

Recovery Point Objectives

The RPO is determined based on the acceptable data loss in case of disruption of operations. It indicates the most recent point in time to which it is acceptable to recover the data, which generally is the latest backup. RPO effectively quantifies the permissible amount of data loss in case of interruption. Depending on the volume of data, it may be advisable to reduce the time between backups to prevent a situation where recovery becomes impossible because of the volume of data to be restored. It may also be the case that the time required to restore a large volume of data makes it impossible to achieve the RTO.

While this is typically the scope of BC and DR planning, it is an important consideration when developing a risk management strategy.

Service Delivery Objectives

SDOs are defined as the minimal level of service that must be restored after an event to meet business requirements until normal operations can be resumed. SDOs will be affected by both RTOs and RPOs and must be considered in any risk management strategy and implementation. Higher levels of service will generally require greater resources and more current RPOs.

Maximum Tolerable Outage

MTO refers to the maximum time an enterprise can operate in alternative (or recovery) mode. Various factors may affect the MTO, such as availability of fuel to operate emergency generators, accessibility of a recovery site that might be located remotely, and limited operational capacity of the recovery site. This variable will affect the RTO, which, in turn, affects the RPO.

From a risk management perspective, the relationship among the MTO, RTO and RPO must be considered to minimize risk of inadequate recovery to the enterprise.

Allowable Interruption Window

AIW is the amount of time the normal operations can be down before the enterprise faces major financial difficulties that threaten its existence. The MTO should in any event be as long as the AIW to minimize the risk to the enterprise in the event of a disaster.

4.7.3 Performance Measurement

The performance measurements for incident management and response focus on achieving the defined objectives and optimizing cost-effectiveness. KGIs and KPIs for the activity should be defined and agreed on by stakeholders and ratified by senior management. The typical range of KGIs encompasses the successful handling of incidents whether by live testing or under actual conditions. Key performance measures can be identified by successfully handling incidents that threaten business operations within the RTOs.

4.7.4 Updating Recovery Plans

Because enterprises constantly evolve and change, the response and recovery plans also need to change. The information security manager must establish a process in which recovery plans are updated as changes occur within an enterprise. Assessing the response and recovery plan requirements during the change management process within an enterprise is an essential part of effective response management.

Plans and strategies for response and recovery should be reviewed and updated according to a schedule to reflect continuing recognition of changing requirements. The following factors, along with others not listed, may impact requirements and the need for the plan to be updated:

- A strategy that is appropriate at one point in time may not be adequate as the needs of an enterprise change.
- New applications may be developed or acquired.
- Changes in business strategy may alter the significance of critical applications or result in additional applications being deemed critical.
- Changes in the software or hardware environment may make current provisions obsolete or inappropriate.
- Changing physical and environmental circumstances may also need to be considered.

The responsibility for maintaining the BCP/DRP often falls to a BCP coordinator and the information security manager may be responsible for maintaining the IRP. However these responsibilities are allocated, specific plan maintenance activities include:

- Developing a schedule for periodic review and maintenance of the plan and advising all personnel of their roles and the deadline for receiving revisions and comments.
- Calling for revisions when significant changes have occurred.
- Reviewing revisions and comments and updating the plan within a reasonable period (e.g., 30 days) after the review date.
- Arranging and coordinating scheduled and unscheduled tests of the plan to evaluate its adequacy.
- Participating in scheduled plan tests, which should be performed at least once each year. For scheduled and unscheduled tests, the coordinator should write evaluations and integrate changes to resolve unsuccessful test results into the response plan within a reasonable period (e.g., 30 days).
- Developing a schedule for training personnel in emergency and recovery procedures, as set forth in the plan. Training dates should be scheduled within a reasonable period (e.g., 30 days) after each plan revision and scheduled plan test.
- Maintaining records of plan maintenance activities, such as testing, training and reviews.
- Updating, at least quarterly, the notification directory to include all personnel changes, such as changes to phone numbers and responsibilities or status within the enterprise.

4.7.5 Testing Incident Response and Business Continuity/Disaster Recovery Plans

In order to ensure success in incident response, all aspects of the IRP should be tested regularly. The main objective of testing is to ensure that executing the plans will result in the successful recovery of the infrastructure and critical business processes.

Testing should focus on:

- Identifying gaps
- Verifying assumptions
- Testing timelines
- Determining the effectiveness of strategies
- Evaluating the performance of personnel
- Determining the accuracy and currency of plan information

Testing promotes collaboration and coordination among teams and is a useful training tool. Many enterprises require complete testing annually. In addition, testing should be considered on the completion or major revision of each draft plan or complementary plans and following changes in key personnel, technology or the business/regulatory environment.

Testing must be carefully planned and controlled to avoid placing the business at increased risk. To ensure that all plans are regularly tested, the information security manager should maintain a testing schedule of dates and tests to be conducted for all critical functions.

Prior to each test, the security manager should ensure that:

- The risk and impact of disruption from testing is minimized.
- The business understands and accepts the risk inherent in testing.
- Fallback arrangements exist to restore operations at any point during the test.

All tests must be fully documented with pretest, test and posttest reports. Test documentation should be retained for audit review and reference. The security manager must ensure that information security is also tested and not compromised during testing.

4.7.6 Periodic Testing of the Response and Recovery Plans

As discussed in prior sections, the scope and nature of incident response and recovery teams and their capabilities will vary with different enterprises as will BC and DR operations. The exact relationship between these functions must be clearly defined and their scope and capabilities understood and integrated. Regardless of the specific scope at any particular enterprise, it is essential for the information security manager to have a good understanding of the entire BC process, including incident management and disaster recovery.

Whatever the structure, the full scope of incident management responsibilities must be tested up to the point of a disaster declaration, including the escalation, and the involvement of, or handover to, the disaster management and recovery operation if it is the responsibility of another group. The discussion in this section includes full disaster recovery, which the information security manager should understand regardless of the specific scope of incident management and response responsibilities.

The information security manager, helped by the recovery team's organization, should implement periodic testing of response and recovery plans. Testing should include:

- Developing test objectives
- Executing the test
- Evaluating the test
- Developing recommendations to improve the effectiveness of testing processes and the response and recovery plans
- Implementing a follow-up process to ensure that the recommendations are implemented

Untested response and recovery plans leave an enterprise with a false sense of security as there is the strong likelihood that plans will not work, even though care is taken in developing and documenting the plans. Because testing plans is costly in terms of time and resources, an enterprise should carefully plan tests and develop test objectives to be methodical, and should help ensure that measurable benefits can be achieved.

Once test objectives have been defined, the information security manager should ensure that an independent third party is present to monitor and evaluate the test. Internal or external audit or other assurance personnel can assume this role. A result of the evaluation step should be a list of findings and corresponding recommendations that an enterprise should consider completing to improve its response and recovery plans. It is extremely unlikely that no recommendations will result, and everything will work as planned. If it does, it is likely that a more challenging test should be planned.

The information security manager should also implement a tracking process to ensure that any recommendations resulting from testing are implemented in a timely fashion. Personnel should be tasked with making the necessary changes.

4.7.7 Testing for Infrastructure and Critical Business Applications

Testing recovery and response plans must include both infrastructure and critical applications, although not necessarily at the same time. With enterprises relying heavily on IT, the information security manager is tasked with securing these systems not only during normal operations, but also during disaster events.

Based on the risk assessment and business impact information, the information security manager can identify critical applications the enterprise requires and the infrastructure needed to support them. To ensure these are recovered in a timely fashion, the information security manager needs to perform appropriate recovery tests.

4.7.8 Types of Tests

Testing should start simply and increase gradually, stretching the objectives and success criteria of previous tests to build confidence and minimize risk to the business. At a minimum, full-interruption tests should be performed annually after individual plans have been tested separately with satisfactory results. Types of tests are described in **figure 4.9**.

Figure 4.9—Types of Incident Response Plan Tests

Type	Description
Checklist	This is a preliminary step to a real test. Recovery checklists are distributed to all members of a recovery team to review and ensure that the checklist is current.
Structured walkthrough	Team members physically implement the plans on paper and review each step to assess its effectiveness and identify enhancements, constraints and deficiencies.
Simulation test	The recovery team role-plays a prepared disaster scenario without activating processing at the recovery site.
Parallel test	The recovery site is brought to a state of operational readiness, but operations at the primary site continue normally.
Full interruption test	Operations are shut down at the primary site and shifted to the recovery site in accordance with the recovery plan; this is the most rigorous form of testing, but it is also expensive and potentially disruptive.

Tests that are progressively more challenging can include:

- Table-top walkthrough of the plans
- Table-top walkthrough with mock disaster scenarios
- Testing the infrastructure and communication components of the recovery plan
- Testing the infrastructure and recovery of the critical applications
- Testing the infrastructure, critical applications and involvement of the end users
- Full restoration and recovery tests with some personnel unfamiliar with the systems
- Surprise tests

There are three main recovery testing categories:

- **Paper tests**—Paper tests are an on-paper walkthrough of the plan involving the major players in the plan's execution who reason out what might happen in a particular type of service disruption. They may walk through the entire plan or just a portion. The paper test usually precedes preparedness tests.

- **Preparedness tests**—Preparedness tests are usually localized versions of a full test, wherein actual resources are expended in the simulation of a system crash. These tests are performed regularly on different aspects of the plan and can be a cost-effective way to gradually obtain evidence about how good the plan is. They also provide a means to improve the plan in increments.
- **Full operational tests**—These tests are one step away from an actual service disruption. An enterprise should have tested the plan well on paper and locally before endeavoring to completely cut over operations.

Most enterprises start with paper tests before attempting preparedness and operational tests as these pose increasing difficulty and introduce the risk of disrupting operations. Regardless of which tests are being performed, during every phase of the test, detailed documentation of observations, problems and resolutions should be maintained. Each team should have a diary with specific steps and information recorded. This documentation serves as important historical information that can facilitate actual recovery during a real disaster. The documentation aids in performing detailed analysis of the strengths and weaknesses of the plan.

It is common for response and recovery tests to fall short of a full-scale test of all operational portions of the enterprise. This should not preclude performing full or partial testing because one of the purposes of the business continuity test is to determine how well the plan works or which portions of the plan need improvement. Although surprise tests are potentially advantageous from the standpoint that they are similar to real-life incident response situations, they have some potential downsides. They can be very disruptive to production and operations. The information security manager should carefully consider the ramifications before recommending various testing approaches. There have been instances of serious extended outages resulting from the inability to restore systems as planned.

Potentially disruptive testing should be scheduled during a time that will minimize impact on normal operations. Weekends are generally a good time to conduct tests. It is important for all key recovery team members to be involved in the recovery test process. The test should address all critical components and simulate actual prime-time processing conditions, even if the test is conducted during off hours.

4.7.9 Test Results

Each test should yield an expected set of results. In other words, there are specific outcomes that should be expected as a result of running a test.

A recovery test should strive to, at a minimum, accomplish the following tasks:

- Verify the completeness and precision of the response and recovery plan.
- Evaluate the performance of the personnel involved in the exercise.
- Appraise the demonstrated level of training and awareness of individuals who are not part of the recovery/response team.
- Evaluate the coordination among the team members and external vendors and suppliers.
- Measure the ability and capacity of the backup site to perform prescribed processing.
- Assess the vital records retrieval capability.
- Evaluate the state and quantity of equipment and supplies that have been relocated to the recovery site.
- Measure the overall performance of operational and information systems processing activities related to maintaining the business entity.

To perform preparedness or operational recovery testing, each of the following test phases should be completed:

- **Pretest**—The pretest consists of the set of actions necessary to set the stage for the actual test. This ranges from placing tables in the proper operations recovery area to transporting and installing backup telephone equipment. These activities are outside the realm of those that would take place in the case of a real emergency, in which there is generally no forewarning of the event and thus no time to take preparatory actions.
- **Test**—Actual operational activities are executed to test the specific objectives of the plan. Data entry; telephone calls; information systems processing; handling orders; and movement of personnel, equipment and suppliers should take place. Evaluators should review staff members as they perform the designated tasks. This is the actual test of preparedness to respond to an emergency.
- **Posttest**—The posttest is the cleanup of group activities. This phase comprises assignments such as

returning all resources to their proper place, disconnecting equipment, returning personnel to their normal locations and deleting all company data from third-party systems. The posttest cleanup also includes formally evaluating the plan and implementing indicated improvements.

4.7.10 Recovery Test Metrics

Just as with nearly everything else in information security, metrics should be developed and used in measuring the success of the plan and testing against the stated objectives. Results should be recorded and evaluated quantitatively, as opposed to being subjected to evaluation based only on verbal descriptions. The resulting metrics should be used not only to measure the effectiveness of the plan, but more importantly, to improve it. Although specific measurements vary depending on the test and the enterprise, the following general types of metrics usually apply:

- **Time**—Elapsed time for completion of prescribed tasks, delivery of equipment, assembly of personnel and arrival at a predetermined site. This is essential to refine the response time estimated for every task in the escalation process.
- **Amount**—Amount of work performed at the backup site by clerical personnel and the amount of information systems processing operations
- **Percentage or number**—The number of vital records successfully carried to the backup site versus the required number, and the number of supplies and equipment requested vs. actually received. The number of critical systems successfully recovered can be measured with the number of transactions processed.
- **Accuracy**—Accuracy of the data entry at the recovery site versus normal accuracy (as a percentage). The accuracy of actual processing cycles can be determined by comparing output results with those for the same period processed under normal conditions.
- **Plans**—The number of plans tested that cover each critical business process. This is required to ensure that business critical functions are properly accounted for, as criticality of business functions may change over time.

This testing process enables the information security manager to achieve initial successes and modify the plan based on information gained from the initial tests. Performing a preparedness or operational test costs resources and requires coordination among the participating departments.

Page intentionally left blank

Part B: Incident Management Operations

The information security manager needs to be fully aware of and understand the environment in which enterprises operate. The increased use, dependency and pervasive nature of technology when combined with omnipresent connectivity and global accessibility not only introduce, but greatly increase both the probability and impact of an information security incident occurring.

To counter the risk enterprises face, the need for well-defined incident management processes, properly trained personnel and the ability to monitor and alert on what really matters is more important. Enterprises need to ensure that their teams can quickly identify, contain, resolve and recover from incidents, as faster response times reduce the overall impact of incidents, mitigating the damages enterprises may suffer and return systems and services back to operations as needed to achieve defined business goals.

Operational incident management capabilities save the enterprise from larger unplanned losses as incidents that are identified sooner are responded to and resolved faster, ultimately reducing the impact to the enterprise.

4.8 Incident Management Tools and Technologies

The infrastructure needed to enable incident management capabilities is significant—from commercially available suites of tools to homegrown applications and everything in between. As such, the IMT will leverage an assortment of technologies.

4.8.1 Incident Management Systems

The sheer amount of information and activities in increasingly complex systems has driven the development of automated incident management systems in recent years. These systems automate many manual processes that provide filtered information that can identify possible technical incidents and alert the IMT.

Note: Some enterprises may have a designated IMT that determines how to manage incidents and is separate from the IRT. In other enterprises, the IMT and IRT may be the same group of people. For the purposes of this manual, IMT will be differentiated, when necessary, but in many cases, the IRT will perform these duties. An example of a distributed incident management system is one that contains multiple specific incident detection capabilities (e.g., network intrusion detection systems [NIDSs], host-based intrusion detection systems [HIDSs] and server/appliance logs).

An example of a centralized incident management system is a SIEM. This tool is an automated log reader that combines critical events and logs from many different systems and devices and correlates them into more meaningful incident information. This is accomplished by collecting data from many system and device logs that are normalized in a single database where the data are mined using correlation and inference tools to create near-real-time notifications and alerts. The log reader can also identify policy violations. Further processing can be done (e.g., prioritizing incidents based on their potential severity or business impacts or performing specific notifications/escalations based on the impact ratings).

Another significant feature of incident management systems is their ability to track an incident during its life cycle. Tracking is a powerful feature that ensures that incidents are not overlooked but instead receive necessary attention based on criticality. Tracking enables users to provide more information and receive status updates along the event life cycle until it is closed. The system is most often offered in a web-based format for easy accessibility.

An effective SIEM will:

- Consolidate and correlate inputs from multiple sources.
- Identify incidents or potential incidents.
- Notify staff.
- Prioritize incidents based on business impact.
- Track incidents until they are closed.
- Provide status tracking and notifications.
- Integrate with major IT management systems.
- Implement good practices (e.g., configuration, workflows, etc.).

There are potential efficiencies and cost savings that can be realized using automated incident management systems once they are properly configured. However, that is usually a complex and time-consuming activity that often takes several years. Some considerations for the information security manager include:

- **Operating costs**—In the absence of an automated and centralized incident management system, information security staff may be required to monitor different security devices, correlate events, and process information manually. With this approach, there are additional costs for training and maintaining the staff over the long term. There also is a higher probability of human error.
- **Recovery costs**—An automated system, when configured properly, is able to detect and escalate incidents significantly faster than when a manual process is used. The amount of damage can be controlled and further damage prevented when the recovery actions are initiated earlier rather than later. In the case of a manual management system, a longer analysis process may contribute to further damage before incidents are contained.

Another solution that has gained popularity is endpoint security, specifically endpoint detection and response (EDR), extended detection and response (XDR) and managed detection and response (MDR). A 2020 study conducted by Ernst & Young states, "Almost 70 percent of all breaches still originate at endpoints."[31] This is important, considering many enterprises have extended their workforce beyond a centralized office, which has driven information security teams to increase their visibility into their environments and develop capabilities to investigate and remediate events in a timely manner.

Endpoint Detection and Response

Historically, endpoint security tended to be reactive in nature, detecting perceived or potential security threats using signatures for known attack patterns. EDR attempts to be predictive in nature, focusing on identifying threats and malware that are designed to evade traditional security defenses. Most EDR solutions will leverage some type of cyberthreat intelligence with machine learning capabilities in conjunction with file analysis and threat detection.

EDR solutions normally create a historical audit trail in which system/user behavior and security events are captured for follow-on analysis by security analysts. EDR solutions not only aid in incident response efforts but also support root cause analysis.

Extended Detection and Response

An evolved version of EDR, XDR takes a holistic approach to endpoint detection and response. As the name implies, detection and response efforts extend beyond the individual endpoint. XDR not only provides enterprise information security teams a unified view across their endpoints but also performs analysis of servers, the cloud and networks.

XDR builds on the capabilities of EDR, leveraging automation, machine learning and artificial intelligence capabilities to provide context around security events.

Managed Detection and Response

MDR is a hybrid combination of a technology and service provider. The value is for those environments that lack both appropriate expertise and skills or have limited resources needed to adequately monitor potential attack vectors. Normally the service provider will be responsible for providing instrumentation.

4.8.2 Incident Response Technology Foundations

IRTs must be familiar with the following security concepts:

- **Security principles**—Knowledge of security principles is important to understand potential problems that can arise if appropriate security measures have not been implemented correctly or if they fail, and to appreciate the potential impacts to the enterprise systems. These security principles include:
  - Access control
  - Authentication
  - Availability
  - Compliance
  - Confidentiality

[31] EY, "Why a culture change program is key to effective cybersecurity," 3 November 2020, www.ey.com/en_se/giss/why-a-culture-change-program-is-key-to-effective-cybersecurity

- Integrity
- Nonrepudiation
- Privacy

- **Security vulnerabilities/weaknesses**—This entails understanding how any specific attack is manifested against people, processes, software or hardware technology. The most common types of vulnerabilities and associated attacks involve:
  - Cloud security attacks (e.g., misconfigurations, lack of data encryption, etc.)
  - Configuration weaknesses
  - Implementation flaws (e.g., buffer overflow, timing windows/race conditions)
  - Malicious code (e.g., viruses, worms, Trojan horses)
  - Operational errors
  - Phishing resulting from lack of user awareness
  - Physical security issues
  - Protocol design flaws (e.g., man-in-the-middle attacks, spoofing)
  - Software/coding flaws
  - User errors or lack of awareness
- **The Internet**—There must be security in the underlying protocols and services used on the Internet. A good understanding is important to anticipate the threats that might occur in the future. The following technologies that enable the Internet should be addressed in the incident response program:
  - **Network protocols**—Common (or core) network protocols such as Internet Protocol (IPv4 vs IPv6), Transmission Control Protocol (TCP), User Datagram Protocol (UDP), Internet Control Message Protocol (ICMP), Address Resolution Protocol (ARP), Neighbor Discovery Protocol (NDP), and Reverse Address Resolution Protocol (RARP); how they are used; common types of threats or attacks against the protocols; strategies to mitigate or eliminate such attacks; and Internet technologies.
  - **Network applications and services**—For example, domain name system (DNS), network file system (NFS) and secure shell (SSH); how they work; common usage; secure configurations; and common types of threats or attacks against the application or service and mitigation strategies
  - **Network security issues**—To recognize vulnerable points in network configurations. Basic perimeter security, network firewalls (design, packet filtering, proxy systems, demilitarized zone [DMZ], bastion hosts, etc.) and router security are relevant to recognize the potential for information disclosure of data traveling across the network (e.g., packet monitoring or sniffers) or threats relating to accepting untrustworthy information.
- **Operating systems**—Knowledge of operating systems such as UNIX, Windows, Mac, iOS, Linux, Android and any other operating systems used by the team or constituency is important, specifically how to:
  - Configure (harden) the system
  - Review configuration files for security weaknesses
  - Identify common attack methods
  - Determine whether a compromise attempt occurred
  - Determine whether an attempted system compromise was successful
  - Review log files for anomalies
  - Analyze the results of attacks
  - Manage system privileges
  - Recover from a compromise
- **Malicious code (viruses, worms, Trojan horse programs, customized/targeted malware)**—These can have different types of payloads that can result in different outcomes. Some malicious code will consume system resources to the point of resulting in a DoS attack against the system. The code can contain more dynamic payloads that can be configured to result in multifaceted attack vectors. It is important to understand how malicious code is propagated through some of the obvious methods (e.g., CDs, universal serial bus [USB] drives, email, programs, websites) and how it can propagate through other means such as macros, multipurpose Internet mail extension (MIME), peer-to-peer file sharing or viruses that affect operating systems.
- **Programming skills**—This includes the range of programming languages used by the enterprise's system and applications, concepts and techniques for secure programming, and how vulnerabilities can be introduced into code (e.g., through poor programming and design practices, lack of input

validation, susceptibility to structured query language [SQL] injection, cross-site scripting, broken authentication and unvalidated redirects).

Note: Technologies continuously change and evolve. This list is not meant to be all-encompassing; rather, it provides the basis of technical knowledge for incident response. The information security manager should be aware of changes and innovations in the field.

4.8.3 Personnel

An IMT usually consists of an information security manager, steering committee or advisory board, and supporting team members. Team members may be identified ad hoc, dedicated full-time IMT support or engaged temporarily during incidents. The composition of team members assigned and how they will support the IMT will vary from enterprise to enterprise.

The information security manager usually leads the team. In larger enterprises, it may be more effective to appoint a separate IRT leader/manager who focuses on responding to incidents. Above the information security manager, a set of senior management executives are part of a security steering group (SSG), security advisory board or an executive committee. Whatever it is called, the SSG function is responsible for approving the charter and serves as an escalation point for the IMT. The SSG also approves deviations and exceptions to normal practice.

Dedicated team members perform the primary tasks in the IMT/IRT. As information systems are broad and complex, it is inefficient and expensive to have all individuals covering all disciplines in performing tasks in the IMT/IRT. Virtual/temporary team members may have specialized skills and are recruited when necessary to fill gaps within the internal skills portfolio.

Incident Response Team Organization

Incident handlers analyze incident data, determine the impact of the incident and recommend the appropriate actions to limit the damage to the enterprise and restore normal services. Often, the team will collaborate with complementary groups, business managers and general users. IRT models that have proven to work in many enterprises include:

- **Central IRT**—A single IRT handles all incidents for the enterprise, typically used in a small enterprise or one that is centrally located.
- **Distributed IRT**—Each of several teams is responsible for a logical or physical segment of the infrastructure, usually of a large enterprise or one that is geographically dispersed.
- **Coordinating IRT**—The central team may provide guidance to distributed IRTs, develop policies and standards, provide training, conduct exercises and coordinate or support responses to specific incidents. Distributed teams manage and implement incident response.
- **Outsourced IRT**—Successful IRTs may consist entirely of employees of the enterprise or may be fully or partially outsourced.

Permanent team members may include incident handlers, investigators and forensics experts, and IT and physical security specialists. Temporary team members normally consist of business representatives (e.g., middle management), legal staff, communications staff (e.g., PR), HR staff, other security groups (e.g., physical security), risk management and IT specialists.

The composition of incident response staff varies from team to team and depends on a number of factors such as:

- Type (i.e., centralized/decentralized) and size of the enterprise
- Mission and goals of the incident response program
- Nature and range of services offered
- Available staff expertise
- Constituency size and technology base
- Anticipated incident load
- Severity or complexity of incident reports
- Funding

Roles and Responsibilities

Figure 4.10 provides common roles and responsibilities of IRT personnel. Note that each position should have an alternative in case the designee is incapacitated or unavailable.

Figure 4.10—Roles and Responsibilities

Position	Roles	Responsibilities
Security steering group (SSG)	Highest structure of an enterprise's functions related to information security	1. Takes responsibility for overall incident management and response concept 2. Approves incident management team (IMT) charter 3. Approves exceptions/deviations 4. Makes final decisions
Information security manager	IMT leader and main interface to SSG	1. Develops and maintains incident management and response capability 2. Effectively manages risk and incidents 3. Performs proactive and reactive measures to control information risk level 4. Reports on program to senior leadership
Incident response manager	Incident response team (IRT) leader	1. Supervises incident response tasks 2. Coordinates resources to effectively perform incident response tasks 3. Takes responsibility for successful execution of the incident response plan (IRP) 4. Presents incident response report and lessons learned to SSG members
Incident handler	IMT/IRT team member	1. Performs incident response tasks to contain exposures from an incident 2. Documents steps taken when executing the IRP 3. Maintains chain of custody and observes incident handling procedures for court purposes 4. Writes incident response report and lessons learned
Investigator	IMT/IRT team member	1. Performs investigative tasks for a specific incident 2. Finds root cause of an incident 3. Writes report of investigation findings
IT security specialist	IMT/IRT team member; subject matter expert in IT security	1. Performs complex and in-depth IT security-related tasks as part of the IRP 2. Performs IT security assessment/audit as proactive measure and part of vulnerability management (i.e., performing routine vulnerability scans and associated remediation)
Business managers	Business function owners; information assets/system owners	1. Make decisions on matters related to information assets/systems when an incident happens, based on IMT/IRT recommendations 2. Provide clear understanding of business impact in BIA process or in IRP
IT specialists/representatives	Subject matter experts in IT services	1. Provide support to IMT/IRT when resolving an incident 2. Maintain information systems in a good condition per company policy and good practices
Legal representative	Subject matter expert in legal	1. Ensures that incident response actions and procedures comply with legal and regulatory requirements. 2. Acts as the liaison to law enforcement and outside agencies.

Figure 4.10—Roles and Responsibilities *(cont.)*

Position	Roles	Responsibilities
Human resources (HR)	Subject matter expert in HR area	**1.** Provides assistance in incident management/response when there is a need to investigate an employee suspected of causing an incident **2.** Integrates HR policy to support incident management/response (sanctions to employees found to violate acceptable use of policy or involved in an incident)
Public relations (PR) representative	Subject matter expert in PR area	**1.** Provides controlled communication to internal and external stakeholders to minimize any adverse impact to ongoing incident response activities and protects an enterprise's brand and reputation **2.** Provides assistance to IMT/IRT in communication issues, thus relieving the team to work on critical issues to resolve an incident
Risk management specialist	Subject matter expert in risk management	**1.** Works closely with business managers and senior management to determine and manage risk **2.** Provides input (e.g., business impact analysis, risk management strategy) to incident management
Physical security/facilities manager	Knowledgeable about physical plant and emergency capabilities	**1.** Responsible for physical plant and facilities **2.** Ensures physical security during incidents

4.8.4 Skills

To build an IRT with capable incident handlers, enterprises need people with both soft and technical skill sets—abilities that enable them to respond to incidents, perform analysis tasks, and communicate effectively with the constituency and external contacts. They must also be competent problem solvers, easily adapt to change, and effective in their daily activities.

The set of basic skills that IRT members need can be separated into two broad groups: personal and technical skills.

Personal skills are the major parts of the incident handler's daily activity. They include:

- **Communication**—The ability to communicate effectively is a critical component of the skills needed by IRTs. They need to be effective communicators to ensure that they obtain and supply the information necessary to be helpful. They need to be good listeners, understanding what is said (or not said), to enable them to gain details about an incident that is being reported. They also remain in control of these communications to most effectively determine what is happening, what facts are important and what assistance is necessary.
  - Members of an IRT need to communicate with:
    - Team members
    - IT staff
    - Application owners
    - Users of the systems
    - Technical experts
    - Management and other administrative staff
    - HR
    - Law enforcement
    - Media/PR staff
    - Vendors
  - Communication can take many forms, including:
    - Email responses concerning incidents
    - Documentation of event or incident reports, vulnerabilities and other technical information
    - Notifications and guidelines that are provided to the constituency
    - Internal development policies and procedures
    - Other external communications to staff, management or other relevant parties

- **Leadership skills**—Members of an IRT are often faced with directing and getting support of other members of the enterprise, so leadership is an important attribute.
- **Presentation skills**—An IRT's skills are needed for technical presentations, management or sponsor briefings, a panel discussion at a conference, or some other form of public speaking engagement. The specialist member's skills might extend to providing expert testimony in legal or other proceedings on behalf of the team or users.
- **Ability to follow policies and procedures**—Team members need the ability to follow and support the established policies and procedures for incident response management.
- **Team skills**—IRT members must have the ability to work in a team environment as productive and cordial team players; to be aware of responsibilities; to contribute to the goals of the team; and to work together to share information, workload and experiences. Members must be flexible and willing to adapt to change. There may be a need for one or more team members to act in a leadership role to support the smaller groups or technical teams.
- **Integrity**—Team members often deal with information that is sensitive and, occasionally, they may have access to information that is newsworthy. Members must be trustworthy, discreet and able to handle information in confidence.
- **Self-understanding**—Team members must be able to recognize their limitations and actively seek support from their team members, other experts or management.
- **Coping with stress**—The IRT is likely to face stressful situations. The members need to be able to recognize when they are becoming stressed, be willing to make their fellow team members aware of the situation and take the necessary steps to control and maintain their composure.
- **Problem solving**—Without good problem-solving skills, team members could become overwhelmed with the volumes of data related to incidents and other tasks that need to be handled. Problem-solving skills also include an ability to think outside the box or look at issues from multiple perspectives to identify relevant information or data. This includes knowing who else to contact or approach for additional information, creative ideas or added technical insight.
- **Time management**—Team members might be confronted with a multitude of tasks, ranging from analyzing, coordinating and responding to incidents, to performing duties such as prioritizing their workload, attending and preparing for meetings, completing time sheets, collecting statistics, conducting research, giving briefings and presentations, traveling to conferences, providing onsite technical support, and prioritizing tasks. Team members must be able to balance efforts between completing the tasks and recognizing when to seek help or guidance.

Technical skills are the basic skills required by IRT members and are of two types:

- **Technical foundation skills**—These require a basic understanding of the underlying technologies used by the enterprise.
- **Incident-handling skills**—These require an understanding of the techniques, decision points and supporting tools (software or applications) required in daily activities.

4.8.5 Awareness and Education

While high-profile breaches and security incidents have increased the security awareness of most individuals, end users are the first line of defense in preventing security breaches. Therefore, it is essential for the information security manager to ensure that an ongoing awareness campaign highlights the importance of being mindful in order to reduce susceptibility to activities that may lead to a security breach (e.g., phishing attacks, malicious websites).

Periodically, a skills assessment is useful to determine whether the required expertise is available in the enterprise for the IRT. In some cases, relevant training or education may serve to provide the necessary skills. If an enterprise is unable to find internal experts or to hire/train staff to provide the necessary incident response specialist skills, it may be able to develop relationships with experts in the field to provide the necessary skills. When a situation arises in which in-house knowledge is insufficient, these technical specialists can be called on to fill the gap in expertise.

4.8.6 Audits

Internal and external audits are performed to verify compliance with policies, standards and procedures defined by an enterprise. Internal audits are conducted by specialists within the enterprise and are usually intended to support compliance requirements or improve risk and incident management. External audits involve a third party, who performs the tasks. While most external audits are exercised as part of mandatory requirements, they are often imposed as part of business collaboration.

Both types of audits can be useful in reviewing incident management and response plans and capabilities. Periodic audits of the processes and procedures specified in the plans can provide validation that security will not be compromised in the event of an incident, and policy compliance and legal requirements are addressed appropriately. Audits can provide an objective view of the overall completeness and functionality of the incident management and response plans and provide assurance that major gaps in the processes do not exist.

4.8.7 Outsourced Security Providers

Outsourcing incident management capability may be a cost-effective option, especially for smaller enterprises (see Section 3.13.2 Third-Party Service Providers). These enterprises simply may not have the internal resources to adequately provide the necessary IMT/IRT skills.

Enterprises that outsource their IT operations may benefit from close integration if incident management is outsourced to the same vendor. These enterprises still require an IRP overseen by an IRT, even if components of incident management are outsourced. It will be essential to clearly understand the outsourcer's capabilities, response times, etc., and develop proper SLAs containing appropriate indemnity clauses.

The information security manager should consider the following when security functions are fully or partially outsourced:

- **Matching the enterprise's incident reference numbers with the vendors for each applicable incident:** This ensures a common understanding of incident details between enterprises. This also helps to identify the actual organizational recovery time. For example, the vendor may report that service was restored at 4:00 p.m.; however, the outsourcing enterprise may note that the incident ended at 6:00 p.m. This means that it took the enterprise an additional two hours to recover internally from the incident. This can be determined by matching the enterprise's incident reference numbers with the vendor's.
- **Integration of the enterprise's change management functions with the vendor's (to the extent possible):** Depending on the nature of the service provided, the enterprise's change management functions may be linked via leaders on the change advisory board or have a platform where the security group can view the vendor's changes and follow-up with key points of contact from the vendor. Also, this contributes to awareness of system changes by both enterprises.
- **Requirement from the vendor for periodic review of incidents that occurs on a regular basis (e.g., monthly, annually)**: Operational leadership from both the enterprise and the vendor attend these meetings, and all incidents/events are reviewed. Follow-up items are generally taken from these meetings to help prevent incidents from recurring.

4.9 Incident Investigation and Evaluation

Not every event is an incident, and the information security manager must be aware of the subtle difference between the two. An event is something that happens at a specific place or time: an account logon, a door opening, an automated process ending. These are all events, lacking any context, that occur with little to no concern. Contextual data adjacent or related to the event need to be investigated to determine if the event was in fact normal or abnormal.

For example, a user account logging in during business hours is an event that, according to an established baseline (see Section 2.2.1 Security Control Baselines), occurs normally throughout the business day. Any deviation to that, such as a user account attempting to log in after business hours, is an event that may warrant further investigation as it is outside of established norms. Additional contextual information may yield this as being either a legitimate event (i.e., the user is currently traveling abroad, with the login coinciding with the user's local business day) or it could be a malicious event (i.e., credentials were acquired by an unauthorized third-party and are being used to access enterprise resources). Until the event is investigated properly, a determination as to the event's legitimacy is unknown.

Once an event's legitimacy is known, the appropriate action can be taken. The initiation and escalation of an event to an incident is conducted through the initial investigation and then evaluating the impact to the enterprise. As previously mentioned, not all incidents are equal. Consider the following scenario:

> In a perfect world, all endpoints, systems, applications and infrastructure logs are collected and forwarded to a fully staffed security operations center (SOC) that is monitoring the enterprise for threats. With full visibility of the perimeter, endpoints and infrastructure, the SOC is able to identify, triage and respond to threats because the enterprise has established a security baseline in addition to properly tuning all of its enterprise instrumentation. The SOC's manager, Jordan, has five SOC analysts currently on shift: Peyton, Zhang, Kelly, Ushma and Mohamed. Jordan tasks each analyst with investigating five separate events.
>
> Peyton is assigned to review alerts originating from an IDS used in the development environment. The alerts coincide with recent changes made to an internally developed application's port and protocols.
>
> Zhang is assigned to review alerts from a key business application. Its performance has dropped 12 percent over the past 24-hours but is still within the defined performance thresholds.
>
> Kelly is assigned to review alerts originating from directory services reporting a virtual private network account with an excessively high number of failed logon attempts from an external source—a classic brute force attack. The enterprise is in the process of implementing multifactor authentication throughout the enterprise for each account.
>
> Ushma is assigned to review a series of alerts from the perimeter firewalls indicating that a successful login using a privileged account from inside the enterprise has occurred.
>
> Mohamed is assigned to review an alert about installation of unauthorized software onto an end-user account's workstation.

Which of the five events should be evaluated and declared an incident and why? An end-user installing an unauthorized software application should be evaluated against the enterprise's security control baseline, defined policies and architecture. As the event is not part of enterprise standard operations and may cause an interruption or reduce quality of service in addition to exposing the enterprise to unacceptable risks, it should be declared an incident.

Once sufficient, proper context around an event has been investigated and evaluated, then appropriate action can be taken. This may result in implementation and execution of the enterprise response and recovery plans in varying degrees depending upon the severity and impact of the incident to the enterprise.

4.9.1 Executing Response and Recovery Plans

Given that a major incident usually causes considerable confusion and a host of unexpected conditions, it is essential that the incident management and response plans have been tested under realistic conditions. It is possible that untested plans will not work as expected. It is also safe to expect that the more severe the incident, the greater the potential chaos, confusion and problems facing the incident management and response teams. Incidents can range from an attack bringing down IT systems to an earthquake bringing down the building. To provide reasonable assurance that the enterprise is preserved under foreseeable circumstances, all reasonably possible events must be anticipated and prepared for and the planning must be thorough, realistic and tested.

Ensuring Execution as Required

To ensure the response and recovery plans are executed as required, the plans need a facilitator to direct the tasks within the plans, oversee their execution, liaise with senior management and make decisions as necessary. The information security manager may or may not be the appropriate person to act as the recovery plan coordinator but must be certain the role is assigned to someone who can perform this critical function.

Developing appropriate response and recovery strategies and alternatives is an essential component in the overall process of executing the response and recovery plans. It will provide reasonable assurance that the enterprise can recover its key business functions in the event of a disruption and respond appropriately to a security-related incident.

Testing the plans is essential to ensuring that plans can be executed as required. It will also help employees become familiar with the process so when an incident occurs they can respond accordingly.

The information security manager should appoint an independent observer to record progress and document any exceptions that occur during testing and during an actual event. Through a post-event review, the information security manager and key recovery personnel can then review the observations and make adjustments to the plan accordingly.

4.10 Incident Containment Methods

As each incident is unique, methods to contain the incident must be tailored. Understanding the benefits and drawbacks associated with initiating containment is vital. Senior management must be fully aware and understand the implications, as they can have a significant impact on immediate response efforts and may result in unplanned outcomes.

Containment includes all the activities, tasks and steps taken in the attempt of limiting or reducing the impact of an incident. Containment is a short-term, tactical action that is meant to purely to stop the bleeding, not necessarily to identify or correct the root cause that allowed the incident to occur.

Common containment activities performed during a security incident may include, but are not limited to, the following:

- Notification and escalation to relevant stakeholders
- Memory captures and analysis
- Enterprise-wide password changes of all accounts
- Updating firewall rule sets to block/deny/drop traffic
- Updating IDS signatures
- Log collection, review and analysis
- Forensically image impacted systems
- Malware reverse engineering
- Removing the device from the network

For example, if the incident involves a malware-infected system actively being controlled by an adversary, the enterprise may choose to disconnect the system from the network, update firewall rules to block identified IP addresses and domains associated with the adversary or scan for indicators of compromise to identify other compromised systems. The purpose is to identify all potentially impacted systems in order to remove the adversary from the environment.

Weighing the benefits and risk as to when to initiate containment efforts is not a decision that should be made without senior management's full understanding and approval. Ultimately senior management—with recommendations from the legal counsel, the information security manager and the IMT—will need to make a decision at what point and how prepared the enterprise is to contain the incident. This is because once containment efforts are initiated, the adversary will be aware their presence is noticed, and they may retaliate.

4.11 Incident Response Communications

As an incident has the potential for impacting various aspects of an enterprise, clear lines of authorized and authoritative communication channels need to be defined in advance. This is to ensure that chances of misunderstanding and limiting misinformation are reduced as much as possible. Because things can change as an incident unfolds, keep in mind that what was truthful when initially reported may become factually inaccurate upon further investigation and will need to be addressed appropriately.

Given the number of personnel associated with responding to an incident, establishing an authoritative source for communicating is mandatory. Often speculation may be taken for fact or facts downplayed due to misunderstanding or lacking appropriate insight and context. There will be different communication channels and methods that need to be defined prior to an incident being declared. These need to be documented and conveyed to each member to ensure that during an incident everyone knows who and where the authoritative information relating to the incidents is coming from.

There are a number of communication channels that should be established during an incident, as communications will need to occur between the IMT manager and senior management over decisions on whether to communicate with enterprise staff, external third parties and affected business partners. Each communication channel needs to be clearly defined, understood and conveyed to all affected members to ensure the proper messages are communicated to their respective audiences.

From a technical perspective, the IMT members will need a method to facilitate communications out-of-band or to communicate by other than normal communication methods. For example, in responding to a suspected network intrusion, users should not communicate over suspected compromised infrastructure that may alert intruders that they have been identified. This results in the IMT members switching to an approved browser-based email platform (e.g., Google Business) instead of the normal enterprise business email (e.g., Microsoft 365).

4.11.1 Notification Requirements

Notification requirements are key parts of the IRP and incident management. The IRP should include a directory of key decision-making personnel, IRT members, information systems owners, end users and others required to initiate and carry out response efforts. This directory should include multiple communication methods (telephone, cellular phone, texting, email, etc.) in the event of any communications channel failure.

The directory should include, at a minimum, the following individuals:

- Representatives of equipment and software vendors
- Contacts within companies that have been designated to provide supplies and equipment or services
- Contacts at recovery facilities, including hot site representatives or predefined network communications rerouting services
- Contacts at offsite media storage facilities and the contacts within the company who are authorized to retrieve media from the offsite facility
- Insurance company agents
- Contact information for regulatory bodies
- Contacts at HR and contract personnel services
- Law enforcement contacts

Note that the decision to bring in law enforcement during such an incident rests solely with senior management. It is generally not the role of an information security manager to inform external organizations. There are companies that handle automated emergency response communications. However, as with any other outsourced service, careful consideration should be given to the required processes that must be in place to ensure the effectiveness of this solution.

4.11.2 Communication Networks

The plan must contain details of the enterprise's telecommunication networks needed to restore business operations. Because of the criticality of these networks, the procedures to ensure continuous telecommunication capabilities should be given a high priority. Telecommunication networks are susceptible to the same natural disasters as data centers but are also vulnerable to disruptive events unique to telecommunications. These include central switching office disasters, cable cuts, communication software glitches and errors, security breaches from hacking (phone hackers are known as phreakers), and a host of other human errors. The local exchange carrier is typically not responsible for providing backup services. Although many carriers normally back up main components within their systems, the enterprise should make provisions for backing up its own telecommunication facilities.

Telecommunications capabilities to consider include telephone voice circuits, wide area networks (WANs) (connections to distributed data centers), LANs and third-party providers. Options can include satellite and microwave links and, depending on criticality and location, wireless links or even single sideband radiotelephone communications. Critical capacity requirements should be identified for the various thresholds of outage, such as two hours, eight hours or 24 hours, for each telecommunications capability. Uninterruptable power supplies (UPSs) should be sufficient to provide backup for both telecommunications equipment and computer equipment.

4.12 Incident Eradication and Recovery

While containment is a short-term approach to limit an incident and keep it from spreading, eradication includes the activities, tasks and steps taken to correct the root cause that led to the incident occurring. This should be properly planned out and executed once containment efforts have been deemed successful.

4.12.1 Eradication Activities

Common eradication activities performed during a security incident include, but are not limited to, the following:

- Root cause analysis
- Cleanup and removal of any artifacts left behind from the incident
- Application of any outstanding patches
- DNS null routing (sinkhole) of malicious IP addresses and fully qualified domain names
- Additional changes to firewalls and IDSs as needed
- Scanning for additional indicators of compromise (IoCs)
- Removing malicious software
- Wipe/rebuilding impacted systems
- Restoring from backups

4.12.2 Recovery

Recovery efforts follow only after the successful containment and eradication phases of the incident response process life cycle. After the incident has been fully addressed and root cause issues remediated, the focus shifts to ensuring that the business can successfully return to operations, which means restoring impacted systems to normal. During this phase, the information security manager should remain vigilant, as rushing an impacted system back into production may reintroduce the same vulnerabilities and causes that initiated the original incident.

During the recovery phase, the activities should be planned and implemented to prevent similar events from occurring. Common recovery activities performed after a security incident has been successfully eradicated include, but are not limited to, the following:

- Testing and validating the security baseline.
- Monitoring network for known indicators of attack (IoAs) and IoCs.
- Actively searching for identified adversary artifacts across the enterprise.
- Moving impacted systems back into production once recovered and verified to meet the security baseline.

Note: Avoid the rush to recovery. Once a system has been compromised by an adversary, the fidelity in that system is zero. It may appear easier to attempt to remove identified adversary artifacts (e.g., backdoors, tool kits, etc.) from the system in an effort to quickly restore services to the business. However, once a system has been compromised, there is no assurance of what may have gone undetected or missed.

Once recovery efforts are started, most enterprises are satisfied with simply returning to business as usual (BAU) operations. Keep in mind, these are the same BAU operations that allowed the incident to occur initially. The need to properly address and remediate the root cause of the incident is important to ensure that business risk is managed properly. While the immediate incident has been resolved, the work is just beginning.

4.13 Post-Incident Review Practices

Understanding the purpose and structure of post-incident reviews and follow-up procedures enables the information security manager to continuously improve the security program. A consistent methodology should be adopted within the information security enterprise so that when a problem is found, an action plan is developed to reduce/mitigate it. Once the action plan is created, steps should be taken to implement the solution. By following these basic principles, the information security program is able to adapt to changes in the enterprise and the threats it faces. In addition, this reduces the amount of time personnel need to react to security incidents, so they are able to spend more time on proactive activities.

The follow-up process in incident response is potentially the most valuable part of the effort. Lessons learned during incident handling can improve both the security practice and the incident response process itself. Additionally, the information security manager needs to calculate the cost of the incident once all response efforts are completed by adding the cost of any loss or damage plus the cost of labor and any special software or hardware needed to handle the incident. The cost provides a useful metric, especially in justifying the existence of the response team to senior management, and may be used as evidence in a court case.

When concluding and closing out an incident, common post-incident activities need to be planned and carried out. Once the business has successfully recovered, activities may include, but are not limited to, the following:

- Documenting the incident
- Stakeholder review and feedback
- Finalizing the report for senior management
- Identifying changes required
- Identifying any process issues
- Updating procedures as needed
- Developing remediation plans to mitigate incident root cause
- Seeking resource and funding approval

The information security manager should manage post-incident reviews to learn from each incident and the resulting response and recovery effort; this information can then be used to improve the enterprise's response and recovery procedures. The information security manager may perform these reviews with the help of third-party specialists if detailed forensic skills are needed.

4.13.1 Identifying Causes and Corrective Actions

Security incidents can be the result of externally initiated attacks, internally initiated attacks or failures in security controls that have been implemented. For a systematic review of security incidents, the information security manager should appoint an incident review team. This team should review any evidence and develop recommendations to enhance the information security program by identifying root causes of a specific incident and necessary measures to prevent the same/similar events from recurring. The root causes of many system compromises, for example, are weak or nonexistent vulnerability assessment and patch management efforts.

The analysis should be done to determine answers to questions such as:

- Who is involved?
- What has happened?
- Where did the attack originate?
- When (what time frame)?
- Why did it happen?
- How was the system vulnerable or how did the attack occur?
- What was the reason for the attack (i.e., the perpetrator's motivation)?

4.13.2 Documenting Events

During and subsequent to any actual or potential security incident, the information security manager should have processes in place to develop a clear record of events. Preserving this information will enable investigation of events and it can be provided to a forensics team or authorities if necessary. To ensure this record-keeping occurs, one or more individuals should be specifically charged with incident documentation and the preservation of evidence. Documentation of any event that has possible security implications can provide clarity as to whether an incident is an accident, a mistake or a deliberate attack.

A serious incident is typically chaotic. Good documentation will prove invaluable in post-incident investigation and forensics and may also be helpful in incident resolution.

4.13.3 Establishing Legal Procedures to Assist in Post-incident Activities

Having solid, legally defensible procedures in place prior to an incident being declared is key to successful recovery and response.[32] As cybercrime has surged in recent years, regulators, legislatures and plaintiffs' attorneys have placed cyber preparedness and incident response under a microscope. This has led to potentially significant risk and exposure arising from compliance with a myriad of new laws and regulatory reforms. Given this landscape, it is imperative that enterprises involve legal counsel in the preparation for and participation in incident response.

Preparing a comprehensive IRP is an important first step to ensure an efficient and effective response to a security incident and the inevitable swell of legal and regulatory landmines. A good IRP is one that is customized to the enterprise and has been developed, vetted and tested by legal counsel and key internal stakeholders. While it may

[32] In development of this section specifically, the U.S.-based firm Vorys, Sater, Seymour and Pease LLP—recognized experts specializing in IT, privacy and data security—was consulted to identify some key concerns and considerations from the legal aspect, with consideration relating to incident response.

be easy to pull a standard IRP form from the internet, this check-the-box approach is not helpful when an incident actually occurs. An IRP should:

- Identify a core team of responders who will manage the response.
- Provide a procedure for documentation of the events leading up to and following the discovery of a compromise (including third parties who have access to organizational information).
- Establish a clear and immediate communication plan that includes communications to internal contacts, third parties (including law enforcement and regulators), advisors (including legal counsel and insurance carriers), customers and the media.
- Set forth key decision points that need to be made.
- Include forms for notifications that can be quickly modified to send to regulators and customers in sufficient time to comply with notification deadlines.

In a highly regulated environment, an IRP should position the enterprise for the legal and technical hurdles it may encounter when responding to an incident. When a security incident occurs, legal counsel should be consulted immediately, as this will help ensure that an investigation is covered by the attorney-client privilege. Legal counsel is also vital in analyzing and fulfilling any notification requirements within the legally mandated number of hours following discovery. Every state has different notice requirements applicable to both individuals and state agencies, and there may be additional notification requirements to third parties, such as insurance carriers or business partners. Complying with these various notification requirements is a complicated process fraught with significant risk of mistakes and legal and regulatory exposure.

Once an enterprise has developed its IRP, it should be tested with a team including legal counsel. For many enterprises, annual testing of the IRP is required. Tabletop trainings evaluate the enterprise's ability to effectively execute the IRP by simulating a real-world data security incident. Benefits of tabletop tests include reviewing the plan in a real-world scenario, preparing members of executive management for their responsibilities in an incident and identifying and closing any gaps and bottlenecks that are discovered. Tabletop exercises are a modest commitment in terms of time, investment and resources and are critical for key stakeholders, while also encouraging team building among the participants.

The business case for proactive incident response preparedness is a compelling one. According to IBM Security's 2021 report, the average data breach in the United States costs an enterprise $4.24 million, a 10 percent increase from 2020. Remote working increased the average total cost of a data breach. However, enterprises that prepared and tested their IRPs prior to an incident averaged a response cost difference of 54.9 percent less than those with no plan or testing.[33]

Having a good legal framework is important to provide options to the enterprise, including pursuing civil or criminal legal action against the perpetrators. The information security manager should develop data preservation procedures with the advice and assistance of legal counsel, the enterprise's managers and knowledgeable law enforcement officials to ensure that the procedures provide sufficient guidance to IT and security staff. With the assistance of these specialized resources, the information security manager can develop procedures to handle security events in a manner that preserves evidence, ensures legally sufficient chain of custody, and is appropriate to meet business objectives.

There are a few basic actions that the information systems staff must understand, including doing nothing that could change, modify or contaminate potential or actual evidence. Trained forensics personnel can inspect computer systems that have been attacked, but if the enterprise's personnel contaminate the information, the data may not be admissible in a court of law and the forensics staff may be unable to use the data in investigating an incident. Computer forensics and gathering and handling information and physical objects relevant to a security incident in a systematic manner so they can be used as evidence in a court of law should be performed by specially trained staff, third-party specialists, security IRT or law enforcement officials. The initial response by the system administrator should include:

- Determining privileged versus non-privileged investigation by legal counsel.
- Retrieving information needed to confirm an incident.

[33] IBM Security, "Cost of a Data Breach Report 2021," www.ibm.com/security/data-breach?mhsrc=ibmsearch_a&mhq=cost%20of%20a%20data%20breach%20report%202021

- Identifying the scope and size of the affected environment (e.g., networks, systems, applications).
- Determining the degree of loss, modification or damage (if any).
- Identifying the possible path or means of attack.

4.13.4 Requirements for Evidence

The information security manager should understand that any contamination of evidence following an incident could prevent an enterprise prosecuting a perpetrator and limit its options. In addition, the modification of data can inhibit computer forensic activity necessary to identify the perpetrator and all the changes and effects resulting from an attack. It may also preclude the possibility of determining how the attack occurred and how the security program should be changed and enhanced to reduce the risk of a similar attack in the future.

The usual recommendation for a computer that has been compromised is to disconnect the power to maximize the preservation of evidence on the hard disk. This approach is generally the recommendation of law enforcement based on the risk of the evidence being compromised. This can occur as a result of the system swap files overwriting evidence or an intruder or malware erasing evidence of compromise. There is also the risk of contaminating evidence.

This approach is not universally accepted as the best solution. One argument against disconnecting power is that data in memory are lost and sudden power loss may result in corruption of critical information on the hard disk. Because some malware is only memory-resident, the cause of an incident and the avenue of attack may be difficult to establish.

Because the best approach is subject to controversy, the information security manager will need to establish the most appropriate approach for the enterprise and train personnel in the appropriate procedures.

Whichever procedure is used to secure a compromised system, trained personnel must use forensic tools to create a bit-by-bit copy (or physical disk image) of any evidence that may exist on hard drives and other media to ensure legal admissibility. To avoid the potential for alteration or destruction of incident-related data, any testing or data analysis should be conducted using this copy. The original should be given to a designated evidence custodian who must store it in a safe location. The original media must remain unchanged and a record of who has had custody of it—the chain of custody—must be maintained for the evidence to be admissible in court.

When taking a copy of a hard drive, the technician should take a bit-level image of all the data on the drive, using a cable with a write-protect diode to prevent writing anything back onto the source drive. Hash values of both the source and destination drive should be calculated to ensure that the copied drive is an exact image of the original.

4.13.5 Legal Aspects of Forensic Evidence

For evidence to be admissible in legal proceedings, it must have been acquired in a forensically sound manner and its chain of custody maintained. The information security manager in charge of an incident must have established and documented procedures for acquisition of evidence by properly trained independent personnel.

The required documentation to maintain legally admissible evidence must include:

- Chain of custody forms that provide:
  - Name and contact information of custodians
  - When, why and by whom an evidence item was acquired or moved
  - Detailed identification of the evidence (serial numbers, model information, etc.)
  - Where it is stored (physically or logically)
  - When/if it was returned
- Checklists for acquiring technicians (including details of legally acceptable forensic practices)
- Detailed activity log templates for acquiring technicians
- Signed nondisclosure/confidentiality forms for all technicians involved in recovering evidence
- An up-to-date case log that outlines:
  - Dates when requests were received
  - Dates investigations were assigned to investigators
  - Name and contact information of investigators and requestors
  - Identifying case number
  - Basic notes about the case and its requirements and completed procedures
  - Date when completed

- Investigation report templates that include:
  - Name and contact information of investigators
  - Date of investigation and an identifying case number
  - Details of any interviews or communications with management or staff regarding the investigation
  - Details of devices or data that were acquired (serial numbers, models, physical or logical locations)
  - Details of software or hardware tools used for acquisition or analysis (must be recognized forensically sound tools)
  - Details of findings including samples or copies of relevant data and references to their storage location
  - Final signatures of investigator in charge

Procedures for initiating a forensics investigation need to be agreed to, documented, followed carefully and understood by everyone in the enterprise. The information security manager should work with management and HR (and other stakeholders) to establish a process that ensures that all investigations are fair, unbiased and well documented.

It is important to be aware that legal requirements vary in different jurisdictions. As a result, informed legal advice for appropriate processes that meet judicial standards will be required.

Case Study 1

A vendor-supplied, business-critical service provisioning system for internal organizational functions (i.e., not customer-facing) has peak usage between the hours of 7:00 a.m. and 7:00 p.m. on weekdays.

On Monday at 6:00 a.m., the system became unresponsive. The network operations center worked with the IMT and opened a conference bridge at 6:30 a.m. At 11:00 a.m., the application owner on the user-enterprise side was notified of the incident by a user group manager. The application was back online by 1:00 p.m.

Three weeks following the first incident, another application service interruption occurred. On a Wednesday at 2:00 p.m., the system became unresponsive for a portion of the user base (i.e., some areas were unaffected, including the office location of the system operations owner for the user enterprise). The network operations center opened a conference bridge at 2:40 p.m. At 3:00 p.m., the application owner on the user-enterprise side was notified of the incident by the vendor. The application was back online for the complete user community by 4:00 p.m.

Going forward, the application experienced a service interruption on average once a month for the next three months. The impact of the service interruptions varied and included partial availability loss for certain functions, as well as a full-service provisioning loss.

Following the lapse in notification from the first incident and the inconsistency brought about by notification from the second incident, the enterprise began to revamp its internal processes. Internal process revisions occurred through the creation of an incident communication procedure, which was distributed to all IT personnel charged with operating the application. The procedures designated communication goals and required post-incident reviews identifying clear root causes for the incidents no later than a week after resolution.

For a longer-term response, the enterprise enacted several business decisions that resulted in remaining with the current service provisioning system and a reduction in service interruptions following the three-month period. These included cataloging the incident history and meeting with the vendor to establish operational level agreements and a comprehensive service improvement plan, including the monitoring of operational results.

1. Considering the first incident, when should the business owner have been notified about the incident?
   A. Within incident reporting operational level agreements
   B. No later than 6:15 a.m.
   C. Within the vendor's incident reporting service level agreements
   D. No later than 6:30 a.m.

2. In a process-mature enterprise, how should the initial notification for the second incident have been delivered to the business owner?

   A. Through separate notifications upon incident discovery to stakeholders
   B. By the security information and event management tool
   C. By the application vendor
   D. By the network operations center

3. When cataloging incidents in preparation for meeting with the vendor, which of the following is the **BEST** choice for the initial set of actions to be taken by the information security manager?

   A. Create a post-incident review for each incident involved.
   B. Perform a business impact analysis.
   C. Update the incident response and recovery plans.
   D. Perform a risk assessment.

Answers on page 319

Case Study 2

In a major US financial institution, low-level personnel monitoring the network operation center (NOC) noticed unusual network activity on a Sunday evening when the bank was closed. Uncertain of what they were seeing, they decided to watch the event rather than risk disturbing management on a weekend. No severity criteria, notification requirements or escalation processes had been developed by the enterprise. By 3 a.m. on Monday, traffic continued to increase at the main facility and then suddenly began to grow dramatically at the mirror site, hundreds of miles away. The NOC staff remained unconcerned and felt they could still handle the increase in traffic.

By 7 a.m. on Monday, the NOC personnel were sufficiently concerned to notify the IT managers that there was a problem and the monitors showed the network was becoming saturated. An hour later when the external CIRT arrived, the network was totally inoperative and the team determined that the network had been compromised by the Slammer worm. The CIRT team manager informed the IT manager that the Slammer worm was memory-resident and restarting the entire network and mirror facility would resolve the issue. The manager stated that he did not have the authority to shut down the system and the CIO would need to approve the action The CIO could not be located, and current emergency phone and pager numbers were kept only in a new emergency paging system that required network access. When asked about the DRP and what it had to say regarding declaration criteria, three different plans were produced that had been prepared by teams in different parts of the enterprise, unbeknownst to each other. None contained declaration criteria or specified roles, responsibilities or authority. The final resolution ultimately required the CEO, who was traveling overseas and not immediately available, to finally issue instructions the next morning (Tuesday) to shut down the nonfunctioning network. The institution was inoperative for a full day and a half, with over 30,000 employees unable to perform their work. The final direct costs were estimated by the post-incident team to exceed US $50 million.

1. Which of the following could have aided the NOC employees in identifying the severity of the incident?

   A. Updated security policies
   B. Meaningful security metrics
   C. Additional security training
   D. Increased decision-making autonomy

2. Which is an example of a metric that would be **MOST** meaningful to the NOC in this scenario?

   A. Amount of traffic during a typical downtime
   B. Number of transactions per hour
   C. Duration of increased traffic prior to contacting management
   D. The number of systems showing traffic

3. Which of the following **BEST** could have aided the network manager in containing the incident in a timelier manner?

   A. A single, approved disaster recovery plan
   B. Earlier notification from the NOC
   C. Better organizational governance structure
   D. Additional security training for staff

4. Who ultimately should be responsible for ensuring that a single DRP is in place for the enterprise?

5. Who should be accountable for the lack of an effective DRP?

Answers on page 319

Chapter 4 ANSWER KEY

Case Study 1

1. **A. The timeframe for incident response should be determined by internal user-enterprise operational level agreements (OLAs).**

   B. The timeframe for incident response should be determined by internal OLAs. These should be determined based on incident categorizations as applied by the IMT.

   C. The user-enterprise's OLAs take precedence over the vendor's internal SLAs. If the vendor's SLAs are insufficient, then the vendor and the enterprise should work to develop an improved solution to bring those SLAs to a level accepted by the user-enterprise. The vendor can provide notification of a service disruption; however, the enterprise should have internal monitoring systems in place.

   D. The timeframe for incident response should be determined by internal OLAs. These should be determined based on incident categorizations as applied by the IMT. 6:30 a.m. represents the time that the conference bridge was opened; however, that may or may not be commensurate with the user-enterprise's incident reporting OLAs.

2. A. Depending on the way an enterprise's security information and event management (SIEM) tool is set up, it is possible for the same incident to be reported multiple times through numerous sources. However, if reporting comes at multiple times to the business owner, then it stops being an initial notification. In fact, all notifications subsequent to the first become ancillary notifications.

   B. The SIEM tool should have notified the application business owner of the incident.

   C. The application vendor could have notified the user-enterprise's business owner of the incident (as stated in the case); however, this should not have been the first (or initial) notification. The initial notification should have come from the SIEM tool. If the alert first came from the vendor, then the incident is either something of an extreme outlier that the SIEM tool did not catch or the enterprise lacks the process maturity that is presupposed in this question.

   D. The user-enterprise's network operations center could have sent out the initial alert, if that was integrated with the SIEM tool; however, there is not enough information either within the case study or this question to conclude that as a certainty.

3. A. A post-incident review was already created for incidents that occurred over the previous three months, based on the updated documentation that was created following the first incident.

   B. Conducting a business impact analysis is the first step in the incident response management process. In this scenario, the incidents have already occurred and were responded to; however, the combined business impact of the combined incident activity needs to be taken into account prior to discussions with the vendor. The vendor needs to understand the damage that system downtime has caused the business because this, along with the consistency of incidents, will be the basis from which a response strategy can be determined.

   C. Updating the incident response and recovery plans can be performed in tandem with preparation for a vendor meeting. However, the response and recovery plans are to help matters going forward, while the vendor meeting is to address the impact of incidents as they occurred and to form a consolidated response to the pervasiveness in the lack of consistent system availability.

   D. The incidents have already occurred; therefore, an impact assessment, not a risk assessment, needs to be performed.

Case Study 2

1. A. Updated security policies would have helped to establish reporting and escalation procedures; however, meaningful security metrics would better help network operation center (NOC) employees recognize that an incident was occurring, which would have helped them to react in a more effective way.

B. For those monitoring the NOC, metrics indicated a problem, but they were not sufficiently meaningful to the employees for them to make any active decisions, much less the correct ones. Either better metrics or greater proficiency of the personnel could have resolved the issue quickly in the initial stages of the incident before it became a problem.

C. Additional security training would help employees know what to do should an incident occur; however, meaningful metrics should be established in order to make training as impactful as possible so incidents can be recognized and handled in a timely manner.

D. Increased decision-making autonomy is helpful when there are meaningful metrics in place to help employees recognize incidents are occurring. Based on that information, they can make informed decisions on how to best contain and respond to incidents.

2. **A. Knowing the normal traffic occurring at that time of night would have made it clear that the situation was not normal, and a serious problem existed.**

   B. Without a reference point, the number of transactions would not have been particularly meaningful.

   C. The duration of traffic without a point of reference would not have been meaningful.

   D. The number of systems without a point of reference would not be helpful.

3. A. A single disaster recovery plan could have been useful but without clear authority it would not by itself have helped.

   B. Earlier notification would have been helpful but only if authority to act was clear.

   C. Better governance would have vested adequate authority in the network manager to take the appropriate action.

   D. Training of staff would have been useful in recognizing the event but authority to act was essential.

4. A disaster recovery plan (DRP) for the overall enterprise is a governance issue; therefore, it is the responsibility of the board of directors to ensure that a DRP is in place.

5. Better governance would have ensured that risk management was in place; however, those involved in governance direct the program. The CISO or CIO—whomever the information security manager reports to—would be accountable for the ineffective DRP. The information security manager and the IRT would be responsible for periodically reviewing and testing the DRP to make sure it was working as expected.

APPENDIX A: CISM Exam General Information

ISACA is a professional membership association composed of individuals interested in IS audit, assurance, control, security and governance. The CISM Certification Working Group is responsible for establishing policies for the CISM certification program and for developing the exam.

> **Note:** Because information regarding the CISM examination may change, please refer to *www.isaca.org/credentialing/CISM* for the most current information.

Requirements for Certification

The CISM designation is awarded to those individuals who have met the following requirements: 1) achieve a passing score on the CISM exam, 2) adhere to the Code of Professional Ethics, 3) adhere to the continuing education policy and 4) demonstrate the required minimum work experience supporting the governance of the IT-related contribution to an enterprise.

Successful Completion of the CISM Exam

The exam is open to all individuals who wish to take it. Successful exam candidates are not certified until they apply for certification (and demonstrate that they have met all requirements) and receive approval from ISACA.

Experience in Information Security

CISM candidates must meet the stated experience requirements to become certified. Please refer to the *www.isaca.org/credentialing/cism/get-cism-certified*for experience requirements and a list of experience waivers.

Experience must have been gained within the 10-year period preceding the application date for certification or within five years from the date of initially passing the exam. A completed application for certification must be submitted within five years from the passing date of the CISM exam. All experience must be independently verified with employers.

Description of the Exam

The CISM Certification Working Group oversees the development of the exam and ensures the currency of its content. Questions for the CISM exam are developed through a multitiered process designed to enhance the ultimate quality of the exam.

The purpose of the exam is to evaluate a candidate's knowledge and experience in data privacy. The exam consists of 150 multiple-choice questions, administered during a three-hour session.

Registration for the CISM Exam

The CISM exam is administered on a continuous basis at qualifying test sites Please refer to the ISACA Exam Candidate Information Guide at www.isaca.org/credentialing/cism for specific exam registration information including registration, scheduling and languages, and other important key information for exam day. Exam registrations can be made online at www.isaca.org/credentialing/cism.

CISM Program Accreditation Renewed Under ISO/IEC 17024:2012

The American National Standards Institute (ANSI) has voted to continue the accreditation for the CISA, CISM, CGEIT, CRISC and CISM certifications, under ISO/IEC 17024:2012, General Requirements for Bodies Operating Certification Systems of Persons. ANSI, a private, nonprofit organization, accredits other organizations to serve as third-party product, system and personnel certifiers.

ISO/IEC 17024 specifies the requirements to be followed by organizations certifying individual against specific requirements. ANSI describes ISO/IEC 17024 as "expected to play a prominent role in facilitating global standardization of the certification community, increasing mobility among countries, enhancing public safety, and protecting consumers."

ANSI's accreditation:

- Promotes the unique qualifications and expertise ISACA's certifications provide.
- Protects the integrity of the certifications and provides legal defensibility.
- Enhances consumer and public confidence in the certifications and the people who hold them.
- Facilitates mobility across borders or industries.

Accreditation by ANSI signifies that ISACA's procedures meet ANSI's essential requirements for openness, balance, consensus and due process. With this accreditation, ISACA anticipates that significant opportunities for CISAs, CISMs, CGEITs and CRISCs will continue to open in the United States and around the world.

Scheduling the Exam

The CISM exam can be scheduled directly from your My ISACA Certification Dashboard. Please see the Exam Candidate Information Guide for complete instructions. Exams can be scheduled for any available time slot. Exams may be rescheduled a minimum of 48 hours prior to the originally scheduled appointment. If you are within 48 hours of your original appointment, you must take your exam or forfeit the exam registration fee.

Sitting for the Exam

Prior to the day of the exam make sure you:

- Locate the test center and confirm the start time.
- Plan to arrive 15 minutes prior to exam start time.
- Plan to store personal belongings.
- Review the exam day rules.

You must present an acceptable form of identification (ID) in order to enter the testing center. Please see the Exam Candidate Information Guide for acceptable forms of ID.

You are prohibited from bringing the following into the test center:

- Reference materials, paper, notepads, or language dictionaries
- Calculators
- Any type of communication, surveillance or recording devices such as:
  - Mobile phones
  - Tablets
  - Smartwatches or glasses
  - Mobile devices
- Baggage of any kind including handbags, purses or briefcases
- Weapons
- Tobacco products
- Food or beverages
- Visitors

If exam candidates are viewed with any such communication, surveillance or recording devices during the exam administration, their exam will be voided, and they will be asked to immediately leave the exam site.

Personal items brought to the testing center must be stored in a locker or other designated area until the exam is completed and submitted.

Avoid activities that would invalidate your test score:

- Creating a disturbance.
- Giving or receiving help; using notes, papers, or other aids.
- Attempting to take the exam for someone else.
- Possession of communication, surveillance or recording device, including but not limited to cellphones, tablets, smart glasses, smartwatches, mobile devices, etc., during the exam administration.
- Attempting to share test questions or answers or other information contained in the exam (as such are the confidential information of ISACA); including sharing test questions subsequent to the exam.
- Leaving the testing area without authorization. (These individuals will not be allowed to return to the testing room.)
- Accessing items stored in the personal belongings area before the completion of the exam.

Budgeting Your Time

The exam is administered over a three-hour period. This allows for a little over 1.5 minutes per question.

Therefore, it is advisable that candidates pace themselves to complete the entire exam.

Grading the Exam

Candidate scores are reported as a scaled score. A scaled score is a conversion of a candidate's raw score on an exam to a common scale. ISACA uses and reports scores on a common scale from 200 to 800.

A candidate must receive a score of 450 or higher to pass the exam. A score of 450 represents a minimum consistent standard of knowledge as established by ISACA's CISM Certification Working Group. A candidate receiving a passing score may then apply for certification if all other requirements are met.

Passing the exam does not grant the CISM designation. To become a CISM, each candidate must complete all requirements, including submitting an application and receiving approval for certification.

The CISM examination contains some questions that are included for research and analysis purposes only. These questions are not separately identified, and the candidate's final score will be based only on the common scored questions. There are various versions of each exam but only the common questions are scored for your results.

A candidate receiving a score less than 450 is not successful and can retake the exam by registering and paying the appropriate exam fee. To assist with future study, the result letter each candidate receives will include a score analysis by content area.

You will receive a preliminary score on screen immediately following the completion of your exam. **Your official score will be emailed to you and available online within 10 working days**. Question-level results cannot be provided.

In order to become CISM-certified, candidates must pass the CISM exam and must complete and submit an application for certification (and must receive confirmation from ISACA that the application is approved). The application is available on the ISACA website at *www.isaca.org/credentialing/cism*. Once the application is approved, the applicant will be sent confirmation of the approval. The candidate is not CISM-certified, and cannot use the CISM designation, until the candidate's application is approved. A processing fee must accompany CISM applications for certification.

Candidates receiving a failing score on the exam may request a rescoring of their exam within 30 days following the release of the exam results. All requests must include the candidate's name, exam identification number and mailing address. A fee of US $75 must accompany this request.

Page intentionally left blank

APPENDIX B: CISM Job Practice

Knowledge Subdomains

Domain 1—Information Security Governance

A. Enterprise Governance

1. Organizational Culture
2. Legal, Regulatory, and Contractual Requirements
3. Organizational Structures, Roles, and Responsibilities

B. Informational Security Strategy

1. Information Security Strategy Development
2. Information Governance Frameworks and Standards
3. Strategic Planning

Domain 2—Information Security Risk Management

A. Information Security Risk Assessment

1. Emerging Risk and Threat Landscape
2. Vulnerability and Control Deficiency Analysis
3. Risk Assessment and Analysis

B. Information Security Risk Response

1. Risk Treatment/Risk Response Options
2. Risk and Control Ownership
3. Risk Monitoring and Reporting

Domain 3—Information Security Program

A. Information Security Program Development

1. Information Security Program Resources
2. Information Asset Identification and Classification
3. Industry Standards and Frameworks for Information Security
4. Information Security Policies, Procedures, and Guidelines
5. Information Security Program Metrics

B. Information Security Program Management

1. Information Security Control Design and Selection
2. Information Security Control Implementation and Integrations
3. Information Security Control Testing and Evaluation
4. Information Security Awareness and Training
5. Management of External Services
6. Information Security Program Communications and Reporting

Domain 4—Incident Management

A. Incident Management Readiness

1. Incident Response Plan
2. Business Impact Analysis
3. Business Continuity Plan
4. Disaster Recovery Plan
5. Incident Classification/Categorization
6. Incident Management Training, Testing and Evaluation

B. Incident Management Operations

1. Incident Management Tools and Techniques
2. Incident Investigation and Evaluation
3. Incident Containment Methods
4. Incident Response Communications
5. Incident Eradication and Recovery
6. Post-incident Review Practices

Supporting Tasks

1. Identify internal and external influences to the enterprise that impact the information security strategy.
2. Establish and maintain an information security strategy in alignment with organizational goals and objectives.
3. Establish and maintain an information security governance framework.
4. Integrate information security governance into corporate governance.

5. Establish and maintain information security policies to guide the development of standards, procedures and guidelines.
6. Develop business cases to support investments in information security.
7. Gain ongoing commitment from senior leadership and other stakeholders to support the successful implementation of the information security strategy.
8. Define, communicate and monitor information security responsibilities throughout the enterprise and lines of authority.
9. Compile and present reports to key stakeholders on the activities, trends and overall effectiveness of the information security program.
10. Evaluate and report information security metrics to key stakeholders.
11. Establish and maintain the information security program in alignment with the information security strategy.
12. Align the information security program with the operational objectives of other business functions.
13. Establish and maintain information security processes and resources to execute the information security program.
14. Establish, communicate and maintain organizational information security policies, standards, guidelines, procedures and other documentation.
15. Establish, promote and maintain a program for information security awareness and training.
16. Integrate information security requirements into organizational processes to maintain the enterprise's security strategy.
17. Integrate information security requirements into contracts and activities of external parties.
18. Monitor external parties' adherence to established security requirements.
19. Define and monitor management and operational metrics for the information security program.
20. Establish and maintain a process for information asset identification and classification.
21. Identify legal, regulatory, organizational, and other applicable compliance requirements.
22. Participate in and/or oversee the risk identification, risk assessment and risk treatment process.
23. Participate in and/or oversee the vulnerability assessment and threat analysis process.
24. Identify, recommend, or implement appropriate risk treatment and response options to manage risk to acceptable levels based on organizational risk appetite.
25. Determine whether information security controls are appropriate and effectively manage risk to an acceptable level.
26. Facilitate the integration of information risk management into business and IT processes.
27. Monitor for internal and external factors that may require reassessment of risk.
28. Report on information security risk, including noncompliance and changes in information risk, to key stakeholders to facilitate the risk management decision-making process.
29. Establish and maintain an incident response plan, in alignment with the business continuity plan and disaster recovery plan.
30. Establish and maintain an information security incident classification and categorization process.
31. Develop and implement processes to ensure the timely identification of information security incidents.
32. Establish and maintain processes to investigate and document information security incidents in accordance with legal and regulatory requirements.
33. Establish and maintain incident handling processes, including containment, notification, escalation, eradication and recovery.
34. Organize, train, equip and assign responsibilities to incident response teams.
35. Establish and maintain incident communication plans and processes for internal and external parties.
36. Evaluate incident management plans through testing and review, including table-top exercises, checklist review, and simulation testing at planned intervals.
37. Conduct post-incident reviews to facilitate continuous improvement, including root-cause analysis, lessons learned, corrective actions, and reassessment of risk.

Glossary

Note: Glossary terms are provided for reference within the *CISM Review Manual*. As terms and definitions may evolve due to the changing technological environment, please see www.isaca.org/glossary for the most up-to-date terms and definitions.

A

Acceptable interruption window—The maximum period of time that a system can be unavailable before compromising the achievement of the enterprise's business objectives.

Acceptable use policy—A policy that establishes an agreement between users and the enterprise that defines, for all parties, the ranges of use that are approved before gaining access to a network or the Internet

Access control—The processes, rules and deployment mechanisms that control access to information systems, resources and physical access to premises

Access path—The logical route that an end user takes to access computerized information.

Scope Notes: Typically includes a route through the operating system, telecommunications software, selected application software and the access control system.

Access rights—The permission or privileges granted to users, programs or workstations to create, change, delete or view data and files within a system, as defined by rules established by data owners and the information security policy

Accountability—The ability to map a given activity or event back to the responsible party

Administrative control—The rules, procedures and practices dealing with operational effectiveness, efficiency and adherence to regulations and management policies.

Advanced Encryption Standard (AES)—A public algorithm that supports keys from 128 bits to 256 bits in size

Advanced persistent threat (APT)—An adversary that possesses sophisticated levels of expertise and significant resources, which allow them to create opportunities to achieve their objectives by using multiple attack vectors, e.g., cyber, physical, and deception. These objectives typically include establishing and extending footholds within the information technology infrastructure of the targeted organizations for purposes of exfiltrating information; undermining or impeding critical aspects of a mission themselves to carry out these objectives in the future. An advanced persistent threat (APT):

- Pursues its objectives repeatedly over an extended period of time
- Adapts to defenders' efforts to resist it
- Is determined to maintain the level of interaction needed to execute its objectives

Source: CMMC-NIST SP800-39

Alert situation—The point in an emergency procedure when the elapsed time passes a threshold and the interruption is not resolved. The enterprise entering into an alert situation initiates a series of escalation steps.

Algorithm—A finite set of well-defined, unambiguous rules for the solution of a problem in a finite number of steps, it is a sequence of operational actions that lead to a desired goal and is the basic building block of a program

Alternate facilities—Locations and infrastructures from which emergency or backup processes are executed, when the main premises are unavailable or destroyed

Scope Notes: Includes other buildings, offices or data processing centers

Alternate process—Automatic or manual process designed and established to continue critical business processes from point-of-failure to return-to-normal

Annual loss expectancy (ALE)—The total expected loss divided by the number of years in the forecast period yielding the average annual loss

Anomaly detection—Detection on the basis of whether the system activity matches that defined as abnormal

Antimalware—A widely used technology to prevent, detect and remove many categories of malware, including computer viruses, worms, Trojans, keyloggers, malicious browser plug-ins, adware and spyware

Antiphishing—Software that identifies phishing content and attempts to block the content or warn the user about the suspicious nature of the content

Antivirus software—An application software deployed at multiple points in an IT architecture. It is designed to detect and potentially eliminate virus code before damage is done and repair or quarantine files that have already been infected.

Application controls—The policies, procedures and activities designed to provide reasonable assurance that objectives relevant to a given automated solution (application) are achieved.

Application programming interface (API)—A set of routines, protocols and tools referred to as building blocks used in business application software development

Application service provider (ASP)—Also known as managed service provider (MSP), it deploys, hosts and manages access to a packaged application to multiple parties from a centrally managed facility.

Scope Notes: The applications are delivered over networks on a subscription basis.

Architecture—Description of the fundamental underlying design of the components of the business system, or of one element of the business system (e.g., technology), the relationships among them, and the manner in which they support enterprise objectives

Asset—Something of either tangible or intangible value that is worth protecting, including people, information, infrastructure, finances and reputation

Asset inventory—A register that is used to record all relevant assets

Asset value—The value of an asset to both the business and to competitors

Asymmetric key (public key)—A cipher technique in which different cryptographic keys are used to encrypt and decrypt a message

Scope Notes: See public key encryption.

Attack vector—A path or route used by the adversary to gain access to the target (asset)

Scope Notes: There are two types of attack vectors: ingress and egress (also known as data exfiltration).

Audit trail—Data in the form of a logical path linking a sequence of events, used to trace the transactions that have affected the contents of a record

Source : ISO

Authentication—1. The act of verifying identity, i.e., user, system

Scope Notes: Can also refer to the verification of the correctness of a piece of data.

2. The act of verifying the identity of a user, the user's eligibility to access computerized information

Scope Notes: Authentication is designed to protect against fraudulent logon activity. It can also refer to the verification of the correctness of a piece of data.

Authorization—The process of determining if the end user is permitted to have access to an information asset or the information system containing the asset.

Availability—Ensuring timely and reliable access to and use of information

B

Backup center—An alternate facility to continue IT/IS operations when the primary data processing (DP) center is unavailable.

Baseline security—The minimum security controls required for safeguarding an IT system based on its identified needs for confidentiality, integrity and/or availability protection

Benchmarking—A systematic approach to comparing enterprise performance against peers and competitors in an effort to learn the best ways of conducting business.

Scope Notes: Examples include benchmarking of quality, logistic efficiency and various other metrics.

Bit—A contraction of the term binary digit, and the most basic and smallest unit of computing information. A bit may be in one of two states, logic 1 or logic 0. It can be thought of as a switch that is either on or off. Bits are usually combined into computer words of various sizes, named bytes.

Bit copy—Provides an exact image of the original and is a requirement for legally justifiable forensics

Bit-stream image—Bit-stream backups, also referred to as mirror image backups, involve the backup of all areas of a computer hard disk drive or other type of storage media.

Scope Notes: Such backups exactly replicate all sectors on a given storage device including all files and ambient data storage areas.

Blue team—A group that proactively conducts systematic examinations of information systems or products to determine the adequacy of security measures, identify security deficiencies, responds to technical security incidents and confirms the adequacy of such measures after implementation. Blue teams are typically internal security personnel that may or may not be part of an enterprise security operations center.

Botnet—A term derived from robot network; a large automated and distributed network of previously compromised computers that can be simultaneously controlled to launch large-scale attacks, such as a denial-of-service attack, on targeted victims

Brute-force attack—Methodically trying all possible combinations of passwords or encryption keys until the correct one is found

Business case—Documentation of the rationale for making a business investment, used both to support a business decision on whether to proceed with the investment and as an operational tool to support management of the investment through its full economic life cycle

Business continuity—Preventing, mitigating and recovering from disruption

Scope Notes: The terms 'business resumption planning', 'disaster recovery planning' and 'contingency planning' also may be used in this context; they focus on recovery aspects of continuity, and for that reason the 'resilience' aspect should also be taken into account.

COBIT 5 and COBIT 2019 perspective

Business continuity plan (BCP)—A plan used by an enterprise to respond to disruption of critical business processes; depends on the contingency plan for restoration of critical systems

Business dependency assessment—A process of identifying resources critical to the operation of a business process.

Business impact—The net effect, positive or negative, on the achievement of business objectives.

Business impact analysis (BIA)—Process of evaluating the criticality and sensitivity of information assets by determining the impact of losing the support of any resource to an enterprise. Establishes the escalation of that loss over time, identifies the minimum resources needed to recover and prioritizes the recovery of processes and the supporting system.

Scope Notes: This process captures income loss, unexpected expense, legal issues (regulatory compliance or contractual), interdependent processes and loss of public reputation or public confidence.

Business Model for Information Security (BMIS)—A holistic and business-oriented model that supports enterprise governance and management information security, and provides a common language for information security professionals and business management.

C

Capability Maturity Model Integration (CMMI)—An integrated model of best practices that enable businesses to improve performance by improving their processes. Product teams developed the model with global members from across industry. The CMMI provides a best-practice framework for building, improving, and sustaining process capability.

See CMMI product suite

Certificate (Certification) authority (CA)—A trusted third party that serves authentication infrastructures or enterprises and registers entities and issues them certificates

Certificate revocation list (CRL)—An instrument for checking the continued validity of the certificates for which the certification authority (CA) has responsibility

Scope Notes: The CRL details digital certificates that are no longer valid. The time gap between two updates is very critical and is also a risk in digital certificates verification.

Certification practice statement (CPS)—A detailed set of rules governing the certificate authority's operations. It provides an understanding of the value and trustworthiness of certificates issued by a given certificate authority (CA).

Scope Notes: In terms of the controls that an enterprise observes, the method it uses to validate the authenticity of certificate applicants and the CA's expectations of how its certificates may be used.

Chain of custody—The process of evidence handling from collection to presentation that is necessary to maintain the validity and integrity of evidence

Scope Notes: Includes documentation of who had access to the evidence and when, and the ability to identify that evidence is the exact item that was recovered or tested. Lack of control over evidence can lead to it being discredited. Chain of custody depends on the ability to verify that evidence could not have been tampered with. This is accomplished by sealing off the evidence, so it cannot be changed, and providing a documentary record of custody to prove that the evidence was, at all times, under strict control and not subject to tampering.

Challenge/response token—A method of user authentication that is carried out through use of the Challenge Handshake Authentication Protocol (CHAP).

Scope Notes: When a user tries to log into the server using CHAP, the server sends the user a "challenge," which is a random value. The user enters a password, which is used as an encryption key to encrypt the "challenge" and return it to the server. The server is aware of the password. It, therefore, encrypts the "challenge" value and compares it with the value received from the user. If the values match, the user is authenticated. The challenge/response activity continues throughout the session and this protects the session from password sniffing attacks. In addition, CHAP is not vulnerable to "man-in-the-middle" attacks because the challenge value is a random value that changes on each access attempt.

Change management—1. A holistic and proactive approach to managing the transition from a current to a desired organizational state, focusing specifically on the critical human or "soft" elements of change (ISACA)

Scope Notes: Includes activities such as culture change (values, beliefs and attitudes), development of reward systems (measures and appropriate incentives), organizational design, stakeholder management, human resources (HR) policies and procedures, executive coaching, change leadership training, team building and communication planning and execution.

2. A methodical approach for controlling and implementing changes in a planned and structured manner (CMMI)

Checksum—A checksum value is generated by an algorithm and associated with an input value and/or whole input file. The checksum value can be used to assess its corresponding input data or file later and verify that the input has not been maliciously altered. If a subsequent checksum value no longer matches the initial value, the input may have been altered or corrupted.

Chief information officer (CIO)—The most senior official of the enterprise who is accountable for IT advocacy, aligning IT and business strategies, and planning, resourcing and managing the delivery of IT services, information and the deployment of associated human resources.

Scope Notes: In some cases, the CIO role has been expanded to become the chief knowledge officer (CKO) who deals in knowledge, not just information. Also see chief technology officer (CTO).

Chief information security officer (CISO)—The person in charge of information security within the enterprise

Chief security officer (CSO)—The person usually responsible for all physical and digital security matters in an enterprise

Chief technology officer (CTO)—The individual who focuses on technical issues in an enterprise.

Scope Notes: Often viewed as synonymous with chief information officer (CIO)

COBIT—1. COBIT 2019: The current iteration of COBIT builds on and integrates more than 25 years of developments in the field of enterprise governance of information and technology (I&T), not only incorporating new insights from science, but also operationalizing these insights as practices. COBIT is a broad and comprehensive I&T governance and management framework and continues to establish itself as a generally accepted framework for I&T governance.

Scope Notes: Earlier versions of COBIT focused on IT, whereas COBIT 2019 focuses on information **and** technology aimed at the whole enterprise, recognizing that I&T has become crucial in the support, sustainability and growth of enterprises. (See www.isaca.org/cobit for more information.)

2. COBIT 5: Formerly known as Control Objectives for Information and related Technology (COBIT); with this iteration used only as the acronym. A complete, internationally accepted framework for governing and managing enterprise information and technology (IT) that supports enterprise executives and management in their definition and achievement of business goals and related IT goals. COBIT describes five principles and seven enablers that support enterprises in the development, implementation and continuous improvement and monitoring of good IT-related governance and management practices.

Scope Notes: Earlier versions of COBIT focused on control objectives related to IT processes, management and control of IT processes and IT governance aspects. Adoption and use of the COBIT framework are supported by guidance from a growing family of supporting products.

3. COBIT 4.1 and earlier: Formally known as Control Objectives for Information and related Technology (COBIT). A complete, internationally accepted process framework for IT that supports business and IT executives and management in their definition and achievement of business goals and related IT goals by providing a comprehensive IT governance, management, control and assurance model. COBIT describes IT processes and associated control objectives, management

guidelines (activities, accountabilities, responsibilities and performance metrics) and maturity models. COBIT supports enterprise management in the development, implementation, continuous improvement and monitoring of good IT-related practices.

Scope Notes: Adoption and use of the COBIT framework are supported by guidance for executives and management (Board Briefing on IT Governance, 2nd Edition), IT governance implementers (COBIT Quickstart, 2nd Edition; IT Governance Implementation Guide: Using COBIT and Val IT, 2nd Edition; and COBIT Control Practices: Guidance to Achieve Control Objectives for Successful IT Governance), and IT assurance and audit professionals (IT Assurance Guide Using COBIT). Guidance also exists to support its applicability for certain legislative and regulatory requirements (e.g., IT Control Objectives for Sarbanes-Oxley, IT Control Objectives for Basel II) and its relevance to information security (COBIT Security Baseline). COBIT is mapped to other frameworks and standards to illustrate complete coverage of the IT management life cycle and support its use in enterprises using multiple IT-related framework and standards.

Compensating control—An internal control that reduces the risk of an existing or potential control weakness resulting in errors and omissions.

Computer forensics—The application of the scientific method to digital media to establish factual information for judicial review

Scope Notes: This process often involves investigating computer systems to determine whether they are or have been used for illegal or unauthorized activities. As a discipline, it combines elements of law and computer science to collect and analyze data from information systems (e.g., personal computers, networks, wireless communication and digital storage devices) in a way that is admissible as evidence in a court of law.

Confidentiality—Preserving authorized restrictions on access and disclosure, including means for protecting privacy and proprietary information

Configuration management—

Content filtering—Controlling access to a network by analyzing the contents of the incoming and outgoing packets and either letting them pass or denying them based on a list of rules.

Scope Notes: Differs from packet filtering in that it is the data in the packet that are analyzed instead of the attributes of the packet itself (e.g., source/target IP address, transmission control protocol [TCP] flags)

Contingency plan—A plan used by an enterprise or business unit to respond to a specific systems failure or disruption.

Contingency planning—Process of developing advance arrangements and procedures that enable an enterprise to respond to an event that could occur by chance or unforeseen circumstances.

Continuous monitoring—The process implemented to maintain a current security status for one or more information systems or for the entire suite of information systems on which the operational mission of the enterprise depends.

The process includes: 1) the development of a strategy to regularly evaluate selected IS controls/metrics, 2) recording and evaluating IS-relevant events and the effectiveness of the enterprise in dealing with those events, 3) recording changes to IS controls, or changes that affect IS risks, and 4) publishing the current security status to enable information-sharing decisions involving the enterprise.

Control—The means of managing risk, including policies, procedures, guidelines, practices or organizational structures, which can be of an administrative, technical, management or legal nature

Scope Notes: Also used as a synonym for safeguard or countermeasure.

See also Internal control.

Control center—Hosts the recovery meetings where disaster recovery operations are managed.

Corporate governance—The system by which enterprises are directed and controlled. The board of directors is responsible for the governance of their enterprise. It consists of the leadership and organizational structures and processes that ensure the enterprise sustains and extends strategies and objectives.

COSO—Committee of Sponsoring Organizations of the Treadway Commission

Scope Notes: COSO's "Internal Control—Integrated Framework" is an internationally accepted standard for corporate governance. See *www.coso.org*.

Cost-benefit analysis—An analysis that relies on the addition of positive factors and the subtraction of negative factors to determine a net result, and is a method used to build a business case to support a risk response

Countermeasure—Any process that directly reduces a threat or vulnerability

Criticality—The importance of a particular asset or function to the enterprise, and the impact if that asset or function is not available

Criticality analysis—An analysis to evaluate resources or business functions to identify their importance to the enterprise, and the impact if a function cannot be completed or a resource is not available.

Cryptography—The study of mathematical techniques related to aspects of information security, such as confidentiality, data integrity, entity authentication and data origin authentication

Cyclical redundancy check (CRC)—A method to ensure that data have not been altered after being sent through a communication channel

D

Data classification—The assignment of a level of sensitivity to data (or information) that results in the specification of controls for each level of classification. Levels of sensitivity of data are assigned according to predefined categories as data are created, amended, enhanced, stored or transmitted. The classification level is an indication of the value or importance of the data to the enterprise.

Data custodian—The individual(s) and department(s) responsible for the storage and safeguarding of computerized data.

Data integrity—The degree to which a collection of data is complete, consistent and accurate

Data leakage—Unauthorized transmission of data from an organization either electronically or physically

Data loss prevention—Detecting and addressing data breaches, exfiltration or unwanted destruction of data

Data mining—Generally, the use of computers to analyze large data sets to look for patterns that assist people in making business decisions

Data normalization—A structured process for organizing data into tables in such a way that it preserves the relationships among the data.

Data owner—The individual(s) who has responsibility for the integrity, accurate reporting and use of computerized data

Data warehouse—A generic term for a system that stores, retrieves and manages large volumes of data.

Scope Notes: Data warehouse software often includes sophisticated comparison and hashing techniques for fast searches as well as for advanced filtering.

Decentralization—The process of distributing computer processing to different locations within an enterprise

Decryption key—A digital piece of information used to recover plaintext from the corresponding ciphertext by decryption

Defense in depth—The practice of layering defenses to provide added protection. Defense in depth increases security by raising the effort needed in an attack. This strategy places multiple barriers between an attacker and enterprise computing and information resources.

Degauss—The application of variable levels of alternating current for the purpose of demagnetizing magnetic recording media.

Scope Notes: The process involves increasing the alternating current field gradually from zero to some maximum value and back to zero, leaving a very low residue of magnetic induction on the media. Degauss loosely means to erase.

Demilitarized zone (DMZ)—A small, isolated network that serves as a buffer zone between trusted and untrusted networks

Scope Notes: A DMZ is typically used to house systems, such as web servers, that must be accessible from both internal networks and the Internet.

Denial-of-service attack (DoS)—An assault on a service from a single source that floods it with so many requests that it becomes overwhelmed and is either stopped completely or operates at a significantly reduced rate

Digital certificate—Electronic credentials that permit an entity to exchange information securely via the Internet using the public key infrastructure (PKI)

Digital code signing—The process of digitally signing computer code to ensure its integrity.

Disaster declaration—The communication to appropriate internal and external parties that the disaster recovery plan (DRP) is being put into operation.

Disaster notification fee—The fee that the recovery site vendor charges when the customer notifies them that a disaster has occurred and the recovery site is required.

Scope Notes: The fee is implemented to discourage false disaster notifications.

Disaster recovery—Activities and programs designed to return the enterprise to an acceptable condition. The ability to respond to an interruption in services by implementing a disaster recovery plan (DRP) to restore an enterprise's critical business functions.

Disaster recovery plan (DRP)—A set of human, physical, technical and procedural resources to recover, within a defined time and cost, an activity interrupted by an emergency or disaster

Disaster recovery plan (DRP) desk checking—Typically a read-through of a disaster recovery plan (DRP) without any real actions taking place.

Scope Notes: Generally involves a reading of the plan, discussion of the action items and definition of any gaps that might be identified

Disaster recovery plan (DRP) walk-through—Generally a robust test of the recovery plan requiring that some recovery activities take place and are tested. A disaster scenario is often given and the recovery teams talk through the steps that they would need to take to recover. As many aspects of the plan as possible should be tested.

Discretionary access control (DAC)—Logical access control filters that may be configured or modified by the users or data owners

Disk mirroring—The practice of duplicating data in separate volumes on two hard disks to make storage more fault tolerant. Mirroring provides data protection in the case of disk failure because data are constantly updated to both disks.

Distributed denial-of-service attack (DDoS)—A denial-of-service (DoS) assault from multiple sources.

Dual control—A procedure that uses two or more entities (usually persons) operating in concert to protect a system resource so that no single entity acting alone can access that resource.

Due care—The level of care expected from a reasonable person of similar competency under similar conditions

Due diligence—The performance of those actions that are generally regarded as prudent, responsible and necessary to conduct a thorough and objective investigation, review and/or analysis

Dynamic Host Configuration Protocol (DHCP)—A protocol used by networked computers (clients) to obtain IP addresses and other parameters such as the default gateway, subnet mask and IP addresses of domain name system (DNS) servers from a DHCP server.

Scope Notes: The DHCP server ensures that all IP addresses are unique (e.g., no IP address is assigned to a second client while the first client's assignment is valid [its lease has not expired]). Thus, IP address pool management is done by the server and not by a human network administrator.

E

Electronic data interchange (EDI)—The electronic transmission of transactions (information) between two enterprises. EDI promotes a more efficient paperless environment. EDI transmissions can replace the use of standard documents, including invoices or purchase orders.

Electronic funds transfer (EFT)—The exchange of money via telecommunications. EFT refers to any financial transaction that originates at a terminal and transfers a sum of money from one account to another.

Encryption—The process of taking an unencrypted message (plaintext), applying a mathematical function to it (encryption algorithm with a key) and producing an encrypted message (ciphertext).

Enterprise governance—A set of responsibilities and practices exercised by the board and executive management with the goal of providing strategic direction, ensuring that objectives are achieved, ascertaining that risk is managed appropriately and verifying that the enterprise's resources are used responsibly.

Eradication—When containment measures have been deployed after an incident occurs, the root cause of the incident must be identified and removed from the network

Exposure—The potential loss to an area due to the occurrence of an adverse event.

External storage—The location that contains the backup copies to be used in case recovery or restoration is required in the event of a disaster.

F

Fail-over—The transfer of service from an incapacitated primary component to its backup component.

Fail-safe— A system or component that automatically places itself in a safe operational mode in the event of a failure

Source: IEEE

Fall-through logic—An optimized code based on a branch prediction that predicts which way a program will branch when an application is presented.

Firewall—A system or combination of systems that enforces a boundary between two or more networks, typically forming a barrier between a secure and an open environment such as the Internet

Forensic examination—The process of collecting, assessing, classifying and documenting digital evidence to assist in the identification of an offender and the method of compromise.

G

Guideline—A description of a particular way of accomplishing something that is less prescriptive than a procedure

H

Harden—To configure a computer or other network device to resist attacks.

Hash function—1. An algorithm that maps or translates one set of bits into another (generally smaller) so that a message yields the same result every time the algorithm is executed using the same message as input

2. Fixed values derived mathematically from a text message

Help desk—A service offered via telephone/Internet by an enterprise to its clients or employees that provides information, assistance and troubleshooting advice regarding software, hardware or networks.

Scope Notes: A help desk is staffed by people who can either resolve the problem on their own or escalate the problem to specialized personnel. A help desk is often equipped with dedicated customer relationship management (CRM) software that logs the problems and tracks them until they are solved.

Honeypot—A specially configured server, also known as a decoy server, designed to attract and monitor intruders in a manner so that their actions do not affect production systems

Hot site—A fully operational offsite data processing facility equipped with both hardware and system software to be used in the event of a disaster.

Hypertext Transfer Protocol (HTTP)—A communication protocol used to connect to servers on the World Wide Web. Its primary function is to establish a connection with a web server and transmit hypertext markup language (HTML), extensible markup language (XML) or other pages to client browsers.

Hypertext Transfer Protocol Secure (HTTPS)—A protocol for accessing a secure web server, whereby all data transferred are encrypted. Standard port number is 443.

I

Identity and access management (IAM)—Encapsulates people, processes and products to identify and manage the data used in an information system to authenticate users and grant or deny access rights to data and system resources. The goal of IAM is to provide appropriate access to enterprise resources.

Impact analysis—A study to prioritize the criticality of information resources for the enterprise based on costs (or consequences) of adverse events. In an impact analysis, threats to assets are identified and potential business losses determined for different time periods. This assessment is used to justify the extent of safeguards that are required and recovery time frames. This analysis is the basis for establishing the recovery strategy.

Incident—A violation or imminent threat of violation of computer security policies, acceptable use policies, guidelines or standard security practices

Incident response—The response of an enterprise to a disaster or other significant event that may significantly affect the enterprise, its people or its ability to function productively. An incident response may include evacuation of a facility, initiating a disaster recovery plan (DRP), performing damage assessment and any other measures necessary to bring an enterprise to a more stable status.

Incident response plan— Also called IRP. The operational component of incident management.

Scope Notes: The plan includes documented procedures and guidelines for defining the criticality of incidents, reporting and escalation process, and recovery procedures.

Information security—Ensures that, within the enterprise, information is protected against disclosure to unauthorized users (confidentiality), improper modification (integrity) and nonaccess when required (availability). Information security deals with all formats of information—paper documents, digital assets, intellectual property in people's minds, and verbal and visual communications.

Information security governance—The set of responsibilities and practices exercised by the board and executive management with the goal of providing strategic direction, ensuring that objectives are achieved, ascertaining that risk is managed appropriately and verifying that the enterprise's resources are used responsibly.

Information security program—The overall combination of technical, operational and procedural measures and management structures implemented to provide for the confidentiality, integrity and availability of information based on business requirements and risk analysis

Infrastructure as a Service (IaaS)—Offers the capability to provision processing, storage, networks and other fundamental computing resources, enabling the customer to deploy and run arbitrary software, which can include operating systems (OSs) and applications

Integrity—The guarding against improper information modification or destruction, and includes ensuring information nonrepudiation and authenticity

Internal controls—The policies, procedures, practices and organizational structures designed to provide reasonable assurance that business objectives will be achieved and undesired events will be prevented or detected and corrected

Internet service provider (ISP)—A third party that provides individuals and enterprises with access to the Internet and a variety of other Internet-related services

Interruption window—The time that the company can wait from the point of failure to the restoration of the minimum and critical services or applications. After this time, the progressive losses caused by the interruption are excessive for the enterprise.

Intrusion detection—The process of monitoring the events occurring in a computer system or network to detect signs of unauthorized access or attack

Intrusion detection system (IDS)—Inspects network and host security activity to identify suspicious patterns that may indicate a network or system attack

Intrusion prevention system (IPS)—A system designed to not only detect attacks, but also prevent the intended victim hosts from being affected by the attacks

IP Security (IPSec)—A set of protocols developed by the Internet Engineering Task Force (IETF) to support the secure exchange of packets

ISO/IEC 17799—This standard defines information's confidentiality, integrity and availability controls in a comprehensive information security management system.

Scope Notes: Originally released as part of the British Standard for Information Security in 1999 and then as the Code of Practice for Information Security Management in October 2000, it was elevated by the International Organization for Standardization (ISO) to an international code of practice for information security management. The latest version is ISO/IEC 17799:2005.

ISO/IEC 27001—Information Security Management—Specification with Guidance for Use; the replacement for BS7799-2. It is intended to provide the foundation for third-party audit and is harmonized with other management standards, such as ISO/IEC 9001 and 14001.

IT governance—The responsibility of executives and the board of directors; consists of the leadership, organizational structures and processes that ensure that the enterprise's IT sustains and extends the enterprise's strategies and objectives.

IT steering committee—An executive-management-level committee that assists in the delivery of the IT strategy, oversees day-to-day management of IT service delivery and IT projects, and focuses on implementation aspects.

IT strategic plan—A long-term plan (i.e., three- to five-year horizon) in which business and IT management cooperatively describe how IT resources will contribute to the enterprise's strategic objectives (goals).

IT strategy committee—A committee at the level of the board of directors to ensure that the board is involved in major IT matters and decisions.

Scope Notes: The committee is primarily accountable for managing the portfolios of IT-enabled investments, IT services and other IT resources. The committee is the owner of the portfolio.

K

Key goal indicator (KGI)—A measure that tells management, after the fact, whether an IT process has achieved its business requirements; usually expressed in terms of information criteria.

Key performance indicator (KPI)—A performance indicator or key performance indicator is a type of performance measurement

Key risk indicator (KRI)—A subset of risk indicators that are highly relevant and possess a high probability of predicting or indicating important risk

Scope Notes: See also Risk indicator.

M

Mail relay server—An electronic mail (e-mail) server that relays messages so that neither the sender nor the recipient is a local user.

Malware—Short for malicious software. Designed to infiltrate, damage or obtain information from a computer system without the owner's consent. Examples of malware include computer viruses, worms, Trojan horses, spyware and adware.

Man-in-the-middle attack (MITM)—An attack strategy in which the attacker intercepts the communication stream between two parts of the victim system and then replaces the traffic between the two components with the intruder's own, eventually assuming control of the communication

Mandatory access control (MAC)—Logical access control filters used to validate access credentials that cannot be controlled or modified by normal users or data owners

Masqueraders—Attackers that penetrate systems by using the identity of legitimate users and their logon credentials.

Maximum tolerable outages (MTO)—Maximum time that an enterprise can support processing in alternate mode.

Media access control (MAC)—Lower sublayer of the OSI Model Data Link layer

Message authentication code—An American National Standards Institute (ANSI) standard checksum that is computed using Data Encryption Standard (DES).

Message digest—A cryptographic hash function takes an input of an arbitrary length and produces an output (also known as a message digest) that is a standard-sized binary string. The output is unique to the input in such a way that even a minor change to the input results in a completely different output. Modern cryptographic hash functions are also resistant to collisions (situations in which different inputs produce identical output); a collision, while possible, is statistically improbable. Cryptographic hash functions are developed so that input cannot be determined readily from the output. See Hash.

Mirrored site—An alternate site that contains the same information as the original.

Scope Notes: Mirrored sites are set up for backup and disaster recovery and to balance the traffic load for numerous download requests. Such download mirrors are often placed in different locations throughout the Internet.

Mobile site—The use of a mobile/temporary facility to serve as a business resumption location. The facility can usually be delivered to any site and can house information technology and staff.

Monitoring policy—Rules outlining or delineating the way in which information about the use of computers, networks, applications and information is captured and interpreted

N

Net present value (NPV)—Calculated by using an after-tax discount rate of an investment and a series of expected incremental cash outflows (the initial investment and operational costs) and cash inflows (cost savings or revenues) that occur at regular periods during the life cycle of the investment.

Scope Notes: To arrive at a fair NPV calculation, cash inflows accrued by the business up to about five years after project deployment also should be taken into account.

Network address translation (NAT)—A methodology of modifying network address information in IP datagram packet headers while they are in transit across a traffic routing device for the purpose of remapping one IP address space into another

Nonintrusive monitoring—The use of transported probes or traces to assemble information, track traffic and identify vulnerabilities.

Nonrepudiation—The assurance that a party cannot later deny originating data; provision of proof of the integrity and origin of the data and that can be verified by a third party

Scope Notes: A digital signature can provide nonrepudiation.

O

Offline files—Computer file storage media that are not physically connected to the computer; typical examples are tapes or tape cartridges used for backup purposes.

Open Source Security Testing Methodology—An open and freely available methodology and manual for security testing.

Outcome measure—Represents the consequences of actions previously taken; often referred to as a lag indicator.

Scope Notes: Outcome measure frequently focuses on results at the end of a time period and characterize historic performance. They are also referred to as a key goal indicator (KGI) and used to indicate whether goals have been met. These can be measured only after the fact and, therefore, are called "lag indicators."

P

Packet—Protocol data unit that is routed from source to destination in a packet-switched network

Scope Notes: A packet contains both routing information and data.

Packet filtering—Controlling access to a network by analyzing the attributes of the incoming and outgoing packets and either letting them pass, or denying them, based on a list of rules

Packet switching—The process of transmitting messages in convenient pieces that can be reassembled at the destination.

Paper test—A walk-through of the steps of a regular test, but without actually performing the steps.

Scope Notes: Usually used in disaster recovery and contingency testing; team members review and become familiar with the plans and their specific roles and responsibilities

Partitioned file—A file format in which the file is divided into multiple sub files and a directory is established to locate each sub file.

Passive response—A response option in intrusion detection in which the system simply reports and records the problem detected, relying on the user to take subsequent action.

Password cracker—A tool that tests the strength of user passwords by searching for passwords that are easy to guess. It repeatedly tries words from specially crafted dictionaries and often also generates thousands (and in some cases, even millions) of permutations of characters, numbers and symbols.

Penetration testing—A live test of the effectiveness of security defenses through mimicking the actions of real-life attackers

Personally identifiable information (PII)—Any information that can be used to establish a link between the information and the natural person to whom such information relates, or that is or might be directly or indirectly linked to a natural person

Phishing—A type of electronic mail (email) attack that attempts to convince a user that the originator is genuine, but with the intention of obtaining information for use in social engineering

Scope Notes: Phishing attacks may take the form of masquerading as a lottery organization advising the recipient or the user's bank of a large win; in either case, the intent is to obtain account and personal identification number (PIN) details. Alternative attacks may seek to obtain apparently innocuous business information, which may be used in another form of active attack.

Platform as a Service (PaaS)—Offers the capability to deploy onto the cloud infrastructure customer-created or -acquired applications that are created using programming languages and tools supported by the provider

Policy—A document that communicates required and prohibited activities and behaviors

Port—A process or application-specific software element serving as a communication endpoint for the transport layer IP protocols (UDP and TCP)

Privacy—The right of an individual to trust that others will appropriately and respectfully use, store, share and dispose of his/her associated personal and sensitive information within the context, and according to the purposes for which it was collected or derived

Private key—A mathematical key (kept secret by the holder) used to create digital signatures and, depending on the algorithm, to decrypt messages or files encrypted (for confidentiality) with the corresponding public key.

Procedure—A document containing a detailed description of the steps necessary to perform specific operations in conformance with applicable standards. Procedures are defined as part of processes.

Proxy server—A server that acts on behalf of a user

Scope Notes: Typical proxies accept a connection from a user, make a decision as to whether the user or client IP address is permitted to use the proxy, perhaps perform additional authentication, and complete a connection to a remote destination on behalf of the user.

Public key—In an asymmetric cryptographic scheme, the key that may be widely published to enable the operation of the scheme.

R

Reciprocal agreement—Emergency processing agreement between two or more enterprises with similar equipment or applications.

Scope Notes: Typically, participants of a reciprocal agreement promise to provide processing time to each other when an emergency arises.

Recovery action—Execution of a response or task according to a written procedure.

Recovery point objective (RPO)—Determined based on the acceptable data loss in case of a disruption of operations. It indicates the earliest point in time that is acceptable to recover the data. The RPO effectively quantifies the permissible amount of data loss in case of interruption.

Recovery time objective (RTO)—The amount of time allowed for the recovery of a business function or resource after a disaster occurs

Red team—A group authorized and organized to emulate bad actors using similar tactics, techniques, and procedures to provide feedback from an offensive perspective. Red teams are typically employed by organizations with larger security teams and differ from penetration testing. While both have a similar goal of improving security, penetration testing mainly focuses on identifying technical vulnerabilities narrowly scoped by rules of engagement, whereas red teaming is more in-depth and often longer duration. Red teaming better assesses detection and response capabilities largely by leveraging social engineering and exploitation of applications, network services and physical facilities. Red teams are also employed in other fields such as airport security, the military and intelligence agencies.

Redundant array of inexpensive disks (RAID)—Provides performance improvements and fault-tolerant capabilities via hardware or software solutions, by writing to a series of multiple disks to improve performance and/or save large files simultaneously.

Redundant site—A recovery strategy involving the duplication of key IT components, including data or other key business processes, whereby fast recovery can take place.

Request for proposal (RFP)—A document distributed to software vendors requesting them to submit a proposal to develop or provide a software product.

Residual risk—The remaining risk after management has implemented a risk response

Return on investment (ROI)—A measure of operating performance and efficiency, computed in its simplest form by dividing net income by the total investment over the period being considered

Risk—The combination of the likelihood of an event and its impact

Risk acceptance—Decision to accept a risk, made according to the risk appetite and risk tolerance set by senior management where the enterprise can assume the risk and absorb any losses

Risk analysis—1. A process by which frequency and magnitude of IT risk scenarios are estimated.

2. The initial steps of risk management: analyzing the value of assets to the business, identifying threats to those assets and evaluating how vulnerable each asset is to those threats.

Scope Notes: It often involves an evaluation of the probable frequency of a particular event, as well as the probable impact of that event.

Risk appetite—The amount of risk, on a broad level, that an entity is willing to accept in pursuit of its mission.

Risk assessment—A process used to identify and evaluate risk and its potential effects

Scope Notes: Risk assessments are used to identify those items or areas that present the highest risk, vulnerability or exposure to the enterprise for inclusion in the IS annual audit plan.

Risk assessments are also used to manage the project delivery and project benefit risk.

Risk avoidance—The process for systematically avoiding risk, constituting one approach to managing risk

Risk mitigation—The management of risk through the use of countermeasures and controls

Risk response—Risk avoidance, risk acceptance, risk sharing/transfer, risk mitigation, leading to a situation that as much future residual risk (current risk with the risk response defined and implemented) as possible (usually depending on budgets available) falls within risk appetite limits.

Risk tolerance—The acceptable level of variation that management is willing to allow for any particular risk as the enterprise pursues its objectives

Risk transfer—The process of assigning risk to another enterprise, usually through the purchase of an insurance policy or by outsourcing the service

Scope Notes: Also known as risk sharing

Robustness—The degree to which a software system or component can function correctly in the presence of invalid inputs or stressful environmental conditions

See Software reliability.

Root cause analysis—A process of diagnosis to establish the origins of events, which can be used for learning from consequences, typically from errors and problems

Rootkit—A software suite designed to aid an intruder in gaining unauthorized administrative access to a computer system

S

Secure Shell (SSH)—Network protocol that uses cryptography to secure communication, remote command line login and remote command execution between two networked computers

Security as a Service (SecaaS)—The next generation of managed security services dedicated to the delivery, over the Internet, of specialized information-security services.

Security information and event management (SIEM)—SIEM solutions are a combination of the formerly disparate product categories of SIM (security information management) and SEM (security event management). SIEM technology provides realtime analysis of security alerts generated by network hardware and applications. SIEM solutions come as software, appliances or managed services, and are also used to log security data and generate reports for compliance purposes. Capabilities include:

- **Data aggregation:** SIEM/LM (log management) solutions aggregate data from many sources, including network, security, servers, databases and applications, providing the ability to consolidate monitored data to help avoid missing crucial events.
- **Correlation:** Looks for common attributes, and links events together into meaningful bundles. This technology provides the ability to perform a variety of correlation techniques to integrate different sources, in order to turn data into useful information.
- **Alerting:** The automated analysis of correlated events and production of alerts, to notify recipients of immediate issues.
- **Dashboards:** SIEM/LM tools take event data and turn them into informational charts to assist in seeing patterns, or identifying activity that is not forming a standard pattern
- **Compliance:** SIEM applications can be employed to automate the gathering of compliance data, producing reports that adapt to existing security, governance and auditing processes.
- **Retention:** SIEM/SIM solutions employ long-term storage of historical data to facilitate correlation of data over time, and to provide the retention necessary for compliance requirements.

Security metrics—A standard of measurement used in management of security-related activities.

Segregation/separation of duties (SoD)—A basic internal control that prevents or detects errors and irregularities by assigning to separate individuals the responsibility for initiating and recording transactions and for the custody of assets.

Scope Notes: Segregation/separation of duties is commonly used in large IT organizations so that no single person is in a position to introduce fraudulent or malicious code without detection.

Sensitivity—A measure of the impact that improper disclosure of information may have on an enterprise

Service delivery objective (SDO)—Directly related to the business needs, SDO is the level of services to be reached during the alternate process mode until the normal situation is restored.

Service level agreement (SLA)—An agreement, preferably documented, between a service provider and the customer(s)/user(s) that defines minimum performance targets for a service and how they will be measured

Shell programming—A script written for the shell, or command line interpreter, of an operating system; it is often considered a simple domain-specific programming language.

Scope Notes: Typical operations performed by shell scripts include file manipulation, program execution and printing text. Usually, shell script refers to scripts written for a UNIX shell, while command.com (DOS) and cmd.exe (Windows) command line scripts are usually called batch files. Many shell script interpreters double as a command line interface such as the various UNIX shells, Windows PowerShell or the MS-DOS command.com. Others, such as AppleScript, add scripting capability to computing environments lacking a command line interface. Other examples of programming languages primarily intended for shell scripting include digital command language (DCL) and job control language (JCL).

Sniffing—The process by which data traversing a network are captured or monitored

Social engineering—An attack based on deceiving users or administrators at the target site into revealing confidential or sensitive information

Software as a service (SaaS)—Offers the capability to use the provider's applications running on cloud infrastructure. The applications are accessible from various client devices through a thin client interface, such as a web browser (e.g., web-based email).

Split knowledge/split key—A security technique in which two or more entities separately hold data items that individually convey no knowledge of the information that results from combining the items; a condition under which two or more entities separately have key components that individually convey no knowledge of the plain text key that will be produced when the key components are combined in the cryptographic module.

Spoofing—Faking the sending address of a transmission in order to gain illegal entry into a secure system

Standard—A mandatory requirement, code of practice or specification approved by a recognized external standards organization, such as International Organization for Standardization (ISO).

Symmetric key encryption—System in which a different key (or set of keys) is used by each pair of trading partners to ensure that no one else can read their messages. The same key is used for encryption and decryption. See also Private Key Cryptosystem.

System owner—Person or organization having responsibility for the development, procurement, integration, modification, operation and maintenance, and/or final disposition of an information system

T

Threat—Anything (e.g., object, substance, human) that is capable of acting against an asset in a manner that can result in harm

Scope Notes: A potential cause of an unwanted incident (ISO/IEC 13335)

Threat agent—Methods and things used to exploit a vulnerability

Scope Notes: Examples include determination, capability, motive and resources.

Threat analysis—An evaluation of the type, scope and nature of events or actions that can result in adverse consequences; identification of the threats that exist against enterprise assets

Scope Notes: The threat analysis usually defines the level of threat and the likelihood of it materializing.

Threat event—Any event during which a threat element/actor acts against an asset in a manner that has the potential to directly result in harm

Threat vector—The path or route used by the adversary to gain access to the target

Token—In security systems, a physical device that is used to authenticate a user, typically in addition to a username and password; in programming languages, a single element of the language

Total cost of ownership (TCO)—Includes the original cost of the computer plus the cost of: software, hardware and software upgrades, maintenance, technical support, training, and certain activities performed by users.

Transmission Control Protocol (TCP)—A connection-based Internet protocol that supports reliable data transfer connections

Scope Notes: Packet data are verified using checksums and retransmitted if they are missing or corrupted. The application plays no part in validating the transfer.

Trusted system—A system that employs sufficient hardware and software assurance measures to allow their use for processing a range of sensitive or classified information.

Tunneling—Commonly used to bridge between incompatible hosts/routers or to provide encryption, a method by which one network protocol encapsulates another protocol within itself.

Scope Notes: When protocol A encapsulates protocol B, a protocol A header and optional tunneling headers are appended to the original protocol B packet. Protocol A then becomes the data link layer of protocol B. Examples of tunneling protocols include IPSec, Point-to-point Protocol Over Ethernet (PPPoE) and Layer 2 Tunneling Protocol (L2TP).

Two-factor authentication—The use of two independent mechanisms for authentication (e.g., requiring a smart card and a password); typically the combination of something you know, are or have

U

Uniform resource locator (URL)—The string of characters that form a web address

V

Virtual private network (VPN)—A secure private network that uses the public telecommunications infrastructure to transmit data

Scope Notes: In contrast to a much more expensive system of owned or leased lines that can only be used by one enterprise, VPNs are used by enterprises for both extranets and wide areas of intranets. Using encryption and authentication, a VPN encrypts all data that pass between two Internet points, maintaining privacy and security.

Virus signature—The file of virus patterns that are compared with existing files to determine whether they are infected with a virus or worm

Virus signature file—The file of virus patterns that are compared with existing files to determine whether they are infected with a virus or worm.

Voice-over Internet Protocol (VoIP)—Also called IP Telephony, Internet Telephony and Broadband Phone, a technology that makes it possible to have a voice conversation over the Internet or over any dedicated Internet Protocol (IP) network instead of over dedicated voice transmission lines

Vulnerability—A weakness in the design, implementation, operation or internal control of a process that could expose the system to adverse threats from threat events

Vulnerability analysis—A process of identifying and classifying vulnerabilities

W

Warm site—Similar to a hot site but not fully equipped with all of the necessary hardware needed for recovery.

Web hosting—The business of providing the equipment and services required to host and maintain files for one or more web sites and provide fast Internet connections to those sites.

Scope Notes: Most hosting is "shared," which means that web sites of multiple companies are on the same server to share/reduce costs.

Web server—End-point hardware or software that serves web pages to users

Wi-Fi Protected Access II (WPA2)—Wireless security protocol that supports 802.11i encryption standards to provide greater security. This protocol uses Advanced Encryption Standards (AES) and Temporal Key Integrity Protocol (TKIP) for stronger encryption.

Wide area network (WAN)—A computer network connecting multiple offices or buildings over a larger area

Worm—A programmed network attack in which a self-replicating program does not attach itself to programs, but rather spreads independently of users' action

Write blocker—A device that allows the acquisition of information on a drive without creating the possibility of accidentally damaging the drive

Z

Zero-day exploit—A vulnerability that is exploited before the software creator/vendor is even aware of its existence. May also refer to known flaws that do not have a patch available.

Page intentionally left blank

Acronyms

AIW	Acceptable interruption window
ALE	Annual loss expectancy
API	Application programming interface
ASP	Application service provider
BCP	Business continuity plan
BIA	Business impact analysis
BYOD	Bring your own device
CA	Certificate authority
CEO	Chief executive officer
CERT	Computer emergency response team
CFO	Cheif financial officer
CIO	Chief information officer
CIRT	Computer incident response team
CISO	Chief information security officer
CMMI	Capability maturity model integration
CMU/SEI	Carnegie Mellon University Software Engineering Institute
COO	Chief operating officer
COSO	Committee of Sponsoring Organizations of the Treadway Commission
CPO	Chief privacy officer
CPU	Central processing unit
CSF	Critical success factor
CSIRT	Computer security incident response team
CSO	Chief security officer
CRO	Chief risk officer
CTO	Chief technology officer
CVE	Common vulnerabilities and exposures
DAC	Discretionary access controls
DBMS	Database management system
DDoS	Distributed denial of service
DHCP	Dynamic Host Configuration Protocol
DMZ	Demilitarized zone
DNS	Domain name system
DoS	Denial of service
DR	Disaster recovery
DRP	Disaster recovery plan
EDI	Electronic data interchange
EGIT	Enterprise governance of information & technology
EGRP	External Gateway Routing Protocol
FAIR	Factor analysis of information risk
FAR	False-acceptance rate
HARM	Holistic approach to risk management
HIDS	Host-based intrusion detection system
HIPAA	Health Insurance Portability and Accountability Act (USA)
HR	Human resources
HTML	Hypertext Markup Language
HTTP	Hypertext Transfer Protocol
HTTPS	Secure Hypertext Transfer Protocol
I/O	Input/output
I&T	Information and technology
IaaS	Infrastructure as a service
ICMP	Internet Control Message Protocol
ID	Identification
IDS	Intrusion detection system
IEC	International Electrotechnical Commission
IMT	Incident management team
IoT	Internet of Things
IP	Internet Protocol
IPF	Information processing facility
IPS	Intrusion prevention system
IPSec	Internet Protocol Security
IRP	Incident response plan
IRT	Incident response team
IS	Information systems
ISO	International Organization for Standardization
ISP	Internet service provider
IT	Information technology
ITIL	Information Technology Infrastructure Library
KCI	Key control indicator
KGI	Key goal indicator
KPI	Key performance indicator
KRI	Key risk indicator
LAN	Local area network
MAC	Mandatory access control
MIME	Multipurpose Internet mail extension
MitM	Man-in-the-middle
MTD	Maximum tolerable downtime
MTO	Maximum tolerable outage
NAT	Network address translation
NCP	Network Control Protocol
NDA	Nondisclosure agreement
NIST	National Institute of Standards and Technology (USA)
NPV	Net present value
OS	Operating system
OSI	Open system interconnectionPlat
PaaS	Platform as a service
PAN	Personal area network
PCI DSS	Payment Card Industry Data Security Standard
PDCA	Plan-do-check-act
PKI	Public key infrastructure
POS	Point-of-sale
PRA	Probablistic risk assessment
QA	Quality assurance
RACI	Responsible, accountable, consulted, informed
RAID	Redundant array of inexpensive disks
ROI	Return on investment
ROSI	Return on security investment
RPO	Recovery point objective
RTO	Recovery time objective
SaaS	Software as a service
SABSA	Sherwood Applied Business Security Architecture
SCADA	Supervisory Control and Data Acquisition
SDLC	System development life cycle
SDO	Service delivery objective
SEC	Securities and exchange Commission (USA)
SIEM	Security information and event management

SIM	Security information management
SLA	Service level agreement
SMART	Specific, measurable, achievable, relevant, time-bound
SOAP	Simple Object Access Protocol
SOP	Standard operating procedure
SQL	Structure Query Language
SSH	Secure Shell
SSL	Secure sockets layer
SSO	Single sign-on
SWOT	Strengths, weaknesses, opportunities, threats
TCO	Total cost of ownership
TCP	Transmission Control Protocol
TLS	Transport layer security
UDP	User Datagram Protocol
URL	Uniform resource locator
USB	Universal serial bus
VAR	Value at risk
VoIP	Voice-over IP
VPN	Virtual private network
XML	Extensible Markup Language
XSS	Cross-site scripting